I0824292

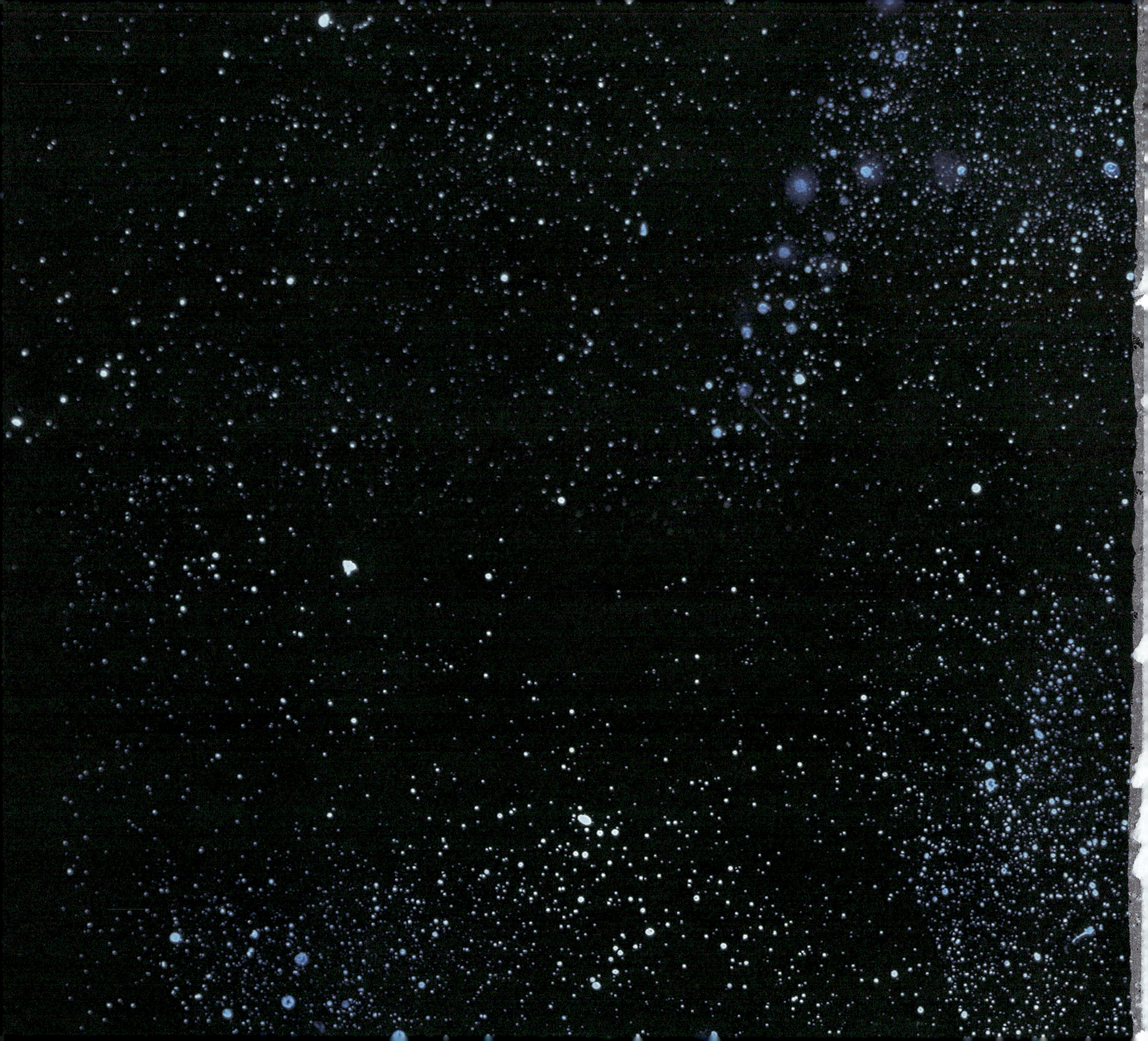

STAR TREK™ III
THE SEARCH FOR SPOCK

THE MAKING OF THE CLASSIC FILM

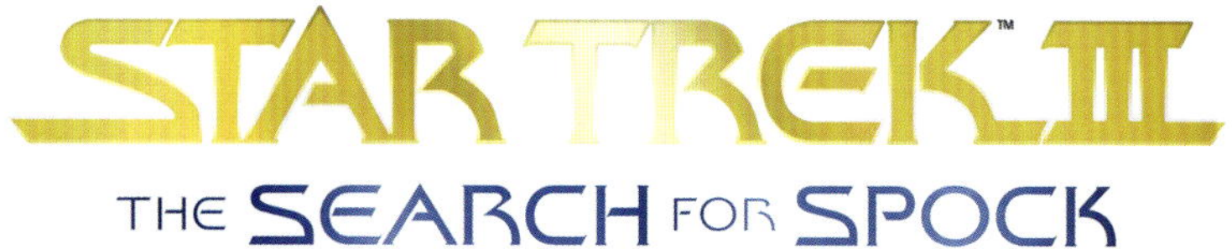

THE MAKING OF THE CLASSIC FILM

ISBN: 9781835412893

Published by
Titan Books
A division of Titan Publishing Group Ltd
144 Southwark St
London
SE1 0UP

www.titanbooks.com

First edition: September 2025
2 4 6 8 10 9 7 5 3 1

EU RP (for authorities only)
eucomply OÜ Pärnu mnt 139b-14 11317
Talinn, Estonia
hello@eucompliancepartner.com
+3375690241

Did you enjoy this book? We love to hear from our readers.
Please e-mail us at: readerfeedback@titanemail.com or
write to Reader Feedback at the above address.

To receive advance information, news, competitions, and exclusive offers online, please sign up for the Titan newsletter on our website: www.titanbooks.com

A CIP catalogue record for this title is available from the British Library.

Printed and bound in China.

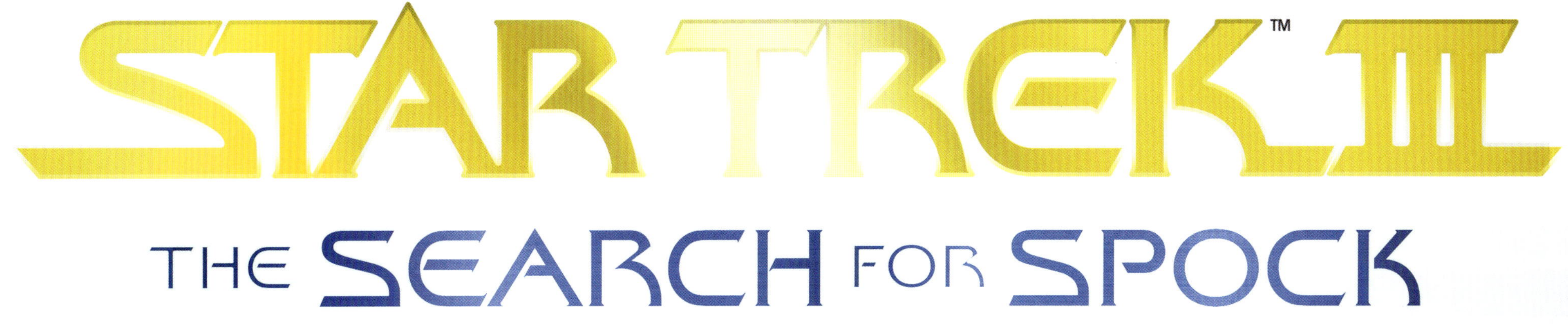

THE MAKING OF THE CLASSIC FILM

JOHN TENUTO AND MARIA JOSE TENUTO

TITANBOOKS

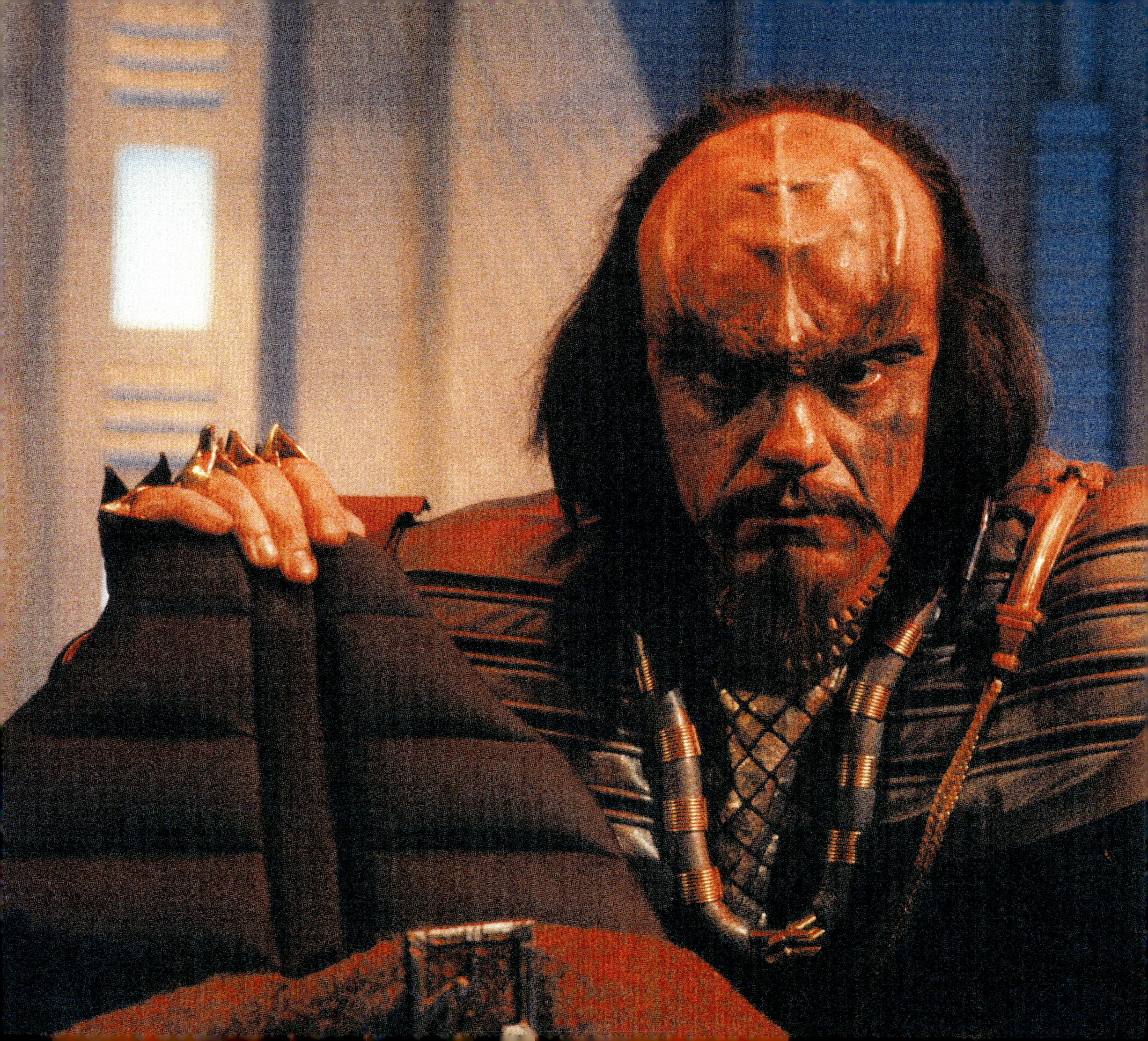

CONTENTS

FOREWORD

BY ROBIN CURTIS

Star Trek III changed my life. I'd give a kidney to thank Leonard Nimoy in person. But Leonard and Harve Bennett died within days of each other in 2015. Well, John and Maria Jose Tenuto's book *Star Trek III: The Search for Spock: The Making of the Classic Film* brings them to life!

The Tenutos' carefully curated book is an impeccably researched retelling of the dazzling thought processes and countless clever decisions made by some of the brightest minds in show business whose collective alchemy created *The Search for Spock*. Leonard Nimoy was the right man for the right film at the right moment. Every page made me feel like I was eavesdropping on his production meetings, were they at Paramount, Industrial Light & Magic or Nimoy's own home! It was a hell of a ride when I lived it in 1983. And all these decades later, *The Making of* is still a hell of a ride filled with fascinating observations and insights, some before now unknown, penned by this talented husband and wife writing team. And right here, I will steal my chance to say, "Thank you, Mr. Nimoy, from the bottom of my heart!"

Beam the Tenutos' book into your *Star Trek* collection! It is logical!

BELOW LEFT: Nimoy confers with Curtis on the planet Genesis set.

BELOW RIGHT: Nimoy, Curtis, and William Shatner discuss how much emotion Saavik should convey when telling Kirk about David's sacrifice.

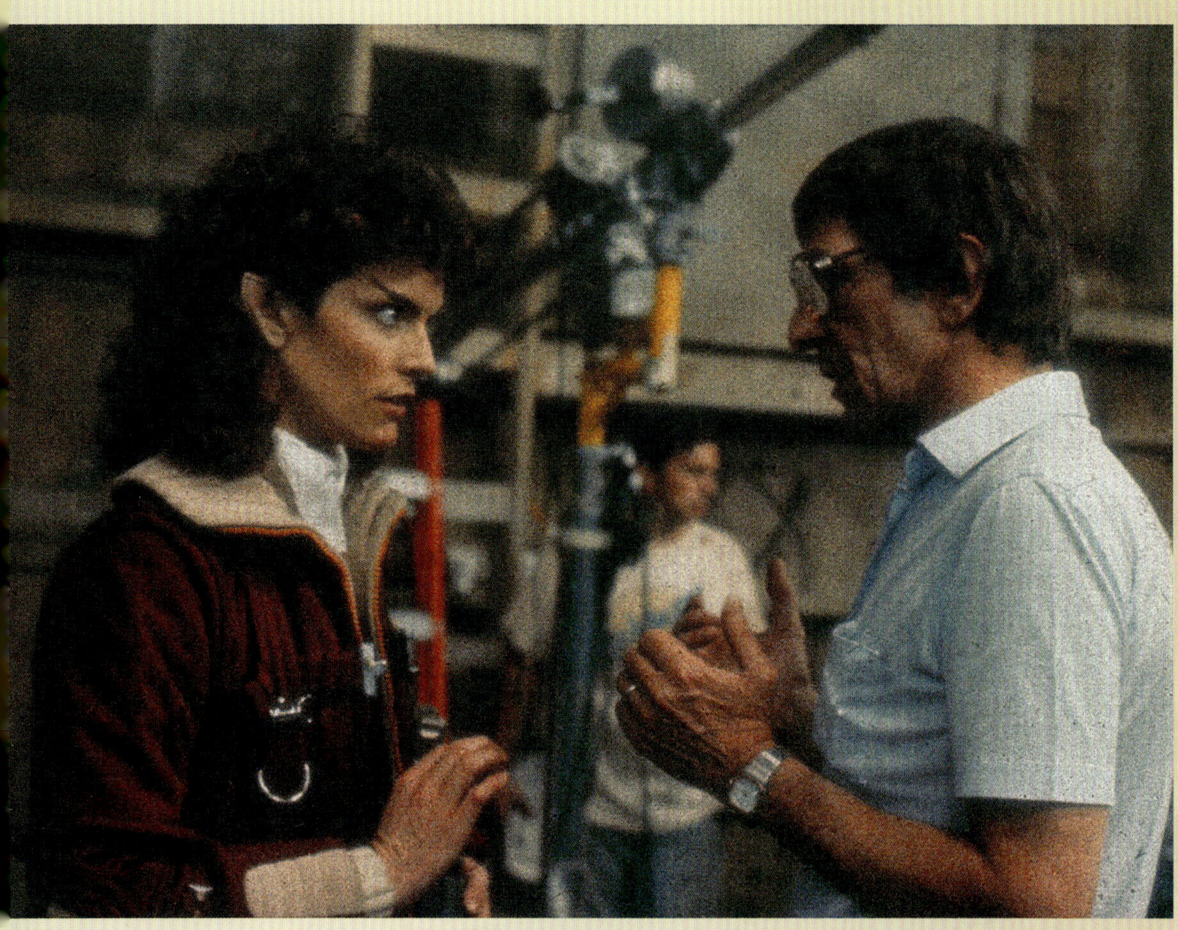

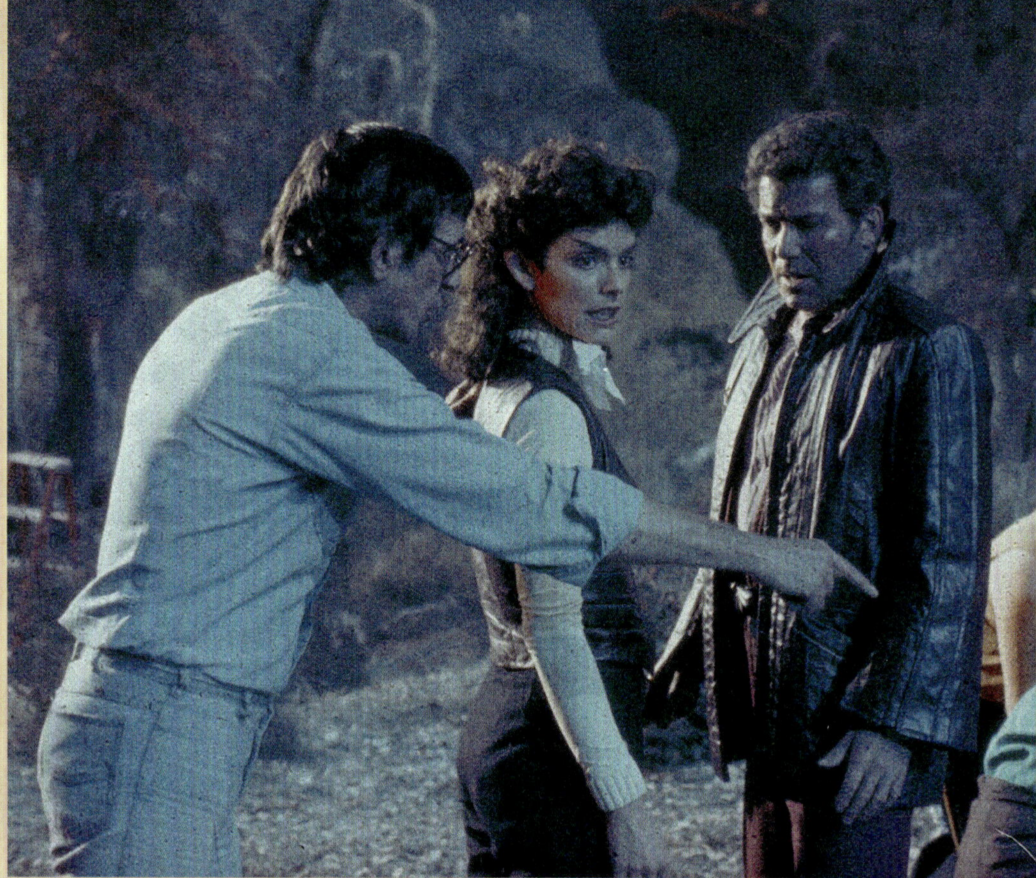

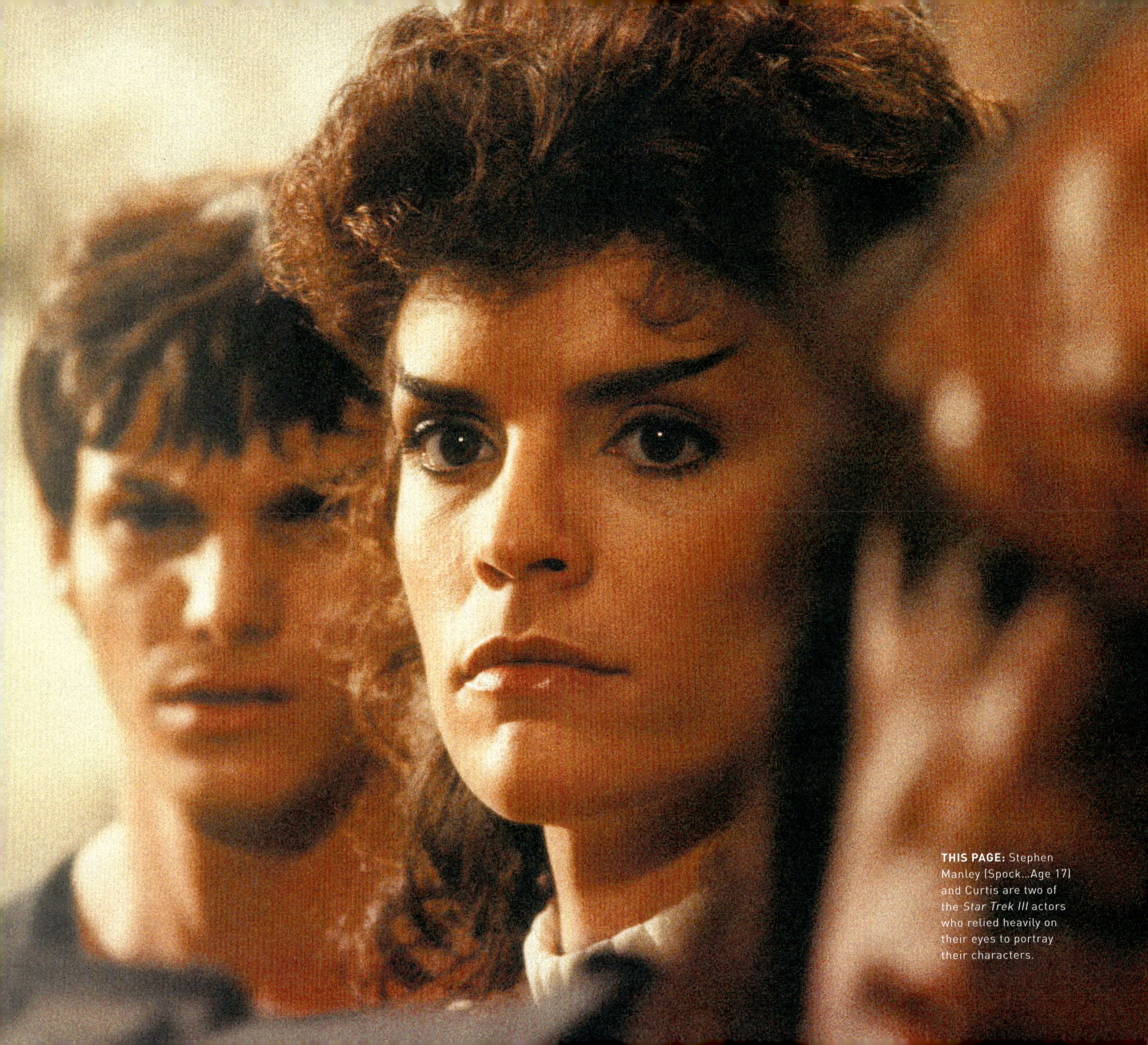

THIS PAGE: Stephen Manley (Spock...Age 17) and Curtis are two of the *Star Trek III* actors who relied heavily on their eyes to portray their characters.

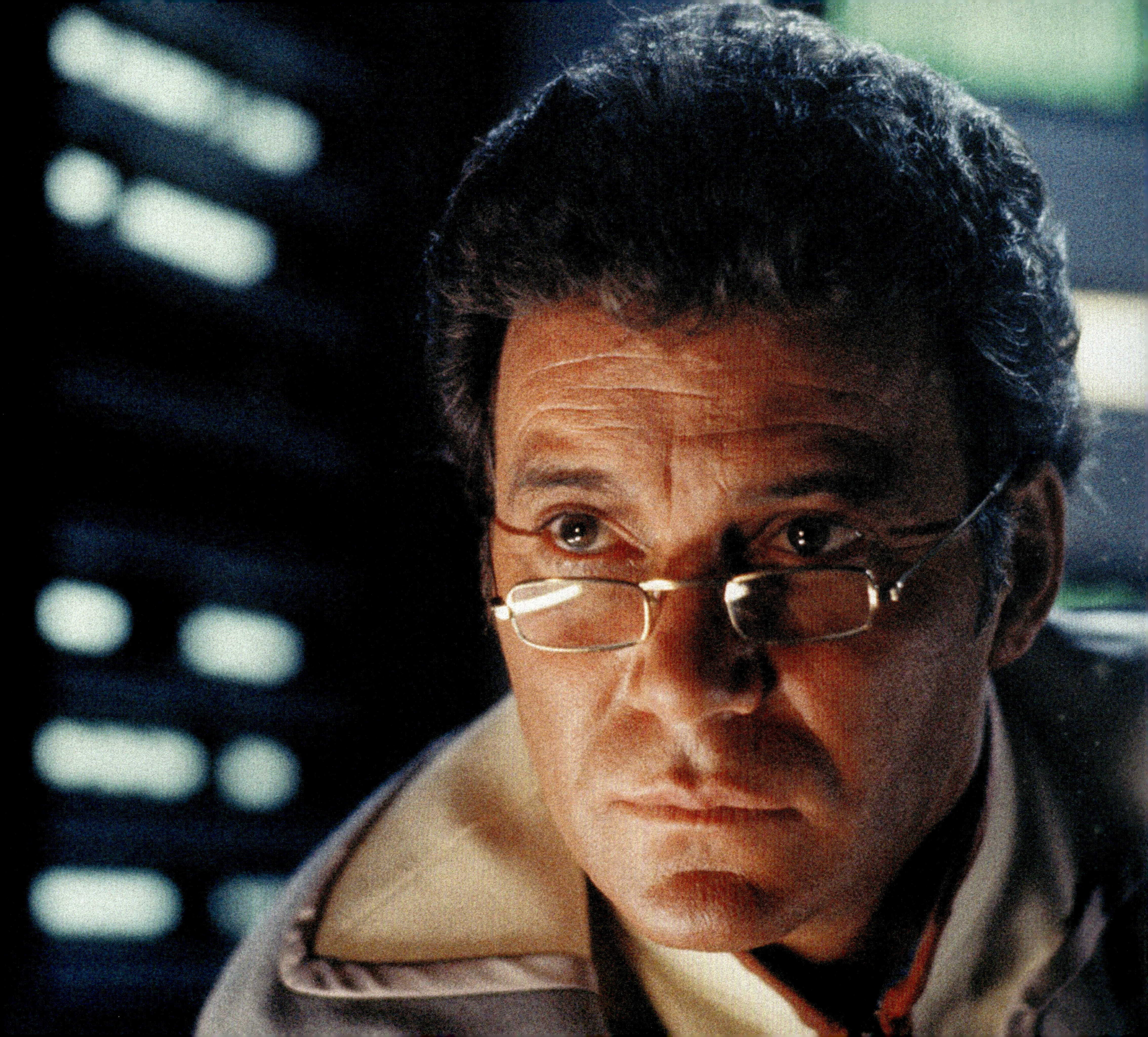

CHAPTER 1

RETURN TO GENESIS

All that they've loved
All that they've fought for
All that they've stood for
Will now be put to the test

Narrator Chuck Riley's words, which usher in the *Star Trek III: The Search for Spock* theatrical trailer, were an invitation for 1984 movie audiences to "join us, on this, the final voyage of the *Starship Enterprise*." In reality, his words could easily have applied as much to the creatives who produced the film as they did to Admiral James T. Kirk and crew. Each of the previous *Star Trek* films had their own trials. *Star Trek: The Motion Picture* (December 7, 1979) was a proving ground, challenged with the pioneering task of converting a ten-year-old television series into a feature film. *Star Trek II: The Wrath of Khan* (June 4, 1982) was commissioned with the goal of restoring the spirit of the television show with its emphasis on characters.

The tests for *Star Trek III*, both personal and existential, would be just as daunting. For some, *Star Trek III* constituted their first time working on a major motion picture. For others, it was a test to see if they could meet, and exceed, the expectations set by previous productions. Challenges of time, budget, and technology needed to be resolved, and the production would face a literal trial by fire as a massive blaze threatened the soundstages only a few weeks after the start of filming. Chiefly, the film itself was to be a test of sustainability: was *Star Trek* a viable film franchise? Were the successes of the previous films mere curiosities or could the characters sustain a continuing series of big screen adventures? The ending of *Star Trek III*, with Kirk on the run, a fragile Spock, and the crew without a ship, was a promise of more adventures to follow. But that promise was never guaranteed. For writer and producer Harve Bennett and his team, like Kirk and company, there would be many tests to meet if any further adventures were to take place.

Premiering on June 4, 1982, and earning $14,347,221 in its first weekend, *Star Trek II* had been a genuine blockbuster met with critical and fan acclaim. The film broke the contemporary record for the highest grossing three-day opening in cinema history. Only a few days later, Paramount president and CEO Michael Eisner asked Bennett to begin

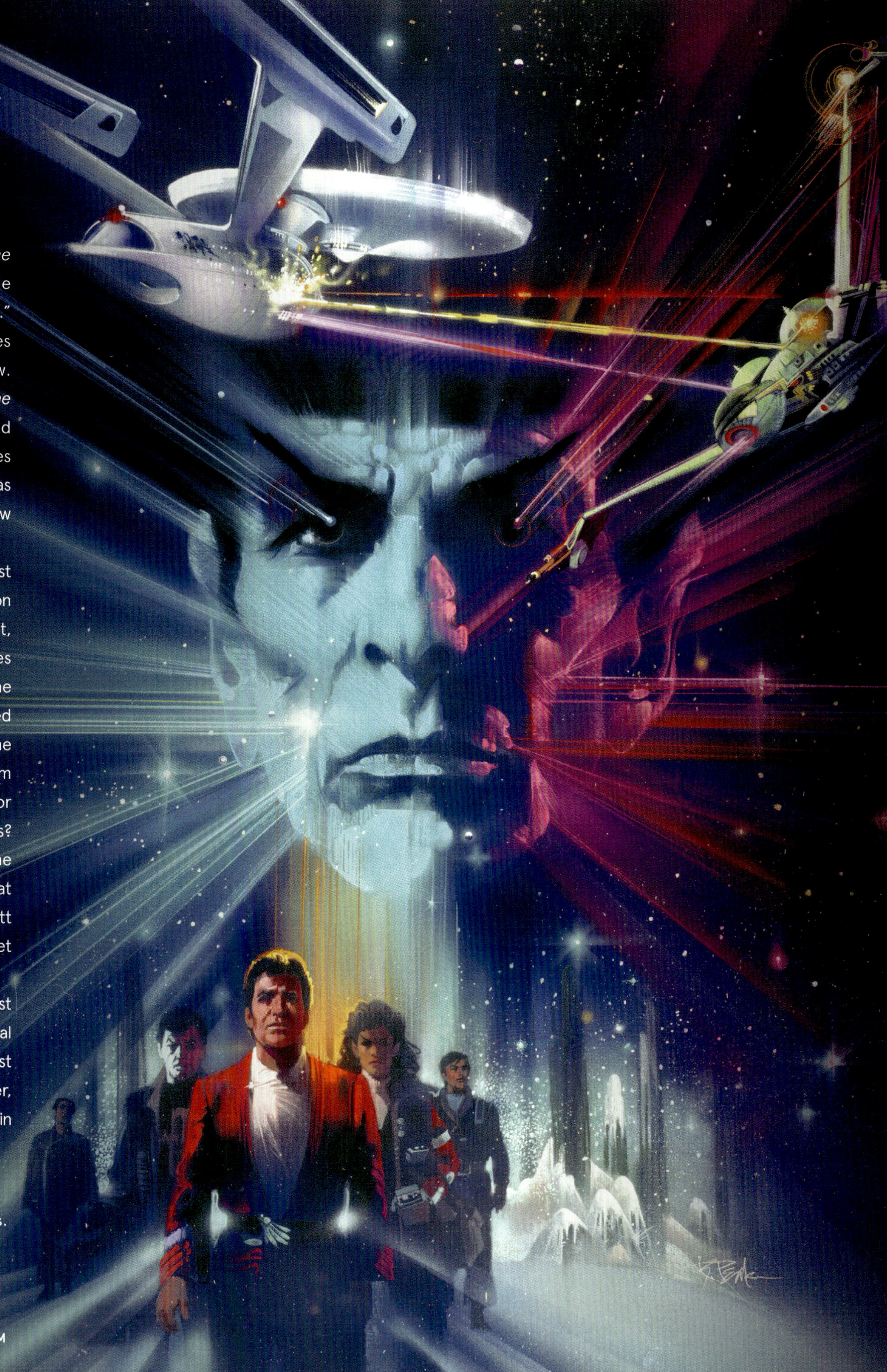

THIS PAGE: Artist Bob Peak consistently produced amazing art for the *Star Trek* films which continues to be reproduced decades later by licensees and riffed by modern *Star Trek* television and film productions. This is his unobscured art for the *Star Trek III* poster which newspaper advertisements featured throughout the summer of 1984.

work on a sequel. According to Bennett, "That is the fastest greenlight on any project I've ever had."[1]

The tests would start immediately. The film needed to be ready in a mere eighteen months with a budget of $16 million. As Bennett did not have a lot of time, he decided to forgo one of the lengthier delays of the previous film – finding the right screenwriter – and do it himself. Despite decades of producing, show creation, and television writing, Bennett had never scripted a major motion picture before. He had contributed the story outline for *Star Trek II*, but the actual script writing had been left to others.

While Socrates argued in favor of divine inspiration, the spark of imagination that set the tone for *Star Trek III* would come from a more prosaic, yet quite appropriate, source: fan fiction. As part of his preparation for the previous movie, Bennett had embraced the fan community, frequently seeking the opinions of fans and immersing himself in the reading of fanzines – popular, unofficial magazines produced by Trek aficionados containing their own stories, poetry, and ruminations.

The general narrative goal of the film was obvious: resurrect Spock. But how to do that, both emotionally and believably, was the challenge. During the summer of 1982, as Bennett was formulating the outline of *Star Trek III*, he thought back upon a fanzine poem he had recently read. It had been scribed in Kirk's voice, with the moral, as Bennett remembered, of "You are my friend. I must return to find you, to do all I can to help you, even at the cost of my own soul."[2] That fan poem would become the theme permeating every outline, script, and the film itself. For Bennett, *Star Trek III* was to be a film about sacrifice and the responsibilities of friendship.

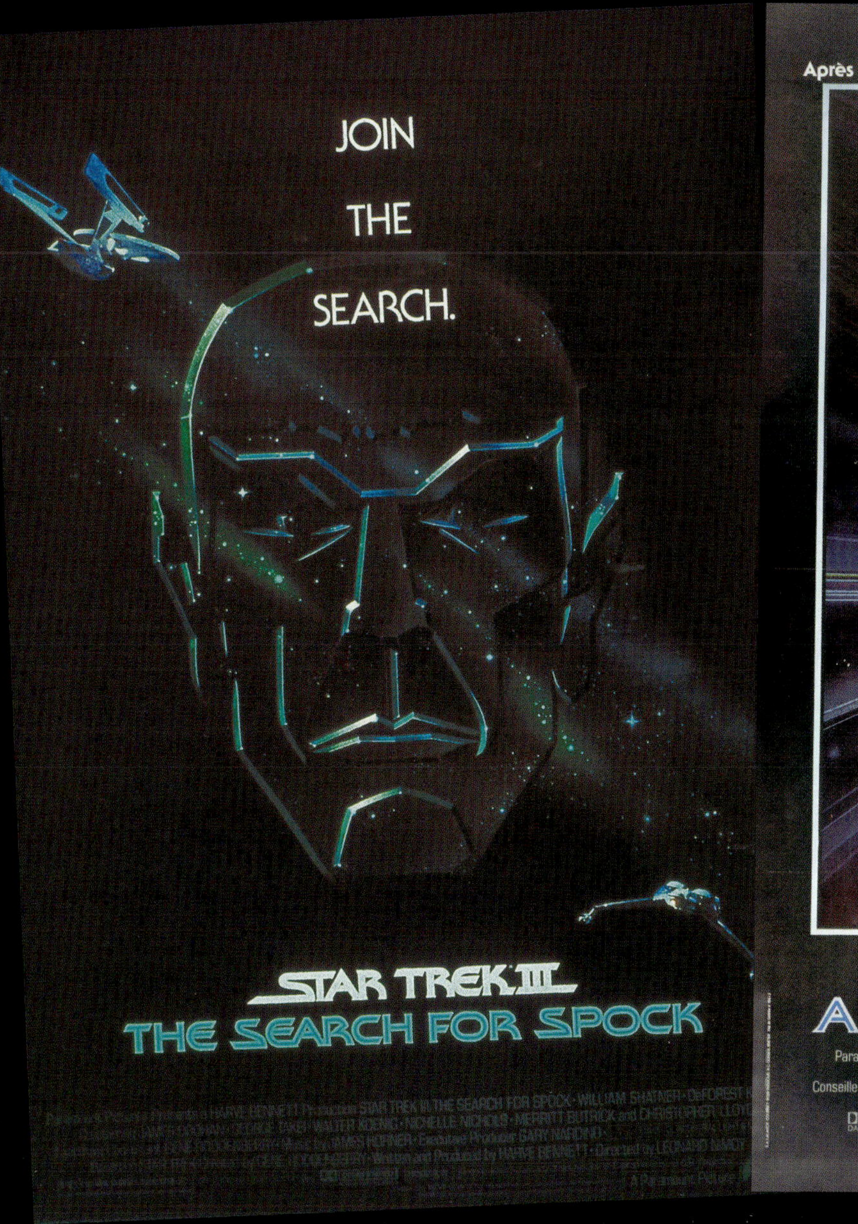

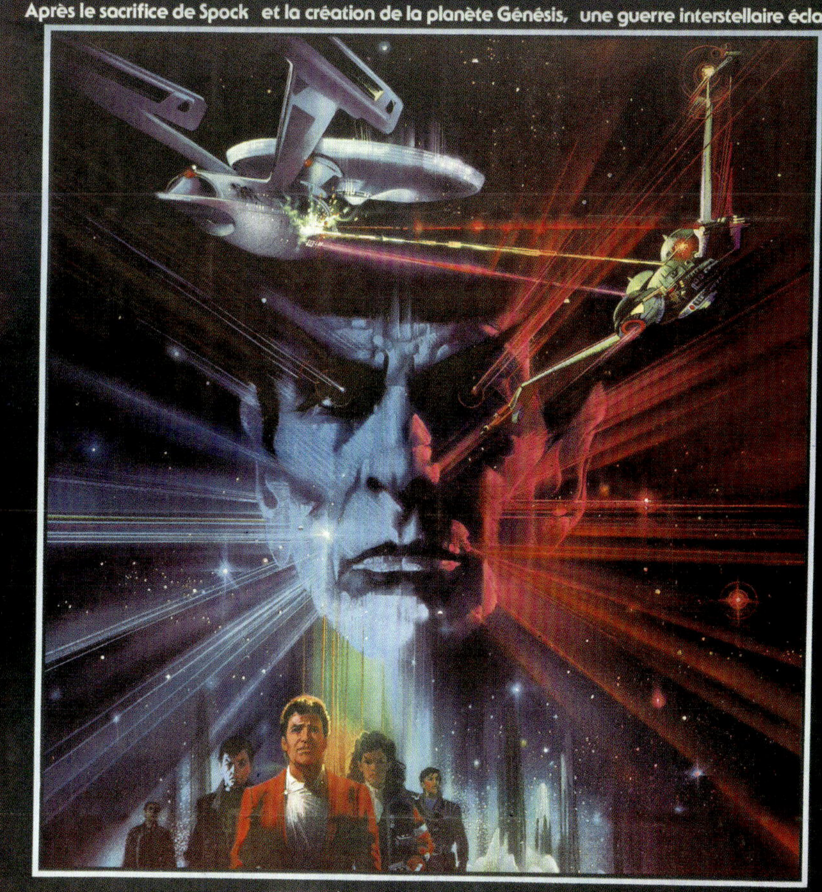

LEFT: The French theatrical poster using Peak's art. The tag line at the top of the poster translates to English as, "After the sacrifice of Spock and the creation of the planet Genesis, an interstellar war breaks out." The literal title can be translated as "In Search of Spock."

FAR LEFT: One-sheet poster art by Roger Huyssen and Gerard Huerta. The iconic design would also be featured as the soundtrack cover. The image of Spock, rendered in mixed media, evokes Bennett's original idea of Spock appearing as an apparition. The *Enterprise* and the Bird-of-Prey were added to give the poster an action vibe in a summer movie season filled with competition from the likes of *Ghostbusters*, *The Karate Kid*, and *Indiana Jones and the Temple of Doom*.

FLIGHT RECORDER VISUAL:

HARVE BENNETT, WRITER AND PRODUCER

Harvard Bennett Fischman was born August 17, 1930, in Chicago, Illinois. Audiences first became aware of Bennett as a literal whiz kid. Recognizing his academic abilities, Bennett's grammar school principal arranged for his star pupil to audition for a new radio program, *Quiz Kids*. From June 1941, starting at age ten, until age sixteen, Bennett starred in 212 episodes, winning $17,800 worth of war bonds as his prize total.[3] The program gave Bennett an expansive world view, traveling to all the states, where he met luminaries such as Presidents Franklin D. Roosevelt and Harry Truman. Most importantly, it introduced him to the entertainment industry. After earning a film degree from the University of California, Los Angeles and two years in the United States Army, he began a career that focused on producing. Many of his programs became iconic: *The Mod Squad*, *The Six Million Dollar Man*, *The Bionic Woman*, and the pioneering mini-series *Rich Man, Poor Man*. Although he had been brought to Paramount in 1980 to help shepherd their television division, he was asked to executive produce the second *Star Trek* feature film because he knew how to produce cost-conscious, yet popular, science fiction.

Bennett would never forget his radio roots, frequently providing voice cameos in his productions. Along with actor Richard Anderson, Bennett gives the narration for the opening credits of *The Six Million Dollar Man*. In *Star Trek II*, Bennett was the voice of the computer during the Kobayashi Maru simulation scene and played the Flight Recorder computer voice in *Star Trek III*.

Bennett died on February 25, 2015, two days before Leonard Nimoy.

REMEMBER...

Adam Nimoy (son of Leonard Nimoy): "There was a warmth and enthusiasm about Harve. He had a childlike wonder about everything. An energy. He was still the *Quiz Kid*. He had a gleam in his eye, a real kind of circus ringleader. He thrived on that energy. I think that is important to the entertainment industry in particular, and life in general."[4]

Stephen Manley (Spock...Age 17): "I had a nice relationship with Harve. I went to art school after I did *Star Trek*, eventually earning a film degree. I made a short film and Harve invited me to the Paramount lot. We discussed what I was doing and he took the film, saying he would critique it. And he did. He gave me a detailed, great critique. It was obvious he watched every detail and asked why I filmed certain scenes as I did. He was fantastic."[5]

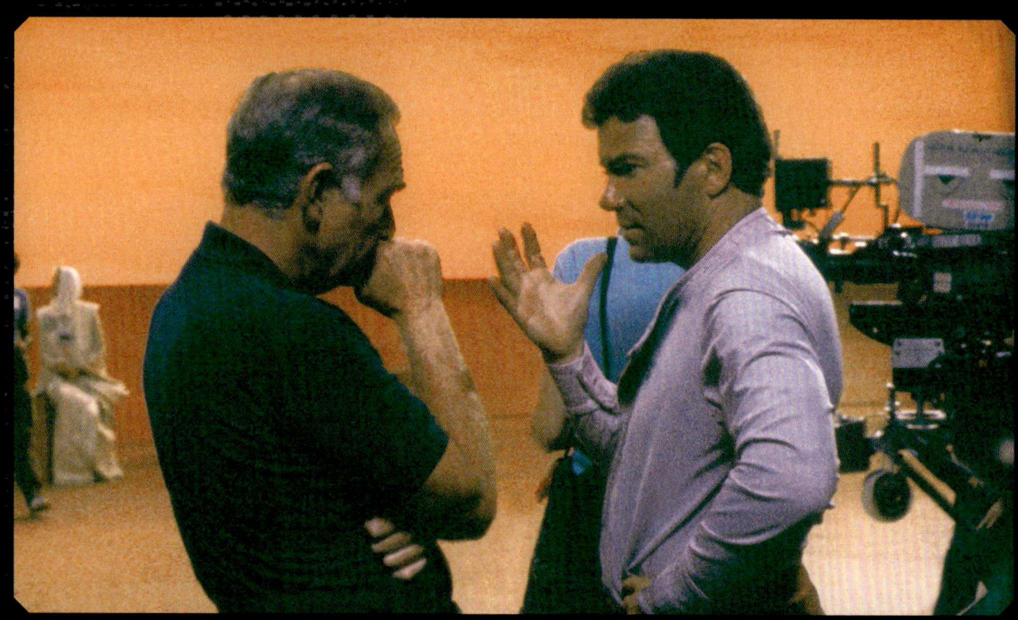

ABOVE: For Bennett, writing scripts for movies was a new experience. He shared, "One of the major frustrations of writing for television is that you can't mess with characters; you can't kill your stars, because they have to be there next week. After all those years of being constrained by the de facto rules of television, I guess I was like a kid in a candy store."[6]

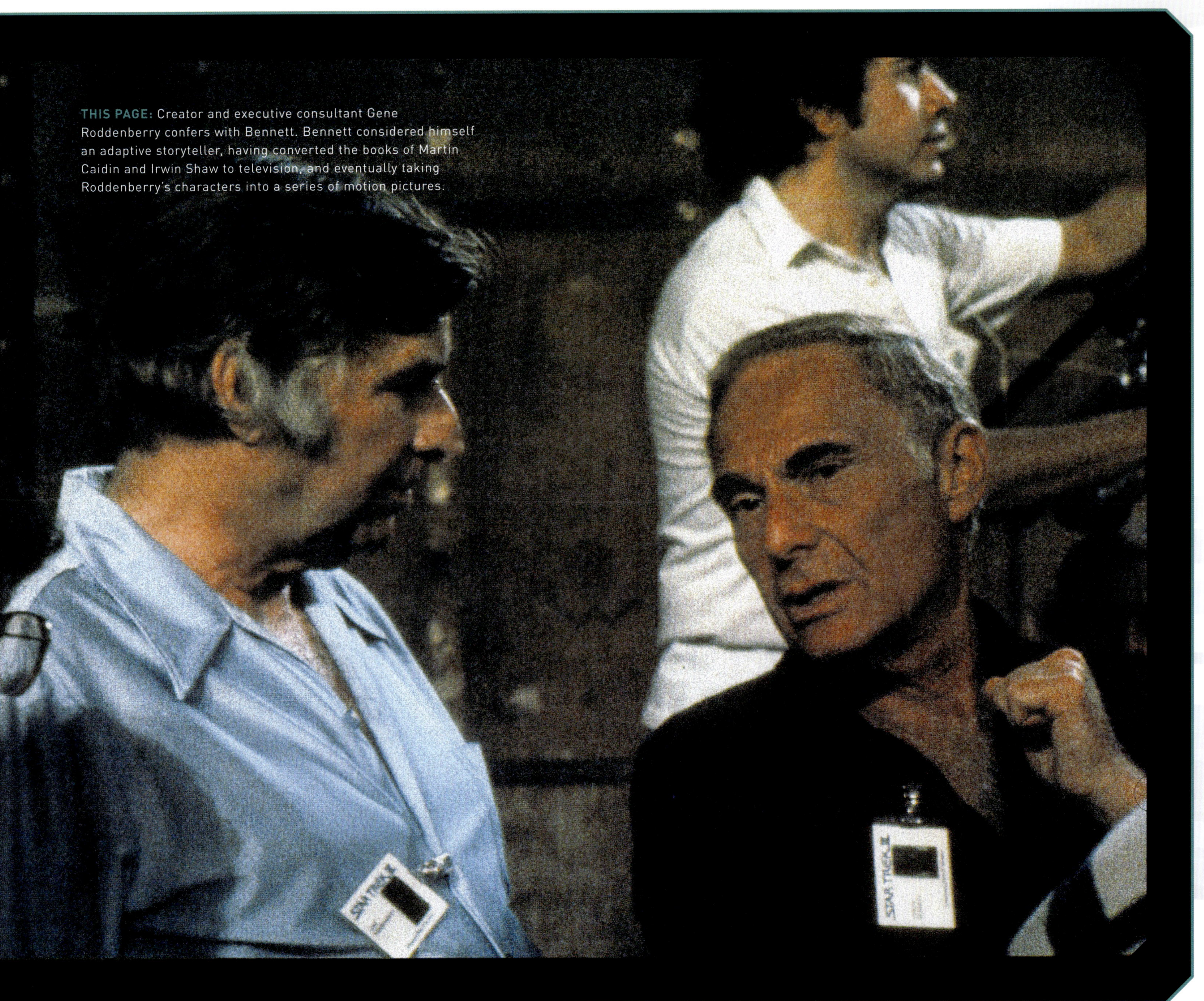

THIS PAGE: Creator and executive consultant Gene Roddenberry confers with Bennett. Bennett considered himself an adaptive storyteller, having converted the books of Martin Caidin and Irwin Shaw to television, and eventually taking Roddenberry's characters into a series of motion pictures.

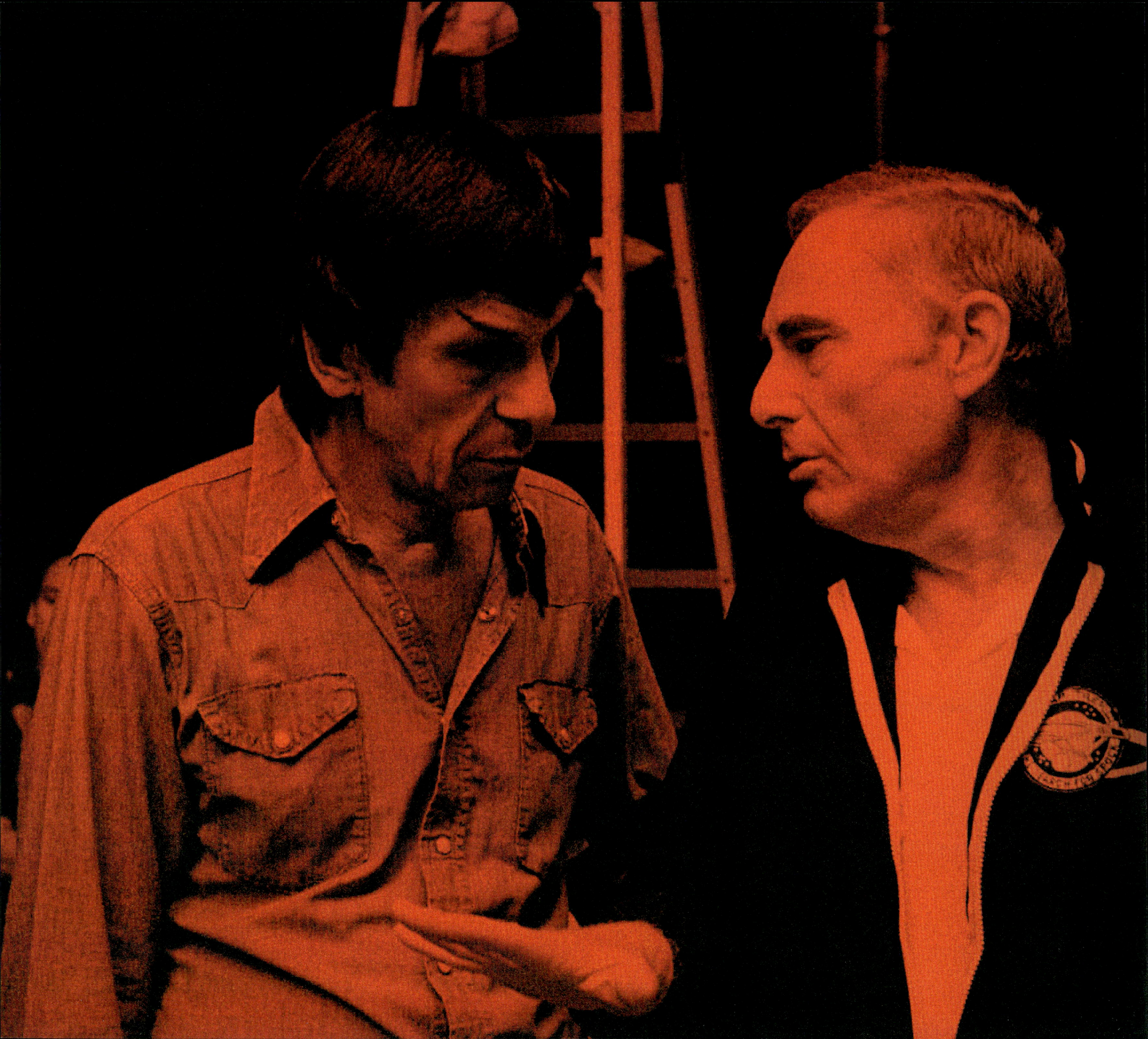

STAR TREK III: RETURN TO GENESIS

On September 16, 1982, Bennett submitted a twenty-page outline that begins on Genesis, with Spock's casket, the Mark IV photon torpedo casing, last seen in *Star Trek II*. As the camera pans to the heavens, then to space, a Romulan Bird-of-Prey decloaks. A spy vessel, the Bird-of-Prey is more advanced than the ones from the original television series. Bennett wrote that its Commander is "a handsome, swarthy man with a dignity reminiscent of the 20th Century actor Omar Sharif." The Romulans beam down to the surface of Genesis to discover nearly unlimited deposits of raw dilithium energy sources on the newly formed planet. In many subsequent drafts, dilithium was the catalyst for the antagonist's actions. The Romulans make another discovery: Spock's sarcophagus. And it is startlingly empty.

The outline then shifts to the *U.S.S. Enterprise* on its way home. While Kirk shares much of the same exposition as he does in the final film's version of his Admiral's Log, there are important differences. David Marcus is not exploring Genesis. Rather, he is back with his mother Carol Marcus on Regula I and is not featured otherwise. With everyone reeling from the loss of Spock, Hikaru Sulu suggests that Kirk rests a while. Kirk is surprised to find Saavik in his quarters, and he jokes that there is likely some command regulation applying to this situation, a humorous comment that harkens back to Saavik's fascination with quoting Starfleet rules. She is nervous, a condition blamed on her half-Romulan nature. Saavik reveals to Kirk that she has seen Spock and that he is alive. Montgomery Scott interrupts with an ominous request that Kirk go to sickbay and to "hurry" – a mirror echo of *Star Trek II* when Dr. Leonard McCoy tells Kirk that he "better hurry" to the dying Spock in engineering.

When Kirk arrives in sickbay, McCoy is "drunk as a skunk.' McCoy blames himself for not saving Spock and begs Kirk to bring him to Vulcan. McCoy "is haunted by a memory he can't reach – something Spock told him that he cannot remember." A version of this scene, minus the inebriation, will be part of the final film. After Kirk leaves, McCoy tries to sober up, splashing water on his face. He sees Spock in the mirror, but when he spins around, Spock is gone. In the film, there is a line where Kirk says to Chekov, "This entire crew seems on the edge of obsessive behavior concerning Mister Spock," despite the audience not really seeing any of that in the movie yet. The line is a relic from this earlier version of the story where the crew was seeing apparitions of Spock.

BELOW: Several photos from set. Far right is from October 1983: A family portrait featuring artists from both Paramount and Industrial Light & Magic (ILM), including Eugene Roddenberry. Set photographer John Shannon captured the making of the film through hundreds of images.

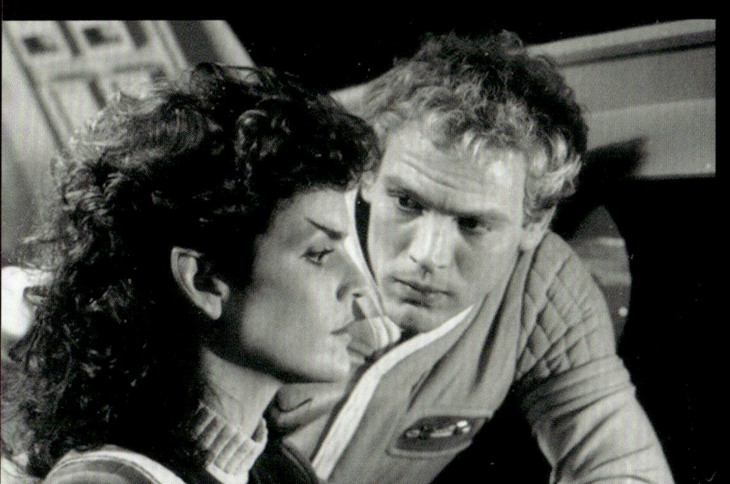

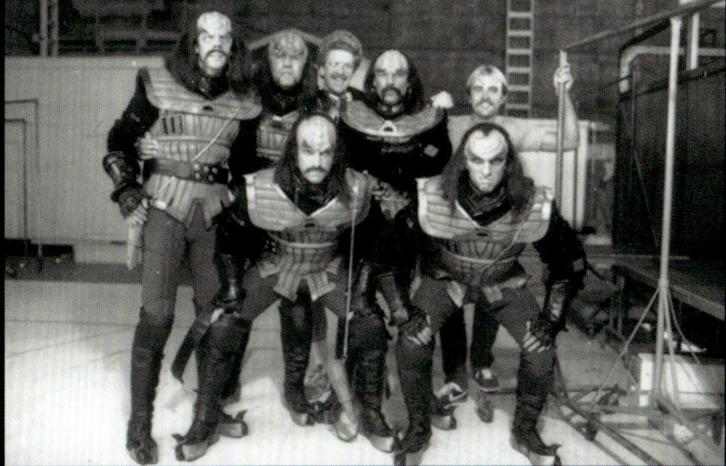

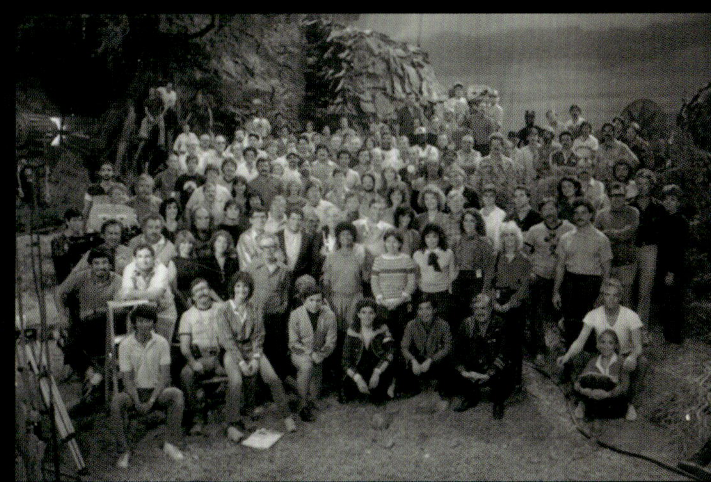

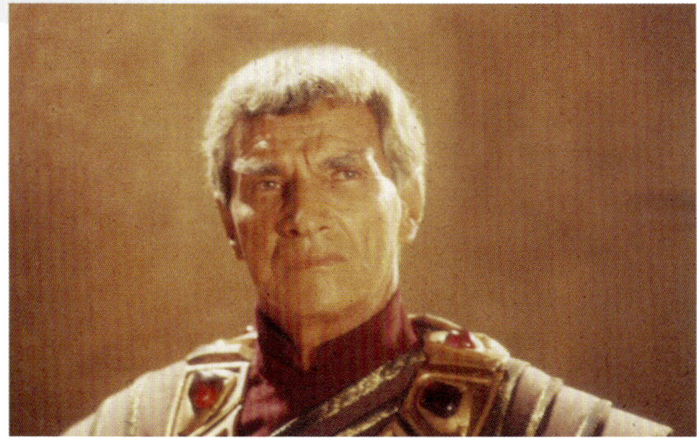

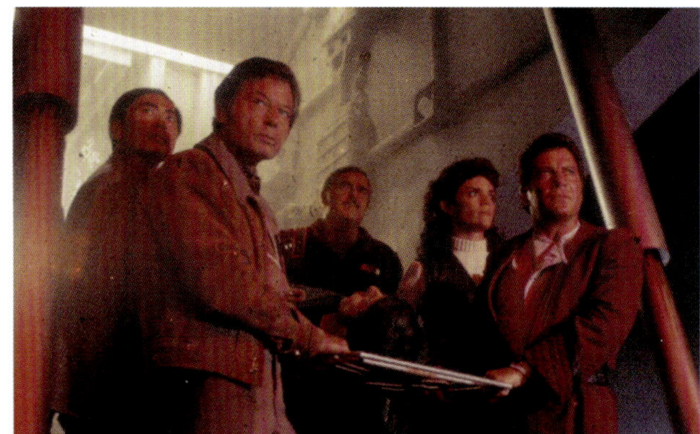

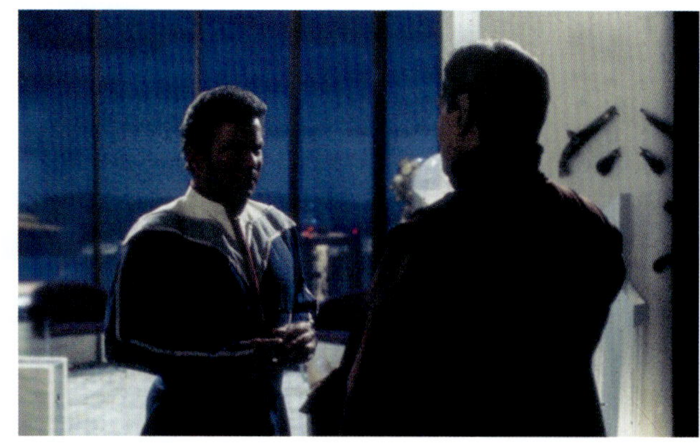

Kirk asks Starfleet for permission to go to Vulcan but is rebuffed. Worried about McCoy, Kirk orders the *Enterprise* to Vulcan anyway. Kirk, McCoy, and Saavik beam down and, upon their arrival, are met by hostile Vulcans armed with lirpas, first seen in the second season episode 'Amok Time.' Help arrives in the form of Prime Minister Sarek who brings with him Vulcan Regulars. Sarek's first words are not reassuring as he tells Kirk, "This is all your doing." It is explained that Genesis, with its Armageddon possibilities, and the death of Spock, have caused young Vulcans to question logic and the alliance with the Federation. Sarek is trying to maintain the peace, but without much success. The scene that follows does not reference the katra, and it hints that perhaps there is an immortality to Vulcans of which Kirk is unaware. Sarek chastises Kirk, "What makes you think he was 'in death'? How dare you presume, with your primitive science, to understand Vulcan physiology and the Vulcan ways!" Kirk promises to find Spock and return him to Vulcan, but first he must get his crew to Earth. In this version, it is McCoy, not Nyota Uhura, who stays on Vulcan, believing there is important medical information for him to learn that could help.

On Earth, Kirk is read the proverbial riot act by the Starfleet Commander and is told that Genesis has become an intergalactic crisis, with Romulan and Klingon ambassadors demanding parity. As Kirk explains himself, he sees Spock sitting in the Commander's office. Kirk says, "Thank God! Now you'll understand...See him there!" But only Kirk can see Spock and the Commander orders Kirk to rest in his quarters.

In his San Francisco apartment, Kirk again sees Spock. He says, "Why are you doing this to me? This is one hell of a mess you've got us in, and the least you could do is talk to me." The image of Spock dissipates as Sulu arrives. He shares with Kirk that the rest of the crew have been reassigned.

THIS PAGE: The character of Sarek was always an essential part of Bennett's story, from his earliest drafts to final script.

BELOW RIGHT: The Vulcan guards that will be featured in the film have their origins as Prime Minister Sarek's Vulcan Regulars from the September 16, 1982 outline.

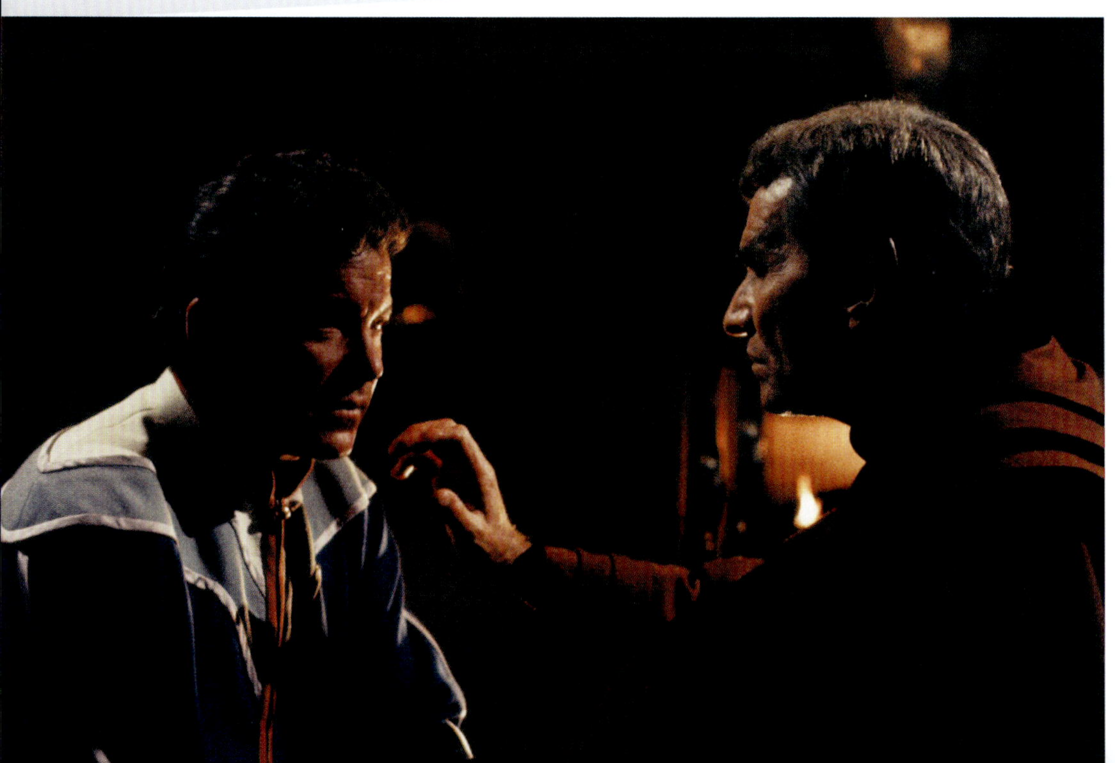

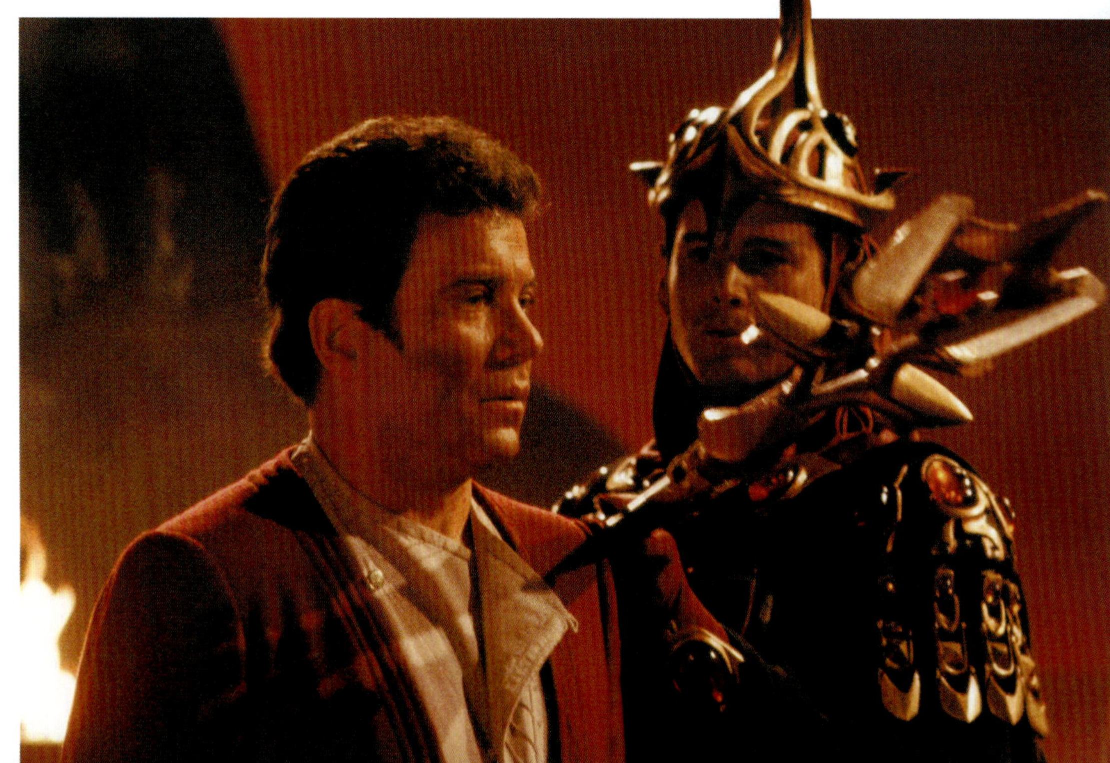

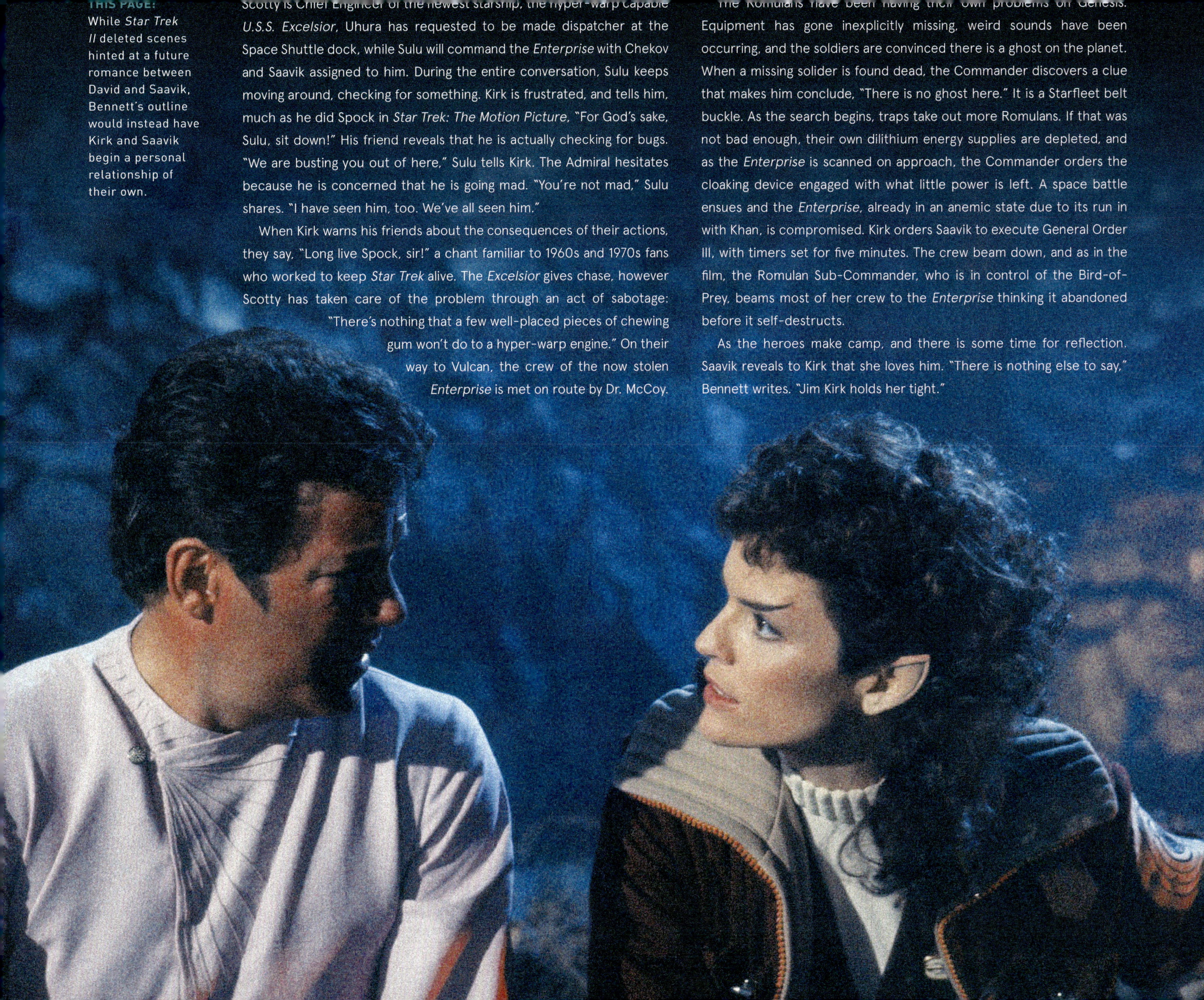

THIS PAGE: While *Star Trek II* deleted scenes hinted at a future romance between David and Saavik, Bennett's outline would instead have Kirk and Saavik begin a personal relationship of their own.

Scotty is Chief Engineer of the newest starship, the hyper-warp capable *U.S.S. Excelsior*, Uhura has requested to be made dispatcher at the Space Shuttle dock, while Sulu will command the *Enterprise* with Chekov and Saavik assigned to him. During the entire conversation, Sulu keeps moving around, checking for something. Kirk is frustrated, and tells him, much as he did Spock in *Star Trek: The Motion Picture*, "For God's sake, Sulu, sit down!" His friend reveals that he is actually checking for bugs. "We are busting you out of here," Sulu tells Kirk. The Admiral hesitates because he is concerned that he is going mad. "You're not mad," Sulu shares. "I have seen him, too. We've all seen him."

When Kirk warns his friends about the consequences of their actions, they say, "Long live Spock, sir!" a chant familiar to 1960s and 1970s fans who worked to keep *Star Trek* alive. The *Excelsior* gives chase, however Scotty has taken care of the problem through an act of sabotage: "There's nothing that a few well-placed pieces of chewing gum won't do to a hyper-warp engine." On their way to Vulcan, the crew of the now stolen *Enterprise* is met on route by Dr. McCoy.

The Romulans have been having their own problems on Genesis. Equipment has gone inexplicitly missing, weird sounds have been occurring, and the soldiers are convinced there is a ghost on the planet. When a missing solider is found dead, the Commander discovers a clue that makes him conclude, "There is no ghost here." It is a Starfleet belt buckle. As the search begins, traps take out more Romulans. If that was not bad enough, their own dilithium energy supplies are depleted, and as the *Enterprise* is scanned on approach, the Commander orders the cloaking device engaged with what little power is left. A space battle ensues and the *Enterprise*, already in an anemic state due to its run in with Khan, is compromised. Kirk orders Saavik to execute General Order III, with timers set for five minutes. The crew beam down, and as in the film, the Romulan Sub-Commander, who is in control of the Bird-of-Prey, beams most of her crew to the *Enterprise* thinking it abandoned before it self-destructs.

As the heroes make camp, and there is some time for reflection, Saavik reveals to Kirk that she loves him. "There is nothing else to say," Bennett writes. "Jim Kirk holds her tight."

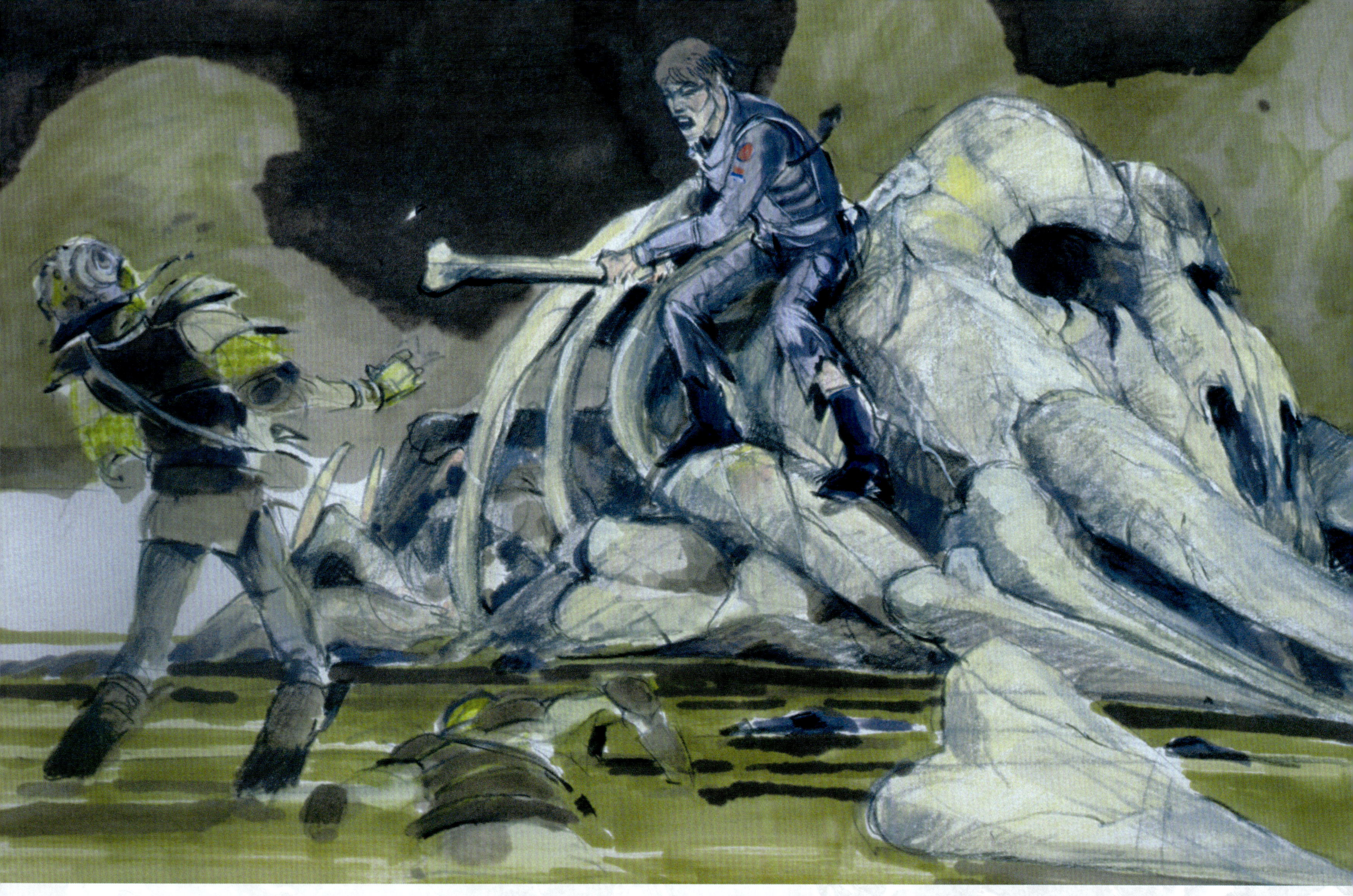

The next morning, the planet has started to rumble and signs of decay are increasing. As Kirk and McCoy reconnoiter, they discover the Romulan dilithium mining operation as the rest of the *Enterprise* officers are taken prisoner. The Romulan Commander and Kirk meet to discuss terms, and it is revealed the Romulans want to create unlimited dilithium resources. Kirk responds "philosophically, and historically...Once, he says, it was gold. Again, it was spices. Then it was oil. Why do civilizations destroy themselves over resources which should be shared?" The Romulan Commander will have none of it, telling Kirk that he wants the secret of how such a planet was formed. He will give Kirk one more day to think about it and leaves, knowing he holds the cards since he has Kirk's crew as captives.

Back at the camp, Saavik is freed by an unseen helper. She releases the others and brings them to a part of the forest where she reveals that her helper was Spock. As they joyously run to him, he lets out an animal roar. Bennett writes, "Spock is bearded, ragged, and half

ABOVE: ILM visual effects art director Nilo Rodis-Jamero, then credited as Nilo Rodis, created this visualization of Spock in his primeval mental state based on Bennett's early ideas.

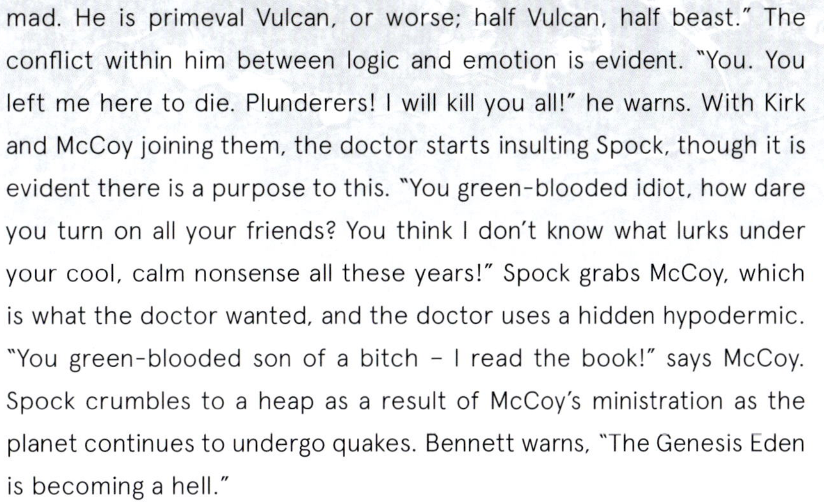

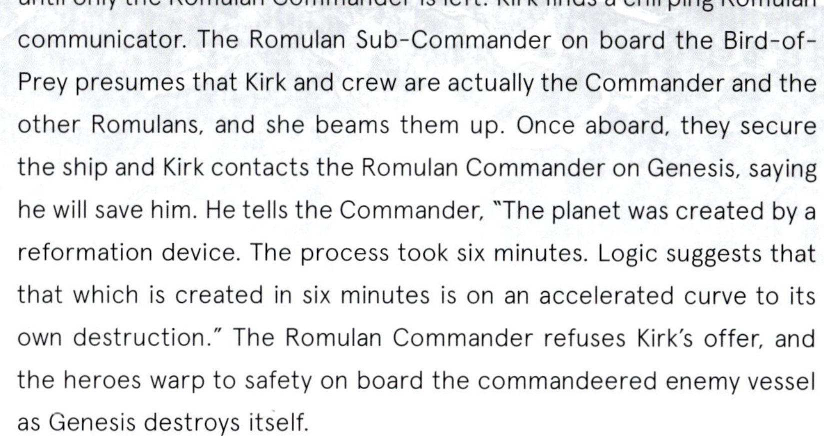

mad. He is primeval Vulcan, or worse; half Vulcan, half beast." The conflict within him between logic and emotion is evident. "You. You left me here to die. Plunderers! I will kill you all!" he warns. With Kirk and McCoy joining them, the doctor starts insulting Spock, though it is evident there is a purpose to this. "You green-blooded idiot, how dare you turn on all your friends? You think I don't know what lurks under your cool, calm nonsense all these years!" Spock grabs McCoy, which is what the doctor wanted, and the doctor uses a hidden hypodermic. "You green-blooded son of a bitch – I read the book!" says McCoy. Spock crumbles to a heap as a result of McCoy's ministration as the planet continues to undergo quakes. Bennett warns, "The Genesis Eden is becoming a hell."

Romulan soldiers succumb to the dangers of the dying planet until only the Romulan Commander is left. Kirk finds a chirping Romulan communicator. The Romulan Sub-Commander on board the Bird-of-Prey presumes that Kirk and crew are actually the Commander and the other Romulans, and she beams them up. Once aboard, they secure the ship and Kirk contacts the Romulan Commander on Genesis, saying he will save him. He tells the Commander, "The planet was created by a reformation device. The process took six minutes. Logic suggests that that which is created in six minutes is on an accelerated curve to its own destruction." The Romulan Commander refuses Kirk's offer, and the heroes warp to safety on board the commandeered enemy vessel as Genesis destroys itself.

In a reversal of the scene from *Star Trek II*, Kirk and Saavik are in the turbo-lift. Kirk explains to Saavik that their romance on the planet was only the result of rules that had changed. But now the rules and regulations were back in effect. Saavik tells Kirk,

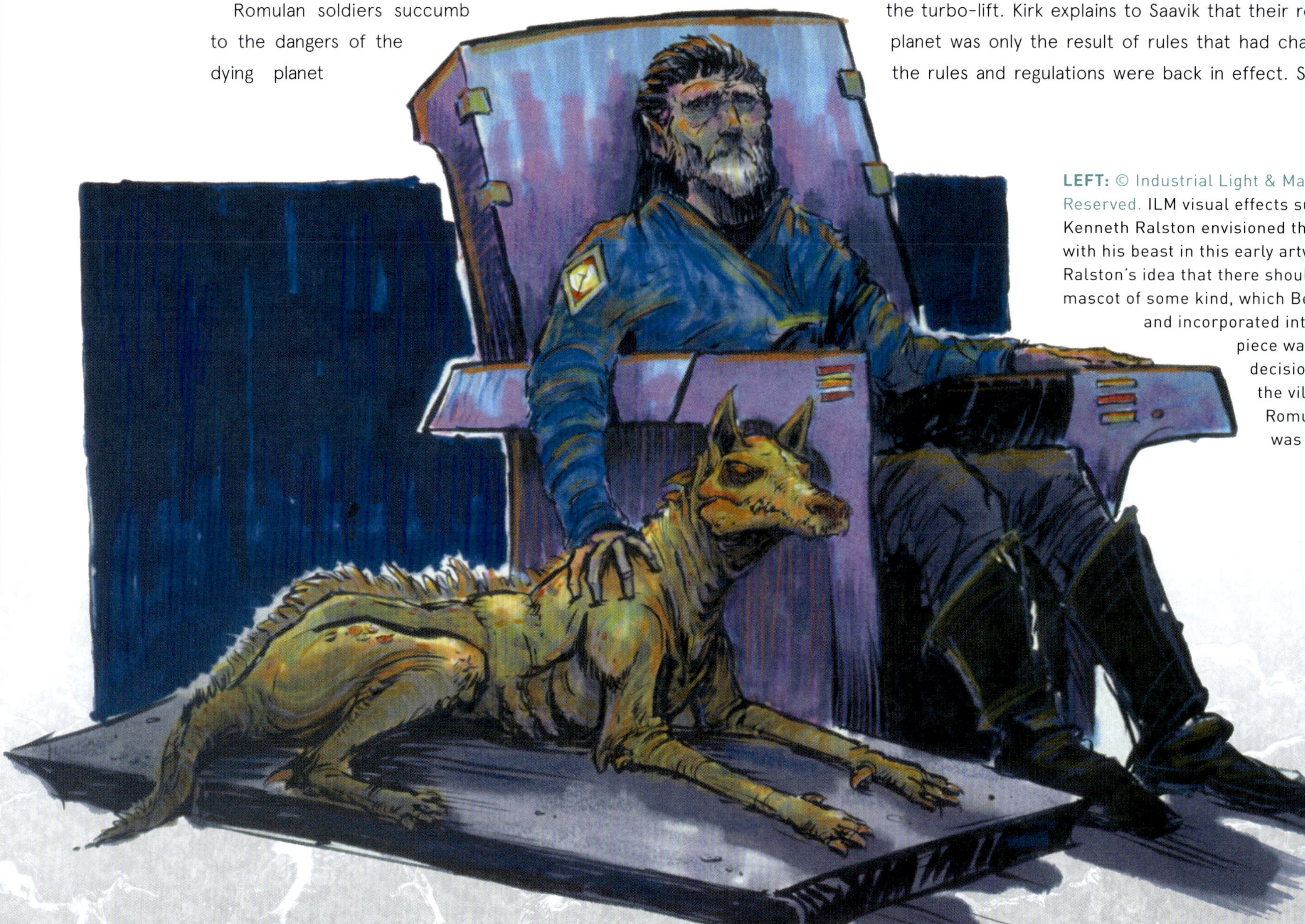

LEFT: © Industrial Light & Magic. All Rights Reserved. ILM visual effects supervisor Kenneth Ralston envisioned the antagonist with his beast in this early artwork. It was Ralston's idea that there should be a pet or mascot of some kind, which Bennett approved and incorporated into the story. This piece was done while the decision of whether the villains should be Romulans or Klingons was in flux.

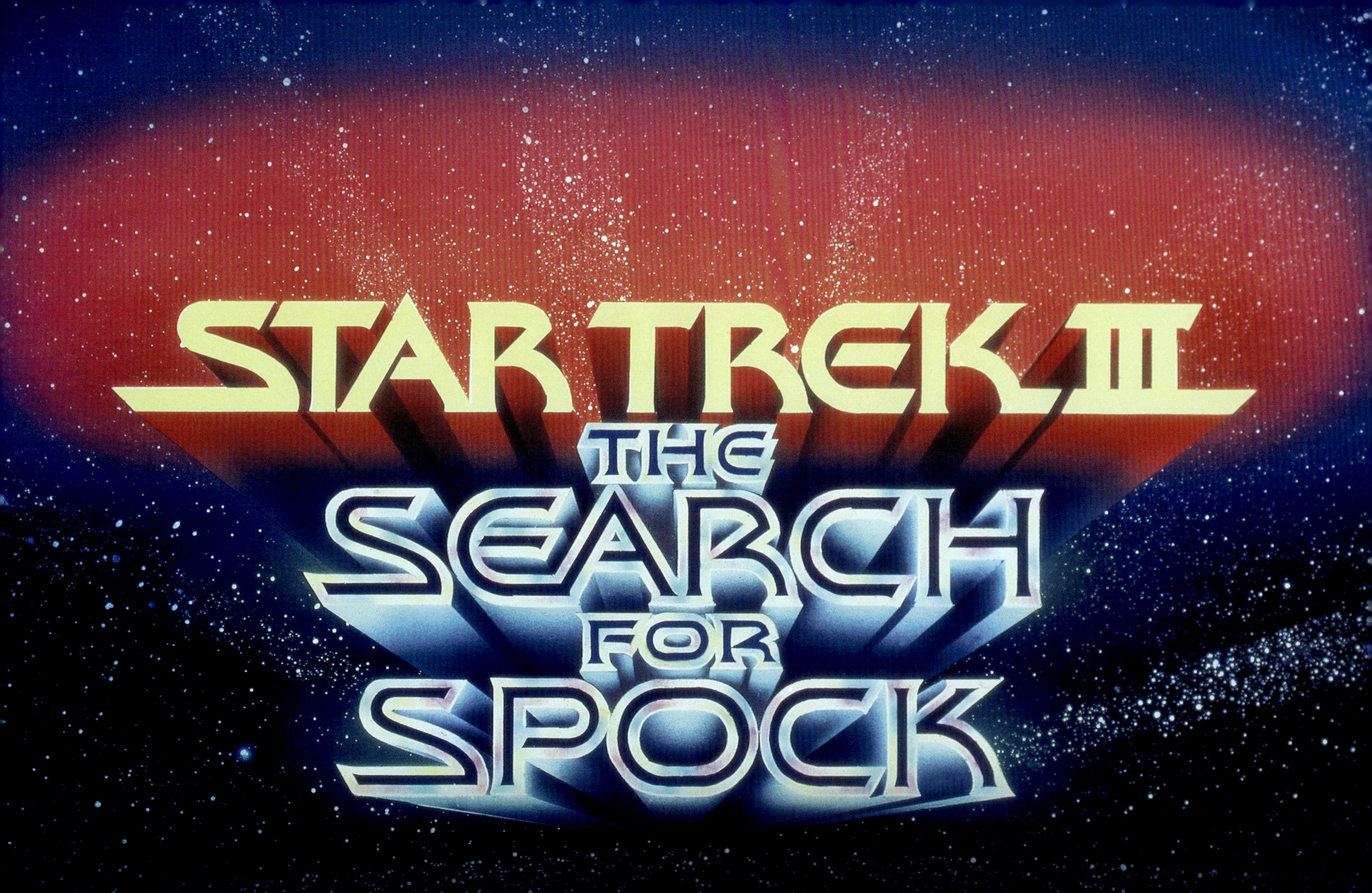

THIS PAGE: An early logo design that utilizes the *Star Trek II: The Wrath of Khan* graphic style. A variation, using different colors, would appear at the end of the *Star Trek III* trailer.

"Self-expression has never been one of your problems, Admiral" and that while she always plays by the rules, Kirk always bent them. Kirk smiles and shrugs in agreement, hinting the romance will continue. In the Romulan sickbay, Spock is now restored thanks to the medicine McCoy had administered on the planet which he learned about consulting books on Vulcan. Spock warns Kirk that he will have to pay a price for what he did to rescue him. Kirk agrees, saying he hopes they demote him to Captain and give him a new mission. "In a new *Enterprise*," adds Spock. Spock thanks Jim for the sacrifices he made to save him, a reflection of the fan poem's theme that first inspired Bennett.

The original outline didn't feature Spock's transformation from youth to adult, there was no katra, and the villains were Romulans instead of Klingons. But it did have many of the same big ideas: McCoy suffering from the mind meld, the stealing and destruction of the *Enterprise*, an unstable planet, the return of a classic TV series alien culture to menace the heroes, and most especially, the camaraderie and loyalty of friends who risk it all to save Spock.

Bennett was wise enough to recognize that the outline needed revision and he would turn to trusted sources for advice. But first, *The Search for Spock* needed a search for its director.

A MOVIE BY ANY OTHER NAME

While *Return to Genesis* was the outline moniker, it was meant as a placeholder title for the film. It was never seriously considered because there were concerns that it was too similar to *Return of the Jedi*. Once Nimoy was considered as director, what started as a joke would transform into the final title. From 1977 until 1982, Nimoy was host of the Alan Landsburg docuseries *In Search Of...*. Bennett explained that *Star Trek III: In Search of Spock* was the title, "for about thirty seconds. We weren't serious, just laughing about it, but Leonard did call his friend, Alan Landsburg."[2] Bennett was speaking hyperbolically because there were documents sent to licensees during December, 1982, with the *In Search of Spock* title. There were concerns about legal problems using *In Search of Spock*, so it was reworked to what Bennett considered a better, stronger *The Search for Spock*. Nimoy also liked the title. He told Dan Scapperotti of *Cinefantastique* right before the film's release that, "The title suggests something. It suggests that there is some question about Spock's condition."[7]

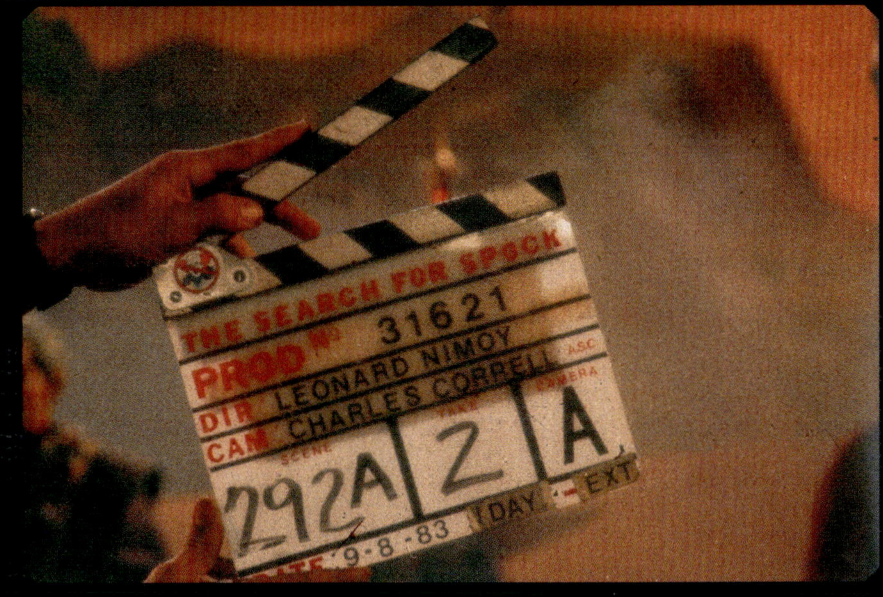

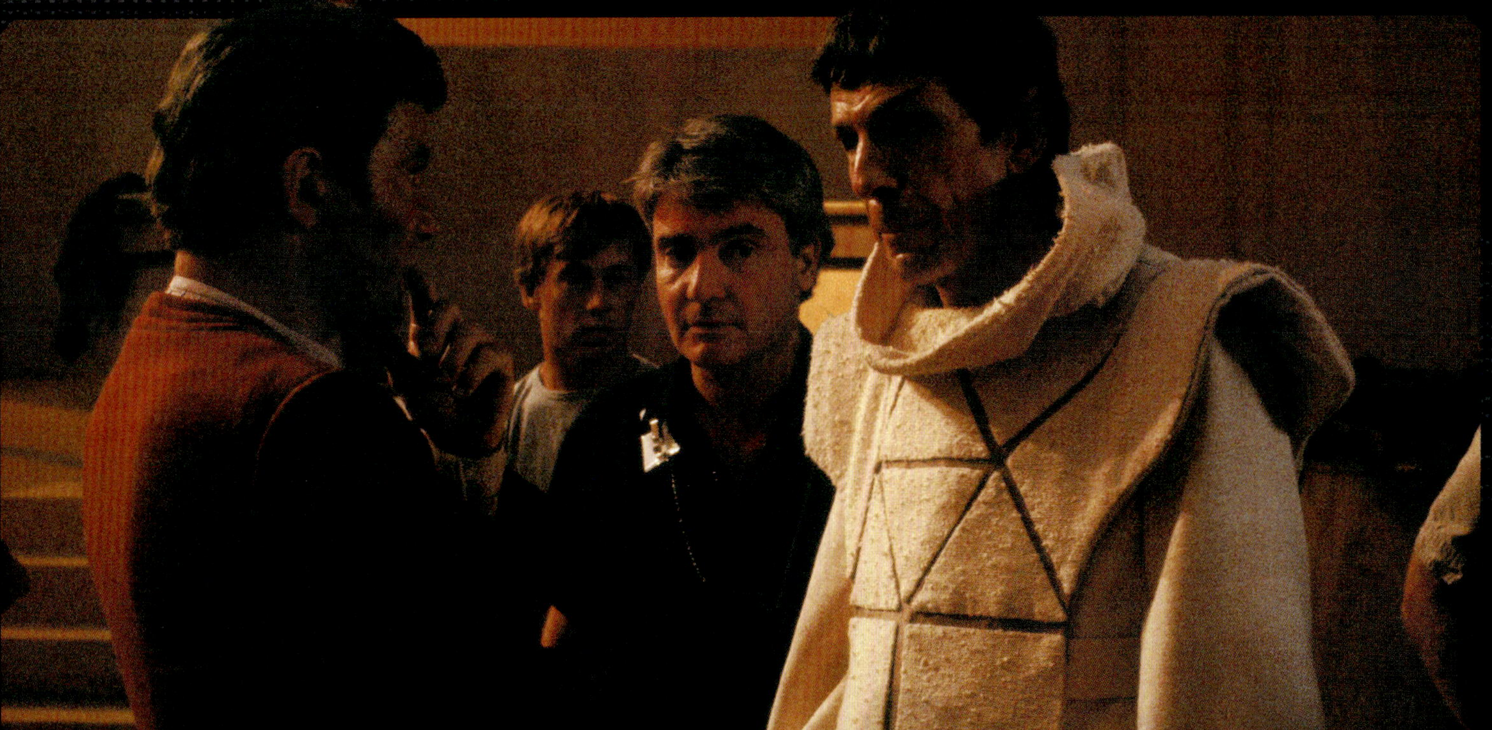

ABOVE: Clapperboards help editors more easily find and catalog various takes of scenes filmed on different days. This clapperboard had a very special date: September 8, 1983, which was the 17th anniversary of the premiere of the original *Star Trek* television series.

LEFT: Acting and directing in the same movie was one of several challenges Nimoy faced. Shatner, cinematographer Charles Correll, and Nimoy discuss Kirk and Spock's reunion scene.

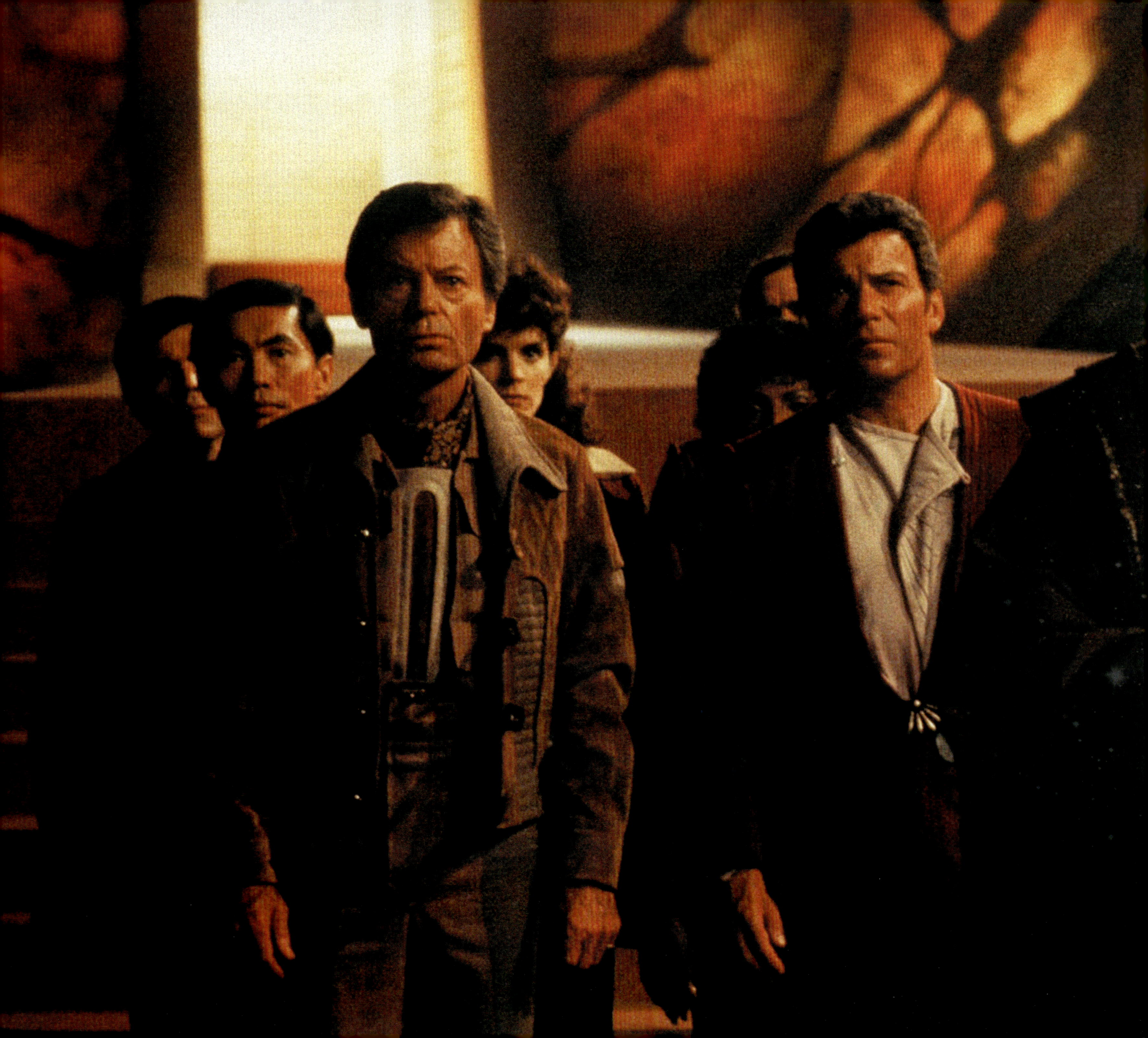

CHAPTER 2

YOU CAME BACK FOR ME

LEONARD NIMOY AS DIRECTOR

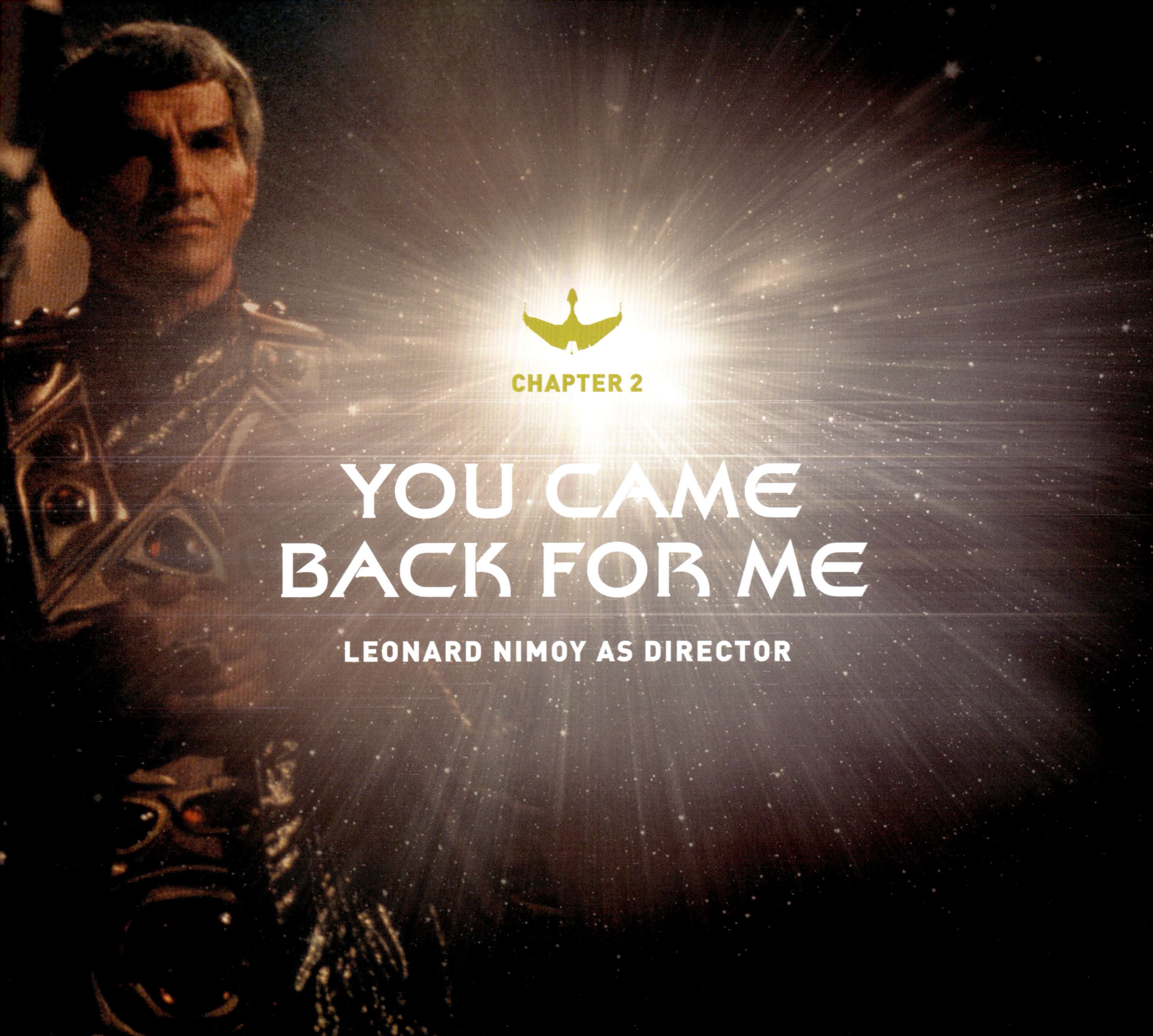

Director Francis Ford Coppola famously believed, "A movie is a little like a question, and when you make it, that's when you get the answer."[1] An essential question for *Star Trek III* was who gets to make it in the first place. As Bennett continued to write, he and executive producer Gary Nardino took on the task of answering that question. The most logical choice for director, however, was intransient. Nicholas Meyer was asked but had no interest in resurrecting Spock. In his autobiography, *The View from the Bridge*, Meyer wrote, "I still felt passionately that Spock ought not to be brought back to life and in any case, bringing dead people back to life was something I didn't know how to do, because, I suppose, I have trouble believing such a thing is possible."[2]

Nimoy had not considered directing the sequel because it had been presumed that Meyer would return. A meeting between Nardino and Nimoy was scheduled for October, 1982. While Bennett's outline had Spock appear, as both apparition and atavist, Nimoy knew going into the meeting that he did not want to contribute only by making a glorified cameo or by getting a play-or-pay contract. "The meeting was really to explore the possibility of my being involved in some way with *Star Trek III*. They wanted to discuss the possibility of Spock making a comeback. There had been no previous discussion or thought given to any other kind of job. It wasn't until we were sitting in the outer office waiting to talk with Gary Nardino that we thought of directing the picture," Nimoy said.[3]

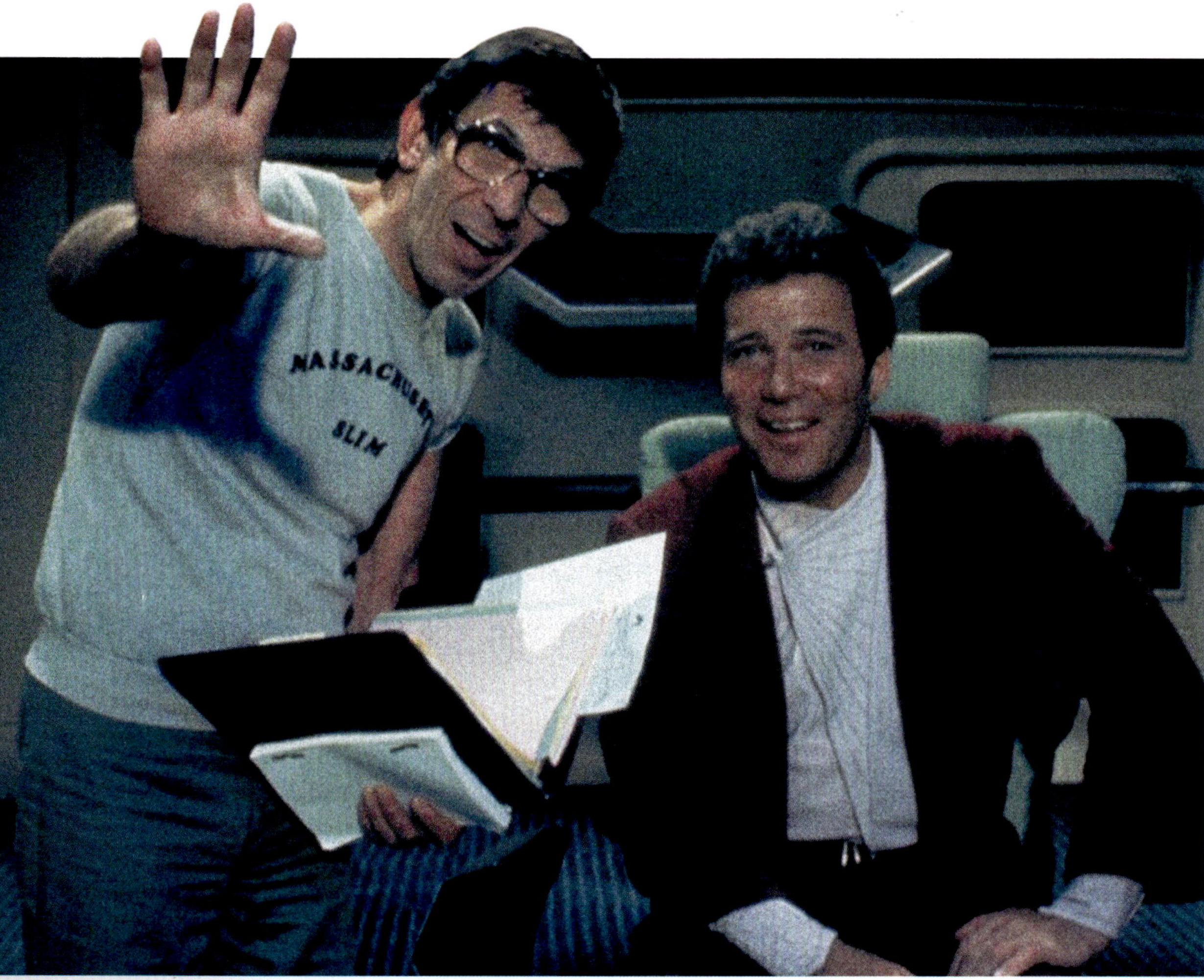

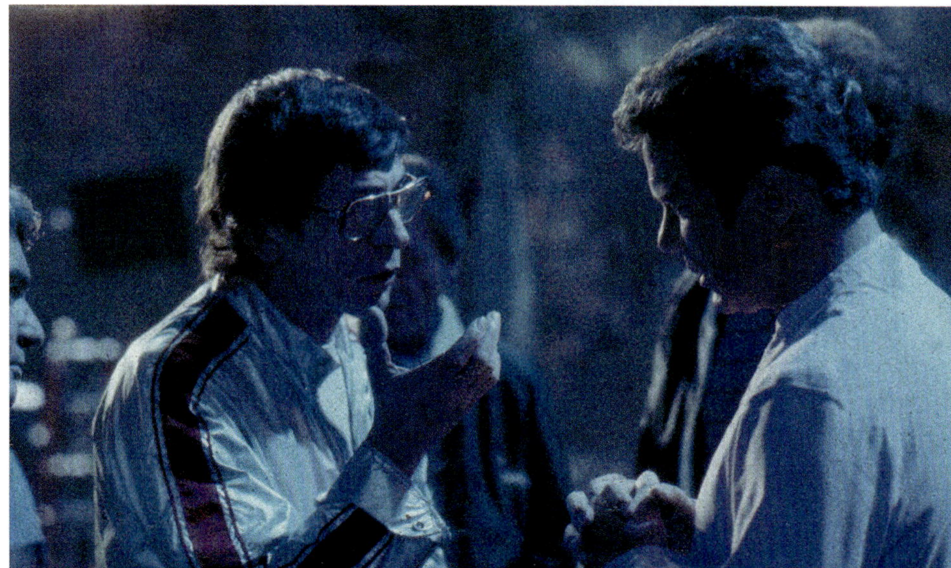

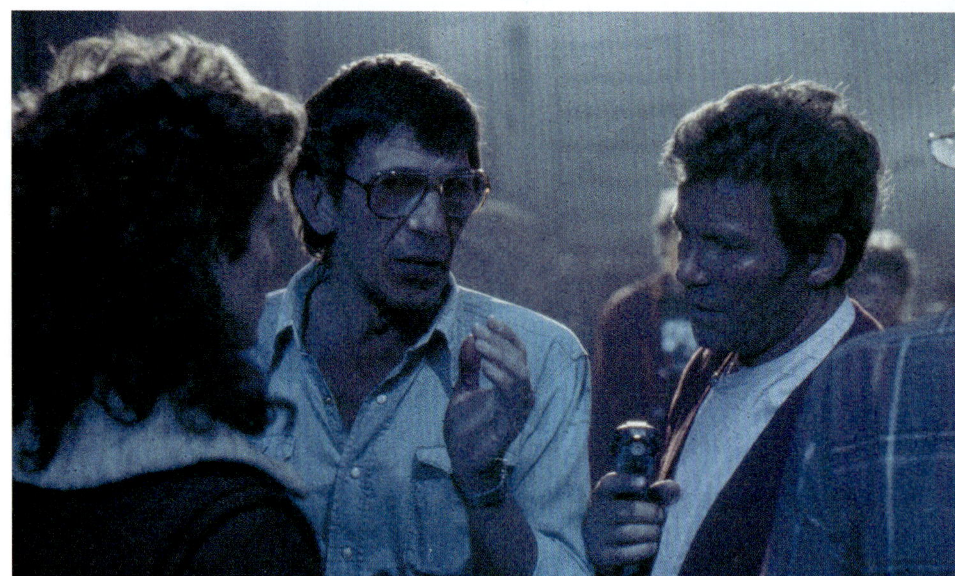

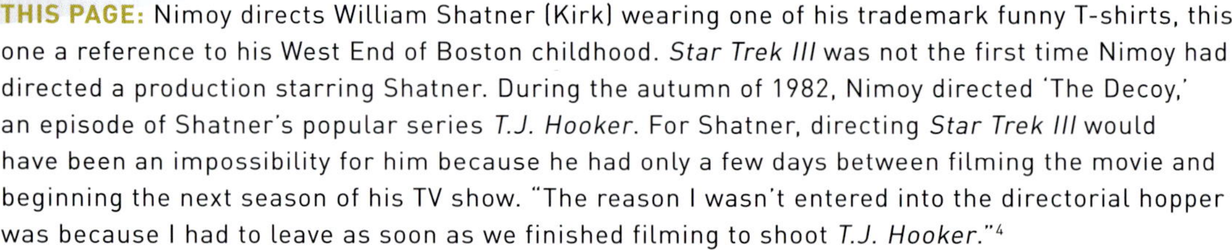

THIS PAGE: Nimoy directs William Shatner (Kirk) wearing one of his trademark funny T-shirts, this one a reference to his West End of Boston childhood. *Star Trek III* was not the first time Nimoy had directed a production starring Shatner. During the autumn of 1982, Nimoy directed 'The Decoy,' an episode of Shatner's popular series *T.J. Hooker*. For Shatner, directing *Star Trek III* would have been an impossibility for him because he had only a few days between filming the movie and beginning the next season of his TV show. "The reason I wasn't entered into the directorial hopper was because I had to leave as soon as we finished filming to shoot *T.J. Hooker*."[4]

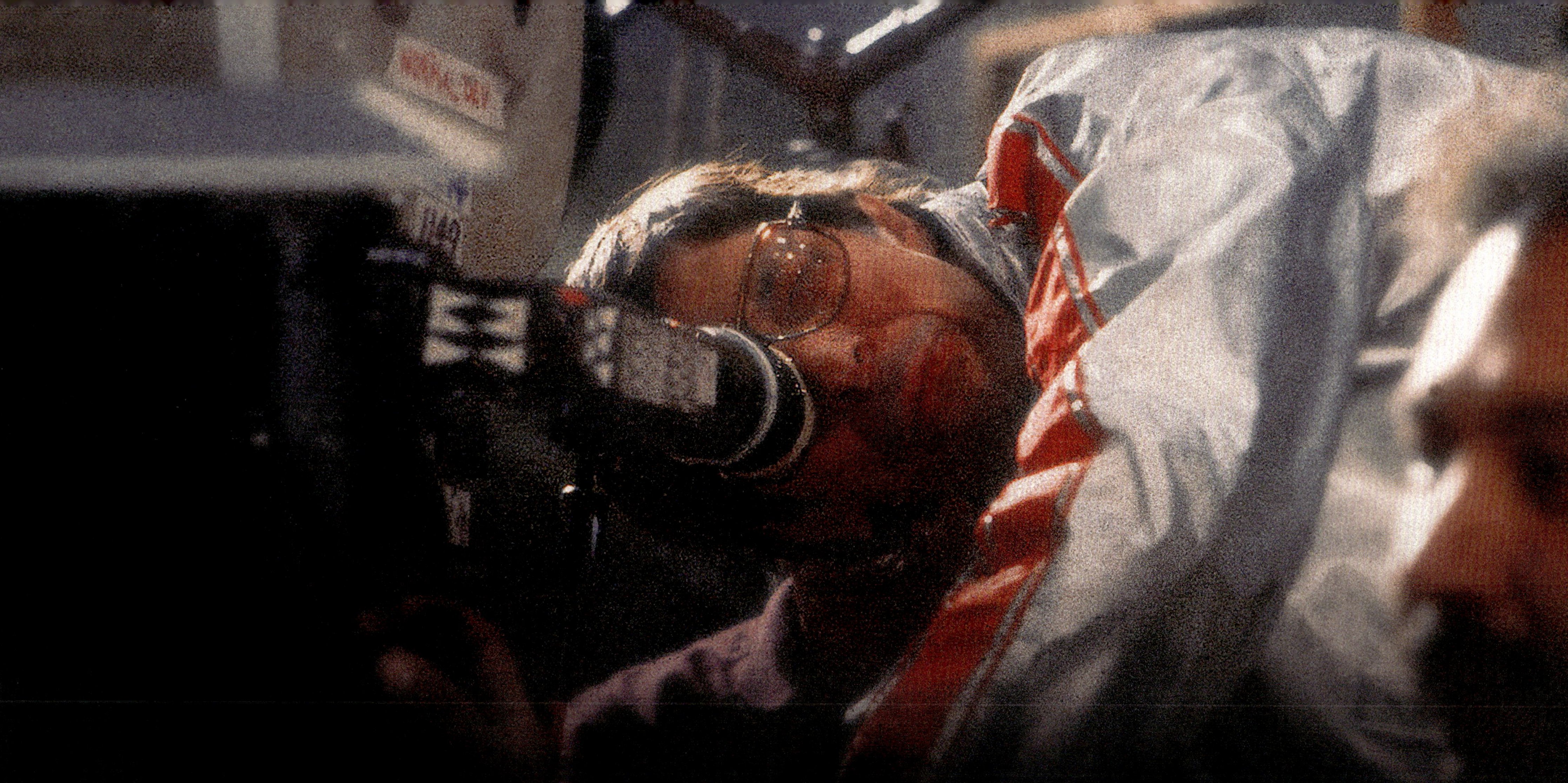

THIS PAGE: Nimoy's lifelong affinity for cameras served him well as a director, allowing him to appreciate how camera movements can help tell a story. He was so passionate about his fine art photography that he seriously considered refocusing his professional career on that during the 1970s.

Others, however, had been privately thinking of Nimoy as a director. During late summer 1982, Bennett had asked Nimoy to direct 'The Triangle,' an episode of a new science fiction show he was producing, *The Powers of Matthew Star*. It became a kind of proving ground and confidence builder for Nimoy. Nardino, too, had been thinking about Nimoy directing, so when the idea was broached during the meeting, there was genuine enthusiasm. Another meeting was set, this time with Paramount president Michael Eisner, who also agreed that Nimoy was a good choice. Nimoy thought that Eisner, "was thinking promotion, he was thinking publicity, great story to tell to the press."[5] Then, nearly six weeks went by with no communication, all the while the clock was ticking with a December, 1983, premiere date looming.

The delay occurred because of concerns brewing among executives about having any actor, let alone the actor playing the popular Spock character, direct an important and expensive film. Further complicating the situation, according to Nimoy, was the mistaken belief that Nimoy disliked playing Spock and that his *Star Trek II* contract stipulated the character's demise. Nimoy told Eisner this simply wasn't true. "I said, 'Michael, the contract is in a file in the building that you're in. Would you go to the trouble of having somebody pull it out of the file, and take a look at it and see if it's in that contract?'. 'No,' he said, 'I take your word for it if it's not in there.' I don't know how this word got out that it was in the contract, because it was not. 'Well, okay, this is a different story.'"[5] Nimoy and Eisner had another meeting, with Nimoy telling Eisner that hiring him solved two problems – the issue of whether he would return to play Spock and the question of who would direct the picture. He had a vision for the film and thought he could do something special with it. Within days, the contract was signed.[6] In January, 1983, Nimoy was officially announced as director with only eleven months until the film's originally planned premiere.

Nimoy's first order of business was an advisory assist to Bennett's scripting. Their relationship mirrored that of Bennett and Meyer, with Bennett explaining, "On *Trek II*, I functioned very much as an editor, helping to rework the script. Strangely enough, on this film, Leonard served that purpose, giving input, telling me, the writer, what worked or didn't work. Gene Roddenberry was intimately involved in the same process."[7]

THE RETURN OF NICHOLAS MEYER

While Meyer did not want to help resurrect Spock, he was more than willing to help his friends when asked. During the delays in negotiation, Nimoy turned to Meyer for counsel. Meyer asked Nimoy, "Are you prepared to let this ship sail without you?" When Nimoy said absolutely, Meyer responded, "Then sit tight; you're gonna direct the movie."[2] Meyer contributed two pages of notes on Bennett's outline when his friend asked for his thoughts. In a September 24, 1982, letter, Meyer wrote that he, "loved the blowing up and loss of the *Enterprise* because the thing I hate most about 'Star Trek' which I suppose I hate most about television is the everything-must-be-where-it-was-at-the-beginning dictum that governs all endings." Meyer did question Bennett about the meaning of the story: "With RETURN TO GENESIS, I am unable to determine beyond its sort of purely entertainment value what it is you are trying to say and talk about." It is a question that Bennett took to heart as he continued various drafts. The move from dilithium as the motivator of Kruge to the story being about the implications of a doomsday weapon is directly the result of Meyer's contribution.

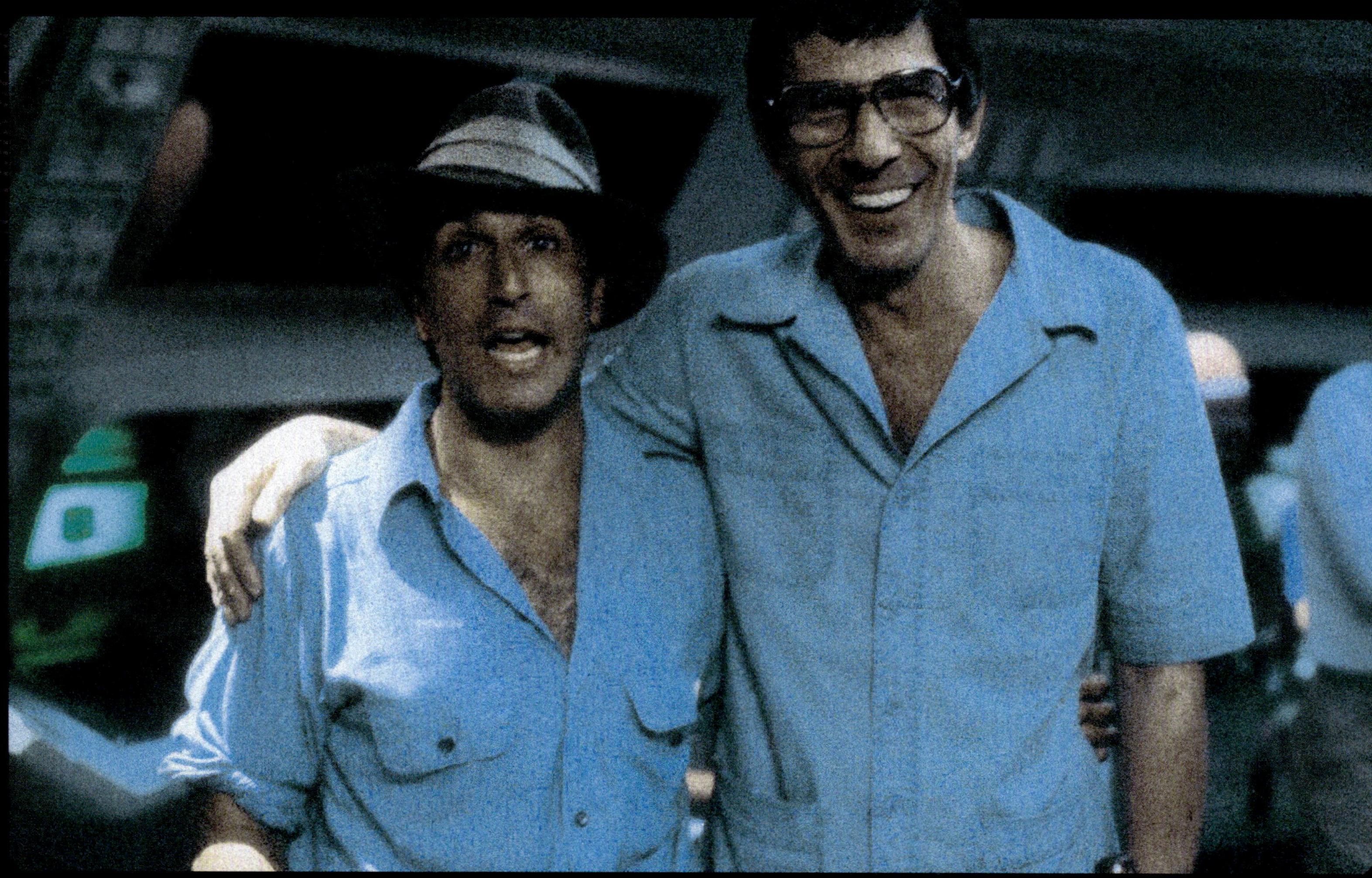

LEFT: Meyer visits Nimoy during the filming of *Star Trek III*.

Bennett began writing the formal script using ideas from his December outline as a guide. Within six weeks, he had written the first draft script, dated March 23, 1983. In transforming *Star Trek III* from outline to script, Bennett began at the end. "I remember totally and vividly that I wrote that last scene first. The scene came out of my mind in a few blurred minutes, like I had written it before. Later, I realized that like all writers I had 'borrowed from the best,' in this case William Gibson. The last scene in *Star Trek III* is the last scene of Gibson's masterpiece, *The Miracle Worker*. It's when Helen Keller finally 'gets it.' With wonder and puzzlement, the deaf, mute, and blind girl says, 'Water,' and her teacher and friend Annie Sullivan confirms, 'Yes!' That's our scene too. Spock says, 'Your name is Jim.' And Kirk says with joy, 'Yes. Spock. Yes.'"[8]

Bennett planned to have the movie start with the words, "It was Shakespeare, a Sixteenth Century Earth poet, who observed: 'What is past...is prologue,'" followed by sequences from *Star Trek II* that 'will be treated in some unique visual way' using some kind of half color, filtration, and possible aspect ratio reduction to suggest 'the recent past as seen through the glass of memory.' Bennett makes commentaries during the script, some of which are humorous, others of which demonstrate he never really removed his producer's hat while writing. One example is his line, "The writer suggests to the producer and director that no acting credit be given for the role of SPOCK until the END CREDITS."

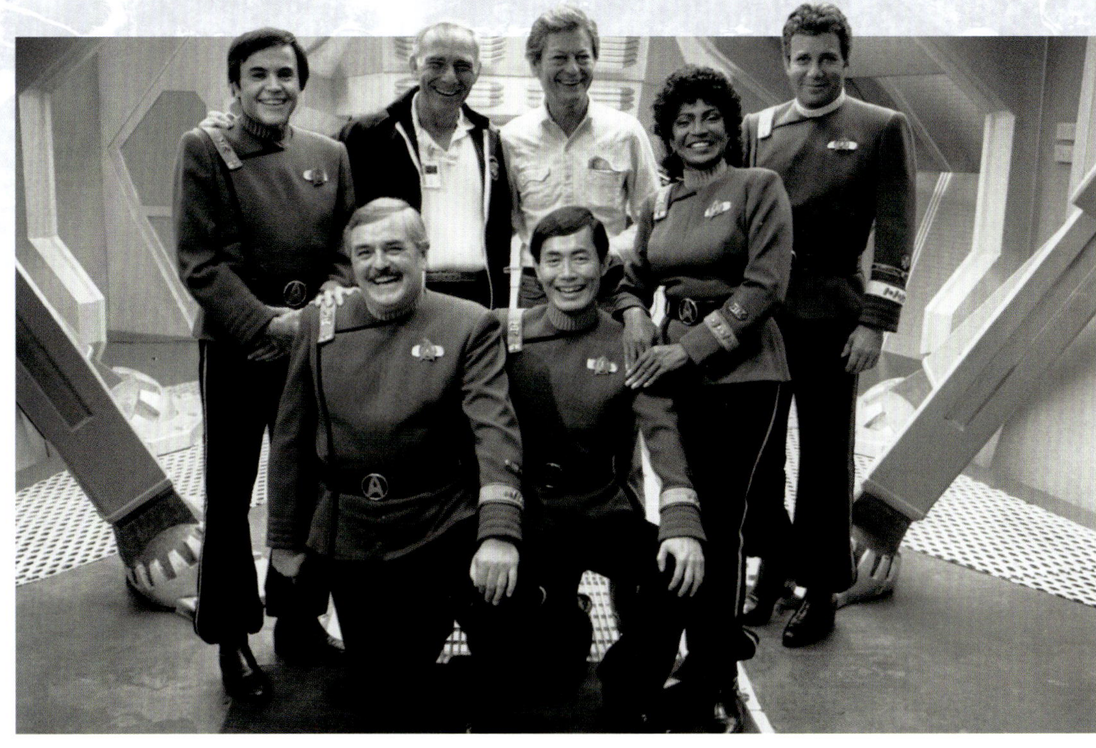

ABOVE: Thinking of his challenge of being a first-time feature film director, Nimoy said of his co-stars, "I had the good fortune of starting in movies with a cast that knew their characters."[3] This picture was taken during a break filming the scene when Admiral Morrow inspects the *Enterprise*. Returning to their roles are actors Walter Koenig (Chekov), James Doohan (Scotty), Leonard Nimoy, not pictured (Spock; director), George Takei (Sulu), DeForest Kelley (McCoy), Nichelle Nichols (Uhura), and William Shatner (Kirk).

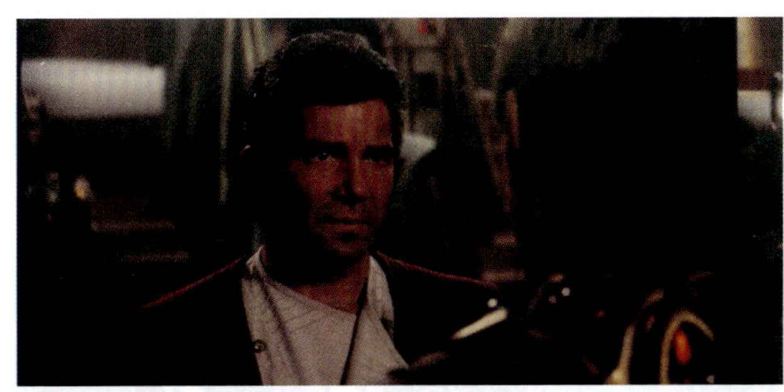

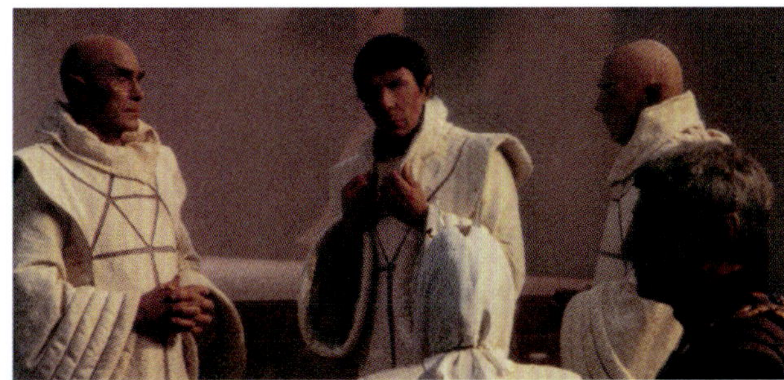

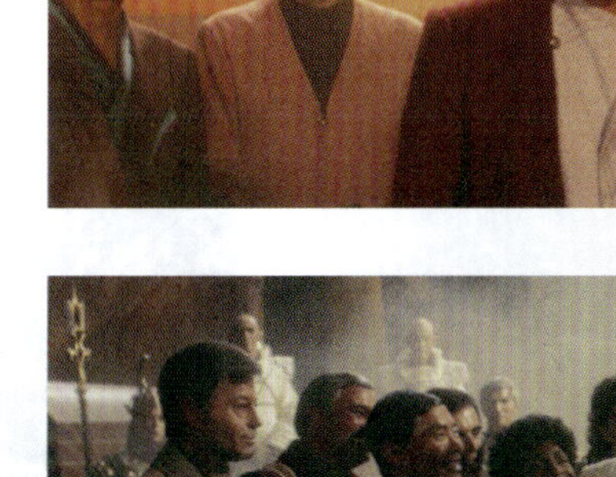

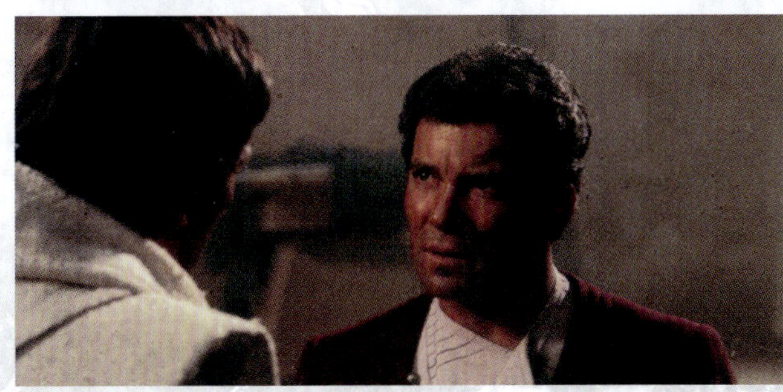

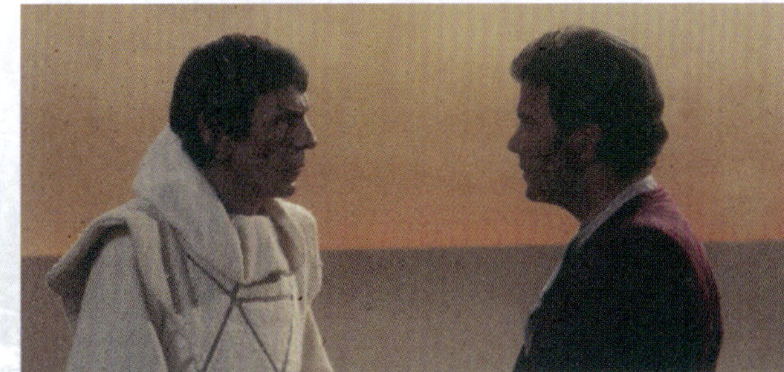

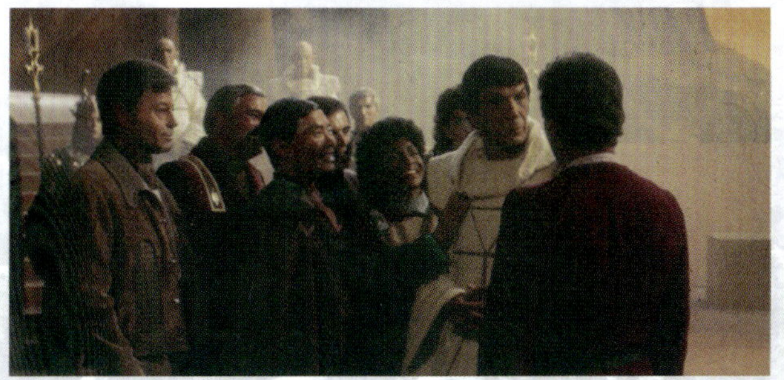

ABOVE: Although there are significant differences in the various versions of Bennett's scripts, one constant can be found in every story: the love and loyalty shared by the crew of the *Enterprise* for each other.

FLIGHT RECORDER VISUAL:

LEONARD NIMOY, DIRECTOR

Star Trek III would be Leonard Nimoy's first motion picture as director, but it was not his first time directing. He brought with him many experiences from which to draw upon. His relationship with using a camera goes back to age thirteen while in Boston, when his grandfather, Samuel Spinner, gave him his first Kodak Bellows Autographic. Of course, he had been an actor for more than forty years, earning an Emmy nomination for Spock each year of the original series, and a fourth nomination for his role as Morris Meyerson in the Harve Bennett produced *A Woman Called Golda*. He had begun directing while stationed at Fort McPherson during his 1950s Army service, and was in the MGM director's training program during the 1960s. Once he joined the Director's Guild of America in the early 1970s, Nimoy directed TV, including Rod Serling's *Night Gallery* and *T.J. Hooker*. His one-man play, *Vincent: The Story of a Hero*, gave Nimoy experience acting and directing in the same production. Nimoy felt ready to take on the challenge of directing a feature: "I became convinced that I could direct a *Star Trek* movie which would make sense. I believe I could take *Star Trek* a step further. I could make a contribution which no other director could. And after 18 years, I felt it was time I made the move. Otherwise, I would be avoiding what I should be doing."[7]

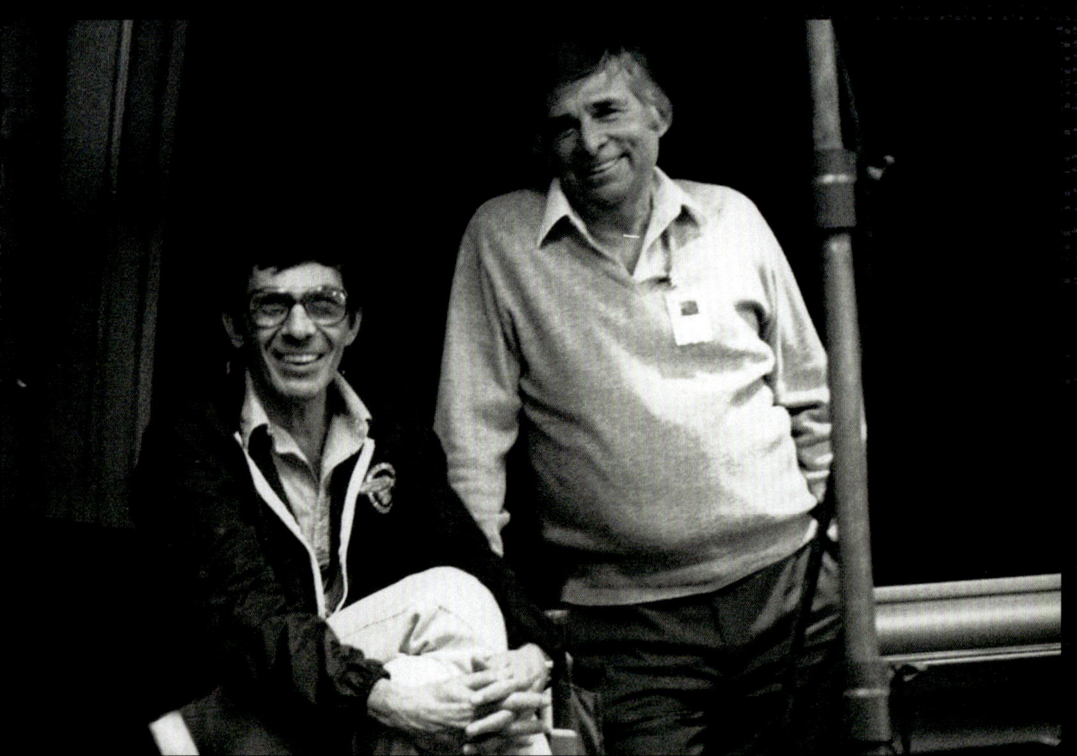

ABOVE: Nimoy and Roddenberry had begun their professional relationship back in 1964 when the actor guest starred on the first television show created by Roddenberry, *The Lieutenant*. During filming of the episode "In the Highest Tradition," Roddenberry approached Nimoy about perhaps playing an alien in a new series he was planning. The rest is science fiction history.

REMEMBER...

Merritt Butrick (David Marcus): "It seemed so natural for him to be the director. Not only is he patient and kind and very humorous but he just seemed to be the right choice. It seemed so logical for him to be there in that capacity. He knew what he was talking about. There was a difference between his and Nick Meyer's job. Nick was really hired to give an outside eye and try to give Star Trek some of the charisma and life that it had on the original series. Leonard's job, once they found the track they wanted to follow, was to bring back some of that magic of the actual cast, and I think he did that."[9]

Gene Roddenberry: "I was hesitant at first about him doing Star Trek III because I thought he didn't have the broad background of experience. But then I began to think, 'well, he does know the show, this way you don't have to break in a new director.'"[10]

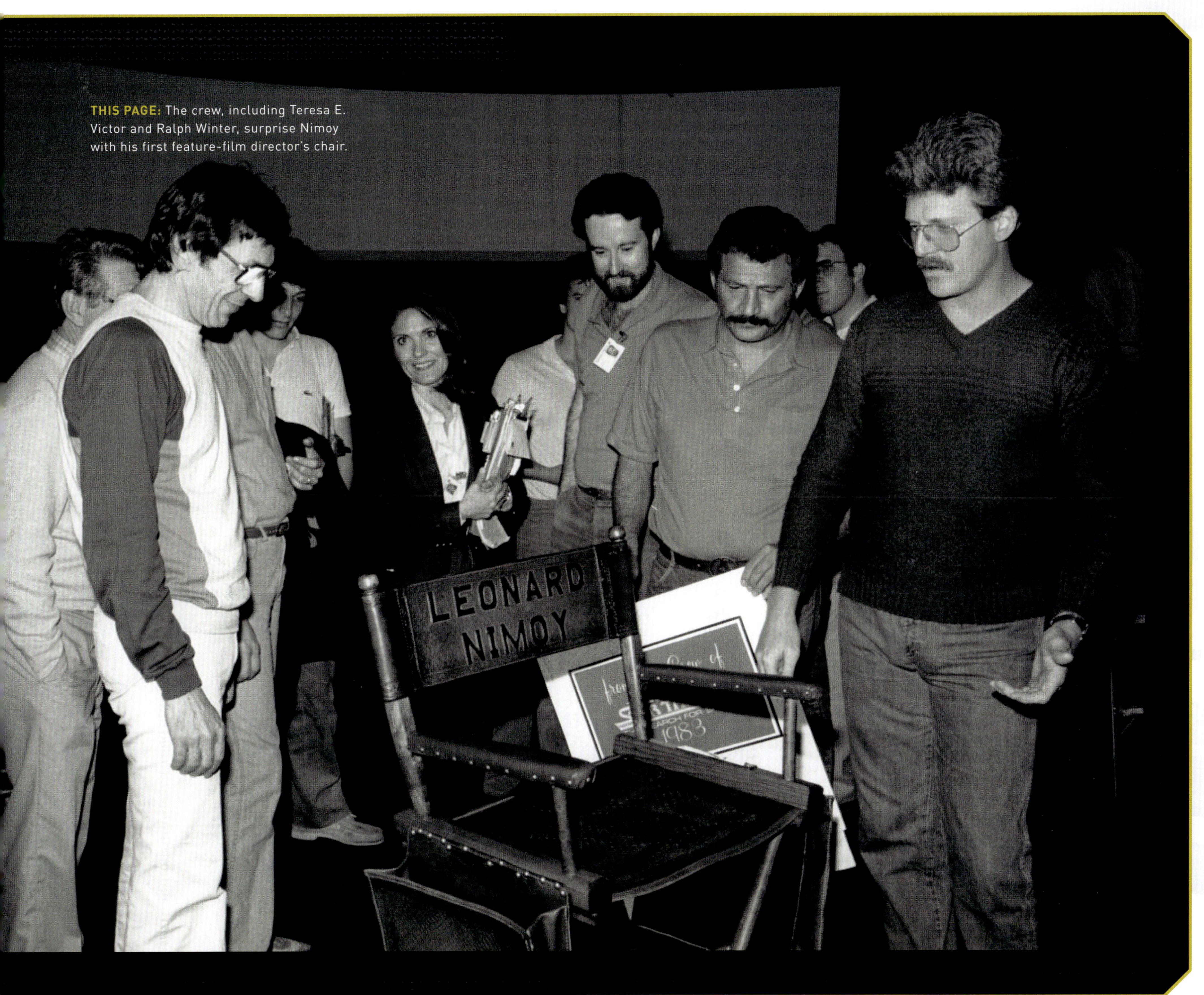

THIS PAGE: The crew, including Teresa E. Victor and Ralph Winter, surprise Nimoy with his first feature-film director's chair.

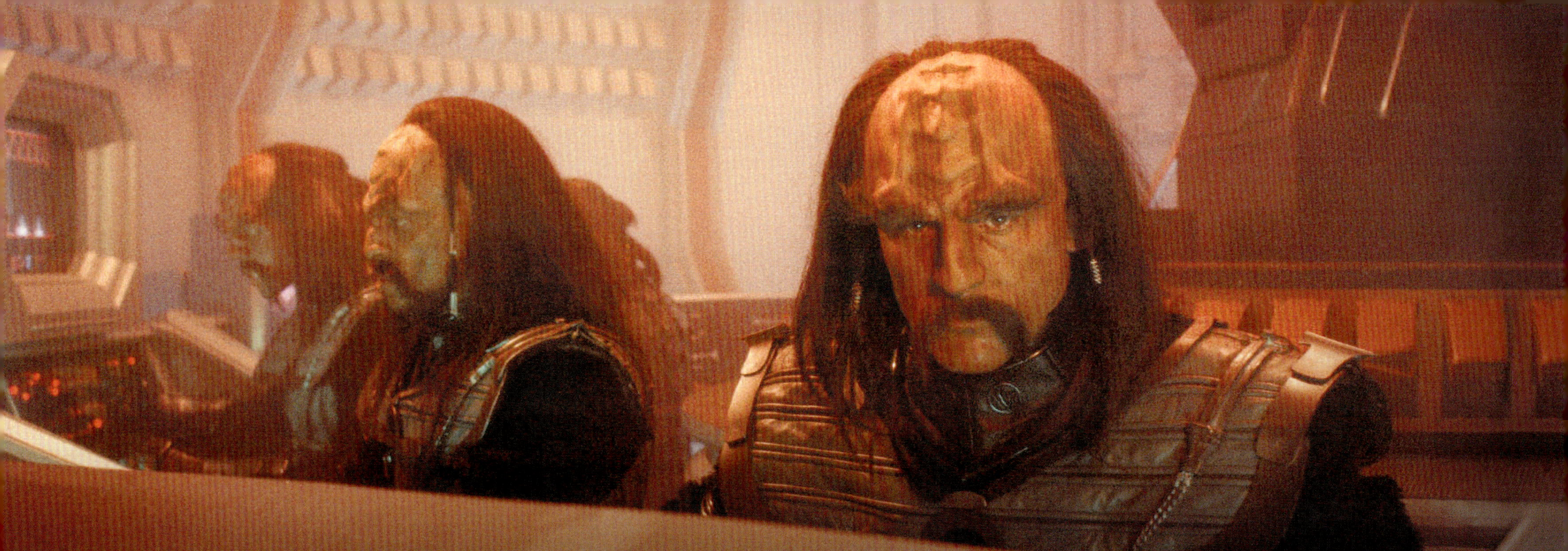

The film settles into a new adventure that begins "SOMEWHERE IN THE KLINGON EMPIRE." It was Nimoy who recommended that the Klingons would make a more cinematic and dramatic villain than the Romulans. In *I Am Spock*, Nimoy explains, "I've always been more intrigued by the Klingons, so I suggested the switch, which Harve readily embraced. To this day, I wish I could have done a serious study of Klingon culture in one of our films."[7] Interestingly, this version of the script does exactly that. There is a great deal of time spent exploring the Klingons and their political structure. The film was going to address the difference between the original series version of the Klingons, sans the bumpy foreheads, and their more elaborately designed film counterparts. Bennett believed that the bumpy forehead Klingons were considered wise, a mark of distinction that was not common amongst most Klingons. The audience is introduced to the First Lord of the Klingon Empire who is gathering his fleet together. One ship, under the command of Kruge, is missing from the flotilla until he makes a grand entrance. Kruge is "universally attractive. Some of that comes from his arrogance, his relative youth, and by Klingon standards, his charm." His crew is "the most awesome collection of large, cruel, and piratical men since the Pittsburgh Steelers of the Seventies." Kruge speaks to them as a pirate would, calling them "my jolly lads." The Klingons have gathered together to consider a preemptive invasion of the Federation. Through the efforts of a Vulcan spy named Galt, they have obtained a video, narrated by Kirk, describing the Genesis device and its awesome power.

Kruge hatches a plan to use his stolen Romulan Bird-of-Prey ship with its cloaking device to determine if the video is real. The First Lord agrees, however Kruge has two conditions. First, he wants to be master of the fleet if he succeeds. Second, he wants the spy Galt to accompany him. If the video is fake, he will make certain Galt suffers the consequences. The idea to keep Kruge's ship a Bird-of-Prey, first in its original Romulan design, and then reengineered as a Klingon vessel, was something that

MAIN IMAGE: *Star Trek III* provided filmmakers with a chance to further explore the Klingon culture through Kruge and his crew.

BELOW: Both Leonard Nimoy and son Adam would direct Christopher Lloyd after *Star Trek III* on different episodes of the same show, the 1995 series *Deadly Games*.

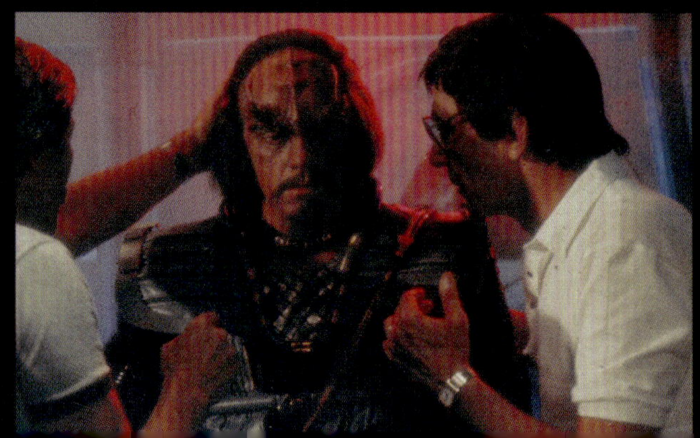

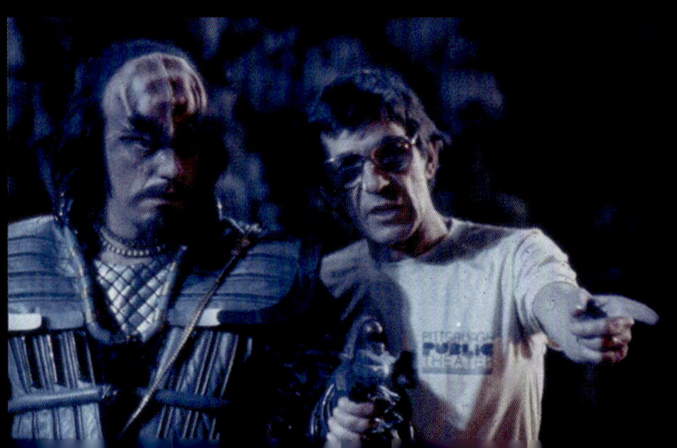

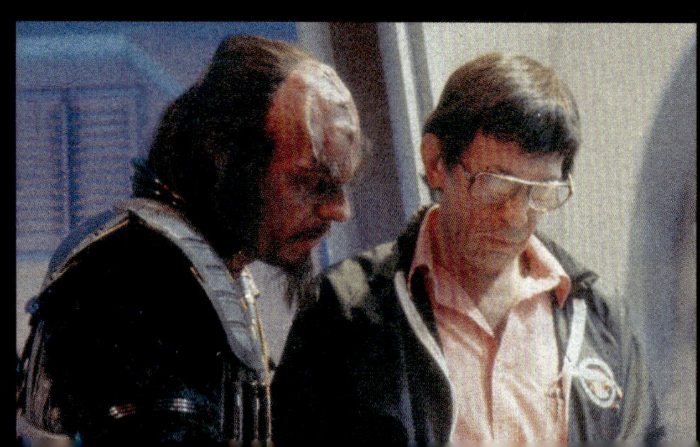

A BRIDGE NOT TOO FAR: THIRD REVISED OUTLINE

On December 9, 1982, Bennett submitted a third revised outline, six pages in total, that begins to bridge his original ideas with that of the final script. This is the outline that would be shared with ILM, inspiring recommendations from the visual artists that further improved the story. Much of the outline reads the same as the story fans know, with important differences. The Romulan Commander from the original outline is now a Romulan Battlelord named Kruge, described as the "most famous warrior in the Empire." It is the *U.S.S. Valiant* rather than *U.S.S. Grissom*. Sulu accompanies McCoy to the bar where the doctor imbibes too much and gets arrested for talking about Genesis. When Sarek meets Kirk at his apartment, he reveals he has studied the Genesis Effect, and that he believes it could restore Spock. This is a shift from the idea in the original outline that Vulcans were immortal to the explanation that the planet caused Spock's restoration. They learn that McCoy has Spock's "essence" and Kirk vows to return them to Vulcan, but the outline does not use the word "katra." There is no pon farr scene between Saavik and Spock, although the outline has a strong bond form between them. Saavik does try to initiate a mind-meld with the young Spock unsuccessfully.

What plays most differently are the scenes after the destruction of the *Enterprise*. Although Spock is still disoriented, he affects an escape. Kruge tortures Saavik for information and as a lure for Kirk. After watching the destruction of the *Enterprise* from the planet, Kirk begins a search for Saavik and Spock, but Spock finds them first. Kirk says the name "Saavik" to Spock in the hopes he will understand despite his diminished mental capacity. Spock does respond and he leads his compatriots to the last place he saw her. As the heroes try to make a rescue, Kruge appears and an all-out fight between everyone occurs. Kruge eventually gets the better of Kirk during their fight until Spock intervenes and helps save the day.

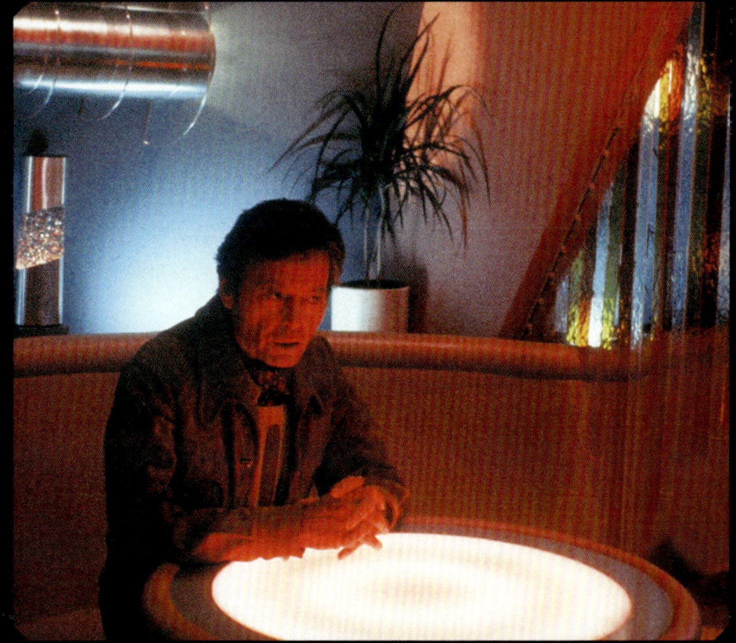

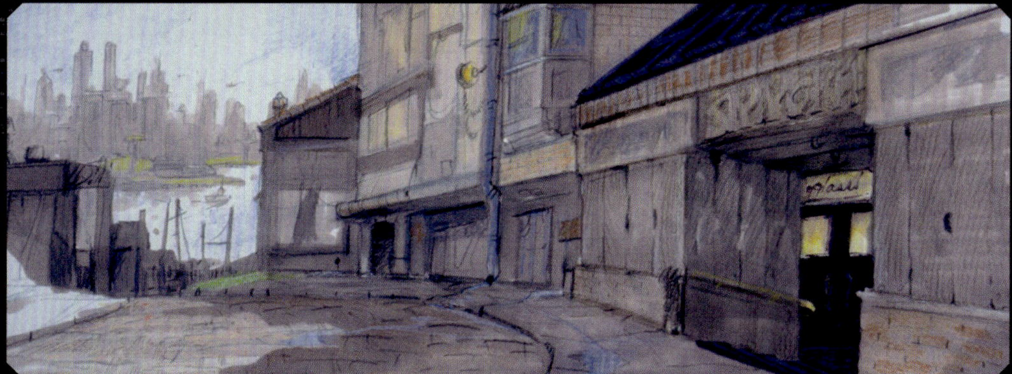

ABOVE: Bennett, with a wink, describes the bar which McCoy goes to. "This feels like an English Pub of the Eighteenth Century, except for its population of Twenty-Third Century clientele. a smattering of civilians, Starfleet personnel, visitors from strange and far off civilizations: it does not have the bizarre qualities of the 'STAR WARS BAR' which is across the street." Carson rendered this unused vision of the exterior of the bar, "My idea was, you can see San Francisco across the bay, and this was kind of a rundown part of town where this bar was."[11]

RIGHT: ILM art director Nilo Rodis' notes on page six of Bennett's outline. The notes capture some of the themes that Bennett and Nimoy wanted for the scene, to create a planet that was "marvelous, heavenly," and "dreamy." Associate producer Ralph Winter, who worked closely with ILM artists, is mentioned. *Time Bandits*, the 1981 film by Terry Gilliam which featured impressive visuals of the Fortress of Ultimate Darkness, is referenced as a possible inspiration.

BELOW: ILM art director David Carson envisions the original scale of Spock's processional. Roddenberry was concerned that an excessive processional could make Spock appear to be a celebrity. He wondered if critics may argue that the filmmakers had confused Nimoy's celebrity with that of Spock. He suggested that the reason many Vulcans would be curious about the ceremony could be that it was something unusual. Bennett would use Roddenberry's idea, making the fal-tor-pan refusion ceremony something that had not been practiced "since ages past, and then only in legend."

Concepts: Vulcan has made it: exterior designs / wonderful / heavenly / some remnants of the past

6.

27. THE TEMPLE OF VULCAN. A wonderful, cathedral-like setting. Sarek is there. And Bones. An ancient ritual is performed by Sarek in which the final moment calls for Bones' hand to be placed upon Spock's temple. It is a stunning and holy moment, the likes of which we have never seen before.

Symbol, bells – Tibetan?

WOW

sensuality dreamy sequence

[Check out connection on Time Bandit]

28. OUTSIDE THE TEMPLE. Kirk and the crew are waiting, uncertain. Then, the distant door opens. Sarek and Bones exit, flanking a hooded figure. They walk toward the waiting Enterprise crew, and stop. Sarek says to Kirk: "Thank you for bringing my son back to me. I know what it cost you." Kirk nods. Then Sarek gestures to the hooded figure, who steps forward to the line of Enterprise personnel. The hood is thrown back. It is Spock. Impassive, but clearly Spock. His eyes convey intelligence and recognition. He walks down the line of each of his old comrades, who behold him with wonder. To each there is a little flicker of recognition. And finally he stops at Kirk. An intense moment. Then Spock raises his hand in Vulcan salute. Kirk returns it. And then, soft wonder of wonders... Spock smiles.

Ralph will send copy of ST Tape on Vulcan exterior.

THE END

no optical. awe inspiring (T.bit). religious. metaphysical

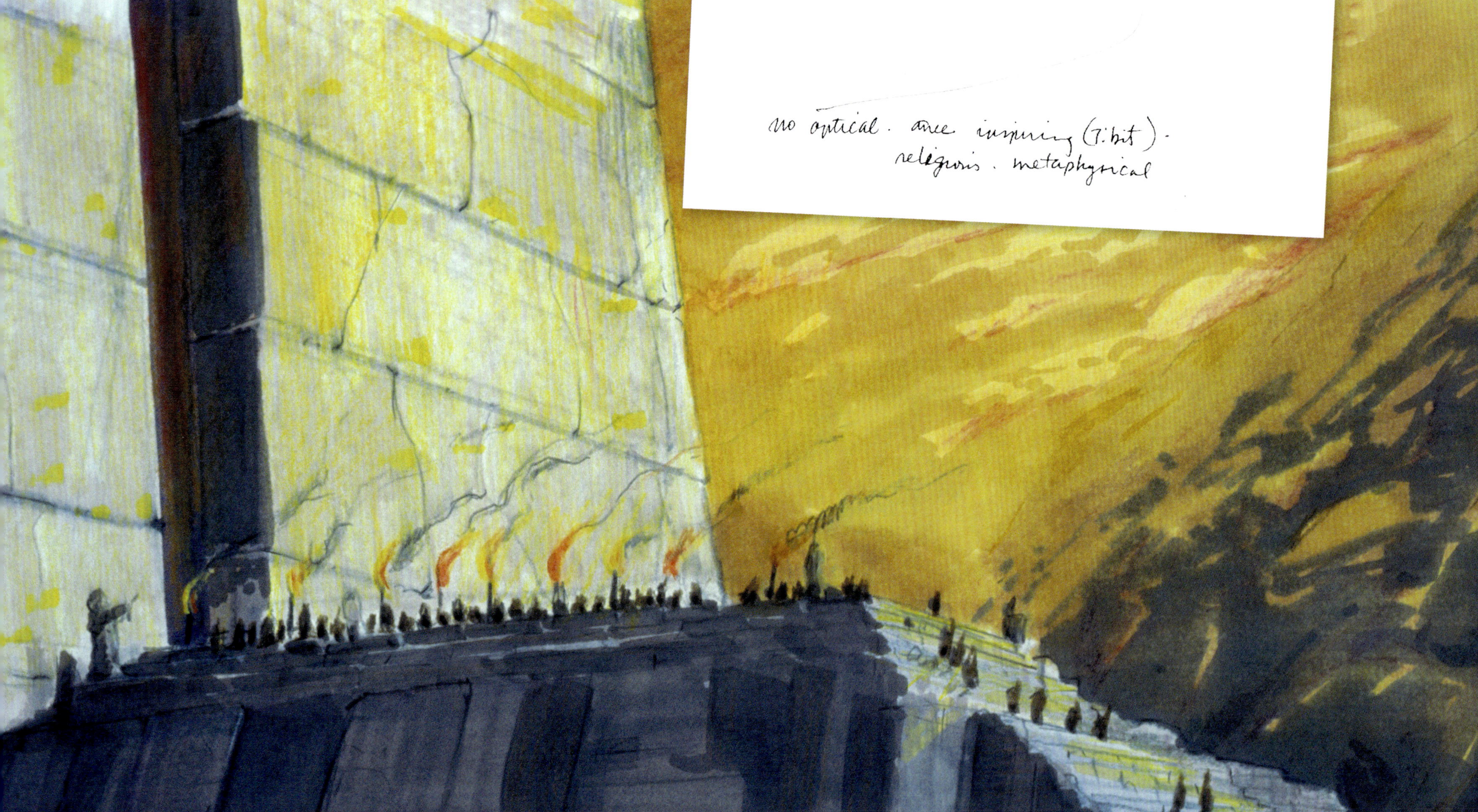

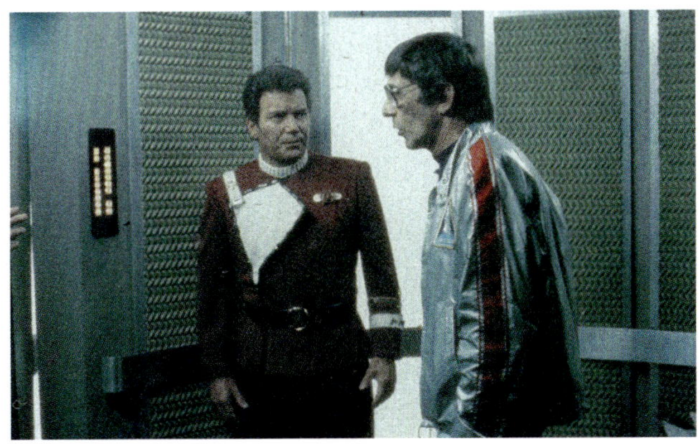

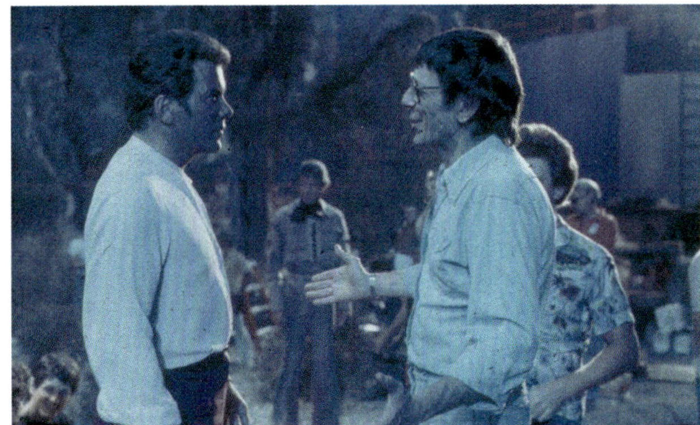

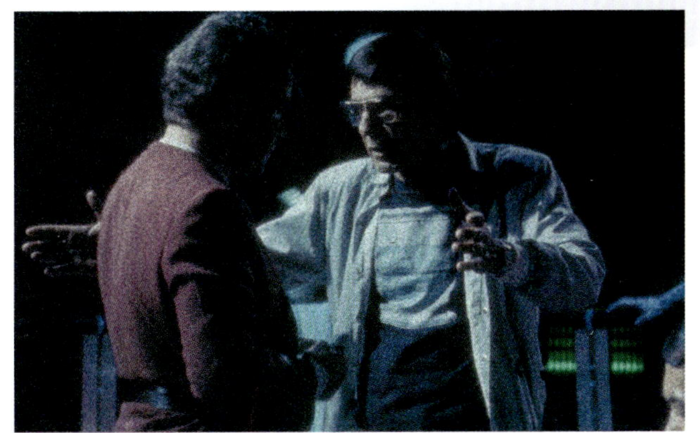

THIS PAGE: Directing on *Star Trek III* required Nimoy to engage with actors in environments both small, like the crowded turbo lift set, and expansive, like the Genesis set. The bridge of the *Enterprise* was always a challenge to film on because of its shape and size, appearing much larger on screen than the actual set.

Bennett discussed with Nimoy, "I always bowed to Leonard on these things. He was, after all, the senior Vulcanologist of the franchise, in addition to being director of the picture. After due consideration, he said, 'The hell with it.' We agreed that the Klingons would steal the best from anybody, though we didn't have time to show it in the story."[8]

Drunk McCoy returns again, this time in the turbo-lift with Kirk. The script has no apparitions of Spock appearing to anyone; however, McCoy does speak in Spock's voice and with his personality in this scene. He even says a line that only Kirk and Spock would know, saying, "Jim, you proceed from a false assumption. I have no ego to bruise." David and Saavik contact Kirk directly and speak with him to get Captain Esteban to let them investigate the strange readings they are getting from Genesis. During the conversation, David says that Saavik has developed a sense of humor because she keeps calling him "the dumb bastard." Kirk asks if David has talked with Carol. Later, Admiral Morrow tells Kirk, "Every civilization in the galaxy thinks we have developed a Doomsday Weapon." Kirk learns he is to be the scapegoat because the Federation was going to share all their data with the other governments before testing, but that is impossible because of the events with Khan. He will be watched by Federation security.

Meanwhile, the story shifts again to Kruge nearing Genesis, as it is revealed that he has slaves aboard his ship and that he learns about his enemies through their art. Kruge is playing 'When We Sail Against Far England' sung by a 1914 U-boat crew as he tries to understand humans. Galt is appalled by slavery, saying, "Whenever I hear anyone justifying slavery, I feel a strong impulse to see it tried on him personally." Kruge shares that he was, indeed, once a slave. There is something familiar about a line Galt says to Kruge, "You should really learn to regulate your passions, Kruge. They blind you." That hint will play an important role in the story.

Sarek arrives on Earth and explains about Vulcan law. Fahn-Lo is the "imprint of Spock's Essence. It must be reunited with Spock before it is too late." Kirk vows to help McCoy and Spock. Nimoy and Bennett had originally thought to include Amanda in the scene, but once the mind-meld was added, it was thought she would not have a meaningful function. Fahn-Lo would be renamed to katra in future scripts, and the idea was inspired loosely on the Dybbuk, a spirit from Jewish folklore which could possess people.

Stealing the *Enterprise* plays differently in this script, especially because Uhura stays with the team the entire time and there is a chase through San Francisco. Kirk and company hide under a traditional dragon costume during a Year of the Boar parade as part of their escape. Carson commented, "One of the very first meetings ILM had with Harve's team is when they came up to the Bay Area because it was Chinese New Year and they wanted to get some reference photos of the traditional dragon."[11]

During the scenes on Genesis, audiences learn more about Saavik who shares her fears with David that she cannot help Spock. She reveals that she does not know which of her parents was Romulan and that Spock found her on the Hellguard Colony.

Near the end of the script, Galt joins forces with Kirk, and tells him that Spock, who he believes he knows, could help build a dilithium converter which they need to escape Genesis. Luckily, Sarek supplied McCoy with medicine to help Spock. After defeating Kruge, the crew beams to the stolen Romulan Bird-of-Prey. Sarek sends them a coded message, "We are waiting, but urge caution. Great bird from home flies between us." While he is referring to the *U.S.S. Excelsior*, Sarek is making a sly Easter egg reference to Roddenberry, who was known as "The Great Bird of the Galaxy." Sarek acts as the priest of the ceremony to restore his son. A surprise is revealed at the end of the script. Galt is Spock's brother, although the revelation is not explored any further. Galt would not appear in further revisions, but the idea was recycled with the character Sybok in *Star Trek V: The Final Frontier* (1989).

THE RODDENBERRY REACTION

One of the challenges making *Star Trek II* had been balancing the various opinions of stakeholders. Eugene Roddenberry had been moved into a consultancy role which meant that his opinions on the films were to be considered, but did not have to be followed. That led to conflicts between Meyer, Bennett, and Roddenberry. By the time of *Star Trek III*, those relationships had smoothed somewhat, although not entirely. However, with Nimoy as director, Roddenberry took on a more active role. His contributions to the film included script notes, casting advice, and commentary on dailies. He was much more present on set than he had been with *Star Trek II*. Of the relationship, Nimoy said, "Each draft of the story and screenplay went to him. He responded with very constructive feedback. We discussed his ideas and his reactions to the script. Gene even watched the dailies with me. He was very supportive. His most frequent comment was that the characters were vividly coming to life."[7] For example, the invention of proto-matter as a mechanism to solve what Bennett considered "the Genesis problem" of having an ultimate weapon that could be used in future films to solve all problems was Roddenberry's idea. He believed if the device was somehow flawed, that would negate its value or ease of its reproduction by any other scientist besides David Marcus. It was Gene, too, who was concerned that Vulcans should not be presented as immortal, which is why the alternative of the katra was established.

The collaborative spirit sometimes turned contentious. In the summer of 1983, Roddenberry met with Bennett and Nimoy, and on August 1, 1983, he put his thoughts to paper. He begins with a warning that speaks directly to the most important test faced by the production: *Star Trek*'s sustainability as a franchise. "If shot without revisions, this draft would create some fairly serious problems for me, and in my opinion, also for Paramount as regards the continuing viability of the *Star Trek* property." He did not think it wise to destroy the *Enterprise*, which was, to many fans, an actual character. He recommended that only the saucer section be destroyed, or if destruction was to occur, there be a promise of a new *Enterprise*, perhaps with a rechristening of the *Excelsior*. Roddenberry's goal was that these "recommendations will center around preventing our audience feeling resentful or cheated by hard-hearted Paramount or Harve Bennett or whoever it was that thought so little of this old friend and format 'character.'" He also worried that Starfleet was presented as "plain dumb" and questioned, "When are we going to stop portraying Kirk's beloved Starfleet as a 'Pirates of the Penzance' admiralty?" Both the destruction of the *Enterprise* and Kirk running circles around Starfleet were kept in the script. Despite this, Roddenberry's *Star Trek III* contributions were significant.

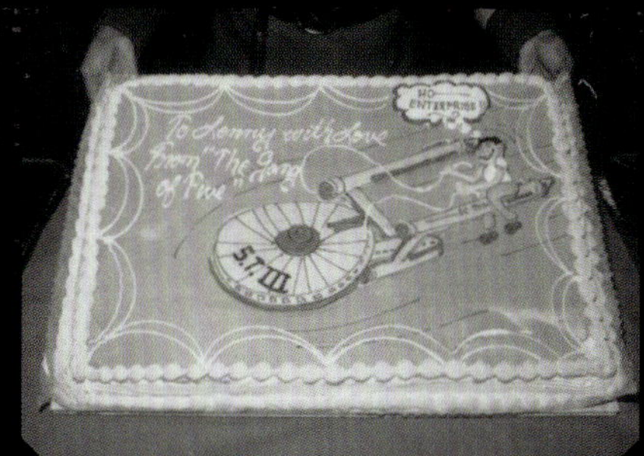

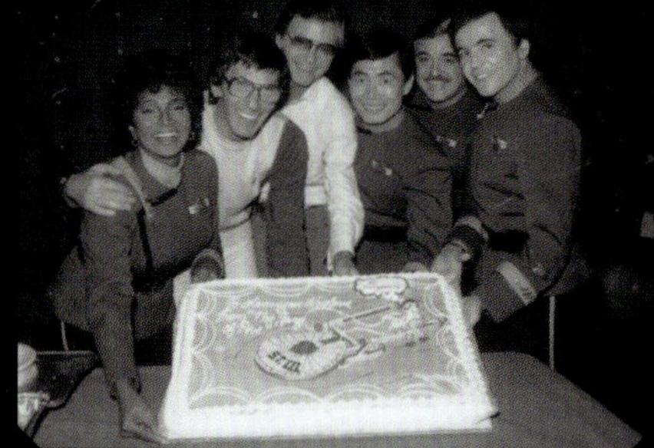

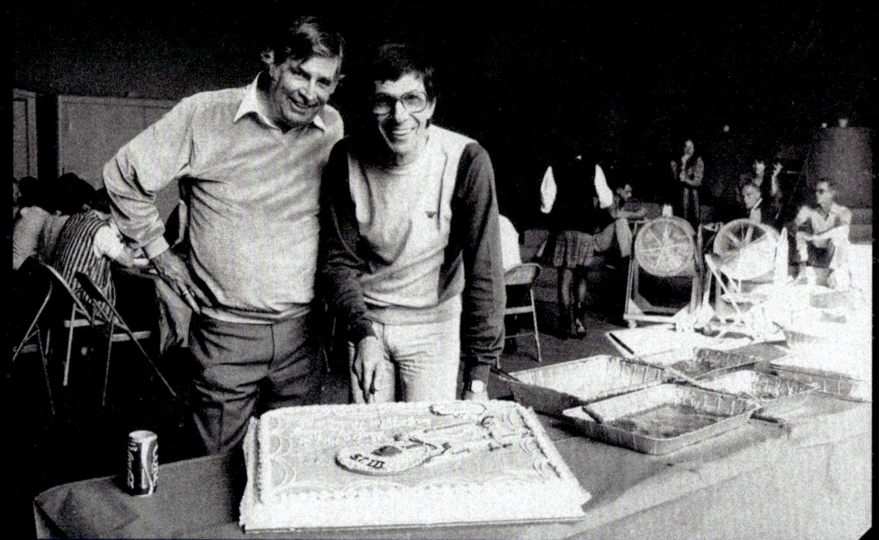

THIS PAGE: Roddenberry and Nimoy share a congratulatory cake given to Nimoy. The decoration reads, "To Lenny, with love from 'The Gang of Five,'" the nickname given to James Doohan, DeForest Kelley, Walter Koenig, Nichelle Nichols, and George Takei.

FLIGHT RECORDER VISUAL:

TERESA E. VICTOR

Teresa E. Victor, born in New York in 1943, was Nimoy's personal assistant for nearly 20 years. She started her tenure during the very first season of the original series, answering fan mail and arranging appearances. Her many years association with Nimoy gave her insight into not only the actor and director as a person, but the characters he played. Her understanding of Spock and *Star Trek* was a help to many *Star Trek III* prospective actors, including Robin Curtis and Stephen Manley, because she made them feel more relaxed as they prepared for auditions and meetings. Victor had many cameos in the *Star Trek* films, including voicing the bridge in *Star Trek II* and playing the usher greeting guests at the Cetacean Institute in *Star Trek IV*. In that same film, Victor also was one of the bee-like Aamaarazan councilors, a role which required her to wear a bald cap, have her arms painted yellow, and wear an intricate mask. Perhaps most notably, Victor supplied the voice of the Computer in *Star Trek III*, whose countdown marks the impending destruction of the *Starship Enterprise*. Victor became a trusted confidant, and Nimoy described her as "extremely loyal" and "dedicated."[12]

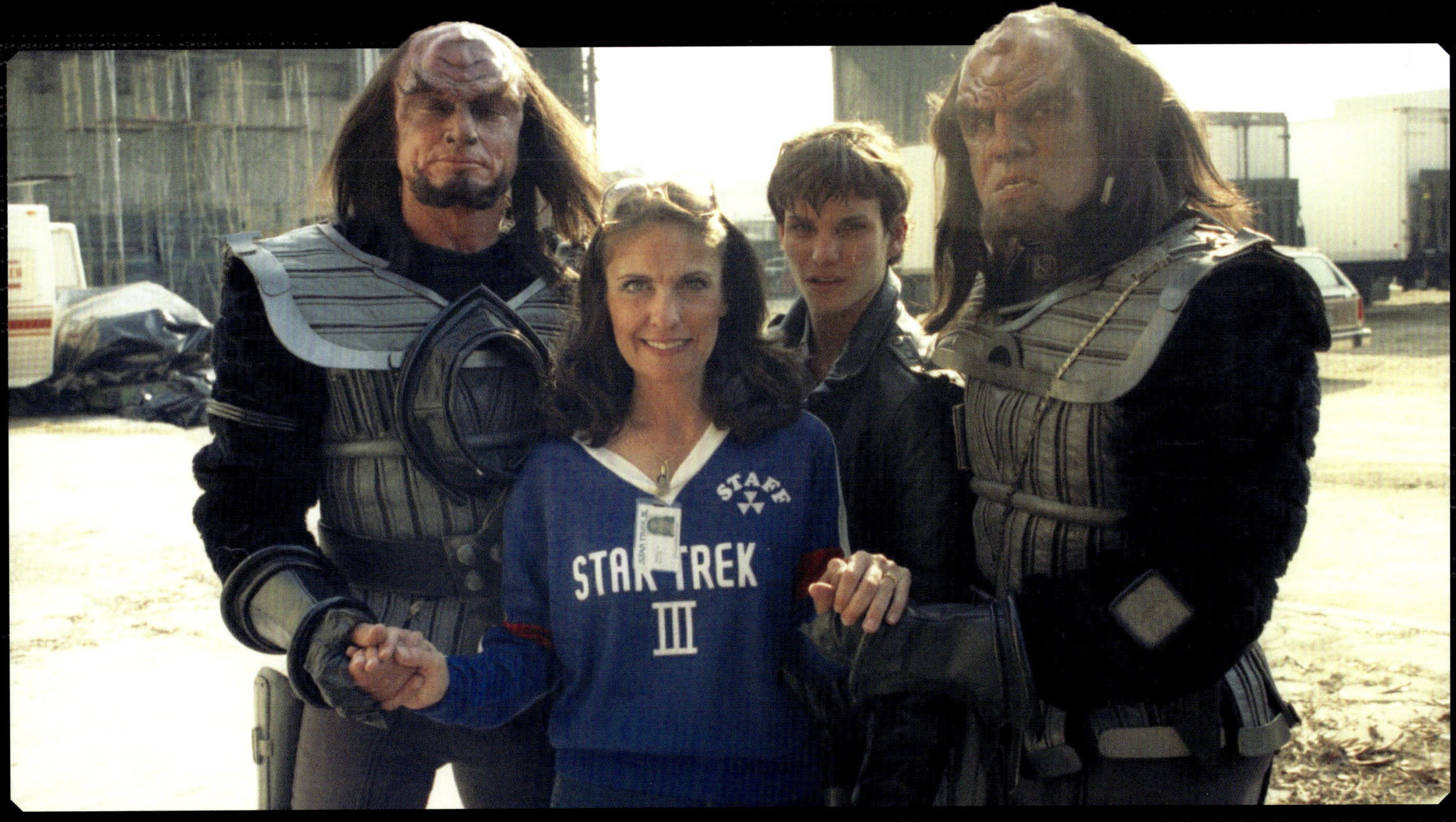

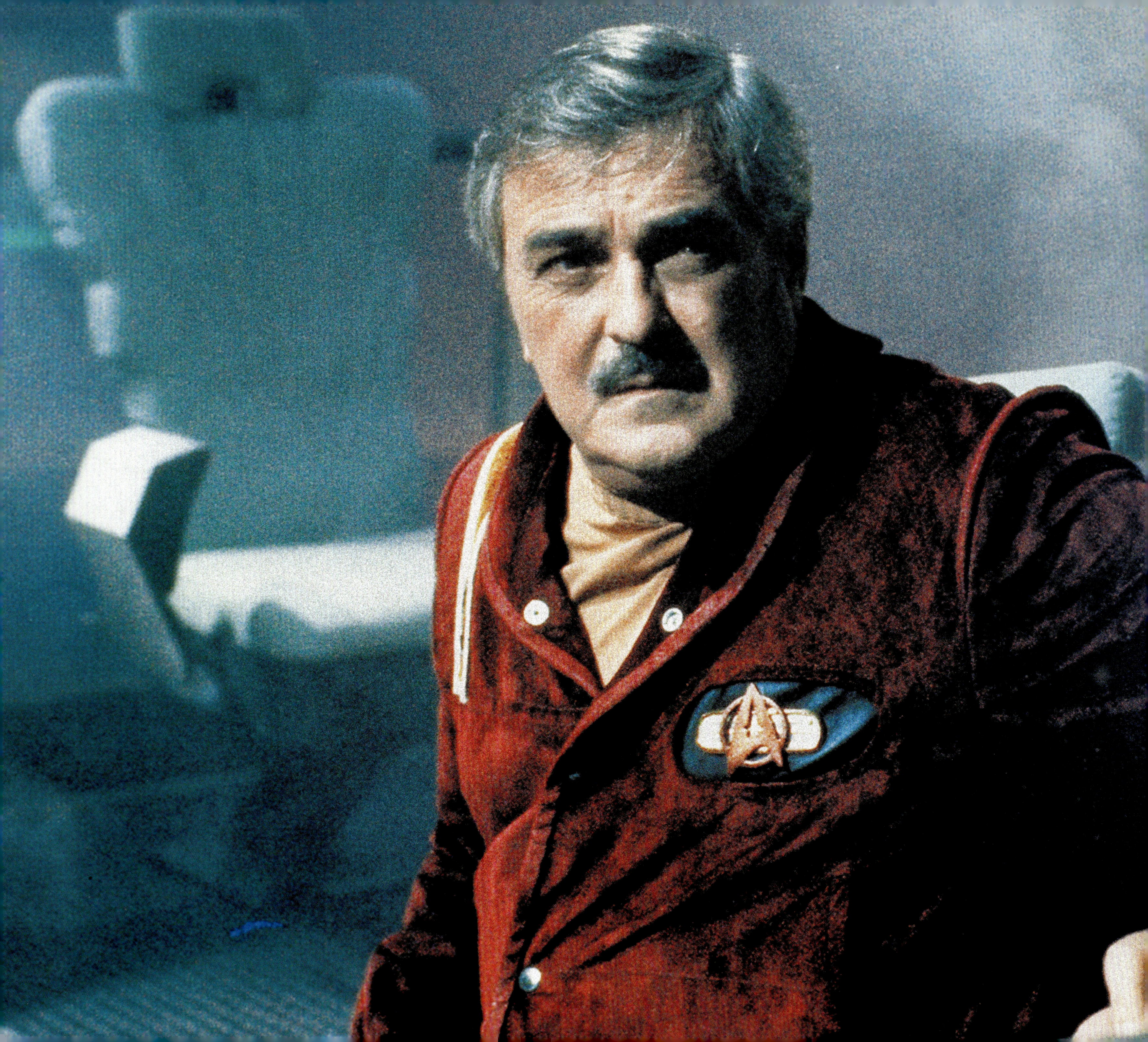

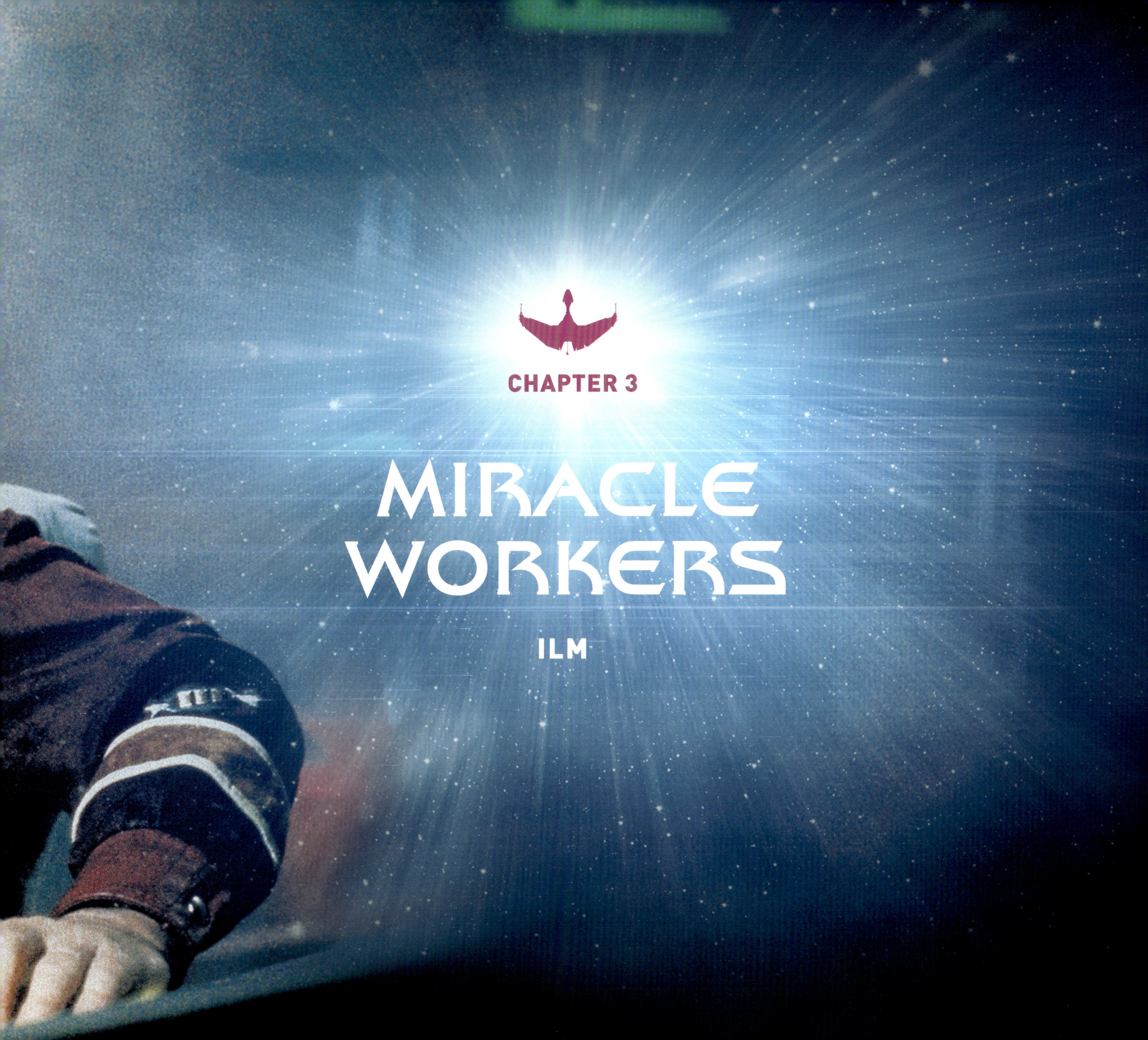

CHAPTER 3

MIRACLE WORKERS

ILM

Two years and a day before the premiere of the original *Star Wars*, on May 26, 1975, George Lucas founded Industrial Light & Magic, so named because its original headquarters were in an area zoned for "light industrial" businesses. The move was out of necessity. The visual effects required for his film had become something of a lost art at the big Hollywood studios, most of which had closed their permanent effects departments in favor of hiring ad hoc artists from independent companies. Many of those independent artists were applying their craft in the world of television commercials at places like Cascade Studios. Hollywood of the 1970s preferred gritty realism, and few and far between were large-scale science fiction films. The new generation of artists were inspired by the likes of Roger Corman and Ray Harryhausen and they had shared biographies of scouring *Famous Monsters* magazines as kids trying to learn how their favorite films were made. By the early 1980s, ILM had become a standard bearer. While initially assigned exclusively to Lucasfilm projects, ILM started producing effects for other films, beginning with 1981's *Dragonslayer* and 1982's *Star Trek II*. As *Return of the Jedi* neared completion, ILM was looking for their next project. It would turn out to be *Star Trek III*.

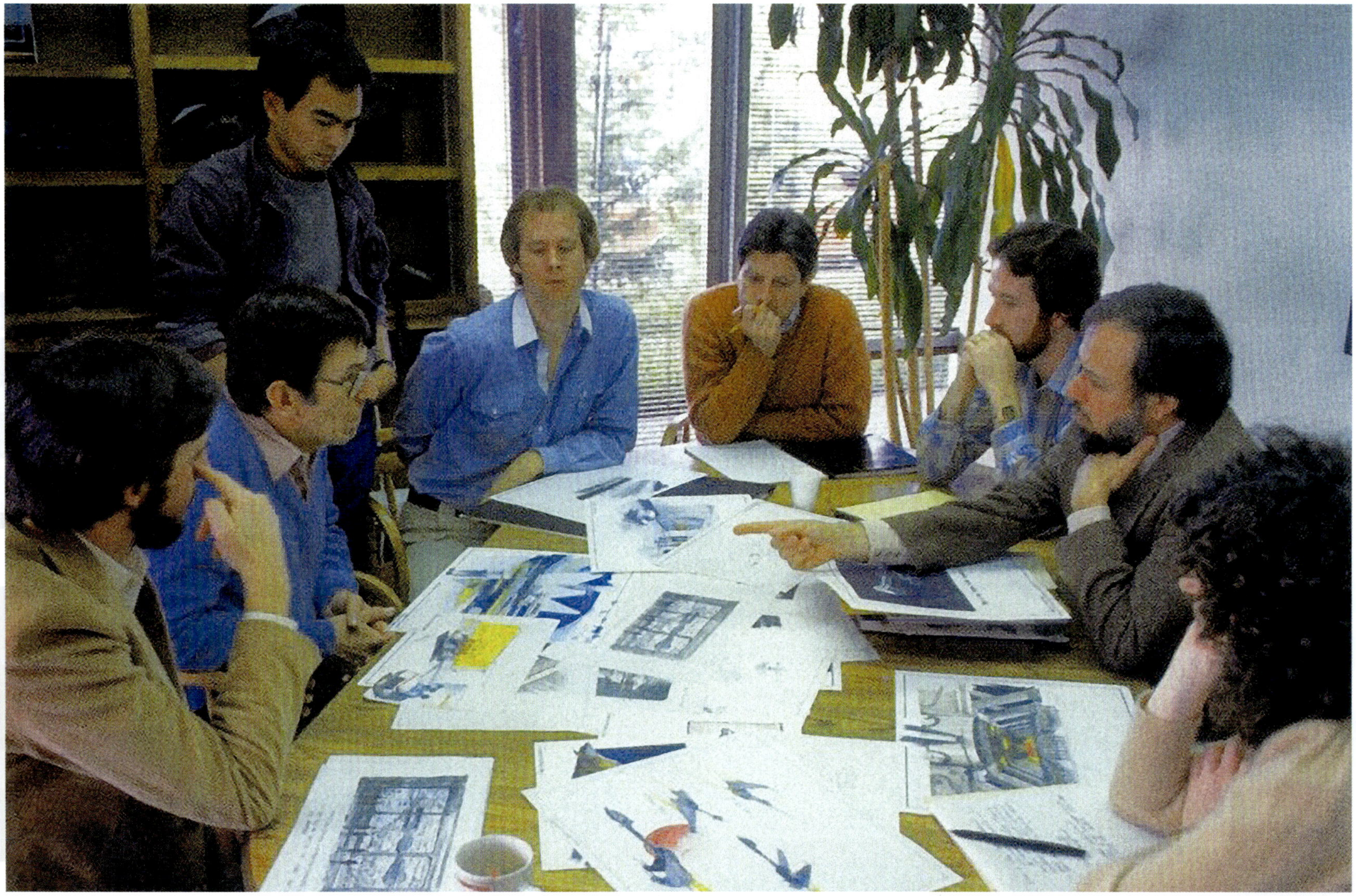

ABOVE: An early 1983 meeting ILM with director Nimoy, associate producer Ralph Winter, and the ILM team – including Ralston and art directors Nilo Rodis and David Carson – to discuss conceptual art. Nimoy found these meetings invaluable: "We exchanged sketches, exchanged conversations, looked at different coloration possibilities, looked at artwork of fantasy literature, science fiction literature, to find elements that might be useful and integrate them into the film."[1]

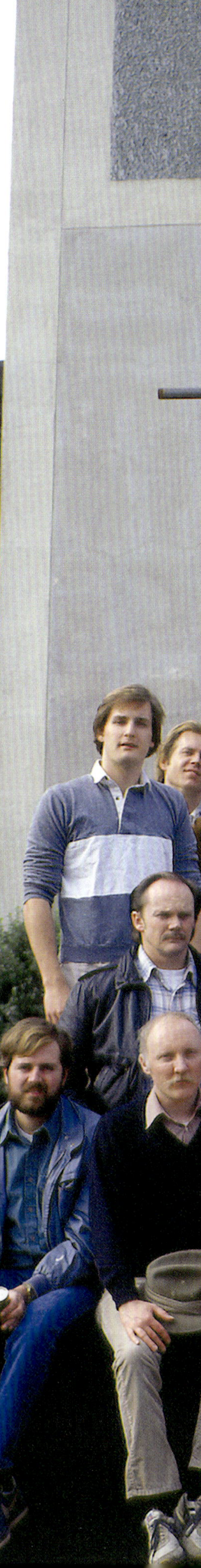

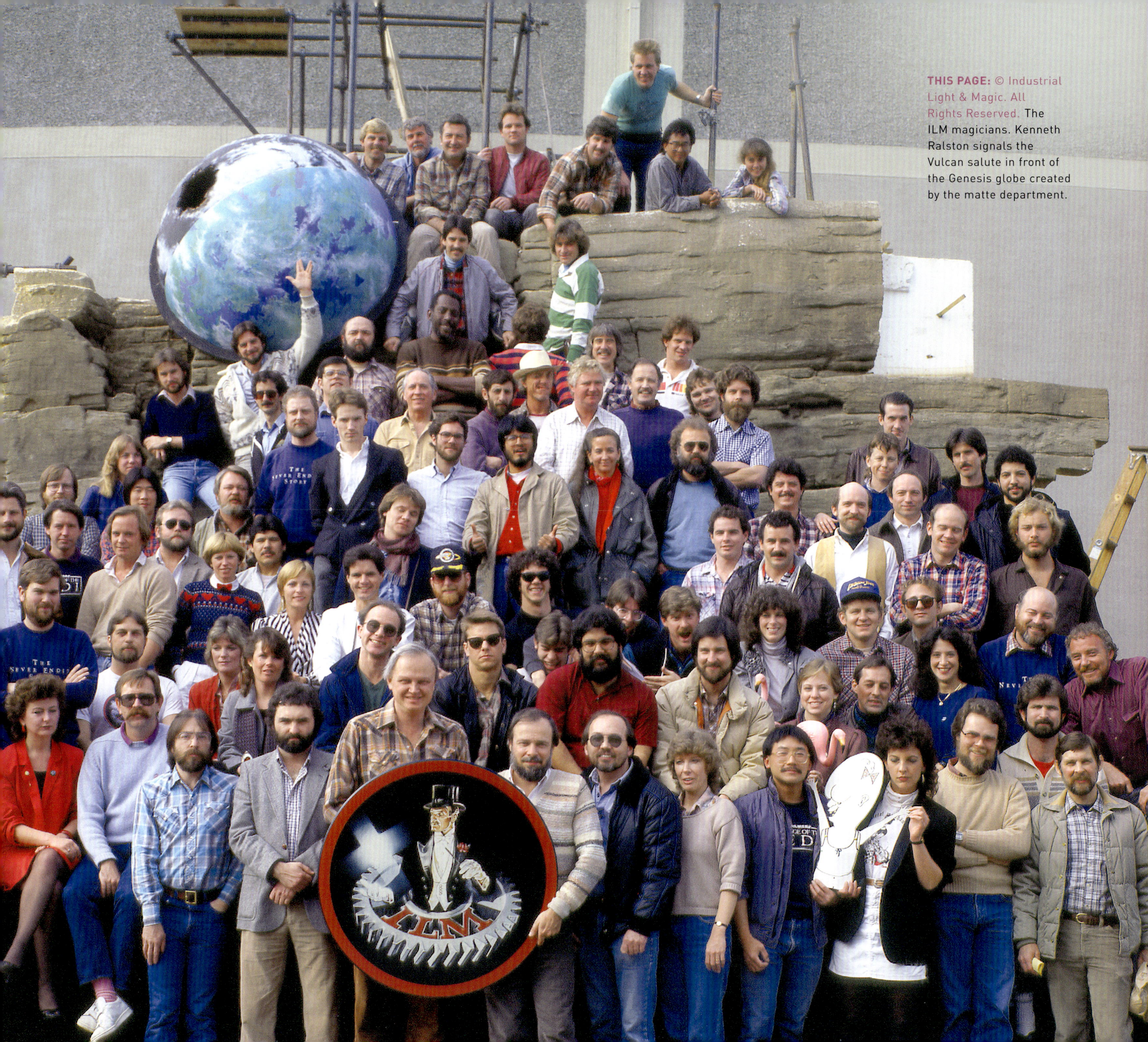

THIS PAGE: © Industrial Light & Magic. All Rights Reserved. The ILM magicians. Kenneth Ralston signals the Vulcan salute in front of the Genesis globe created by the matte department.

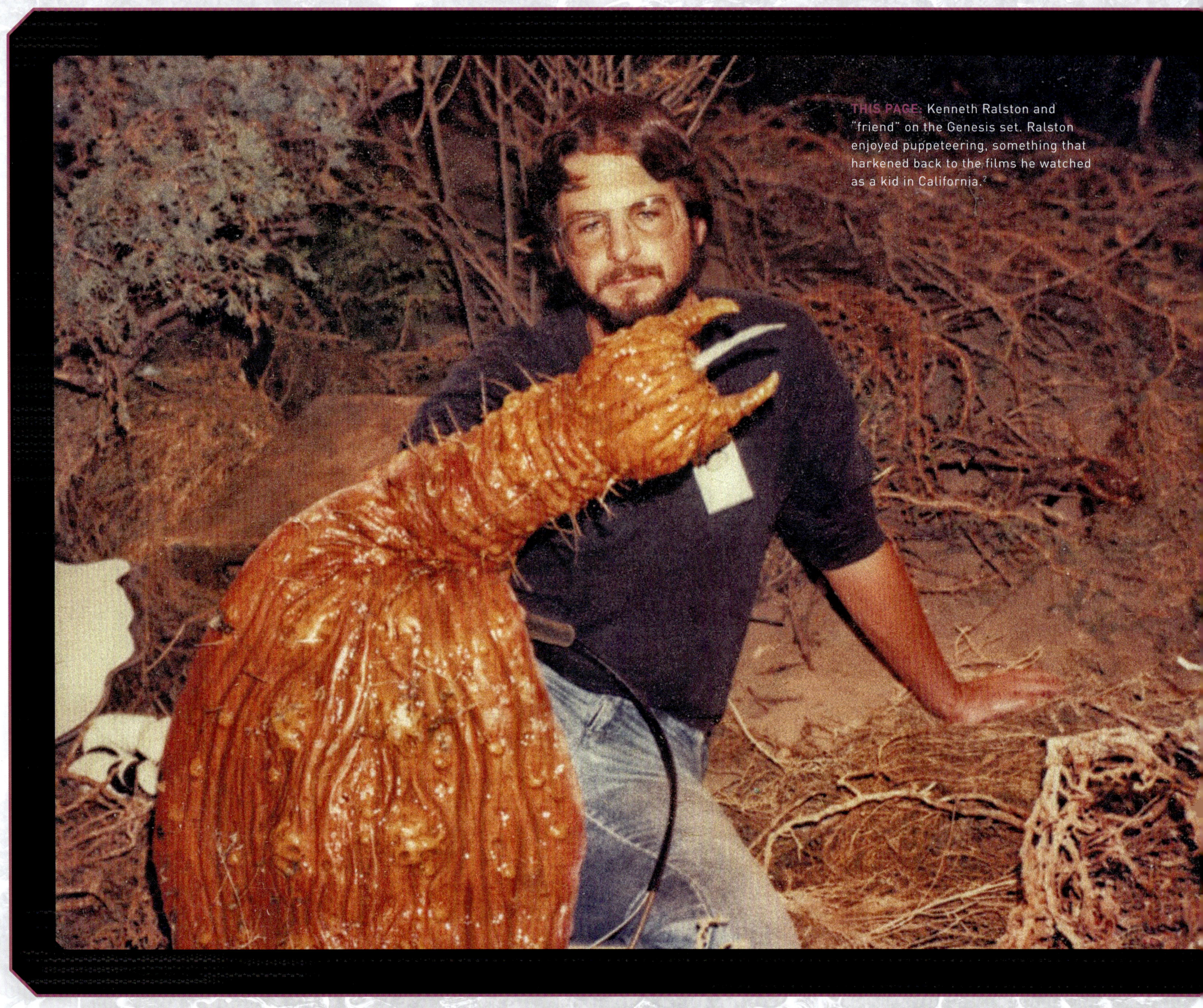

THIS PAGE: Kenneth Ralston and "friend" on the Genesis set. Ralston enjoyed puppeteering, something that harkened back to the films he watched as a kid in California.[2]

FLIGHT RECORDER VISUAL:

KENNETH RALSTON, VISUAL EFFECTS SUPERVISOR

"You never think, in a million years, how people slowly guide you through to what your future will be," believes Kenneth Ralston. Born 1954, Ralston was one of the artists inspired by Harryhausen, films like *King Kong*, and the animation of Chuck Jones and Tex Avery. He wrote letters while in junior high school to Forrest J. Ackerman, who published *Famous Monsters* and who opened his home, a veritable museum of classic Hollywood visual effects memorabilia, to anyone with a passion for effects. "I went to Forrest Ackerman's. He had a couple of people meet me there, Jon Berg and Bill Hedge, two guys that were working at Cascade Studios making commercials. That was the first time we'd ever met, and they were there to answer our questions. We got an invitation by Forry [Ackerman] to go back again, and Harryhausen was there. So, wow! All of that was exciting and we got to talk with him a little bit. There was a book or magazine I looked at years later and there was a picture of Harryhausen at Forry's and Phil Tippett is behind him. I had no idea Phil was there that day!"

At age seventeen, Ralston began working at Cascade where he met many artists who would inspire him. "Obviously Jon Berg, Dave Allen, Dennis Muren, and Phil Tippett were inspirations to me. Phil Kellison and Joe Rayner who ran Cascade were mentors. When I was at Cascade, Tex Avery was there. I got to work with Tex. You know, what a weird deal. I would never have thought in a million years how all these things came together. It was a constant learning experience and especially for me, it was important having the kind of people around us that were more experienced. I learned so much from them about just being a good person."[3]

Ralston would parlay those inspirations into a five-time Academy Award® winning career. In addition to his work on *Star Wars* and *Star Trek*, Ralston produced and supervised effects for more than thirty films, from the *Back to the Future* trilogy – where he would reunite with Christopher Lloyd – to *Alice in Wonderland*.

REMEMBER...

Don Dow (effects cameraman): "When you're working for Ken Ralston, you have a lot of latitude. He's more interested in what works than anything else. He has it thought out, sure, and he knows what he wants, but we work pretty well in conjunction. If somebody comes up with something – 'It would be neat to do this or that, what about when the ship gets hit, what about this type of electricity or lighting effect' – he's very open to it."[4]

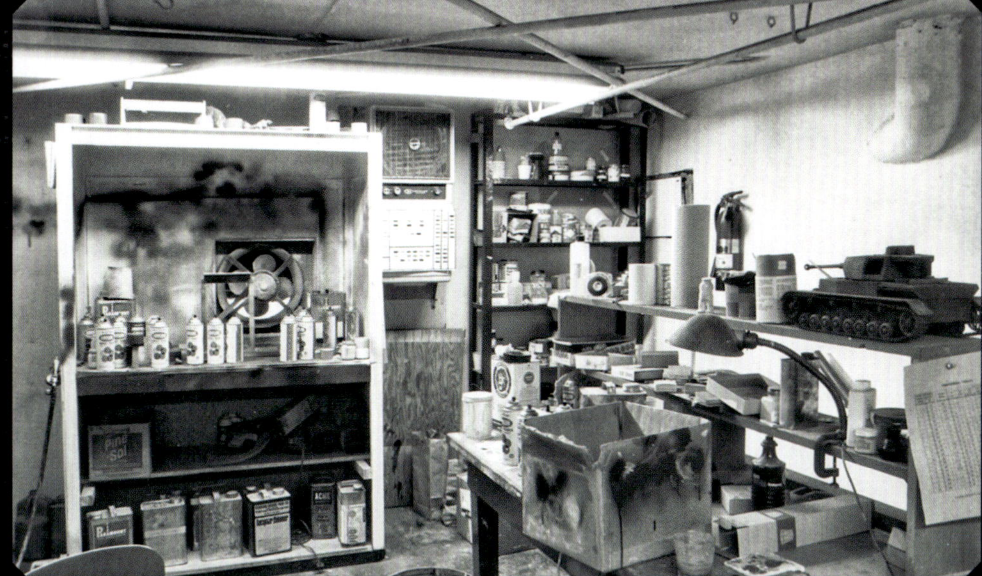

LEFT: A corner of Cascade Studios.[2]

THE SCRIPT IS FINALIZED

Bennett would continue to work on the final script, incorporating ideas from Nimoy, Roddenberry, Meyer, ILM, actors, and even fans. The October 7, 1983, script was a third revision of the final draft. Differences between the film and this final version of the script are:

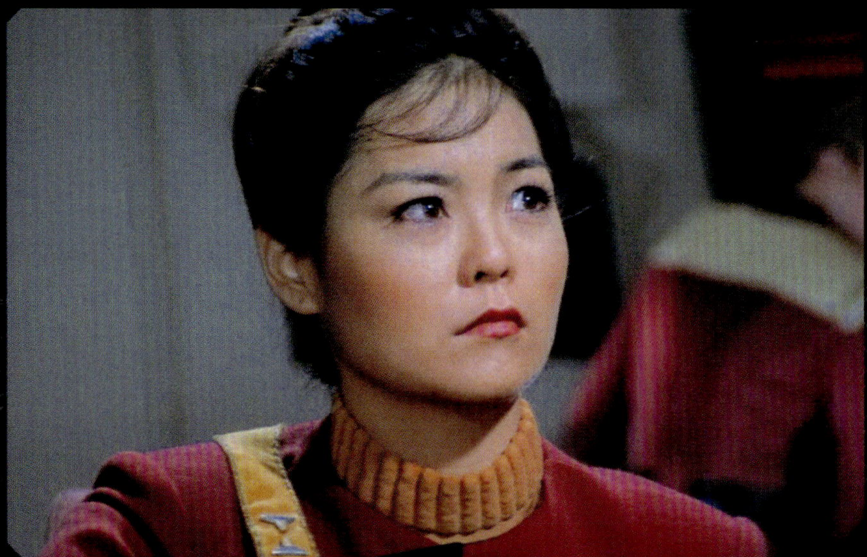

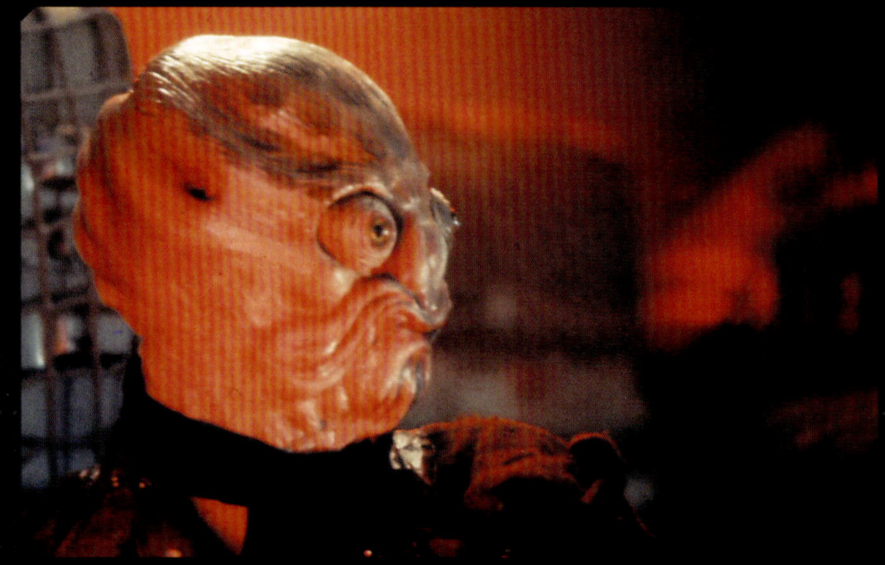

- The script starts with the *U.S.S. Grissom*'s arrival at Genesis. This was the intention during filming, but sequences were shifted during editing.
- Kirk knows at the start of the script that Spock's casket has been located on Genesis.
- Valkris and the merchant ship are said to be in Organian Space, a nod to the episode 'Errand of Mercy.'
- Valkris and the merchant ship captain have more dialog, with him complaining about "Klingon mumbo-jumbo" when Valkris says that Kruge has, "been here for some time. I can feel his presence."
- There is a bar fight caused by McCoy's attempt to escape Federation security. The scene was filmed, but not included in the film.
- Carol Marcus is mentioned. David confirms that Carol was unaware of his use of proto-matter: "My mother knew nothing about it. That's why I asked her to leave Genesis in my hands."
- Kirk eulogizes David with a Shakespeare quote.
- Saavik compares the normal katra ritual and the unusual fal-tor-pan refusion.
- Kirk joins McCoy after the doctor admits to Spock he couldn't bear to lose him again.

ABOVE: Bennett's description in the script of the reaction by the crew of the *U.S.S. Grissom* to the news that Spock is alive further exemplifies his humor. Bennett writes, "There is a moment of uncertainty between Esteban and his science officers that should be one of the grand laughs of this film." Jeanne Mori delivered a performance that evoked exactly that response from audiences. It is a fun, but important, moment that helps the audience buy the conceits of the script.

LEFT: Stuntman and actor Tom Morga played an alien officer of the merchant ship. The character, barely visible in the final film, had more screen time due to the lengthier original destruction scene. Morga was impressed by the specialized makeup: "They had wires under the makeup. They could make the eyebrows move and make expressions. They could control the character almost like puppetry. It was kind of disappointing that it didn't really make any showing in the movie much except a brief moment, but it was pretty cool makeup."[5]

With rapidly changing technology, the artists and technicians at ILM played an important role in keeping directors and producers in the know about what is possible and what is not. Shatner shared, "The new technology is so incredible. You've got to be with it. You've got to be aware of the changes month to month. If you are a director and you lose six months of what's happening, you're kind of out of it because it's changing so rapidly."[6] This was especially true during the early 1980s as computer effects were beginning to reshape cinema. One of the luxuries to the budget limitations on *Star Trek*, from its very beginning, had been to constrain the use of effects merely because they looked cool. There is always the danger that visual effects become a substitute for story or character rather than a support and enhancement of it. Those from Paramount making *Star Trek III* understood the value of effects and the help that ILM could provide in maintaining that balance. Of this, Nimoy said, "The effects in this film are so integrated. By that I mean they flow naturally out of the drama that's taking place in such a wonderful way. I think that enhances the appeal."[7]

Facilitating that collaboration was how unusually early ILM was brought into the process on *Star Trek III*. Bennett knew the dangers of going to ILM too late. Bennett was not about to let the same kind of delays that had plagued the previous films happen again if possible, so a deal was reached early and ILM came aboard in November, 1982. Used to dealing primarily with final scripts on non-Lucasfilm projects, ILM artists were excited to start with early outlines instead, giving them a chance to contribute more. Bennett's idea was fortuitous, because ILM not only contributed their trademark visual effects, but also would help reshape the story. "It was all too rare at ILM," recollected visual effects art director David Carson, "that we had an opportunity for visual input so early in the process."[8]

One example of ILM's contributions is Fifi Rebozo. After reading Bennett's script, Ralston thought that it would fun if Kruge had a pet, the equivalent of the parrot on the pirate's shoulder. "I drew the dog, did a 12-inch maquette of it with fake fur. I did this whole number to sell the look of it, which they went for," Ralston remembered.[9] The final

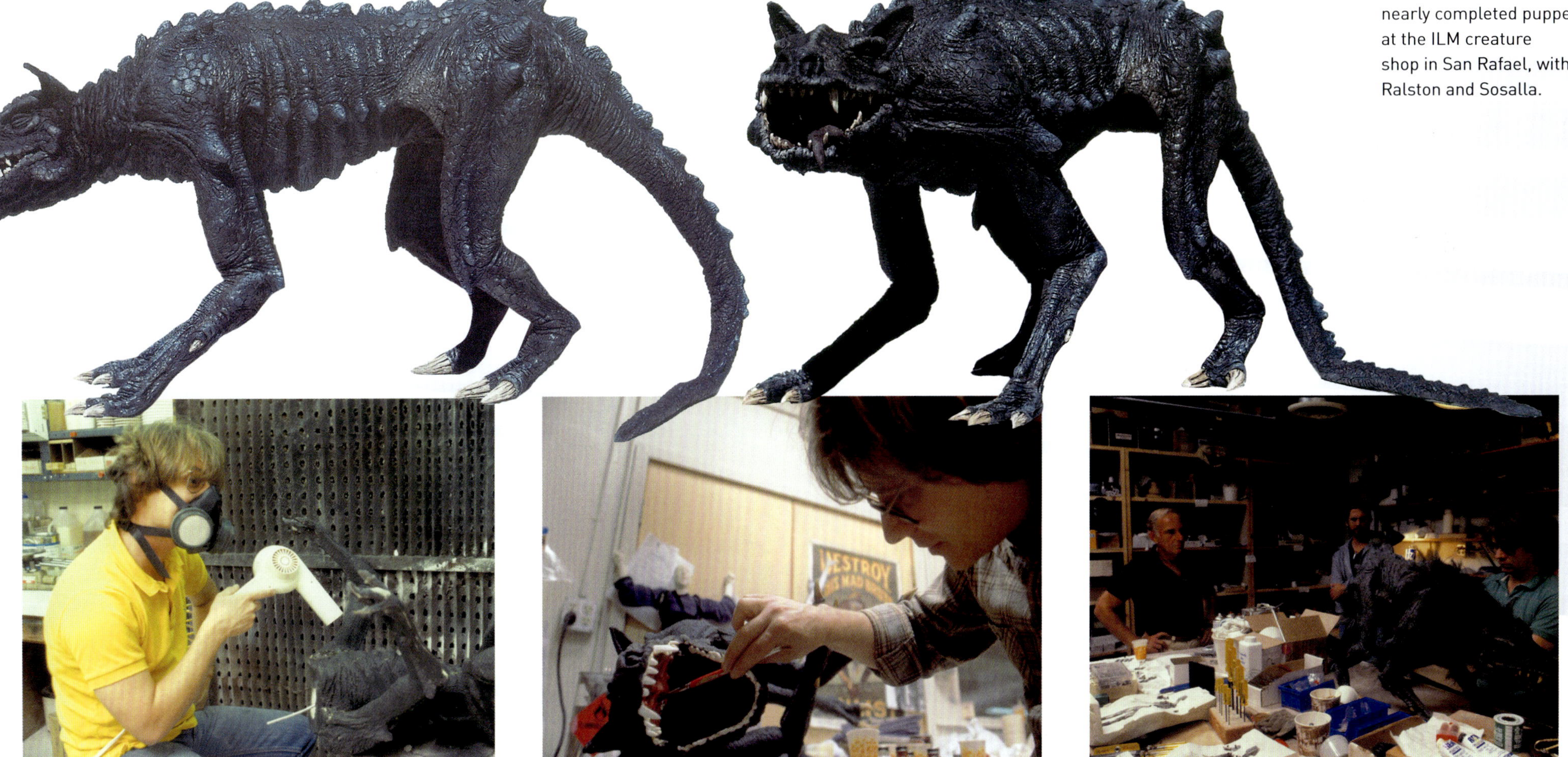

BELOW LEFT AND RIGHT:
ILM in-progress reference photos of Fifi Rebozo, before hair is added. The hair would come from wigs.

BOTTOM LEFT AND MIDDLE: Creature supervisor David Sosalla works on the beast puppet. He contributed to the previous *Star Trek* films as a sculptor.

BOTTOM RIGHT:
Bennett inspects the nearly completed puppet at the ILM creature shop in San Rafael, with Ralston and Sosalla.

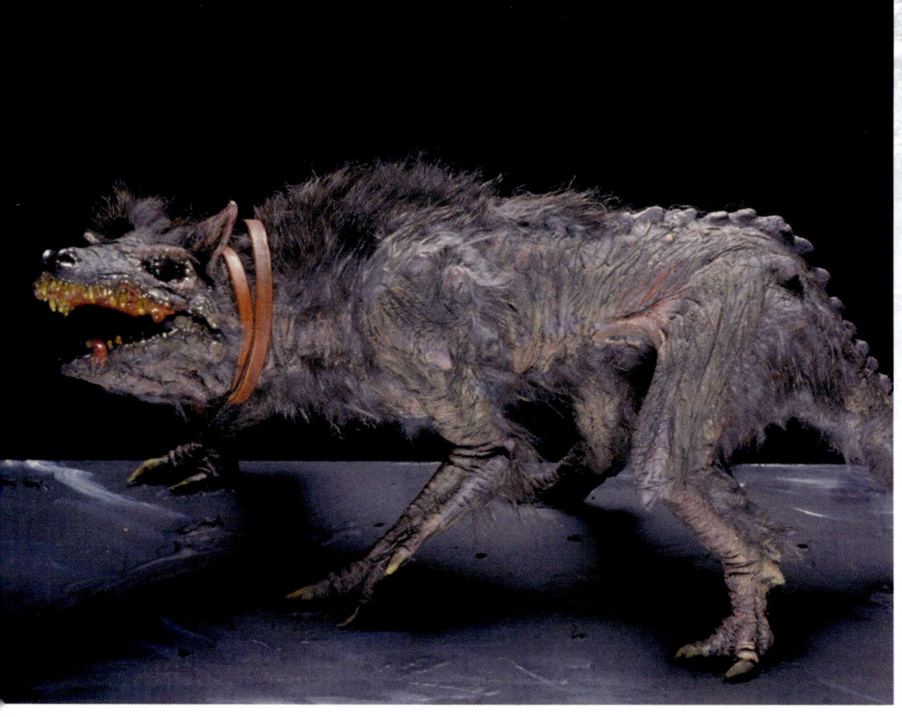

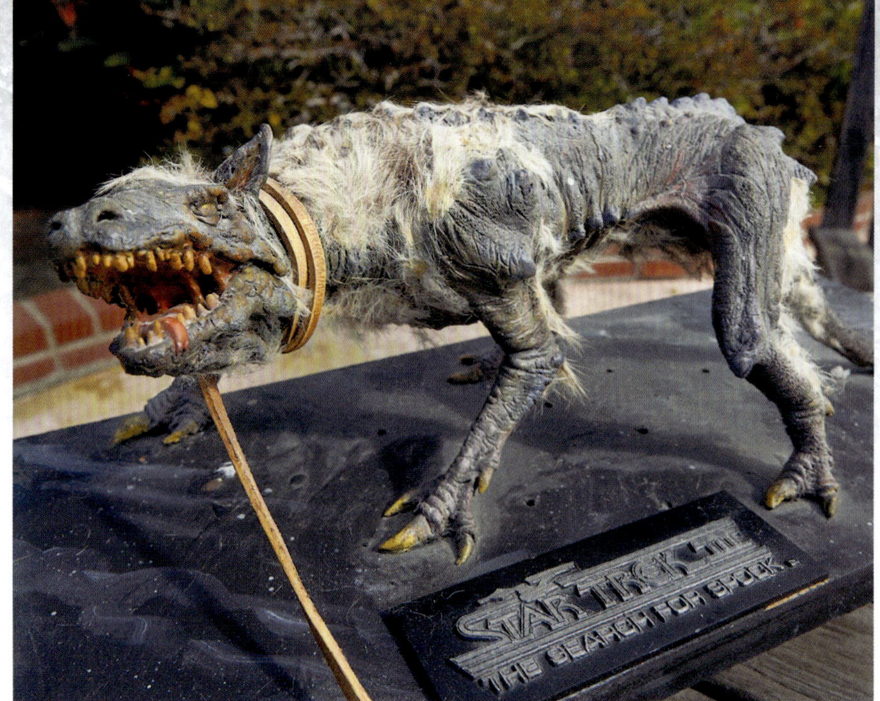

FAR LEFT: © Industrial Light & Magic. All Rights Reserved. Fifi Rebozo in his final form, 1984.

LEFT: Fifi Rebozo in 2024 where he resides with creator Ralston.[2]

version was sculpted by Ralston, David Sosalla, John Reed, and Kirk Thatcher, who went on to play the punk rocker on the bus in *Star Trek IV: The Voyage Home*. The ILM team nicknamed the beast Fifi Rebozo, albeit unofficially.

Christopher Lloyd (Kruge) would find the beast not only a humorous addition, but one that he incorporated to show dimensions to his character. His genuine sympathy for the animal when it dies contrasts his more ruthless actions in other parts of the film. Ralston explained, "We had a second dog. It was basically a stand-in to get the shot set up, so I didn't have to sit there with that on my arm inside the chair Kruge sits on. It had aluminum wiring. You could bend it around. We were having a rehearsal with Chris Lloyd. This is when the *Enterprise* attacks, there are explosions, and the Klingon dog dies. Chris did something that we never thought that he'd ever do, that wasn't scripted. He picks up the stand-in dog and holds it. I'm sitting there thinking 'Oh, no. Now what? He can't do that with the actual puppet.' During lunch, we grabbed that thing, tore it to shreds to make it limper, put weights in it, and glued stuff together with its tongue sticking out. What a race to the finish line that was! It's still not that convincing. But luckily you don't see it too much."[3]

BELOW LEFT: Ralston would operate the Fifi Rebozo puppet on stage with access on the left side of the creature. Ralston was hidden from view under Kruge's chair.

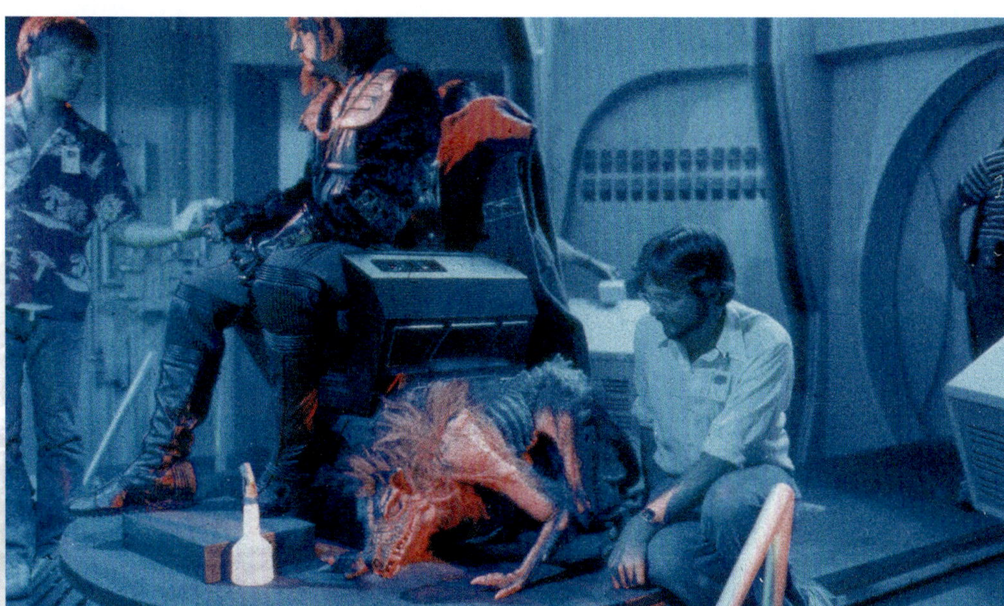

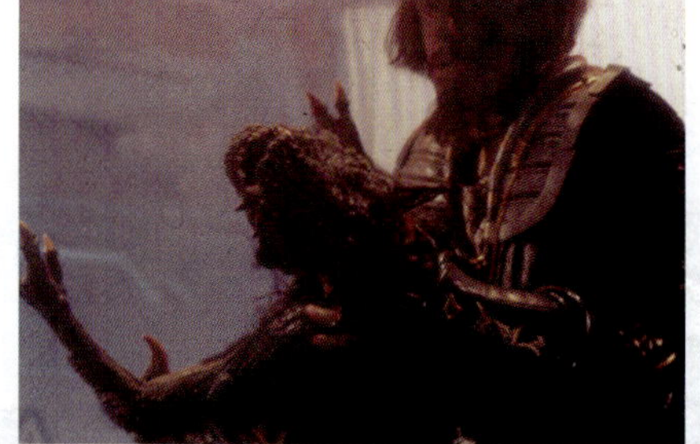

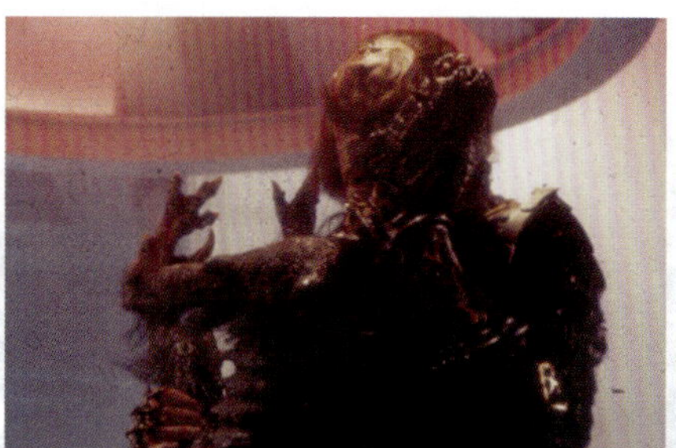

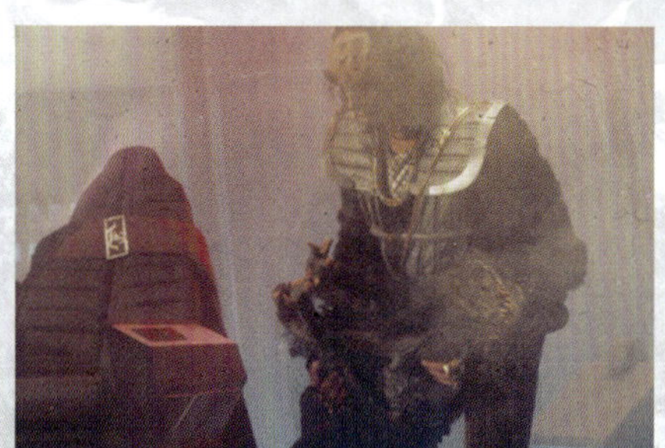

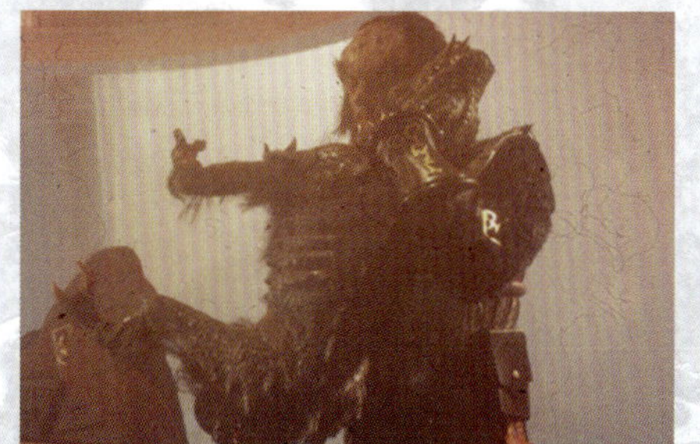

DELETED SCENE: KRUGE'S CRUELTY

There was more of the merchant ship crew and Valkris filmed than was featured in the film. Valkris' introduction included her wearing a ritual Klingon veil. She removes it, revealing she is Klingon to the audience as she begins to speak to Kruge. The veil can be seen for a brief moment above the merchant ship Captain in the final film. The first volley by the Bird-of-Prey does not destroy the merchant ship as in the film. Rather, the crew survives, and pleads for their life with Kruge, "For God's sake, help us! Please! We'll keep your damn secrets, just don't let us die in space!" As they ask for mercy, Valkris returns the veil to her face, knowing her and their fate is sealed. Kruge then commands their destruction.

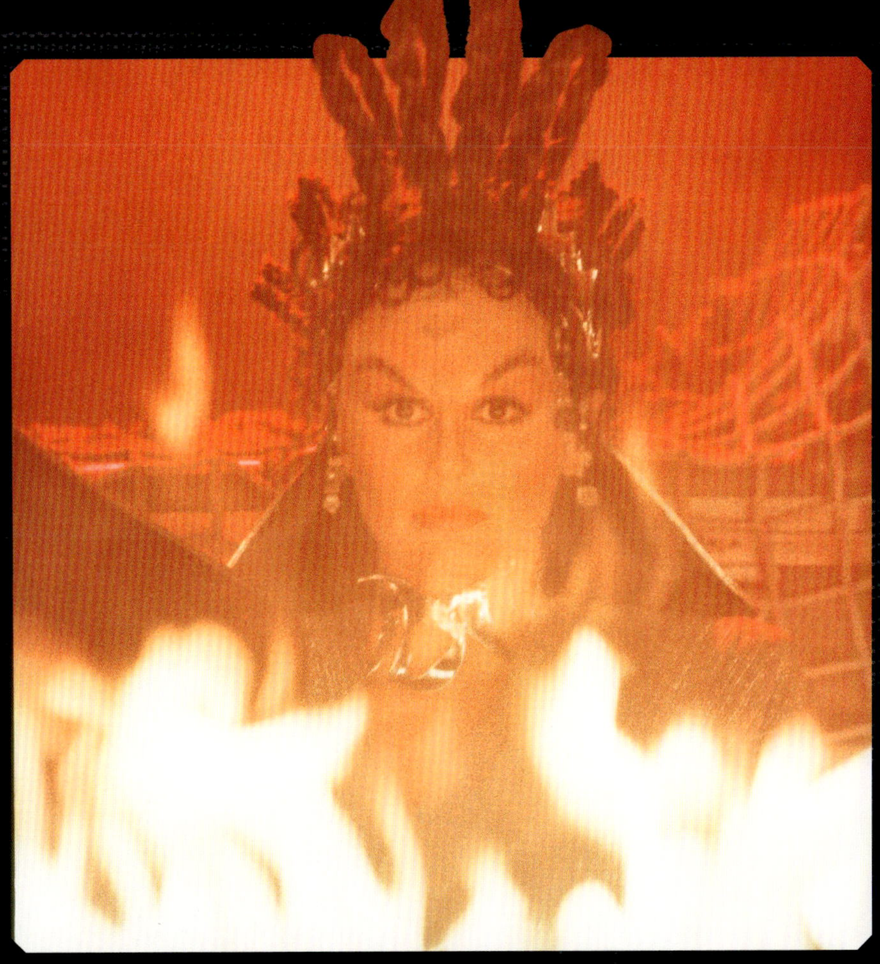

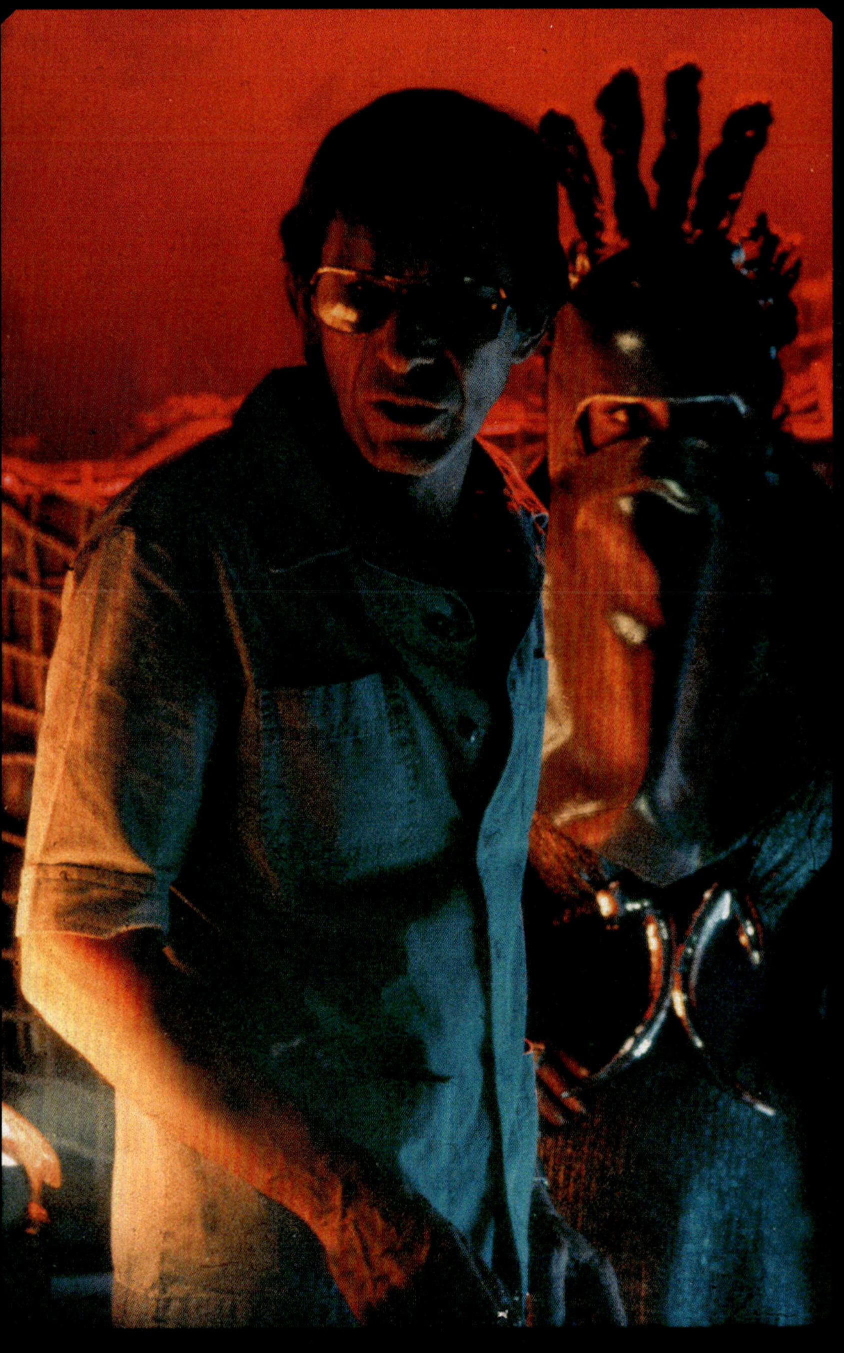

ABOVE: Nimoy directs Catherine Shirriff (Valkris) in the deleted scene.

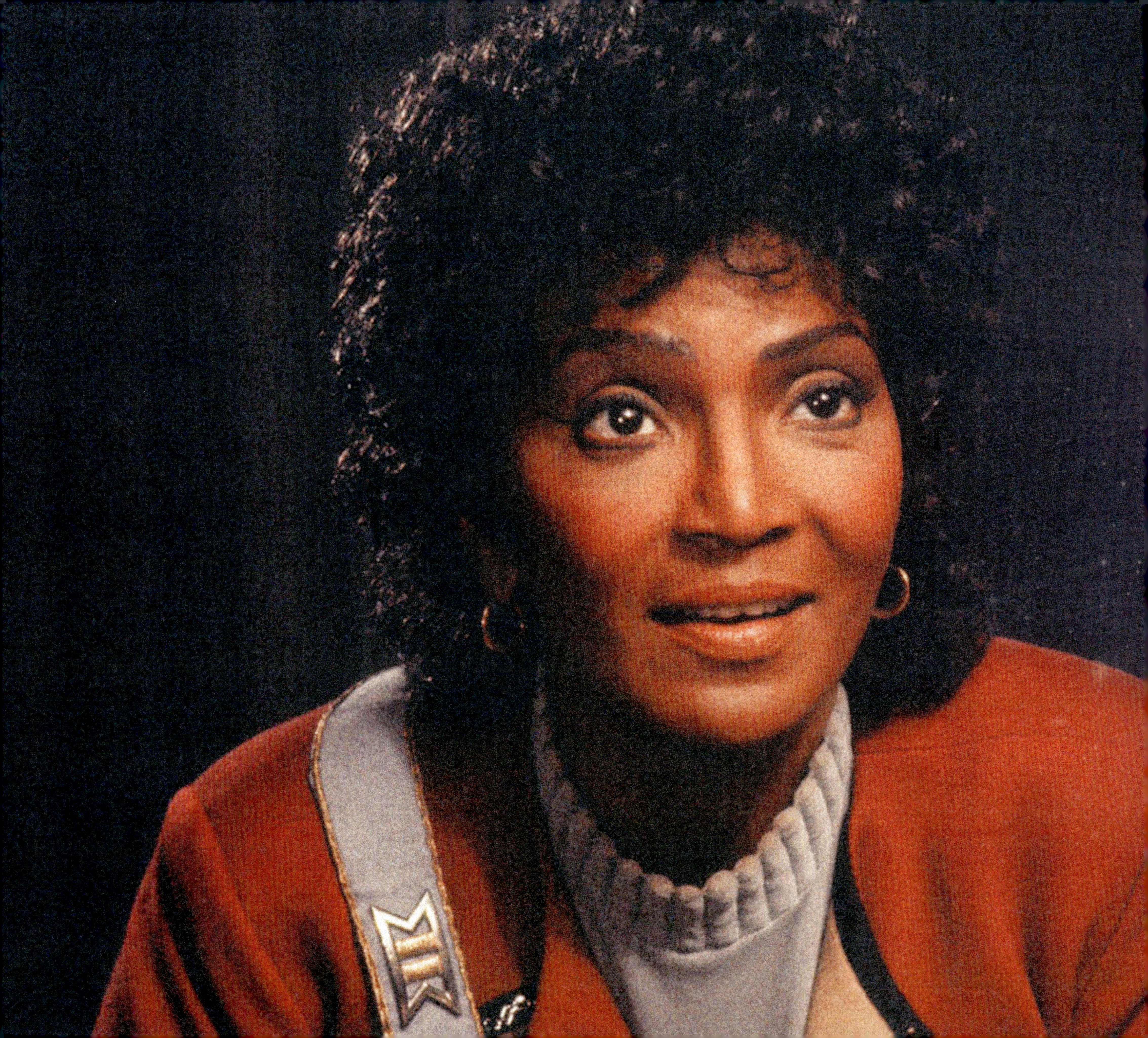

CHAPTER 4

ALL MY HOPES

NEW FACES OF THE FEDERATION

Although the character of David Marcus did not appear in early versions of the story, Saavik was always considered an essential player. Harve Bennett explained why, stating, "We needed to have someone in the crew to replace Vulcan knowledge, and that ultimately decided for us that she had to be in the story."[1] During negotiations with actress Kirstie Alley, who originated the role in the previous film, Bennett and Nimoy would be given yet another test. One of the unique qualities of *Star Trek* was its continuity of performers. Unlike franchises such as *James Bond*, the same troupe of actors had always played the main character roles. For the first time, *Star Trek III* required a fan-favorite main character actor to be replaced, because Alley was not returning.

In *I Am Spock*, Nimoy wrote about what occurred. "It looked like everything would work out, so when the script was ready, we sent it along for Kirstie and her agent to read. Shortly thereafter, her agent called us back, and said, 'Look, we didn't realize how large a role Saavik was going to have in this film. So we're withdrawing our earlier figure. Here's what we have to have now.'"[2] The price left Nimoy stunned: "I'm sure neither he nor Kirstie realized it, but the salary he wanted for her second *Star Trek* appearance was higher than what was being paid to De Kelley after seventeen years."[2]

Recasting did have a benefit. It would allow Nimoy to find an actress who could play a more traditional Vulcan, which he preferred to the emotional interpretation seen in *Star Trek II*. Even though *Star Trek III* occurs only days after the previous film, it was thought that Saavik's experiences had been transformative. The script described a Saavik that was less of an inexperienced cadet and more of a mature Vulcan expert. No Alley meant another search for Spock, this time to find a new Saavik.

BELOW: The novelization of the film by Vonda McIntyre posits that J.T. Esteban and James Kirk were friends, something that is hinted at in the film when Kirk sends Esteban his compliments.

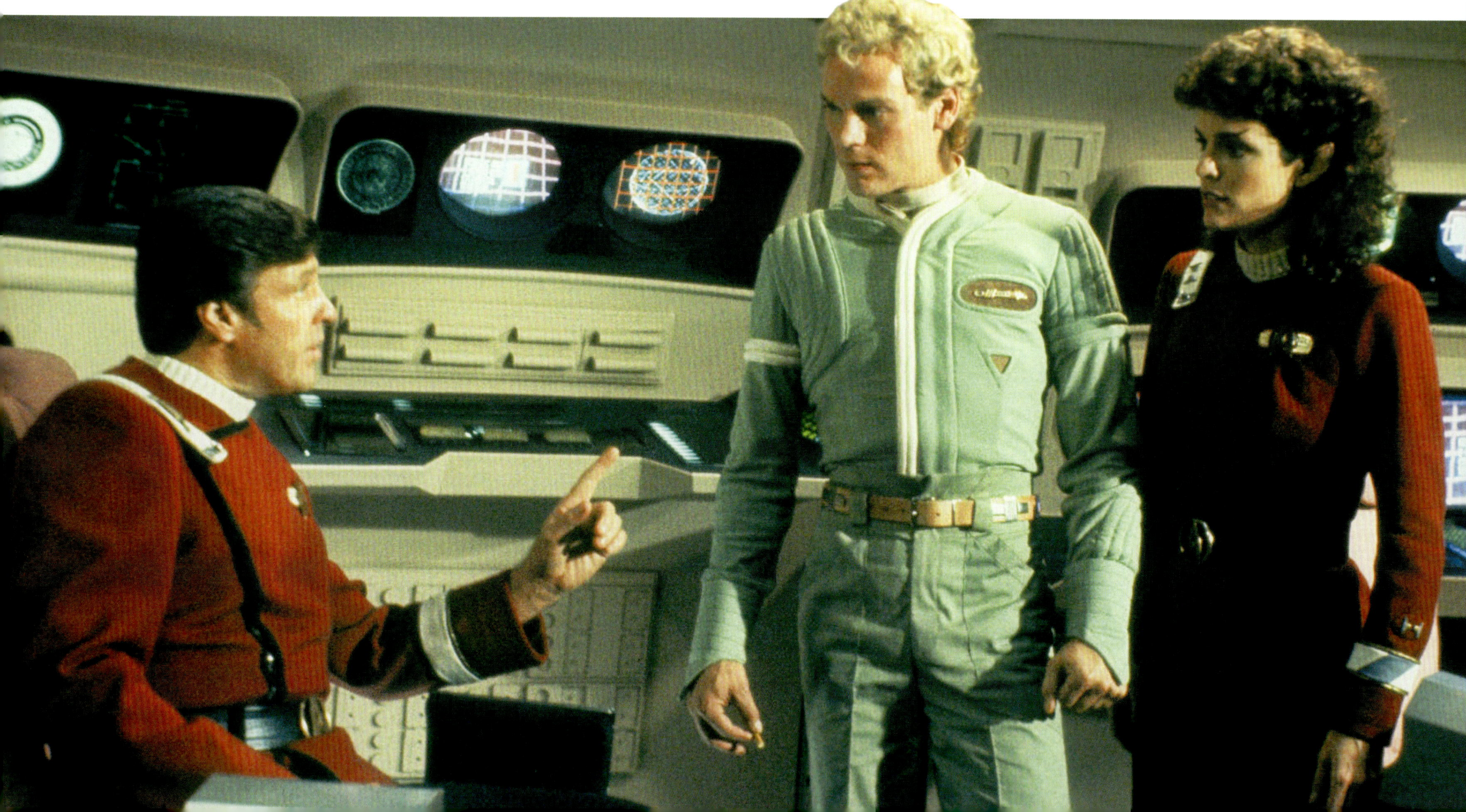

NEW FACES

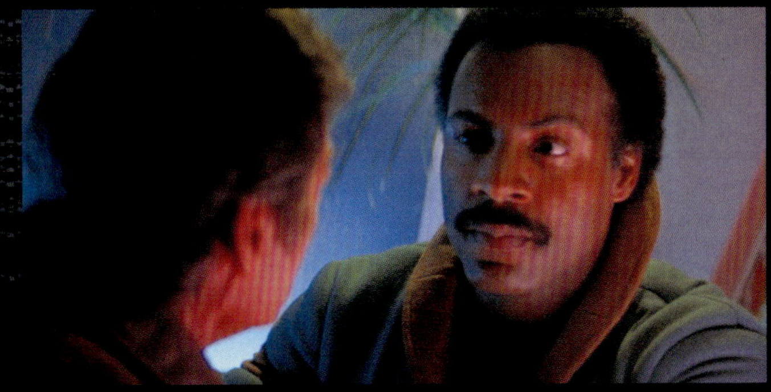

ABOVE: The civilian Federation Security officer who invites McCoy to take a nice, long rest is played by Conroy Gedeon. Had the bar fight scene been included in the final film, Gedeon's character would have had a larger role trying to navigate the crowd in order to capture McCoy.

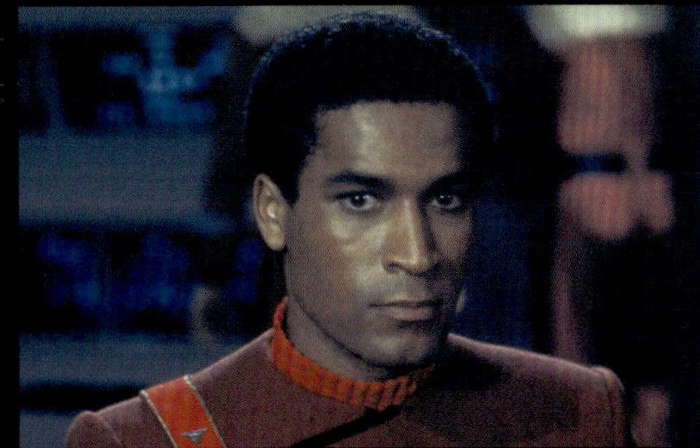

ABOVE: Phil Morris, who played Cadet Foster, is no stranger to *Star Trek*. He would play four more roles during thirty years on various *Trek* series, a child in the original series episode 'Miri' wearing an Army helmet, Klingon Thopok in *Deep Space Nine*'s 'Looking for par'Mach in All the Wrong Places' and Jem'Hadar Remata'Klan in 'Rocks and Shoals,' and astronaut John Kelly in *Voyager*'s 'One Small Step.'

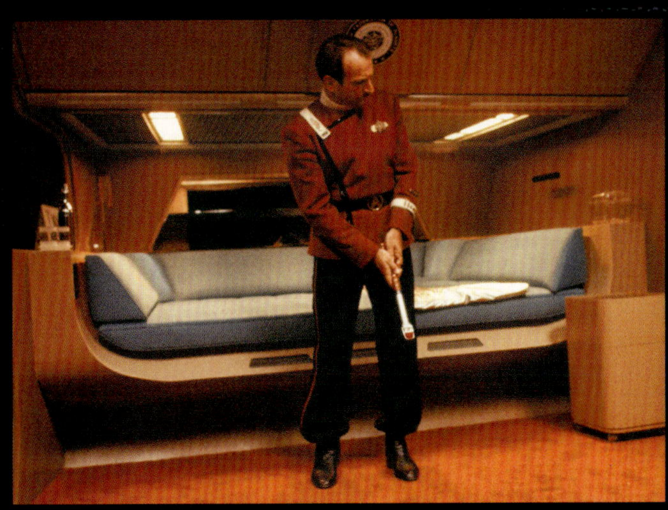

ABOVE: Emmy-nominated for his performance of Howard Hunter on *Hill Street Blues*, James B. Sikking took on the role of Captain Styles when asked by his friend Nimoy. The taciturn Styles proved so popular that he would be included in novels, comic books, and role-playing games. His first name, Lawrence, is visible on the *U.S.S. Excelsior* dedication plaque in the *Star Trek: Picard* episode 'The Star Gazer.' Pictured is an alternate version of the scene where Styles relaxes in his cabin, practicing golf instead of filing his nails.

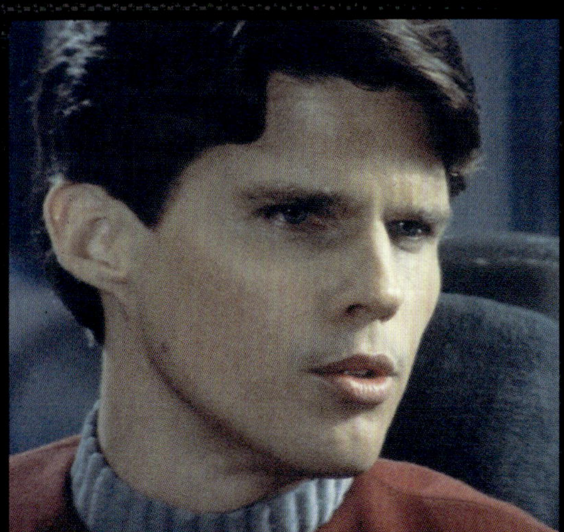

ABOVE: Colloquially known as "Mr. Adventure," the young Lieutenant literally put in his place by Uhura was played by actor Scott McGinnis. Author Vonda McIntyre invented the name Heisenberg for the character in the film's novelization, a nod to physicist Werner Heisenberg who, like his unofficial namesake in *Star Trek III*, was not above challenging the status quo.

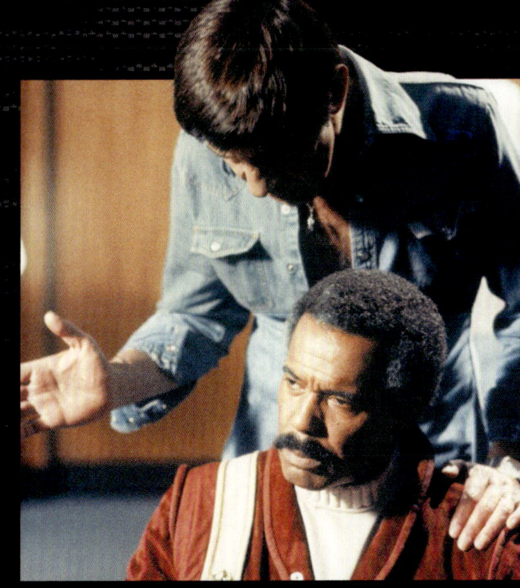

ABOVE: Robert Hooks played Admiral Morrow, a friend of Kirk who tries to refocus his colleague's priorities. The character was scripted to return in *Star Trek IV: The Voyage Home*, but Hooks was busy performing in a series of guest TV roles and in the TV movie *D.C. Cops*. Hooks would play a supervisor to a Shatner character again on *T.J. Hooker*.

ROBIN CURTIS (SAAVIK)

Saavik may have been born on the Romulan Hellguard Colony, but Robin Curtis was born June 15, 1956, in the small town of New York Mills, New York. "I think what was unique about my childhood, as my former partner would say, is that it is an example of how many hairs make a fine brush," she said. Many people shaped her journey, including music teacher Jo Gatsa, mother Carol, a musician, and father, Robert. New York Mills was a small enough school district, Curtis could participate in many, if not all, extracurricular activities - sports, cheerleading, choir, band, and school plays. After graduating from the *State University of New York at Oswego*, she moved to New York City to join friends seeking careers in the theater. An invitation from a fellow alum to join the cast of a new off-off Broadway musical led her to an introduction to her first talent agents, Lester and Juliet Lewis. Within weeks, she scored her first commercial for *Oil of Olay*. "There I was with an apartment, a great waitressing job, an agent, and my first national commercial! From then on, I worked pretty consistently but never let go of my waitressing job. And three years later, my agents encouraged me to go to Hollywood."

In the early spring of 1982. Curtis' LA manager, Michael Mann, introduced her to the various casting offices at the major studios. At Paramount, Robin met Elza Bergeron who thought of Robin a year later when the character of Saavik appeared in the breakdowns. By this time, Robin had guest starred on a *Knight Rider* episode and a movie-of-the-week, *In Love with an Older Woman*. "When the role of Saavik came across her desk, Elza remembered me and brought me in to see her and Stuart Jensen, head of casting. I understood I was there for *Star Trek* but beyond that, it was all very clandestine. I left the meeting still not knowing the name of the character!" To her surprise, Curtis was given an appointment the following day to meet the director, Leonard Nimoy. "*Star Trek* was familiar to me because I watched it as a kid back in the late sixties. My brother, who is two years older than me, loved it; he understood the science and the allegory in Roddenberry's storytelling. I was more enthralled by the weekly romantic escapades of Kirk and Spock. Spock's dilemma whether to leave or stay in the cave with Mariette Hartley? Now, that's erotic!"

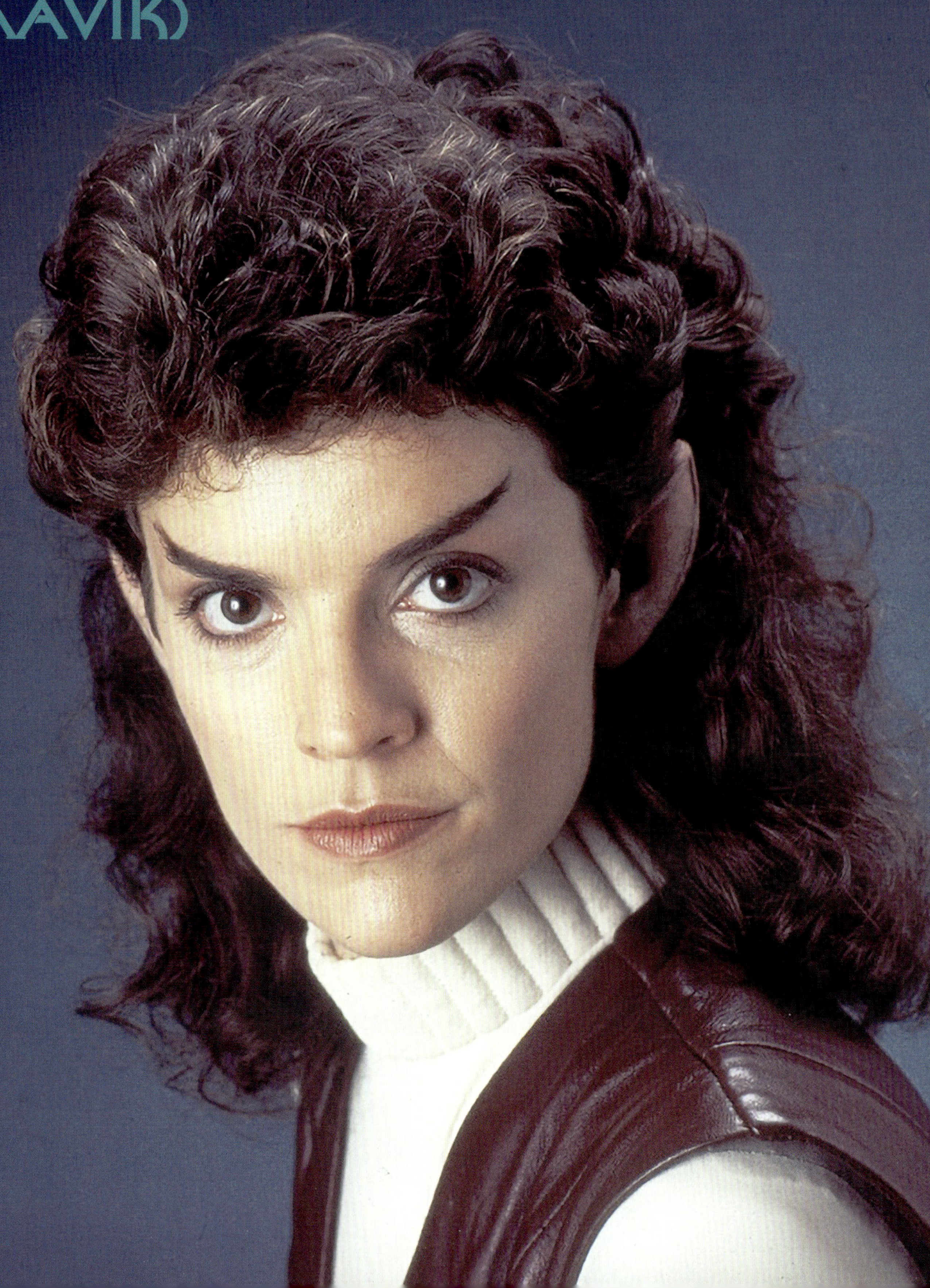

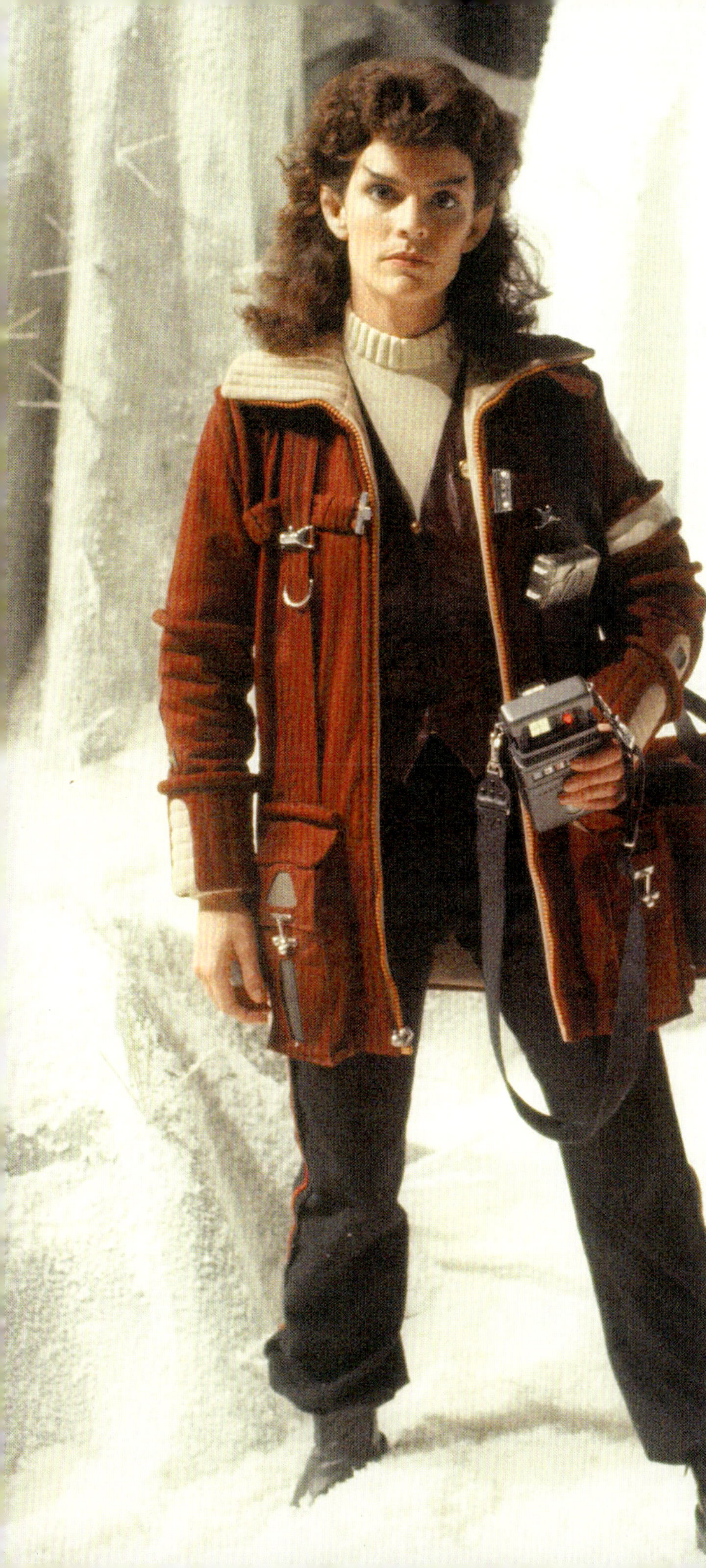

THIS SPREAD: Saavik is seen without her uniform jacket (opposite page) briefly at the end of the film when the crew disembarks on Vulcan. The casual look helps convey that Saavik feels comfortable around her *Enterprise* family, as contrasted to her wearing the more formal uniform when the ceremony led by T'Lar actually begins.

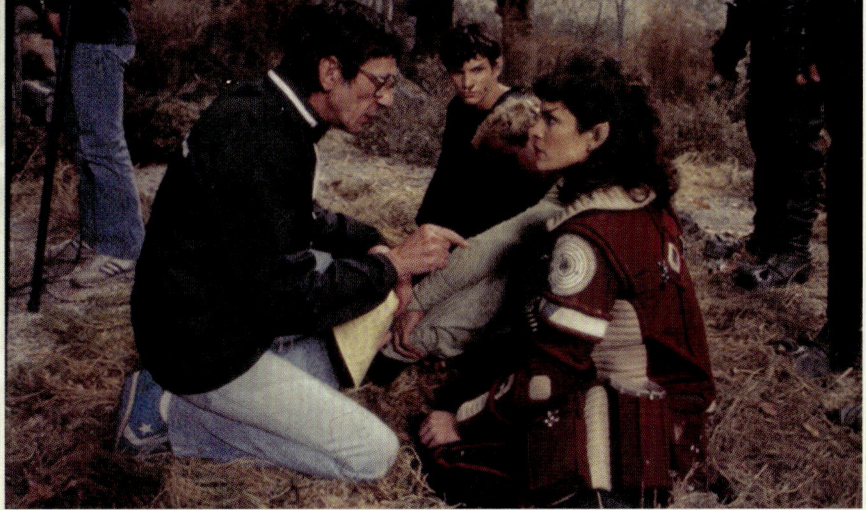

Nearly every *Star Trek III* actor that Nimoy auditioned remembers the experience more like a conversation than a formal audition. Curtis reminisced, "I wore a white jumpsuit, with this really cool, tie-dyed, multicolored short sleeved V-neck overlay with a belt across my hip. I hoped I appeared somewhat futuristic! What made my initial meeting with Mr. Nimoy unique and special was that rather than meeting a roomful of people to whom I wouldn't be introduced, I met with him one on one. This kind, articulate man might have intimidated me but he didn't because he was so charming and put me at ease immediately. He asked if I minded if he videotaped our conversation. Of course, I didn't mind. Capturing our meeting on tape saved me from having to return for a callback, what people in the industry call an actor's second audition – which can be very stressful. I finished the audition, Mr. Nimoy walked me to the door, shook my hand and said, he had no doubt I could play the part. 'Now it's up to the powers that be.' I walked out of there on Cloud 9!"

Once cast, getting the role of Saavik in August of 1983 meant more to Curtis then Nimoy could know. "*Star Trek III* was not only my first leading role in a major motion picture; it was a boon to my family at a very difficult time. My father had lung cancer in 1978 and five years later, in June of '83, the cancer metastasized to his brain. We were grief stricken. *Star Trek* became this magical and novel distraction for me and for my family from the sadness and fear we lived with daily. *Star Trek* brightened our lives like a beacon and I will always be most grateful for that. Contrary to most of my friends' parents, mine actually rooted for me as I pursued a very competitive field. When I called home, I always heard on the other end of the line, 'What do you need? Are you okay? Can we send you anything?' So blessed." Curtis' father lived to see the premiere in June of 1984. And Curtis remembers the film and all of its promise was a way of saying to her father, "I'm going to be okay, Dad."[3]

A SPOCK SCRAPBOOK

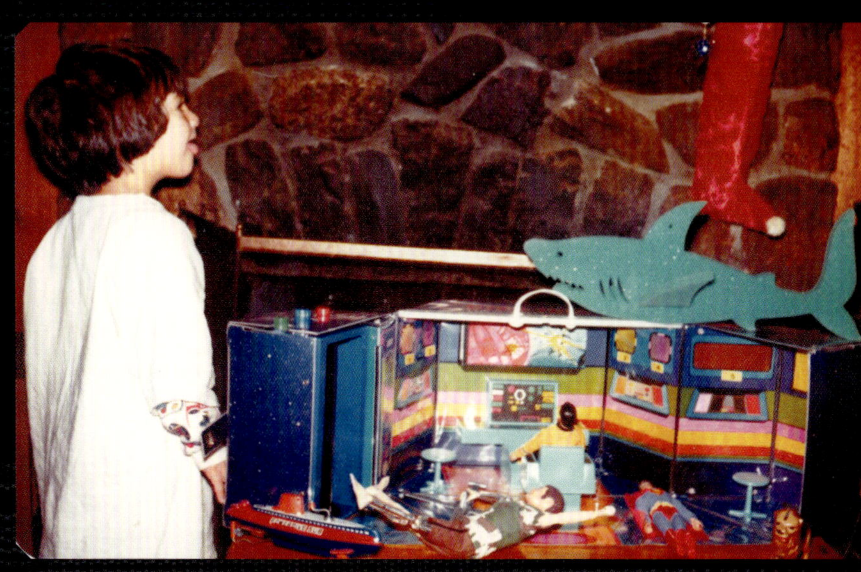

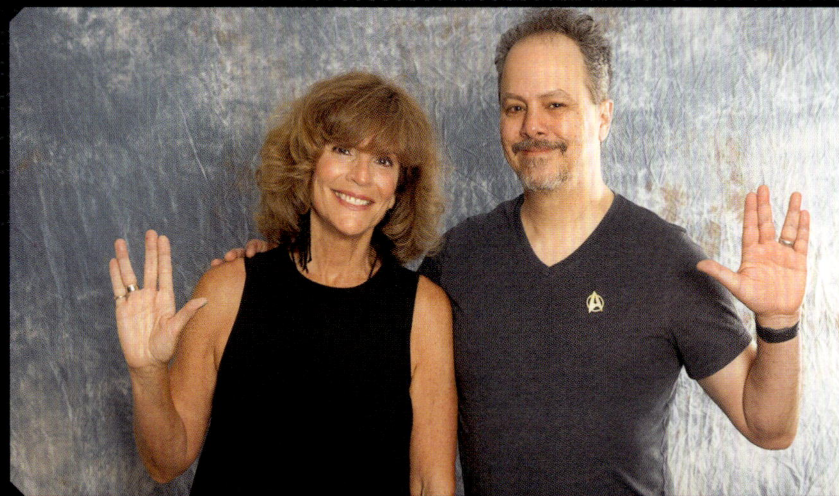

STAR TREK III - Rev. 8/10/83 71.

145 BACK TO DAVID 145

He reacts in wonder.

146 INT. THE CAVE AT GENESIS PEAK - CLOSE - MOVING - NIGHT 146

Saavik is ministering to the O.S. boy. We do not yet see his face. We hear his SOFT SOUNDS, the aftermath of cries which we heard earlier. CAMERA CONTINUES MOVING as Saavik takes off her tunic and throws it as an added cover on the O.S. figure. Then she stops, looks at the boy in wonder, as CAMERA completes its arc to reveal the BOY. *

We are shocked to see the Boy is changed. He is now unquestionably older, perhaps 13 or 14. He is breathing heavily as his pain recedes.

SAAVIK
(... Sleep...)

She rises, and slowly steals out. HOLD on the Boy.

257

147 EXT. GENESIS PROMONTORY - CLOSE - DAVID - NIGHT 147

Looking out over the darkened planet, lost in thought. WIDEN to admit Saavik. She too looks outward. A distant, FAINT RUMBLE. No tremor felt. Then:

DAVID
(taking tricorder readings)
This planet is aging in surges.

Saavik steps forward seeking eye contact and an explanation. David looks at her now.

DAVID
The Genesis wave started a life clock ticking for him and the planet. But at the rate things are going now... *

(CONTINUED)

TOP: Christmas Day: Potenza playing with his MEGO *Star Trek* bridge playset and action figures. "I was already a big *Star Trek* fan and I was as traumatized as everyone else from Spock's death in *Star Trek II*. I was wondering if and how they were going to bring him back."[4 10]

BOTTOM: Curtis and Potenza reunited at a convention nearly forty years later. "Robin, I cannot sing her praises enough. I remember feeling very safe and comfortable around her," Potenza said. "Movie sets could be intimidating. Robin was a very reassuring presence."[4 10]

ABOVE: Potenza's actual script page: "You know they were so secretive. I was given only a single script page. I didn't know if I was a flashback or some other Vulcan boy that just happened to find his ceremonial robe. After I was done filming, someone said to me, 'Don't tell anyone what happens.' And I was like, 'I have no idea what happened!' I have a vivid memory of sitting in the makeup chair next to Merritt Butrick. We were waiting for our next scene. I asked him, 'Does Spock live?' And he said, 'No one knows!'"[4]

THE MANY FACES OF SPOCK

Before the era of de-aging computer effects and AI fakes, multiple actors were required to play a given character at different ages in the same production. Six actors would play the role of Spock in *Star Trek III*, in addition to stunt performers and even a puppet (see Chapter 6).

CARL STEVEN (SPOCK…AGE 9)

Carl Steven, born Carlo Steven Krakoff on November 7, 1974, appeared in shows such as *Simon & Simon* and *Little House on the Prairie* before *Star Trek III*. Spock would not be the only time Steven played a younger version of a Nimoy character. Seven years later in *Never Forget*, he played the young version of Nimoy's Mel Mermelstein. Steven died at age thirty-four in 2011. Vadia Potenza who played Spock at age thirteen fondly thinks of his time on stage with Steven, "I have a very sweet memory of him. We were both little kids, and we were just kind of being goofy and laughing on set."[4]

VADIA POTENZA (SPOCK…AGE 13)

Vadia "Vaj" Potenza was born on April 22, 1971, in New York before moving to Los Angeles when he was four years old. "My mom was an off-Broadway actress for about ten years, and that is the way I got into acting. When I was a baby, I had done a commercial with my mother for a cold product. When I was ten years old, I told my mom, 'I think I want to try acting.' I was lucky enough to get an agent relatively quickly."

Potenza, actually twelve when he got the role of Spock, joked, "I could play thirteen, because I was, you know, very mature for twelve! They said it was *Star Trek*, yet didn't say anything else other than that. The audition meeting was Leonard Nimoy and myself. We exchanged pleasantries and found out that we shared ancestry from a similar area in Ukraine. When we discovered that commonality, I remember us sharing a smile and in my mind, that's when he decided to let me be Spock because it seemed like we had a rapport."[4]

BELOW LEFT: Nimoy with Steven, Curtis, and Butrick."In the rehearsal of that scene," Curtis remembered, "Leonard suggested that young Spock reach out and touch my nose as a recognition of sorts."[3] A Ritter fan stands ready in the background to blow plastic snow all around the Genesis set.

BELOW RIGHT: Potenza as Spock…Age 13.

BOTTOM RIGHT: Carl Steven (Spock…Age 9) and Robin Curtis.

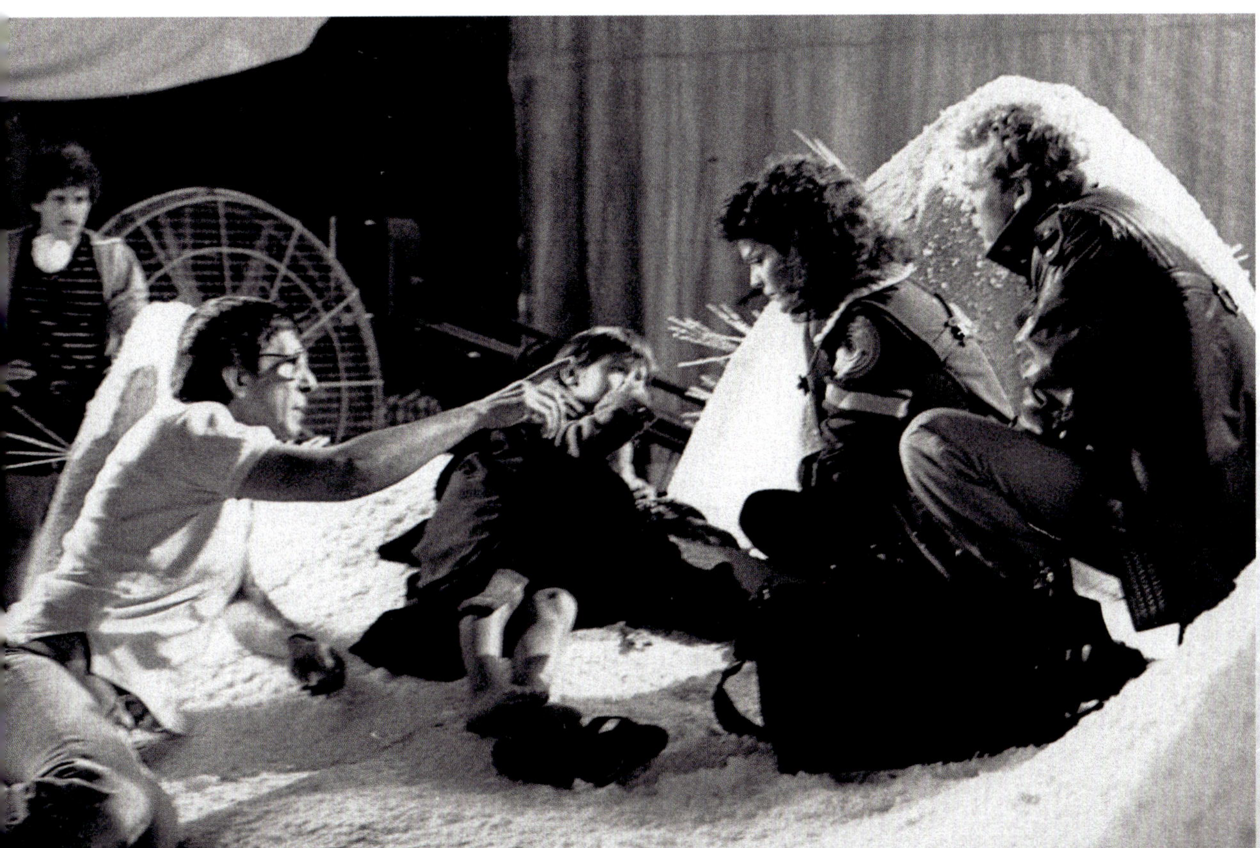

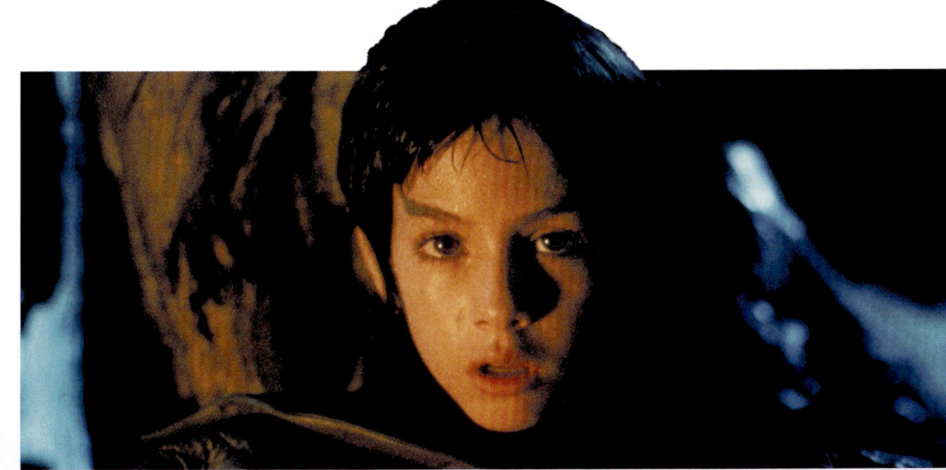

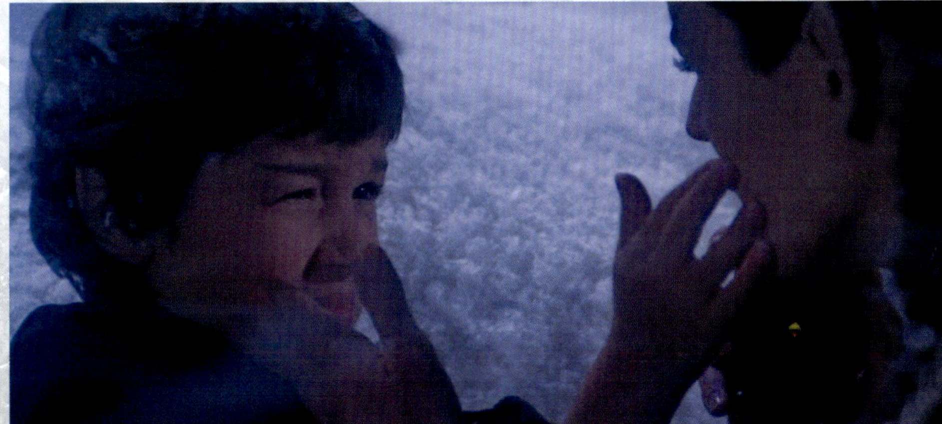

STEPHEN MANLEY (SPOCK...AGE 17)

"My grandfather, Stephen Soldi, was an actor, starting in the silent film era. He worked with the Marx Brothers and he is the actor who takes the umbrella from Gene Kelly in *Singing in the Rain*. He was my hero. He taught me how to read by reading scripts, about set etiquette, makeup, camera placement, and the various kinds of artists who worked on a set. I wanted to make my grandfather proud, carry on his tradition, and do good work and be responsible," remembered Stephen Manley. Born February 13, 1965, Manley was one of the 1970s and 1980s most popular child actors, guest starring on *The Carol Burnett Show*, *The Love Boat*, *The Streets of San Francisco*, and in the Robert Wise movie *The Hindenburg*, a production on which he suffered terrible second-and-third-degree burns due to an accident on set.

Nimoy had recently watched Manley's performance in the David Jacobs-produced television show *Secrets of Midland Heights*. According to Manley, "I played a young person trying to come to terms about losing my mom with the help of a fortune teller played by the famous stage actress Zohra Lampert. She was a very heavy method actor and people were intimated by her. I fell in love with her and thought she was wonderful. A few years later, when I was eighteen, I was called to a meeting with Leonard Nimoy. It wasn't really an audition. It was more of a conversation. Leonard said to me, 'I've seen you before. How did you like working with Zohra?' I knew it was a test because of how many actors were intimidated by her. I said, 'I loved her. I learned a great deal from her.' He said, 'That's great because she is a friend of mine and I know what kind of an actress she is.' Leonard told me that I would not have dialog in the role and that he wanted me to bring the same kind of work ethic I did with Zohra to what he wanted me to do. That's what got me the job as Spock."

As with the other Spocks, Manley was also given very little information. "I never did get any script pages. Those who had script pages had infrared coding on their pages. I did not know I was playing Spock until they brought Joe Davis in, who plays Spock at twenty-five. Harve Bennett and [Gene Roddenberry's assistant] Richard Arnold arrived at the meeting. They had myself, Joe, and Leonard stand together. They thought we all looked good. Leonard said, 'Stephen, could you wear brown contact lenses because your eyes are too blue?' I said, 'Yes, no problem. I'll wear whatever you want.' It was then I realized that I would be playing a younger Spock."[5]

JOE W. DAVIS (SPOCK...AGE 25)

An actor and musician, Davis was born February 27, 1959. Although brief, his role of Spock required him to have a life-mask made by the makeup department so they could design a puppet that would transform his visage to that of Nimoy. The role of Spock at this age was originally offered to Adam Nimoy, who said, "My father asked me if I wanted to play the part of the younger Spock. It was nice of him to offer but it wasn't something I cared to pursue."[6]

BELOW LEFT: Stephen Manley as Spock...Age 17.

BELOW RIGHT: Joe W. Davis as Spock...Age 25.

RIGHT: Although Manley performed his own screams on set, tapping into the real pain he had suffering from migraines, the voice of Frank Welker was used instead to give the sound an otherworldliness and consistency actor to actor. Curtis, Manley remembered, was such an empathetic person that she screamed along with him in the scene silently.[5]

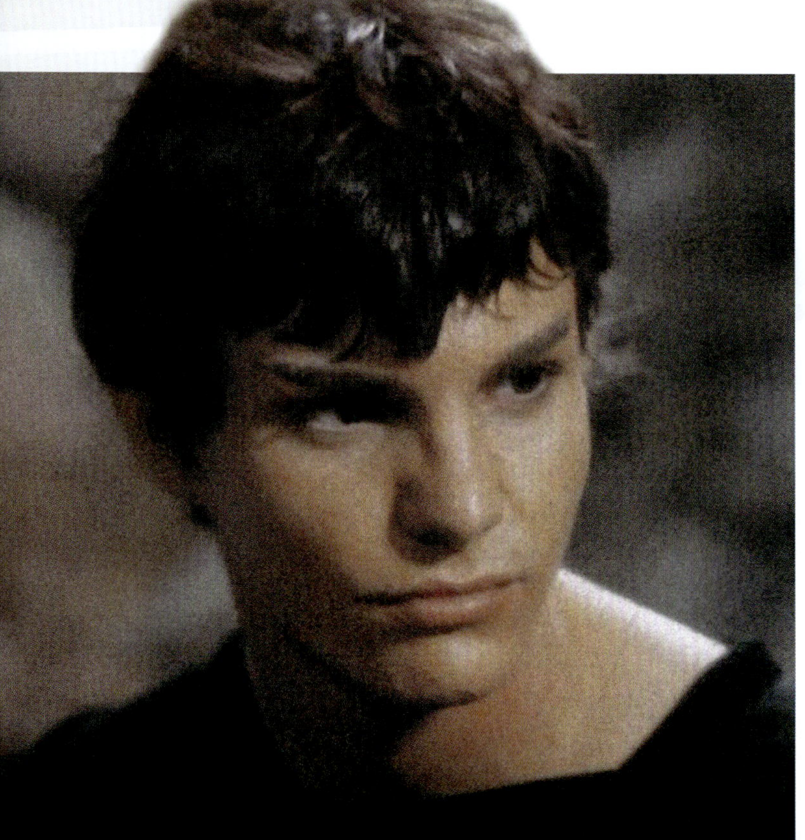

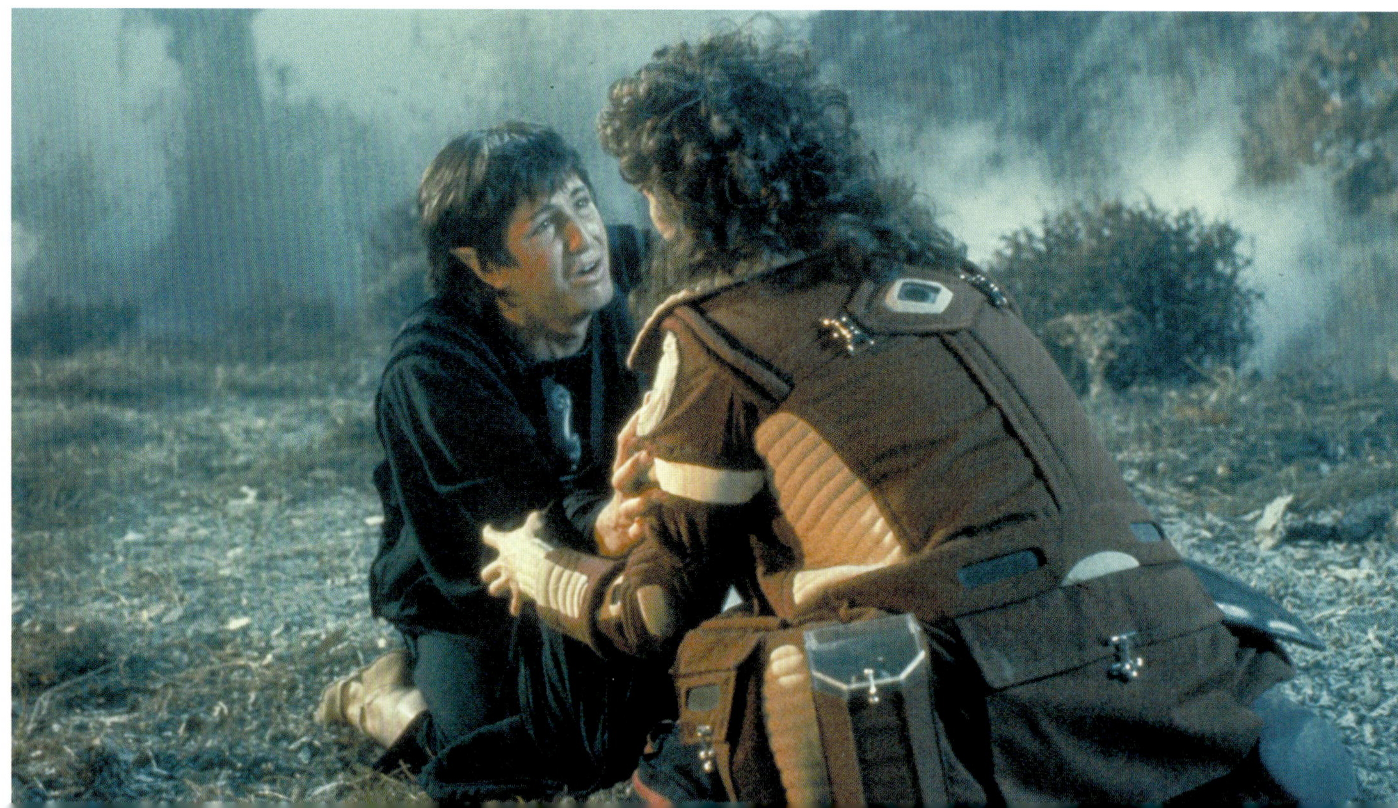

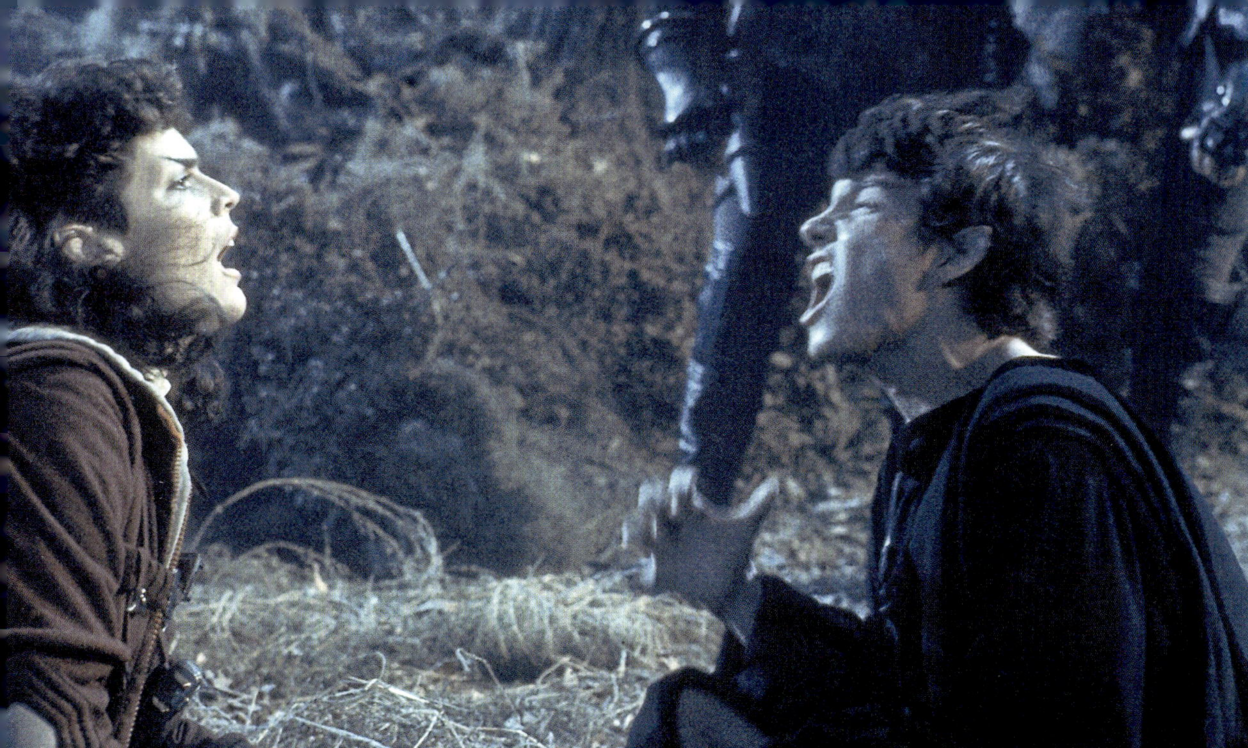

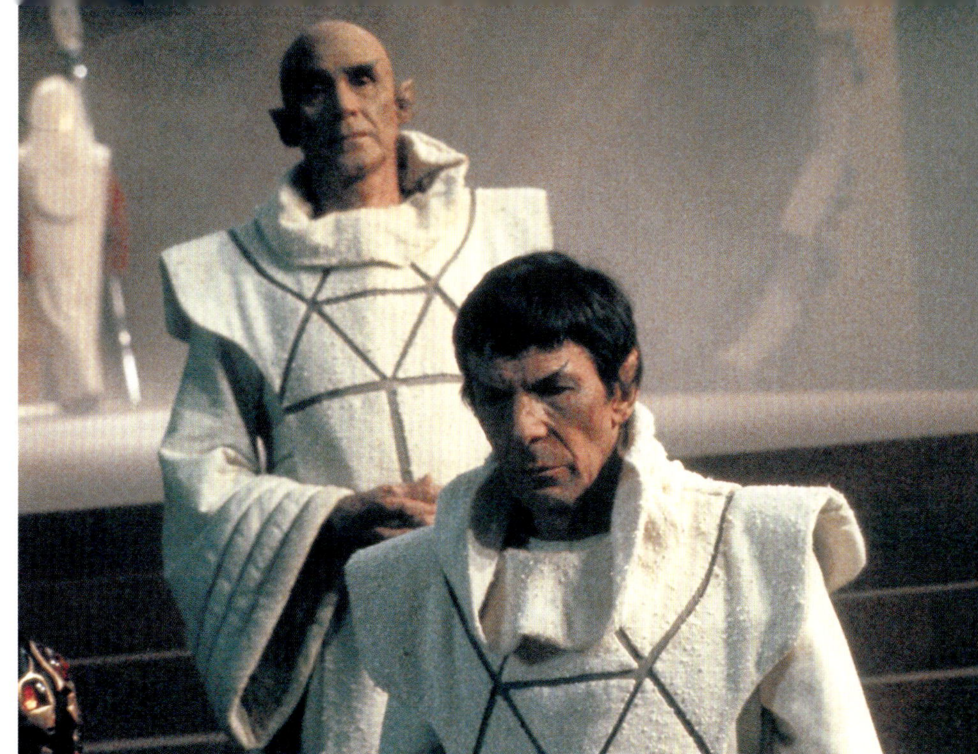

FRANK WELKER (SPOCK SCREAMS)

With close to 900 performances in films and television shows, from Scooby-Doo to Megatron, there are few voice actors as iconic as Frank Welker. He literally is the man of a thousand voices. Welker was very happy to join *Star Trek III*: "I was just asked if I was available and wanted to do it. Of course, when I heard the details and that I would be working with Leonard, I was at the studio before they opened the gate!"

Nimoy directed Welker's session himself. "He was an excellent director; he knew what he wanted and yet he was open to any ideas I had," said Welker. "I told him it is best for me to just watch the scene and react to what I saw. He liked this approach and was delighted that there was not much direction to be given, it was obvious and on screen in front of me. He was very protective and concerned with my voice and comfort, and only asked for another take when he felt he really needed it. It was the two of us and the sound editor. A funny aside, these sound stages are absolutely quiet. You can literally hear a pin drop. Well, the poor sound editor kept ruining our takes because of a noisy stomach. Leonard politely turned to him and asked him to leave the room and get something to eat. With tail between his legs, he gurgled his way to the sound booth and took his notes from there. Leonard looked at me and we both chuckled at the irony of the situation."

Welker would also provide the sounds of the creatures in the film. "After doing the screams of the young Nimoy character, he asked me if I would like to try to do some sound effects for the creature… Of course, I was delighted since it is what I do… [Nimoy] laughed after the take and said, 'That was just wonderful!' My weird and slightly disgusting sounds were just what he wanted. Thinking back, I may have been channeling the sound editor's stomach growling!"[7]

FRANK FORCE (SPOCK)

Trying to find a credit list for the actor Frank Force who played Nacluv in *Star Trek III* would be a daunting challenge – because he doesn't exist! To preserve the secret of if and how Spock returned, call sheets and crew referred to Nimoy as Frank Force and Spock as Nacluv (Vulcan backwards.) Nimoy, as Frank Force in the film's credits, also performed the *Excelsior* "Elevator Voice" which Scotty rebuffs with, "Up your shaft!"

ABOVE: This is Frank Force in his one and only movie!

BELOW: The September 16, 1983, call sheet required a closed set to help preserve the secret that Frank Force and Nacluv were really Nimoy and Spock.

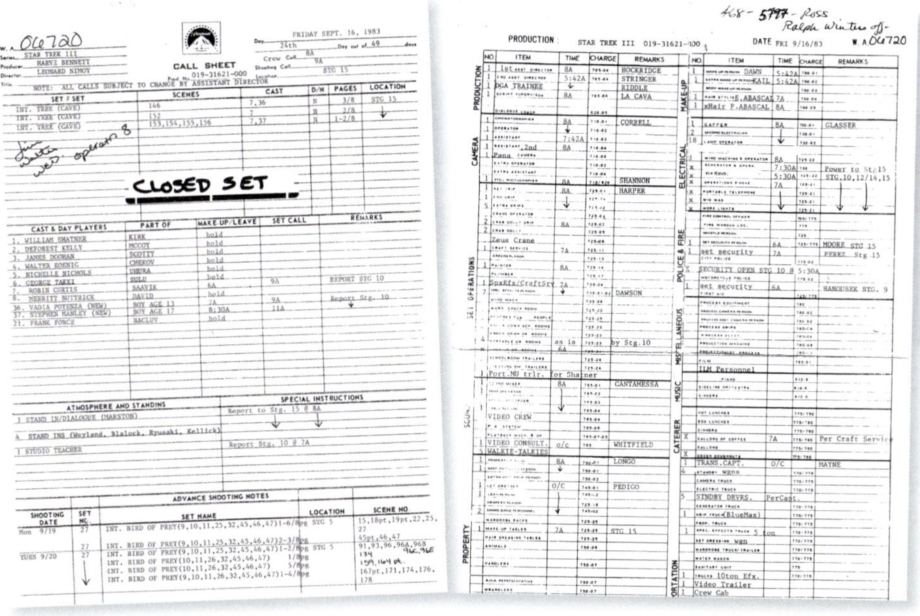

W. A. 06720

Series: STAR TREK III
Producer: HARVE BENNETT
Director: LEONARD NIMOY

CALL SHEET
Prod. No. 019-31621-000

FRIDAY SEPT. 16, 1983
Day 24th Day out of 49 days
Crew Call 8A
Shooting Call 9A
Location STG 15

NOTE: ALL CALLS SUBJECT TO CHANGE BY ASSISTANT DIRECTOR

SET / SET	SCENES	CAST	D/N	PAGES	LOCATION
INT. TREE (CAVE)	146	7,36	N	3/8	STG 15
INT. TREE (CAVE)	152	7	N	2/8	↓
INT. TREE (CAVE)	153,154,155,156	7,37	N	1-2/8	

CLOSED SET

CAST & DAY PLAYERS	PART OF	MAKE-UP/LEAVE	SET CALL	REMARKS
1. WILLIAM SHATNER	KIRK	hold		
2. DEFOREST KELLY	MCCOY	hold		
3. JAMES DOOHAN	SCOTTY	hold		
4. WALTER KOENIG	CHEKOV	hold		
5. NICHELLE NICHOLS	UHURA	hold		
6. GEORGE TAKEI	SULU	hold	9A	REPORT STG 10
7. ROBIN CURTIS	SAAVIK	6A		
8. MERRITT BUTTRICK	DAVID	hold		Report Stg. 10
36. VADIA POTENZA (NEW)	BOY AGE 13	7A	9A	↓
37. STEPHEN MANLEY (NEW)	BOY AGE 17	8:30A	11A	
21. FRANK FORCE	NACLUV	hold		

ATMOSPHERE AND STANDINS	SPECIAL INSTRUCTIONS
1 STAND IN/DIALOGUE (MARSTON)	Report to Stg. 15 @ 8A
4 STAND INS (Weyland, Blalock, Ryusaki, Kellick)	↓
1 STUDIO TEACHER	Report Stg. 10 @ 7A

ADVANCE SHOOTING NOTES

SHOOTING DATE	SET NO.	SET NAME	LOCATION	SCENE NO.
Mon 9/19	27	INT. BIRD OF PREY(9,10,11,25,32,45,46,47)1-6/8pg	STG 5	15,18pt,19pt,22,25,27
		INT. BIRD OF PREY(9,10,11,25,32,45,46,47)2-3/8pg		45pt,46,47
	27	INT. BIRD OF PREY(9,10,11,25,32,45,46,47)1-2/8pg	STG 5	91,93,96,96A,96B 96C,96E
TUES 9/20	27	INT. BIRD OF PREY(10,11,26,32,45,46,47) 1/8pg		134
	↓	INT. BIRD OF PREY(10,11,26,32,45,46,47) 5/8pg		159,164 pt.
		INT. BIRD OF PREY(9,10,11,26,32,45,46,47)1-4/8pg		167pt,171,174,176,178

PRODUCTION STAR TREK III 019-31621-000 DATE FRI 9/16/83

A SON REMEMBERS

PHILLIP R. ALLEN BY KEEGAN ALLEN

A successful actor in his own right, Keegan Allen (*Pretty Little Liars* and *Walker*), son of Phillip and Joan, was not even born when his father starred as Captain Esteban. This didn't stop Keegan from playing the VHS tape of his father's appearance in *Star Trek III* so many times that he wore the tape out. Keegan remembers his dad and the lessons he taught him.

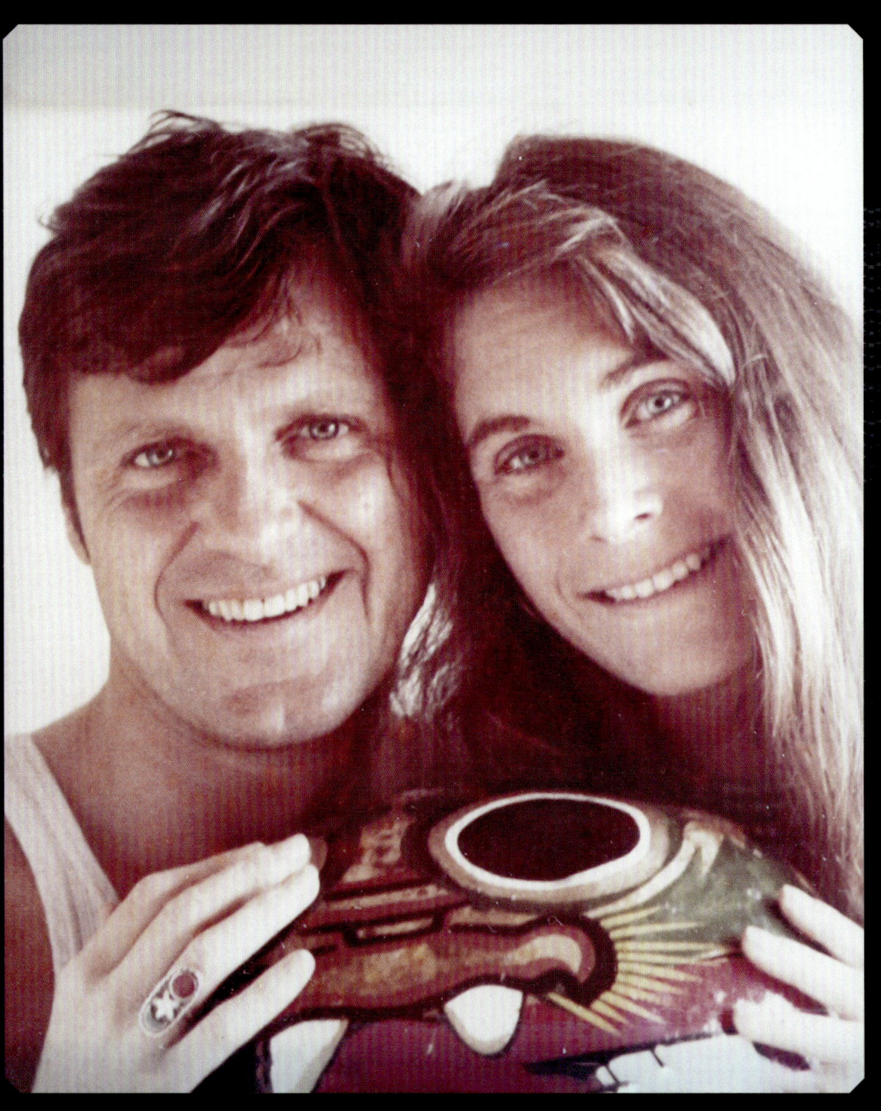

"Dad told the story of how he got into acting. He would say, 'I had 11 bucks in my pocket and a dream.' That is such an actor thing to say! He started acting at a young age and got into the Neighborhood Playhouse in New York. My dad had that bug that I often have of pursuing art, the love of theater, TV, movies. The passionate actor. There is a part of me that always wished I could be what he was, but he had this magic with people. He was in the Korean War as a paratrooper. I recently found some of his medals. Dad was highly decorated, yet never really discussed it because the war really affected him. He was an artist at heart and a man of faith. Sometimes we'd be out in the forest or fly fishing and he would say, 'Thank you, God.' As an actor, he had a way of finding a lot of humanity in a small moment. I think a lot of that came from the deeper pain he witnessed during the war and his beliefs.

There was a part of him that realized that the struggle of rejection that every actor faces was important. He would say to me, 'It is beautiful to be rejected because it means something better is coming.' He was trying to teach me to be grateful.

There was a *Star Trek* picture signed by my dad online recently. I bought it. My dad would always answer fan mail and talk with fans. He was a great raconteur. He was very close friends with Leonard Nimoy. My father and William Shatner got along very well. Whenever I have been a guest at conventions and Bill is there, he is just the most pleasant, amazing person. *Star Trek* was albeit one of many projects my dad did, but it is one that really did shape my father's life in a beautiful way because of the fandom.

[Soon after] Dad passed, I did an off-Broadway show in 2013 called *Small Engine Repair* and my mom was there on opening night. And I felt like Dad was there, too. When I looked out, I knew, I felt that he would be proud of me in what I had pursued. He was my best friend."[8]

LEFT: Phillip Allen and his wife Joan, provided by Keegan Allen.

PHILLIP R. ALLEN (J.T. ESTEBAN)

The character of Captain J.T. Esteban was a contrast to James T. Kirk. He shared Kirk's compassion and exploratory enthusiasm, however Esteban was a by-the-book, cautious leader while Kirk had a more risk-taking, imaginative style. Symbolically, Esteban serves an example of the kind of leader Saavik could become if she continued with her focus on regulations. The actor who played the role would need to express both stringent composure and likeability at the same time.

Nimoy found that in his friend Phillip R. Allen, with whom he happened to share the birthday of March 26. Audiences knew Allen from guest appearances on televisions shows, including *The Bionic Woman*, produced by Bennett, *Happy Days*, and *The Mary Tyler Moore Show*, in addition to his regular role as Roy Turner on *The Bad News Bears* TV series and his many stage performances. Allen would appear in more than eighty movies and television programs before passing in 2012.

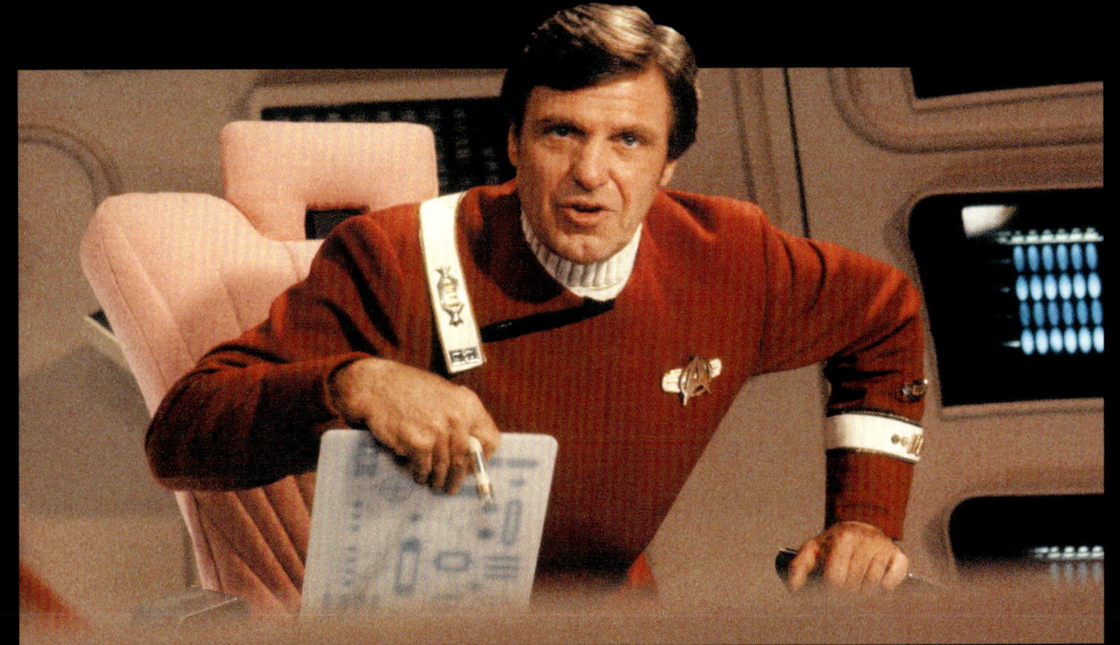

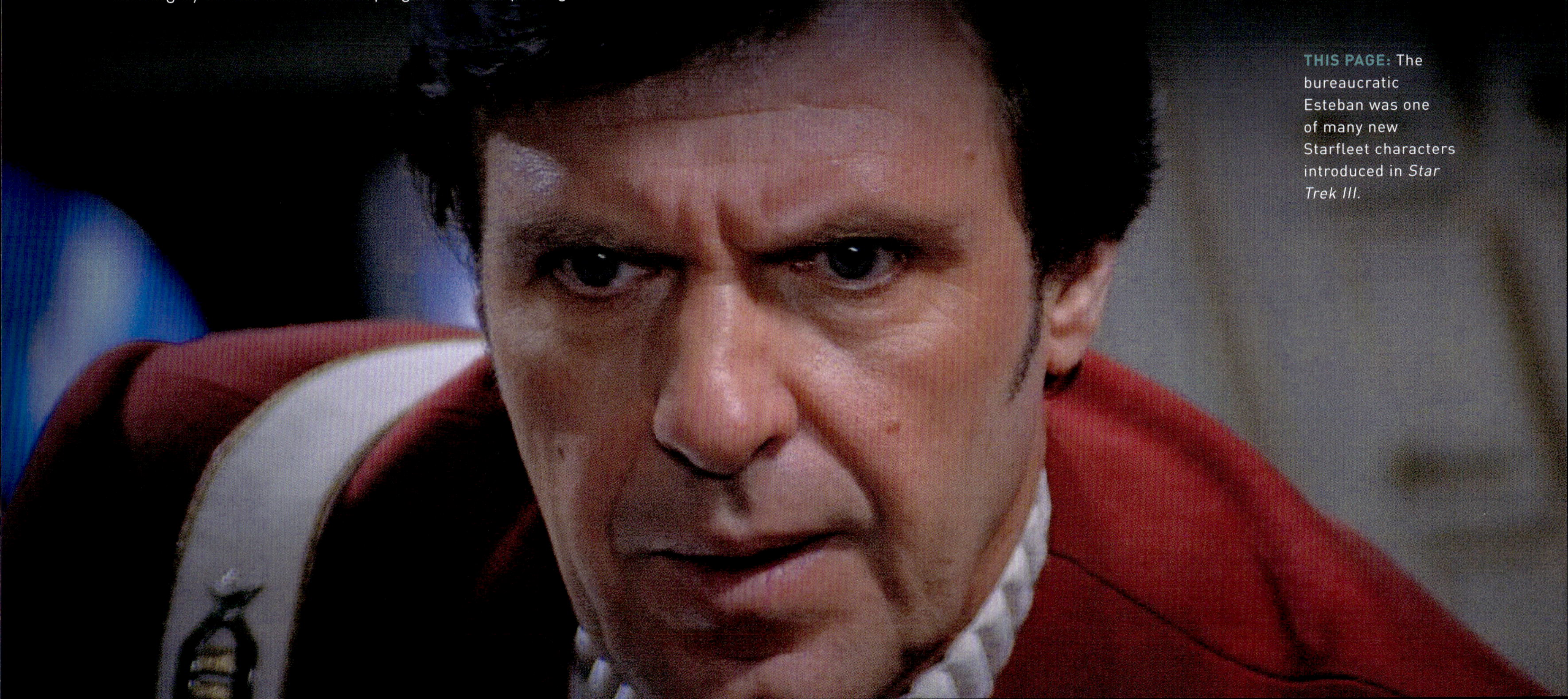

THIS PAGE: The bureaucratic Esteban was one of many new Starfleet characters introduced in *Star Trek III*.

DAME JUDITH ANDERSON (T'LAR)

Dame Judith Anderson may have been new to *Star Trek*, but she was a veteran actor whom Nimoy greatly admired. Born Frances Margaret Anderson on February 10, 1897, in South Australia, Anderson would go on to earn a Tony Award, two Emmy Awards, and be nominated for both a Grammy and Academy Award®. Her roles in *Rebecca* (1940), *Laura* (1944), and in the stage play *Medea* (1947) demonstrated her range, and her career would encompass more than fifty television and film appearances in addition to scores of theater roles.

Nimoy had been affected by the performance of Celia Lovsky as another matriarchal Vulcan named T'Pau from the original series episode 'Amok Time' and knew T'Lar similarly required someone of great stature. Anderson's voice and theatrical personality were perfectly suited to the role. The question was whether she would come out of semi-retirement to play the part. Nimoy asked Anderson to lunch, explaining his vision of the character and her importance to the movie. Two days after their meeting, she told Nimoy, "I've just had the most remarkable trip!' And Nimoy said, 'Where did you go?' She said, 'I just read your script!'"[9] Despite this endorsement, Anderson was going to decline until her nephew, a fan of Spock, learned she had lunch with Nimoy. He told his aunt she absolutely had to play the role. Anderson was eighty-six at the time she filmed *Star Trek III*.

THIS SPREAD: T'Lar may have been a matriarch of Vulcan, but Anderson was a matriarch of the theater, admired by the actors on set who all wanted pictures with her.

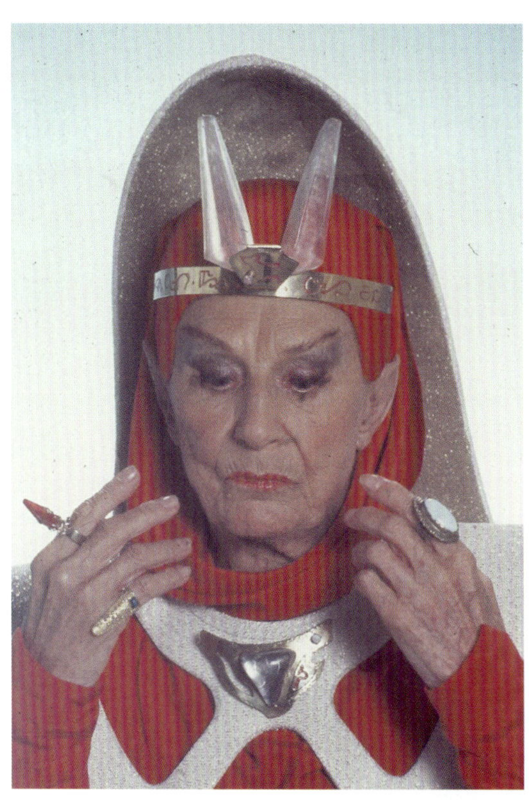

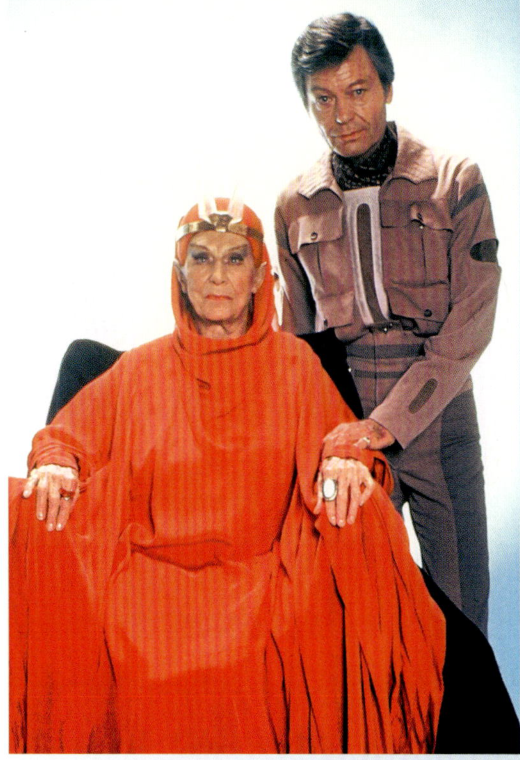

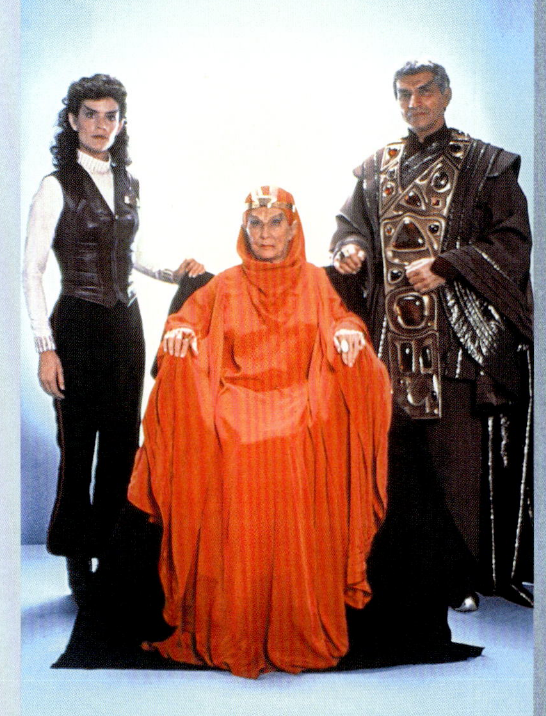

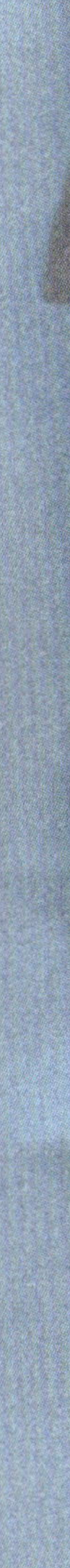

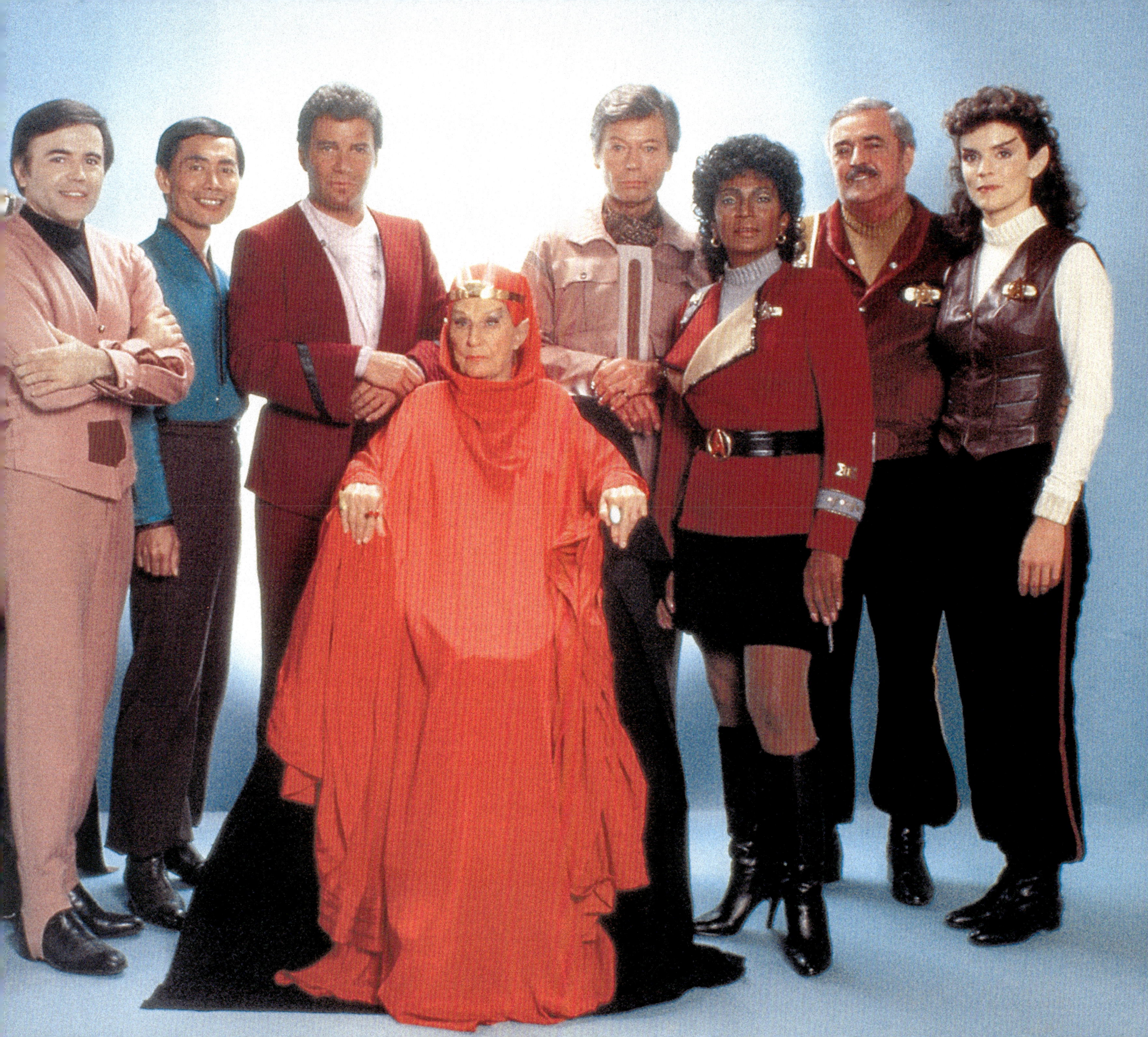

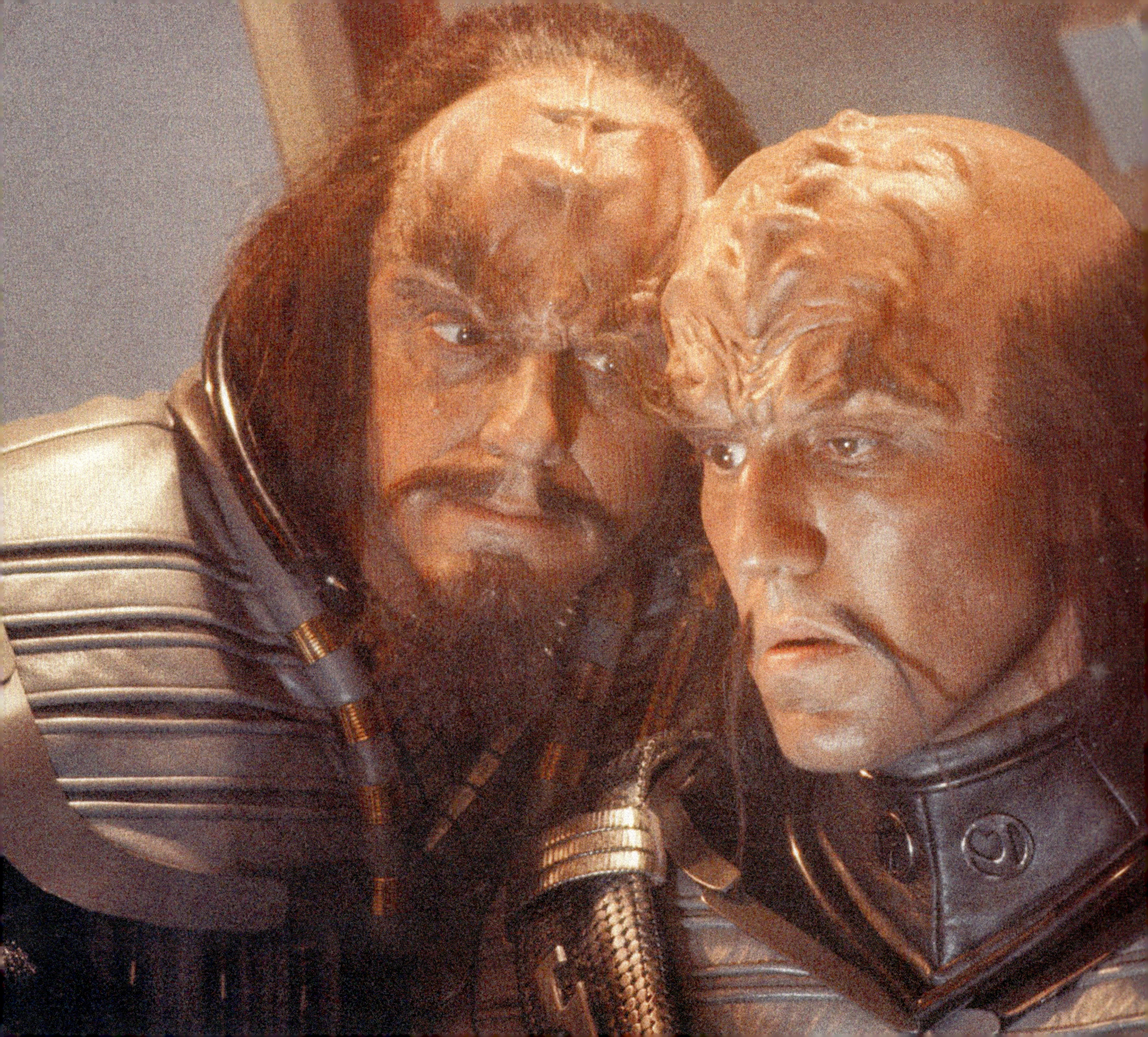

CHAPTER 5

THIS IS YOUR OPPONENT SPEAKING

KRUGE AND THE KLINGONS

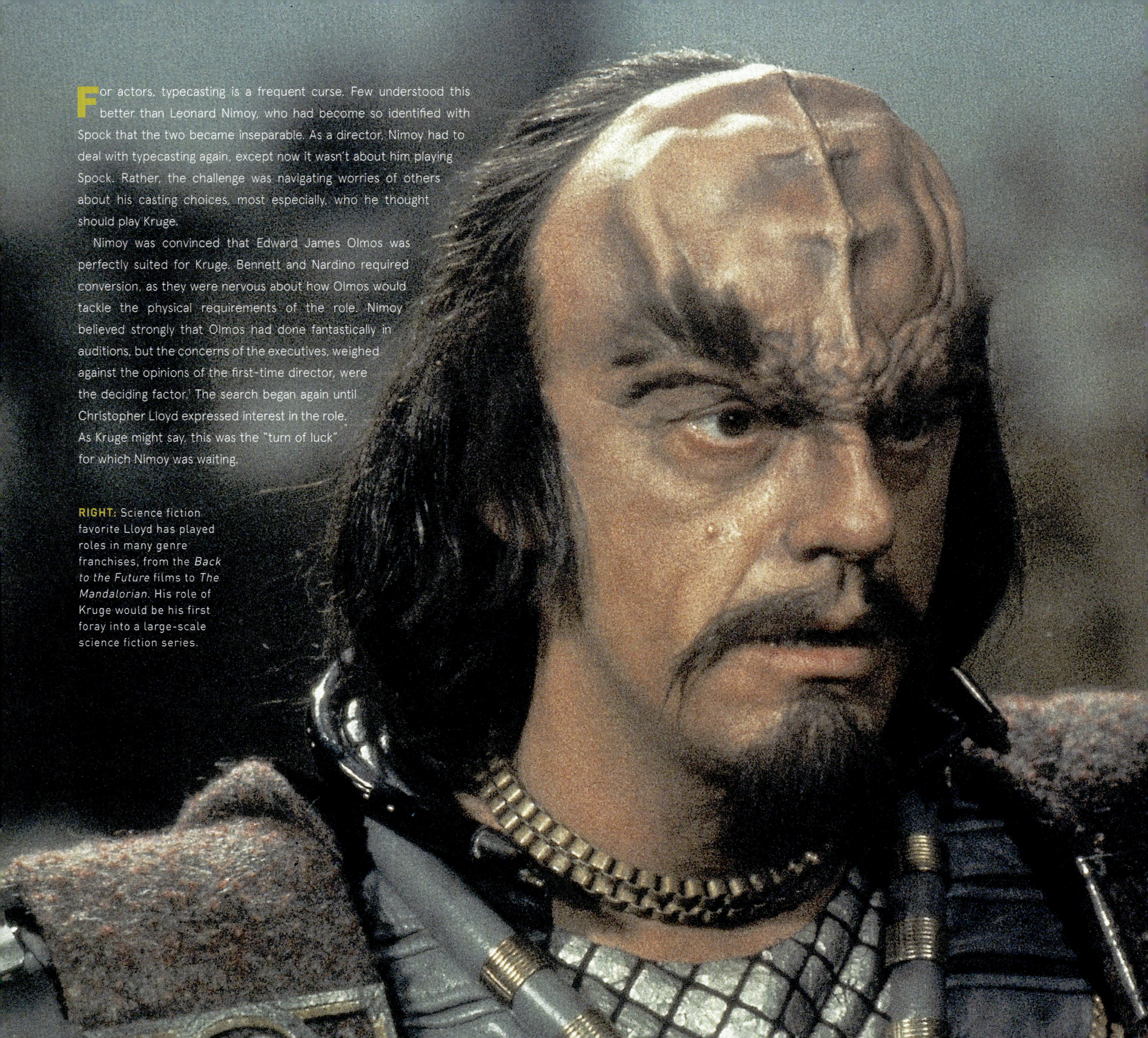

For actors, typecasting is a frequent curse. Few understood this better than Leonard Nimoy, who had become so identified with Spock that the two became inseparable. As a director, Nimoy had to deal with typecasting again, except now it wasn't about him playing Spock. Rather, the challenge was navigating worries of others about his casting choices, most especially, who he thought should play Kruge.

Nimoy was convinced that Edward James Olmos was perfectly suited for Kruge. Bennett and Nardino required conversion, as they were nervous about how Olmos would tackle the physical requirements of the role. Nimoy believed strongly that Olmos had done fantastically in auditions, but the concerns of the executives, weighed against the opinions of the first-time director, were the deciding factor.[1] The search began again until Christopher Lloyd expressed interest in the role. As Kruge might say, this was the "turn of luck" for which Nimoy was waiting.

RIGHT: Science fiction favorite Lloyd has played roles in many genre franchises, from the *Back to the Future* films to *The Mandalorian*. His role of Kruge would be his first foray into a large-scale science fiction series.

CHRISTOPHER LLOYD (KRUGE)

Born October 22, 1938, in Stamford, Connecticut, Lloyd made his cinematic debut in *One Flew Over the Cuckoo's Nest* (1975). He won two Emmy Awards, one given while he was filming *Star Trek III*, for his role of Reverend Jim Ignatowski on *Taxi* which he played from 1978 until 1983. By happenstance, his character Jim was a *Star Trek* fan. In the episode 'Jim Joins the Network,' he questions a network executive why *Star Trek* was cancelled. Of the *Taxi* scene, Lloyd said, "I don't think that I had any anticipation then that I would be involved in a *Star Trek* film. It ties it in a very nice kind of way though."[2] Like his character Jim, Lloyd appreciated the original series: "I always liked *Star Trek* stylistically and visually. It's more of a thinker's adventure. It has action, but it's more of a thoughtful kind of dialogue than in most of these films. Ideas are presented and worked out. They think out their problems as they go along."[3]

By the summer of 1983, Lloyd was looking to explore other character types. Nimoy was thrilled to have Lloyd join the film, thinking him to be "a chameleon actor if there ever was one. This is a guy who can really change persona, character, from one performance to another."[4] Despite Nimoy's support, there were concerns among some executives about having Lloyd, so identified in audience's minds with Jim, play the menacing Kruge. Nimoy explained, "There was some concern, which I recognized, and the concern was, won't people think he's funny because of the character that he played in *Taxi*? He was so brilliantly, wonderfully funny as this dazed kind of guy in *Taxi*. I said, 'I'm not the person you should be talking to about typecasting issues, because I've had my share of those. And I think I've managed to play other characters besides Spock without people saying, 'Oh, he can only do Spock.' So, let's not get into that. Christopher Lloyd can do this, and it's gonna work.'"[4]

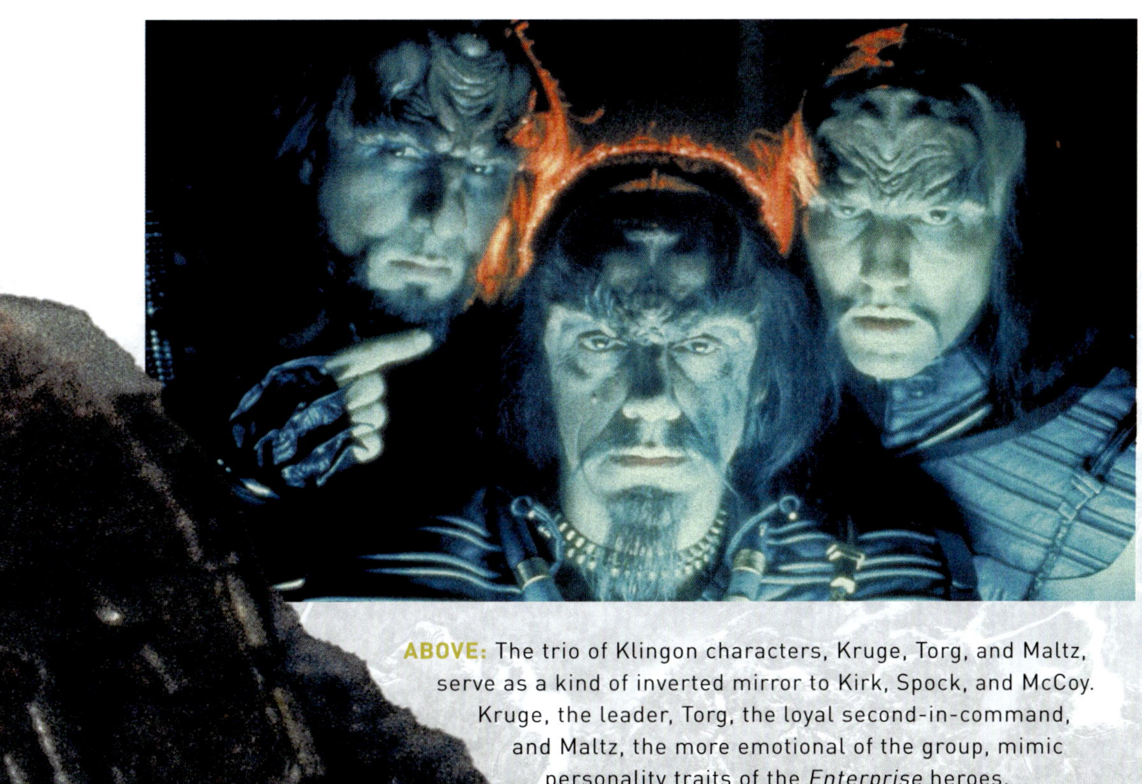

ABOVE: The trio of Klingon characters, Kruge, Torg, and Maltz, serve as a kind of inverted mirror to Kirk, Spock, and McCoy. Kruge, the leader, Torg, the loyal second-in-command, and Maltz, the more emotional of the group, mimic personality traits of the *Enterprise* heroes.

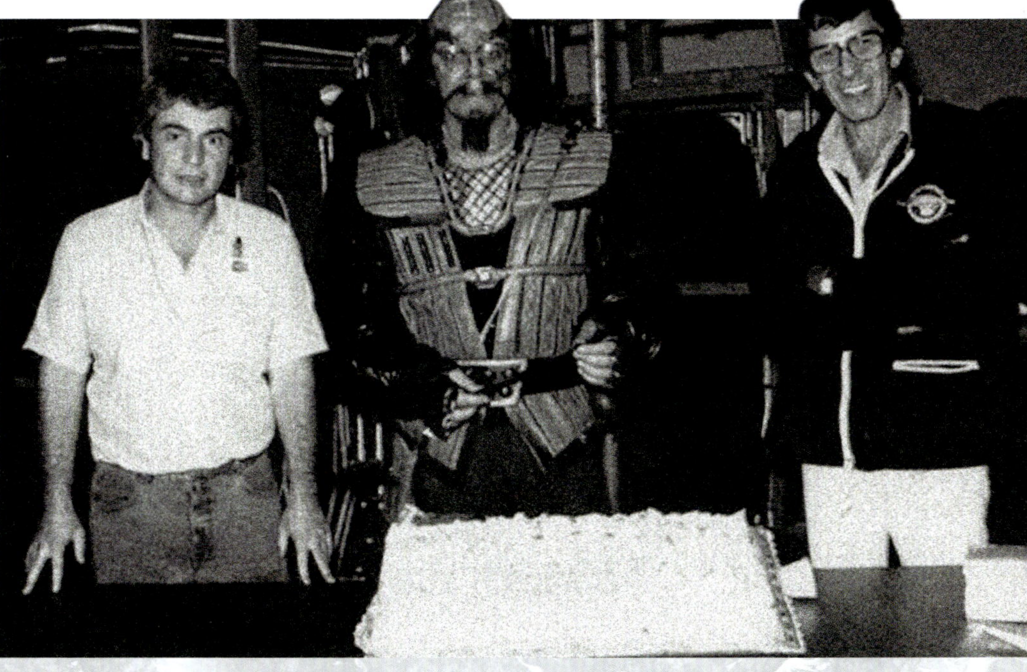

ABOVE: Director of photography Charles Correll, Lloyd, and Nimoy take a break from filming to celebrate Lloyd's September 25, 1983 Emmy win for Outstanding Supporting Actor in a Comedy or Variety or Music Series.

STEPHEN LISKA (TORG)

As the outlines and scripts evolved, the character of Spock's brother Galt would eventually morph into Torg, Kruge's second-in-command. "I was born in Pittsburgh, Pennsylvania. I went to a small Catholic school. I had a nun teaching about Shakespeare which I had never heard of before," said Liska, who played Torg. "One day, after class, I said to her, 'Could we talk a little more about acting?' Later, I tried to get into Carnegie Mellon but couldn't afford it. So what I did was check out all the state colleges around Pittsburgh and found that the state school Slippery Rock University had many teachers who had graduated from Carnegie. I figured I would get a similar education because of that."[5] Liska met his wife, also an actor, and they moved to L.A. where he earned roles in various plays and TV shows such as *Hill Street Blues*, *Knight Rider*, and *T.J. Hooker*. He was also the stand-in for actors like Robert Urich on *Vega$*.

Liska's agent, who worked for the same agency that represented Nimoy, told him about a possible role in *Star Trek III*. The audition was unusual, according to Liska. "They held the auditions for the Klingons at Leonard's house. His wife Sandra was very helpful. Sandra opened the front door and has all these guys coming in to audition, yet she was a doll. She offered us food and drinks, and then Leonard would call out your name and you would go up the steps and he auditioned us upstairs. There were about six of us there."[5]

Liska was as fond of Leonard himself. He explained, "Thinking of my approach to acting back then, I was young, and I tried to come in with some ideas on what to do. I saw the Klingons as being more like snakes. We did a couple of rehearsals. Leonard said, 'Steve, come on. Let's go here.' And we went to the side where there were table and chairs. He said, 'Let's sit down and we're going to do this scene like we were having coffee and just talking.' We did the scene once and Leonard said, 'That's it. That's how you do it.' And ever since then, every time I do a film I'll work on a character, but I try to realize that it is about what is happening right there at that time while filming. Leonard taught me a very interesting way to approach acting. I learned a lot from him and had a great time with him."

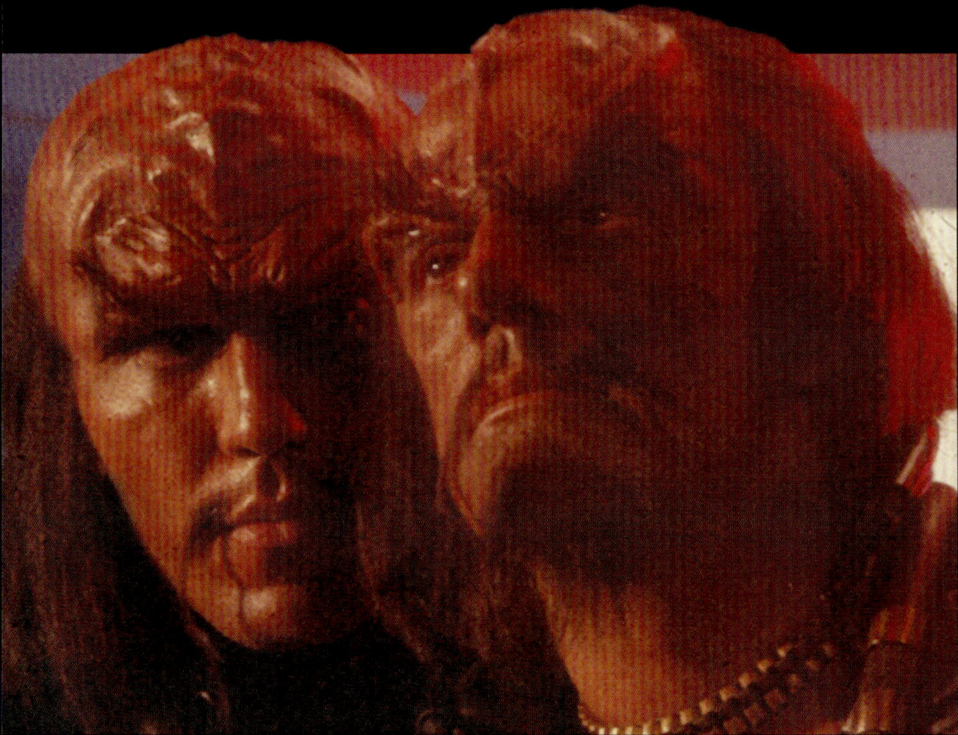

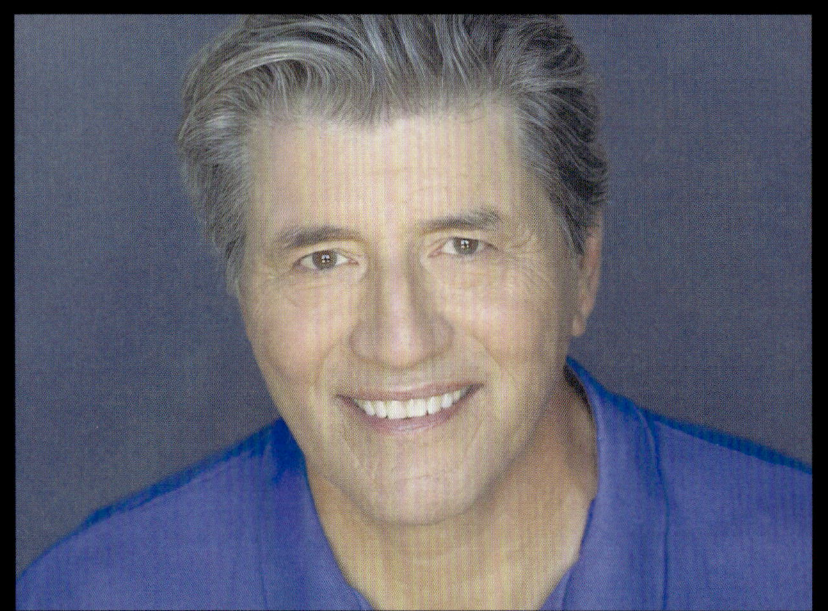

THIS SPREAD: Photos of Liska as Torg and out of makeup.

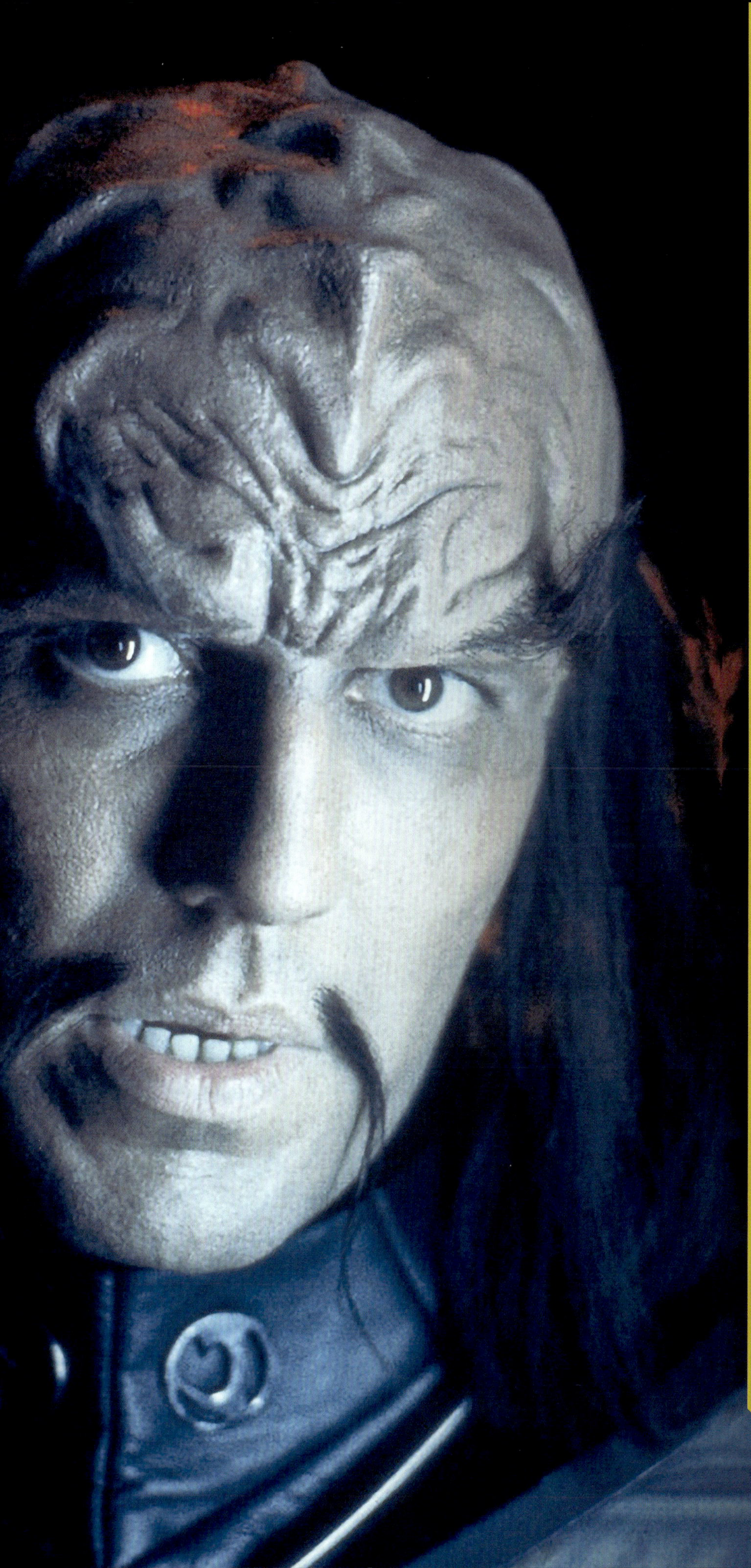

SANDRA "SANDI" ZOBER NIMOY

Of Liska's memory of Sandra Zober Nimoy being a kind hostess during auditions, Adam Nimoy reflected, "My mom is, I think, an unsung hero in the story of Leonard Nimoy and his success. She never deviated in her support of him. For many years my parents struggled to make ends meet but my mother always believed in my dad. She read through all those *Star Trek* scripts with him, running lines with him every night. I can still hear them in my head. My mom was a warm, generous, sensitive, loving, and caring person. I like to say she was a Flower Power Priestess and wife of Mr. Spock! She was a gracious hostess who welcomed people into our house all the time. She had the best dinner parties."[6]

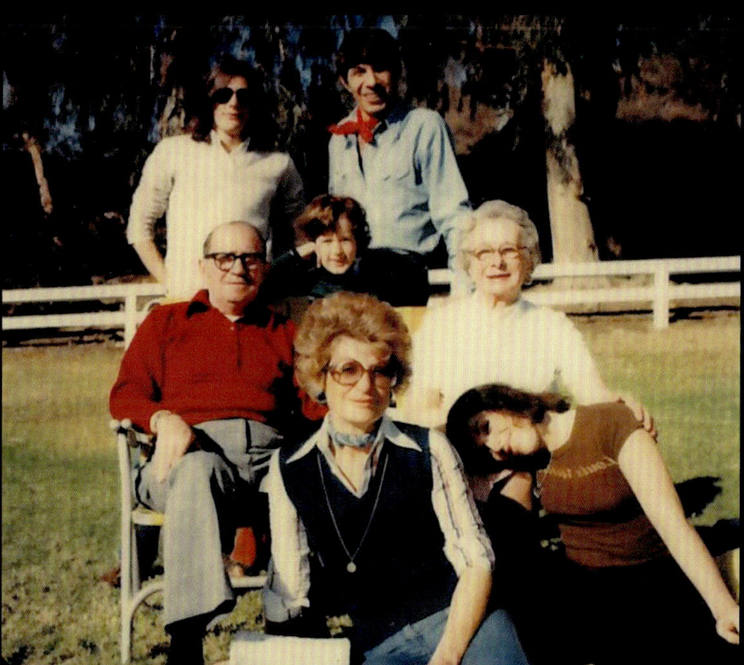

ABOVE: The Nimoys during a 1970s family gathering. From top: Leonard Nimoy, son Adam; father Max, nephew David, mother Dora; Sandi Nimoy and daughter Julie. Photograph provided by the Nimoy Family.

JOHN LARROQUETTE (MALTZ)

Whilst Lloyd was departing the popular sitcom *Taxi* as filming on *Star Trek III* began, John Larroquette was about to begin a nine-year run on *Night Court*, winning four consecutive Emmy Awards for his role of Dan Fielding. As Maltz, Larroquette would play the only survivor of Kruge's crew. According to *The Klingon Dictionary* by Marc Okrand, it was Maltz who provided the Federation with its understanding of the Klingon language. Larroquette auditioned by meeting with Nimoy and was enthusiastic about playing such a fun role. He joked to *Starlog* magazine that he wanted Kruge to say at some time in the film, "Bring me some chocolate, Maltz."[7] Larroquette would again don Klingon makeup in his role of Fielding on the 2024 *Night Court* in the episode 'Wrath of Comic-Con' as his character goes to a science fiction convention.

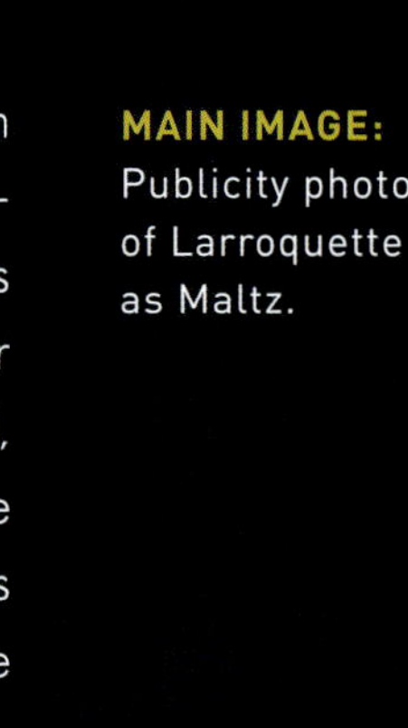

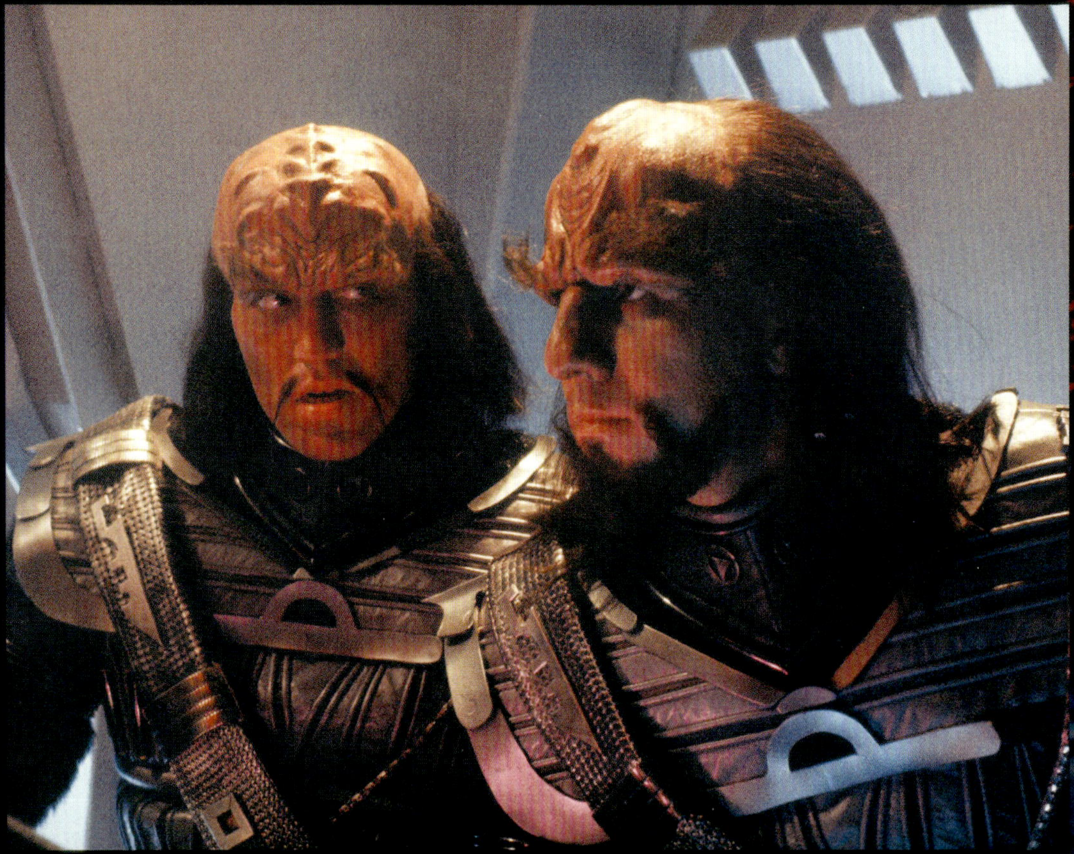

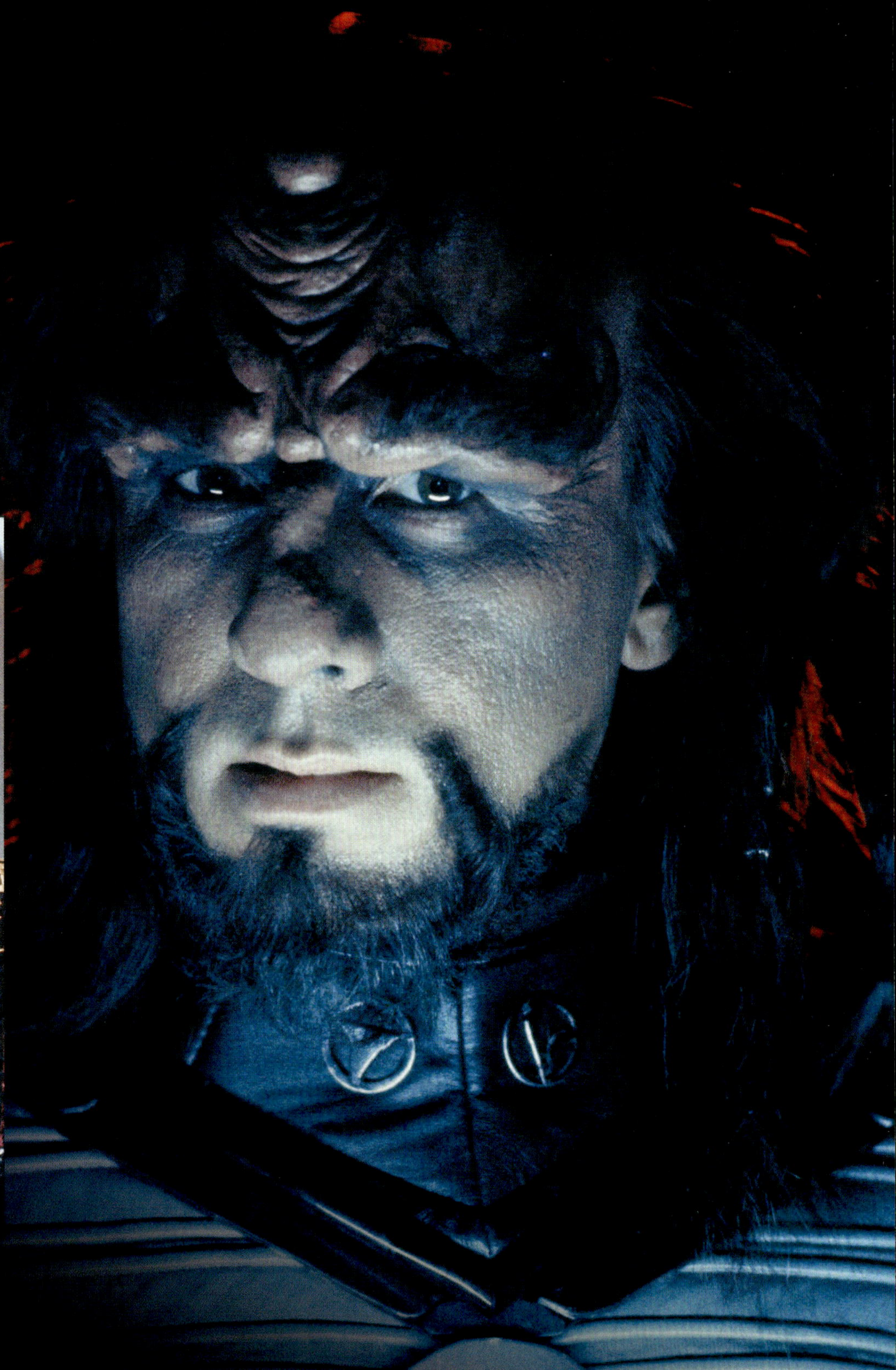

MAIN IMAGE: Publicity photo of Larroquette as Maltz.

CATHIE SHIRRIFF (VALKRIS)

If *Taxi* was an alternate timeline of *Star Trek*, it could explain how Valkris and Kruge first met. In a 1983 *Taxi* episode that is coincidentally named 'Alex Gets Burned by an Old Flame,' Shirriff and Lloyd first played lovers a year before the actors would reunite for *Star Trek III*. In addition to guest roles on shows such as *Taxi* and *Magnum P.I.*, Shirriff was a model and host of *Ripley's Believe it or Not* TV show. Speaking to *The Twilight Zone Magazine* in 1984, Shirriff described Valkris as "fiercely proud and very strong and completely dedicated to the film's villain."[8]

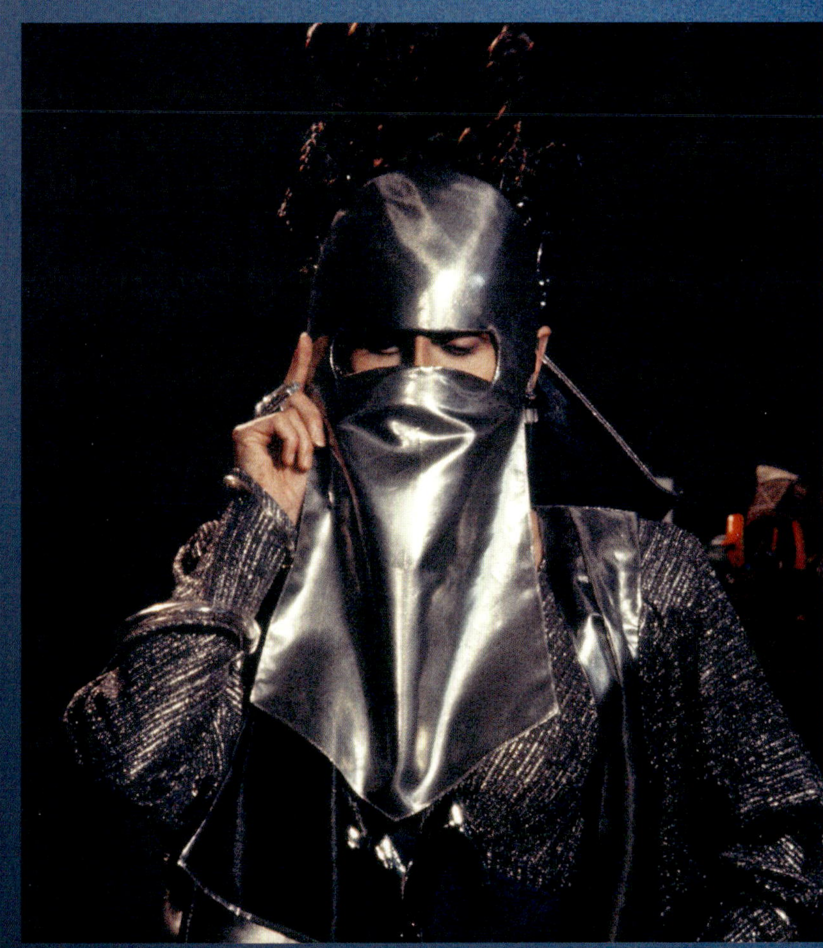

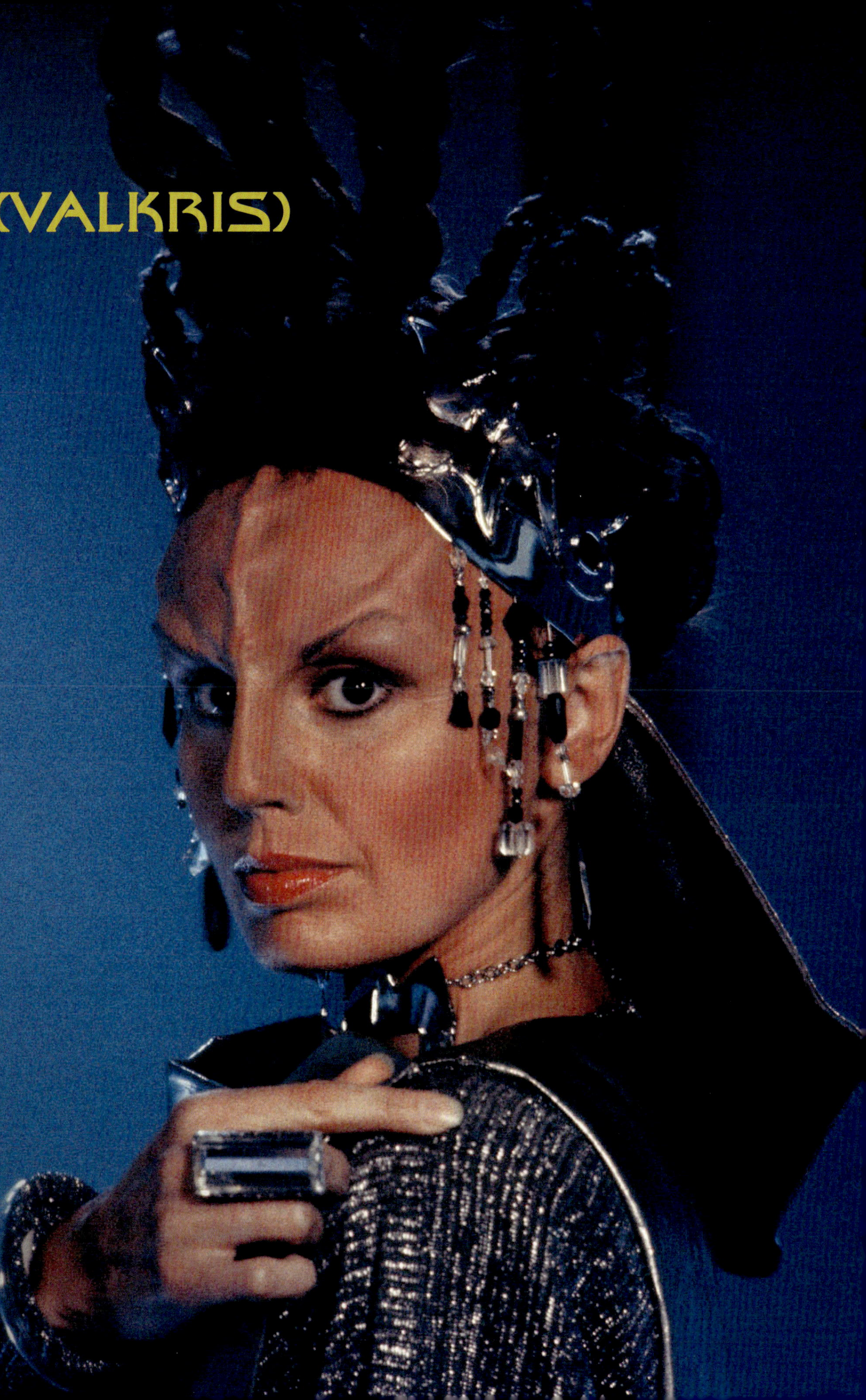

MAIN IMAGE: Publicity photo of Shirriff as Valkris.

MARC OKRAND (LINGUIST)

Dr. Marc Okrand could have never imagined that his interest in Earth's languages would take him deep into outer space. In 1982, his job helping to pioneer and advance the then-new technology of closed captioning had brought Okrand to Los Angeles on a unique mission. The Academy Awards® television program was going to be a proving ground for whether closed captioning technology had developed far enough to accurately transcribe live broadcasts. Okrand explained that the Oscars® had been chosen for the test because, "It had high publicity value and a relatively low probability of error because much of the Oscars® are scripted. Not the winners, which no one knows until the envelope is opened, or the acceptance speeches, but everything else is scripted. We could get the scripted parts before and type the text into the computer. And then we could switch to live captioning when needed." Because the script was always under revision, Okrand was selected to go to L.A. to coordinate.

On March 22, 1982, events transpired that would eventually lead to the Klingon language as fans know it. Okrand shared, "One of my friends – Sylvia Rubinstein – invited me to lunch where she works while I was in L.A. Her boss was Harve Bennett, who I knew from when I worked at a radio station with his wife before I went to college." Okrand, Rubinstein, and Deborah Arakelian, who was an assistant to the *Star Trek II* producers, went to lunch at the Paramount commissary. Okrand continued, "Deborah said, 'Oh, I understand you have a degree in linguistics. That's interesting because we're in touch with the linguistics department at UCLA.' I asked why and she said, 'There's a scene in the film where Mr. Spock and another Vulcan character have a short conversation in the Vulcan language. When we filmed it, they were speaking English because that is what is in the script. For a number of reasons, people think they should be speaking their own language.'" The plan was that the UCLA linguist was supposed to create words that sounded alien yet matched the lip movement of the actors. However, logistics delayed the process and Paramount needed the work done by the end of the week. Okrand laughed, saying, "That was exactly how long I was in town for the Oscars®. So I said, 'I can do that.' My friend said, 'Yeah, he can do that. He has the same kind of degree as the people from UCLA.' At that time, associate producer William Phillips came by and they turned to him and said, 'We just solved

BELOW RIGHT: The Kolinahr scene from *Star Trek: The Motion Picture* was filmed in English, then dubbed in Vulcan. Hartmut Scharfe from UCLA created the Vulcan words that would be lip synched in post-production. The Klingon spoken in that film was created by James Doohan and associate producer Jon Povill.

BELOW LEFT: Marc Okrand in 2024, photo provided by him.

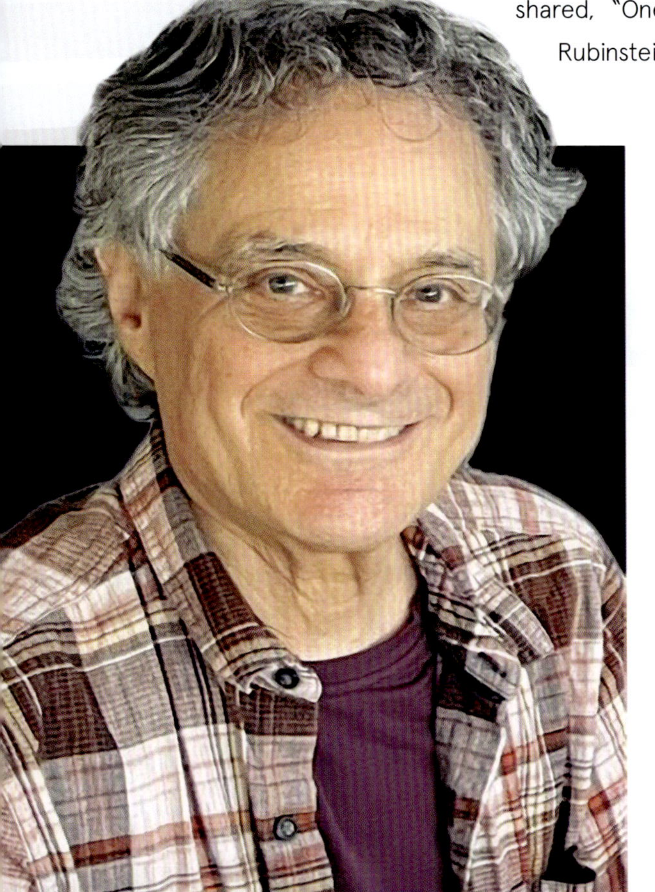

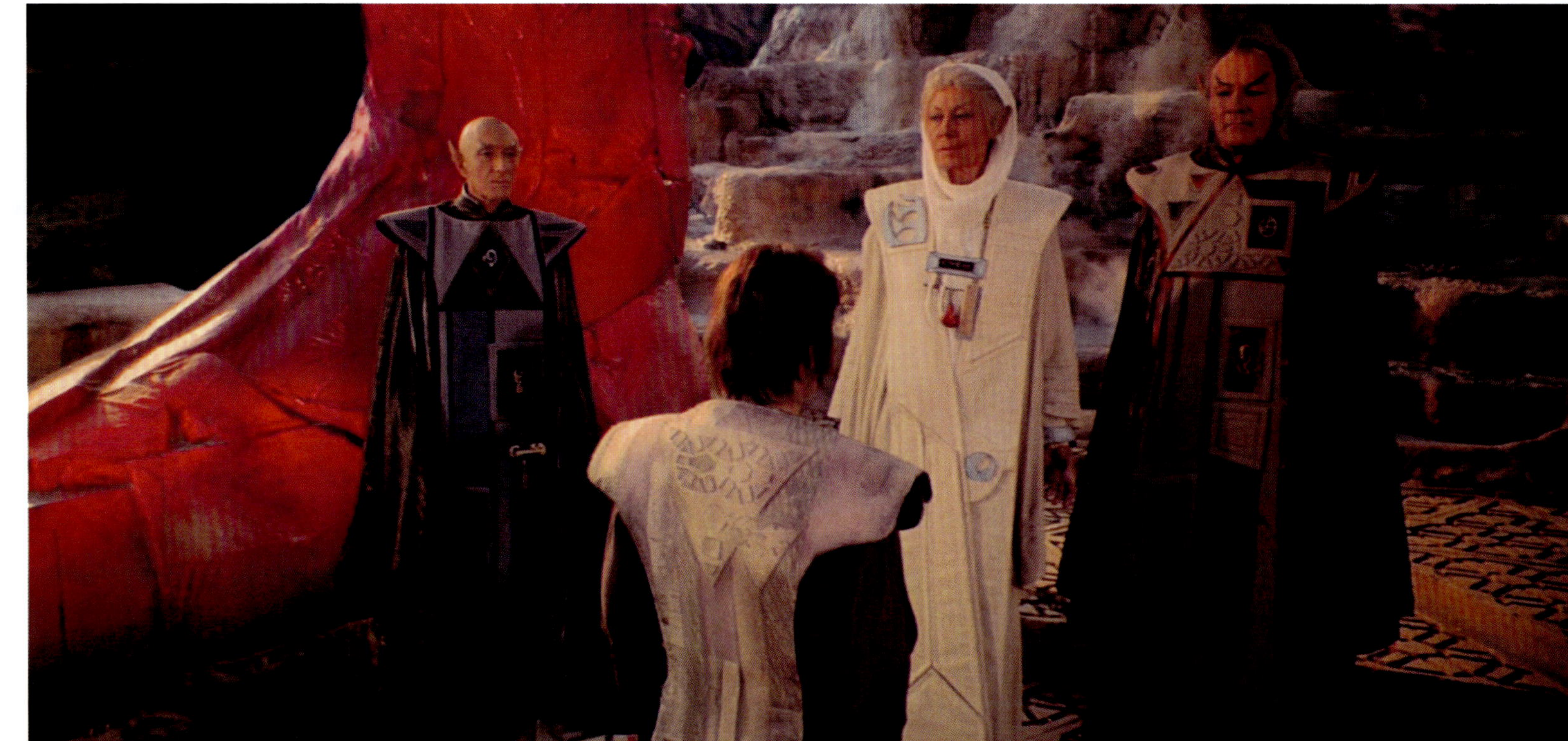

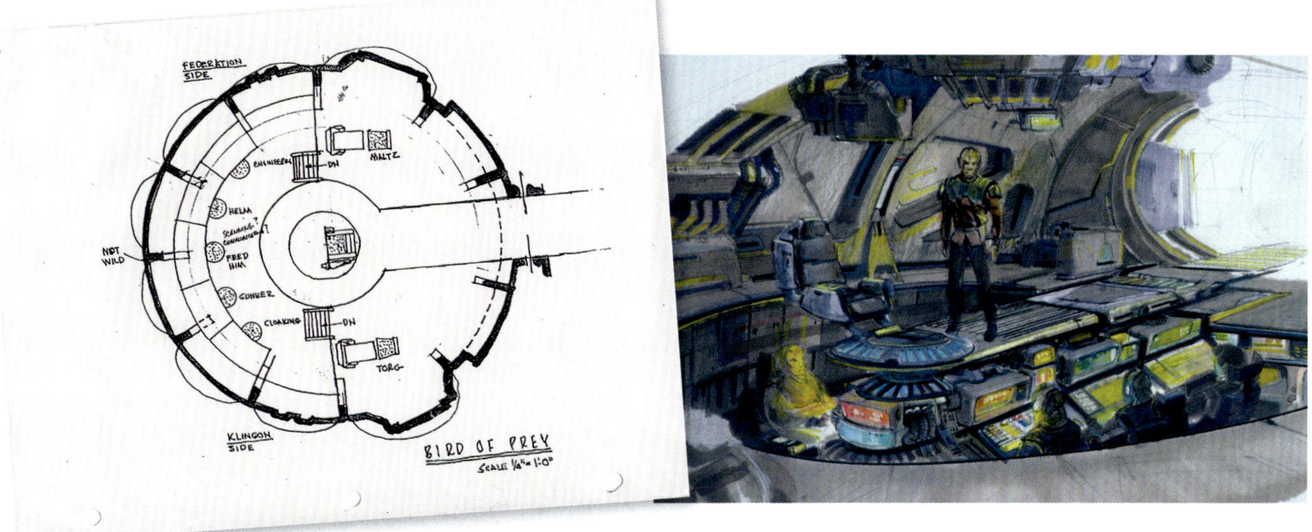

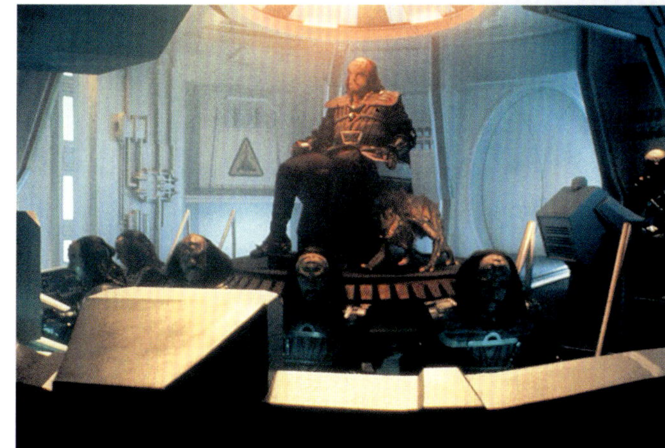

ABOVE LEFT: The art department at Paramount was led by John E. Chilberg II, with set designs by Cameron Birnie and Blake Russell, and set decoration by Tom Pedigo. Paramount supplied ILM this blueprint of the Bird-of-Prey bridge to help with their exterior designs.

ABOVE MIDDLE AND RIGHT: © Industrial Light & Magic. All Rights Reserved. Art by Rodis featuring an original design of the Bird-of-Prey bridge as compared to its final appearance in the film. Kruge's chair would need to be redesigned to accommodate Ralston who hid under it while puppeteering the Klingon beast.

the Vulcan problem.' He told me to see him after lunch. The fact that Harve knew me ahead of time is not irrelevant to the story because it was really his decision whether to hire me or not. You know, I went there to have a sandwich, not to get a job!"[9]

To create the Vulcan words for *Star Trek II*, Okrand said, "I wrote down the dialogue in English and I looked at their lips to see if they were doing anything with their lips that I might take advantage of, even if it didn't make any English noise." Okrand realized that Nimoy had closed his mouth at the end of both of his lines. "I knew that whatever I came up with for him should end with an 'um' sound, although, really, all he was actually doing was closing his mouth and not making a sound." Okrand found Nimoy to be interested in the language, making recommendations and asking questions. "He was involved in that process. After we had recorded his part, he jokingly crumpled the paper we had worked with and tossed it at me saying, 'Did anyone ever tell you that you are out of your mind!' and we both laughed. About a decade later, I created the language for the animated film *Atlantis: The Lost Empire* which featured Leonard. I wasn't there when Leonard recorded his Atlantean lines, but I was told by the producer or one of the directors that Leonard asked, 'Where did this come from?' When they told him it was me, he said, 'Marc Okrand! I know him. He is out of his mind!'"[9]

When production began on *Star Trek III*, Bennett called Okrand and asked if he wanted to create and teach the Klingon language. Of his answer, Okrand said, "Every once in a while you are presented with a decision that is easy to make and that was one of them!"[9]

Okrand did not want Klingon to resemble any real language because, "The Klingons at the time of *Star Trek III*, they were horrible and despicable and awful. If I made Klingon sound like a real language, I would have people mad at me." However, he revealed there was an exception to his rule, with a suffix phonetically similar to one in the language he wrote about in his PhD dissertation. "That was on purpose, a kind of Alfred Hitchcock cameo thing." He also discussed the rationale Bennett had thought of for why Klingons sometimes canonically speak English. "Klingon society is a hierarchical society. There are higher classes and the lower classes. The higher classes get a better education which includes a foreign language like English, or Federation Standard. They use it in part to show off that class distinction and in part to keep secrets from underlings."[9]

Developing the language was not the only responsibility Okrand had. He had to teach the actors the language and be on set to correct any discrepancies or mispronunciations. "The procedure I used for teaching an actor Klingon was to write out the lines in a transcription system I devised and provide the actors with a phonetic key so they knew how the words were supposed to sound. I also made a cassette tape of me saying all the lines, sent it to Paramount and then they reproduced it to give to the different actors who learned their lines by listening to it. When I was on the set, I would sit down with the actors who by now would have already heard it and seen it. We would refine it. I would then watch them film the scene and approve or correct their pronunciation. In almost every scene where they speak Klingon, I'm just outside the frame."[9]

Because of the importance of his role as Kruge, Lloyd spent a good deal of time with Okrand. He found the language a challenge to learn, saying, "It was invented by a doctoral student of linguistics – with its own grammar, vocabulary, everything. I had to sit down and learn it. It was difficult to memorize because you couldn't relate it to *anything*; it was only sounds."[3] Whatever Lloyd's challenges with the language, he met them fantastically according to Okrand who was impressed with Lloyd's commitment. "Some actors are there on set all the time. Some do their

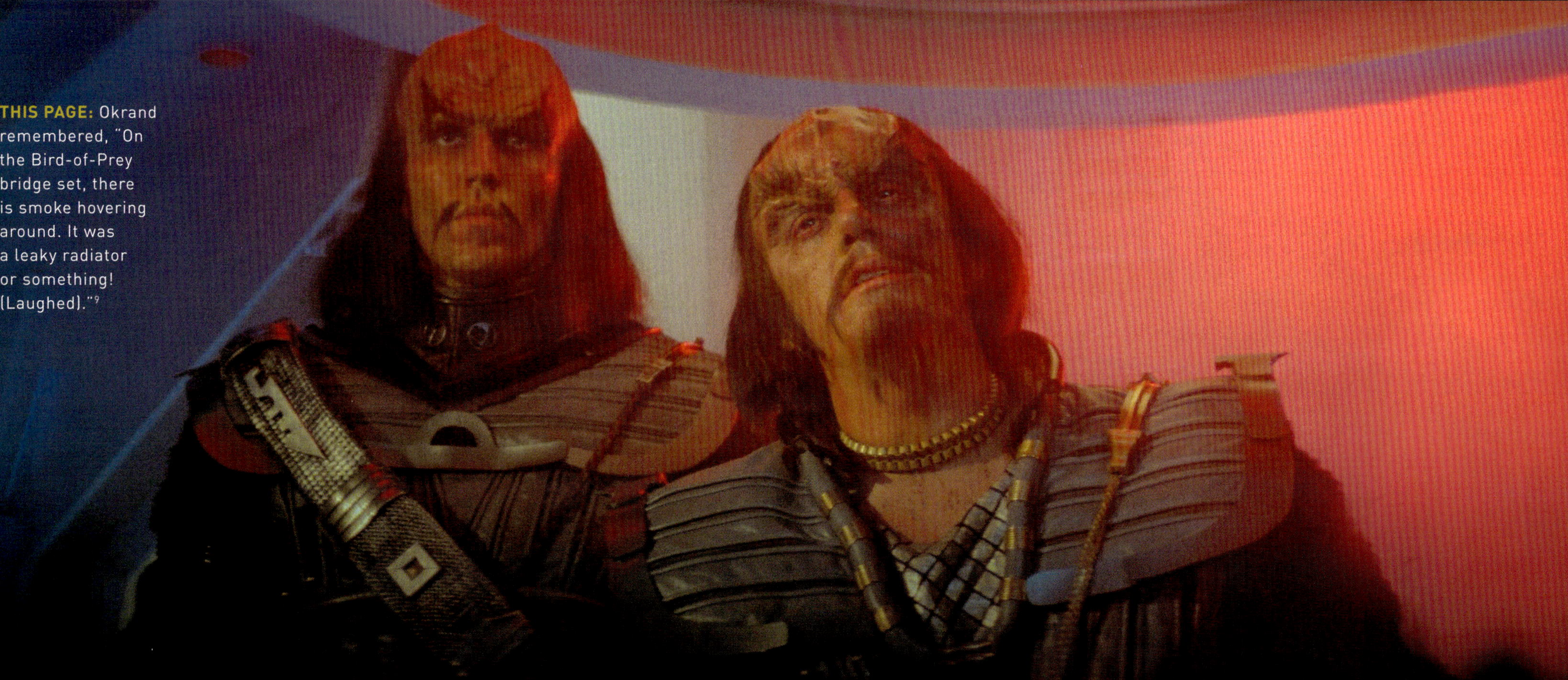

THIS PAGE: Okrand remembered, "On the Bird-of-Prey bridge set, there is smoke hovering around. It was a leaky radiator or something! (Laughed)."[9]

thing and then leave until they have more to do," observed Okrand. "Christopher Lloyd was there all the time, on set from whatever time he arrived until he was done for the day. We would talk and practice." Their practice sessions were not confined only to the set; the first lesson was in a room above Lloyd's garage. Okrand laughed remembering, "We started practicing, and then all of a sudden Christopher Lloyd says, 'Wait, I need to get my teeth.' I thought, 'Oh, I didn't even notice this poor guy doesn't have any teeth.' That's not what he meant. He meant his Klingon teeth appliance because he said, 'If I'm going to become comfortable saying these words, I better become comfortable wearing these.' I went back to Paramount and someone asked me how Chris did with the language. I said, 'He's great. He is going to do a really good job with this language.' Then they asked, 'Is he like Jim?' I said, "Jim? Jim who?' They said, 'Jim from *Taxi*.' And I said, 'Oh, my God! That's who that was!' He was such a great actor and chameleon in his roles that the first time I met him I did not recognize him from his character."[9]

As frequently happens with any teacher, Okrand learned a few important Hollywood lessons himself. "Whenever a scene was filmed that involved the Klingon language, I was asked if everything was good. I answered either yes or no. I learned very quickly not to give that second answer frequently because they would have to film again." Instead of making them reshoot, Okrand would just adjust the rules of the language because – at that time – no one knew the language but him. An example is Kruge ordering his soldiers, "Kill one of them. I don't care which." The Klingon translation is *Ha' yIHoH! vay' jISaHbe'*. "Christopher Lloyd and I practiced the line again and again," said Okrand. "The set was enclosed in plastic to accommodate the atmospheric smoke. They had this device that looked to me like a backwards vacuum cleaner that would shoot this oil-based steam into the set then they had to wait for it to settle. When it got to the right level, it was time to shoot the scene. It was quite a process. After filming, Leonard asked everyone how it was. Chris shared, 'I said the Klingon wrong.' And he had. He left out two words, *Ha'* and *vay'*. Leonard asked me, 'Marc, how did the Klingon sound to you?' I knew there was only one answer I could give. 'The Klingon sounded fine.' I had to reconfigure the rules. We had lost the word *Ha'*, meaning 'one,' which was important to the scene. I changed the grammar of the language so that *yIHoH* is a command meaning 'kill!' but used only with a singular object so that the word 'one' was not needed. I also adjusted the grammar of the second sentence. Sometime later, and for unrelated reasons, the word for 'one' was changed to *wa'*."[9]

The bestselling *The Klingon Dictionary* book by Okrand was the result of the filmmaking crew frequently asking him how something could be said in Klingon. This gave Okrand the idea of a dictionary, which he proposed to Bennett. By chance, Bennett was having a meeting with licensees. Later that day, Bennett told Okrand, "Don't be surprised if you get a call from Pocket Books." Typing Klingon for the manuscript, it turned out, was more complicated than Okrand anticipated. He was using underlined letters to indicate non-English sounds, but, he explained, "on what was at that time a modern word processor, underlining was a major problem. You had to do all kinds of stuff to get an underline. I thought, 'This is ridiculous. I'm never going to get through this if I have to type it like this.' So, instead of using underlines, I used capitals because that was easier. That's why all the capital letters are there, and then I stuck with it, even though you can make up a Klingon writing system very easily, with no capital letters."[9]

MAKING THE BIRD-OF-PREY

The ships in *Star Trek* have always been more than mere vessels. They are characters in their own right. Furthermore, the ships and their design elements reveal traits about those who command them and the cultures from which they derive. The Bird-of-Prey had been a part of every outline and script. Now it was time to create it.

The collaboration and constant communication between ILM and Paramount would be a major factor in why the final design turned out successfully. So iconic was the Bird-of-Prey that it, or designs inspired by it, would be featured in nearly every version of Star Trek that followed. Both Roger Ebert and Gene Siskel, famed movie reviewers, mentioned the impressive Bird-of-Prey in their reviews of *Star Trek III*. For ILM visual effects art director Nilo Rodis, who had never seen *Star Trek*, the process began by asking questions. "There was a line in the movie, when Sulu said, 'It's a Bird-of-Prey.'' I'm reading this, and I go, 'What the heck is a Bird-of-Prey?' and nobody was really able to give me an answer. I remember talking to George [Takei] about it. His eyes lit up and he acted it out to me, like, 'My God. It's a Bird-of-Prey!' And I go, 'OK, yeah. Well, that's not going to help.' But, I figured it must be very scary. (Laughing)."[10] Rodis also turned to Nimoy, who sparked more inspiration. "Leonard gave me a picture of a Klingon and said, 'OK, this is who they are, and they fly the Bird-of-Prey.' I looked at that and I thought, 'OK, I think I understand.'"[10] Nimoy even acted out with his arms his vision of the ship's profile.

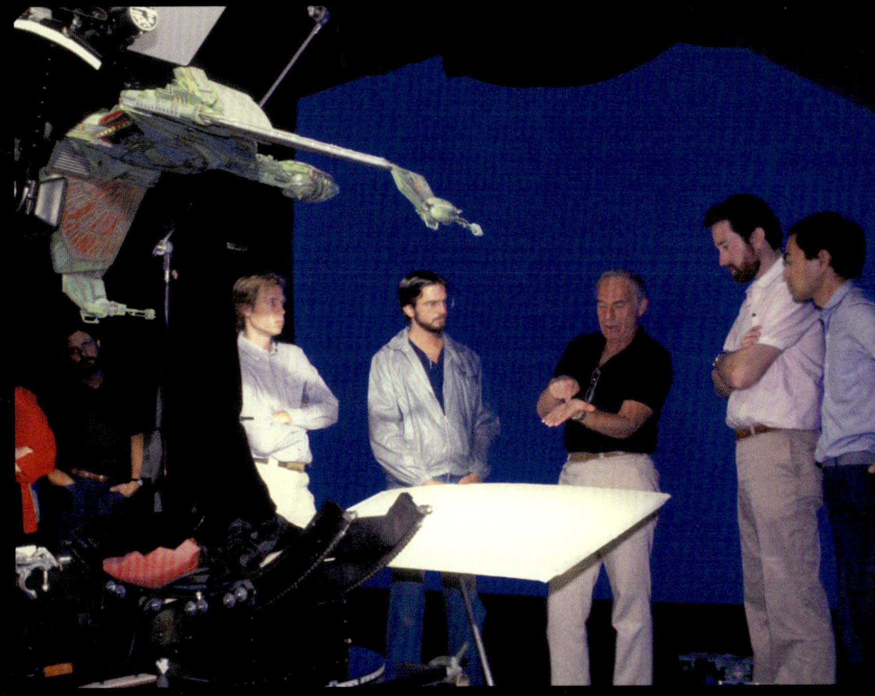

Rodis began formulating drawings and as the process evolved, an appreciation of the Klingon culture and how it could affect the story and the ship began. Rodis explained, "In fact, when Harve started talking about the cloaking device, I pitched them the idea that when they decloak, the first thing that forms is their guns! In other words they want to make sure they arrive with weapons."[10]

Model maker Bill George spoke about the teamwork that existed between the art directors and the model team. "Nilo was coming up with the kind of bird proportions, the head, the neck, and the wings. The interesting thing about it is that he gave me some sketches, none of which looked like the final product, and said, 'Kind of like this; kind of like that.' Then he started describing what he wanted it to feel like."[11]

"I knew exactly what the proportions were and the overall detail," said Rodis, "so I gave [George] a couple of sketches of that. He was so good that you could give him an abstract drawing and he would apply it to the design you had in mind. So, I actually drew a guy flexing his muscles. If you look at the Bird-of-Prey, it looks like Arnold Schwarzenegger doing his pose, so I did bunch of drawings of that and said, 'Bill, I want it to look like this when you're done.'"[11]

LEFT: Carson, Ralston, Bennett, associate producer Ralph Winter, and Rodis confer on the Bird-of-Prey at ILM. It was Bennett's idea to have the crew disembark from the back of the vessel instead of the front as early production drawings had originally planned.

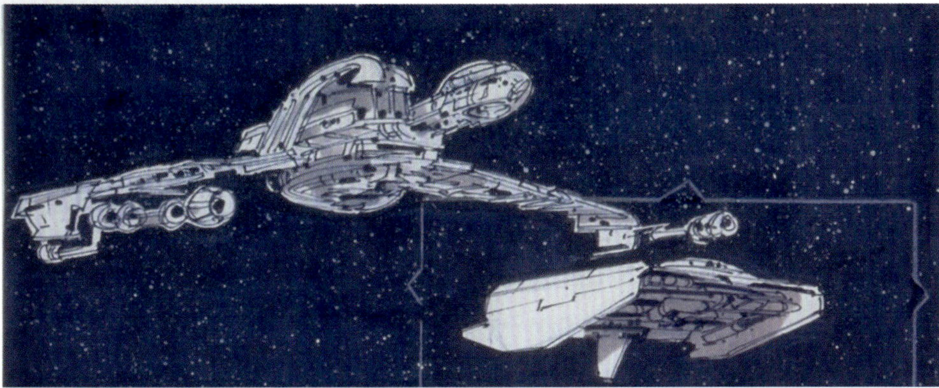

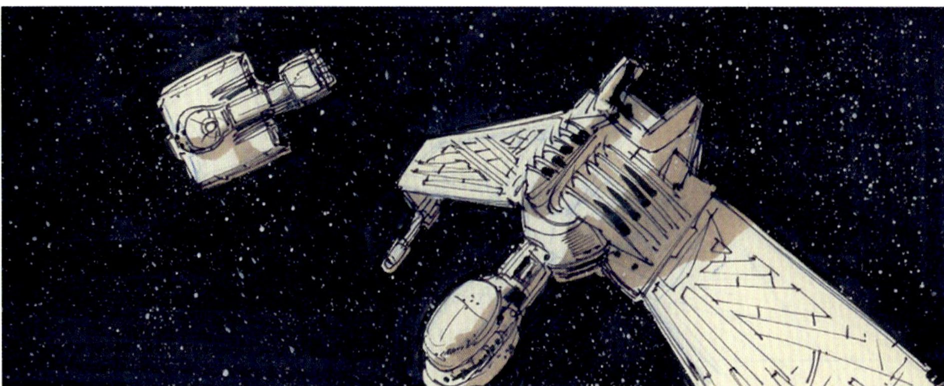

ABOVE: Storyboards by ILM's visual effects art director David Carson showing the Bird-of-Prey engaging the merchant ship. Rodis created the merchant ship design, saying, "I didn't want it to be fancy; I wanted it to be lumpy so that when the Bird-of-Prey hovered over it, you just felt sorry for these guys. They don't have a good-looking ship, and they are about to be blown up!"[10]

ABOVE: Carson revealed a change that needed to occur to his original storyboards: "The idea is that the camera starts on the merchant ship and pulls back to reveal the Bird-of-Prey as it materializes. I wanted to do it as an actual pullback, not a zoom. It turns out, you can't do a pullback in space because the stars stay at infinity. So when you do a pullback, it makes the ship look like it is shrinking. You have to do it as a zoom."[12]

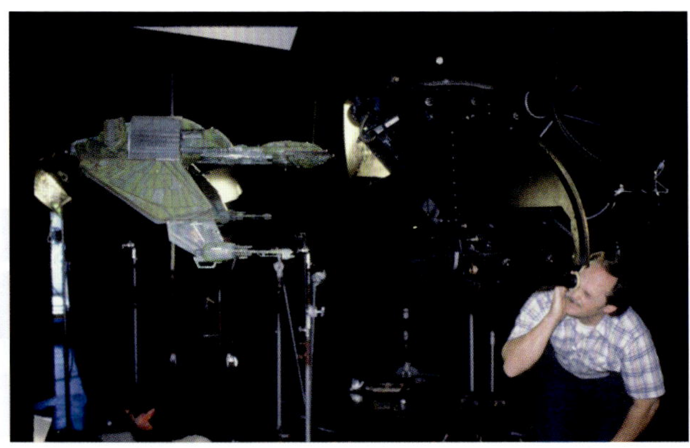

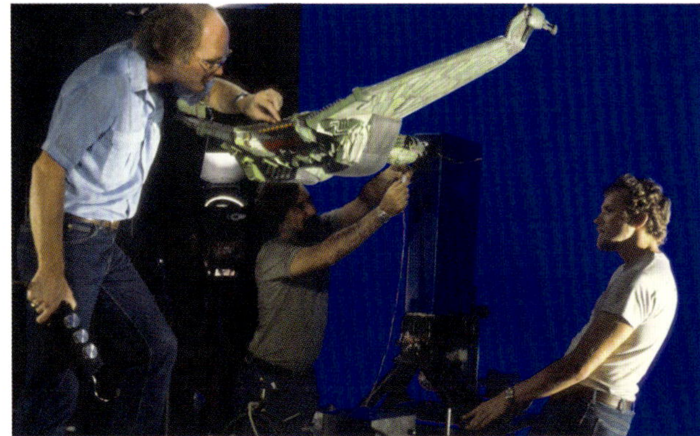

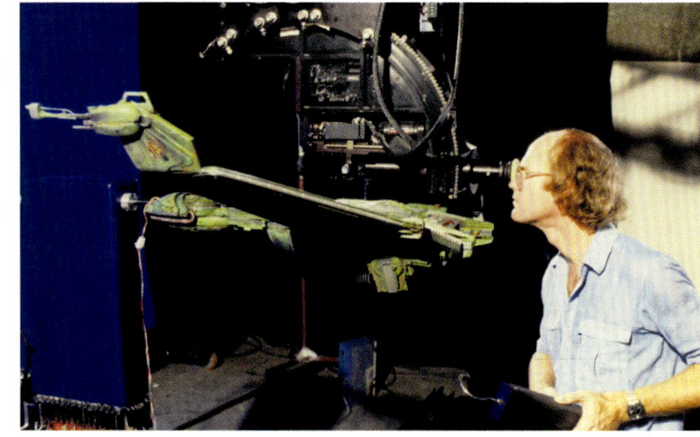

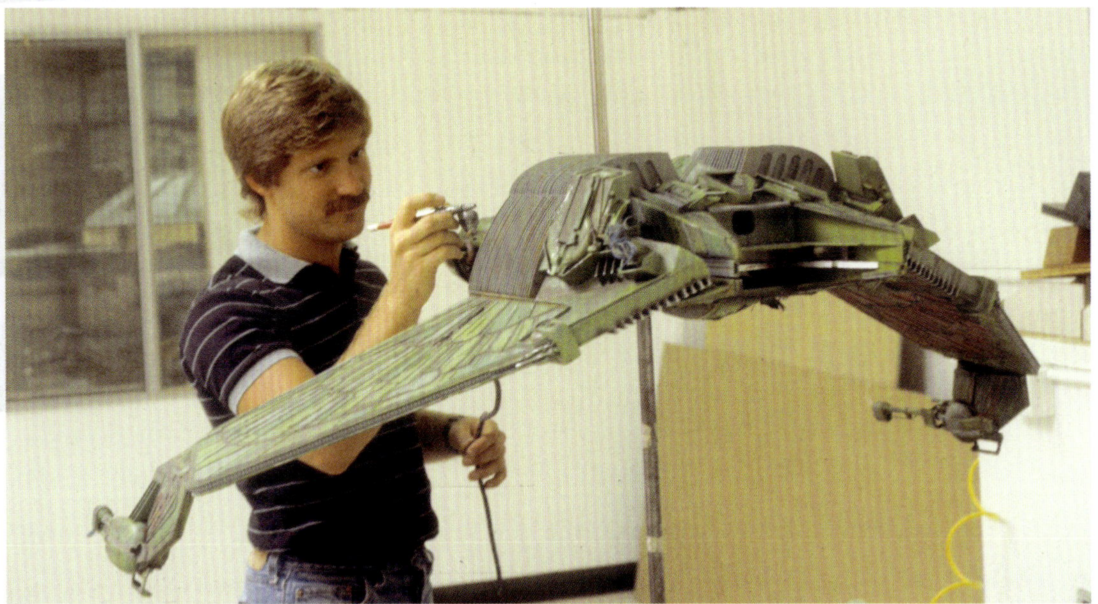

ABOVE LEFT: Visual effects cameraman Don Dow is checking the Vista Cruiser camera. The Bird-of-Prey is bracketed in the back for this shot.

ABOVE MIDDLE AND RIGHT: Special visual effects cameraman Scott Farrar prepares to film the Bird-of-Prey in front of a blue screen. The model was unique because it could be bracketed from either the front or the rear, giving it a wider range of angles from which to choose, a gift of sorts to ILM that the *Enterprise* model could not provide. Here, the model is front bracketed. Supervising modelmaker Steve Gawley said, "There is something about the whole design of the ship. It was very graphic. It was a really fun model to photograph."[13]

LEFT: Of the Bird-of-Prey, Gawley shared, "Bill came up with the interesting concept of a radio tuner. If you look at old radios, they have plates that lock inside other plates. They are all on a single shaft. The wing assembly of the Bird-of-Prey was very similar. It was a really clever innovation but, when we built the final model, I had to make that thing work!"[13]

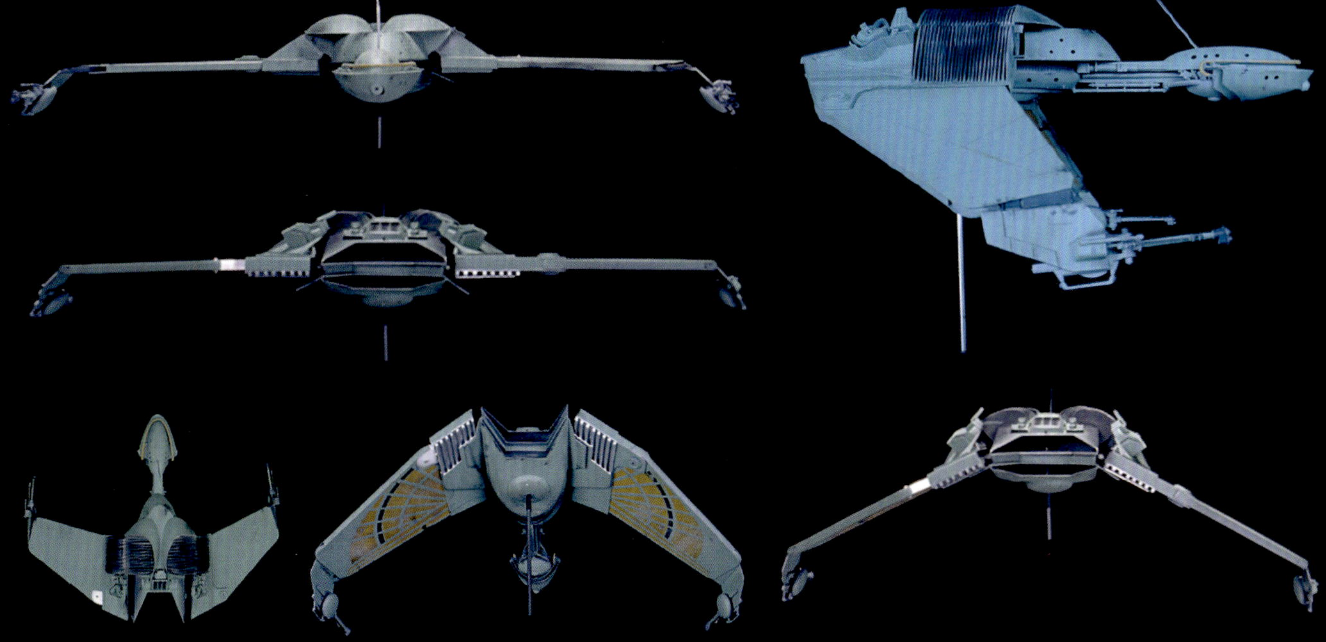

LEFT: Various views of Bill George's original study models. Ralston explained, "These illustrate the brilliant idea that Leonard had which I don't think anyone had ever done before. He traveled to ILM early to go through all the designs. The model shop had maquettes, little models that they had put together, based on some illustrations that had been done. Leonard would hold the physical model and spin it around. We'd have discussions about, 'What if we changed this? What if we changed that?' The model guys could grab the model and change it while we were in the meeting. They'd change it in half-an-hour. Leonard could look at the model again. It was different than now, looking at a monitor. Maybe I'm wrong, but for me, anyway, that physicality made a difference in what we were doing."[13]

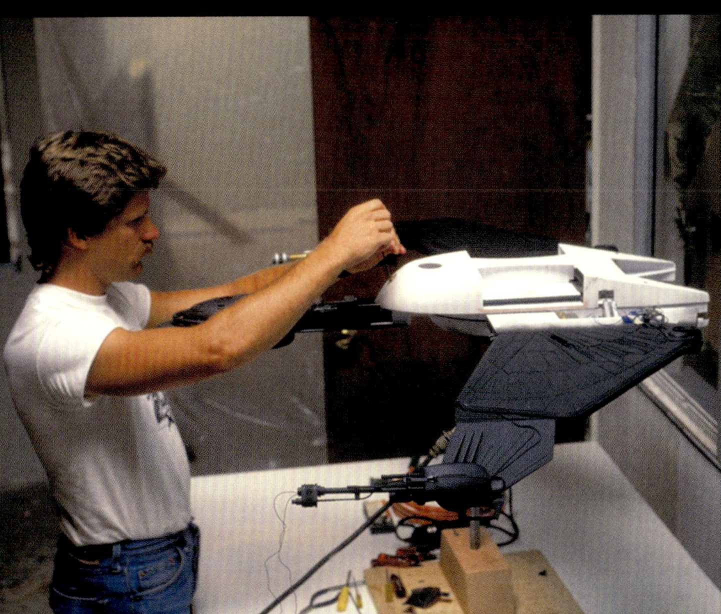

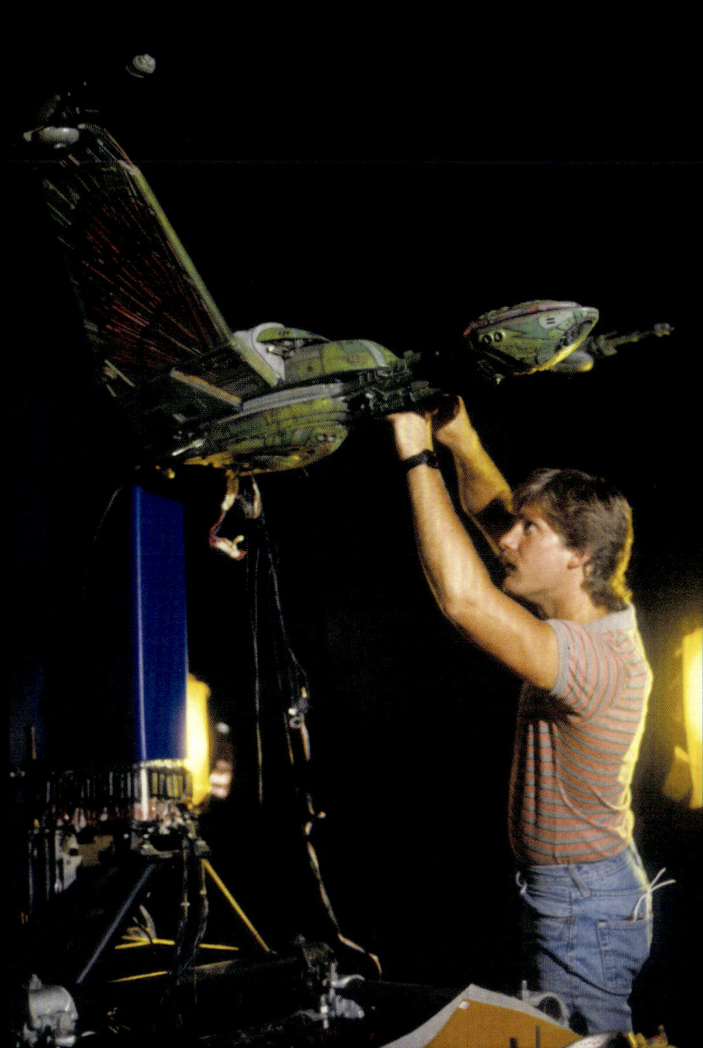

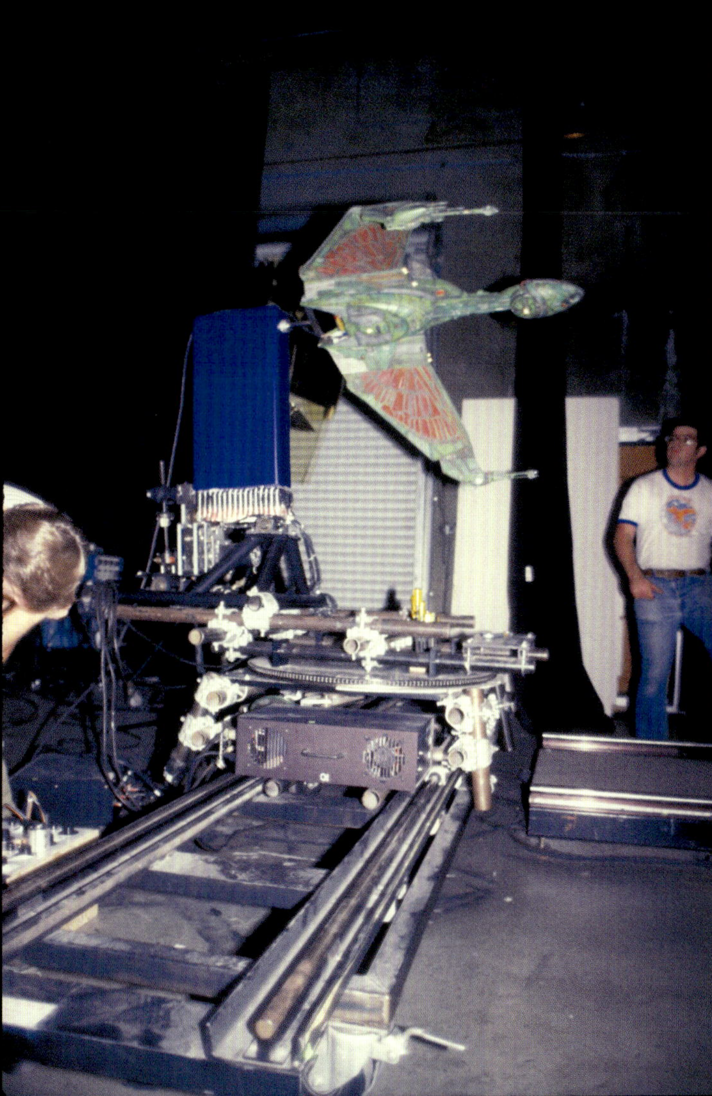

ABOVE AND RIGHT: © Industrial Light & Magic. All Rights Reserved. Bill George and Steve Gawley would be responsible for the filming model. Here, George works on the outside of the ship, while Gawley would design all the internal mechanics.

FAR RIGHT: © Industrial Light & Magic. All Rights Reserved. This image demonstrates the maneuverability of the Bird-of-Prey model, something of a joy for a *Star Trek* production which was accustomed to more cumbersome Federation starships.

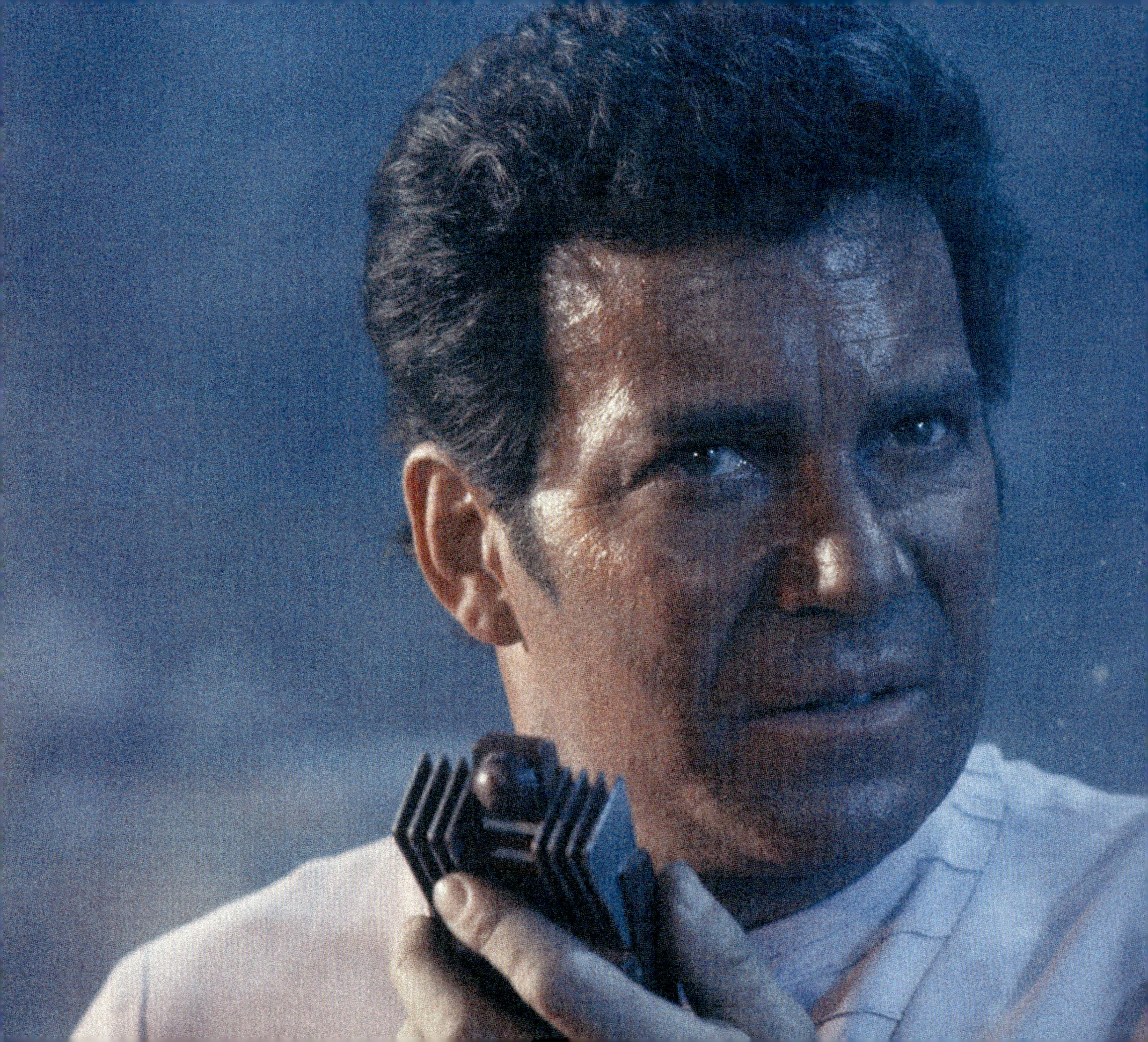

CHAPTER 6

C'EST LA VIE

THE COSTUME AND MAKEUP DEPARTMENTS

While Kruge and Saavik may have little in common, Christopher Lloyd and Robin Curtis had a similar experience with their costumes and makeup. For both, the externals given them by makeup artists and costume designers were essential to shaping their characters. "The costume and makeup, if nothing else, certainly set a tone for me and I just tried to fill it in," Lloyd said. "I liked the character makeup, and with the costume combined, it really gave, in my mind, an image of the character that was fun to play. The costume made me look regal, which I felt Kruge was. When I would put the costume on, immediately I would stand a certain way and walk a certain way and it forced me to take a posture that made me feel good for the character. It helped me become the character even more when I would see myself in the makeup and the costume."[1] Curtis agreed, stating, "It sort of helped you take on the mantle of the character. I love the vest, which was very flattering, and felt good. That big flak jacket, however. I remember asking Leonard, 'What the hell are all these pockets?' It was hot and bulky. But you know, transformation to a character is from the outside in. When you wear those clothes, your posture just changes almost unwittingly. You are becoming the character, and your shoulders square like Saavik would have because of the costume."[2]

Returning for *Star Trek III* would be costume designer Robert Fletcher, who had worked on the previous two films. This time, Fletcher would be coordinating designs and collaborating with the makeup team at The Burman Studio, Inc.

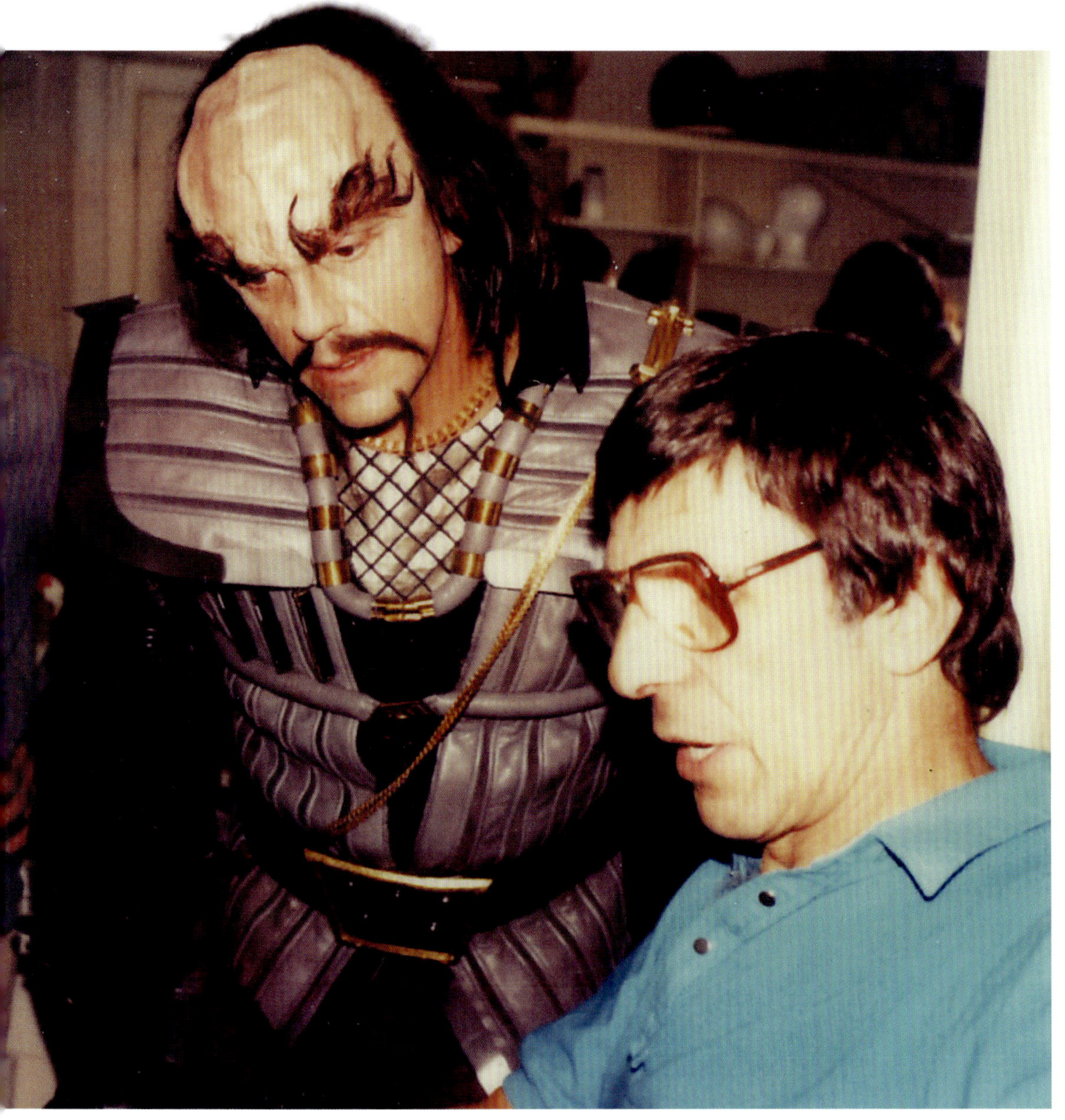

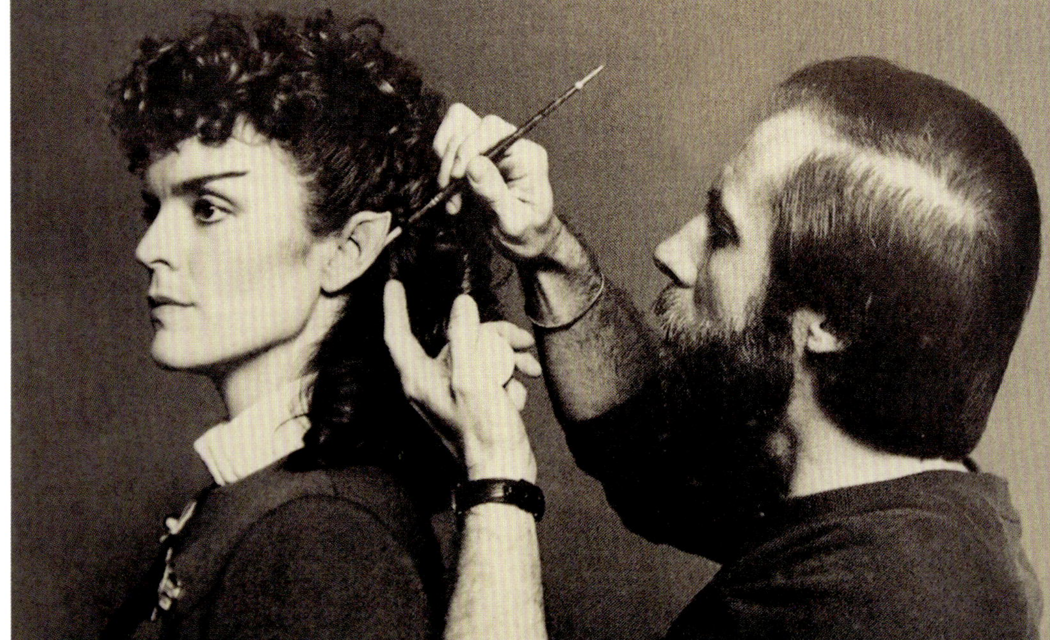

ABOVE: "They actually experimented with green makeup, creating a green tinge to my skin. That idea was rejected pretty quickly. New ears were applied every day because the chemicals used to remove the prosthetic pretty much destroyed the material. The ears were weightless and once applied, I forgot I was even wearing them," shared Curtis.[2] The makeup artists asked Curtis to use antibiotic ointment each night on her ears to avoid an infection. To help avoid damaging or gluing Curtis' real hair, white cardboard was fitted behind her ears during the application process.

LEFT: The makeup department was a social gathering place. Some actors, like the Spock actors and Curtis, would meet for the first time while getting their makeup done. Long hours in the makeup chair would provide time for sleep, memorizing lines, and conversation. Here, Lloyd and Nimoy chat in the makeup department.

FLIGHT RECORDER VISUAL:

ROBERT FLETCHER, COSTUME DESIGNER

There are few artists who have had such a sustained and profound effect on *Star Trek* as Robert Fletcher, who served as costume designer on the first four *Star Trek* films. His costumes would appear not only in those movies, but also the next three, and inspire uses and adaptations in *Star Trek: The Next Generation*, *Star Trek: Voyager*, *Star Trek: Strange New Worlds*, and the 2009 *Star Trek* movie, to name a few. Fletcher's hand can be seen with the look of the Klingons beginning with *Star Trek: The Motion Picture* and on many of the aliens featured in *Star Trek III*. The Klingon ridges were inspired by a design he had done for a 1955 American Shakespeare Festival production of *Julius Caesar* and *The Tempest* starring Jack Palance and Christopher Plummer, who would eventually play Klingon General Chang in *Star Trek VI: The Undiscovered Country*.

He was born Robert Fletcher Wycoff on August 23, 1922, in Cedar Rapids, Iowa. After his military service as a bombardier, he attended *The* University of Iowa, the same school director Nicholas Meyer would graduate from decades later. He began working as an actor, set decorator, and producer on theater, television, and film productions, which gave him a wealth of experience to draw on in his later career. Perhaps Fletcher's successes as a costume designer, including an Emmy nomination, were rooted in the many theater production roles he played before settling on that profession, from actor to set decorator. He never stopped designing costumes during his seventy-five-year career, including one of his last contributions, creating the armor for *Game of Thrones*. Fletcher passed on April 5, 2021, at age 98.

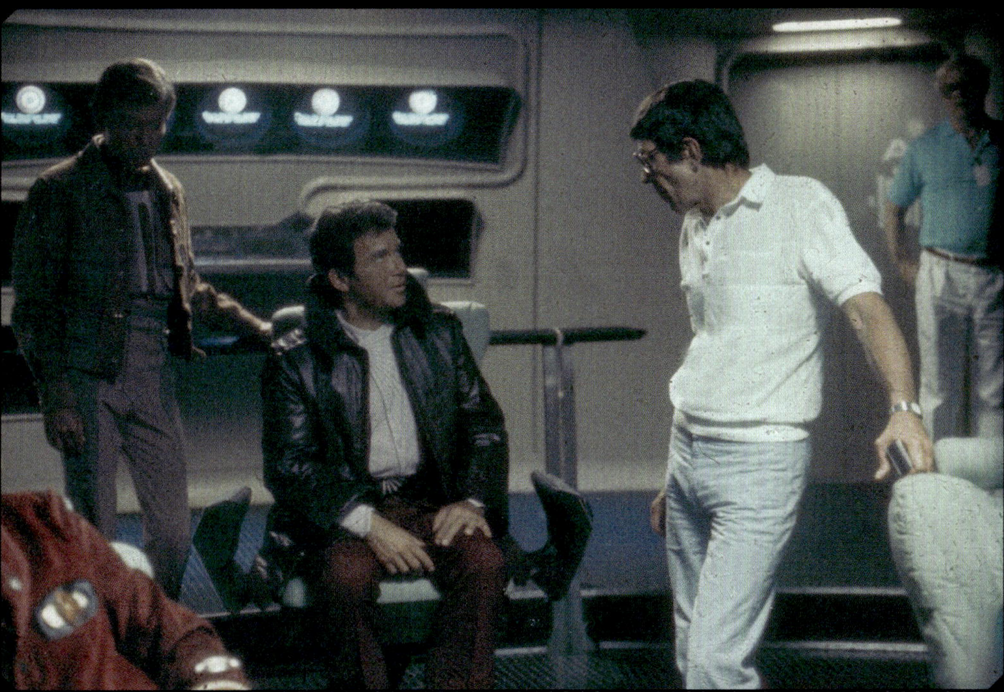

REMEMBER...

Robin Curtis: "I met Robert Fletcher when I was at the Western Costume Company for fittings. Lovely man, lovely man! I was measured and the costume was stitched. It was so much fun, with costumers fussing about you to make you the best character you can be."[2]

LEFT: Fletcher, standing near the turbo-lift, visits the sets to see his costumes in action.

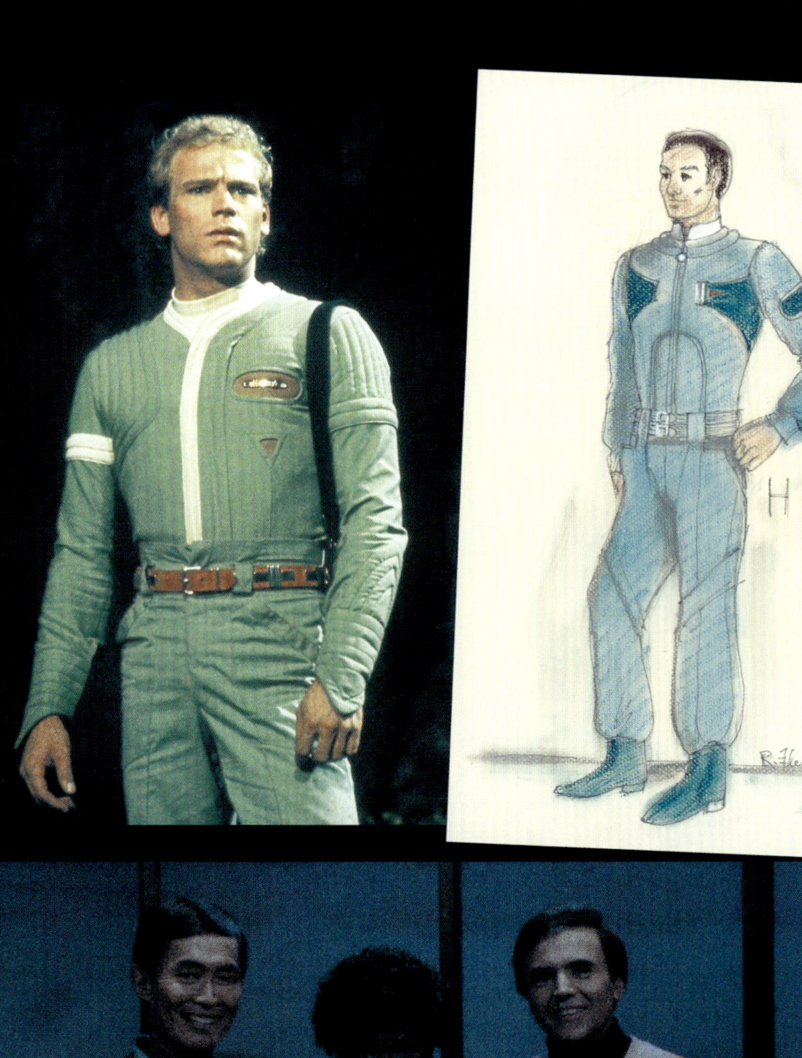

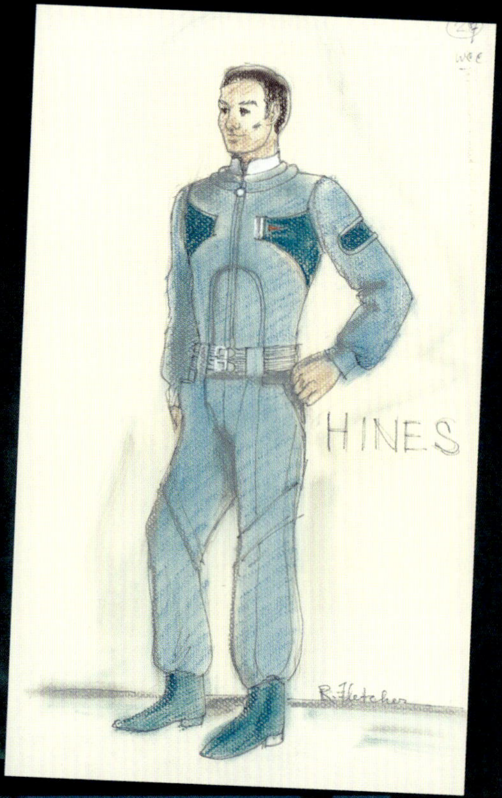

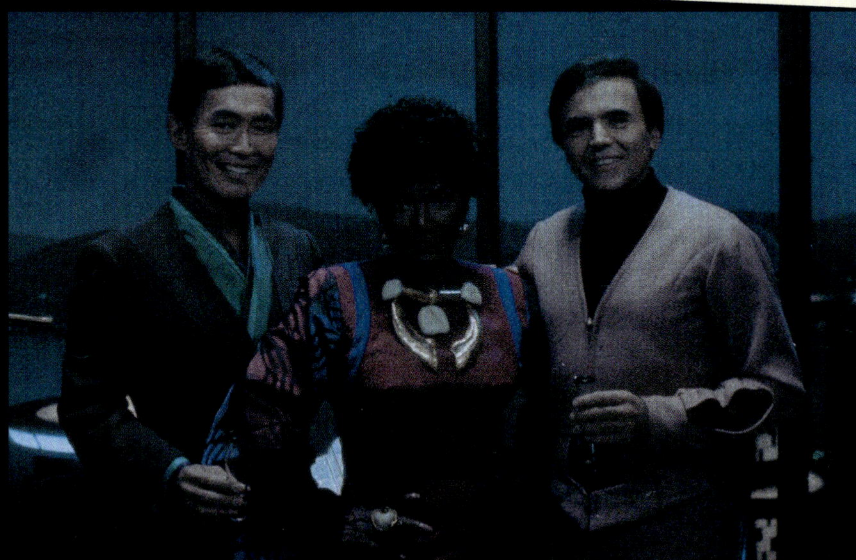

TOP: Illustration © Museum Associates/LACMA. Fletcher designed a costume for the character Hines who was supposed to play a larger role as another scientist helping to study Genesis on the *U.S.S. Grissom*. In the final film, Hines is a background character working next to David Marcus, wearing the Regula I scientist costume from the previous film. Instead, David is given a variation of the Hines costume.[3]

ABOVE: An unused publicity photo showing Sulu, Uhura, and Chekov's civilian costumes. Nichelle Nichols designed the jewelry Uhura is wearing here.

RIGHT: Fletcher's unique design for Kirk's civilian costume.

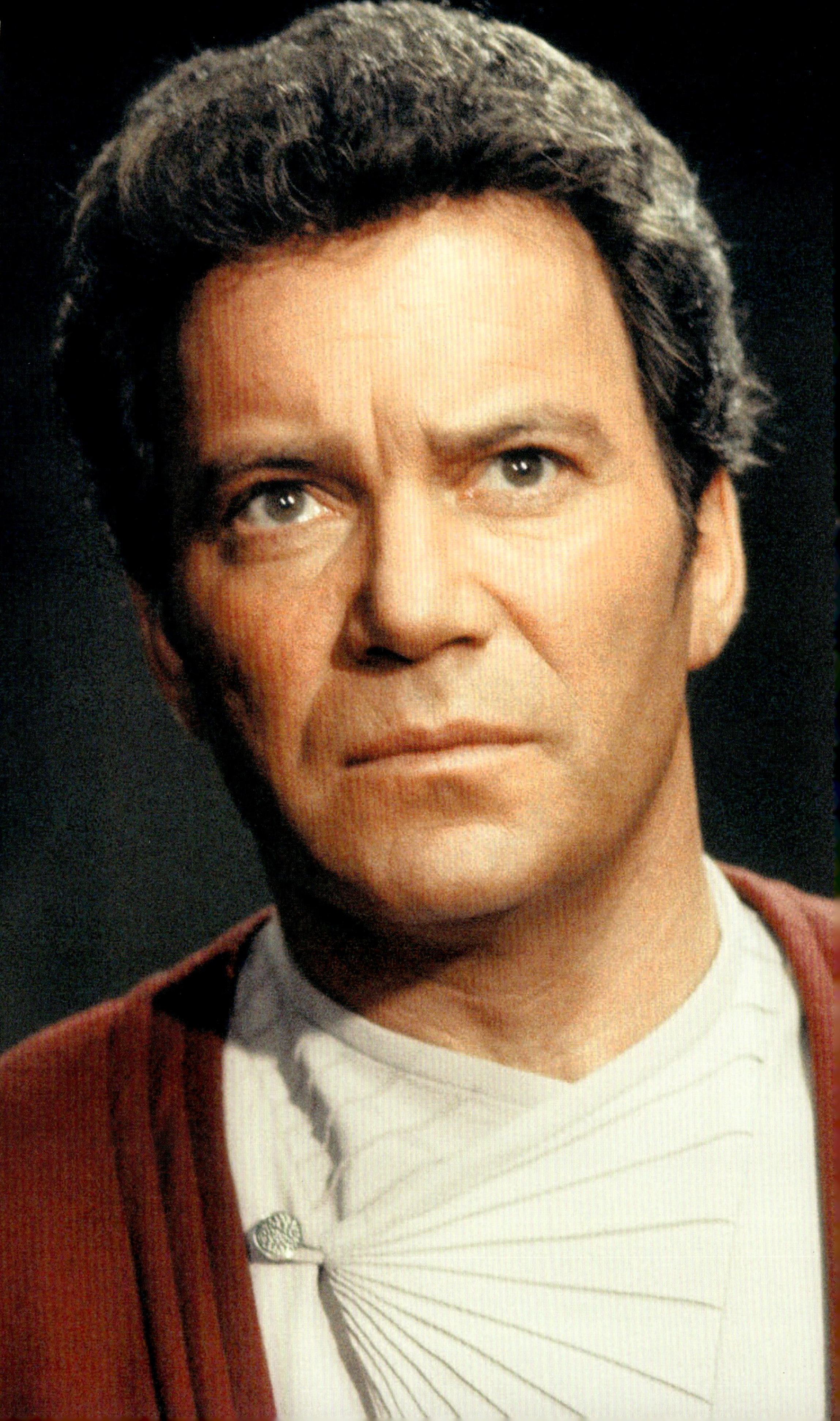

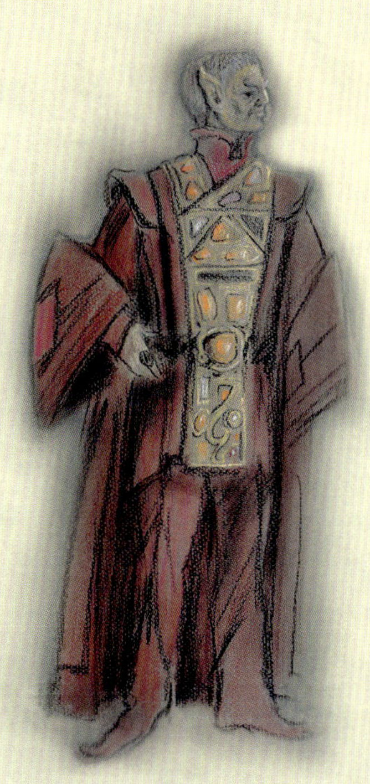
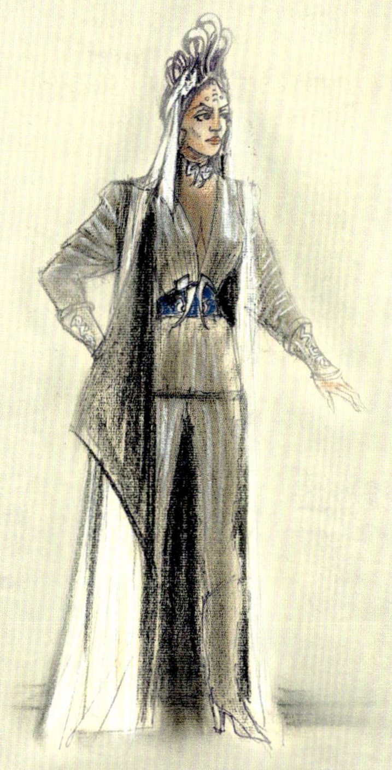
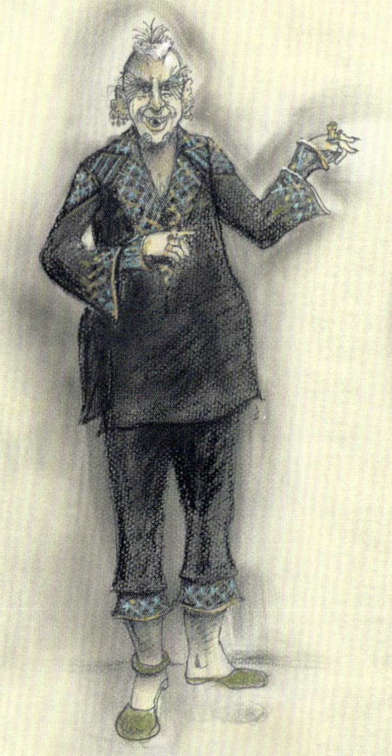
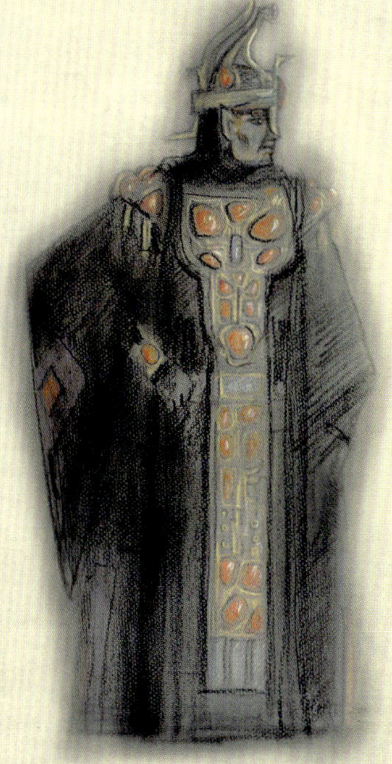
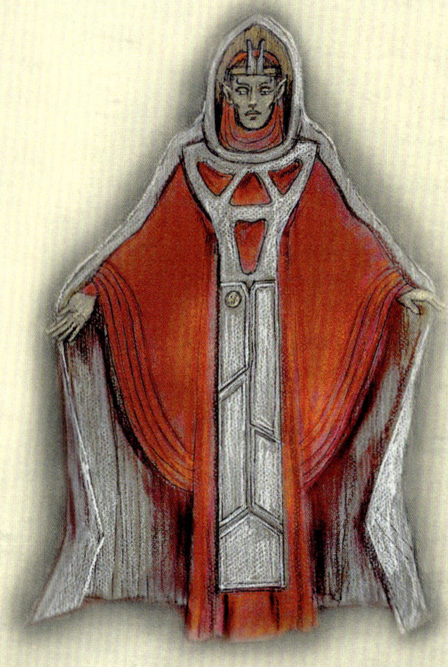
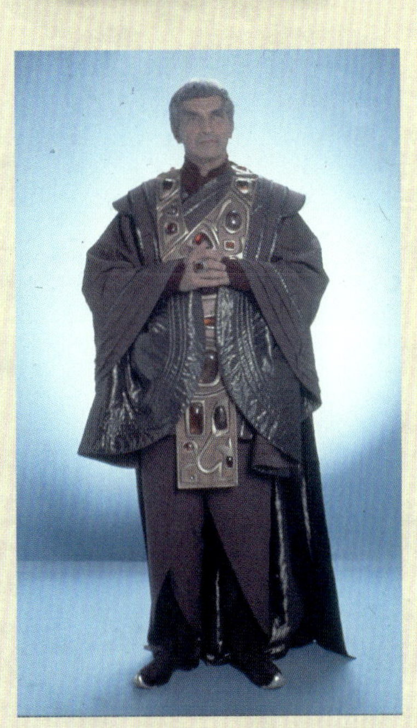
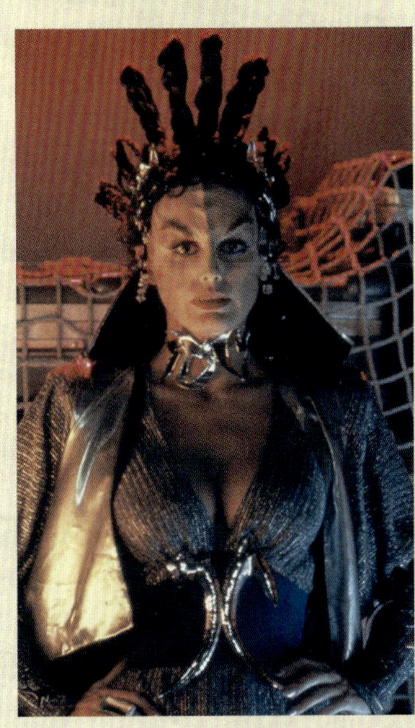
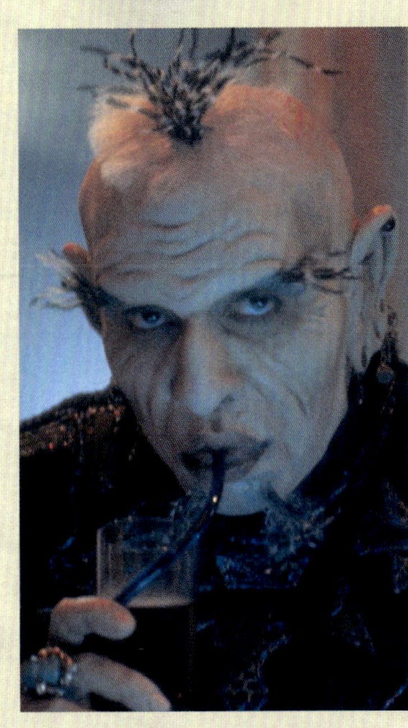
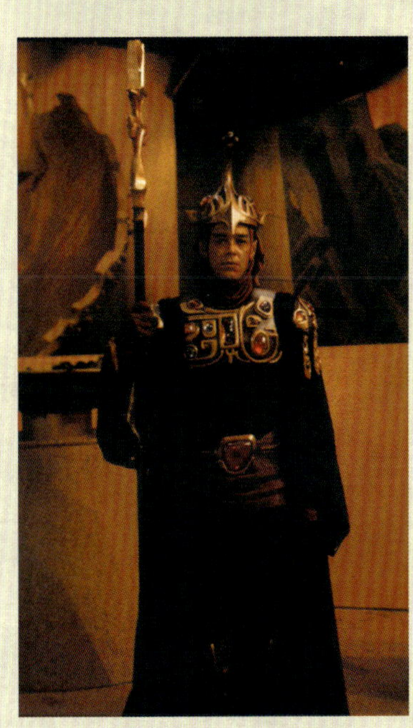
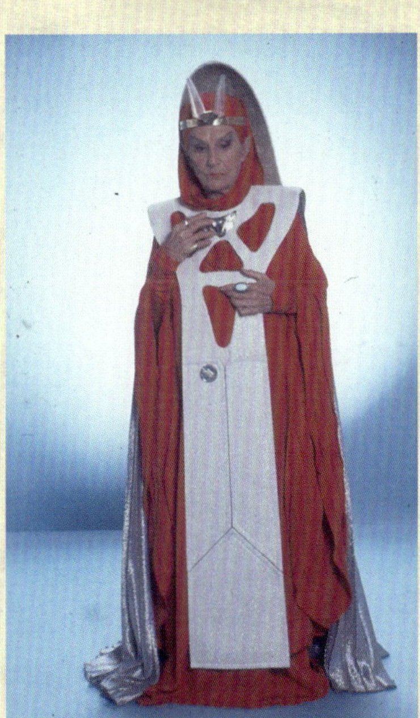

The tests faced by the various production teams always had one element in common: finding strategies to get around budgetary limitations. Fletcher had a total budget of $350,000 to work with on *Star Trek III*, which included Klingon uniforms, various Starfleet costumes, scores of Vulcans at Spock's procession, and numerous bar aliens. The original Klingon costumes which were thought to be recyclable from *Star Trek: The Motion Picture* had been damaged during production or on publicity tours. Fletcher cobbled together some costumes from those originals and created new pieces for Kruge. Torg actor Stephen Liska remembered that he and the other Klingons had to step into the costume to put it on. "Once it was on, it was on. You couldn't sit down comfortably, you couldn't bend, and you couldn't really eat. If you wanted to rest, you had to lean against something."[4] Each "monster maroon" Starfleet uniform cost about $1,950. Sometimes multiples of costumes were required, especially if stunts were part of the equation. For example, the shirts that William Shatner wears during his fight with Kruge cost about $300 each due to the intricate pleating around the collar, and Fletcher originally planned to have three of them on hand in case of emergencies such as ripping during filming or even the deleterious effects of lighting burning out the shirt's color. The production wound up needing twelve.

THIS PAGE: Fletcher's original designs and the final costumes.

THIS SPREAD: All illustrations © Museum Associates/ LACMA.[5]

FLIGHT RECORDER VISUAL:

THE BURMAN STUDIO, INC.

Even though Thomas Burman's father Ellis was a pioneering makeup artist, responsible for the memorable work on *The Twilight Zone*, Thomas had trouble determining what career he wanted to pursue. After service in the United States Marines, he worked various odd jobs before agreeing to help his father on a project for Don Post Studios. It was there that he met John Chambers, who would create the award-winning makeup for *The Planet of the Apes* films and was responsible for making Mr. Spock's ears on the original series. It was then that Burman decided on a career in makeup and special makeup effects that eventually led him to create his own studio during the early 1980s and help revolutionize the industry. His wife is co-owner and makeup artist Bari Dreiband-Burman, and their sons Barney and Rob worked for their parents' studio, and contributed to *Star Trek III*. [6]

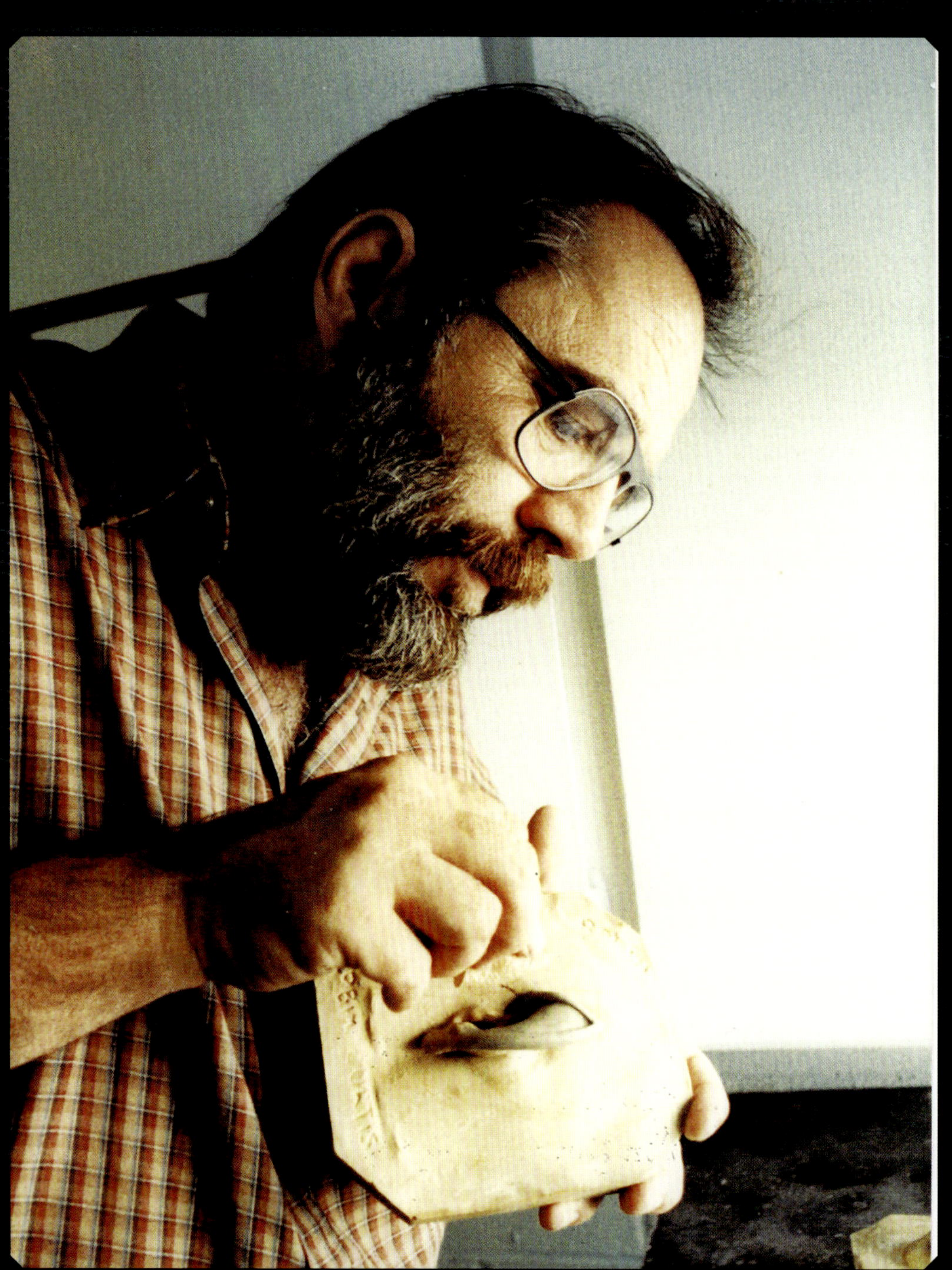

REMEMBER...

Robin Curtis: "I remember meeting Silvia Abascal with regards to the hair. She was lovely. She chose to go with my natural curly hair versus trying to fashion it in some way, and the only adjustment that was made was to cut it so that you could see those fabulous Vulcan ears. It was tamed around my ears. They tried several different hairstyles at the time. I think it was shrewd for them to go with me as 'naturally me' as possible. Much less to be constantly fussing about. You want to create a look that is easy to maintain."[2]

THIS PAGE: Some of the hundreds of Vulcan extras who needed makeup. Due to cuts to the processional scene, in order to advance the narrative, most were not seen in the final film.

Although Fletcher found solutions to these budgetary problems, mostly by reusing and adapting previously made costumes whenever possible, there were some disappointments for him, most especially when costumes they created were edited from the film due to time or story requirements. "As an example," shared Fletcher, "we worked very hard on a whole big processional scene on Vulcan with the body of Spock being carried up the mountainside to the temple. We had hundreds of extras and hundreds of costumes and it's not in the film at all!"[7]

From Klingons to bar patrons, from Vulcan ears and eyebrows to injured Kirk, the number of actors needing makeup on *Star Trek III* would be significant in comparison to the previous film. With preparatory work such as face-masks done at the Burman Studio itself, located in Burbank, a temporary studio, approximately ten by twenty feet, built in the corner of the soundstages handled makeup during filming days. The makeup team included the Burmans, hair stylist Silvia Abascal, and makeup artists Wes Dawn, Jim Kail, *Star Trek II* veteran James L. McCoy, and Tom Woodruff, Jr., among others. The Burman Studio was hired close to production beginning, which necessitated Fletcher, who had designed the movie version of the Klingons, and makeup artists like Don Cash, lending their expertise.

Nimoy frequently spoke about how Vulcan makeup was never an easy process. The Burman Studios were able to meet that challenge thanks in part to having experts such as Nimoy and Mark Lenard, who was reprising his role as Sarek, readily available for consultation. Lenard described how his past experiences were drawn upon. "They asked me what my makeup was like and I brought some pictures in. We even went back and looked at a part of 'Journey to Babel' so that the makeup people could see it."[8]

BELOW RIGHT: Unlike Kirstie Alley, who had her natural eyebrows for *Star Trek II*, Curtis did have her eyebrows shaved for the role. The makeup artists starting shaving beyond the natural arc of her eyebrows.

BELOW LEFT: Shaving half the eyebrow to permit makeup artists to create an upswept shape is usually part of the process of Vulcanizing an actor. While Lenard was able to avoid that when playing Sarek on the television series because of the screen size of TVs then, for the film, the eyebrows had to go. More white was added to Lenard's hair for the role of Spock's father, as he was actually only six years and five months older than Nimoy.

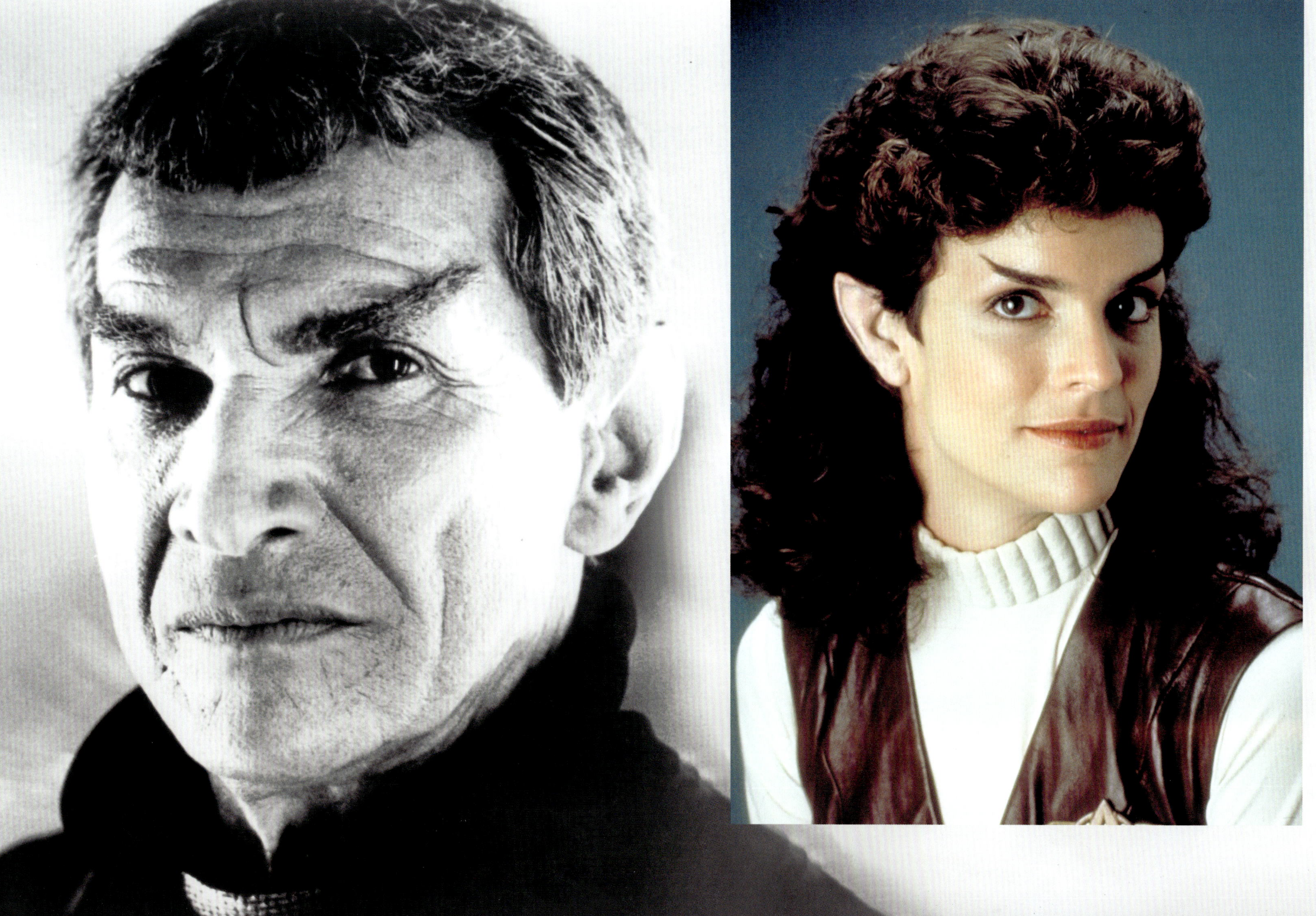

Despite the generally smooth process of creating the makeup and special makeup effects for the film, there were some hiccups occasionally. Stephen Manley, who played Spock at age 17, remembered, "The Spock actors went to The Burman Studios to have our ears molded. Tom Burman and his team were up to their noses in plaster, clay, and foam. He had about a dozen people working for him and then other artists would be added to the shop when needed. There was a mix-up with the ears and they had tried to place Vadia's ears on me, but of course, they did not fit. Wes Dawn, who started my makeup process said, 'Something is going on here. He's got the wrong ears!'"[9]

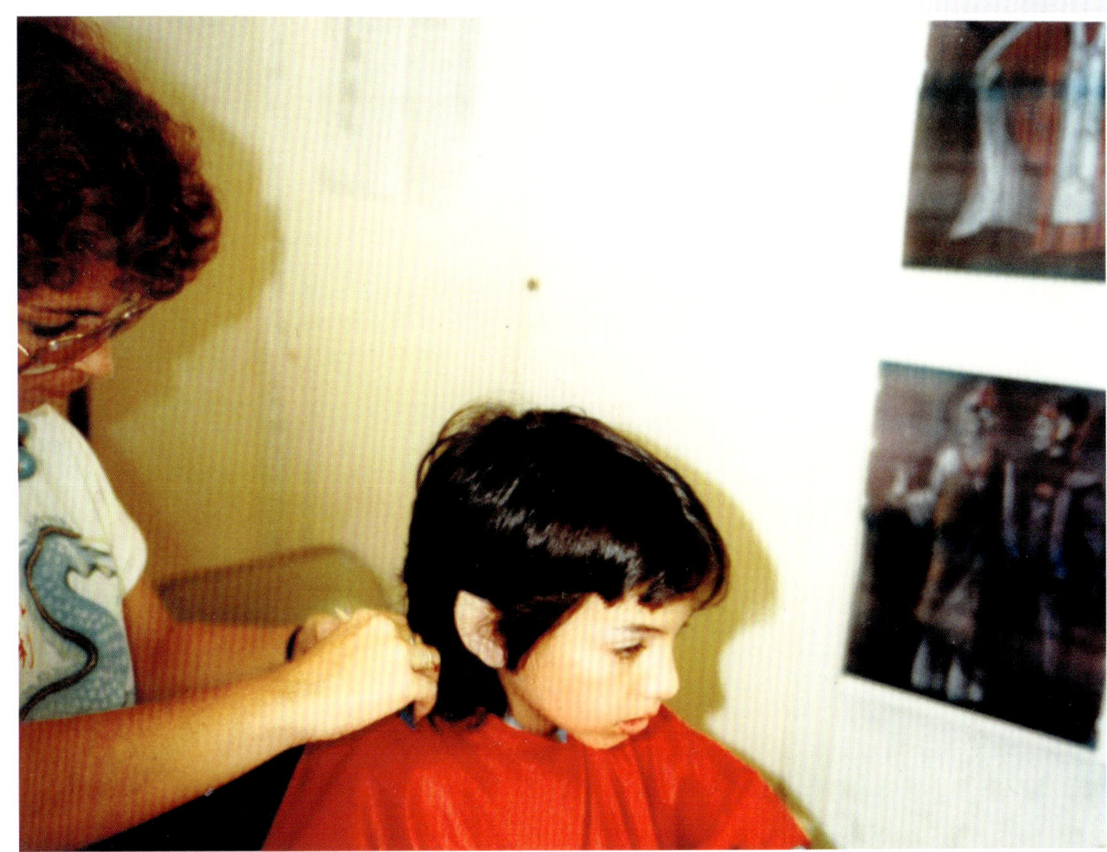

RIGHT: Fletcher's art can be seen on the wall of the makeup department as Vadia Potenza gets his ears. "I had to sit with these big plaster molds on my ears and wait for them to set," said Potenza. "It was like a big plaster kind of Princess Leia thing on my ear. They asked me to grow my hair out long so they could style it however they wanted. I had to wear my hair long for the first month of school and that was not really the style at the time in Southern California, so I caught some flak for that. On the day of filming, I was in makeup for about three hours. They let me go home with the makeup on. And I kept it on, the ears, the eyebrows. I went to the movies with my friends that night in full makeup, just hoping and praying someone would ask me about it. I don't think anyone really noticed!"[10 11]

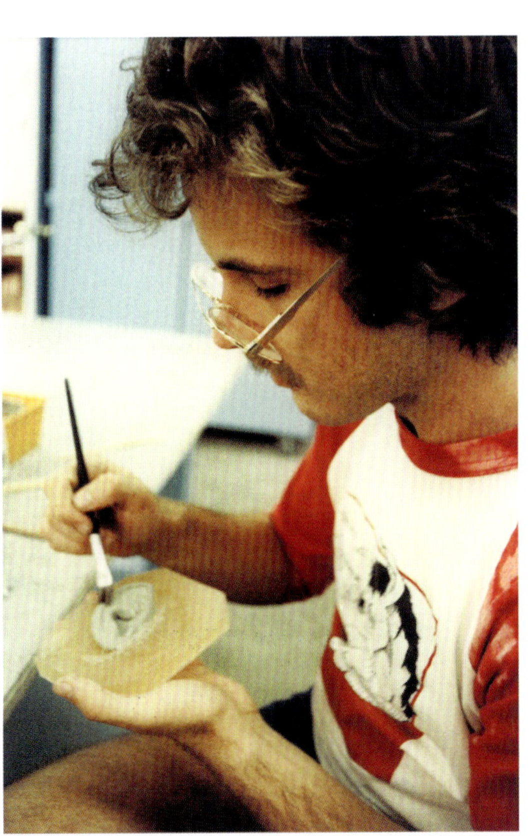

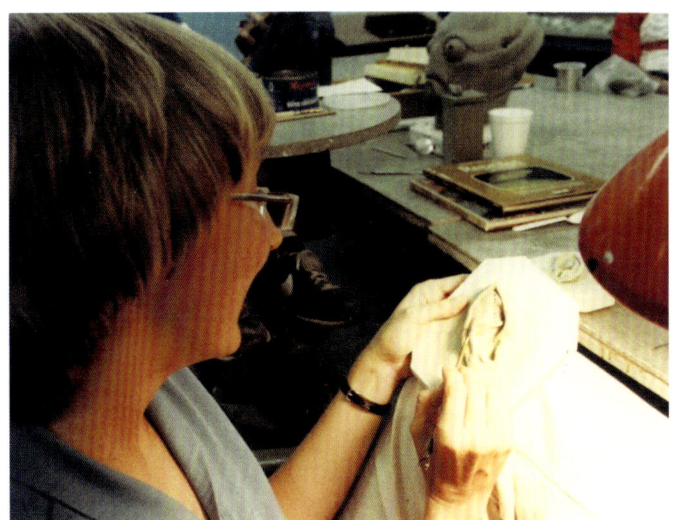

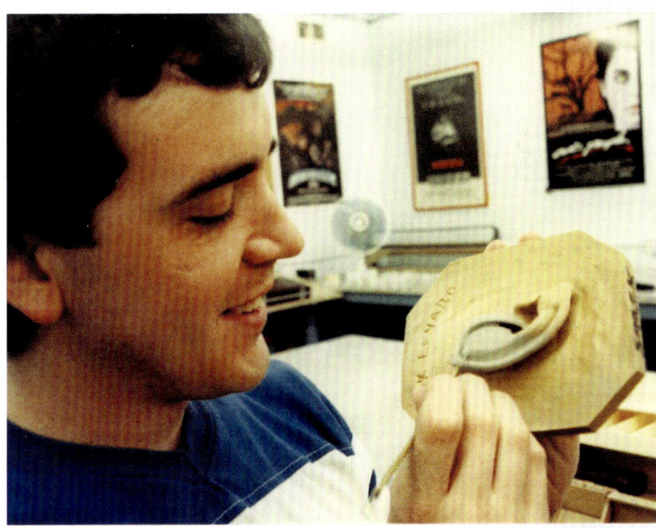

LEFT AND ABOVE: Many Vulcan actors and extras required many hours of work by The Burman Studio artists. Pictured are Scott Wheeler, Linda Frobos, and Thomas Woodruff. Lenard was impressed with the work done by The Burman Studio artists, stating, "They're kind of stylish and they are sort of integrated more with the face than the others. They're still effective but the whole feeling is slightly different. And that had to be done and they had to make casting of the ears and so forth. Because the ears are tricky to put on, in order to look real, the molded rubber has to fit perfectly. There can be no marks or creases on the inside. They have to be colored so they blend in with the skin. I was made very pale. I have a very natural tan so my color bled through and Vulcans are supposed to be pale. You can't have a tanned Vulcan. (Laughter)."[8 6]

SPOCK CHANGE-O-HEAD

Before the era of morphing technology, transitions of aging were handled by other visual and makeup effects. Although computer generated images were starting to be used, with *Star Trek II*'s Genesis effect a pioneering example, *Star Trek III* had to rely on the tried and true. To show audiences Spock's aging as Genesis transformed, what was known as a "Change-O-Head" puppet was built by The Burman Studio artists. Joe Davis, who played Spock at 25, and Nimoy both had molds made of their entire head. The puppets were built with expanding and contracting bladders filled with a liquid creating the illusion of rapid transformation and aging. On the cold set, the liquid would need to be warmed by studio lights to function. One of the puppets showed the transition between Davis and younger Nimoy, and the other between a younger Nimoy and Nimoy almost as he appeared at the time of the film. The mold of Nimoy would do double duty since it was also used to create a mannequin that could be carried during the processional and during scenes where Nimoy was directing himself.

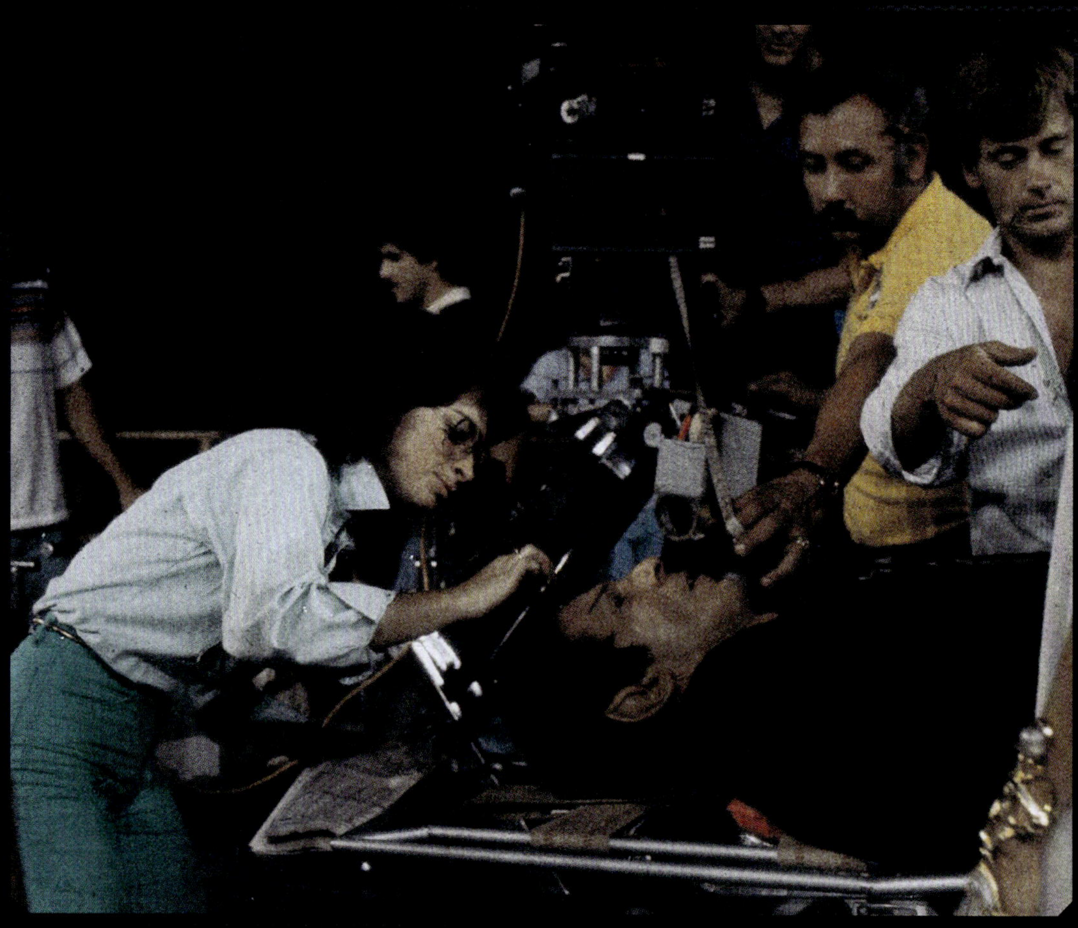

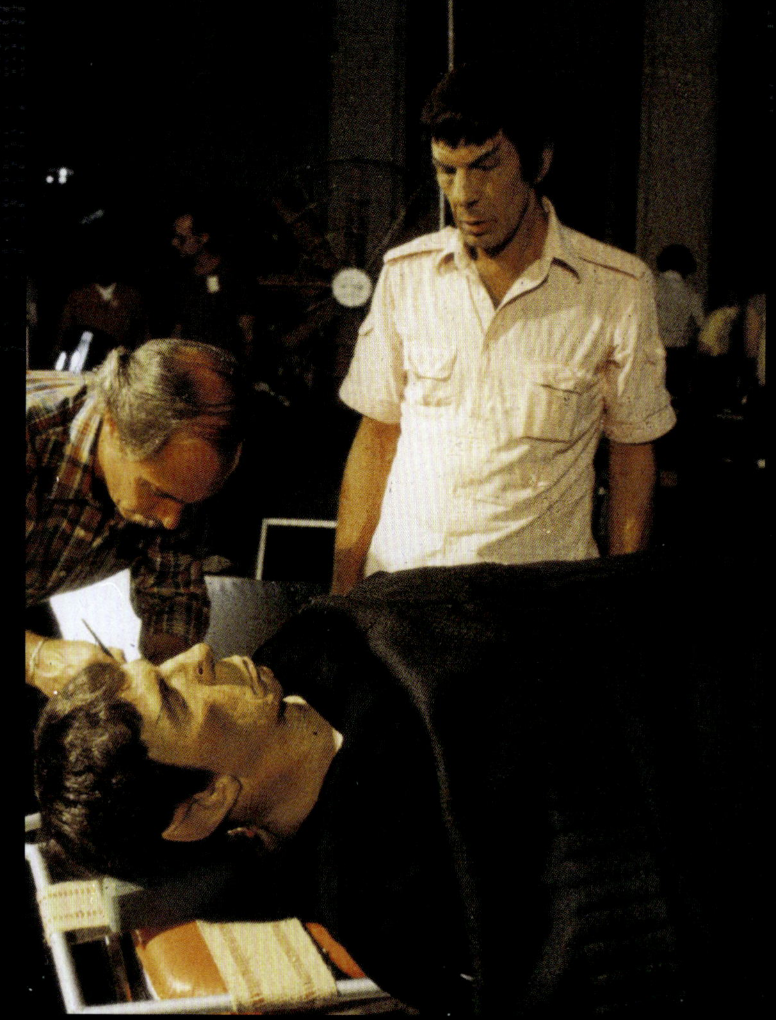

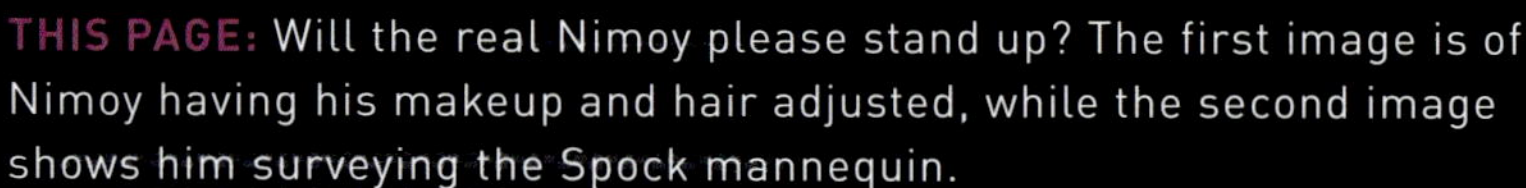

THIS PAGE: Will the real Nimoy please stand up? The first image is of Nimoy having his makeup and hair adjusted, while the second image shows him surveying the Spock mannequin.

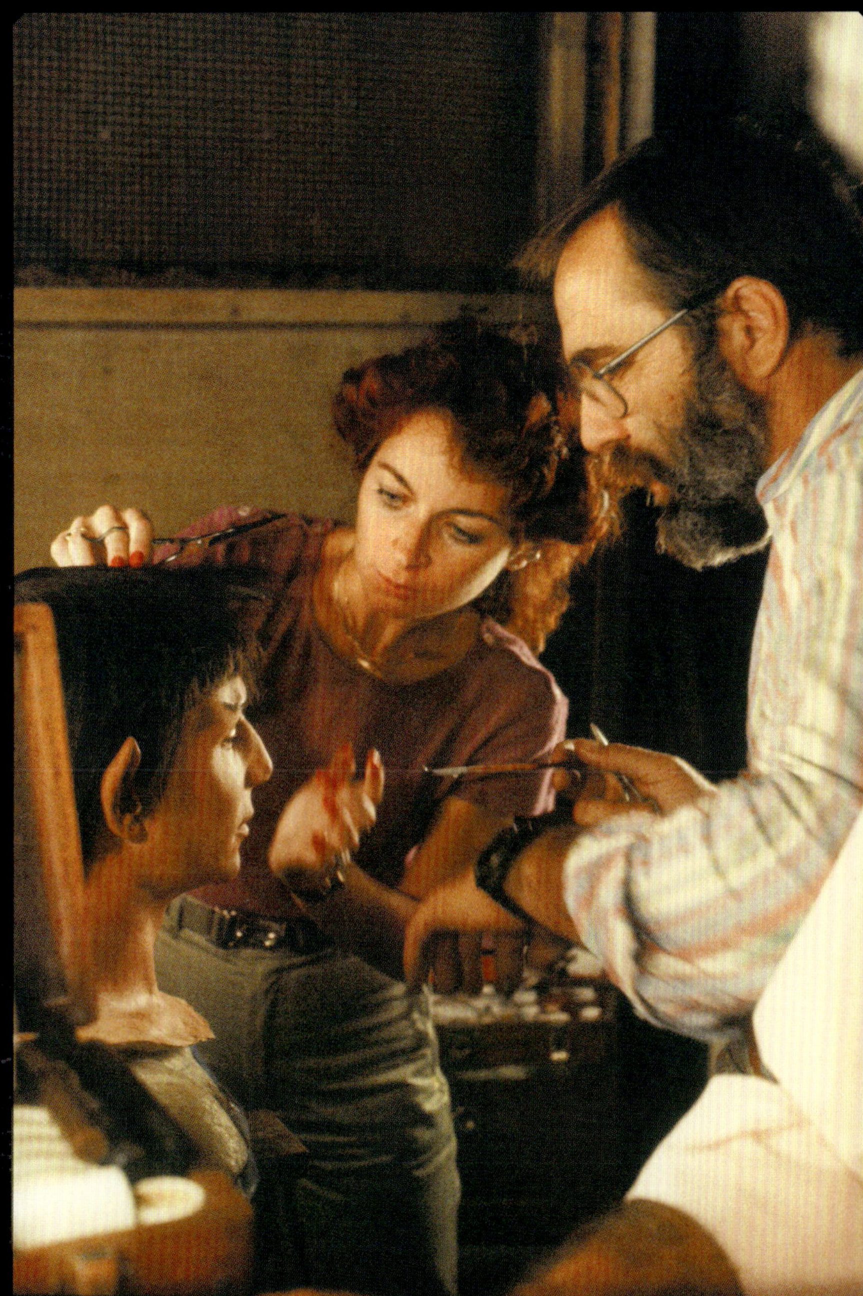

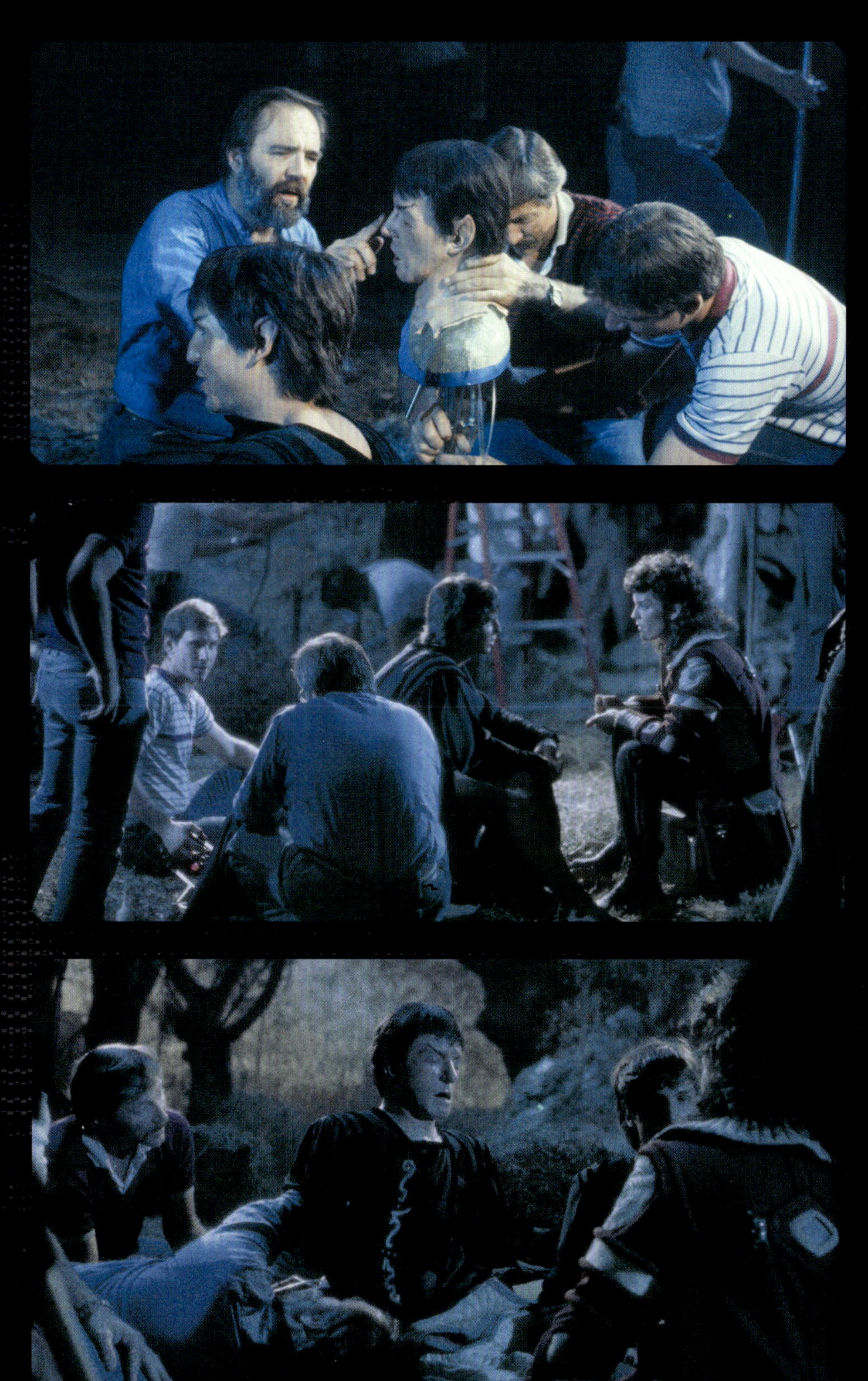

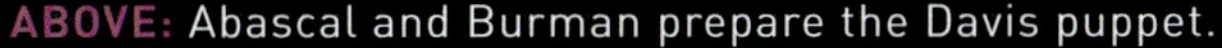

ABOVE: Abascal and Burman prepare the Davis puppet.

TOP RIGHT: The puppet that brings Spock closer to the age of Nimoy.

MIDDLE RIGHT: Davis and Curtis wait as the puppet is prepared.

BOTTOM RIGHT: A close-up will hide the puppet operator during filming.

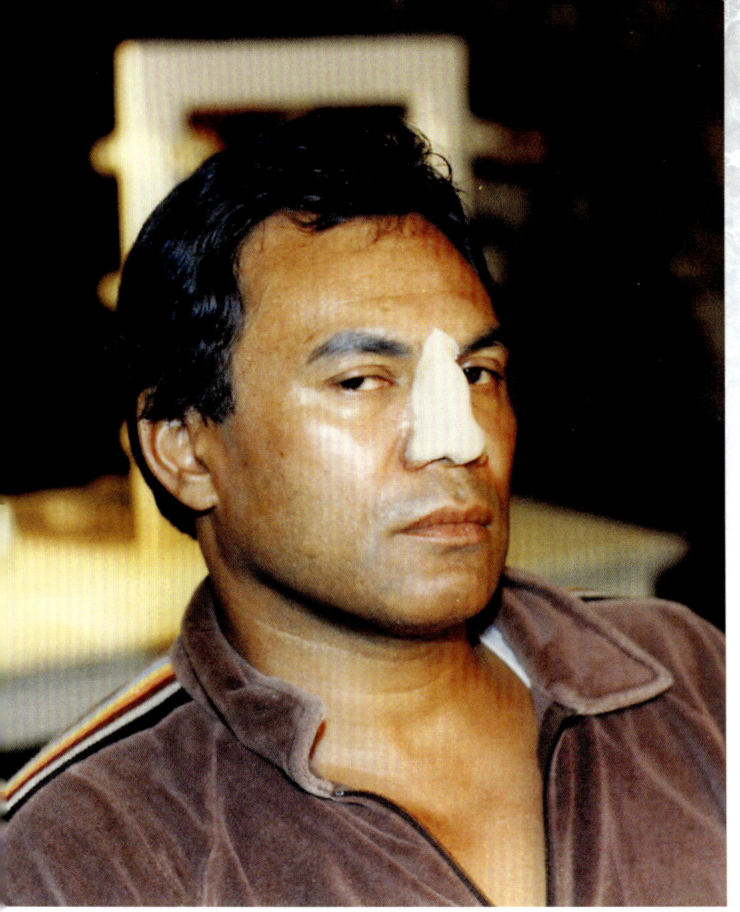
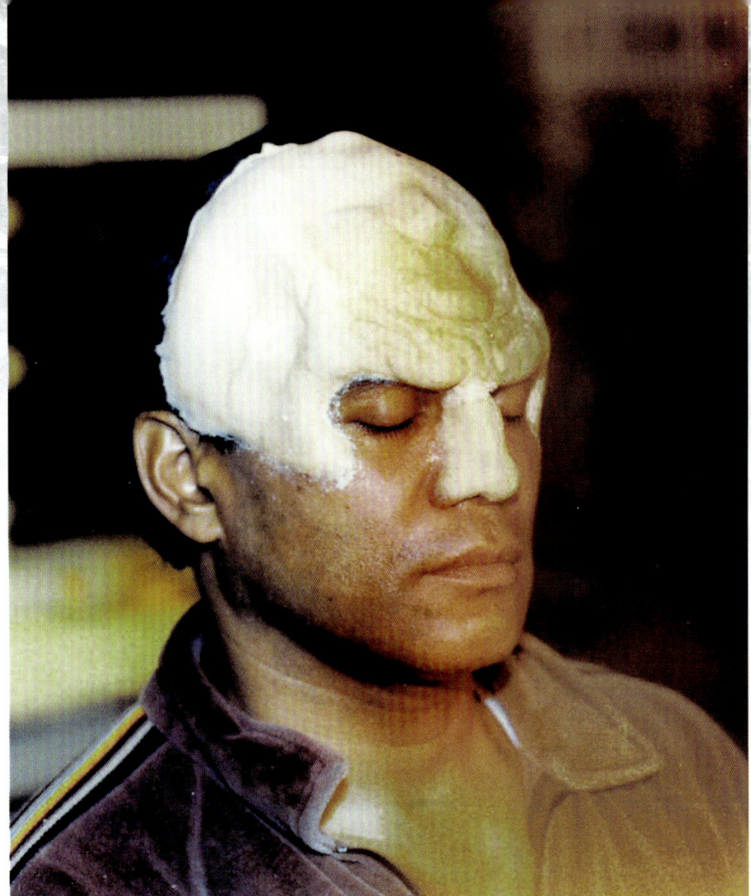
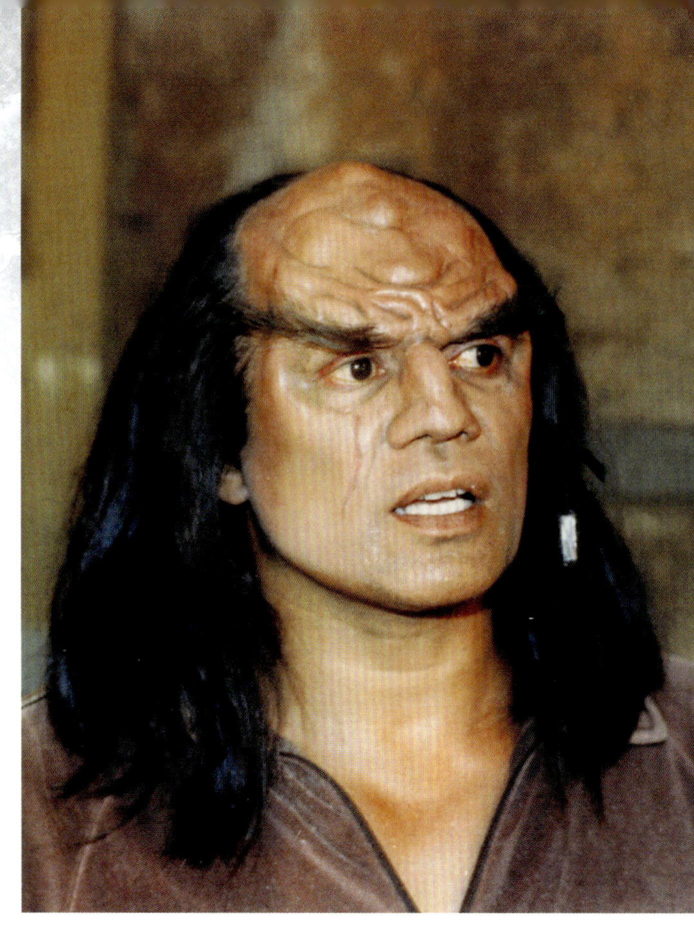
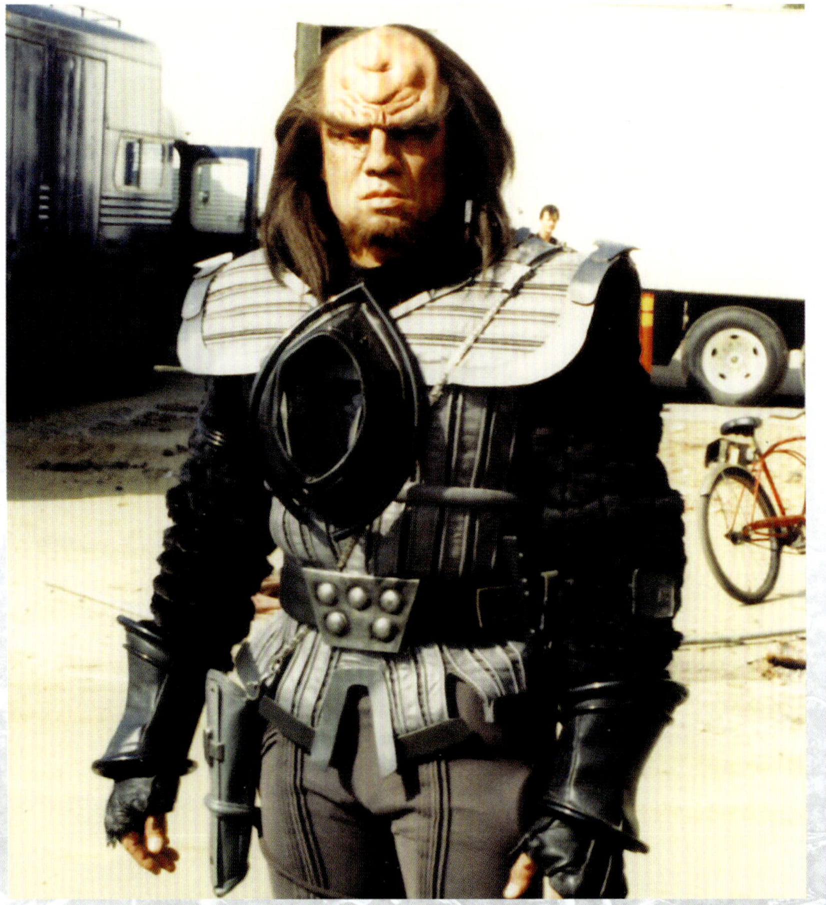
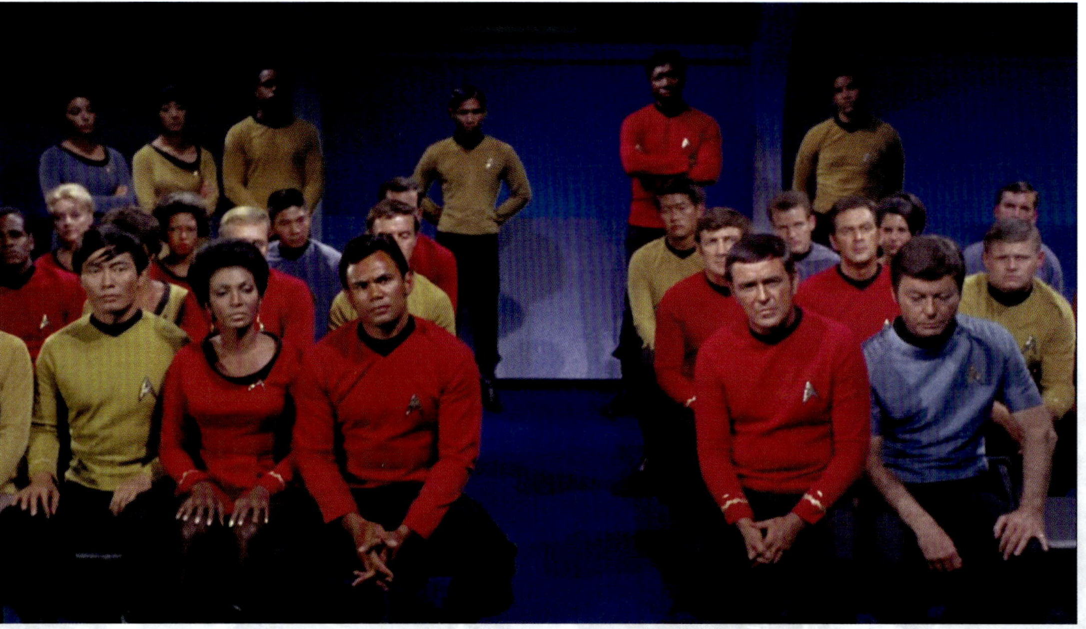

TOP AND LEFT: From makeup fittings to Abascal adjusting the wig to the final results, veteran actor and stuntman David Cadiente underwent hours of makeup to become the Klingon sergeant character in charge of the Genesis planet survey when Kruge returns to his ship.

ABOVE: Cadiente played an *Enterprise* crewman sitting next to Nichols in the original series episode 'The Tholian Web.'

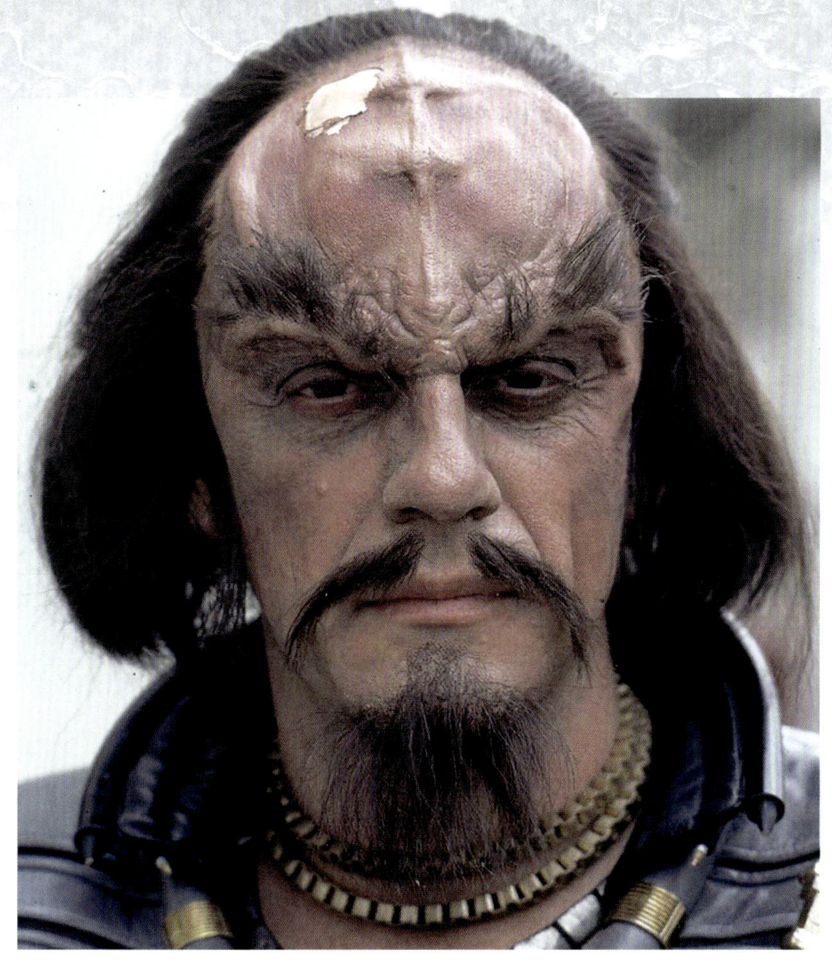

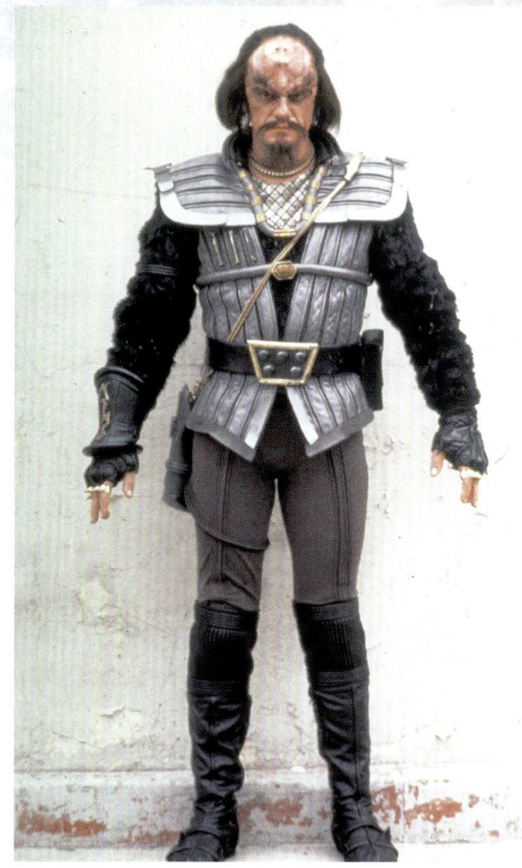

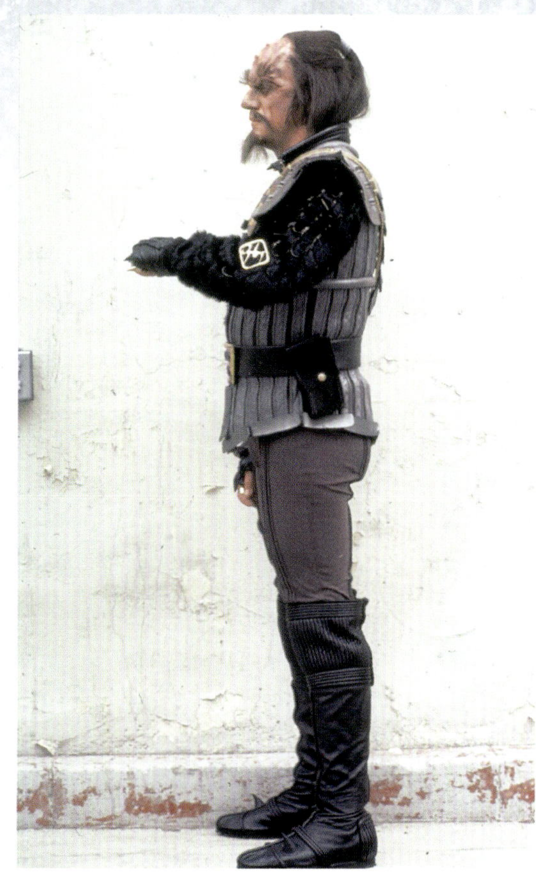

Vulcans weren't the only denizens at The Burman Studio. Stephen Liska spoke about how his Klingon makeup was applied. "The makeup artists first took a mold of my face. This was to design the head molds for the Klingons. I had to breathe out of straws. Then, the actual makeup took about four to five hours to put on each day, and three hours to remove. They had to be very slow and careful with the appliances because they were going to be used again. We Klingon actors would be half asleep getting our makeup on. But once it is on, you fall into the role and you are serious. We are all Klingons! It was my first role in that kind of heavy makeup"[4] So successful was the transformation that linguist Marc Okrand, who had worked closely with Liska and the other Klingon actors, had struggled to recognize him. "I was at the cast and crew premiere and someone said, 'Hi, Marc.' I looked at him quizzically. He said, 'You don't know who I am, do you?' It was Steve Liska who played Torg! I had never seen him out of makeup."[12]

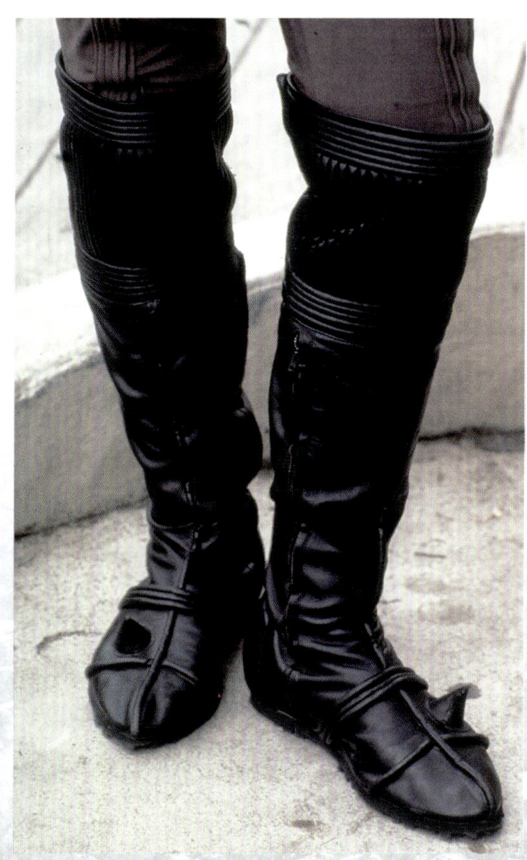

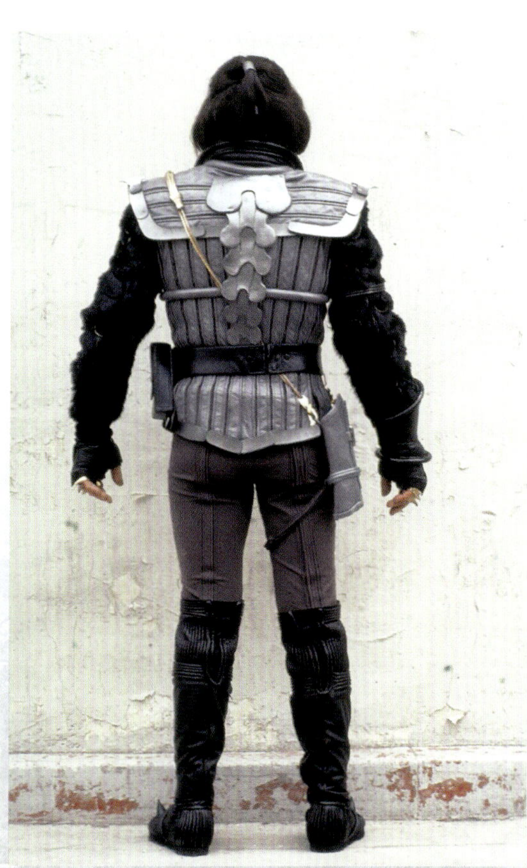

THIS PAGE: Reference photographs taken of Kruge's costume. While Fletcher designed the costumes, it was Rubal Cava, of the Western Costume Company, who measured each of the actors for a custom fit of their wardrobe. Fletcher described Cava as "a genius tailor."[3] Western Costume, which was founded in 1912, supplied costumes for the original *Star Trek* television series.

DELETED CAMEO

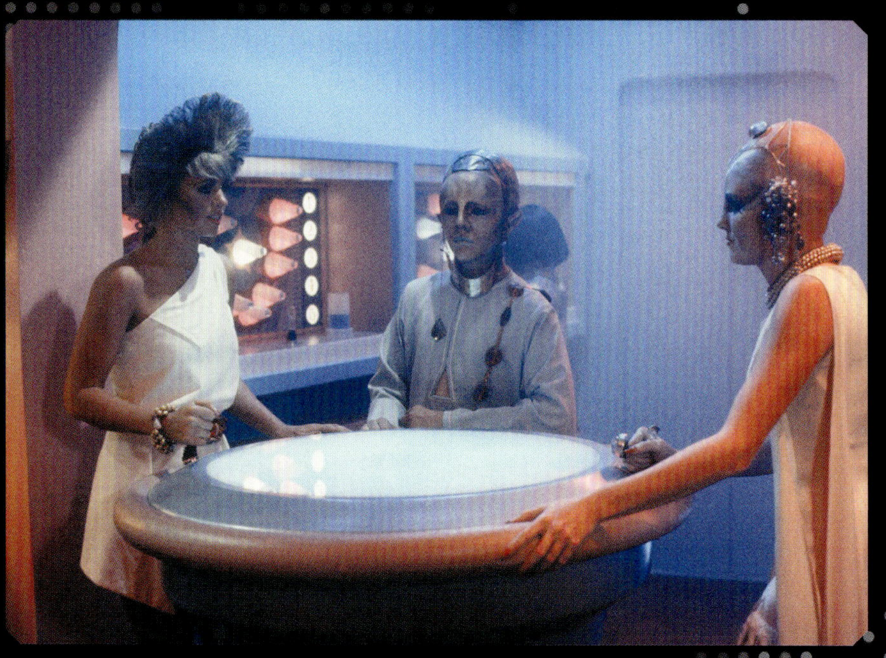

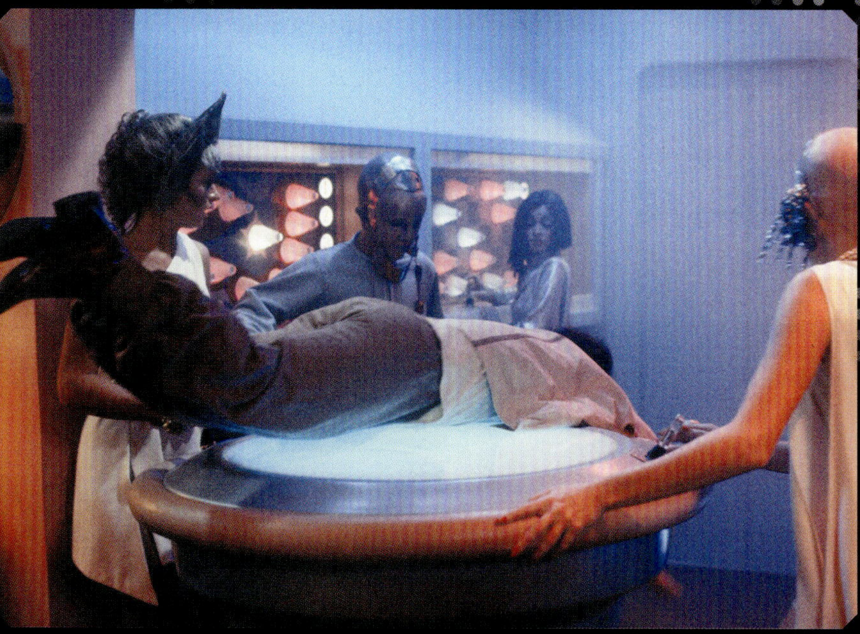

ABOVE: In addition to the bar fight scene, a cameo by Silvia Abascal (left), hair stylist, and Barney Burman (center), makeup effects lab technician, and son of Thomas, was edited from the film.

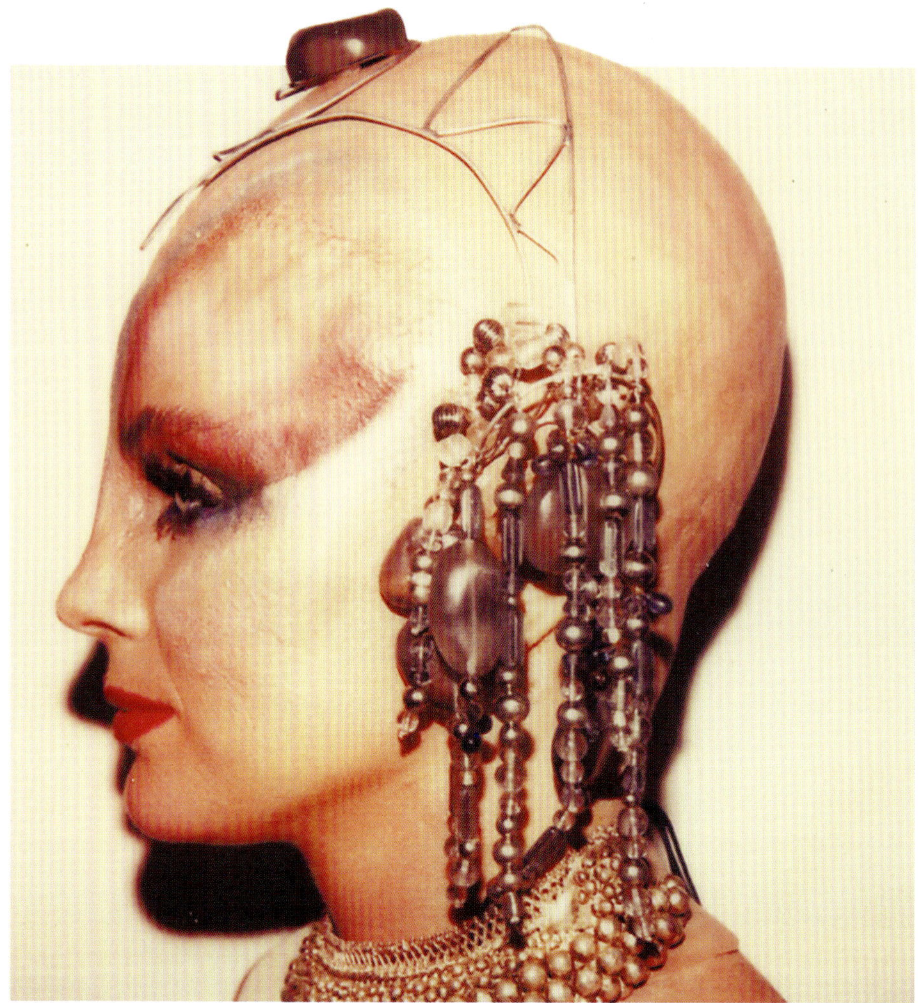

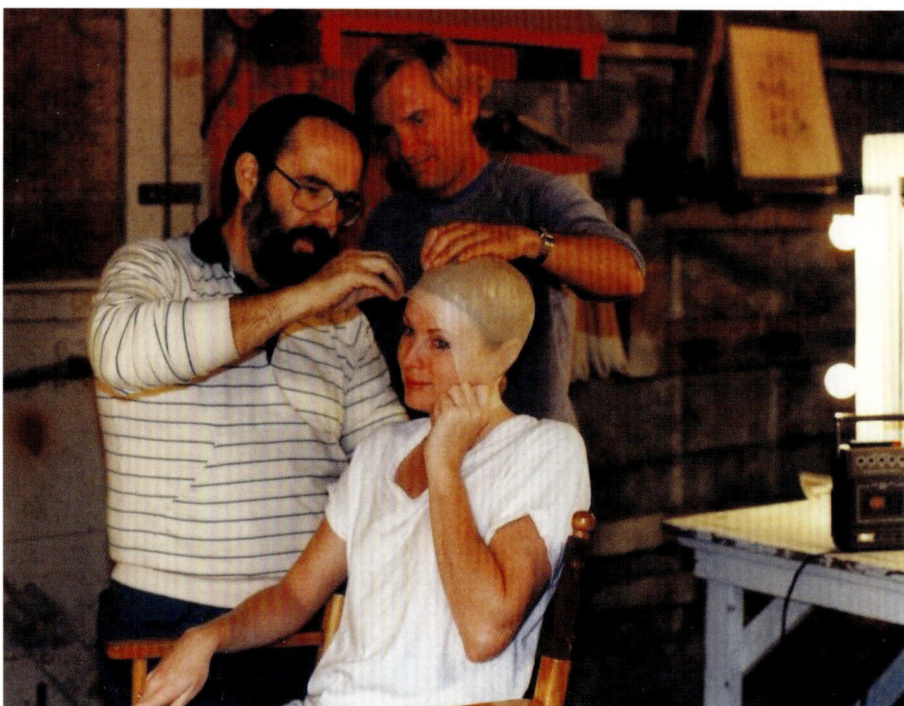

ABOVE: Preparing the makeup for a bar patron.[6]

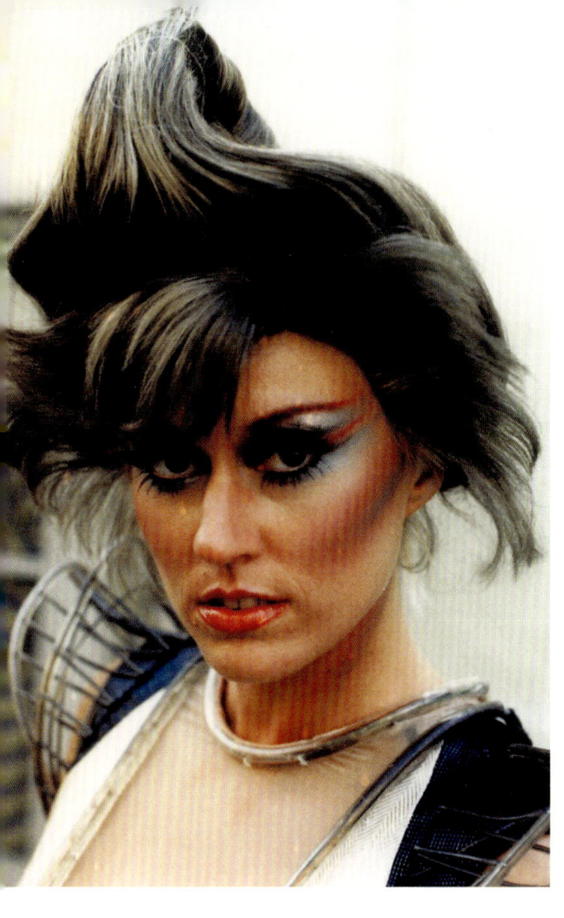

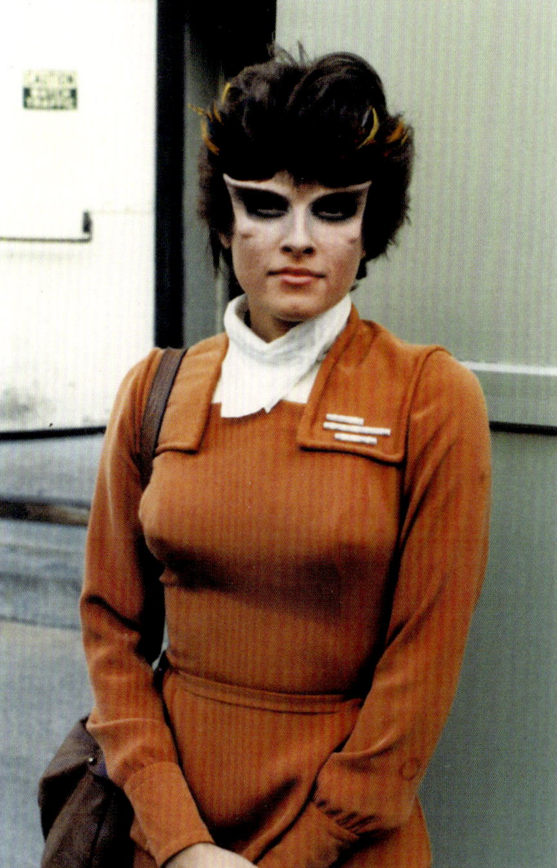

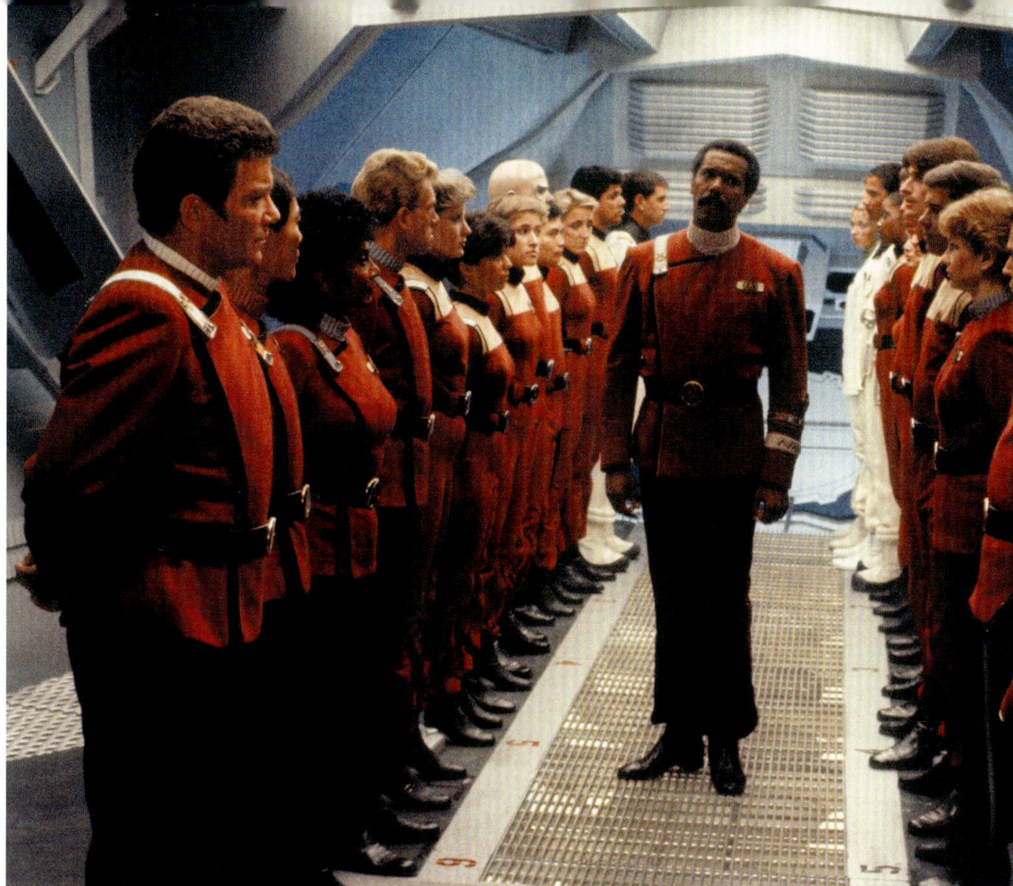

ABOVE LEFT: Eagle-eyed fans may recognize Nanci Rogers, who played one of Khan's followers in the previous film, as the second waitress in the bar scene. A unique feature of her costume is the lights around the collar and neckline.

ABOVE: Kimberly L. Ryusaki, an extra and stand-in who plays many roles, from cadets to aliens, in *Star Trek II*, *III*, and *IV*, is made up as a bar patron for this image. Moments earlier in the film, Ryusaki plays a cadet in the inspection scene. She is five people from Takei's Sulu, next to an alien character. The right hand photo is a moment edited from the film as the crew prepares for Admiral Morrow's arrival.

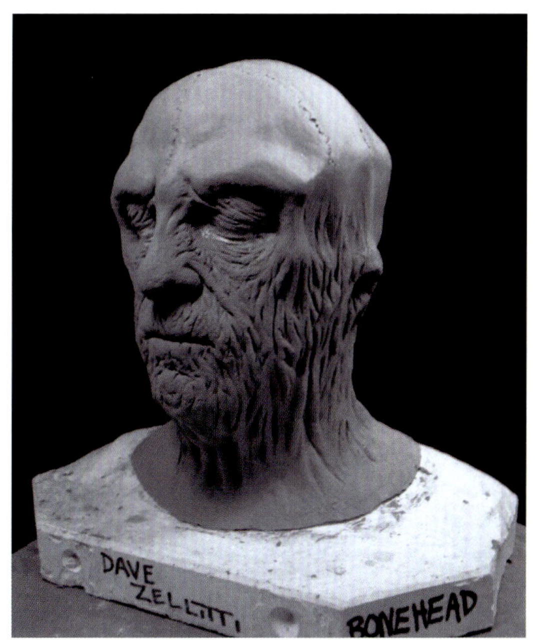

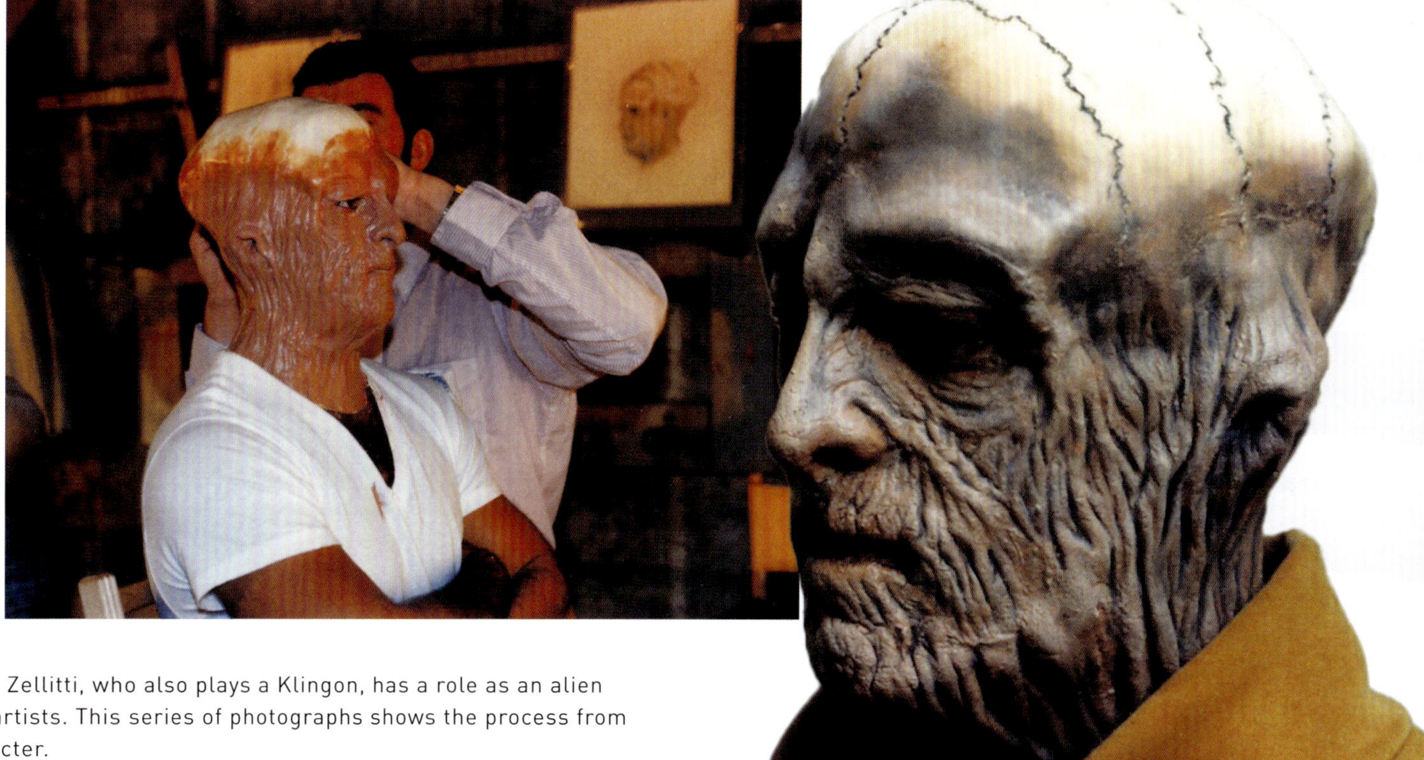

ABOVE AND RIGHT: Evolution of a bar patron: David Zellitti, who also plays a Klingon, has a role as an alien affectionately nicknamed Bonehead by the makeup artists. This series of photographs shows the process from sculpting to makeup to finished and costumed character.

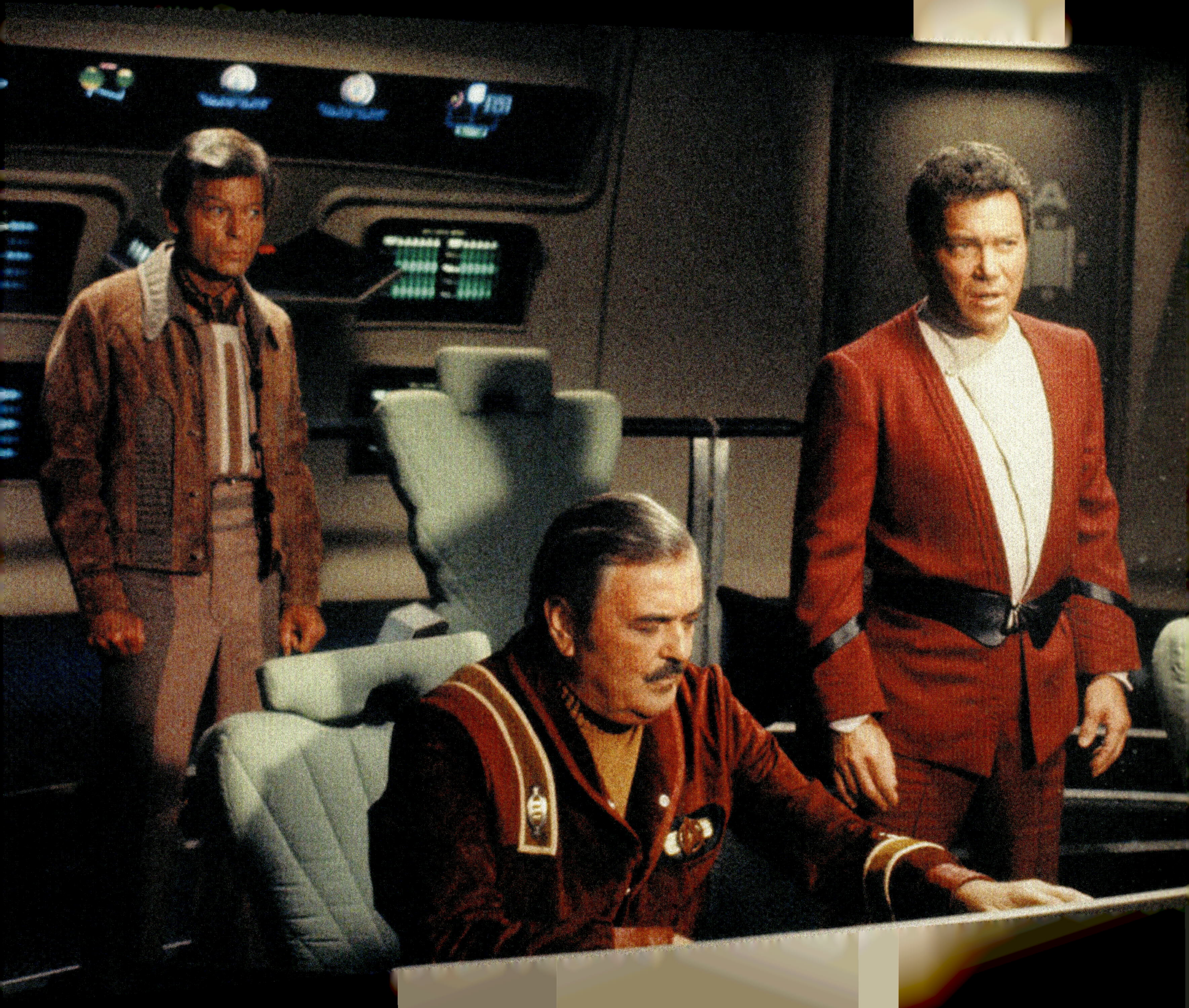

CHAPTER 7

CLEAR ALL MOORINGS

THE CAMERA DEPARTMENT

Filming at Paramount began August 15, 1983. Pre-production delays, including director selection and story revisions, had postponed the start of production, and as a result, a new premiere date of summer 1984 had been selected. While the added six months helped alleviate some of the pressure on filmmakers, there was a personal and professional test that Nimoy faced. As a first-time film director, he wanted to deliver *Star Trek III* on-time and on-budget. As much as Nimoy was respected, he was also going to be watched closely by studio executives, who, as he wrote, "observed my every move and took care lest something go awry in a remarkably expensive way."[1] Additionally, Nimoy had a troupe of actors who, while supportive, were cautious about what kind of director he would be.

Nimoy knew that a proven strategy for achieving his goals and assuaging concerns was proper prior planning. Rehearsals with actors, walk-throughs with department supervisors, close collaboration with ILM, storyboarding, and other forms of pre-planning were time and cost saving measures. Talk really was cheap, especially when compared to the expense of filming, or worse, refilming. "Everything I know has been tapped," Nimoy shared. "My knowledge of acting, of drama, of photography, of production, my taste in color, in composition, in structure, in editing."[2]

BELOW LEFT: The sequence where Sarek and Kirk review the flight recorder visual, learning that Spock gave his katra to McCoy, was a challenge. The original *Star Trek II* footage had to be transferred to videotape, then computerized, then enhanced. The real-time scanning that Kirk and Sarek rely on in the film was timed and filmed on set with the actors watching. Here, Shatner and Nimoy enjoy a moment of levity before filming the scene.

BELOW RIGHT: Originally, the flight recorder visual scene featured Kirk wearing the eye glasses Spock had given him for his birthday. In the final film, Kirk is holding the glasses, although he never wears them. The glasses are barely visible as Kirk turns to speak with Sarek. The scene was filmed with and without the glasses, but the thought was that the audience might wonder when Kirk would have had the time to have the antique glasses repaired because only days have passed since the lenses were broken.

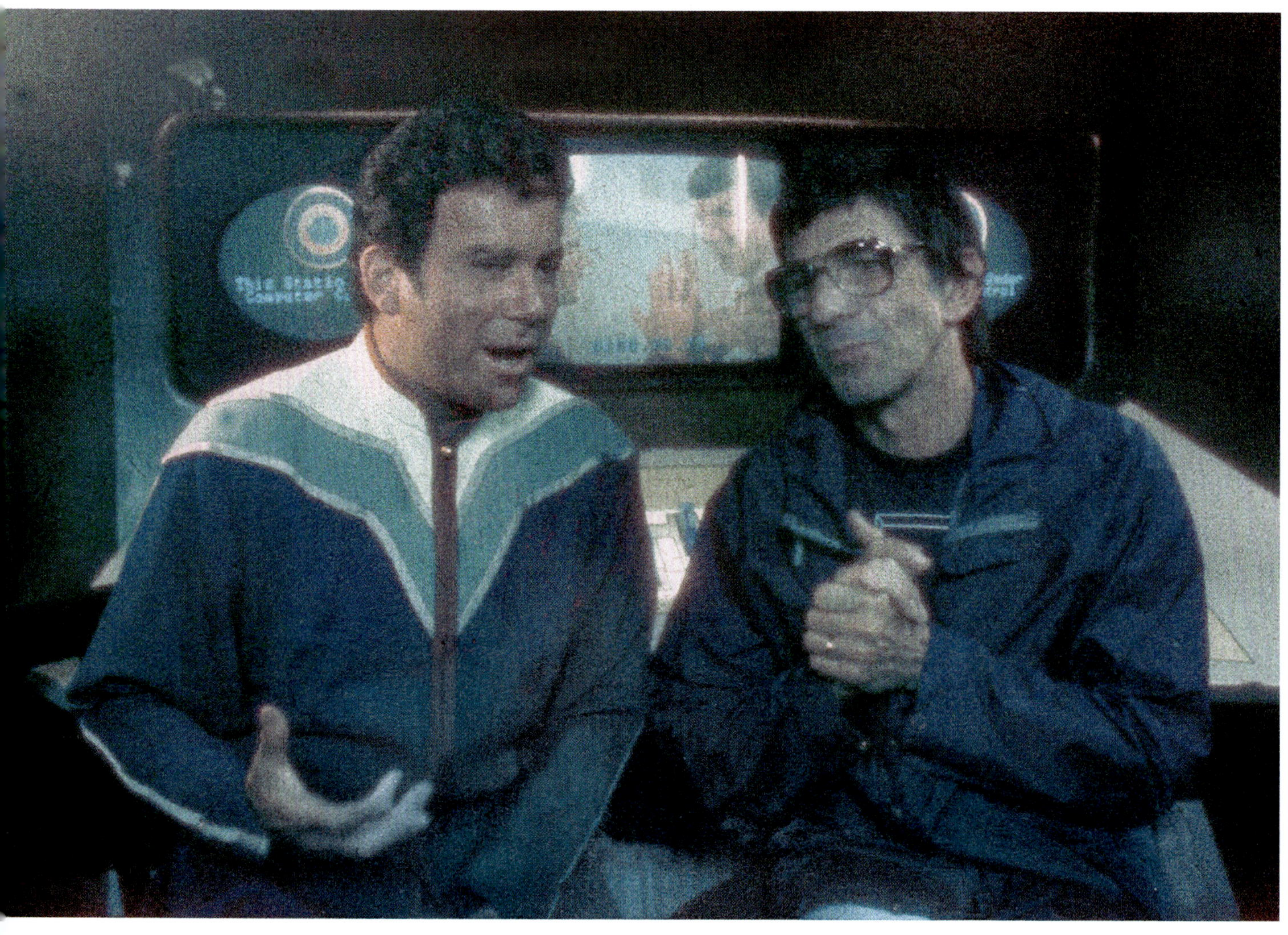

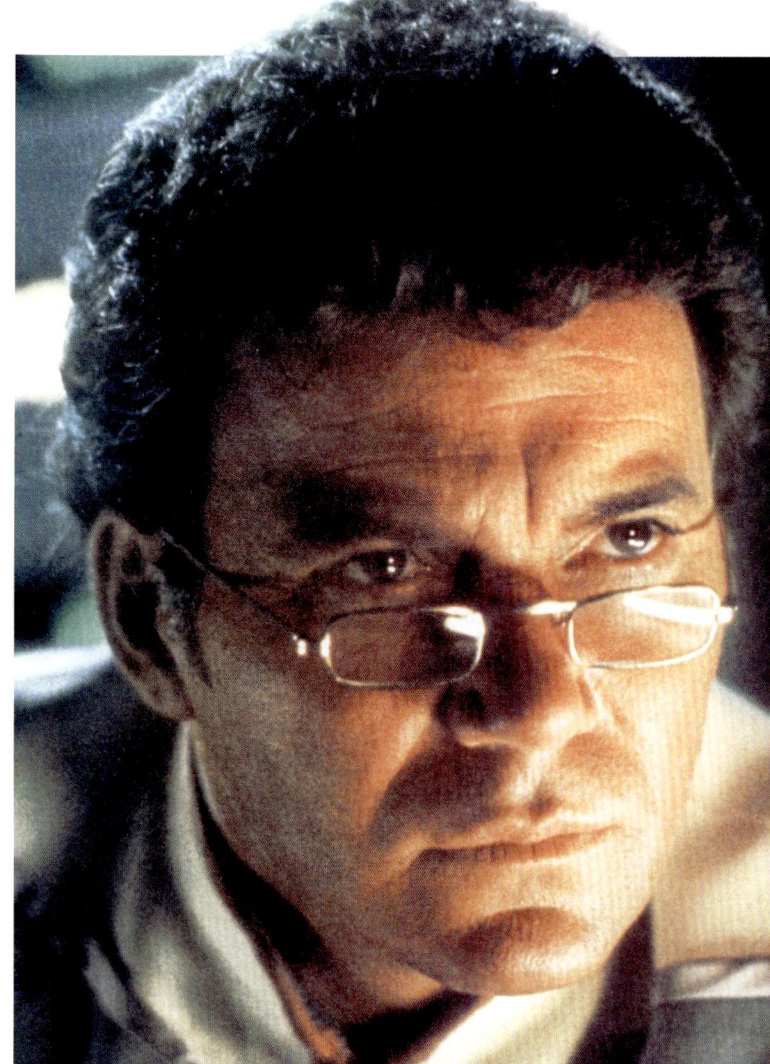

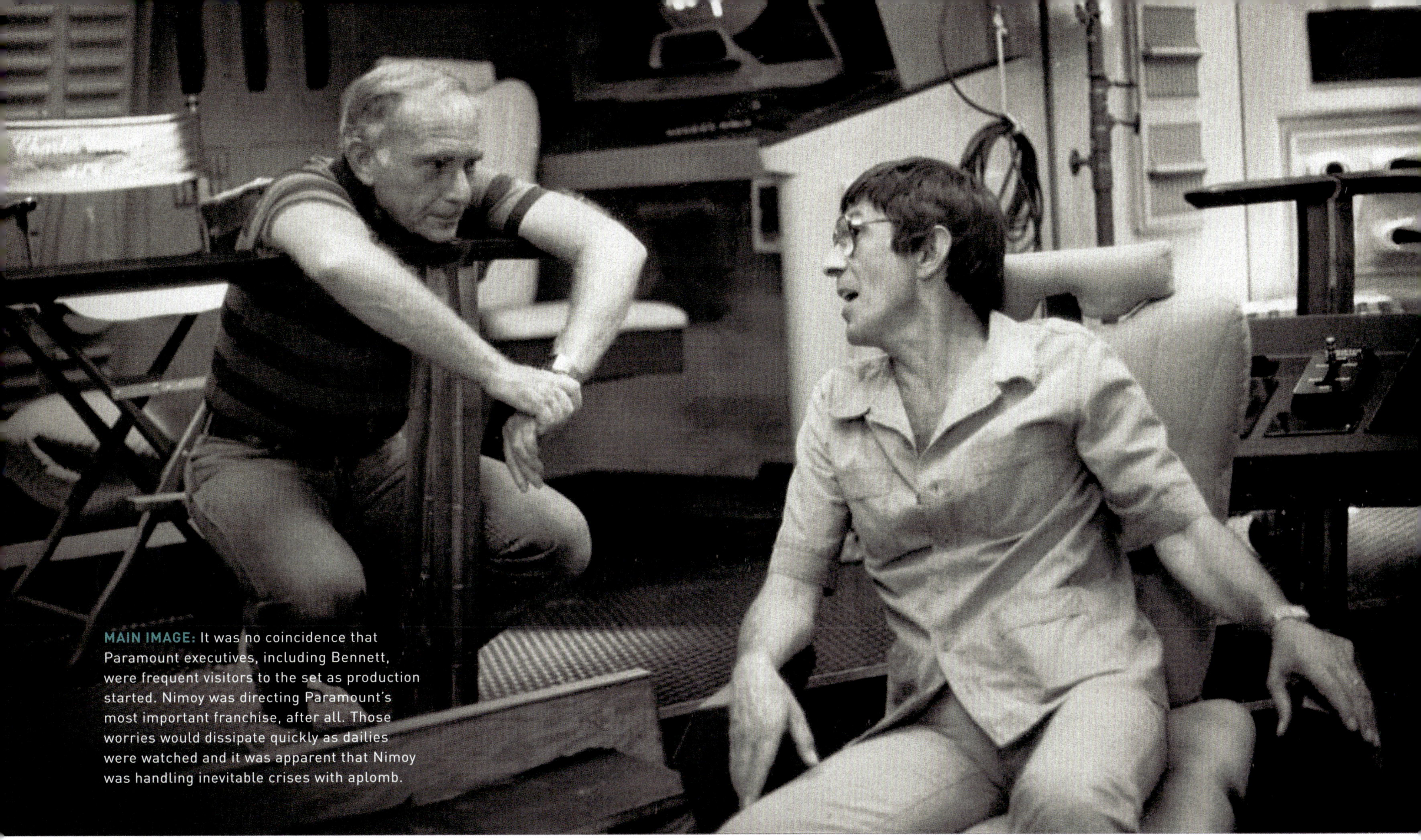

MAIN IMAGE: It was no coincidence that Paramount executives, including Bennett, were frequent visitors to the set as production started. Nimoy was directing Paramount's most important franchise, after all. Those worries would dissipate quickly as dailies were watched and it was apparent that Nimoy was handling inevitable crises with aplomb.

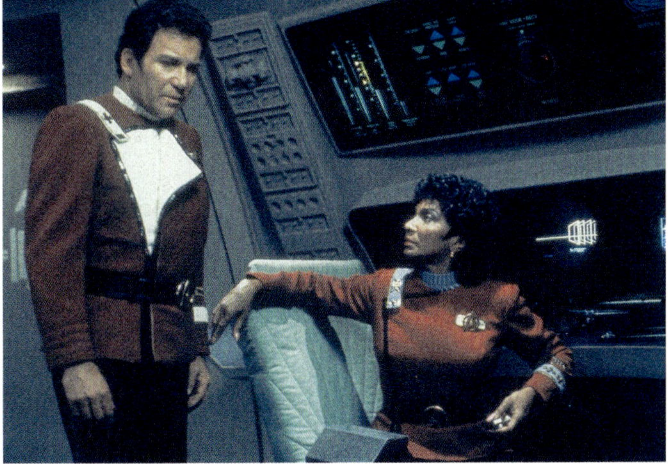

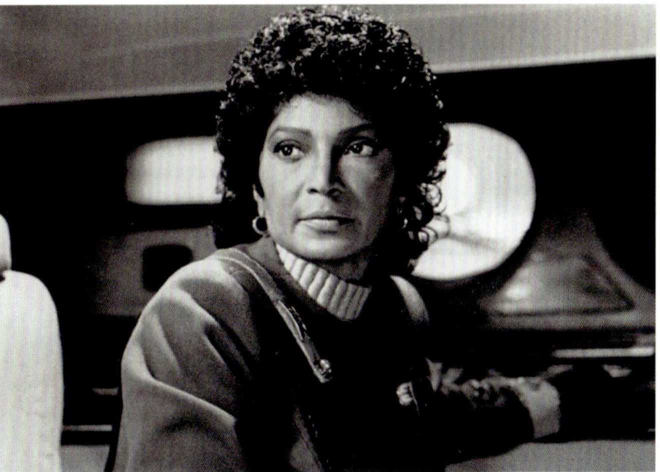

FAR LEFT: Shatner and Nichols on the first day of filming, which began on Stage 9's *Enterprise* bridge set.

LEFT: The video screens behind Nichols were created by Hal Landaker and Alan Landaker of the Burbank Studios, who had innovated a system for displaying video in motion pictures. Their 24-frame color video system had made it possible to film the kind of dynamic visuals on the *Enterprise* bridge set in camera, winning a special Academy Award® for Technical Achievement on March 29, 1982. Their system was used in *Star Trek II*, *III*, and *IV*. Approximately 600 video elements were created for the films.

MCCOY AND KIRK

Those familiar with the film will remember a quiet moment when Kirk, alone in the turbo-lift, is deflated. Spock's death and trying to keep his crew focused is taking its toll. The scene ends with Kirk leaning against the wall. There was more to the scene that was filmed with McCoy and Kirk. Kelley was sad the scene was removed from the final film but understood the reason, "There was a scene that proceeded that where I get on the elevator and Kirk is there with me, and I'm in this very Spock-like attitude. This is where Kirk first thinks, 'What the hell is wrong with this guy?' It was an excellent scene and played very well, but it gave away the secret. It let the audience know who was in McCoy's mind from that scene, so they had to lose it."[3]

RIGHT: The scene 12A as written by Bennett.

(continuing)
Are they planning a ceremony when we get in...? I mean, a reception...?

KIRK
A hero's welcome, son? Is that what you'd like?... Well, God knows, there should be. This time we paid for the party with our dearest blood.

He enters the elevator, and the doors close.

11 OMITTED 11

12 INT. ELEVATOR - KIRK 12

Even as the doors close, his mood changes. The mantle of command falls away and he allows himself the luxury of his deeper feelings. Feelings of aloneness. And grief. CAMERA IN CLOSE to HOLD this anguished moment. Then, an intrusive interruption. Kirk covers hiss feelings as:

12A WIDER ANGLE 12A

The elevator doors open at a floor and "BONES" McCOY steps in. He is disheveled, unshaven -- and in a very odd emotional place. He takes his place in the elevator and gazes at the ceiling as the doors close, and the HUM BEGINS.

KIRK
... Bones.

McCOY
(stiffly)
Jim.

KIRK
(after a pause, with growing irritation)
Are you planning to shave today?

McCOY
Quo vadis, Admiral...

KIRK
What is that supposed to mean?

McCOY
What is our destination?

KIRK
We'll be orbiting Earth in two hours.

McCOY
Then we're headed in the wrong direction.

KIRK
(warning)
Bones, don't do this. This is

Small and grubby; populated by three or four crewmen of mixed special breeds, and a renegade CAPTAIN who suggests a Federation traitor. And, lurking in the shadows, her face concealed by a half-veil, what appears to be an exotically beautiful WOMAN of epic proportions and mystery.

CAPTAIN
Steady... Steady, boys. Keep scanning...
(beat)
I thought you people were reliable... Where the hell is he!

WOMAN
He has been here for some time. I can feel his presence.

CAPTAIN
Don't give me your Klingon mumbo-jumbo -- there ain't another vessel in this whole damn quadrant.

WOMAN
Put me on the hailing frequency.

CAPTAIN
(sourly)
Sure - whatever games you wanna play.

He shakes his head, presses a button and nods to her. She now removes the veil, showing us a fascinating face of Klingon features. The crew stare at her as she speaks into a communication device. She is oddly unemotional.

WOMAN
Commander Kruge: this is Valkris. I have obtained the Federation data, and am ready to transmit.

15 INT. BRIDGE - BIRD OF PREY (CLOAK EFFECT) - CLOSE - KRUGE'S PET 15

A SHOCK CUT to a frightening creature, half timber wolf, half lizard. His head is being rubbed by the hand of the owner. We PAN UP from the beast with Kruge's hand as it snaps switches.

KRUGE (O.S.)
Well done, Valkris... Stand by.

The PAN CONTINUES UPWARD to reveal BATTLE COMMANDER KRUGE, a Klingon War Lord of handsome but frightening presence, and relative youth. Now, in Klingon:

KRUGE
(Disengage cloaking device!)

There is a light change from CLOAK to DE-CLOAKED CONDITION, along with ELECTRONIC WHIRRING SOUNDS. CAMERA PULLS BACK from man and beats during this to reveal the

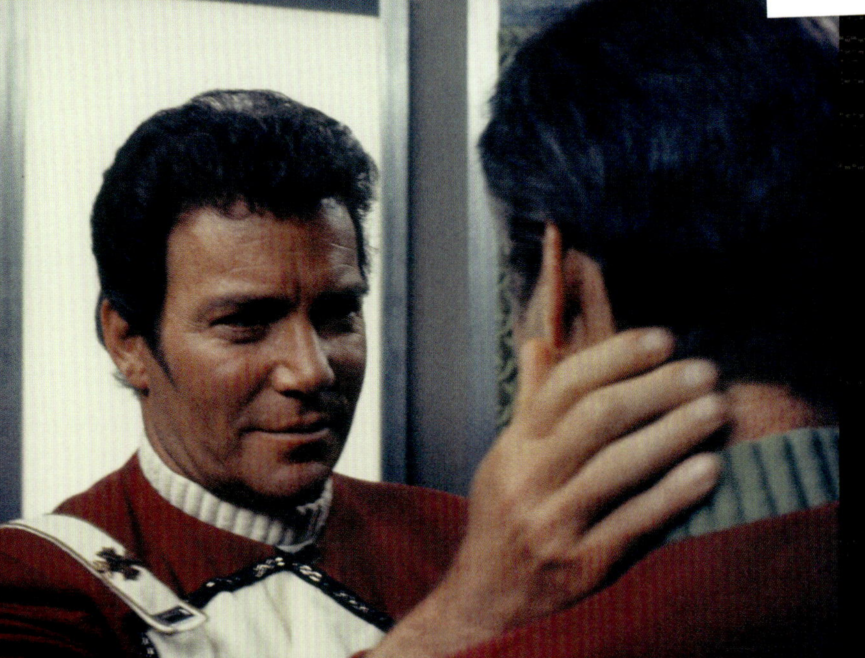

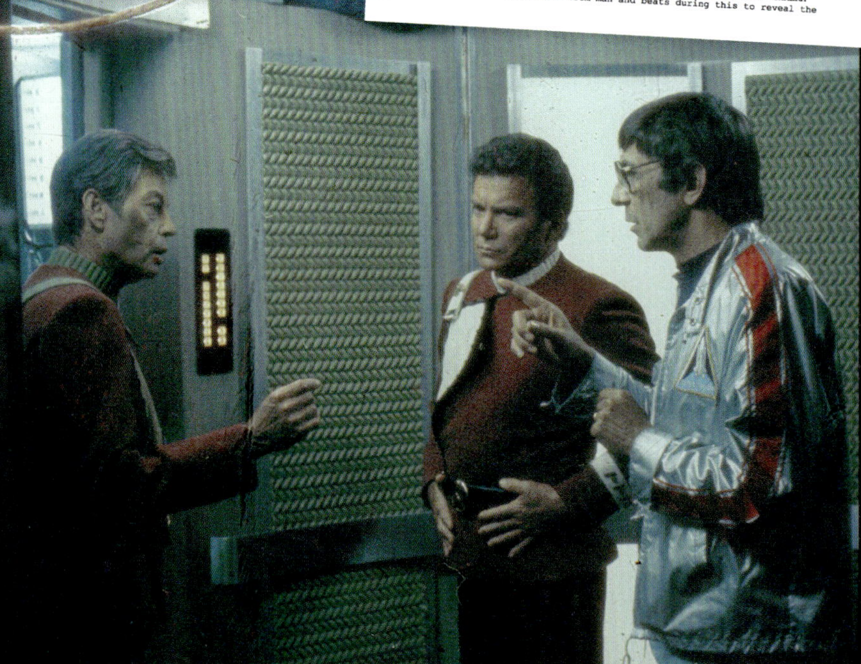

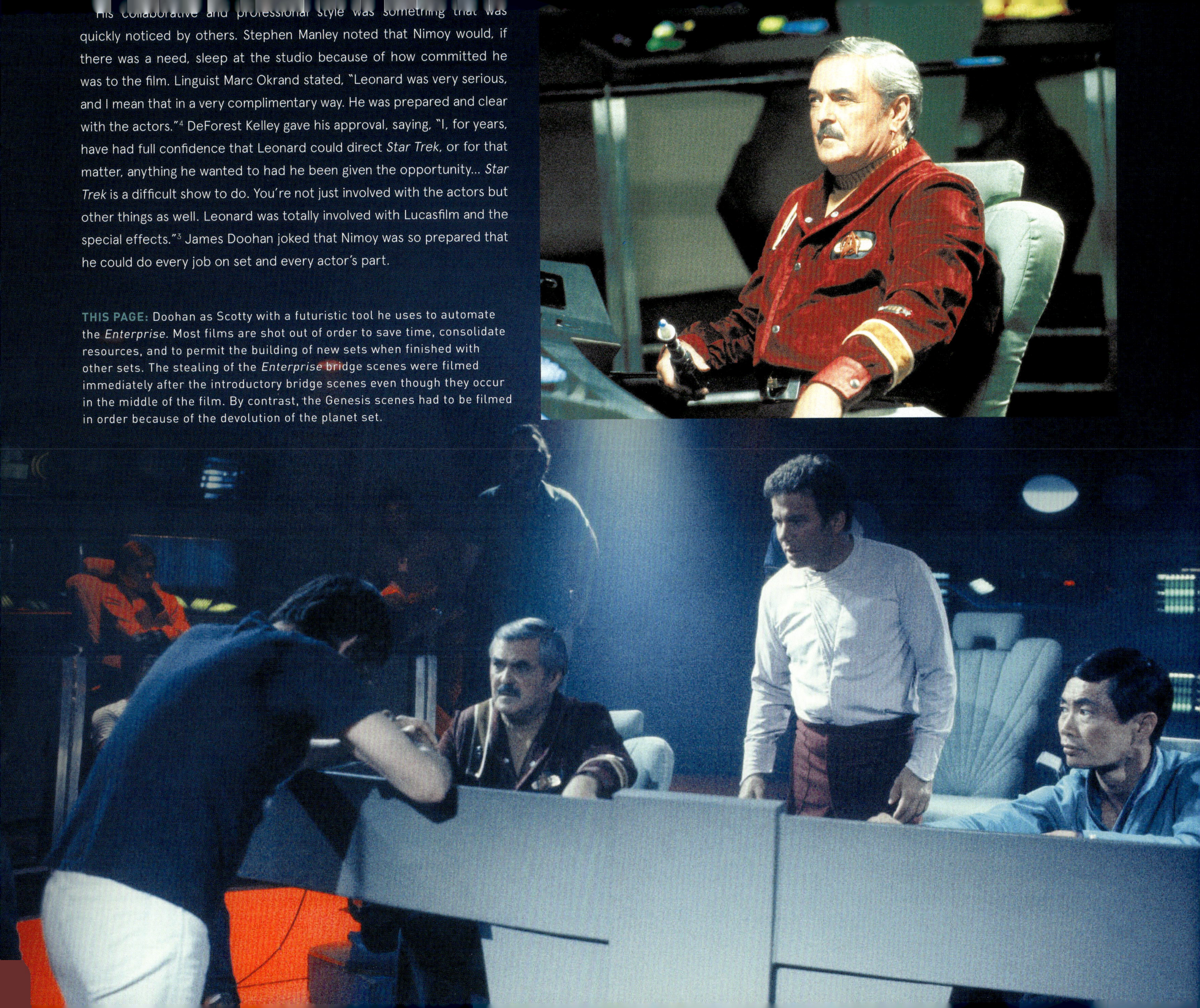

His collaborative and professional style was something that was quickly noticed by others. Stephen Manley noted that Nimoy would, if there was a need, sleep at the studio because of how committed he was to the film. Linguist Marc Okrand stated, "Leonard was very serious, and I mean that in a very complimentary way. He was prepared and clear with the actors."[4] DeForest Kelley gave his approval, saying, "I, for years, have had full confidence that Leonard could direct *Star Trek*, or for that matter, anything he wanted to had he been given the opportunity… *Star Trek* is a difficult show to do. You're not just involved with the actors but other things as well. Leonard was totally involved with Lucasfilm and the special effects."[3] James Doohan joked that Nimoy was so prepared that he could do every job on set and every actor's part.

THIS PAGE: Doohan as Scotty with a futuristic tool he uses to automate the *Enterprise*. Most films are shot out of order to save time, consolidate resources, and to permit the building of new sets when finished with other sets. The stealing of the *Enterprise* bridge scenes were filmed immediately after the introductory bridge scenes even though they occur in the middle of the film. By contrast, the Genesis scenes had to be filmed in order because of the devolution of the planet set.

One of Nimoy's most important decisions would be which cinematographer to hire. With his life-long fascination with photography, Nimoy's selection of cinematographer was both important to the film and him personally. Movies are usually dependent on a good relationship between the director, who directs the performance of the actors and has a meta vision of the film, and the cinematographer, who directs the lighting and camera angles and movements to translate that vision into reality. Nimoy selected veteran cinematographer Charles Correll Jr., a fortuitous decision as they collaborated with ease and a short-hand due to their mutual understanding of photography. An example is how Correll originally recommended that the Genesis planet be filmed in Hawaii to take advantage of its other-worldly beauty. However, he understood that production realities, including budget, the need for the creation of strange, new worlds that had cactus and snow in the same environment, the secrecy factor, and most especially, the ability to control the sets for stunts and for the destruction of Genesis, precluded those location possibilities. Knowing this, whenever needed, Correll collaborated with the ILM matte department to expand the scope of the film through the use of their paintings.

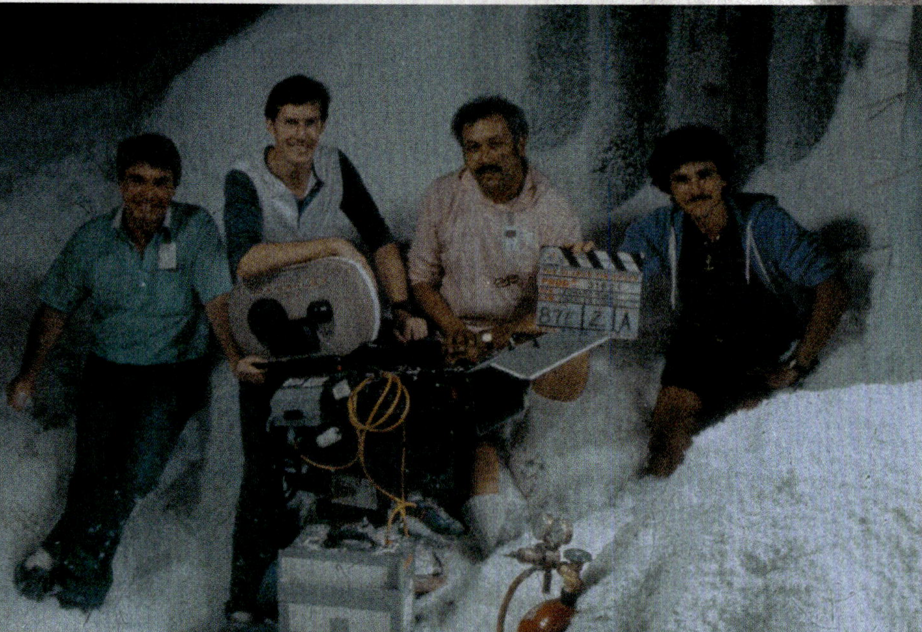

ABOVE: The camera department: Correll, camera operator David Nowell, first assistant camera Robert A. Torres, and second assistant camera Alfredo Sepulveda with a Panaflex camera. Invented during the 1970s, the Panaflex was quieter and lighter than its predecessors, especially of value when navigating sets like the *Enterprise* and the Bird-of-Prey which did not have a great deal of space for bulky equipment.

A MOST UNUSUAL SET VISITOR

On the various *Star Trek* series and films, it was not unusual for people from all kinds of professions to visit the sets. Leaders such as former United States President Ronald Reagan, the Dali Lama, then Prince Abdullah II bin al-Hussein of Jordan, former Secretary of State Madeleine Albright, actor Clint Eastwood, astronaut Mae Jemison, and physicist Stephen Hawking, are just a few of those that visited a *Star Trek* production; some were even there to film a cameo appearance. Bennett and actors would also invite fans, such as when fan artist and fanzine editor Vel Jaeger was given a tour as a thank-you for serving as an advisor. Visitors to the *Star Trek III* set specifically included Jaeger, DC Comic's Robert Greenberger, fan club president Dan Madsen, Nicholas Meyer, and United States General Scott among others.

However, the most unusual set visitor is arguably C.J., the famed orangutan actor who had starred in Eastwood's *Every Which Way but Loose* and *Any Which Way You Can*, and who had guest starred on the 1982 'Thieves' Highway' episode of William Shatner's *T.J. Hooker*. C.J. was currently filming his TV series *Mr. Smith* about an orangutan who, because of an experiment, has an I.Q. of 256 and becomes advisor to the U.S. President at Paramount. As a joke, C.J. was brought on to the bridge to surprise Shatner.

Shatner remembered the experience fondly. "One of the funniest moments I can remember seeing is a Clint Eastwood movie where he pretends to knock an orangutan out. I see how intelligent animals are, and we don't give them enough credit for the intelligence that they have that's unspoken. If you can speak their language a little bit, they talk to you like we do with our dogs. I don't know whether the orangutan was comedic or not. I mean, it could have had a sense of humor. I think that it's possible. In the movie that Clint Eastwood did, if the orangutan just crumpled or anything like that, it wouldn't have been funny. But the way the orangutan fell over, it was hysterical. It was one of the great gags. That was the orangutan who visited the set. So, I admired the orangutan! They bring the orangutan on to the set and I get to meet the orangutan, and I love these animals that can communicate."[5]

BELOW: C.J. vies for the captain's chair during his visit to the *Enterprise* bridge.

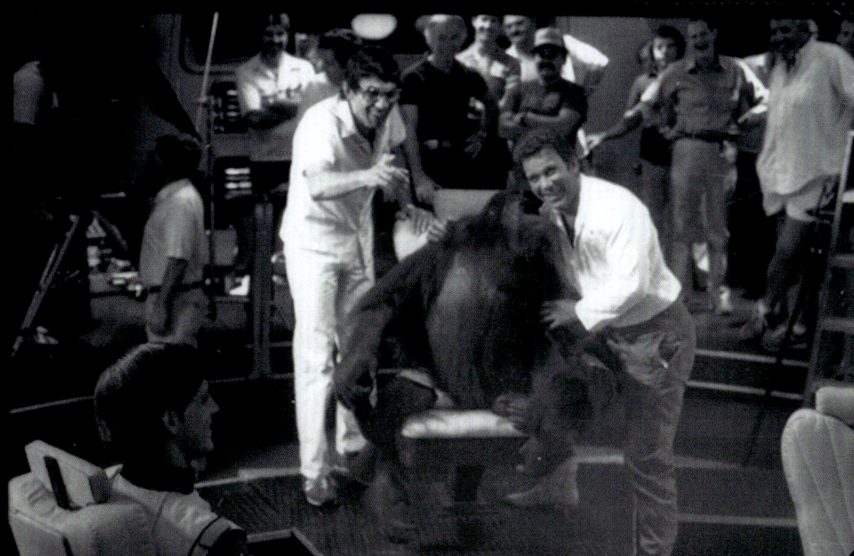

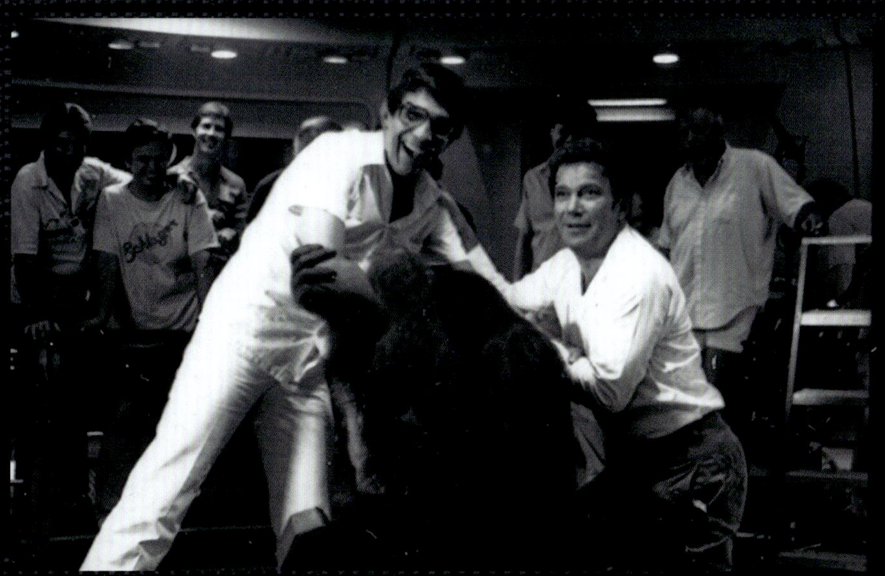

FLIGHT RECORDER VISUAL:

CHARLES CORRELL JR., CINEMATOGRAPHER

Born in Los Angeles on January 23, 1944, Correll was the son of famous voice actor Charles Correll and dancer Alyce McLaughlin. His original artistic endeavor was music. Correll was the drummer for The Cornells, a surf band mostly comprised of the children of athletes and actors. The band appeared on a 1963 episode of *I've Got a Secret*. By the 1970s, however, his interest had shifted to camera work. He was the director of photography or cinematographer on TV shows and films such as *Kojak*, *The Winds of War*, and *National Lampoon's Animal House*. The summer that *Star Trek III* premiered, Correll married Robin Kellick who had been a stand-in on the film. Correll became a director on such programs as *Beverly Hills, 90210* and *Melrose Place*. Correll died in 2004 as a result of pancreatic cancer.

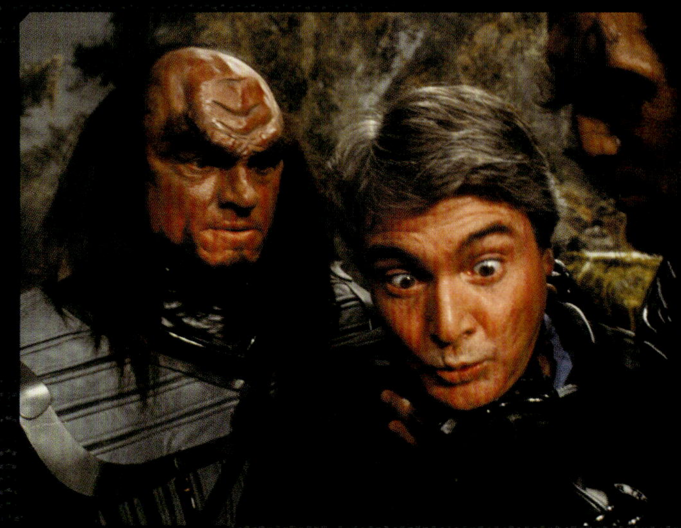

ABOVE: Those that worked with Correll remember his sense of humor as a defining trait. It is on display here as he jokes around with the Klingons.

REMEMBER...

Kenneth Ralston: "During filming, Charlie knew of some great sushi place and we had great meals with him. What a wonderful man. He was hilarious."[6]

Philip Weyland (Stand-in): "As a stand-in, you have many bosses. You have a first assistant director. A second assistant director. The director. You have the cinematographer who is the most important of those as far as the stand-ins. Charlie was sort of a jokester. He is the only cinematographer of the four hundred episodes and films I did who said to me, 'Your skin tone is not right. You need to be in makeup every day.' I went to the makeup artist James McCoy and he said, 'We'll do the makeup for like three or four days and then we won't do it anymore.' We did that and Charlie never said another word. Never knew if Charlie was joking or not about that. But, Charlie liked me because I talked to him about his father. I was very interested in radio history. Later, when I was on *Beverly Hills, 90210*, Charlie directed episodes."[7]

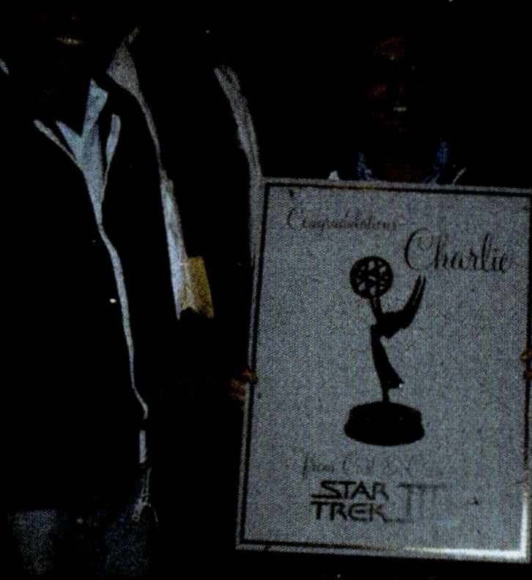

ABOVE: A September 26, 1983 set photo celebrating Correll's Emmy win the day before for his cinematography on *The Winds of War*. Joining the party are Nimoy and Butrick.

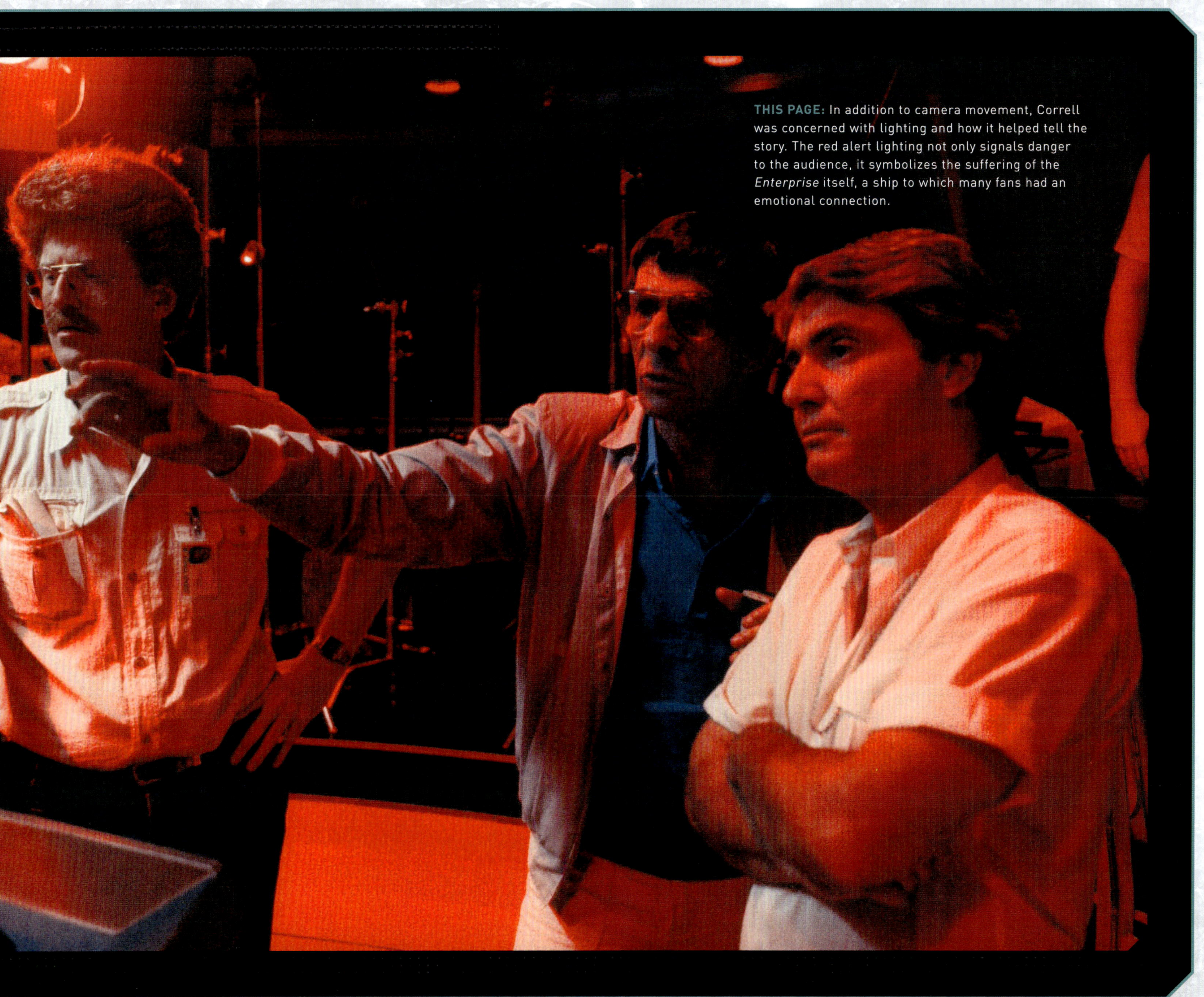

THIS PAGE: In addition to camera movement, Correll was concerned with lighting and how it helped tell the story. The red alert lighting not only signals danger to the audience, it symbolizes the suffering of the *Enterprise* itself, a ship to which many fans had an emotional connection.

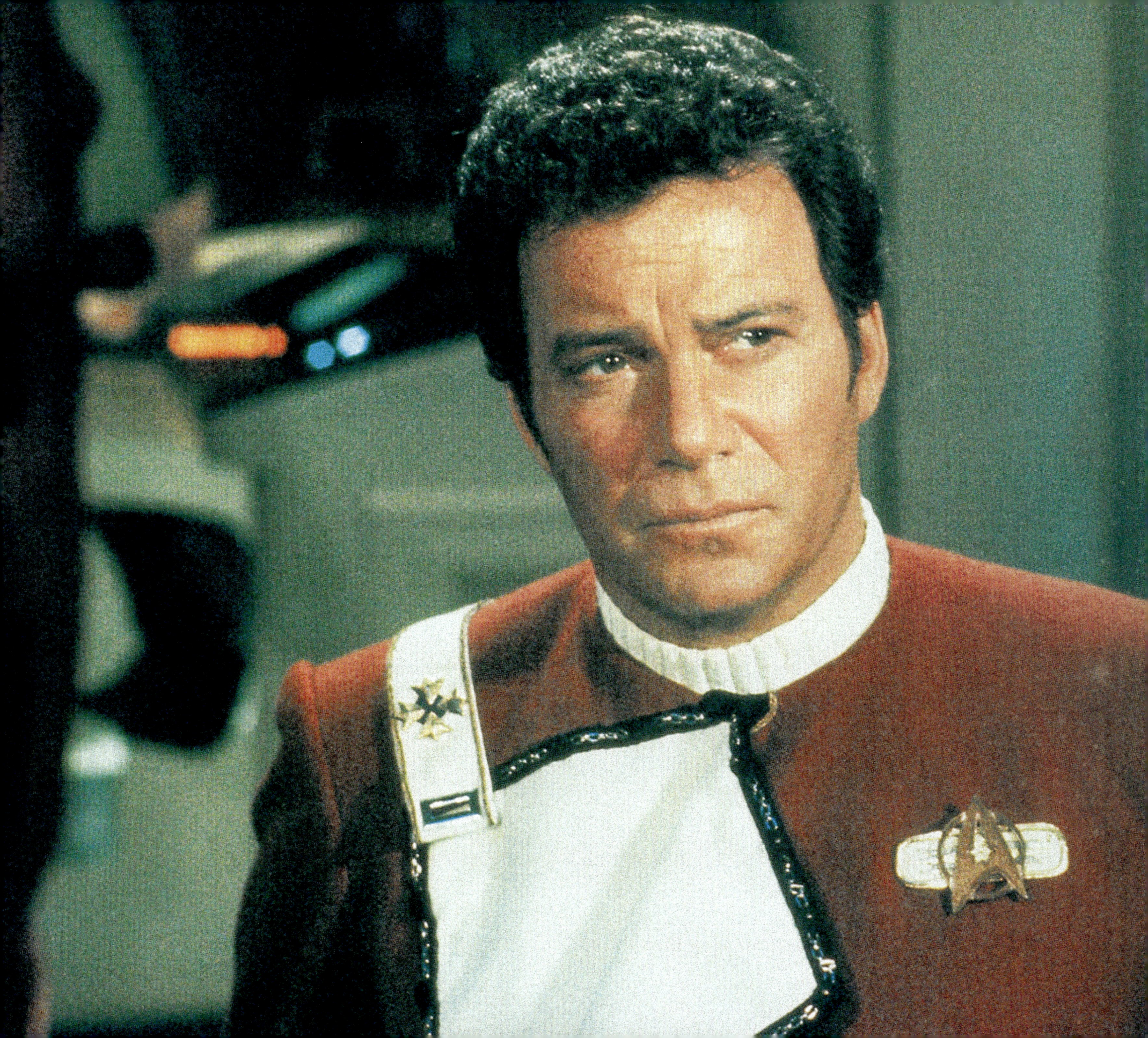

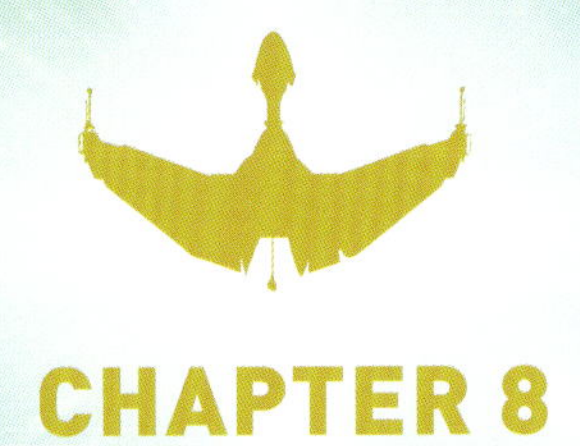

CHAPTER 8

A HERO'S WELCOME

THE FIRE AT PARAMOUNT STUDIOS

August 25, 1983, a mere 10 days after filming began, the most dangerous challenge of the production occurred. At approximately 4:00 p.m., a fire began behind the Tattoo Shop store facade on McFadden Street, part of the outside sets that mimicked cities in many television shows and movies. Quickly, other street facades on the 350,000 square foot sets and various soundstages were on fire. Inspector Ed Reed explained that, "Due to the age and composition of the sets, which are mostly wood and 50 years old, the fire burned very quickly."[1] Described as a wall of fire, the blaze would eventually traverse six acres of the then fifty-acre studio. Destroyed were the McFadden Street, Boston Street, Church Street, and New York Street, two storage buildings, with additional damage to some of the landscaping and graves at the nearby Hollywood Memorial Park Cemetery where the likes of Rudolph Valentino, Cecil B. DeMille, and Charlie Chaplin Jr. were buried. Nearly three million dollars in damage was caused, equivalent today to more than nine million dollars. Of these, the greatest loss in terms of historical value was the New York Street set, which had been built in 1927, and was featured in *Laverne & Shirley* and *The Godfather*. Paramount's chief of set lighting David Pondella – whose name is visible as a tribute on the *U.S.S. Columbia NX-02* dedication plaque in the *Star Trek: Enterprise* episode 'Affliction' – said of the blaze, "There was a solid fire from building to building, a solid sheet, just like a tornado. It was roaring."[2]

Thirty-four fire companies responded, with more than 150 firefighters taking about two-and-a-half hours to put out the blaze. Two firefighters were injured by electrical shocks believed to have occurred because of power lines. The fire was eventually determined to be an act of arson, with Fire Chief Gerald Johnson relaying, "About two weeks ago we did determine that the fire was suspicious. Since that time we have changed the designation on the fire from suspicious to incendiary. That means intentionally set."[3]

While most of the damage was to the outdoor sets, adjacent soundstages were not immune because of the strength and alacrity of the fire. The sprinkler systems caused damage to the sets of *Happy Days*, *Family Ties*, *Mr. Smith*, and *Webster*.

One of the locations that faced the greatest danger was Stage 15 where the *Star Trek III* Genesis set had been built. Much of the planet had been constructed with polyurethane which could cause explosions and release toxic chemicals if

THIS PAGE: While the fictional crew of the *Enterprise* faced many dangers in *Star Trek III*, the real actors and film crew faced a genuine emergency of their own.

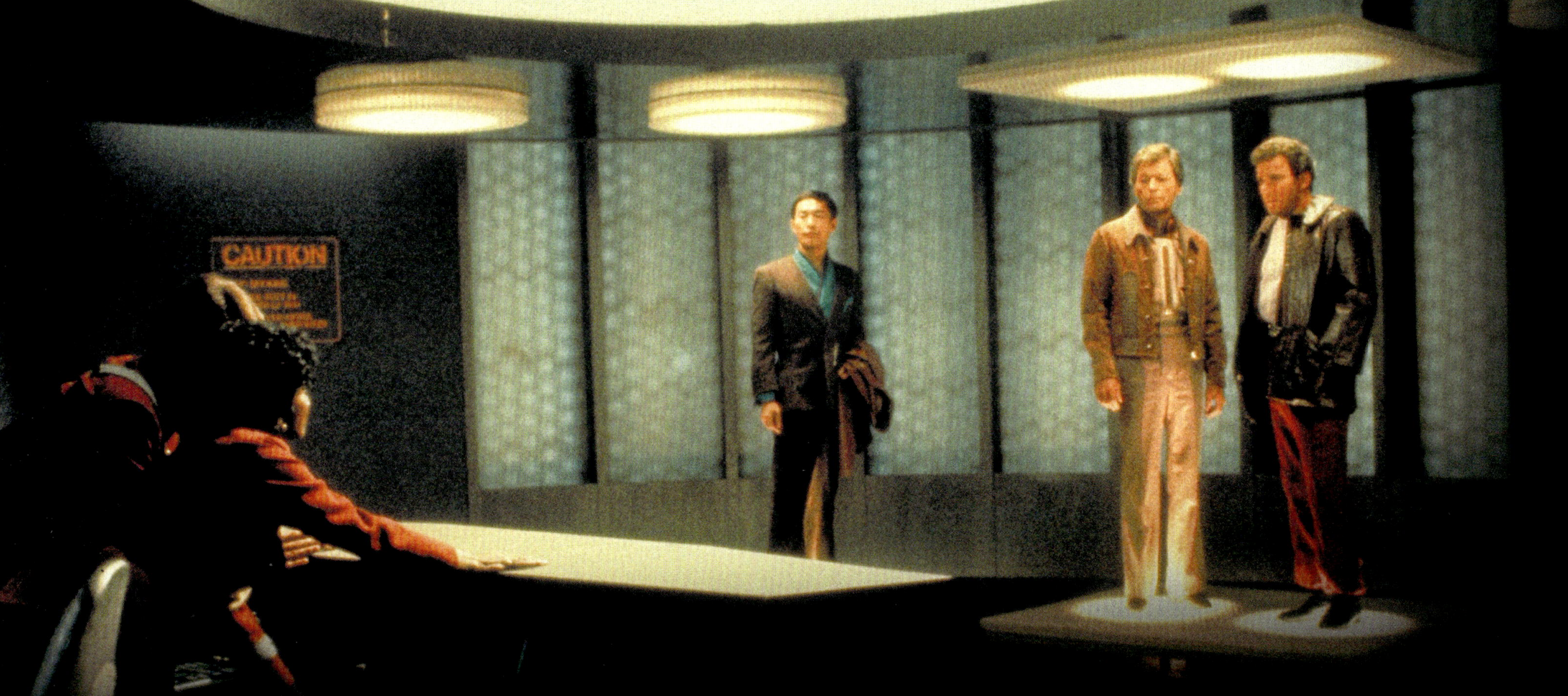

THIS PAGE: Shortly after the Paramount Studio fire, Shatner, Takei, and Kelley joined Nichols and McGinnis to complete the scene on the set nicknamed the "shabby transporter room."

the blaze ever reached it. As the fire inched so close to Stage 15 that ceiling panels would eventually need to be replaced, there was a real possibility of the set being lost entirely or, considering the polyurethane, something worse occurring.

Luckily, William Shatner was there to take action and help contain the blaze until the firefighters arrived. Shatner's stand-in Philip Weyland remembered being outside the stage watching events transpire. "Bill came out of the door in a hurry," Weyland said, "I asked someone, 'Where is Bill going.' They said, 'There is a big fire on the back lot over there and he wants to help!'"[4] Once the firefighters arrived, they instructed Shatner to leave because of the real danger posed by the chemicals.

Shatner detailed his actions, and motivations, that day:

"I was really focusing on making sure we finished our dates shooting *Star Trek III* because the dates of shooting *T.J. Hooker* were coming up, and that was a previous contract. So, I had to be there. Otherwise, you know, they might have sued me. It was uncomfortable. Everything I did was like, 'Let's go! Come on, that's good!' and was pointed towards making sure we finished our shooting schedule." Understandably, he was concerned when he arrived to work one day and learned of the fire. "I thought, 'There can't be a fire. That'll delay us. I've got to put that fire out!' So, I ran into the interior of the stage, and indeed there was a fire. Not large, but large enough. One of the sets, one of the pieces of the set, was burning. And by coincidence, and I don't remember where it was and how I picked it up, but there was a hose and I turned the handle. There was water and I ran to the fire. I started putting it out, and while I was putting it out, in come the fire engines and the firemen come running down into the stage and take me out of there. Literally carry me out of there because that plastic that was burning was poisonous. They ushered me out and they put out the fire, and we didn't lose any time shooting."[5]

In the end, the damage to the set was undoubtedly less than it would have been without Shatner's intervention. Water damage from the sprinklers and holes in the ceiling where the fire broke through were the worst of it, but the set was damaged enough to cause problems for Nimoy, Harve Bennett, and associate producer Ralph Winter. Cinematographer Charles Correll summarized the worst of it. "There were huge holes in [the set]. So, we had to put up these huge black curtains to keep the sunlight from coming in. But the fire at Paramount almost destroyed the stage."[6]

ILM's Kenneth Ralston sympathized with his friends at Paramount, telling Brad Munson of *CineFex* magazine of another incident that occurred. "The gods were against them, I'm telling you," he said. "About

A SON REMEMBERS

ADAM NIMOY AND LESSONS LEARNED FROM LEONARD

Adam Nimoy is a director of shows such as *Nash Bridges, Gilmore Girls, Star Trek: The Next Generation, Babylon 5,* and on the "I, Robot" episode of *The Outer Limits* where he directed his father Leonard. His documentary, *For the Love of Spock* (2016) was a project started with his father and finished in tribute to him after Leonard's passing. His newest book is *The Most Human: Reconciling With My Father, Leonard Nimoy.*

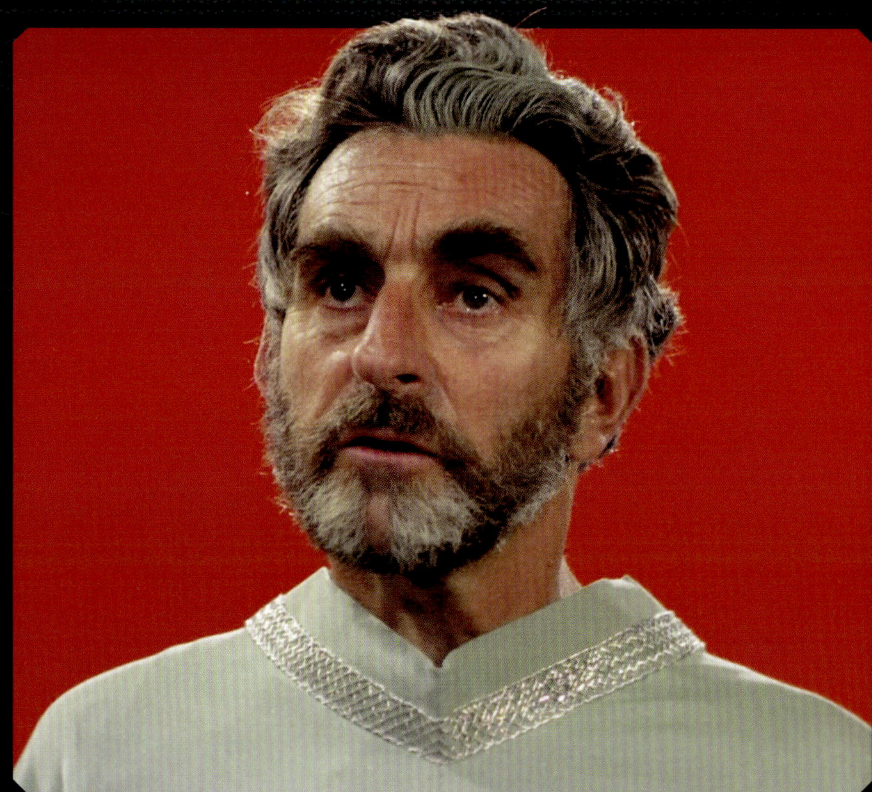

ABOVE: Jeff Corey, who taught both Leonard and Adam Nimoy, starred as Plasus in the *Star Trek* episode 'The Cloud Minders.' Adam, who had been an entertainment lawyer, changed careers after taking Corey's class. "That's when I started to think I may be in the wrong profession."

"My dad came out to Pasadena in 1949. He had saved a bunch of money and sent it to the *Pasadena Playhouse* because he wanted to take acting classes. And this was all against his parents' wishes. 18 years old. A three-day train trip, ending in Pasadena, wearing a wool suit in 80-degree weather. When he got to the Playhouse, he discovered that apparently a lot of the guys in the class were on some sort of G.I. Bill and were required to prove that they were enrolled in an educational institution to get their pension. They really weren't there for the class. My dad was disillusioned and looked for another way to learn his craft which is how he ended up in Jeff Corey's acting class. Jeff was teaching because he was blacklisted and banned from working in Hollywood. My dad was in Jeff's class for a number of years and when Jeff started working again in films and TV, my dad started teaching his class. That was one of the many ways my dad generated cash to keep the family going in the years prior to *Star Trek*."

"My dad taught me about what to focus on as a director. First is story, story, story. Second is performance, playing a role realistically, convincingly, truthfully, and honestly, in the context of imaginary circumstances. And third is technique, everything about camera, lighting, production values, production design, wardrobe, makeup, special effects, and post-production. When I got a script, I would go to my dad's house and we'd break it down. His number one mantra was, 'What is the story about?' He wanted to know: can you clearly articulate it? It was like going to the Leonard Nimoy School of Directing. My dad and Jeff Corey both taught me the same thing: 'Generality is the enemy of art.' You have got to be specific and know what it is you want to say. Everything will be okay once you have a good, clear vision of what it is you are trying to say about the human condition."

"As a director, you are asked questions all day. My dad taught me that sometimes, when you don't know the answer, it's okay to say, 'I don't know. What do you think?' That is not necessarily a sign of weakness but a willingness to collaborate. Directors don't have the answers to everything."[9]

two weeks before the fire, someone was sliding open the huge doors that connect Stage 15 to 14 – where some more of the *Star Trek* sets were – when suddenly the main support beam for the building went 'crack' and the whole roof on the place fell two feet."[7]

Despite these misfortunes, the schedule was salvaged because of two factors. One reason was that the schedule was reconfigured so that time spent repairing Stage 15 would not delay production. In fact, Spock actor Stephen Manley was supposed to start filming his scenes in August, but the dates were moved to five days during the week of October 8 to accommodate, while other scenes not requiring Stage 15 were rescheduled earlier.

The second reason was that, despite the fire, Nimoy kept filming in another part of the lot, on Stage 5, far from the danger. Shatner explained the balance that must occur between art and practicalities when making a film, saying, "There's always something going on when shooting that delays you. Somebody's sick. Somebody's not coming. Can't find the director... Whereas time is money. So, there's this conflict of people who say, 'Well, I'm an artist, and I have to take my time getting ready to do my art' and the economics of getting going."[5]

BELOW LEFT AND BELOW: As firefighters and Shatner battled the Paramount blaze, Nimoy continued to direct Nichelle Nichols and Scott McGinnis in what is known as the "Mr. Adventure" scene.

BOTTOM LEFT: When first glancing at the script, Nichols was concerned that Uhura was not featured in enough of the movie. She related how, "I called Harve Bennett and complained...he was heartbroken and asked, 'Nichelle, did you happen to read your scenes?' I hadn't, I had just looked for my name. Well, I sat down and read the scenes and thought, 'Hmmm, I can do something with this.'"[8]

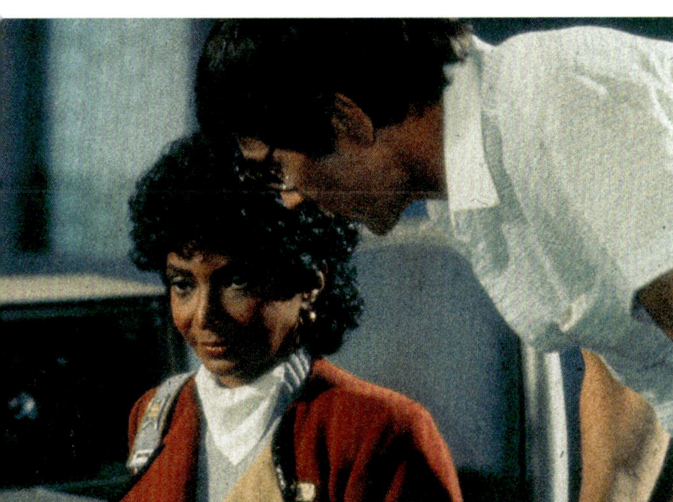

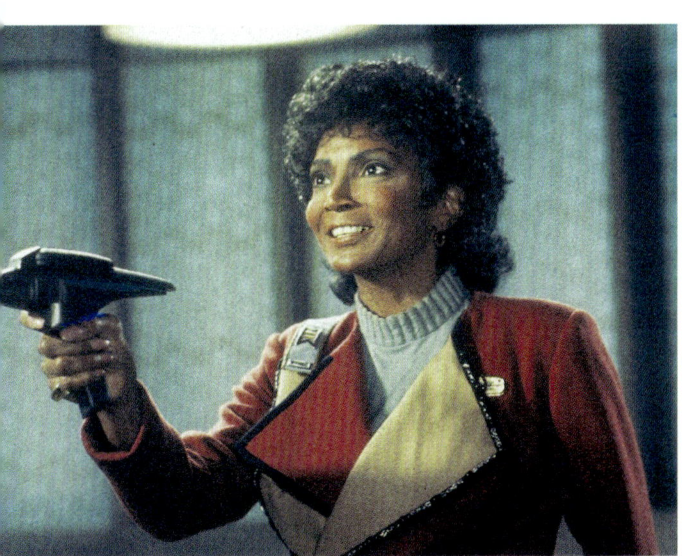

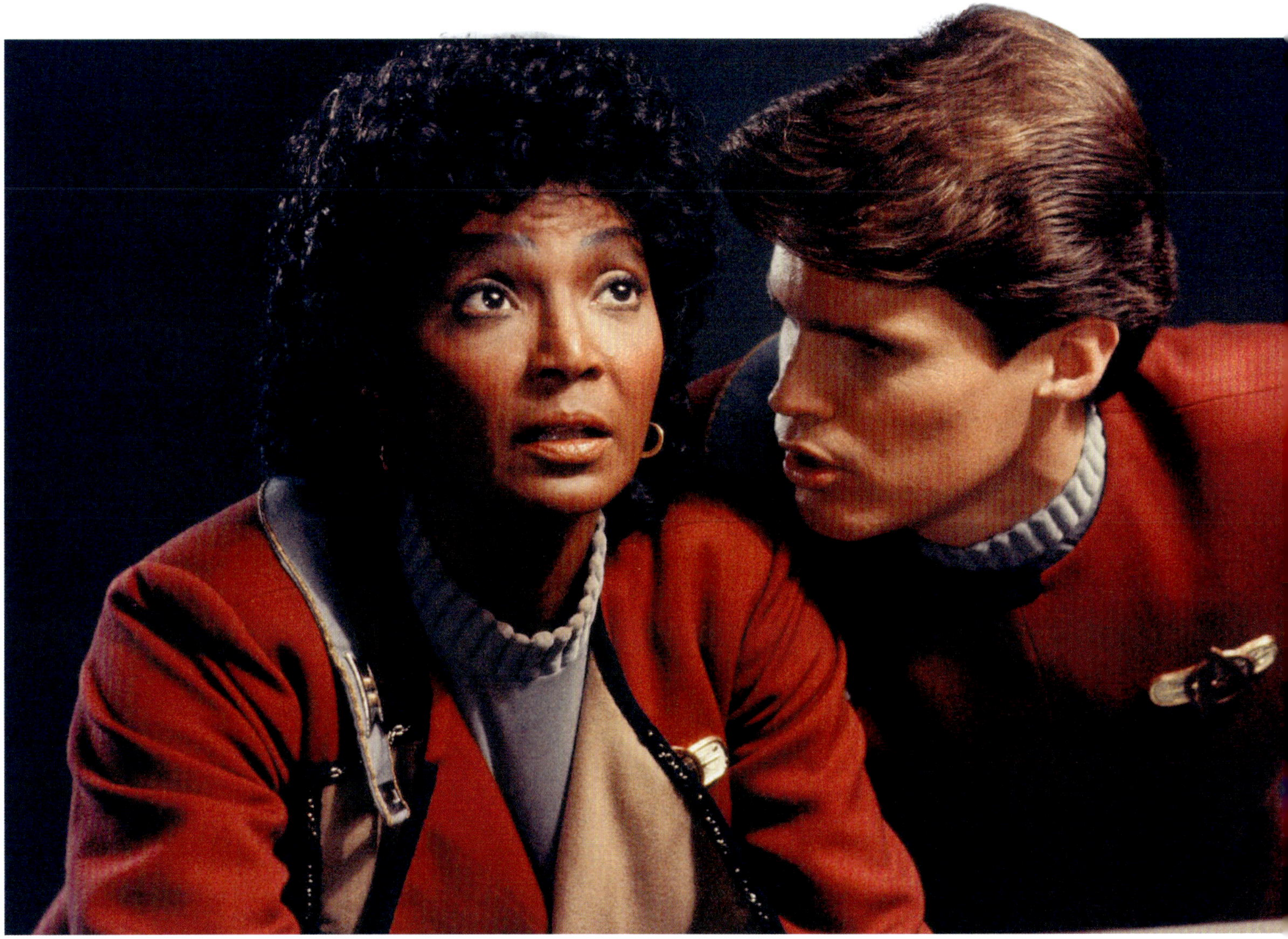

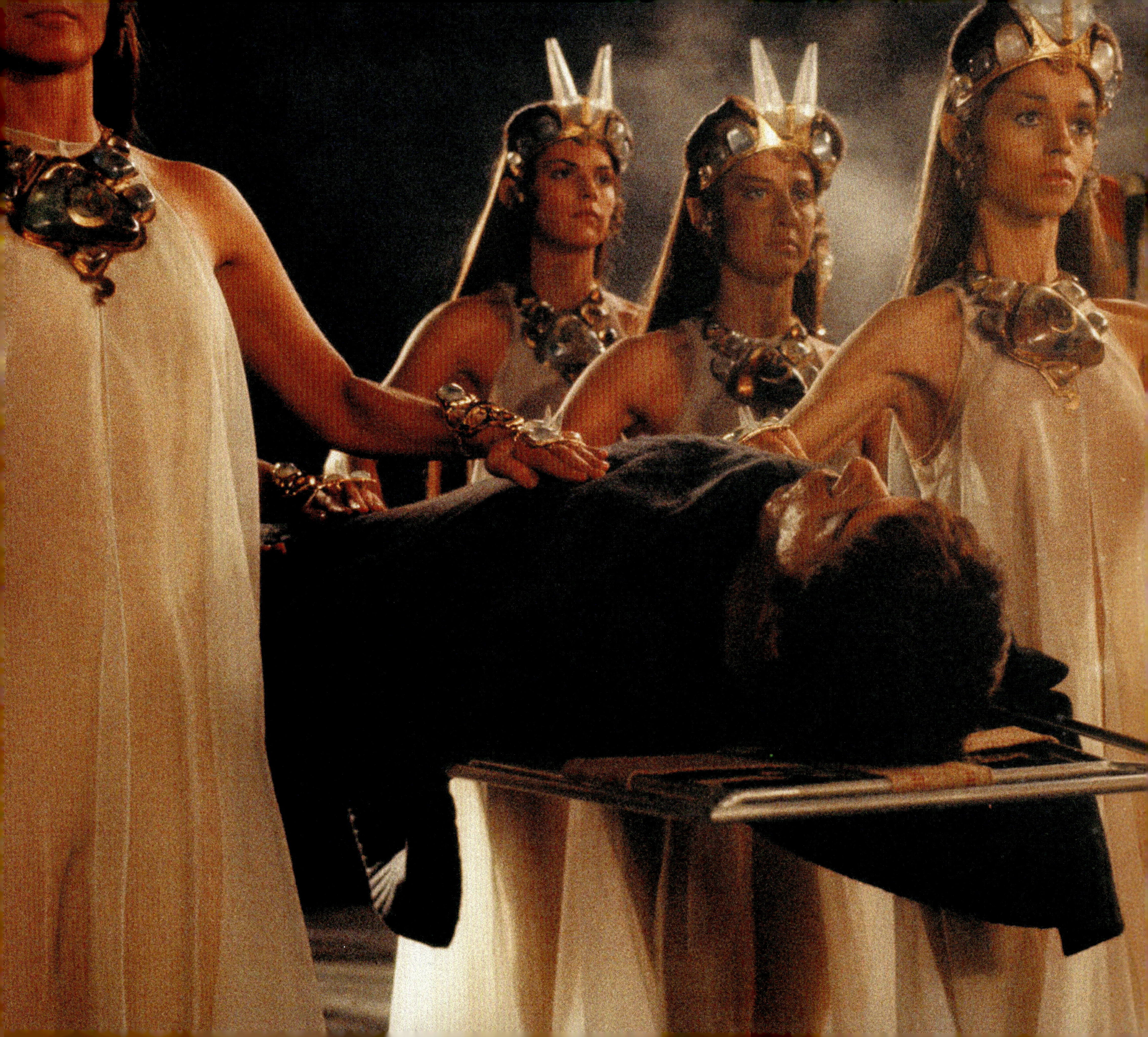

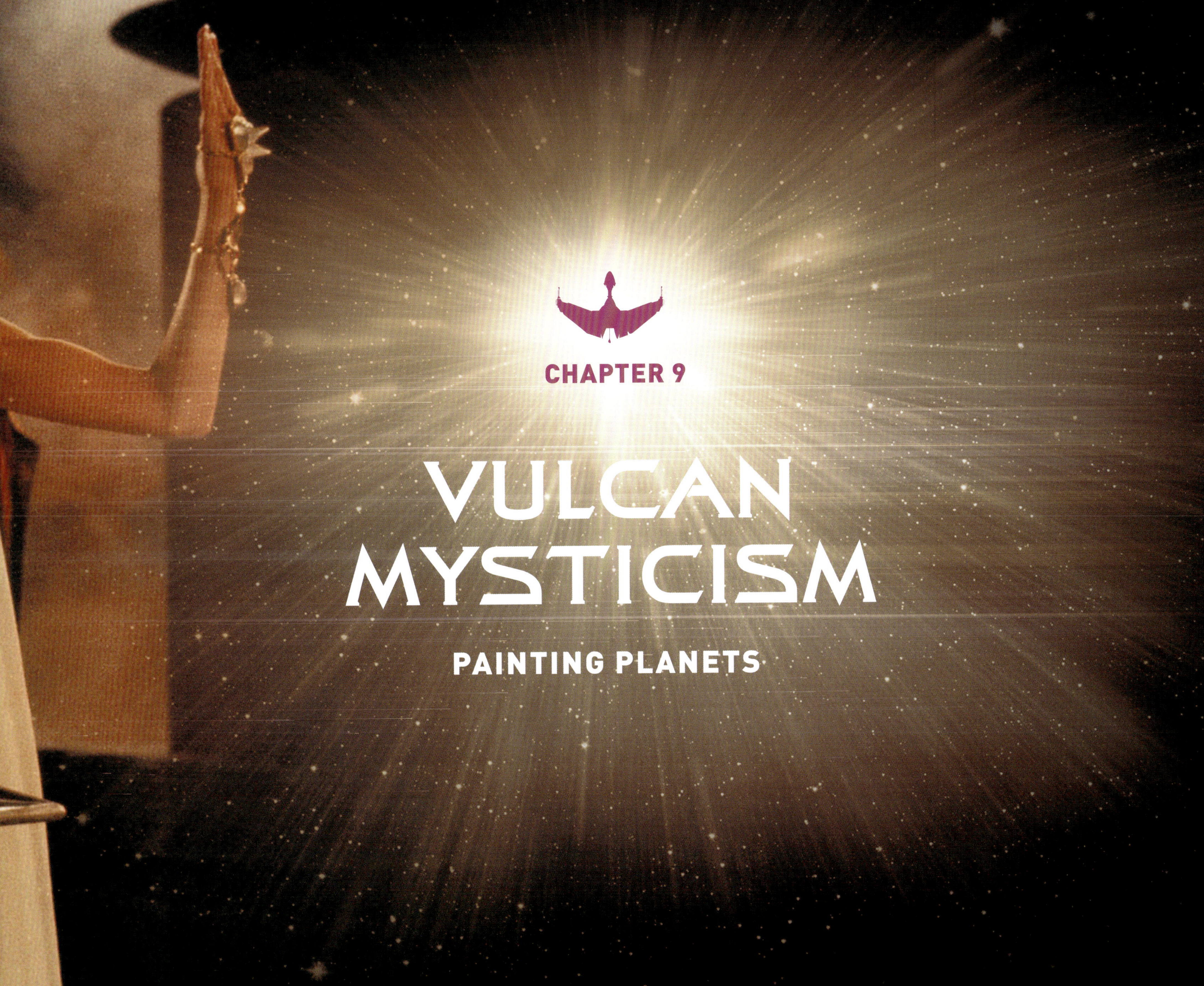

CHAPTER 9

VULCAN MYSTICISM

PAINTING PLANETS

It is only logical that one of the joys creatively for Leonard Nimoy while directing *Star Trek III* was the chance to add to Vulcan by expanding its scope and the audience's understanding of its culture. Nimoy's concerns about Vulcan were contagious, as explained by ILM's matte camera supervisor Craig Barron. "The movie was an opportunity to visit Vulcan and to explore his character in a way that hadn't been done before. We wanted to support him and help make his project successful even under the constraints of budget and vision."[1]

The idea to have the Nevada desert or California Red Rock Canyon State Park substitute for Vulcan had been bandied about, but there were problems, both practical and artistic. Budget was a concern, of course, as was the need to preserve secrecy about Spock, who would be in those sequences. Additionally, there was a desire to honor the art designs that had existed before. Vulcan had been visited four times on screen, in 'Amok Time,' in 'Journey to Babel' by orbit, in the animated series episode 'Yesteryear,' and at the start of *Star Trek: The Motion Picture*. In all productions, the red-orange-brown sky of Vulcan had been dominant and both Correll and Nimoy wanted to preserve that otherworldly quality. *Star Trek III* would serve as a master class in collaboration, as the magicians at ILM worked closely with the Paramount art department, with Correll, and with Nimoy to bring the planet back to the big screen. Matte paintings, set designs, and the film's only real-world location filming combined to create an environment that met Nimoy's Wagnerian vision.

To achieve a common visual theme, Nimoy first worked with ILM's art directors Nilo Rodis and David Carson, and visual effects supervisor Kenneth Ralston, to brainstorm pre-production storyboards and art. Those paintings were a cost saver because ideas could be worked out more easily – and cheaply – than building the sets and discovering mistakes after. They helped inspire lighting and camera angle possibilities before any filming or set construction began.

Storyboards and art from Paramount and ILM's art departments, and the matte department, in addition to study models, gave Nimoy tangible artifacts by which he could determine how best to present his vision.

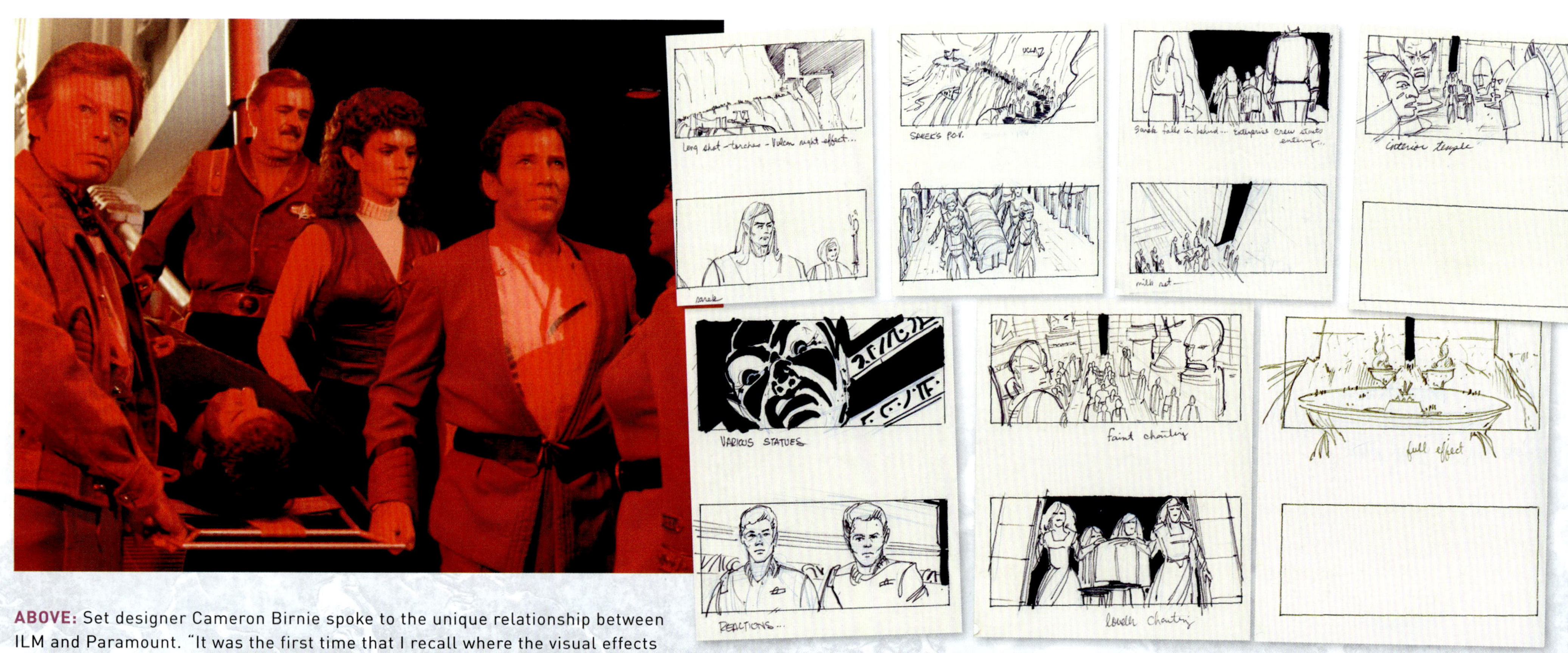

ABOVE: Set designer Cameron Birnie spoke to the unique relationship between ILM and Paramount. "It was the first time that I recall where the visual effects department was giving instructions to the art department rather than the other way round. We did a scene where the Bird-of-Prey lands on Vulcan. I thought we were building the inside of the spaceship, the door, the ramp down, and then the environment that they were coming down to. They said, 'No, you don't have to do any of that. All we need you to do is build the ramp and the doorway.'"[2] The rest would be added through the magic of matte paintings.

ABOVE: Sketches by Carson reveal that it was acceptable to dream big on paper, even if the vision would have to be scaled later to a more budget friendly set. Originally, the idea was to show a procession inside the Hall of Ancient Thought, whose massive structure held remnants of statues from antiquity. The statues were meant to align culturally with those seen during the Kolinahr ceremony from the first movie.

SAREK RETURNS

Fan favorite Mark Lenard played the Romulan Commander in 'Balance of Terror,' Sarek in 'Journey to Babel,' and the Klingon captain in *Star Trek: The Motion Picture*. Although he tried to get a role in *Star Trek II* without any luck, it was at a convention celebrating that film when he learned he might be returning for the next movie. "We were all in Houston at the Ultimate Fantasy Convention and Harve Bennett was there," detailed Lenard. "He approached me after I had come off the stage in the alley way behind the big auditorium. He said he thought it might be a good idea to bring Spock's father back in the next movie because, after all, he had lost his son. I said, 'That's not a bad idea!' (Laughter). And he said, 'let me think about it and mull it over.'"[3]

Lenard would work for two-and-half weeks filming his scenes set on Vulcan for Spock's restoration and on Earth with William Shatner, who he described as "a very fine actor."[3] He was also fond of fellow-Vulcan Robin Curtis, saying, "She's a very dedicated kind of actress and has had more experience than Kirstie has. I think this is her first major movie... I think the fans will like Robin's portrayal."[3] Despite the trust and friendship that Lenard had with the *Star Trek* actors and producers, he still had to first read the script at Paramount in a protected office. Even then, some of the script's most secret moments were missing. "There was about five percent of it left out," Lenard revealed. "I went to see Harve Bennett and Leonard Nimoy afterwards and they described it to me. So the whole thing was very hush-hush and very secret."[3]

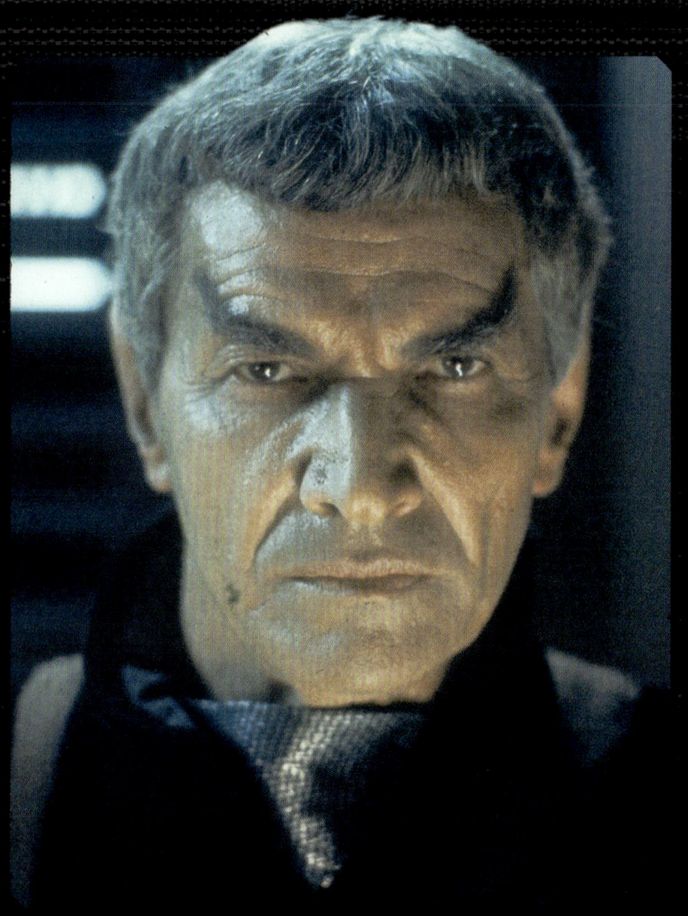

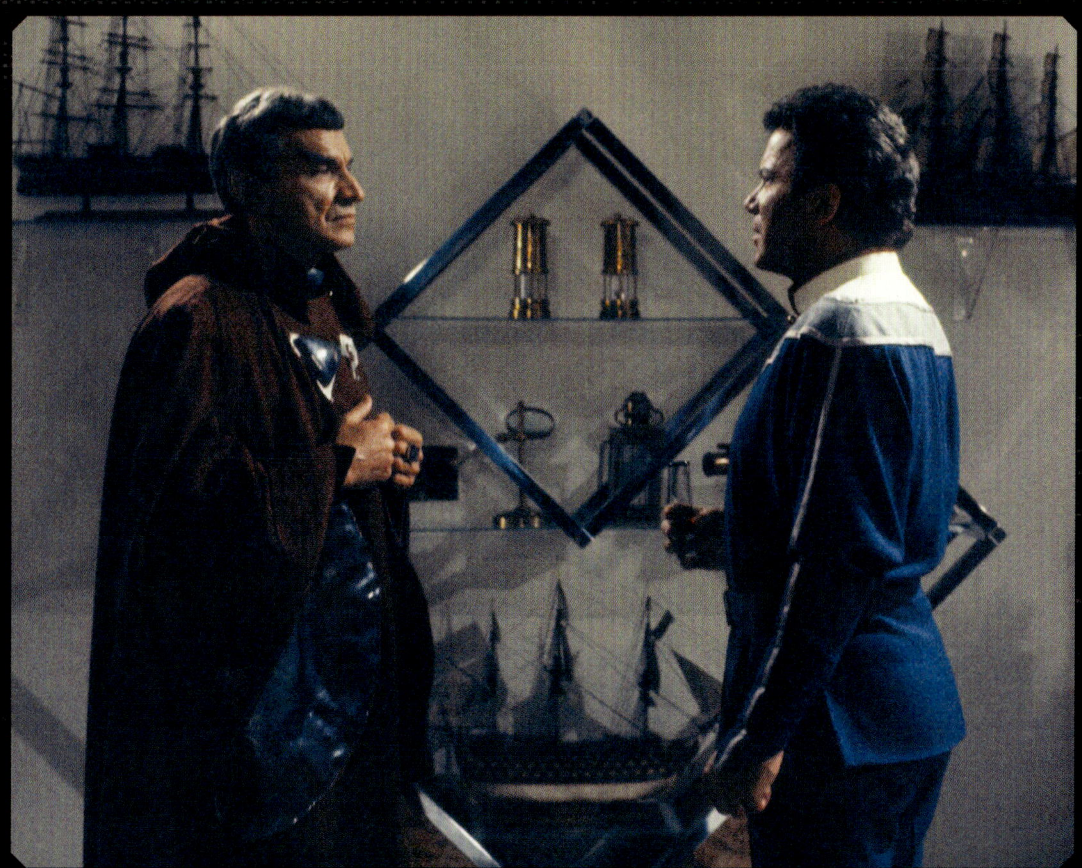

For Nimoy and Bennett, the ILM matte department was the next essential team in bringing the film as close to their imaginings while still being fiscally realistic. The matte department are responsible for creating realistic backgrounds to blend live action with unreal environments. Barron remembered, "During our meetings, Nimoy expressed frustration about the budgetary limitations affecting the Vulcan temple sequence. The creation of Vulcan held great significance for him, and he was particularly concerned about the visual quality of the film's finale. He saw that the matte department's involvement could significantly expand the canvas and the scope of his movie."[1] For both Vulcan and Genesis, the matte department helped make the sky the limit.

BELOW: Many of the early renderings by ILM featured a blue sky instead of the traditional Vulcan patina.

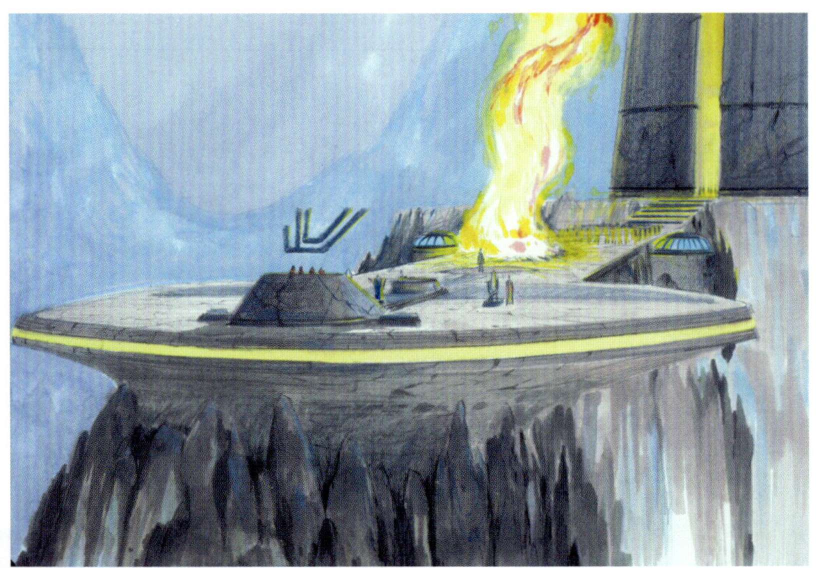

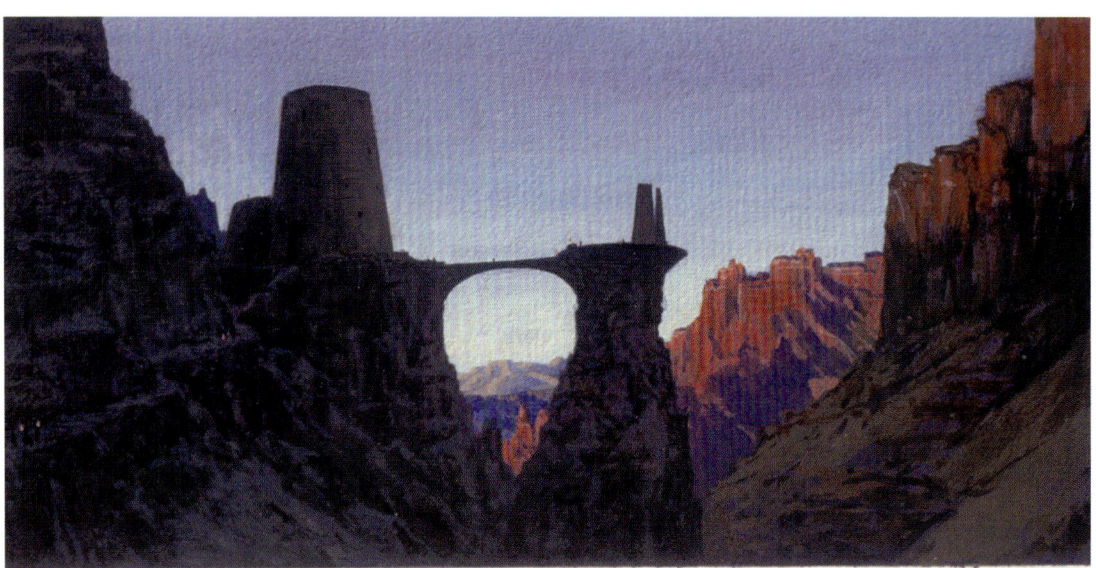

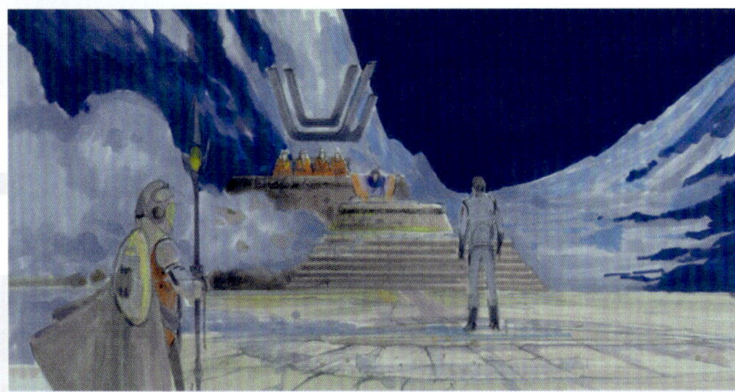

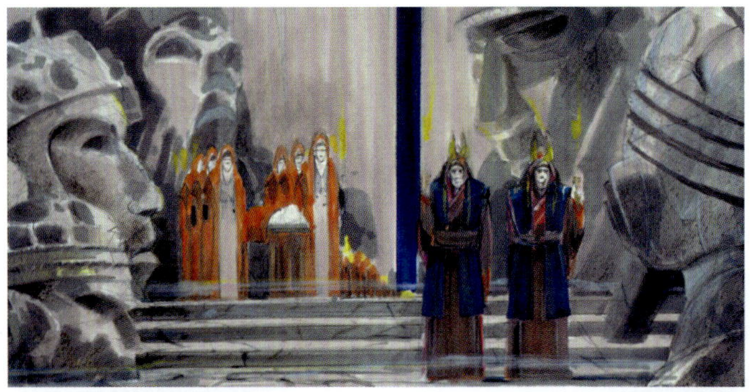

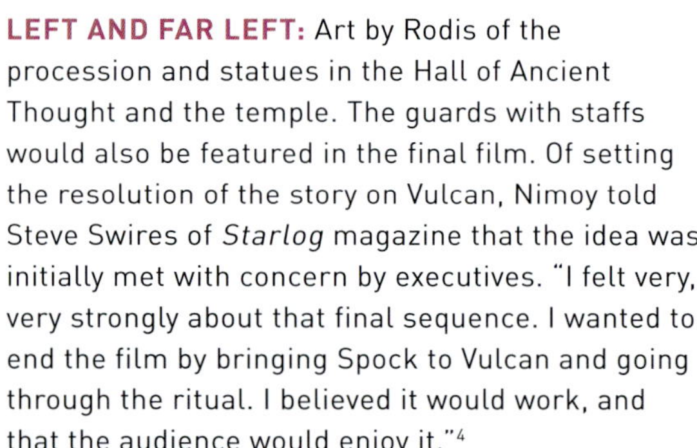

LEFT AND FAR LEFT: Art by Rodis of the procession and statues in the Hall of Ancient Thought and the temple. The guards with staffs would also be featured in the final film. Of setting the resolution of the story on Vulcan, Nimoy told Steve Swires of *Starlog* magazine that the idea was initially met with concern by executives. "I felt very, very strongly about that final sequence. I wanted to end the film by bringing Spock to Vulcan and going through the ritual. I believed it would work, and that the audience would enjoy it."[4]

FAR LEFT: The Vulcan temple as designed by Carson featured a whimsical and stylized version of the Vulcan salute behind the Vulcan priests.

LEFT: Once certain ideas were approved, more elaborate art was created. This is Carson's chalk painting of Mount Seleya, the Hall of Ancient Thought, and the temple where the ceremony would take place.

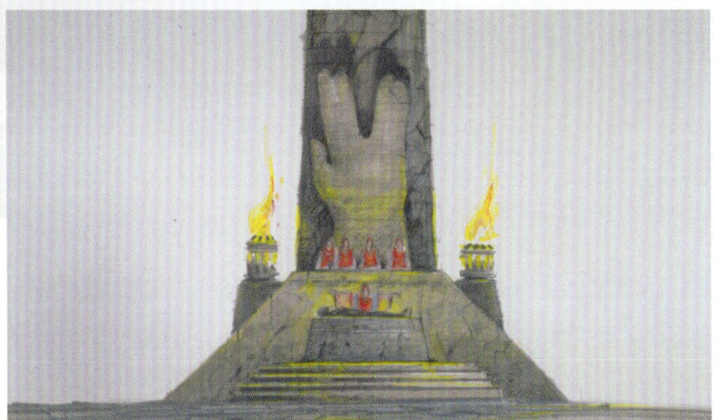

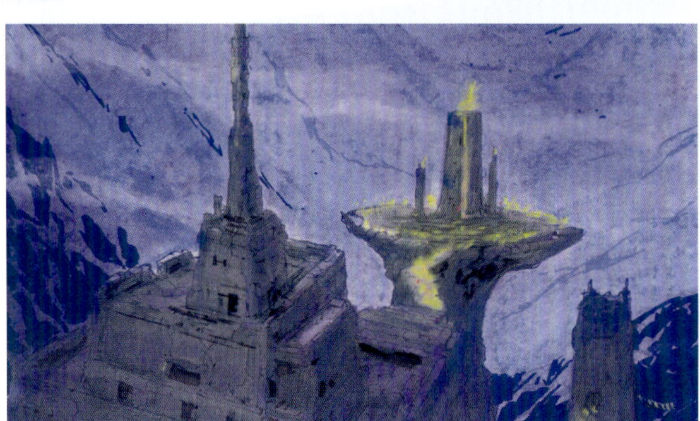

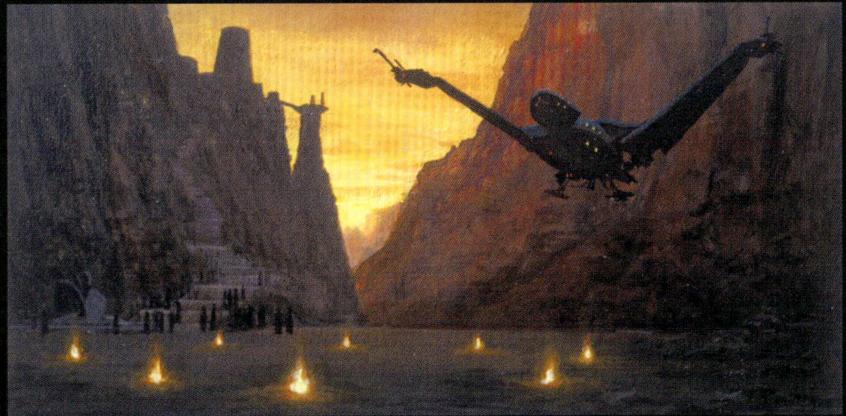

ABOVE: The matte department designed their own production art for the shots they worked on, as with this concept painting by matte artist Chris Evans. They would show Nimoy concepts done in acrylic paint on 8 x 10 illustration board to get an idea of what he liked. Barron relayed Nimoy's sense of humor: "It was kind of funny the way he worked with us. He pretended that he had been to Vulcan before and would say, 'Well, no, the landing area was behind the cliff wall, more to the right.'"[1]

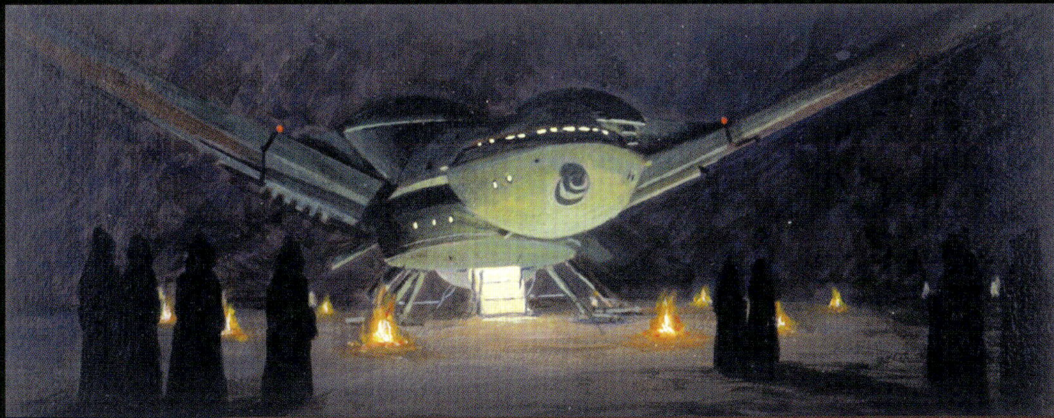

ABOVE: Chris Evans imagined the Bird-of-Prey landing sequences in this production painting, with flames illuminating the ship rather than the spotlights that were eventually featured. Barron said, "I prefer this look to the shot that actually got into the film. At the time, the idea was that Vulcans had technology, but during the traditional and ancient ceremonies, they were more low-tech."[1]

MAIN IMAGE: A composited image that never appears in the film. ILM would produce these kinds of shots for use in publicity materials or licensed products.

FLIGHT RECORDER VISUAL:

CRAIG BARRON, ILM MATTE CAMERA SUPERVISOR

Craig Barron shares a similar love of science fiction as many of his colleagues at ILM. Ray Harryhausen, as always, was an inspiration, and as a young fan, he would make stop-motion amateur films in his garage. After high school, he learned that ILM was moving to Marin County, and he would take a bus there trying to find where the special effects studio was located. He learned instead where George Lucas' home was located and, as an example of the blissful naivety of youth, decided to go there with his amateur reel. "What saved me," Craig said, "was the fact that the lower floor of his house was actually used as his office. George's assistant, Patty Blau, was there at her desk. She asked if she could help and was very nice. She was looking at what I brought to show when George walked down the stairs. Patty said, 'Oh, George, this is Craig, you know, and he's interested in visual effects.' George shook my hand, but I just couldn't say anything because I was petrified with fear."[1]

Blau took pity on Barron, called him a cab, and sent him to ILM, telling them on the phone, "George is sending somebody down for an interview." "She changed my life at that moment. Everyone was there at ILM to meet me: VFX supervisor Richard Edlund, art director Joe Johnston, production manager Jim Bloom, and others. They thought I was going to be some kind of amazing visual artist. After people got the message and started stepping out, concept designer and matte painter Ralph McQuarrie stayed and said he needed someone to help him in the matte department. Of course, I said yes. He would later become a mentor and a good friend. Ralph was as great a human being as he was a teacher and artist."[1]

After learning about matte painting from McQuarrie and serving as matte photographer Neil Krepela's camera assistant on *The Empire Strikes Back*, Barron observed a cultural shift occurring at ILM. Following the completion of *Return of the Jedi* in 1983, Lucas announced a hiatus from *Star Wars* and many of ILM's originating leaders left. ILM itself would need to survive by taking on outside productions. The matte department had already lost McQuarrie after *The Empire Strikes Back* and was now losing its supervisor Krepela. "Those departures left a significant void in our department," remembered Barron.[1]

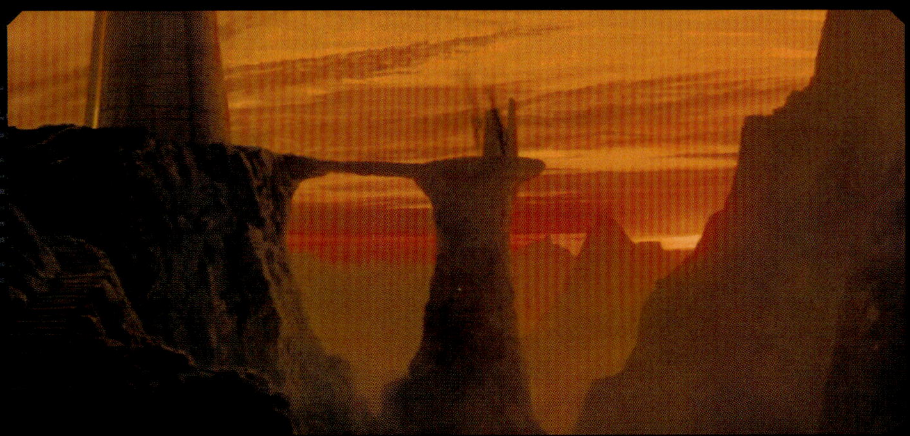

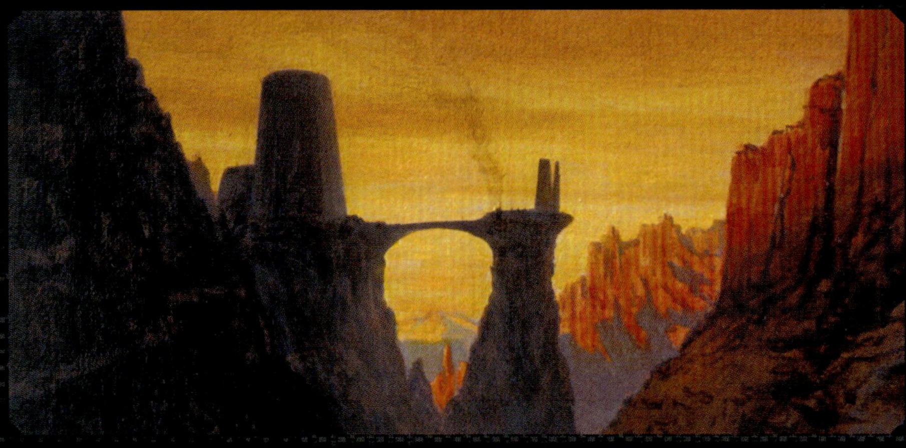

TOP AND ABOVE: The ILM matte department was renowned for producing remarkable works of matte painting art. They began the process by creating quickly rendered production paintings for director Leonard Nimoy's approval, allowing for any adjustments before moving on to the final shots. The first image showcases a production painting by Chris Evans, while the second features the completed matte painting by Mike Pangrazio from the film. This comparison emphasizes the transition from concept to the polished final artwork, highlighting the skill and creativity inherent in the matte painting process.

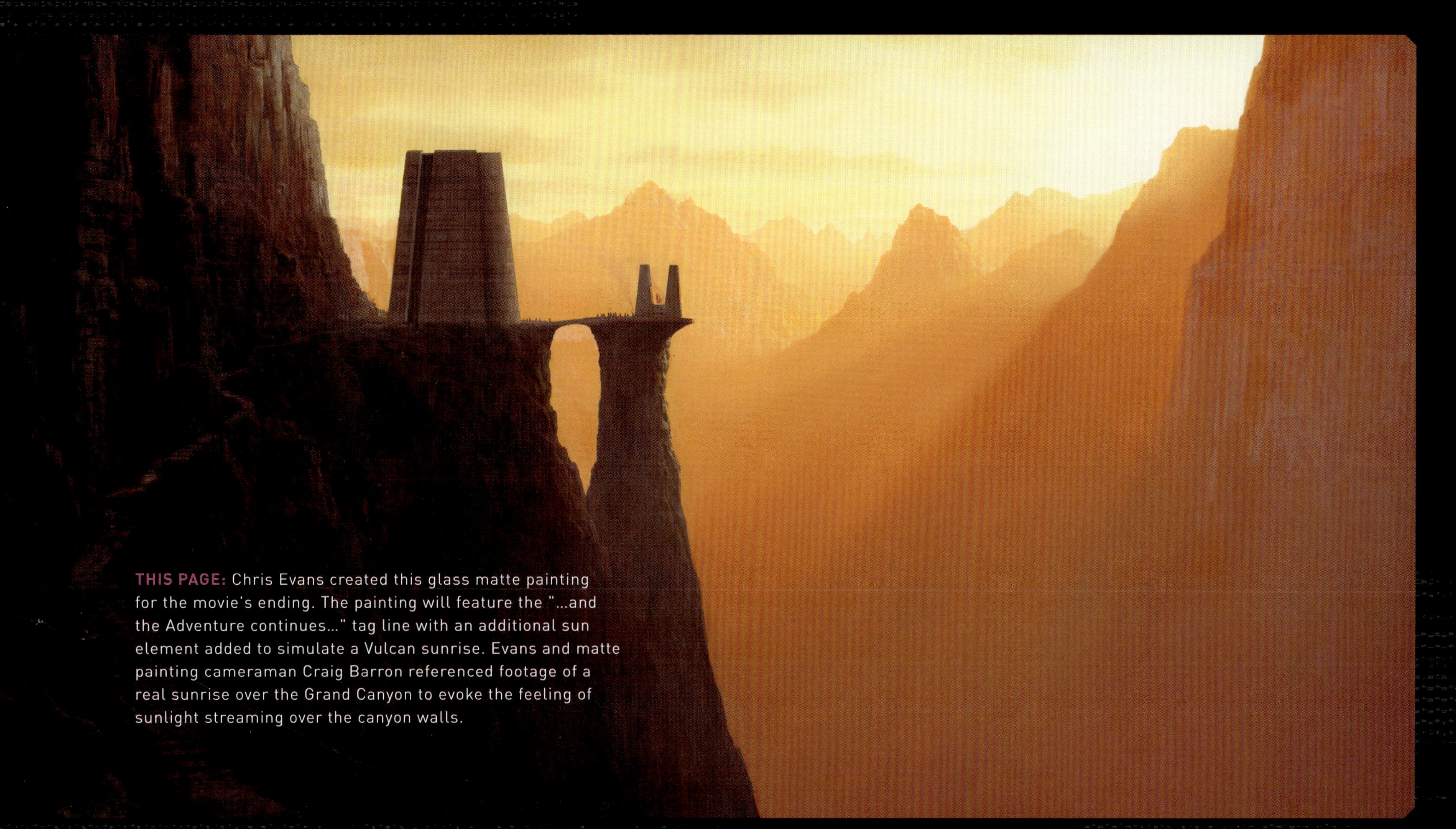

THIS PAGE: Chris Evans created this glass matte painting for the movie's ending. The painting will feature the "...and the Adventure continues..." tag line with an additional sun element added to simulate a Vulcan sunrise. Evans and matte painting cameraman Craig Barron referenced footage of a real sunrise over the Grand Canyon to evoke the feeling of sunlight streaming over the canyon walls.

At only 23, Barron found himself the matte camera supervisor, working closely with the new lead matte artist Michael Pangrazio. Despite his apprenticeships with McQuarrie and Krepela, there were concerns about someone so young being given that kind of responsibility. "Beyond operating the intricate camera systems in the matte department, I would also need to serve as a director of photography for filming original negative live-action scenes that would later be combined with matte paintings, and assist with shot design and technical aspects," explained Barron.[1] For Barron, then, *Star Trek III* represented a proving ground of sorts, giving him and Pangrazio the chance to explore their own ideas and techniques about how to do matte paintings. "A particularly special aspect of working on the *Star Trek* movies was the recognition and appreciation we received for our experience with the *Star Wars* films. The *Star Trek* productions were eager to collaborate with us and hear our ideas, especially from our matte painting department, due to our ability to significantly expand a movie's scope. This became especially important when most of the *Star Trek* movies at that time were made inside sound stages. During the three *Star Trek* films I worked on at ILM, I developed a uniquely close and creative working relationship with their team, more so than on other productions. Being part of a *Star Trek* picture really felt like joining a family. This connection was so strong that I continued working with them on other *Star Trek* productions through my own visual effects company after leaving ILM."[1]

DELETED SCENE

VULCAN GOOD WISHES

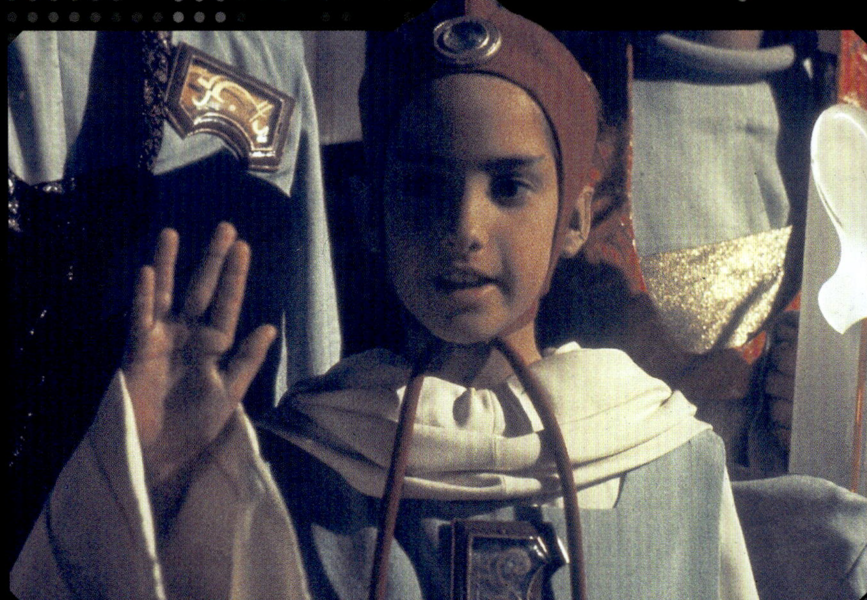

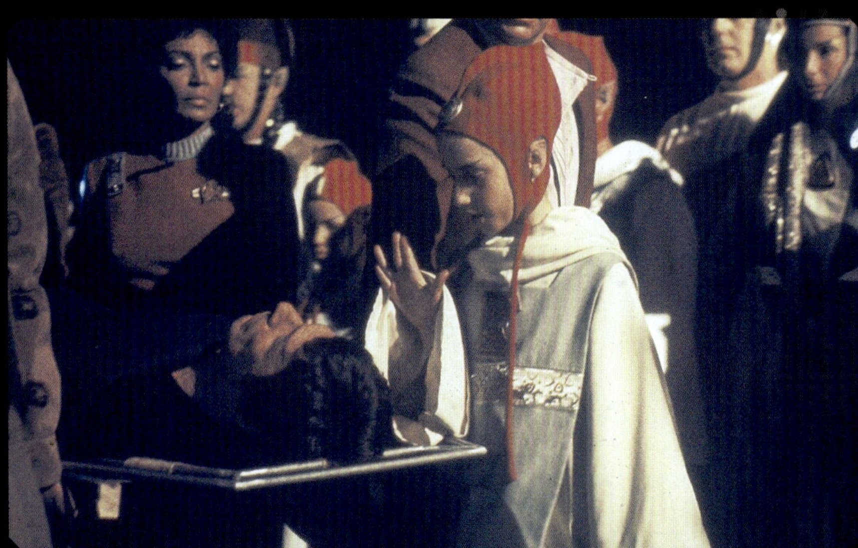

ABOVE: Katherine Blum played a Vulcan girl who gives Spock the Vulcan greeting, telling him "Live Long and Prosper, Spock." The scene was edited from the film, along with most of the processional sequence.

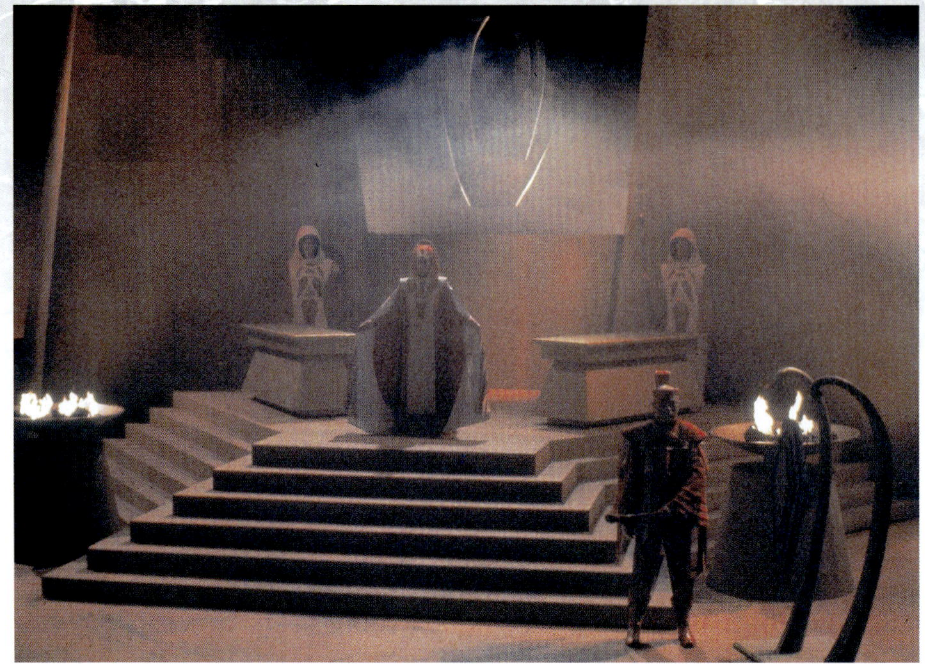

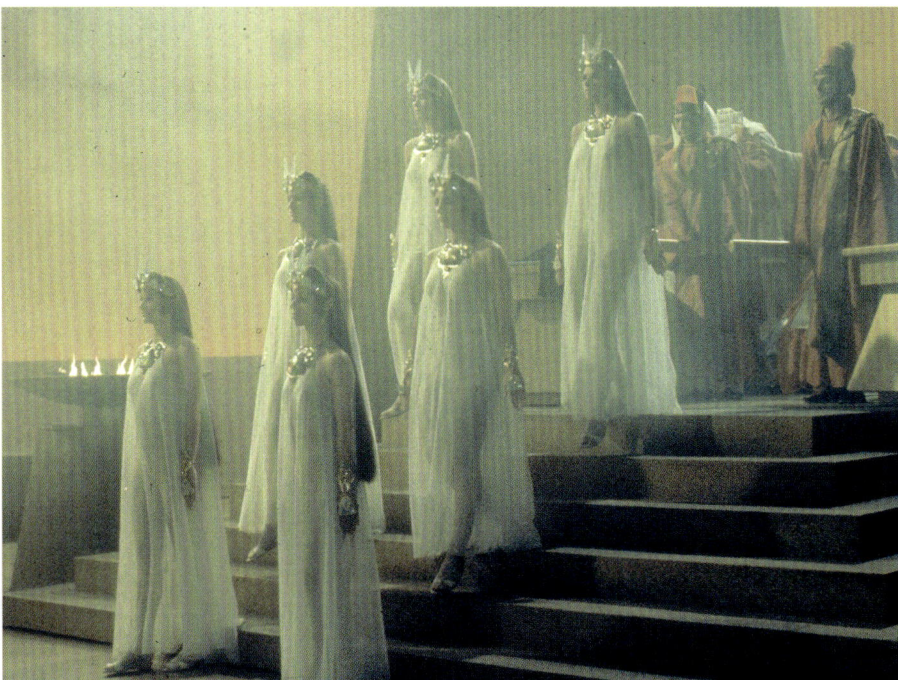

ABOVE: Paramount's Stage 5 with Dame Judith Anderson and Vulcan maidens played by actors including Rebecca Soladay, Jessie Biscardi, and Debra Dilley. In the top image, the ILM stylized Vulcan salute originally imaged by Rodis and Carson can be seen. Without ILM's matte department to expand sets using their paintings, *Star Trek III* would have felt claustrophobic. Barron shared, "We had created a few matte paintings for the previous *Star Trek* film directed by Nick Meyer. Unfortunately, the Eden Cave mattes weren't as successful as we had hoped. This fueled our determination to excel in the next *Star Trek* film, and we were thrilled to have the opportunity to work on location for an important matte shot set on Vulcan."[1]

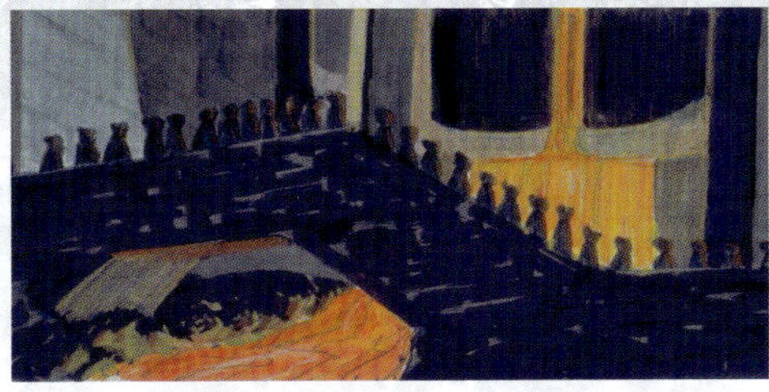
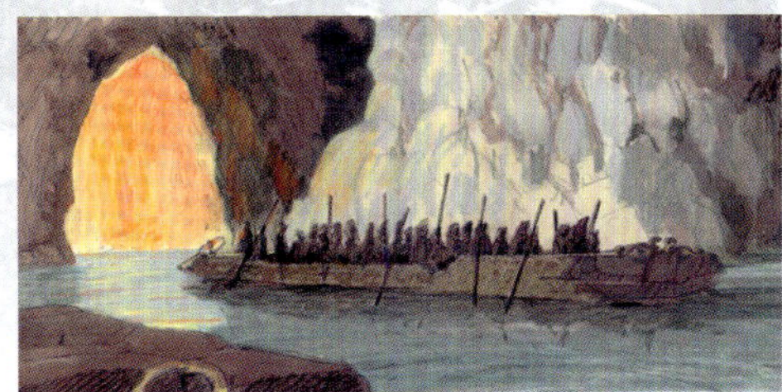
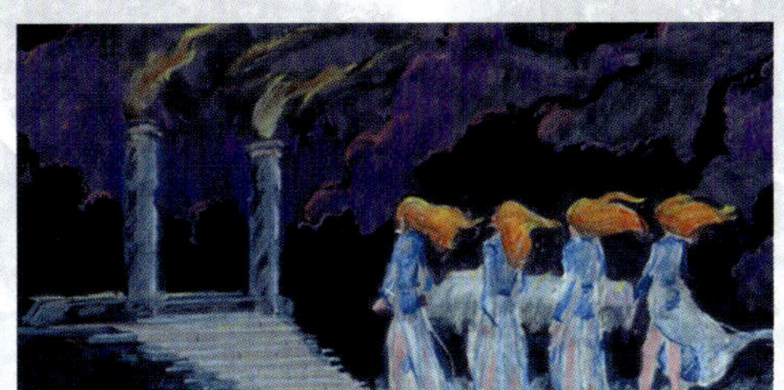
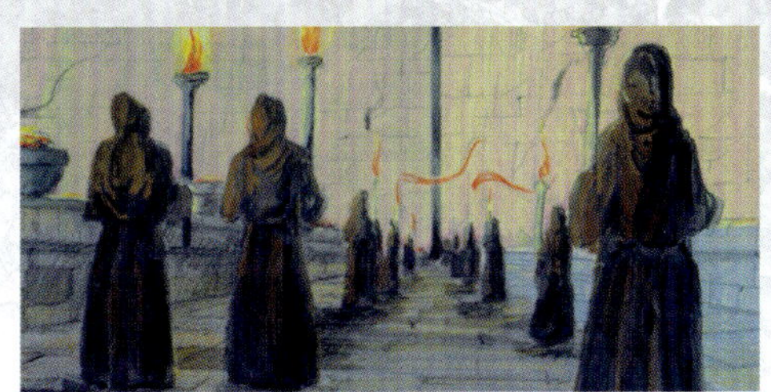

ABOVE: Imaginings by Carson of the processional, which was trimmed significantly in the final film.

BELOW: Occidental College, specifically its Gilman Fountain, was selected to stand-in for the Bird-of-Prey landing site on Vulcan.

In addition to the virtual world of matte paintings, Vulcan existed both as sets on Paramount Stages 5 and 8, and as a redressed real-world location – Occidental College, a private liberal arts college in Los Angeles. The Paramount sets were transformed from script to reality by art director John E. Chilberg II and set designers Cameron Birnie and Blake Russell. The scenes shot at Paramount and Occidental College had to form the substance of any matte painting extensions done by ILM and stand on their own as the characters interacted on screen.

Although Vulcan appears at the end of the film, the scenes on the planet were filmed early in the schedule. The Occidental College footage was completed on August 31 and September 1, 1983. The scenes in the temple and the Hall of Ancient Thought were filmed beginning the next day. The cast and crew were very happy to get out of the studio, even if only for two days. Associate producer Ralph Winter shared, "You know, that was a big deal for us. We were landlocked, we were on sound stages the whole time. And to go outside was like, 'Wow! This is really a big movie!'"[5]

Other colleges and locations were considered, and ILM's David Carson relayed a funny incident that happened while ILM and Nimoy did location scouting for a place that had a large enough area to accommodate the many Vulcan extras and had stairs that could be extended using matte paintings as a starting place for the processional scene. "We did a location scout at USC or UCLA as possible locations for the Vulcan ceremony," he said. "We took a bus there and we trundled from the bus to wander around the campus for a while, making notes and learning what we needed to learn. When we got back to the bus, there was a *Star Trek III* script sitting on the bench next to the bus. Leonard told us all about how important it was to keep our scripts with us. The scripts were numbered and there was high security to keep the movie's secrets. Of course, it turned out to actually be Leonard's script! (Laughs)."[6]

The filming, which took place at night starting around 8 pm, required hundreds of extras in addition to the ILM and Paramount crew and the main actors. The alumni gymnasium was converted into both the wardrobe fitting room and the makeup room. Music advisor John Oliver worked with the extras playing Vulcan musicians, while Andre Tayir worked with the extras and actors to choreograph traditional Vulcan gestures and movements. Visual effects production coordinator Laurie Vermont told *CineFex*'s Brad Munson, "At midnight, they had to serve what was essentially lunch. We had hundreds of Vulcans, all in costume, and they put these bibs on them to cover up their costumes, and everyone was herded into a traditional school cafeteria where they were served ribs about a foot long. So here were all these Vulcans – with the little bibs and big ears – eating ribs. It was incredible."[7]

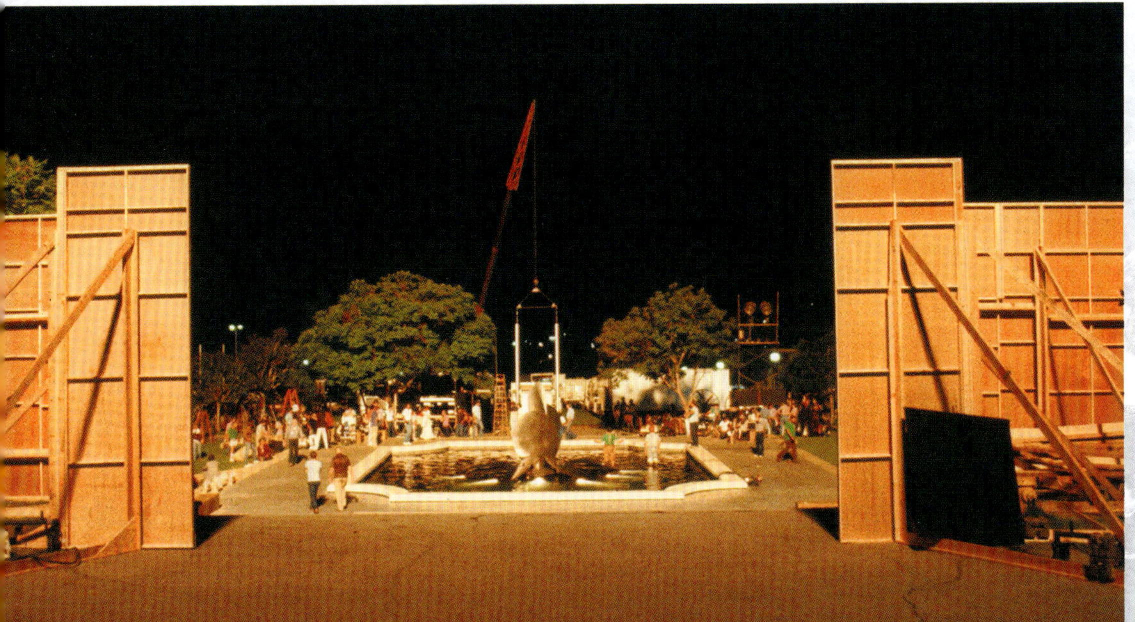
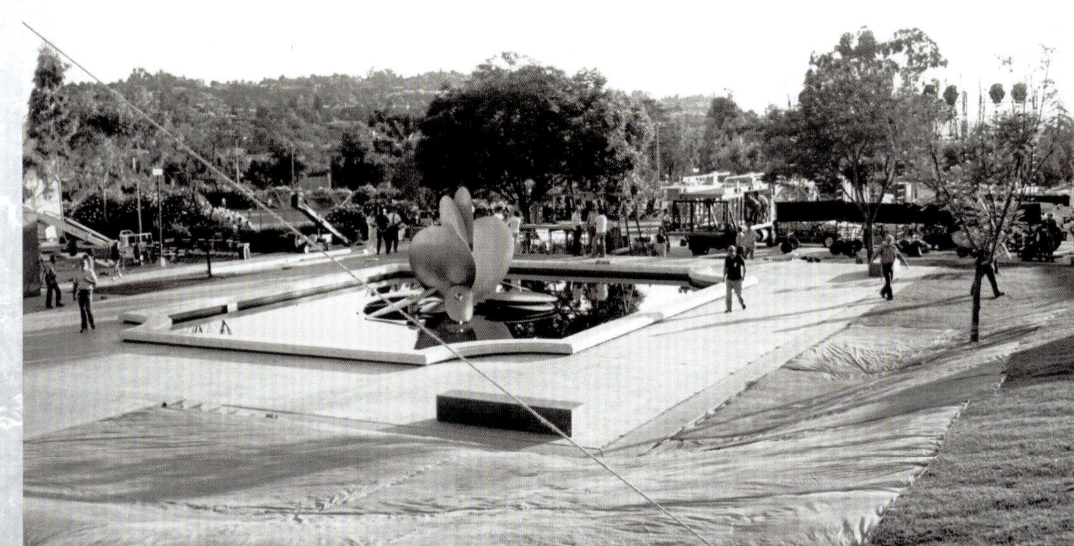

For Barron, his favorite matte shot in *Star Trek III* was the one captured on location at Occidental College. "I collaborated with Director of Photography Charles Correll on the lighting for our Vulcan matte shot. This was a crucial shot for the production, as it was our only location shoot. Correll devised a special lighting setup that allowed us to maintain a sharp focus, even during a night scene," Barron explained. "Typically, during a night shoot, the background might be slightly out of focus. However, that wouldn't have worked here because we needed the steps to be clearly visible, extending back and leading up to Mount Seleya and our distant temple, which would be added through matte painting."

Barron continued, "When rehearsing the shot, I noticed a problem and quickly told Leonard, 'If Nichelle crosses as planned, she will go behind the matte painting, causing her to disappear.'" Barron suggested they could rotoscope her over the matte painting and wanted to swap out cameras to the Vista Vision they had in reserve, but Nimoy had another idea. He proposed editing the film to show Uhura, then cut to a reaction shot of Kirk seeing her, and finally return to Uhura once she cleared the matte painting area. Barron thought it was a great idea, noting, "Nimoy was already thinking about how the film would be edited. It was great how he worked with us, making quick decisions to get the best shot for his film without additional cost."[1]

Barron's favorite matte shot for the movie was photographed as an original negative matte shot. After the initial live-action photography on location, Barron brought back the original negative before development, adding a second exposure for Mike Pangrazio's matte painting and additional exposures for the drifting smoke and flames elements, which were also shot at night in ILM's parking lot. All these elements came together to create the final shot, resulting in a seamless blend of live action, painted artwork, and practical effects—all contributing to the misty, mysterious Vulcan location.

After filming at Occidental College, it was time for Nimoy to play Spock in the final scenes of the film. For Nimoy, balancing his acting and directing responsibilities was certainly a test. "The days when I had to perform as Spock were very difficult for me," opined Nimoy. "The character is demanding and I didn't like jumping in. You have to get into a certain mental condition to do it justice. There was this very energetic person in me that was jumping around, creating ideas for

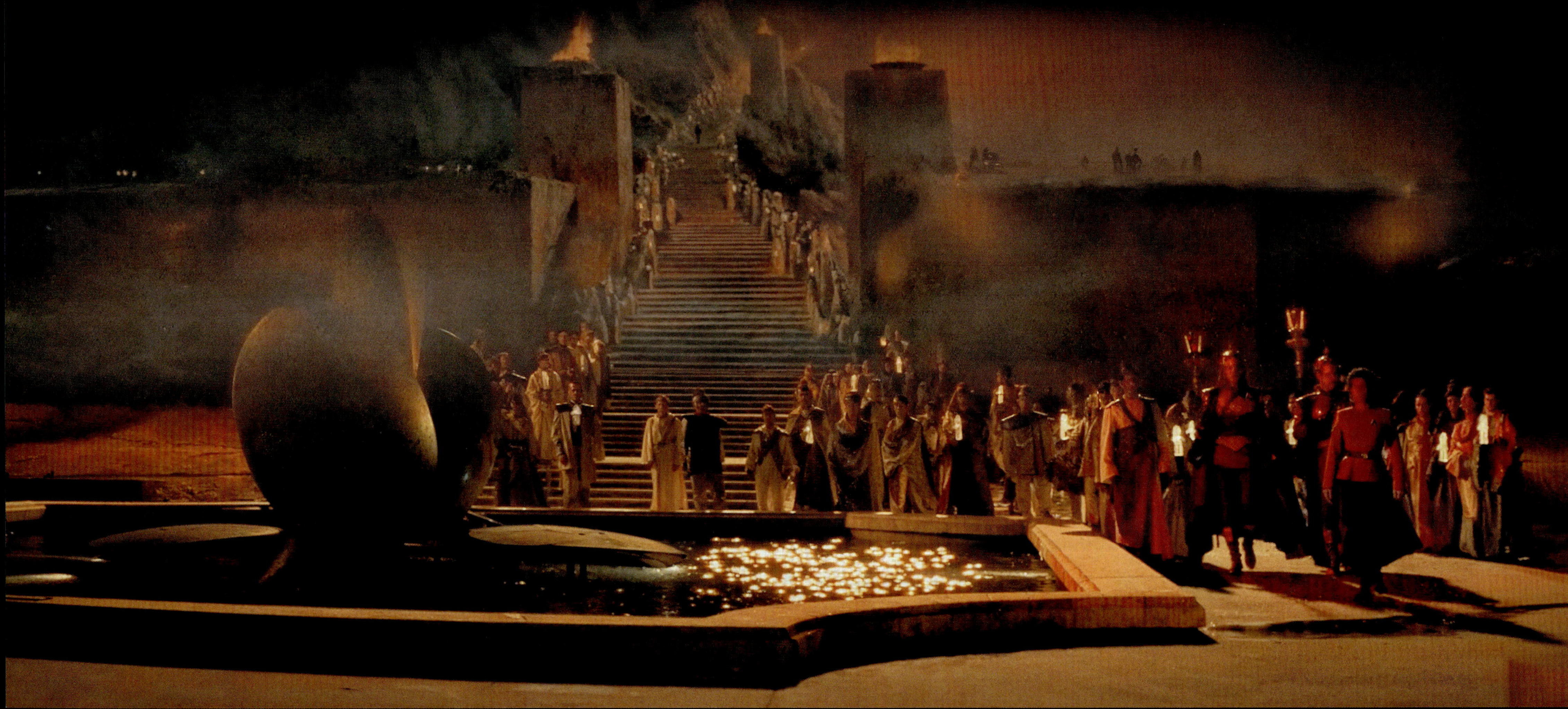

BELOW: Evans is painting on a 2.5 x 6-foot-wide glass panel framed in aluminum. The artists frequently employ a paint originally developed for cartoons called Cartoon Color because it photographs more accurately than traditional acrylic paint and dries faster than oil paints. A photo enlargement of the live action scene is temporarily taped to the center of the temple area, so Evans knows exactly where the live action scene ends and his painting begins. Later, that picture will be removed, leaving empty glass where the real footage will be rear-projected and photographed by Barron. According to Barron, the goal is "to make the transition as seamless as possible, so you can't tell where the live action ends and the matte painting begins."[1]

BELOW: The final result shows the live action sequence visible in the middle of the painting. The matte department was one of the only departments at ILM that could generate a finished shot from start to finish entirely by themselves, although frequently there were additions of spacecraft and blue screen elements added by colleagues in the optical department. "This particular shot is an example of the department's best work. We designed the shot for our Automatte Camera system, a multi-plane track camera originally built for Return of the Jedi to shoot matte paintings with motion control," Barron explained. "I programmed a slight push-in on the shot to simulate camera movement. It worked out nicely, and Leonard was very pleased, as it successfully made the sequence appear more expansive."[1]

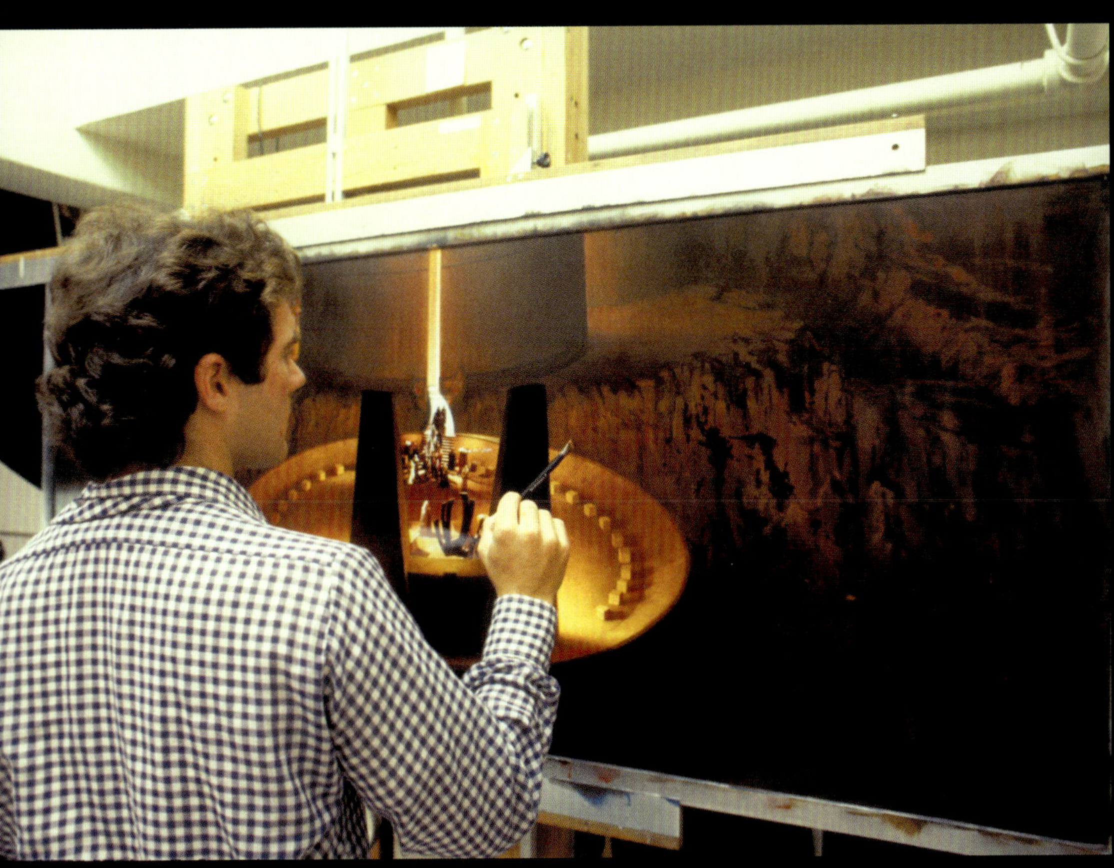

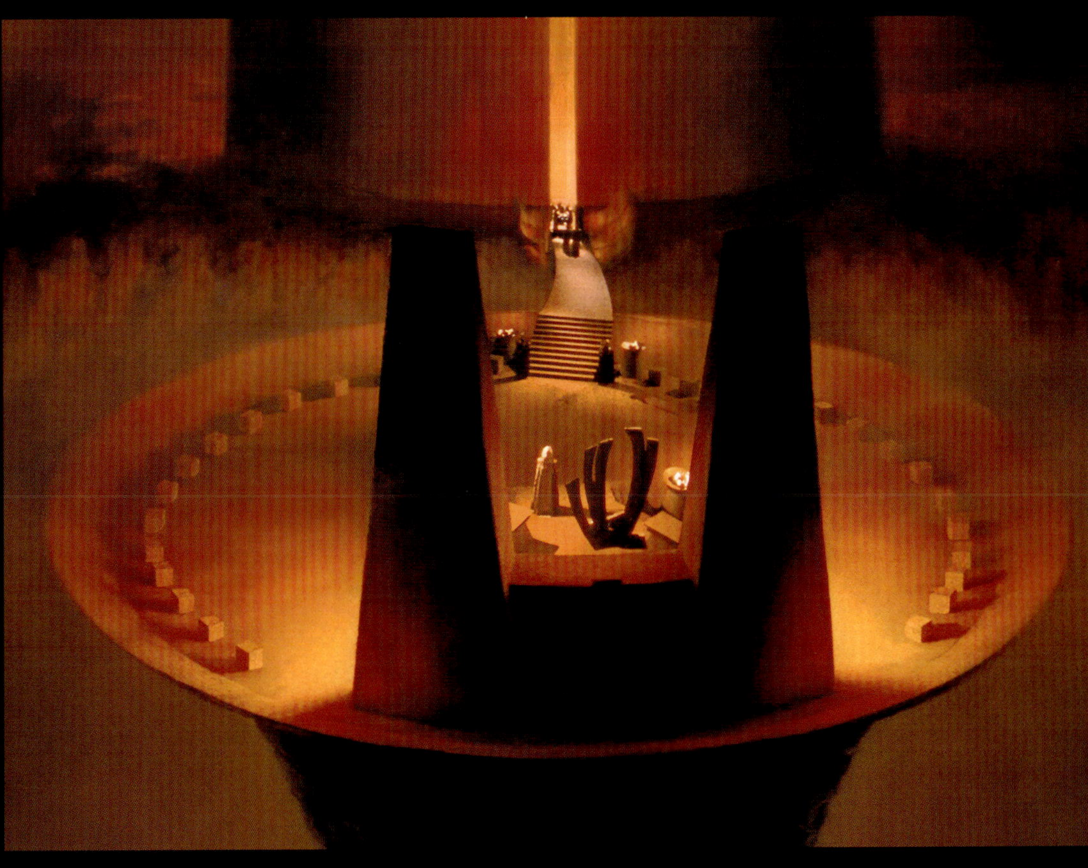

how the scene should play, where the camera should be, how much the explosion should go off, how heavy the rain should be, whether the sun should break through. Then I had to step in front of the camera, erase all that, and become Spock."[8]

Craig Barron had flown to Paramount to get Nimoy's approval on some additional matte painting production sketches, probably for the de-orbit and destruction of the *Enterprise* matte painting added late in the schedule. He was first met by Ralph Winter who said, "'Oh, Craig, I'm so sorry. We tried to stop you from flying down, but today is Leonard's first day playing Spock. He's in character, remembering his persona, being Spock. He can't see you today.'"[1]

Barron understood, gave Winter the production painting for Leonard to review later, and walked around a corner of the Paramount lot. There, walking toward him in full Spock regalia and makeup, was Nimoy. "He was Mr. Spock," said Barron. "Now I'm in his way exactly where I'm not supposed to be. Ralph had just told me not to even try talking to him when he was playing Spock as it could affect his focus. He looks at me, and it's like he doesn't know who I am because although Nimoy knew me, Spock didn't. He was staying in character. So, I did the Vulcan hand salute, and he returned it, nodded, and walked past me to the set. To do the Vulcan hand sign with Mr. Spock...gosh! I met Mr. Spock. My [internal] teenage fanboy went crazy."[1]

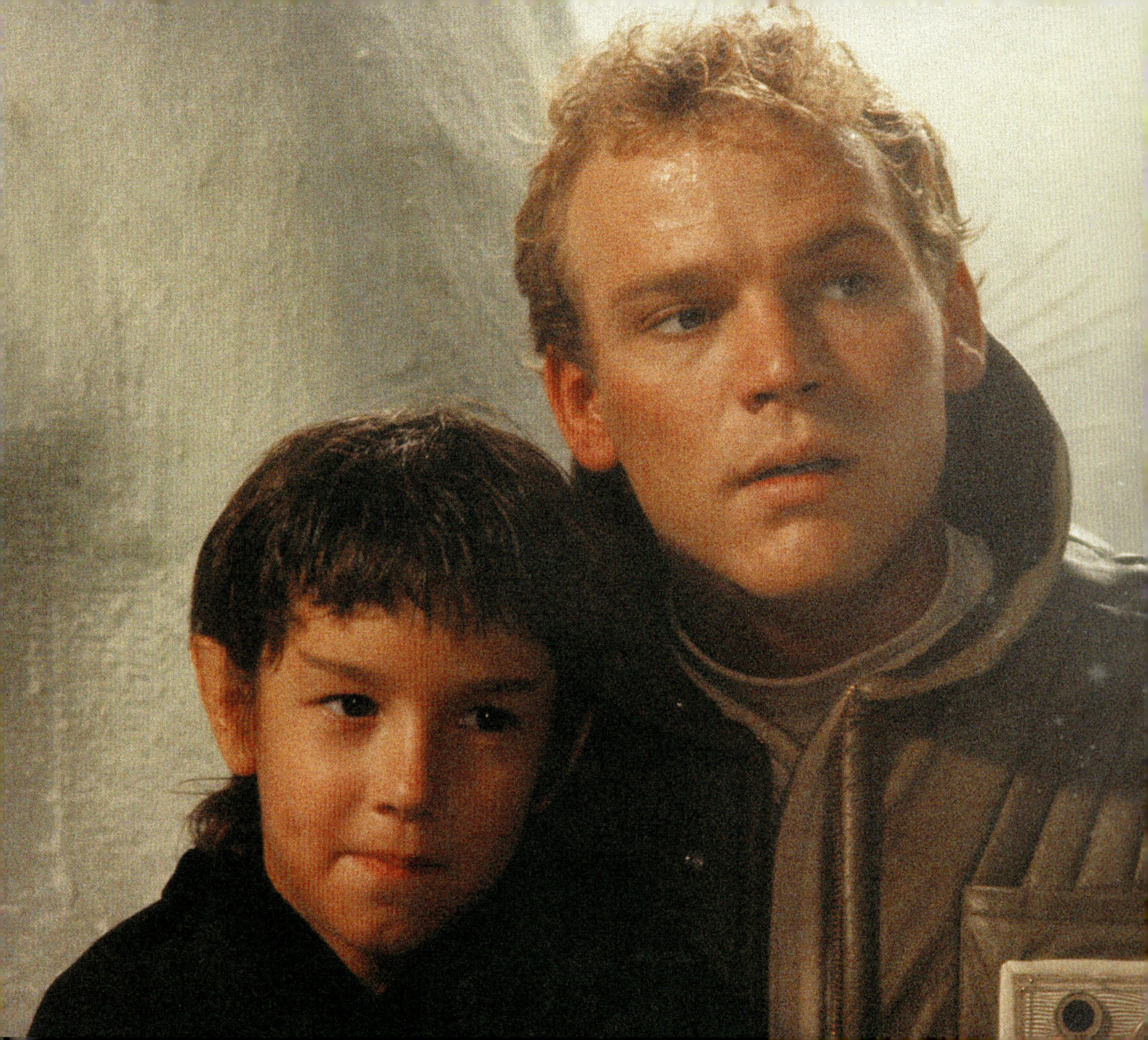

CHAPTER 10

PLANET FORBIDDEN

CREATING AND DESTROYING GENESIS

"Impressive. They can make planets." Maltz's observation to Kruge when viewing the stolen data they have acquired applies as much to the real artists and technicians who built Genesis for the film as it does the fictional terraforming device.

Genesis was created utilizing every means possible: massive sets on Stages 12, 14, and 15 at Paramount, at ILM in miniature scale, and by the matte department's paintings. Filming the Genesis scenes at Paramount occurred mostly in late September and early October, requiring several weeks of shooting because nearly forty-six minutes of the film's one hour, forty-five minute running time takes place either in orbit of, or on the surface of, Genesis.

The Paramount set designs on *Star Trek III* were the responsibility of art director John E. Chilberg II and his team, who collaborated closely with ILM. Chilberg had worked previously with Bennett on *Rich Man, Poor Man* and had been nominated for two Emmy Awards for his outstanding work on *Battlestar Galactica* and *Dynasty*. Set designers Cameron Birnie – who would eventually earn four Emmy nominations – and Blake Russell, along with construction foreman Scott Goodale, set decorator Tom Pedigo, and illustrator Tom Lay – who created the background paintings that would wrap around the set – were responsible for transforming ideas into reality. Beginning with detailed blueprints, practical techniques would have to balance Chilberg's designs, Nimoy's vision, special effects, and actor and stunt movements, the camera department needs, and budget. Most especially, the sets had to serve the story.

At the time, Genesis was one of the largest sets ever constructed for a *Star Trek* production. To achieve even more scale, Chilberg and his team employed forced perspective, a technique that had been used on the original series and previous films. Forced perspective uses set design and camera movement techniques to create a desired optical illusion, usually to make the audience believe that objects or sets are bigger than they are in reality. Sometimes that involves building part

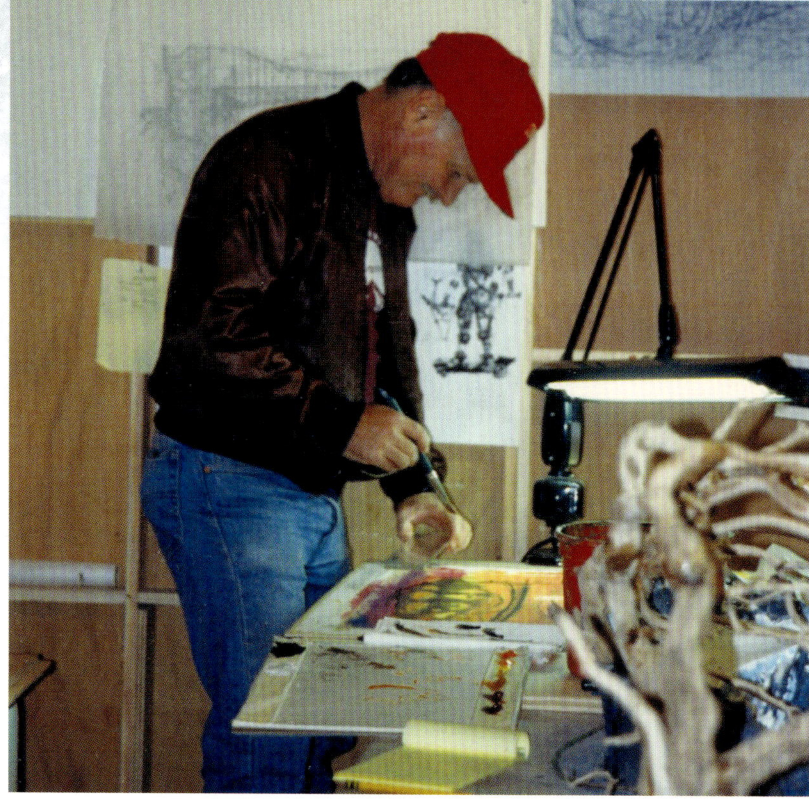

ABOVE: Illustrator Thomas Lay designed and painted the backgrounds for Vulcan and Genesis that would be enlarged on a massive scale to serve as wrap-arounds on set.

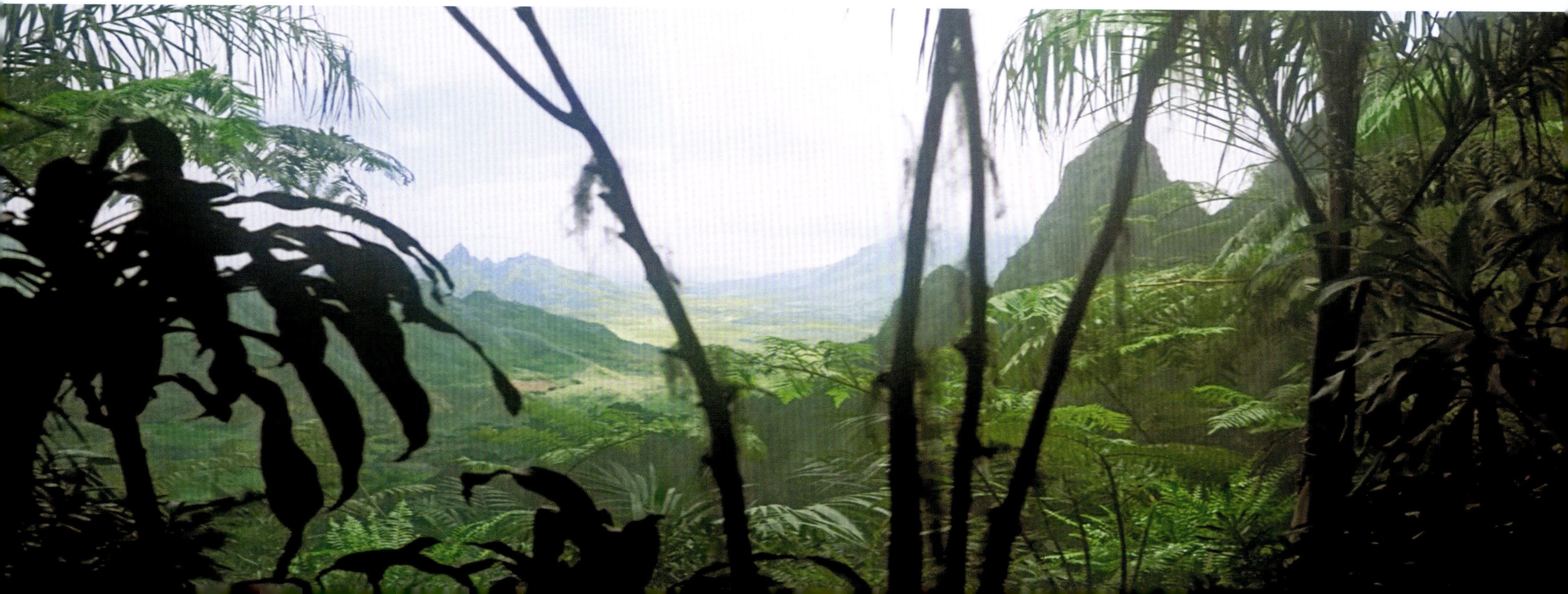

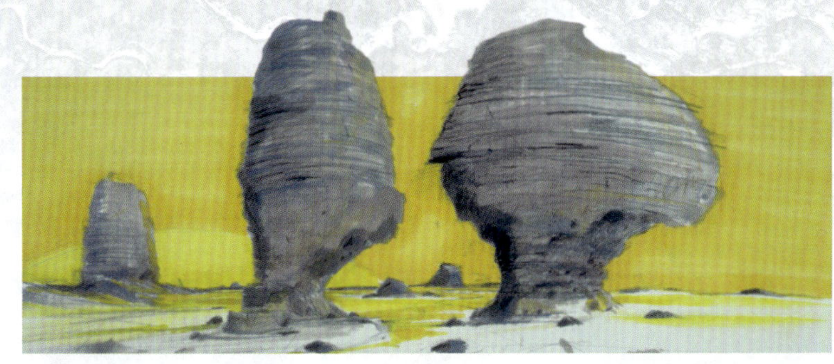

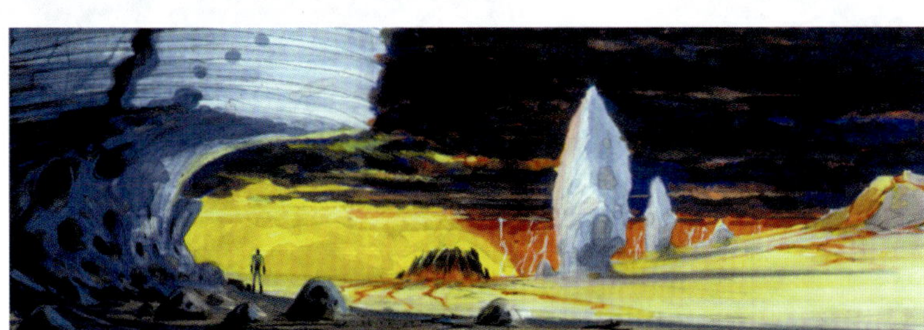

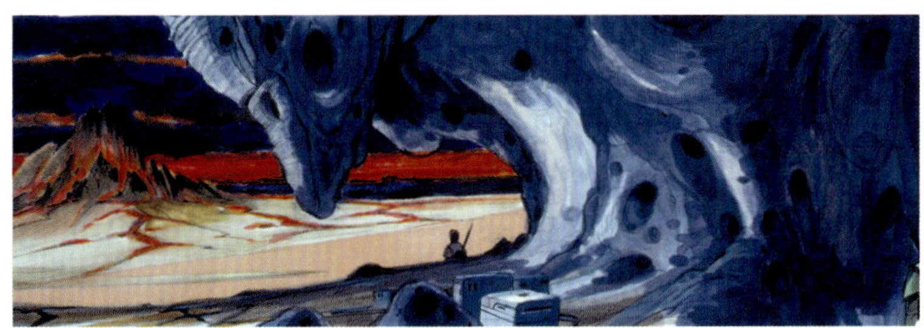

ABOVE: ILM's Nilo Rodis created these visions of Genesis early in pre-production, including unusual rock formations and the Klingon camp.

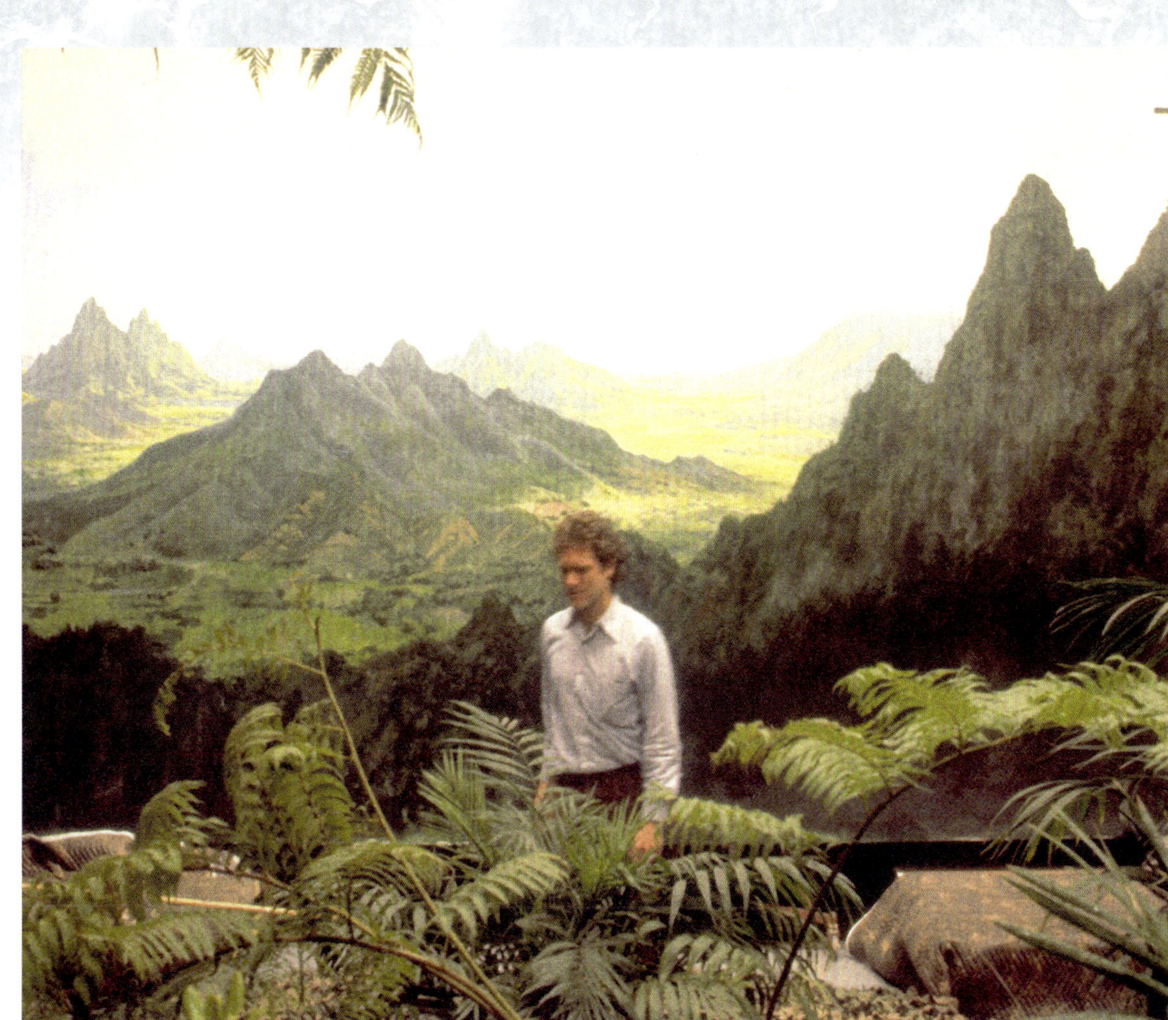

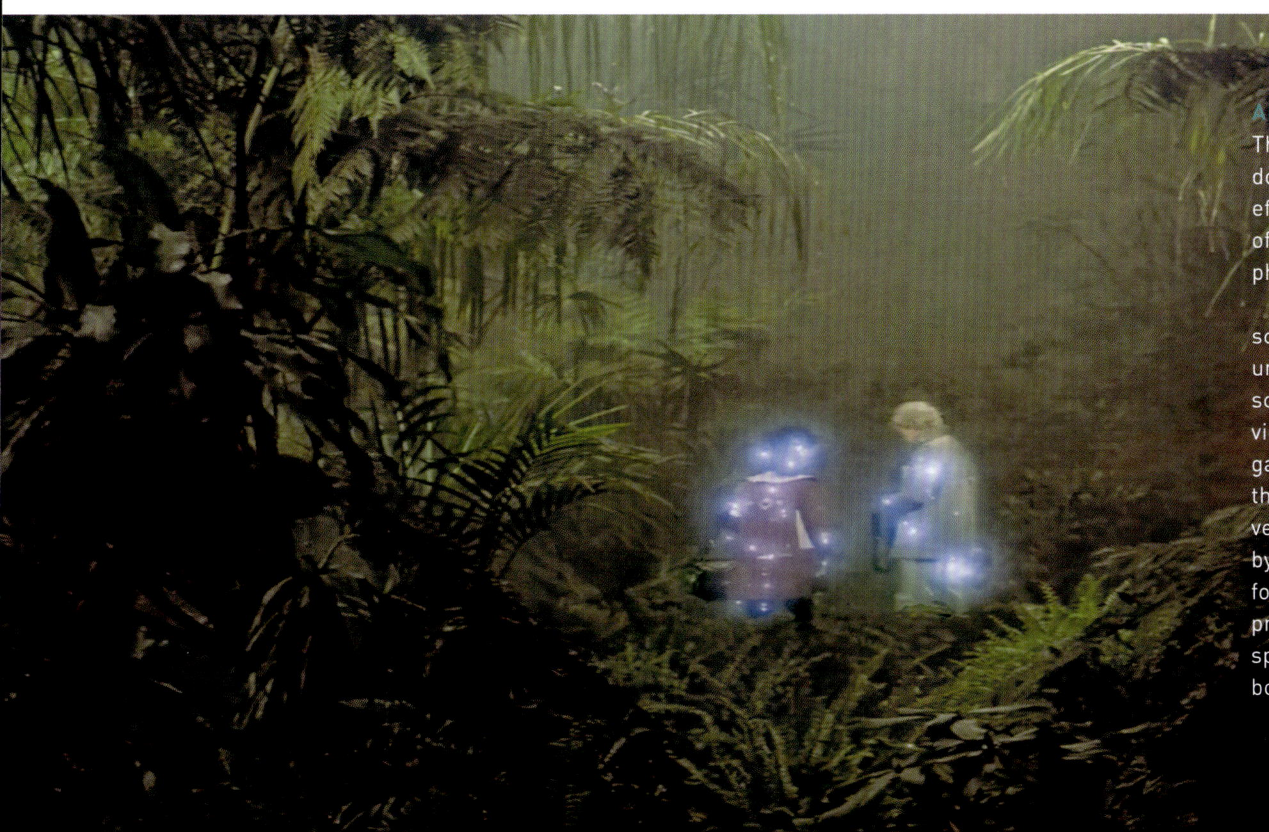

ABOVE AND LEFT:
The first glimpse of Genesis as a paradise occurs when Saavik and David beam down to Sector 1 from the *U.S.S. Grissom*, achieved through a complex composite effect. This effect combines the beam-in sequence with live-action footage of actors Curtis and Butrick filmed at Paramount, along with a Genesis set photographed by Craig Barron at ILM.

Barron explains their unique approach: "Chris and I chose not to use blue screen for the foreground palm trees and ferns. Although it might seem unusual, plants are very reflective, which would have caused issues with blue screen spill for the Optical Department. Instead, we arranged real plants and viewed them directly through the camera. I collaborated with ILM lighting gaffer Pat Fitzsimmons to light the shot, using darker silhouettes of plants in the foreground. This allowed us to see through to the illuminated midground vegetation, which carefully matched the painted backdrop measuring 35 feet wide by 10 feet high and painted by Chris. The size of the backing ensured that the foreground palms appeared to be in proper scale with the background painting. I programmed a pan using motion control, but we actually shot the set at normal speed, introducing subtle wind movement to the plants—many of which were borrowed from various offices at ILM over the Thanksgiving weekend."[1]

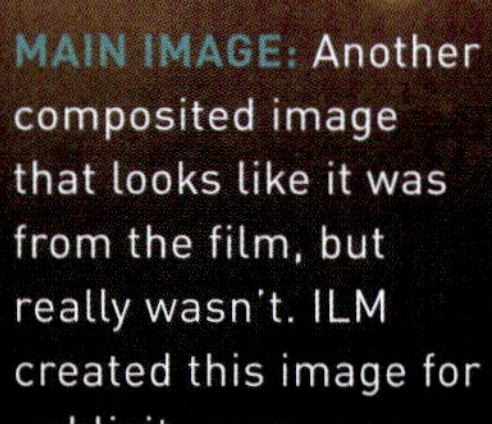

MAIN IMAGE: Another composited image that looks like it was from the film, but really wasn't. ILM created this image for publicity purposes.

of a set smaller in the background and placing actors or extras of shorter stature near those locations. Other times, as with how the art department dealt with the Vulcan temple set and Genesis, parts of the sets or objects were built larger than needed so that when actors were filmed near those, it gave the impression of even more massiveness of scale.

Chilberg's team worked closely with ILM, who created the orbital imagery of Genesis and helped construct scenes of the planet's destruction using a miniature set and visual effects. Additionally, Chilberg coordinated with the stunt department because the set had trap doors, catapults, and specific locations for erupting steam, fire, and rocks which needed to be built into the design. In fact, much of the set was constructed on a kind of scaffolding about sixteen feet above the floor to accommodate technicians working from below to fix and operate those parts where the flames and rocks break through the planet.

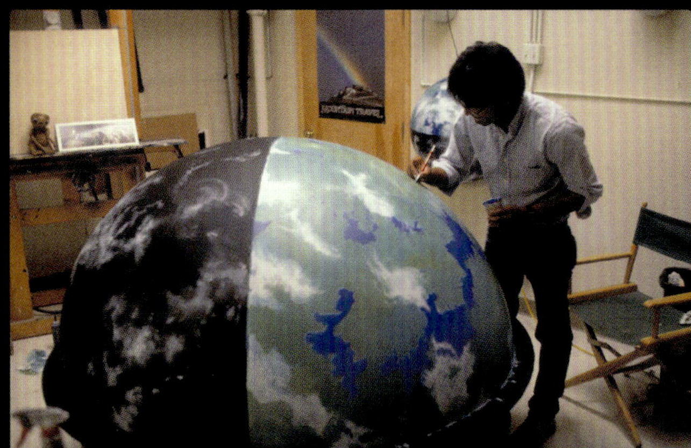

ABOVE: While most matte painting is done on glass, sometimes they are created on other surfaces. Here, matte artist Frank Ordaz puts his spin, literally, on Genesis. Plastic globes, from three to six feet across, would frequently serve as planets. Matte camera supervisor Craig Barron explained, "With these spheres you get that curvature automatically which is more difficult to get with a regular painting. Frank would paint the inside of the plexiglass blue for the ocean, and then paint the white clouds on top."[1]

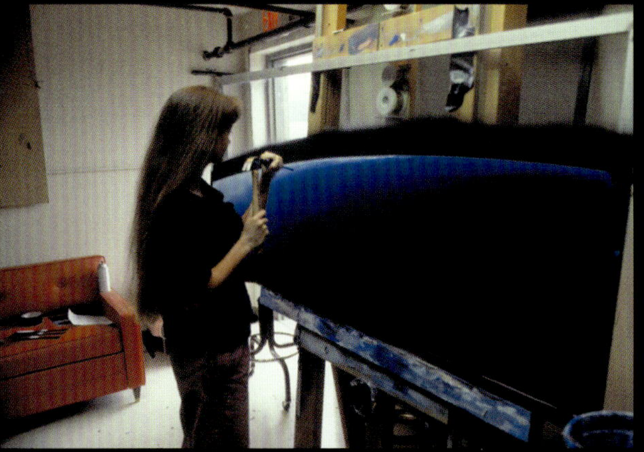

ABOVE: Matte artist Caroleen "Jett" Green was new to ILM around the time of *Star Trek III*. She has since worked on more than fifty films as a matte painter and also on projects as a fine artist. Here, Green is joking around during a break from painting by pretending to break a painting! Matte camera supervisor Craig Barron took this photo. He said, "Sometimes we took zany photos in the department to help us get through the desperation of late nights!"[1]

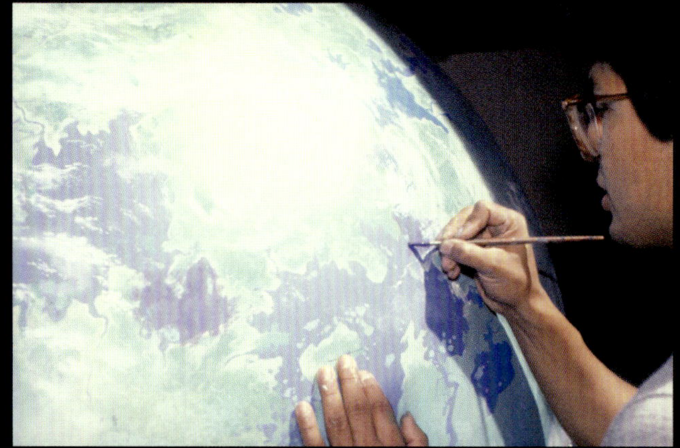

ABOVE: "We also had another idea," Barron shared. "We painted some of the clouds against black. We could first expose the painting slowly rotating as if the planet was rotating, and then we could spin it around and double expose just white clouds over the existing white clouds to make the clouds look like they were moving a little bit. We had to be very subtle with this, because we didn't want the clouds to be moving that fast, it would ruin the scale."[1]

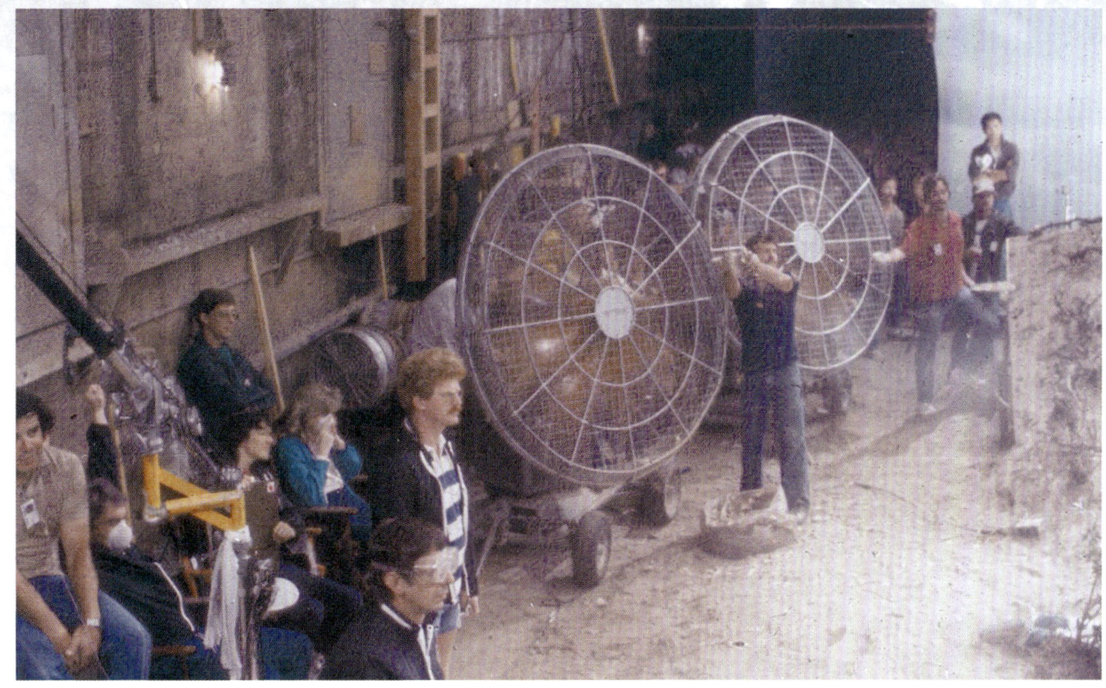

ABOVE: Ritter fans stand ready to create the snow storms on the Genesis set.

To call the Genesis set impressive, as Maltz might, is an archetypal understatement. It was enough to bring out emotion even in Vulcans. Robin Curtis praised the sets, saying, "I was very taken with all of it and very impressed. To be honest, I was just like a little kid, these large cacti laden with snow."[2] Spock actor Vadia Potenza, literally being a little kid, was equally impressed: "The set was amazing, huge and alive. There were bubbling pools and waterfalls. I think there were parts of that set that never even made it on screen. It was stunning. It felt so real to me. The artisans that created that set were amazing people."[3] Potenza was so taken with Genesis that when asked by a producer if he wanted to see the other sets, he immediately said yes, getting to see the *Enterprise* bridge redressed as the *U.S.S. Grissom*. Fellow Spock actor Stephen Manley remembered, "There were real and plastic plants. It smelled an awful lot like potting soil and gravel. They had giant canvases and they built a hillside, which is not easy and takes a great deal of expertise. There was a big, tropical portion of the set and a snowy area where Carl Steven filmed his scenes as Spock. There was a waterfall, but it was not running when I was there. The Genesis set reminded me of the original

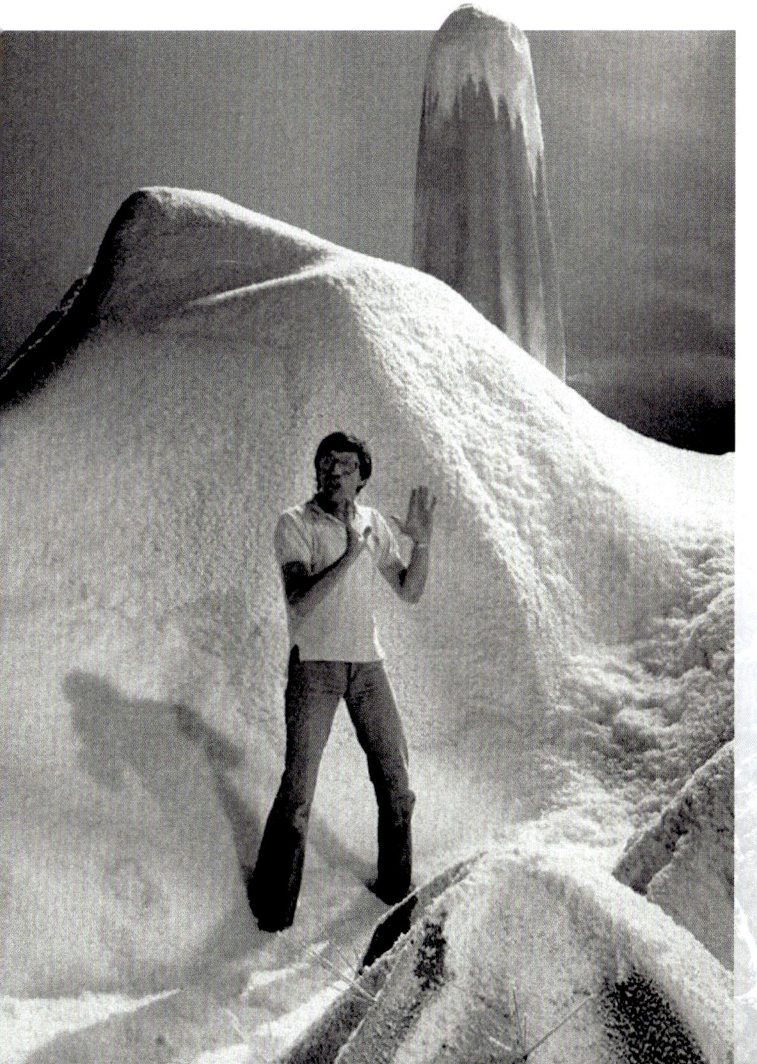

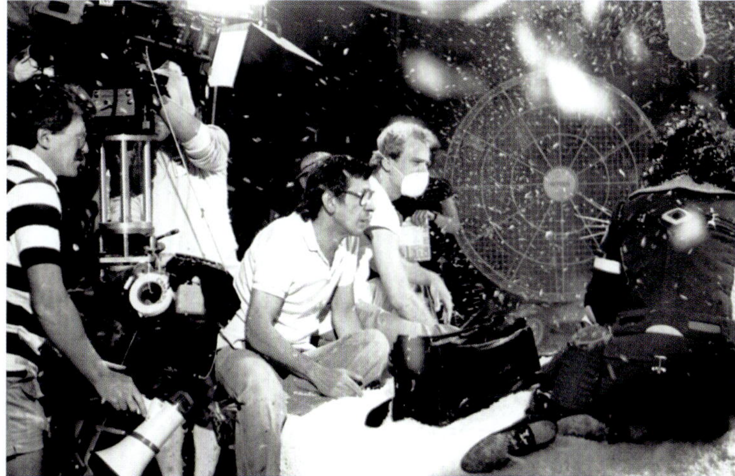

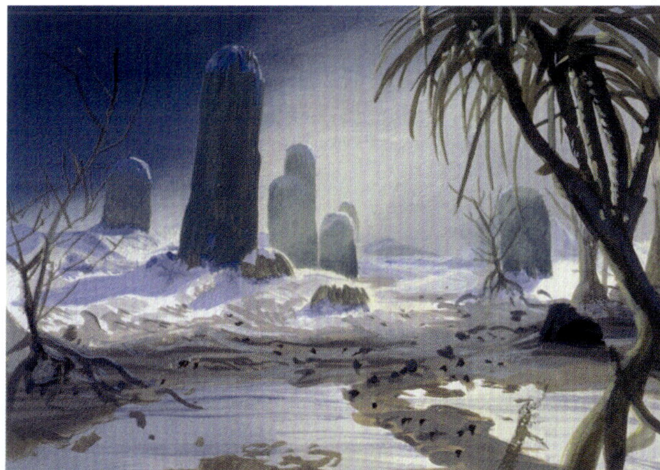

LEFT: By oversizing the cacti, Chilberg gave Gensis scale. Here, Nimoy directs, surrounded by fake cacti and plastic snow.

ABOVE MIDDLE: "The problems I had on *Star Trek III* were basically those of allergies," Merritt Butrick shared. "I've never, to date, done a job that had so many non-real situations. We had fake snow, fake wind, fake dust, fake fire – everything I happen to be allergic to they ended up using on a close soundstage. Originally, in *Star Trek III*, there was a eulogy for David; on the planet Bill would lean down and give this quick speech. I remember sneezing while they were doing this because I couldn't lie there dead with them blowing a huge fan in my face with dust. I was also allergic to the snow. It made my eyes water."[4]

ABOVE RIGHT: A production painting by ILM's matte department was instrumental in helping Nimoy visualize the strange world of Genesis where artic and desert features co-exist.

ABOVE: Ralston supervises the Genesis lava flow which was created using lighting effects under plexiglass and a mixture of charcoal, methacyl, and vermiculite dripping on the surface.

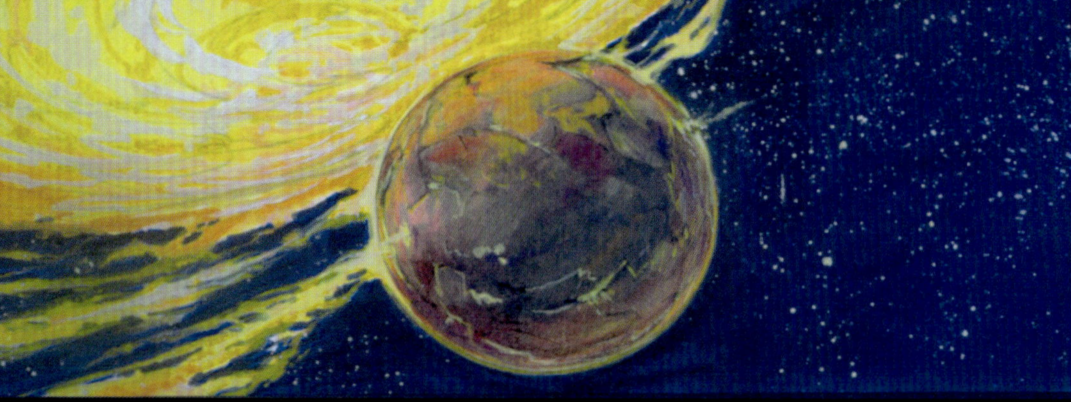

ABOVE: The original idea for the destruction of Genesis was to have the planet move out of its orbit and collide with its sun. The idea was abandoned due to budget and time limitations. Art by Rodis illustrates the beginning of Genesis' end.

show sets, because many scenes of the alien planets were filmed on a sound stage then."[5]

The budget and technology at the time did, however, limit set construction, including Genesis and the bridge of the Bird-of-Prey. Nimoy explained, "We were on a very, very limited budget on *Star Trek III*. The studio belief was 'The third in a series of films will do 25 percent less business than the second in the series.' That's the mythos of studio accounting. I was quite convinced that that would not be the case, and it turned out not to be. But that was the formula that they were projecting and therefore the budget was extremely tight, but we managed."[6] Nimoy spoke about the confining atmosphere that the sets sometime took, even sets as large as Genesis. "The foliage exterior of the planet where we find Spock's tube was extremely limited," he mentioned.[6]

ILM's Kenneth Ralston was dissatisfied with some of the Genesis sequences. The scene where the cliff underneath Kruge breaks from the mountain was disappointing to Ralston, and to Nimoy, because the seam where the break occurs is visible. "We had to hide the practical set effect with flames. The transition is so obvious," Ralston said. Additionally, "There was a camera problem when they filmed Bill Shatner holding Leonard when they are supposed to escape the planet. What I think happened was the film was going through the gate at high speed, but it wasn't quite registering perfectly. The footage was shaking. We had to do our best to make it all blend together using that piece of film because they obviously could not refilm that again as the sets were gone."[7] However, Ralston tried to keep these kinds of disappointments in perspective, even though they are vexations. The lessons he learned from George Lucas about what the audience can and can't see was a help. Ralston explained, "We can waste too much time noodling stuff, which happens a lot now with digital effects. I think there might possibly be some valuable lessons lost in how we learned to make an effect work without taking months to get it done when we could do it in a week. You know where to put that detail and where not to, and it really is good to get the money where your eye is really going to take it in."[7]

BELOW: Ralston was never totally satisfied by these moments. The second image is an early composite test not used in the final film.

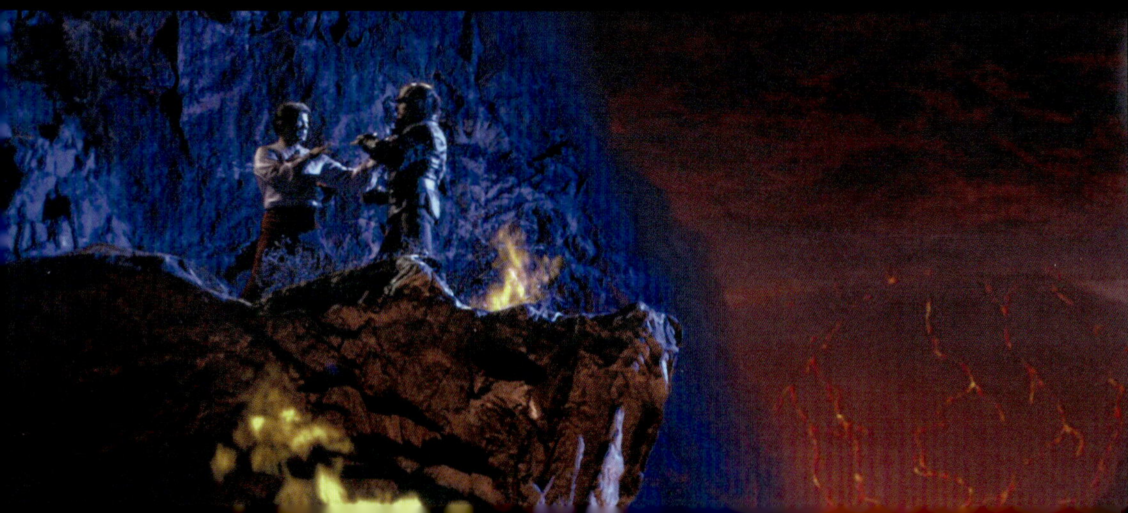

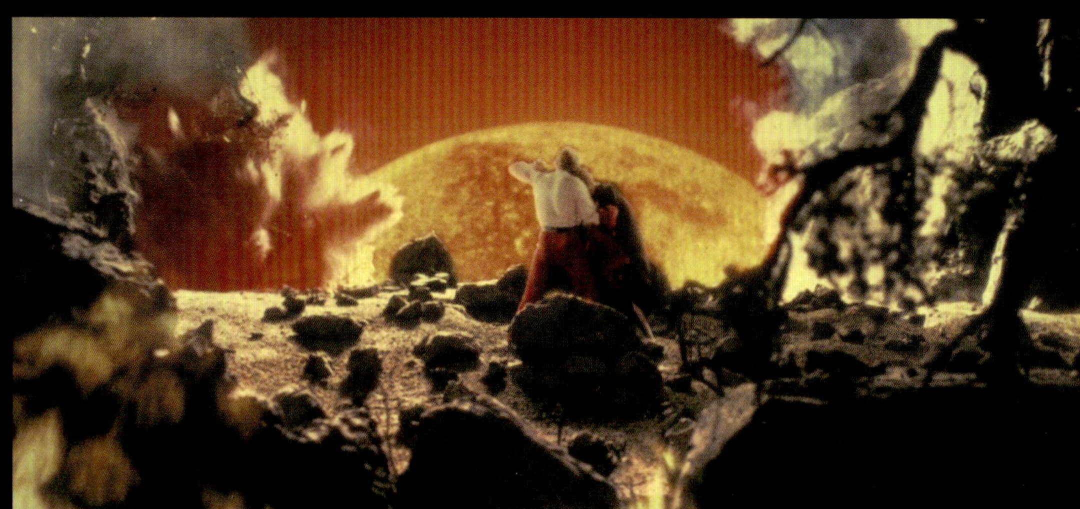

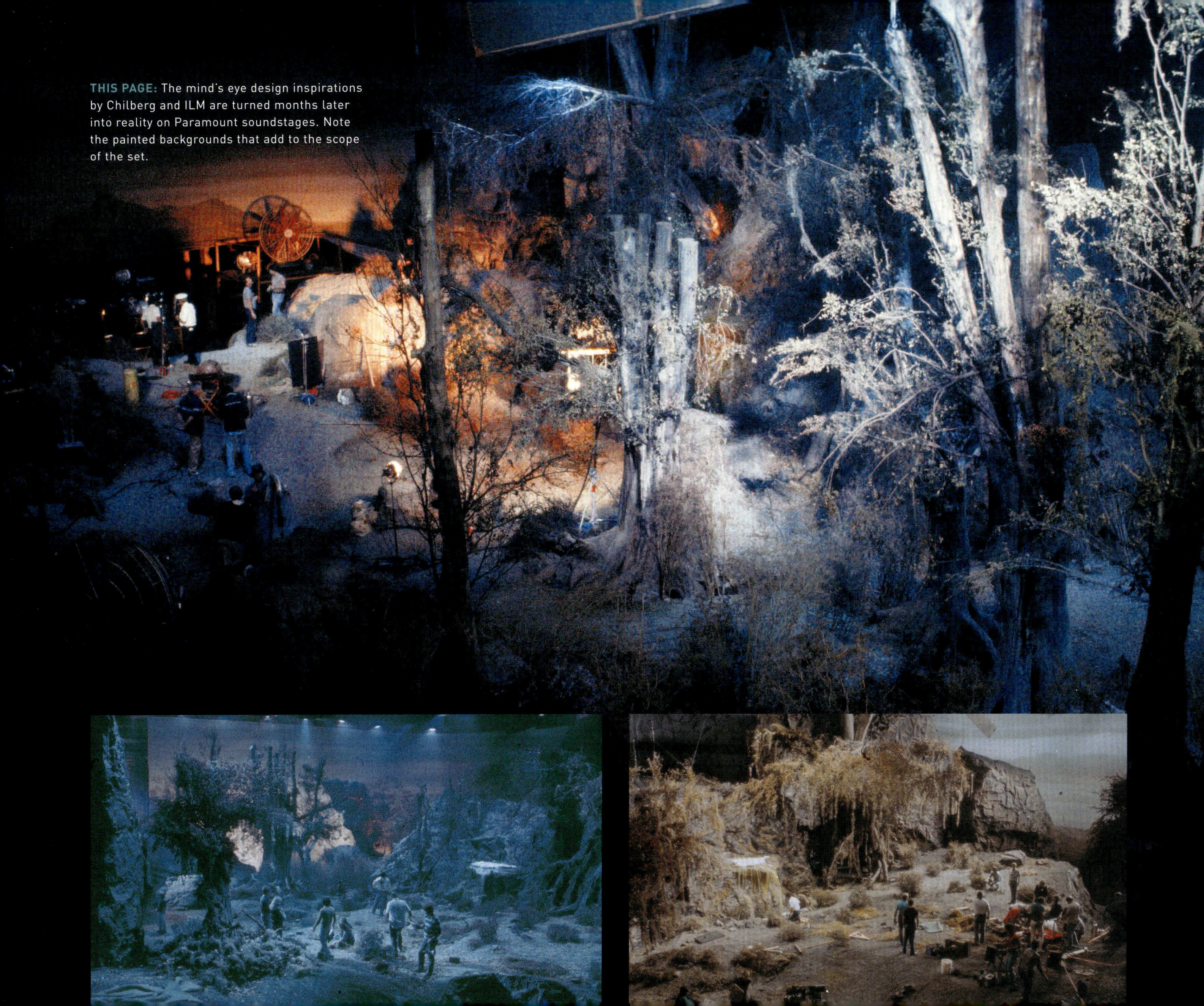

THIS PAGE: The mind's eye design inspirations by Chilberg and ILM are turned months later into reality on Paramount soundstages. Note the painted backgrounds that add to the scope of the set.

Star Trek creatives, however, knew how to turn limitations into strengths. An example is the Bird-of-Prey scenes as it orbits Genesis. To save money, a set from another movie was redressed to double as the Klingon bridge. Nimoy wrote, "...it achieved a certain kind of claustrophobia, which added some element of menace to the whole Klingon notion. I got in tighter and tighter as I went along with the camera. There are some moments where I'm in their noses, particularly in Christopher Lloyd's case. And the fact that he was elevated above them in the way he was gave him a certain amount of ominous power. I tried to make use of it to the best of my ability."[6]

Adding to the challenge of set design and decoration was the ever-changing nature of Genesis as environmental extremes and climate juxtapositions increased as the film progressed. Linguist Marc Okrand revealed an unusual filming requirement caused by the story. "Normally when they make a movie, they film all the scenes that take place in the same location back-to-back regardless of where they come in the film because it is more efficient. But for the Genesis planet, they had to film them in story order because the Genesis planet was falling apart. Once they got a take they liked, everything would pause, they would take the Genesis planet apart a little more, then film the next scene."[8]

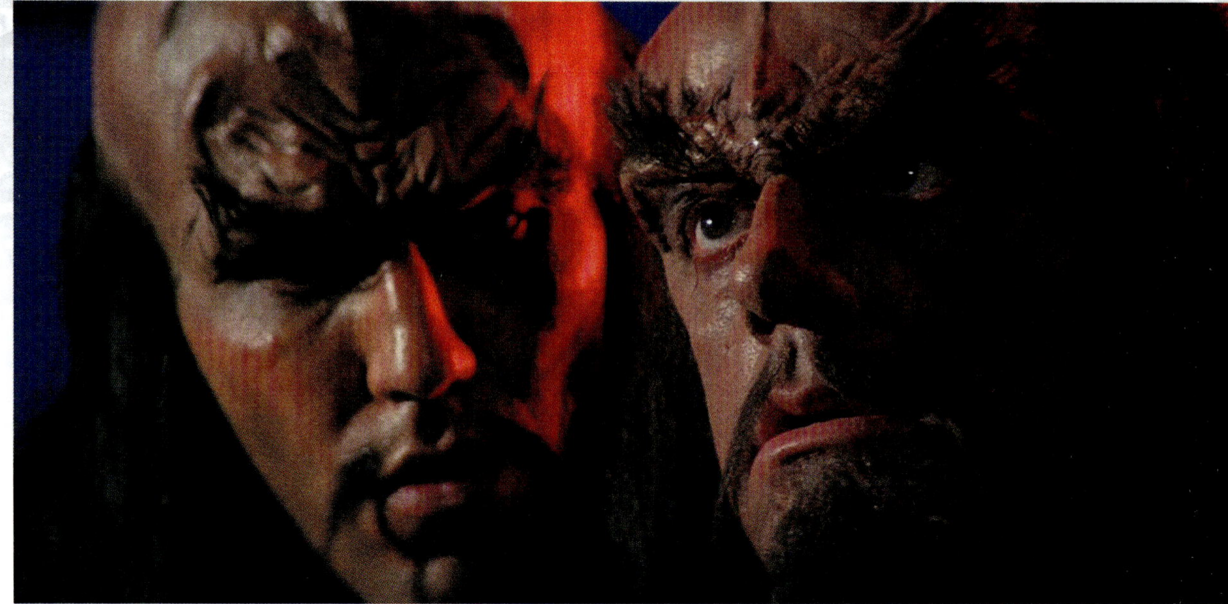

ABOVE: Stephen Liska, who played Torg, described, "The Klingon bridge set was claustrophobic. Christopher Lloyd and I were in a scene where Kruge is looking out and says, 'We are Klingons!' He is getting angry. I am standing behind him. He raises his fist which has spikes on his glove knuckles and he is very close to my face. If you watch the scene, you can see me flinch because it was that close. I thought we were going to have to do another take, but it worked out fine. I didn't realize how tight that set was going to be."[9]

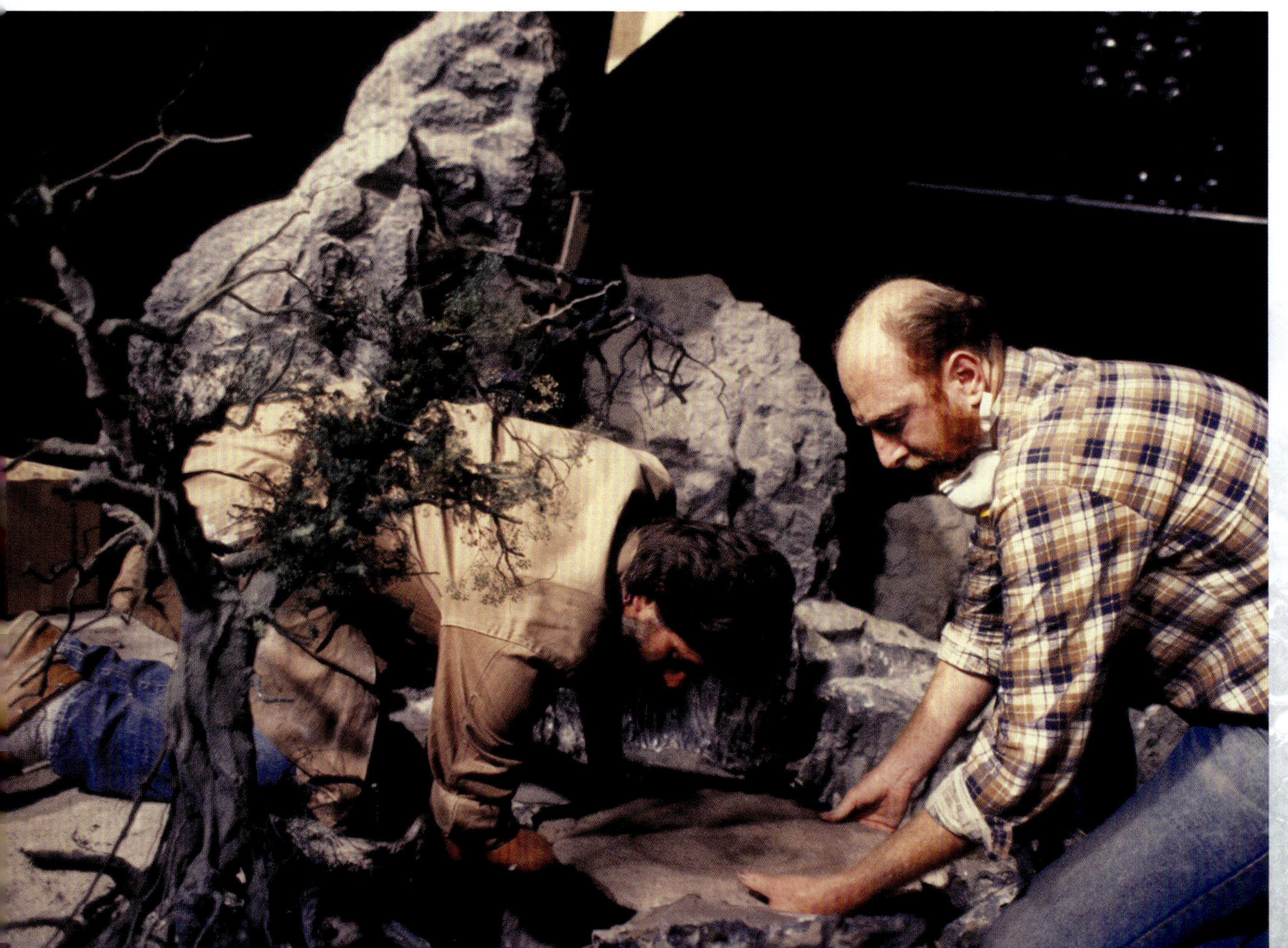

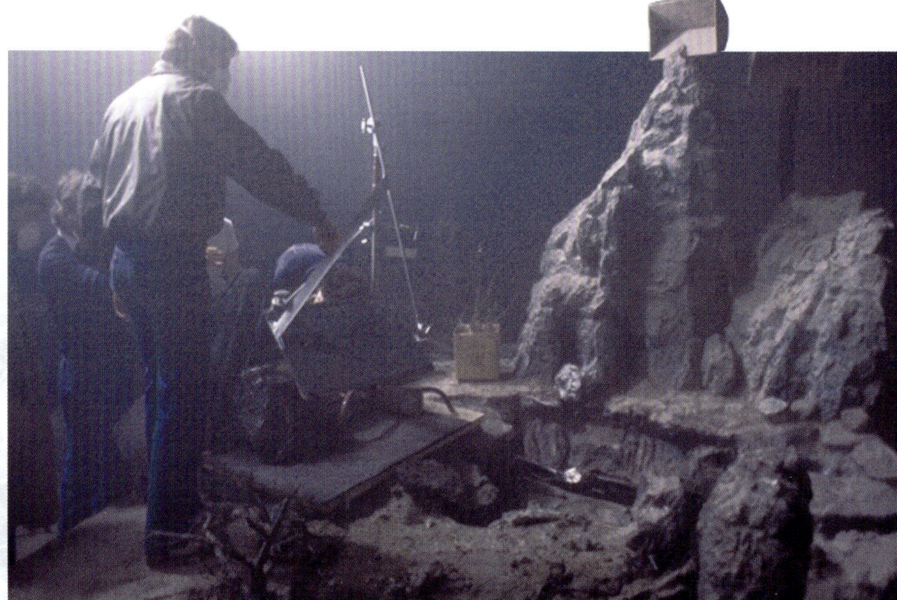

ABOVE AND LEFT: As Genesis decays, the special effects artists would film the destruction in miniature, which would be edited in later with practical, in-camera footage taken on set at Paramount. By changing the frame rate that such miniatures were filmed at, an illusion of reality and scale is created. The miniature set was created under the auspices of ILM stage supervisors Patrick Fitzsimmons and Ted Moehnke.

PON FARR

Nimoy felt very strongly that Saavik helping Spock through his tremulous pon farr experience was important to the story and to fans because it further explored Vulcan culture. And, thinking of the future, it created a possibility; Saavik could have a child as a result of their shared experience, something that would be scripted for the next film. However, some Paramount executives, like Jeffrey Katzenberg, had concerns about the scene, thinking the audience might laugh. Nimoy and Bennett bet Katzenberg $1 each that the scene would work, agreeing to let test audience reaction of the scene determine the winner.

The pon farr scenes were filmed during early October, 1983. Nimoy had been thinking about the scene from his earliest days on the project. Manley remembered Nimoy telling him, "About the pon farr sequence, the TV show took it to a certain stage and then it stopped. I want to continue it and show more in the film. I don't know what I am going to do with it yet. We'll figure it out. But I want you to know, this is important to the fans." On the day of filming, Nimoy asked for a thirty-minute break so that he, Manley, and Curtis could rehearse. "He brought our fingers up as they did during the TV show," Manley said, "I thought, 'Hey, what if I, by gut reaction, respond to what Robin was doing by kind of grabbing her hand.' Leonard liked that idea and it was included in the film."[5]

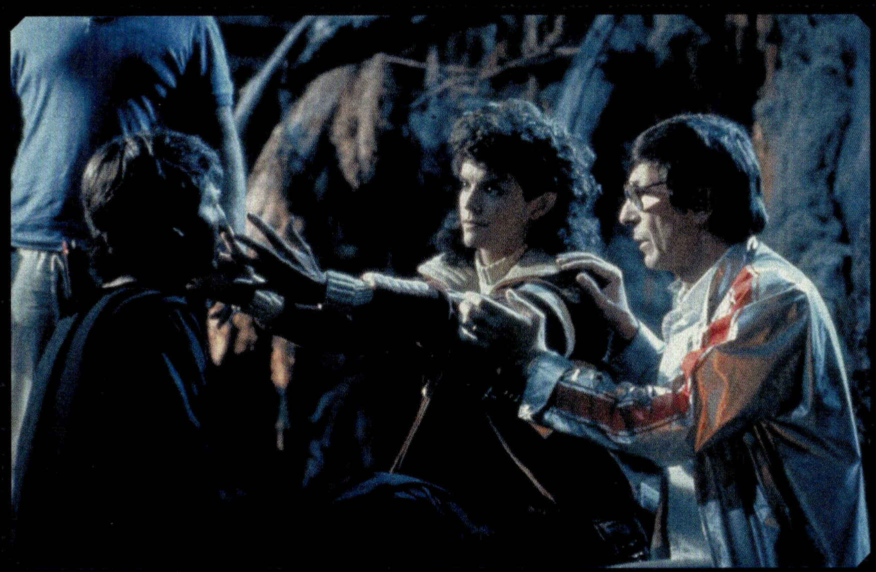

For Curtis, playing a Vulcan was, ironically, an emotional experience because containing herself as an actor was antithetical to both her training and her energetic and empathetic personality. "The meter of speech in the world of *Star Trek* is very specific," explained Curtis. "A Vulcan wouldn't stammer or stutter in search of a word. Conversationally, the dialogue does not overlap as it might elsewhere. In a sense, the restraints on my emotions and manner of expression tended to make me feel straightjacketed. That said, I loved speaking the Vulcan language. Mark Okrand created beautiful sounds and pronouncing the words he composed was such a pleasure. I say composed because I heard his words musically."[2]

The pon farr scene and the moment she informs Kirk of David's death were two of her most challenging scenes. Luckily for Curtis, she had Nimoy to guide her. "I was pretty insecure because the Vulcan demeanor just did not come naturally to me at all! I said to Leonard the first day on set, 'Mr. Nimoy, you seem to think I know what I'm doing but I do not!' And he reassured me, 'Robin, I will take you every step of the way. I will never leave you dangling out on a limb' And he kept his promise. Leonard's sensitive direction allowed me to go as close to the emotional edge without going over. Before every scene, he'd invite me to sit with him in a quiet corner of the sound stage and he'd say, 'Okay, let me hear it.' I'd recite the lines for him and he would modulate my delivery as if he had his hand on the dials of an equalizer for a stereo. He had this way of almost tricking me into the pocket of the moment. And being the person who created the Vulcan mystique, he had my complete trust. Such a gifted director."[2]

When the pon farr scene was finished and it proved successful, Katzenberg made good on his bet. In his book *I Am Spock*, Nimoy shared, "I don't know where Harve keeps his dollar, but mine is hanging on my office wall. It's signed and framed, above a small brass plaque that reads 'I bet the Pon Farr scene gets a laugh. Jeff Katzenberg, April '84.'"[10] According to Adam Nimoy, his father had great affection for Katzenberg, who always made certain that whatever budgetary or other problems occurred, the *Star Trek* production was given what was needed. Nimoy shared, "The other story my father liked to tell about Jeffrey was that whenever Dad would show up early to the lot for work, he would see Katzenberg's car already in the parking lot and would go over to touch the hood. The engine would be cold indicating that Jeff had already been there for some time."[11]

FRUITFUL MICROBES

Described by Bennett's script as "worm-like forms...they are small, horrible, and unquestionably alive," the evolving microbes that accompanied Spock's casket from the *Enterprise* would play an important role in the film, from the McGuffin that brings David and Saavik to the Genesis surface, to serving as an illustration of Kruge's brute strength. Designed by ILM, the microbes in their second-stage evolution were puppeteered by Ralston.

BELOW RIGHT: © Industrial Light & Magic. All Rights Reserved. Ralston operated the second-stage evolved microbe that attacks Kruge, both at Paramount in Los Angeles and for ILM closeups in Marin County. John Reed was responsible for helping to create the second-stage microbes. The other evolved microbes employed a complicated pneumatical system devised by Sosalla.

BELOW MIDDLE: © Industrial Light & Magic. All Rights Reserved. At ILM, visual effects cameraman Don Dow stands-in for Lloyd wearing full Klingon outfit sans the makeup to film the moment when Kruge crushes the microbe.

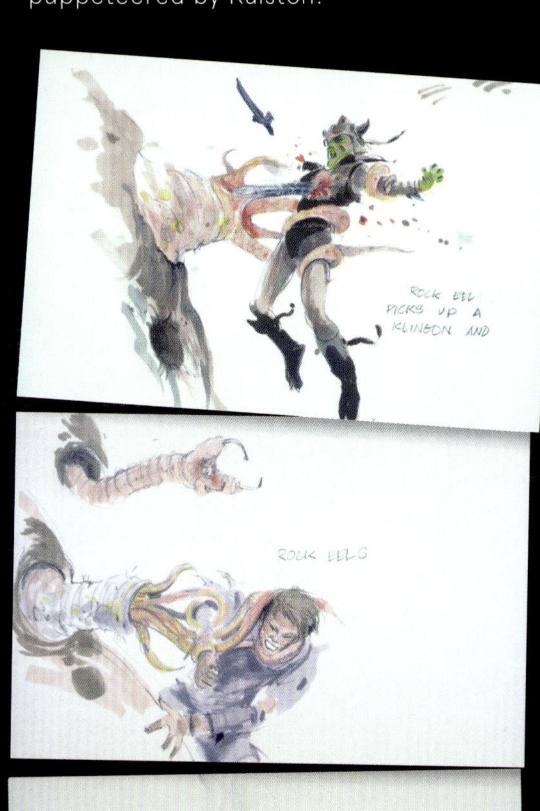

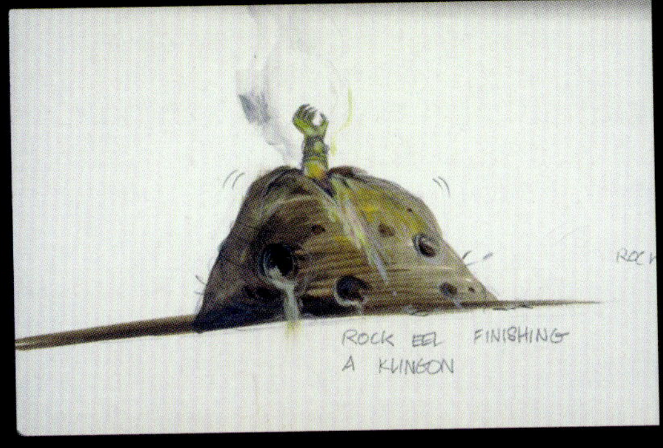

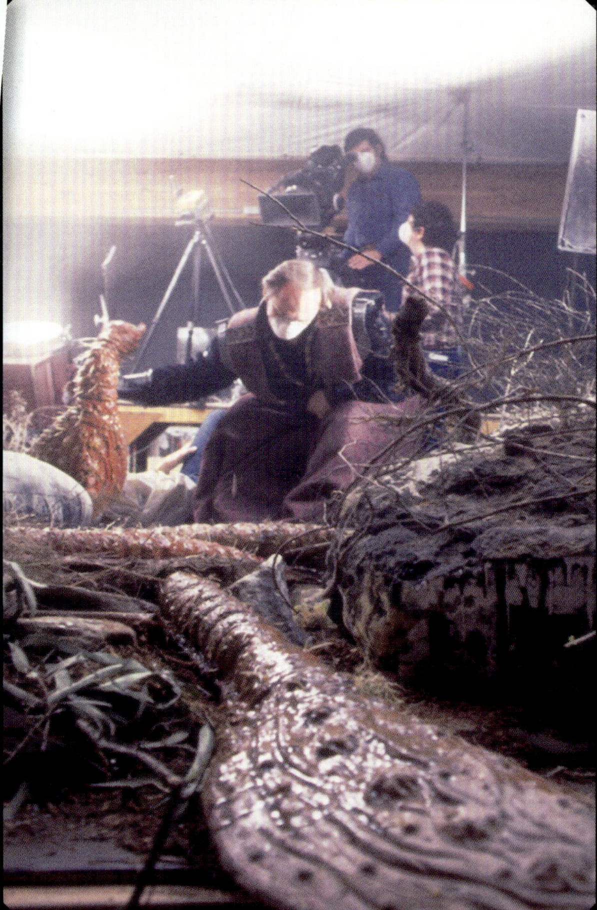

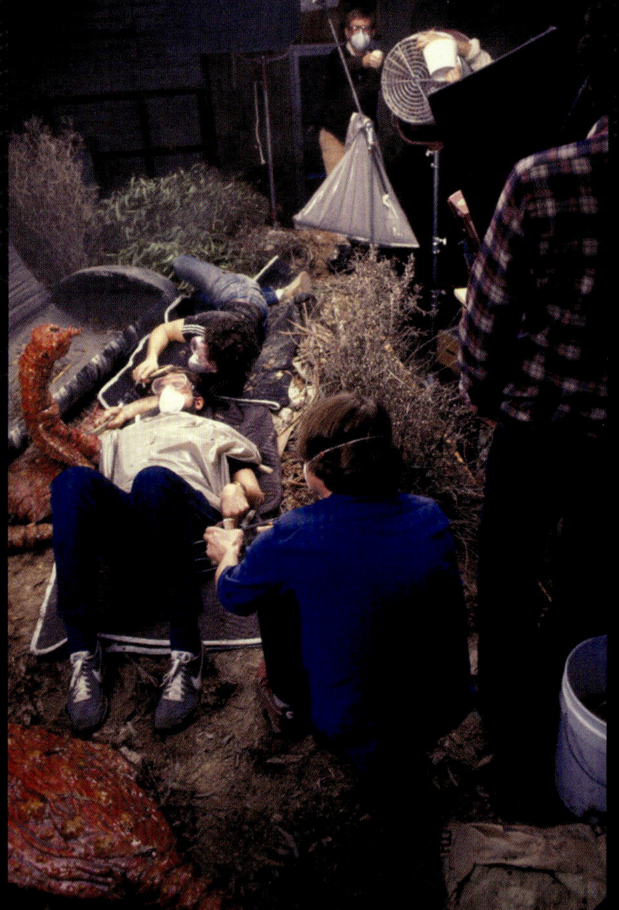

LEFT: ILM art director Nilo Rodis conjures early designs for a rock eel, which will eventually transform into the giant microbe idea.

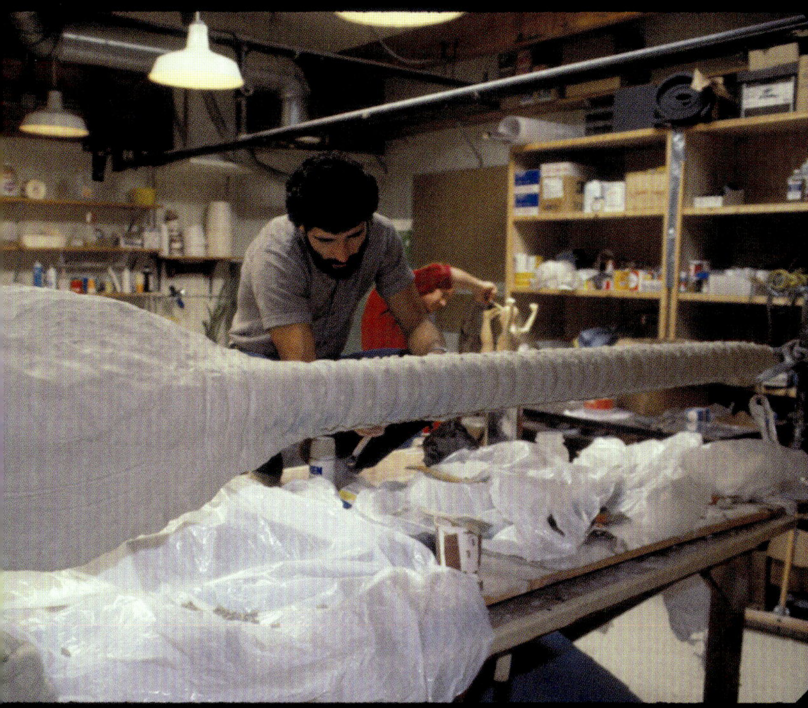

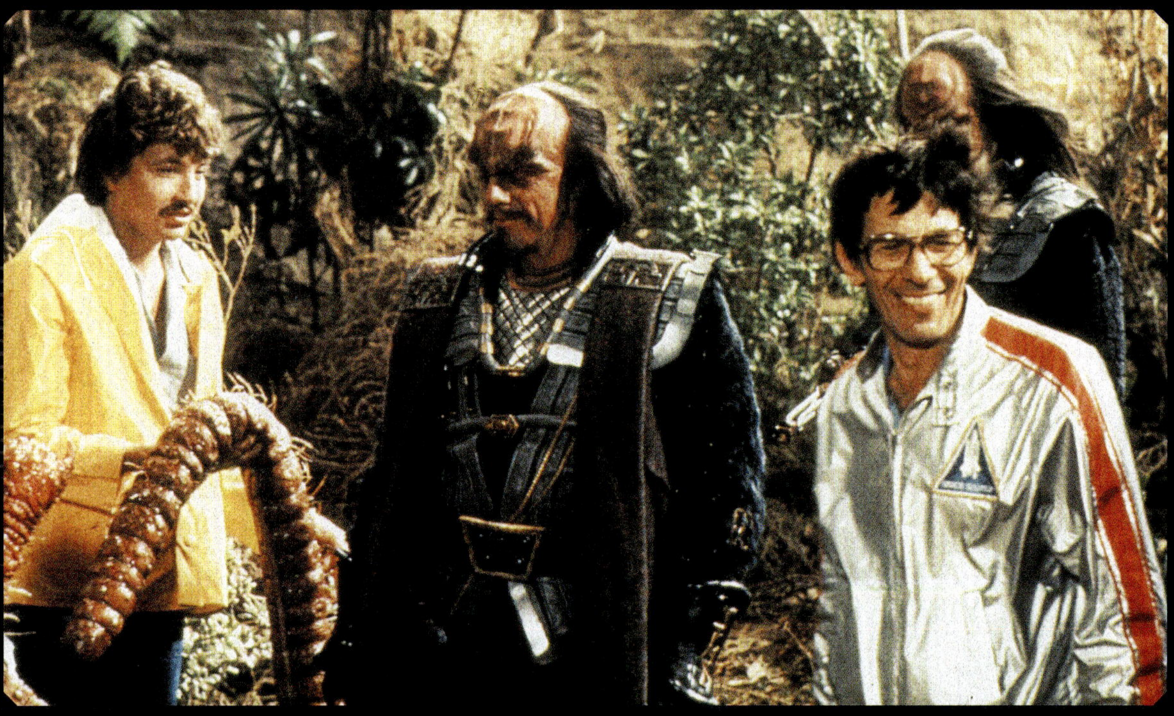

ABOVE: Sculpting work continues on the second-stage evolved microbes which were eight to ten feet in length. Space needed to be left near the mouth of the microbes to permit articulation and movement for added realism.

ABOVE: "What I remember the most about the microbes is Chris Lloyd just crushing my arm, holding that thing on one of the takes. He is a very strong guy," remembered Ralston. "I just like being around him. I have a nice memory of *Star Trek III* on the Genesis set. I was sitting on a tree log with Chris, talking. Not about anything that had to do with the movie. We talked about what was going on with each other and some of his adventures. He is in full costume and makeup. I wish someone had got a photo of that!"[7]

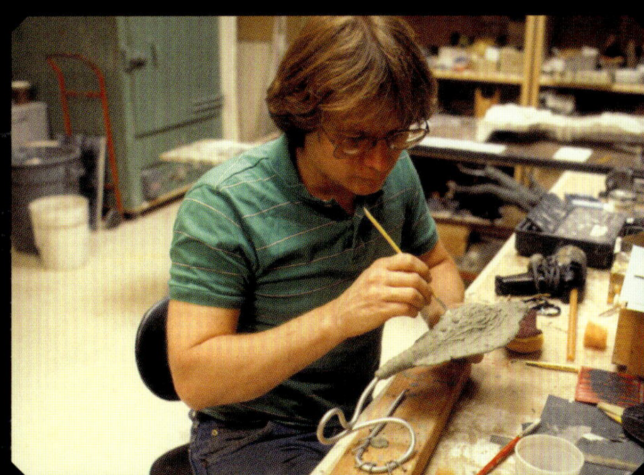

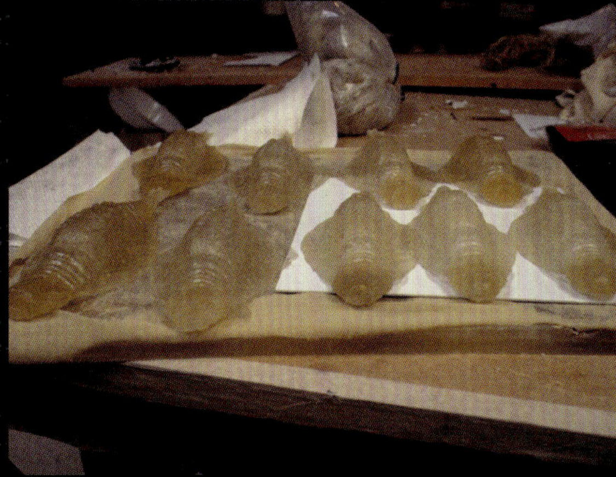

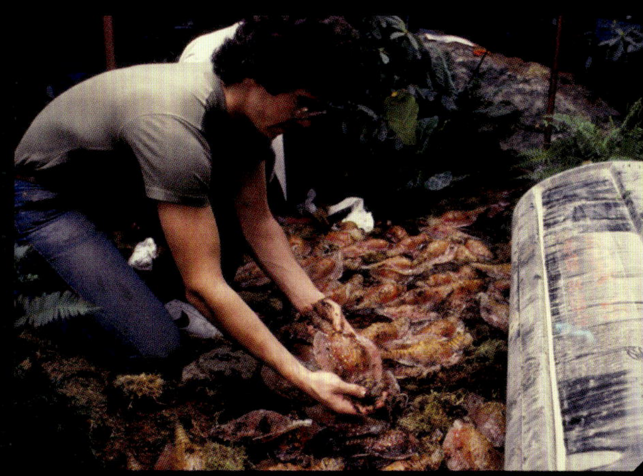

ABOVE: Creature supervisor David Sosalla sculpts a first-stage evolved microbe at ILM's creature shop.

ABOVE: The rubbery translucent first-stage evolved microbes before painting.

ABOVE: Strings and air-bladders would help the first-stage microbes convincingly "shimmy and squirm" as Bennett's script directed.

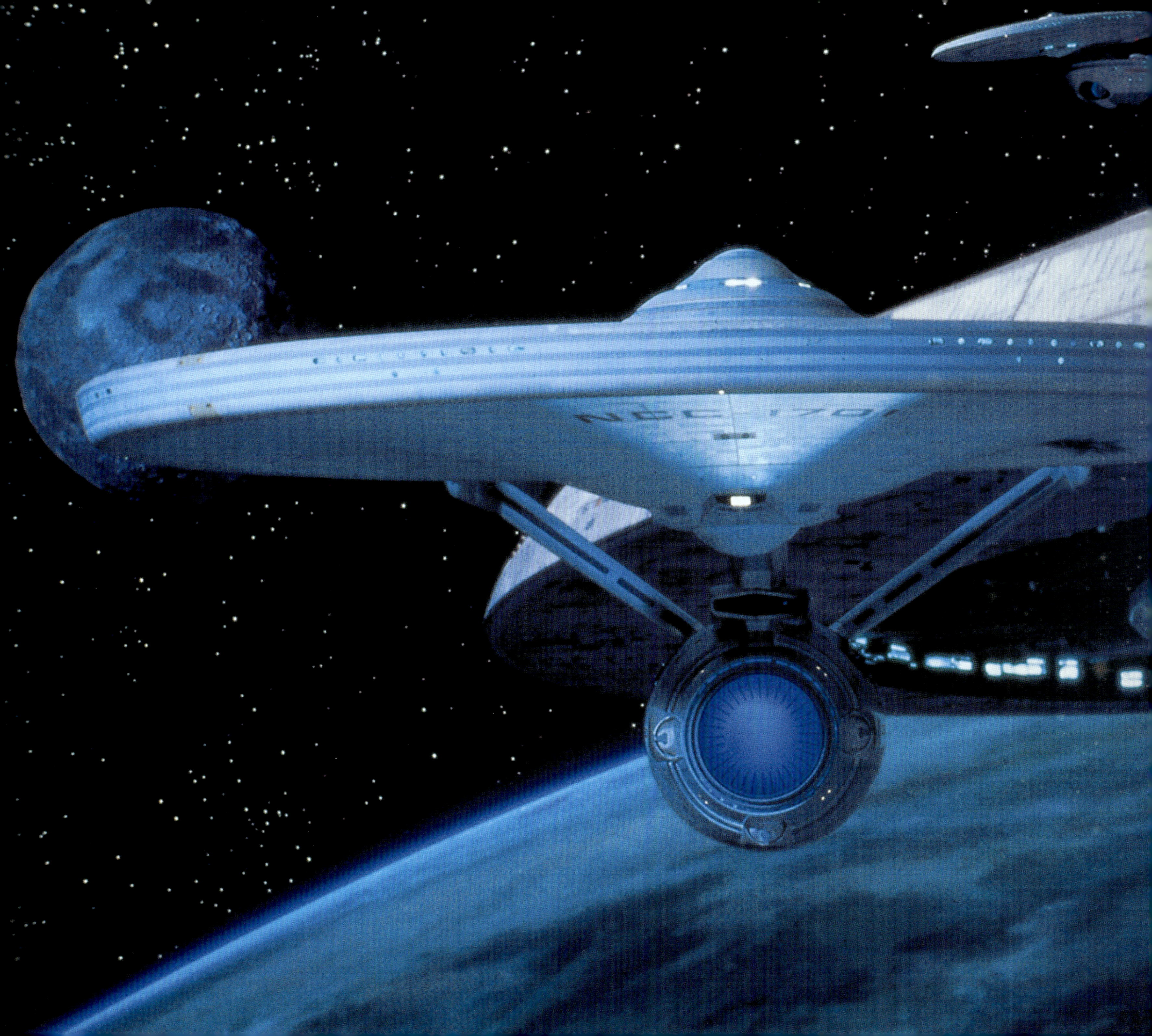

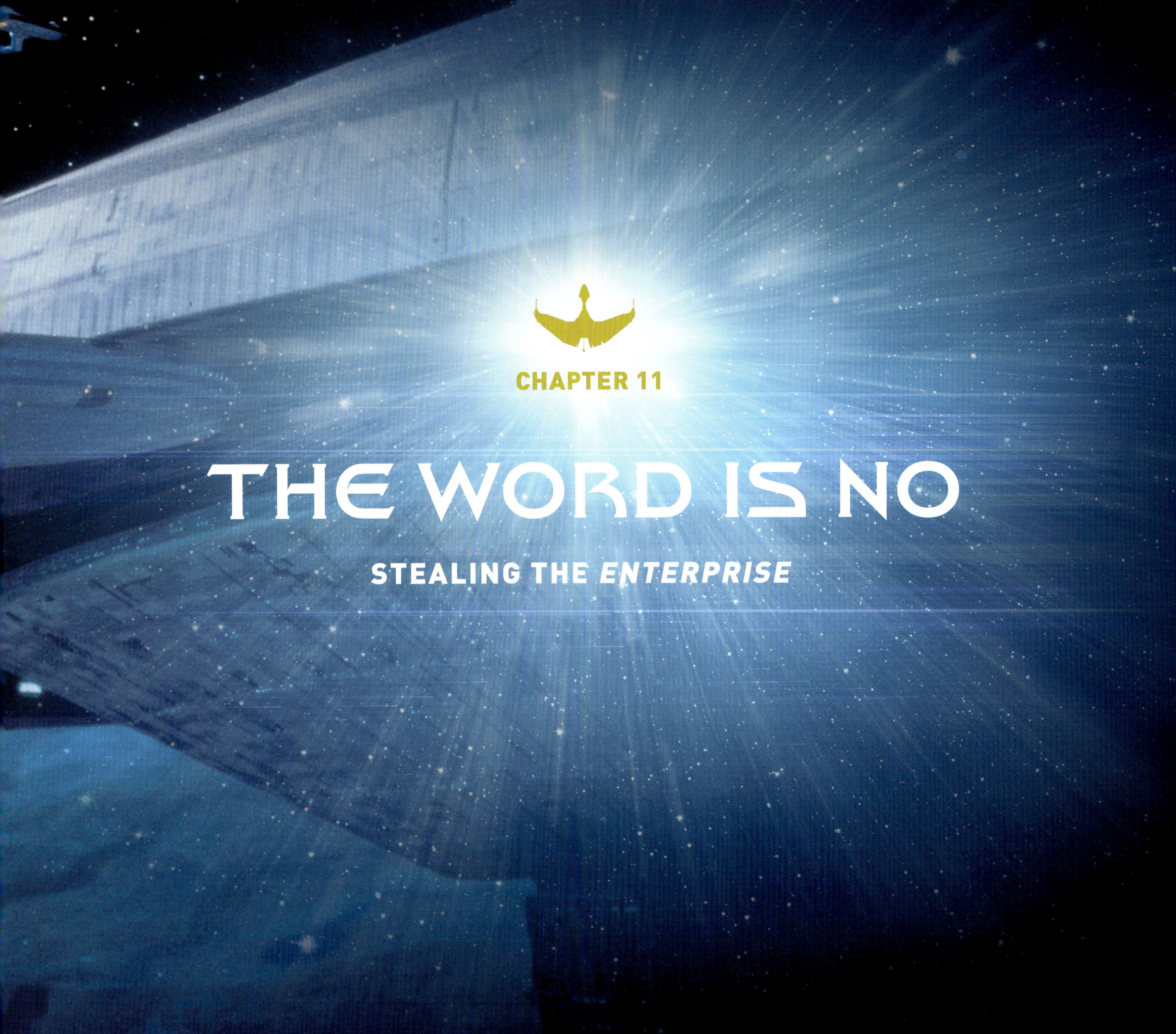

CHAPTER 11

THE WORD IS NO

STEALING THE *ENTERPRISE*

Harve Bennett believed *Star Trek III* to be part space opera and part heist picture. The breakout of McCoy and theft of the *Enterprise* are some of the movie's big set-pieces and, like much of the film, were created as a result of the collaboration between Paramount and ILM.

THIS PAGE: The left image is the spacedock without any ships, while the right is an unused test composite from ILM. The bottom image is of the spacedock as it appears in the film. The ship barely visible near the shuttle is a cameo, meant as a homage to famed *Star Wars* illustrator Ralph McQuarrie. It is the *Enterprise II* study model which McQuarrie designed for Gene Roddenberry's 1976 *Star Trek: Planet of the Titans* movie that was never made.

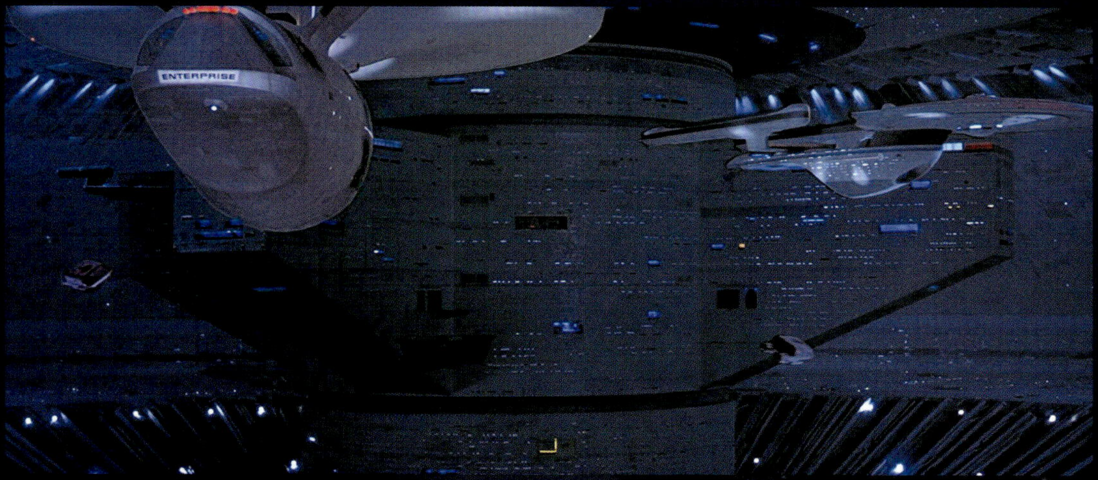

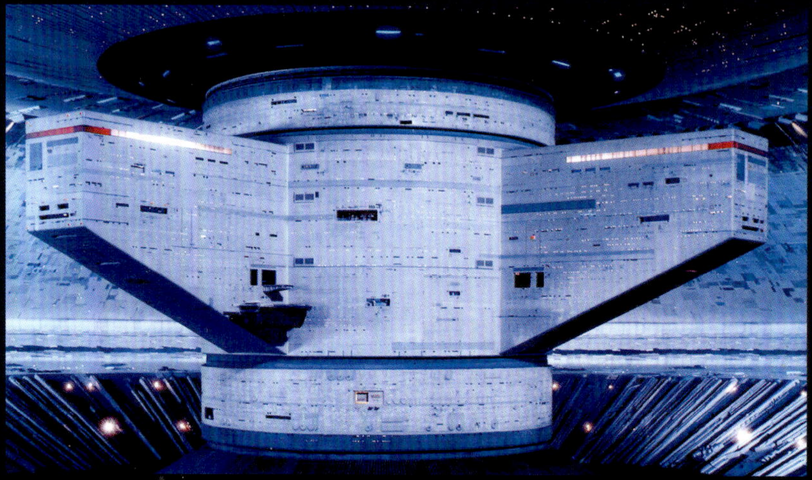

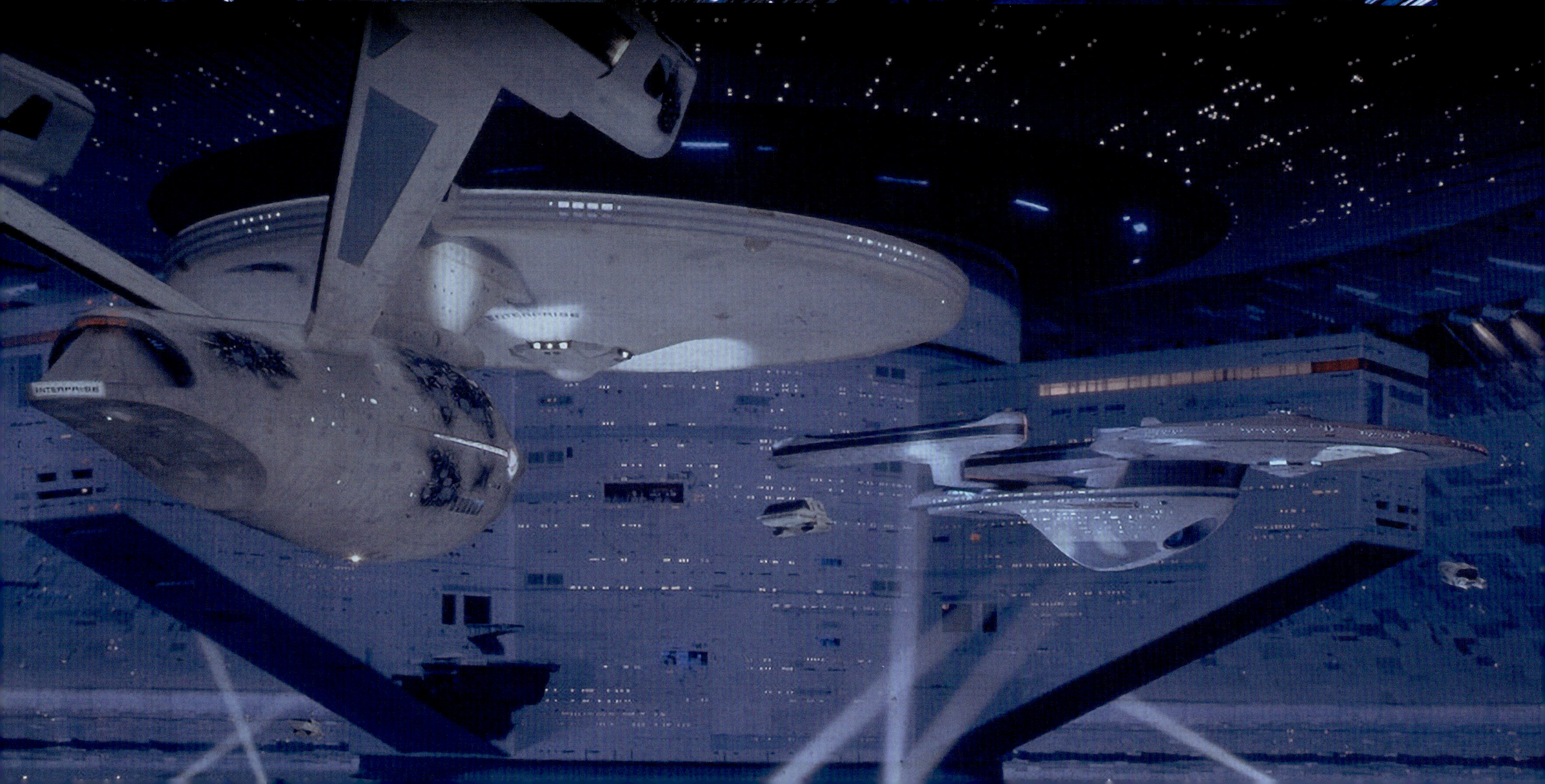

SPACEDOCK

Working from the December 1982 outline by Bennett, the ILM art department went to work imagining new starships and the spacedock. Suggestions by the art department would result in several of the most memorable elements that comprise the escape and theft sequences. ILM Art Directors Nilo Rodis and David Carson were instrumental in this process, as were model makers and visual effects artists. The initial presumption was that the spacedock would be the same as the kind seen in the previous two films. However, Carson was inspired to rethink the concept, wondering what would happen if instead of a dry dock, it was more like an airplane hanger which starships could go into. The space doors that Carson envisioned inspired Bennett to create one of the most exciting moments of the film as Scotty tries desperately, and successfully, to open the "barn door after the horse has come home."

THIS PAGE: Carson's evolving spacedock from sketches to painting.

BOTTOM RIGHT: A composite shot made for publicity purposes showcases a much more vibrant moon than seen in the actual film.

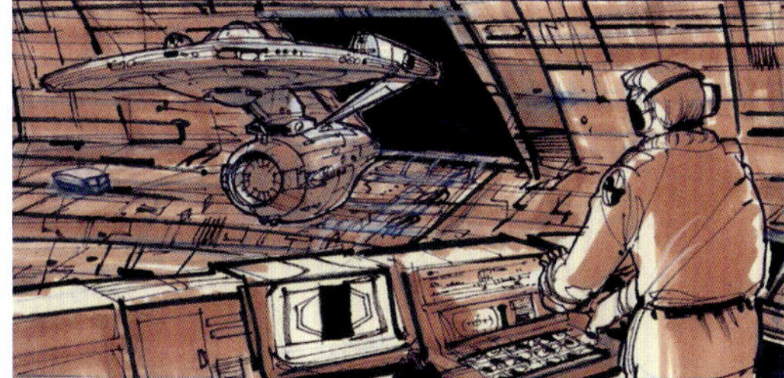

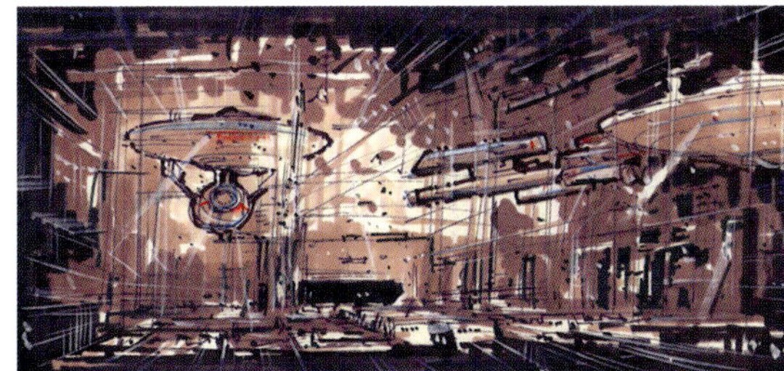

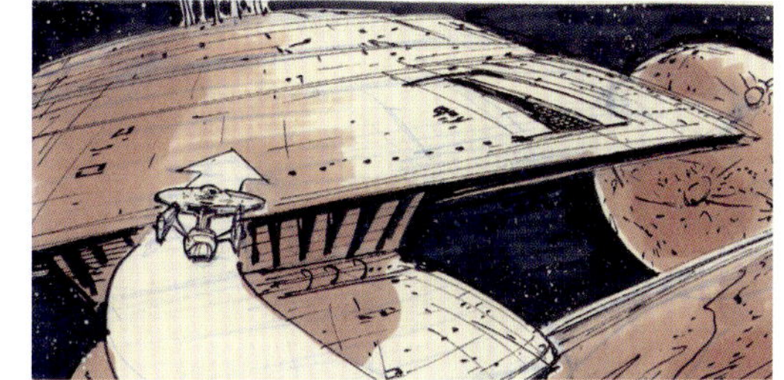

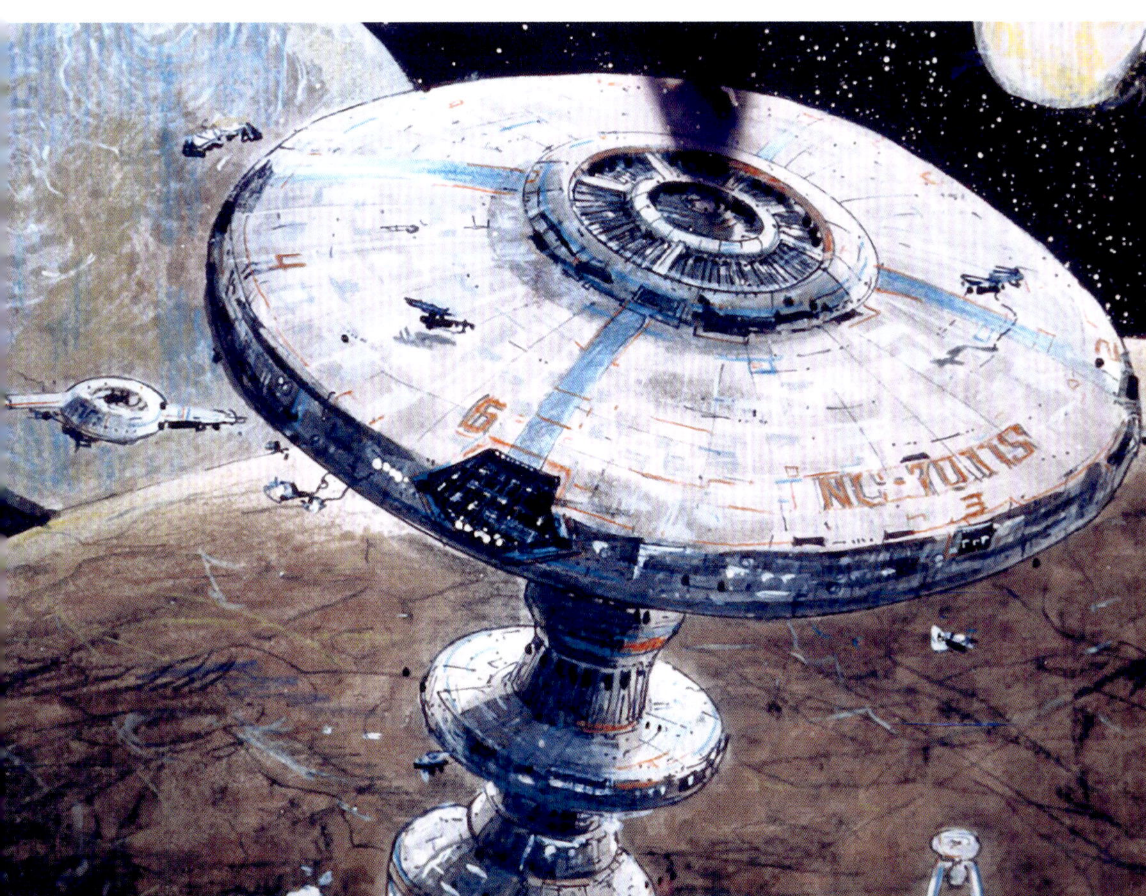

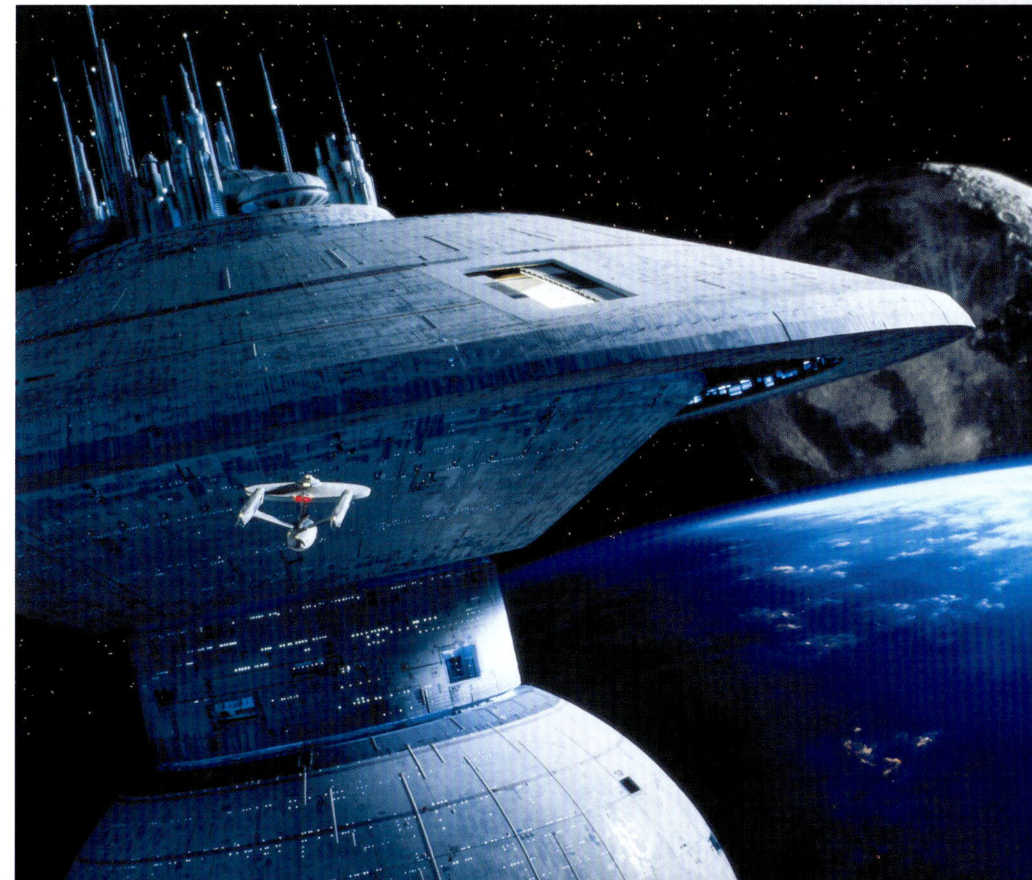

FLIGHT RECORDER VISUAL:

DAVID CARSON, ILM VISUAL EFFECTS ART DIRECTOR

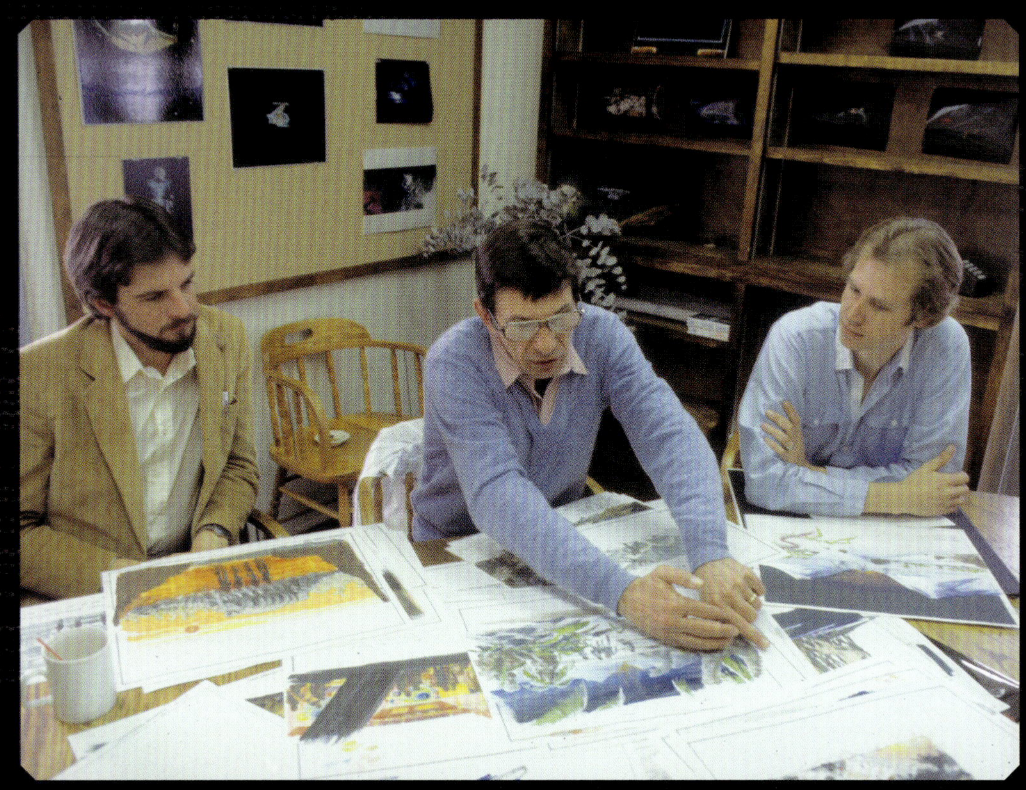

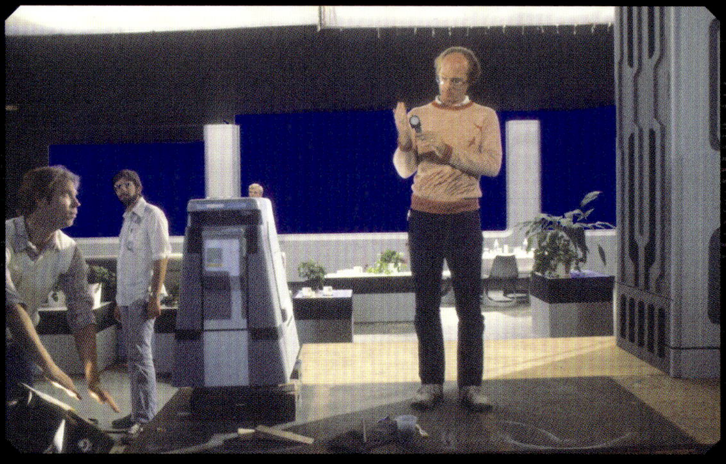

LEFT: Ralston, Nimoy, and Carson discuss the visuals of Genesis.

ABOVE: The cafeteria scene was filmed at ILM with Nimoy and the actors traveling to San Rafael. Only ILM had a bluescreen large enough to accommodate the sequence. Here, Carson, Ralston, and Farrar prepare for the shoot.

"I was like a lot of people who ended up in visual effects," said David Carson. "I started out reading *Famous Monsters* as a twelve- or thirteen-year-old. I saw Ray Harryhausen's films. By the age of fourteen, I had aspirations of working in visual effects someday." Carson started working in visual effects during the mid-seventies in Southern California for David Allen, who was known for his work on special effects for television commercials. Learning stop motion, sculpting, storyboards, art direction, and other skills while working for Allen would be an important experience for Carson.

"That is where I met a lot of the folks who had just come off of the first *Star Wars*," continued Carson. "I got hired to work on *Empire* as a model maker because they had an opening. Then I worked on *Dragonslayer*, and then *Jedi* for about two and half years without any kind of vacation. Nilo Rodis told me he had been asked to be the visual effects art director on *Star Trek III* and he asked me if I would co-direct with him, which was a very generous offer." Laughing, Carson shared, "However, Nilo insisted I take a week vacation, which I did, and then we started. Nilo was really in charge, and he was very gracious, very open. We would all draw whatever inspired us. If one of us seemed to have a better handle on something that was a little more intriguing, then that person would kind of take that and run with it."[1]

Visual effects supervisor Kenneth Ralston, Rodis, and Carson held several meetings at ILM with Bennett and Nimoy to discuss the spacedock. As with the starship designs, Ralston asked supervising model maker Steve Gawley and model maker Bill George to create study models to provide Bennett and Nimoy a tangible representation of the spacedock. After looking at four models, the best features were combined into a fifth study model that was approved. Models of both the exterior of the spacedock and its interior would be built to accommodate story needs.

During filming, ILM had to derive solutions to a most curious issue: the concern that the liminal space of the interior model would not

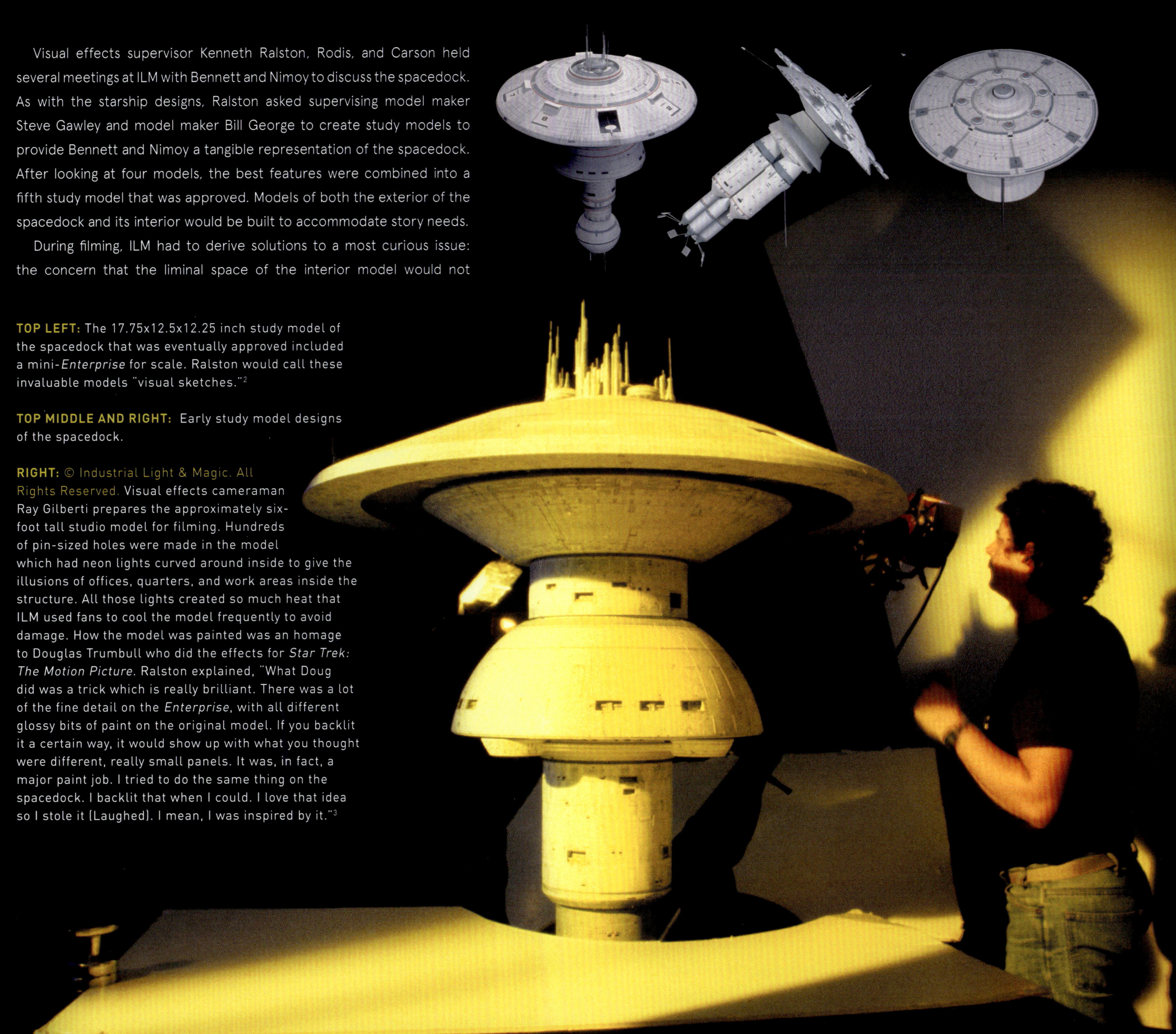

TOP LEFT: The 17.75x12.5x12.25 inch study model of the spacedock that was eventually approved included a mini-*Enterprise* for scale. Ralston would call these invaluable models "visual sketches."[2]

TOP MIDDLE AND RIGHT: Early study model designs of the spacedock.

RIGHT: Visual effects cameraman Ray Gilberti prepares the approximately six-foot tall studio model for filming. Hundreds of pin-sized holes were made in the model which had neon lights curved around inside to give the illusions of offices, quarters, and work areas inside the structure. All those lights created so much heat that ILM used fans to cool the model frequently to avoid damage. How the model was painted was an homage to Douglas Trumbull who did the effects for *Star Trek: The Motion Picture*. Ralston explained, "What Doug did was a trick which is really brilliant. There was a lot of the fine detail on the *Enterprise*, with all different glossy bits of paint on the original model. If you backlit it a certain way, it would show up with what you thought were different, really small panels. It was, in fact, a major paint job. I tried to do the same thing on the spacedock. I backlit that when I could. I love that idea so I stole it (Laughed). I mean, I was inspired by it."[3]

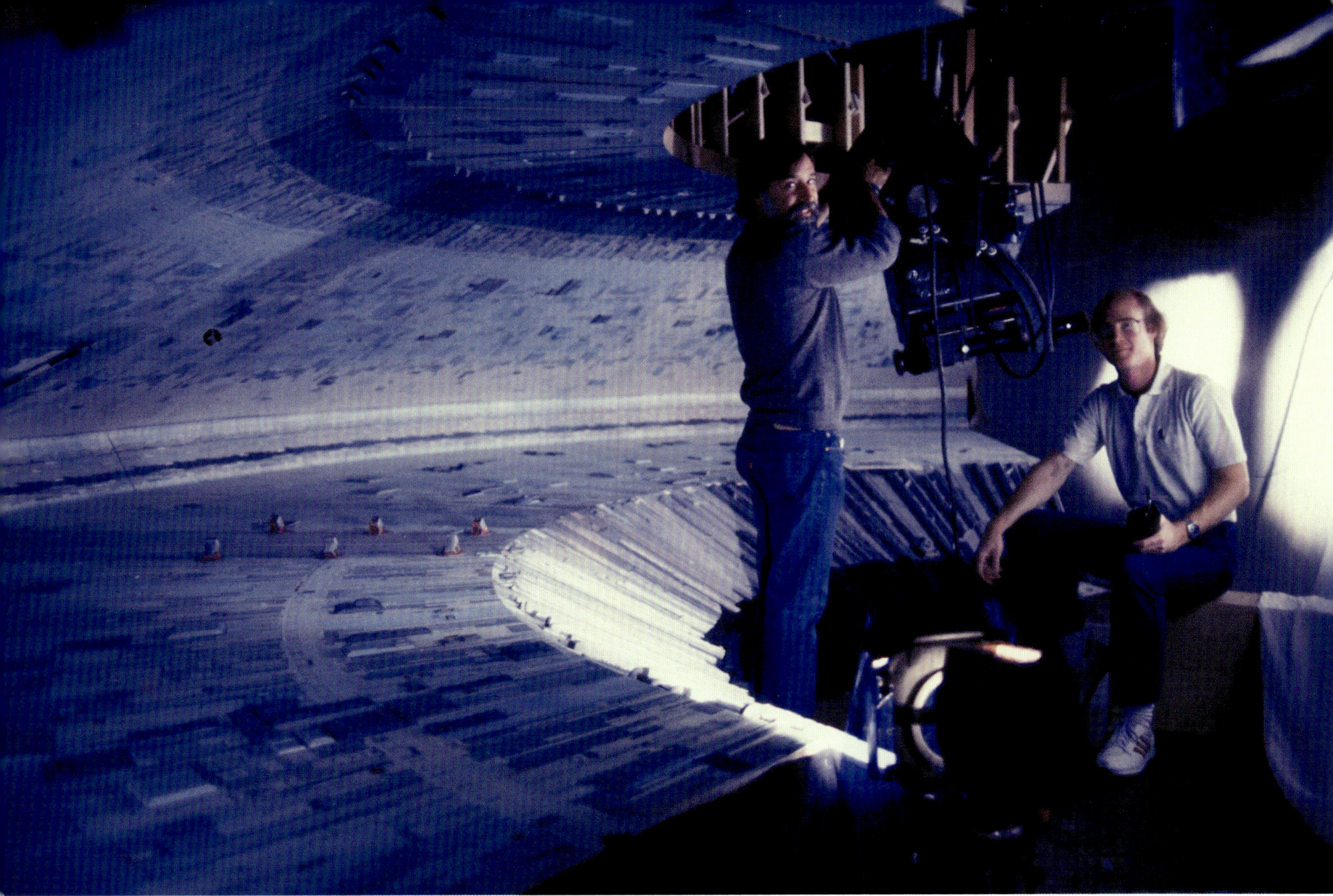

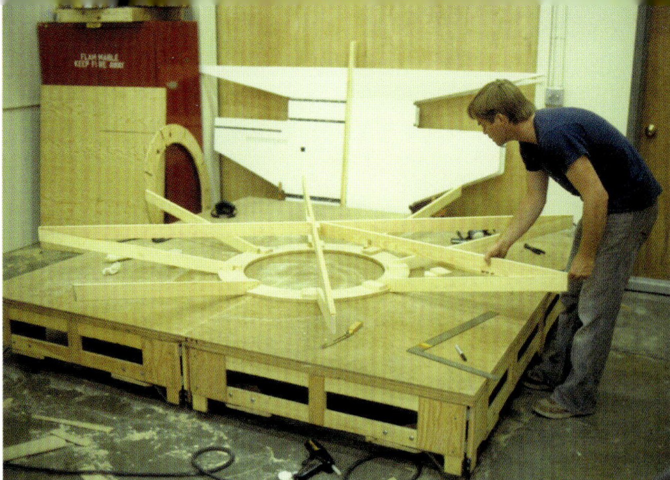

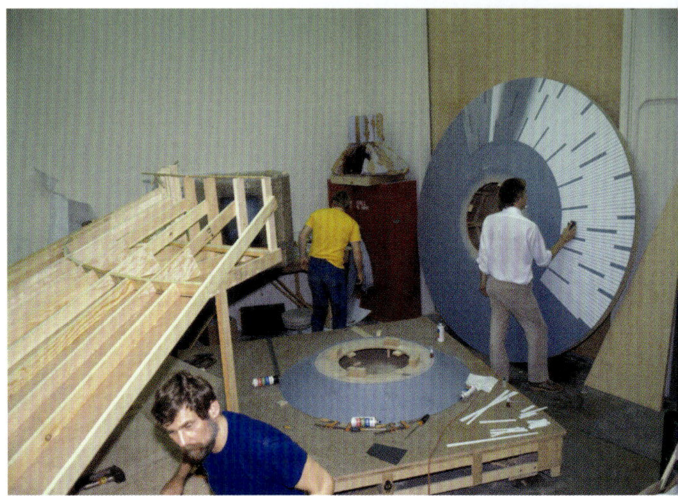

translate to the big screen with a proper sense of scale. Worried that audience eyes would detect the problem, several strategies were employed. First, docking lights were added to the *Enterprise* as it sailed into spacedock. Rodis remembered, "...it's like the docking of the *Queen Mary*. It's beautiful; it's slow; and if it hit anything it would destroy a lot of things. The light that hits the bottom of the dish starts to define that surface as it is coming toward you. Then when it finally drops anchor it feels like it's being supported by these beams of light. Without that element it just wasn't magic."[4] Another strategy was to add a kind of smokey haze to the environment. As explained by Farrar to Brad Munson of *CineFex*, "We tested a lot of different looks to make the interior of the dock seem appropriately vast. After trying various things, we found that the interior demanded some degree of atmospheric haze, even though there probably wouldn't be any in outer space. It just needed help to look slightly degraded – not so crisp and clean."[2]

Another solution was suggested by Carson. "All of us at ILM were frequently taking flights on *PSA Airlines*, flying from Burbank to San Francisco," he explained. "I remember exiting the plane and looking back through the window and seeing the nose of the plane and thinking, 'You know, that's a really interesting idea.' I drew a sketch of the *Enterprise* outside the window as people were disembarking."[1] This inspiration resulted in the cafeteria scene being added where Starfleet personnel are emotionally affected by the return of the damaged *Enterprise*. Now audiences could understand the scale of the *Enterprise* in comparison to the patrons of the cafeteria looking through the window, and of the *Enterprise* to the spacedock environment.

In an example of how effects can enhance the story, Nimoy utilized Carson's idea to showcase Grace Lee Whitney, who fans would recognize from her role in the original *Star Trek* series as Janice Rand. Although not formally named Rand, fans would know who she was and her reaction of pain and incredulousness bring emotion to the moment. Whitney wrote in her autobiography, *The Longest Trek*, "While we were at ILM, a number of us were given a tour of the studio. We were introduced to George Lucas, and we met a lot of the artists, animators, and model-builders. Most of them seemed so young, practically teenagers, yet they were all incredibly talented. They showed us their drawings and paintings and miniatures of starships, Klingons, aliens – a whole bizarre wonderland of movie magic."[5]

ABOVE LEFT: © Industrial Light & Magic. All Rights Reserved. Visual effects cameramen Robert Hill and Scott Farrar prepare to film the interior spacedock model. It took several months to film all the interior elements. Bill George explained how the paneling effect was created, "We printed, and basically made our own wallpaper, that was this kind of Aztec pattern that's very typically *Star Trek*. And so then, myself and a couple other guys, we wallpapered the inside with his texture."[6]

ABOVE RIGHT: © Industrial Light & Magic. All Rights Reserved. Construction begins on the nearly 30-foot interior model of the spacedock.

FAR RIGHT: Call sheet for the November 15, 1983, cafeteria scene. This scene was filmed almost three weeks after regular production had wrapped. Notice both Whitney and cinematographer Charles Correll are listed as the players for this scene. Correll had a cameo as the janitor watching the *Enterprise* escape.

MIDDLE RIGHT: Nimoy wrote of Whitney, "I call her Amazing Grace. She rejects that name and denies that she is amazing, but I insist, because she is."[5] Whitney would appear in all the *Star Trek* films that Nimoy either directed or executive produced.

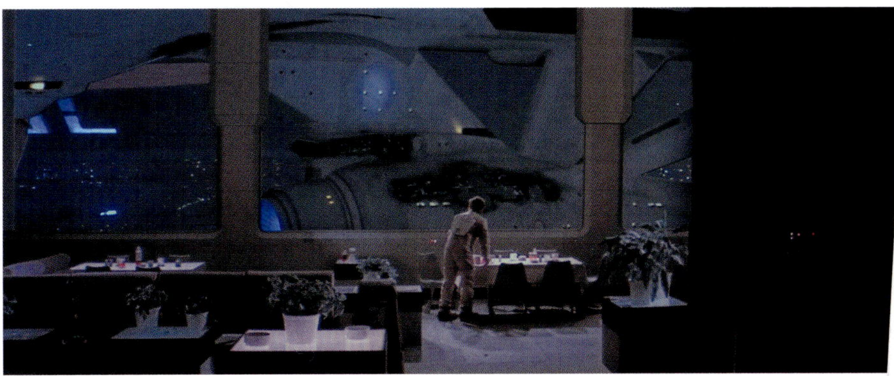

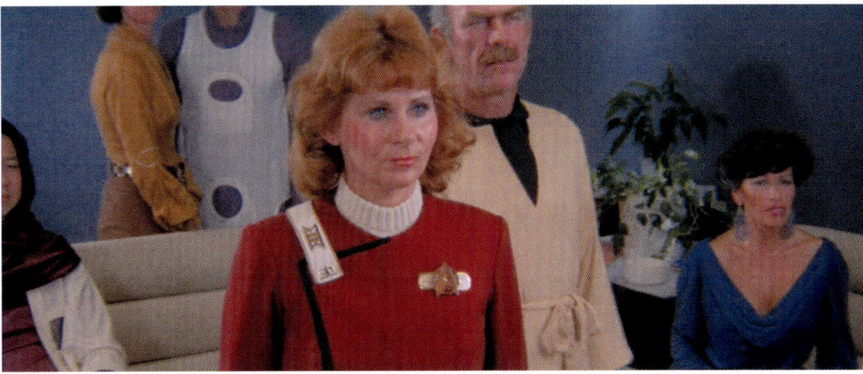

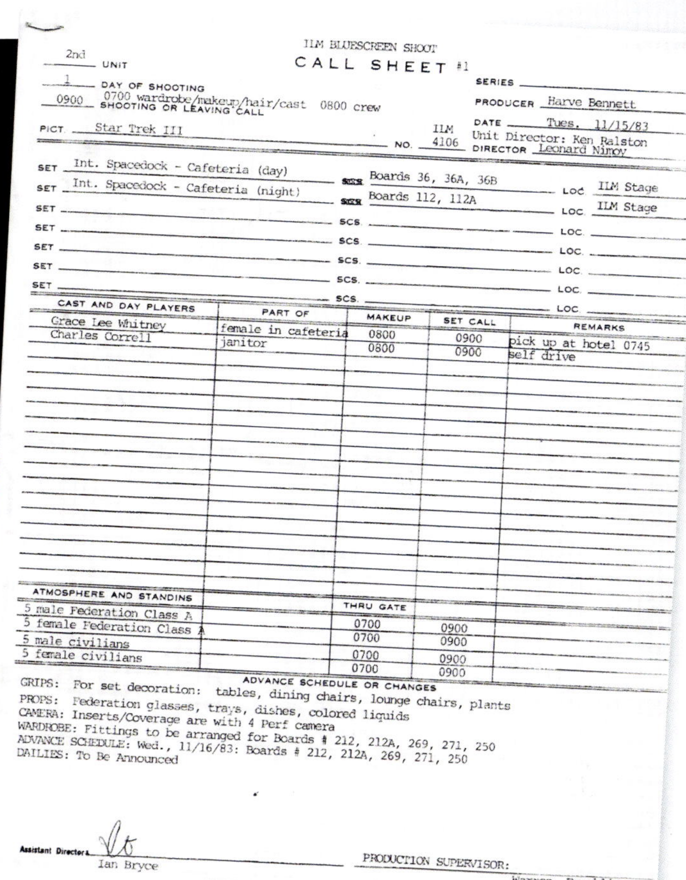

ILM BLUESCREEN SHOOT
CALL SHEET #1

2nd UNIT
1 DAY OF SHOOTING
0900 SHOOTING OR LEAVING CALL — 0700 wardrobe/makeup/hair/cast 0800 crew
SERIES
PRODUCER Harve Bennett
DATE Tues. 11/15/83
PICT. Star Trek III NO. ILM 4106
Unit Director: Ken Ralston
DIRECTOR Leonard Nimoy

SET Int. Spacedock - Cafeteria (day) SCS. Boards 36, 36A, 36B LOC. ILM Stage
SET Int. Spacedock - Cafeteria (night) SCS. Boards 112, 112A LOC. ILM Stage

CAST AND DAY PLAYERS	PART OF	MAKEUP	SET CALL	REMARKS
Grace Lee Whitney	female in cafeteria	0800	0900	pick up at hotel 0745
Charles Correll	janitor	0800	0900	self drive

ATMOSPHERE AND STANDINS		THRU GATE		
5 male Federation Class A		0700	0900	
5 female Federation Class A		0700	0900	
5 male civilians		0700	0900	
5 female civilians		0700	0900	

ADVANCE SCHEDULE OR CHANGES
GRIPS: For set decoration: tables, dining chairs, lounge chairs, plants
PROPS: Federation glasses, trays, dishes, colored liquids
CAMERA: Inserts/Coverage are with 4 Perf camera
WARDROBE: Fittings to be arranged for Boards # 212, 212A, 269, 271, 250
ADVANCE SCHEDULE: Wed., 11/16/83: Boards # 212, 212A, 269, 271, 250
DAILIES: To Be Announced

Assistant Directors Ian Bryce
PRODUCTION SUPERVISOR: Warren Franklin

ENTERPRISE STATIONERS 7401 SUNSET L.A., CA. 90046 (213) 876-3533 FORM NO. 91

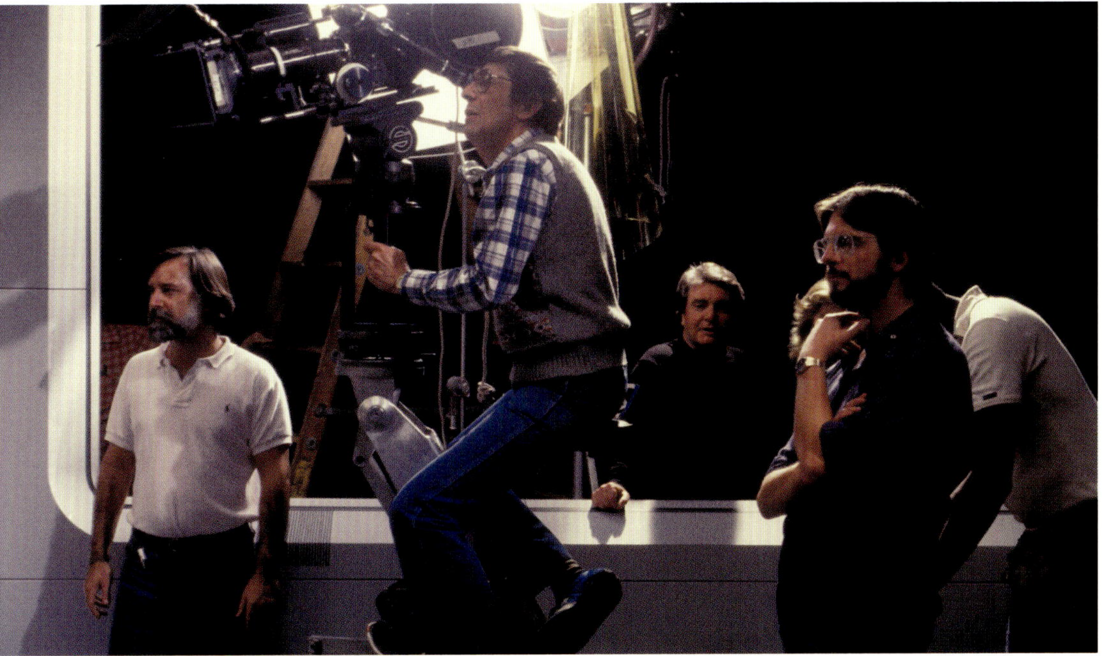

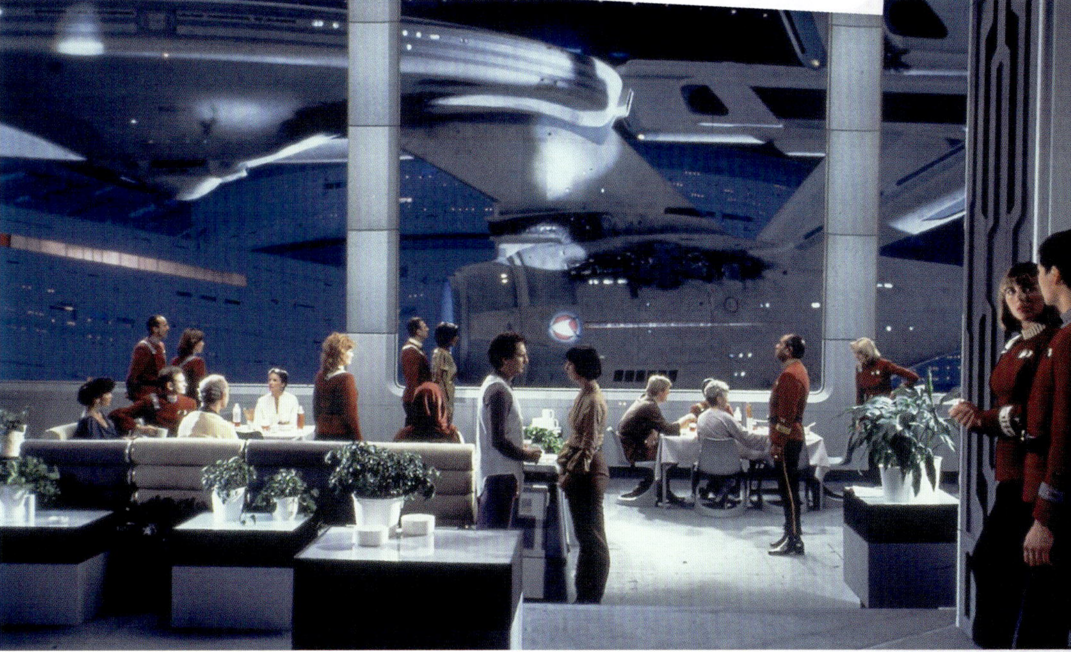

ABOVE LEFT: Nimoy, director of photography Charles Correll, and Ralston prepare the camera at ILM. Nimoy respected the contributions of everyone on the film that even though many of the faces of extras in the cafeteria scene would not been seen on screen, he took time to film each extra because he believed they deserved their moment after working so many long hours.

ABOVE RIGHT: Unused test composite for the cafeteria scene. There would be no extras walking in the foreground in the actual scene. The planters used on set were actually white painter buckets. The matte department had quite a challenge trying to perfectly align the painted columns that extended the set.

THE STARSHIPS

Star Trek III introduced both the *U.S.S. Excelsior* and *U.S.S. Grissom* which gave ILM the rewarding experience of designing, building, and filming iconic additions to the Federation starship lexicon.

The *Excelsior* was mentioned in a deleted scene from *Star Trek II* where Sulu announces that he will soon be given its captaincy. The design, and the mysterious reference to its transwarp capabilities, helped popularize the starship, so much so that it would be seen in four of the original *Star Trek* films, and in *Star Trek: Voyager* and *Star Trek: Picard*. The studio model would be reused and redesigned for other ships on many *Star Trek* productions, most especially, as the *U.S.S. Enterprise-B* from *Star Trek: Generations*. Of course, not everyone was a fan of the new design. Creator Gene Roddenberry had a nickname for the *Excelsior* – "the pregnant duck!"[7]

If the *Excelsior* was akin to a large carrier at sea, then to Nimoy, the *Grissom* was, "to be the equivalent of the Jacques Cousteau's *Calypso*. We talked about *Calypso*. I said, 'This is a peaceful vessel, it is a research vessel. It is not a fighting ship. It should look kind of boyscoutish.'"[8]

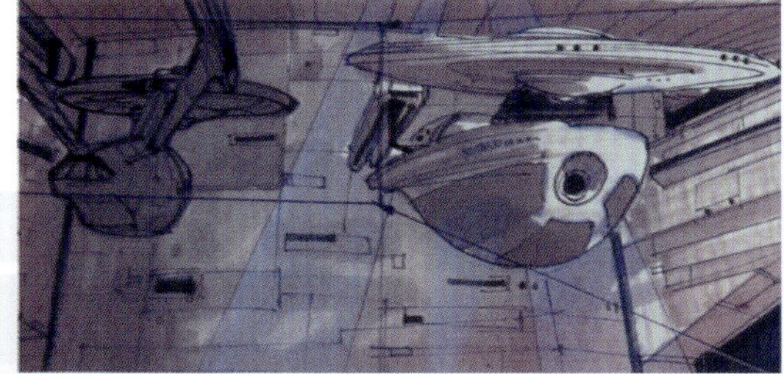

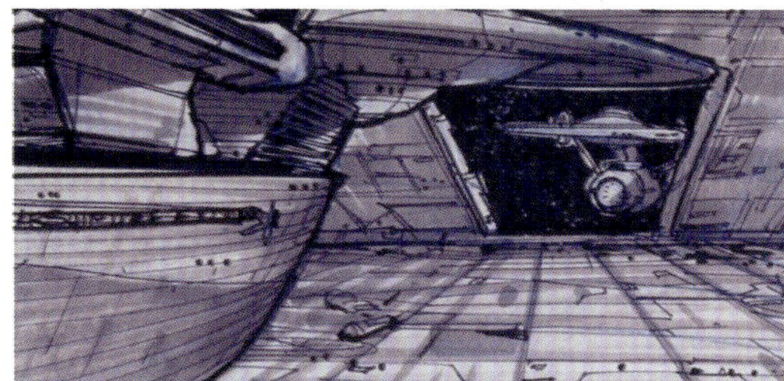

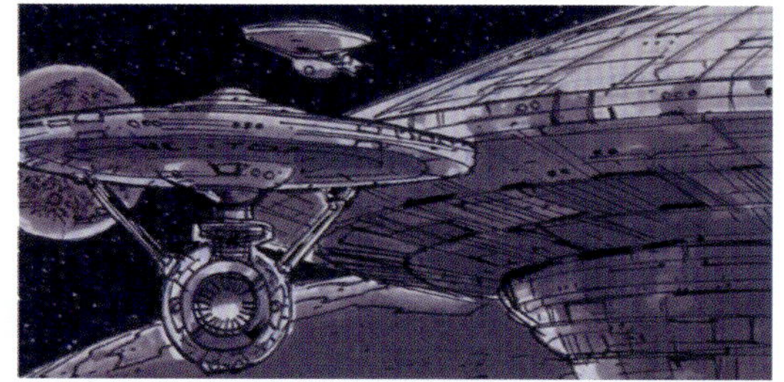

BOTTOM LEFT AND RIGHT: Contributing to the construction of the seven-foot, seven-inch studio model was ILM's Richard Davis. Vacuum forming techniques helped ILM build the model more efficiently than using other processes.

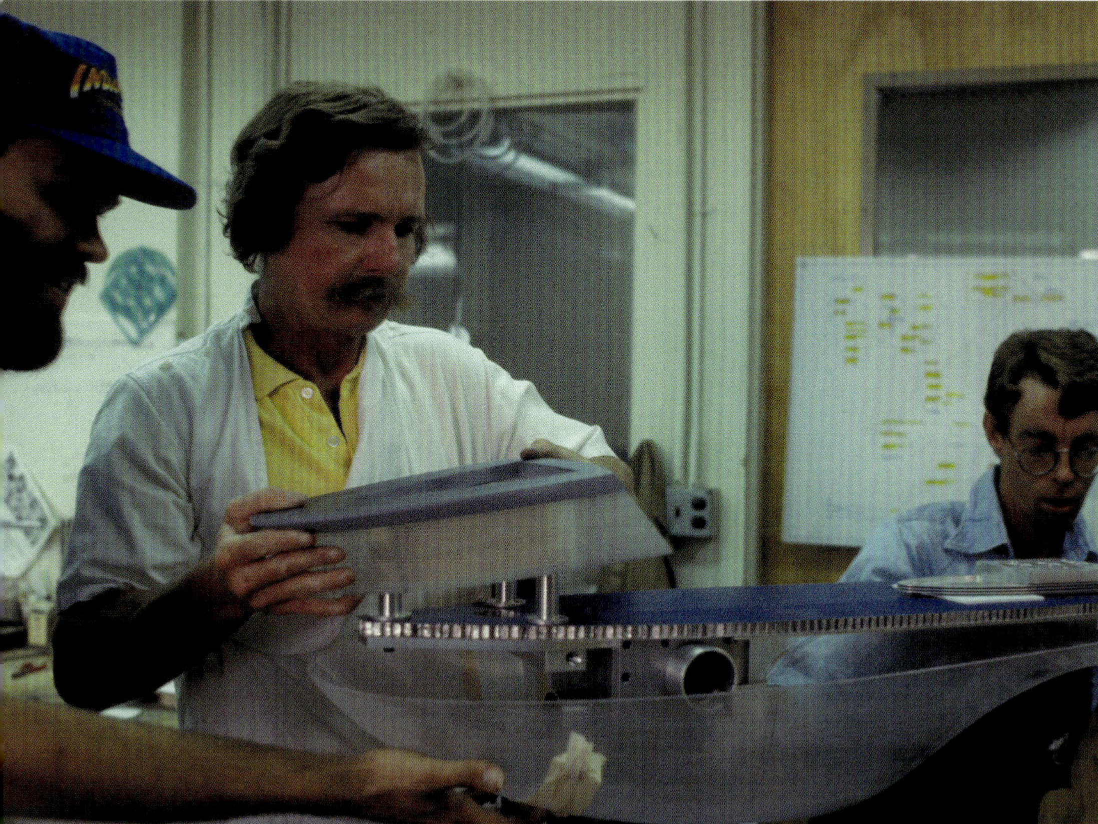

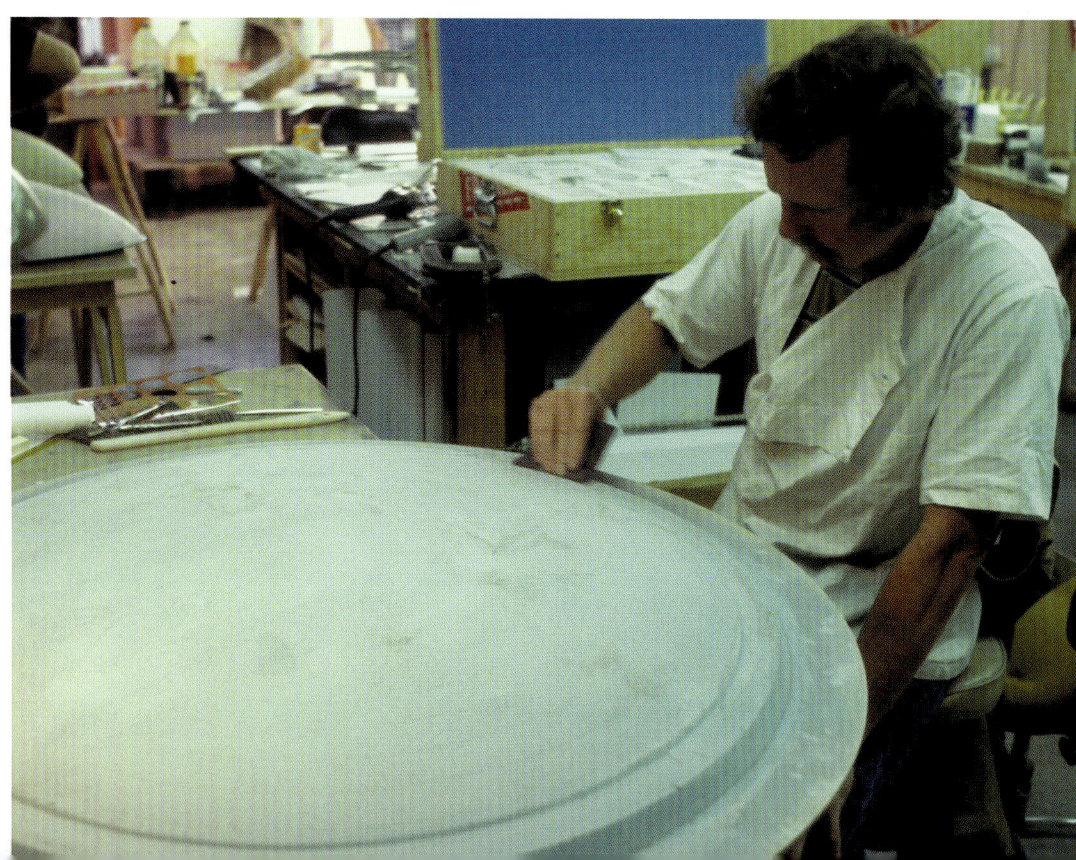

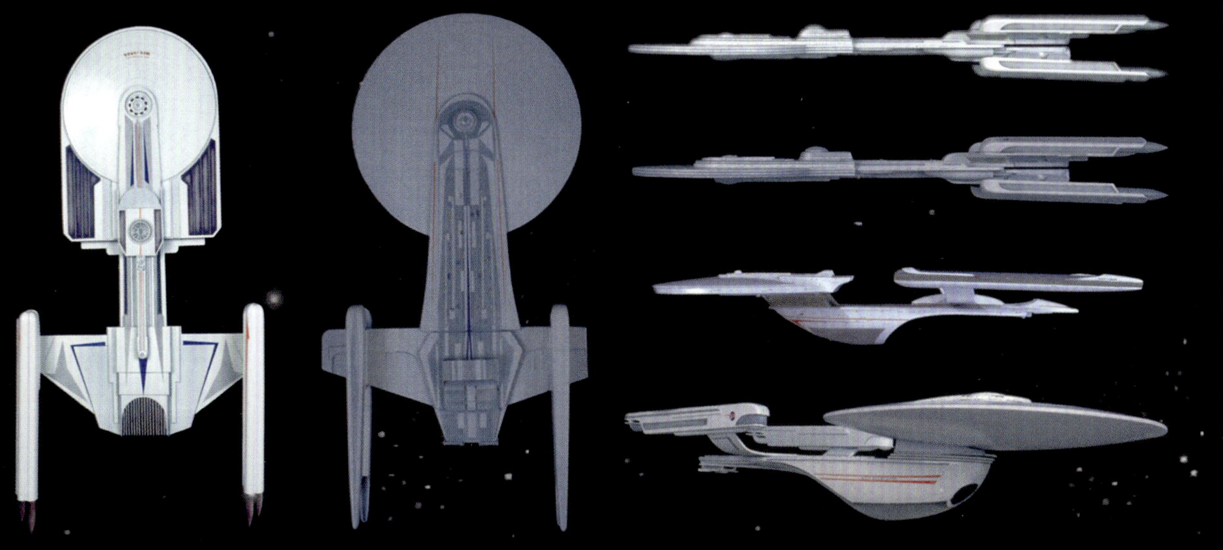

LEFT: Designed by Carson and Rodis with ideas from model makers Gawley and George, these study models of the *Excelsior* show the evolution towards the approved design. George likened the *Excelsior* to a Japanese version of the *Enterprise*.

BELOW: A publicity composite of the *Excelsior*. The various ILM departments had a shared aesthetic mission to make certain the ships of *Star Trek* were different than the ships of *Star Wars*. "The idea behind the *Star Trek* shots was to have these gloriously beautiful, wonderfully lit ships moving slowly," explained Farrar. "That was very different than the movies we had worked on before, especially *Star Wars*. George liked to see how much a person could absorb in 40 frames or so... *Star Trek* was more like large ships at sea that moved slowly, big tankers."[9]

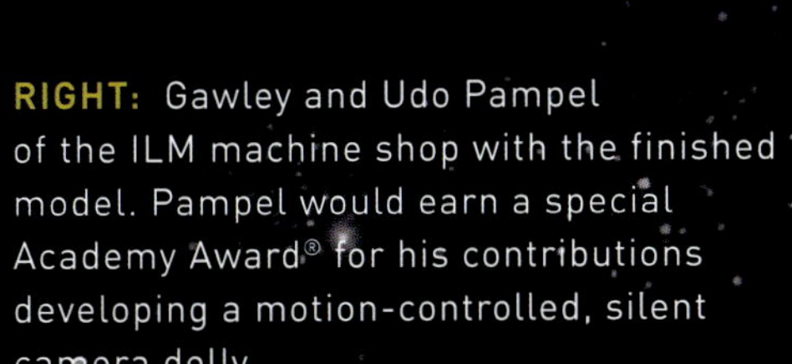

RIGHT: Gawley and Udo Pampel of the ILM machine shop with the finished model. Pampel would earn a special Academy Award® for his contributions developing a motion-controlled, silent camera dolly.

FAR RIGHT: Gawley and model maker Ira Keeler work on the studio model. Keeler died in 2021 and was honored at a memorial service for all his contributions to film, including his work on *Return of the Jedi* and creating the DeLorean time machine model from *Back to the Future*.

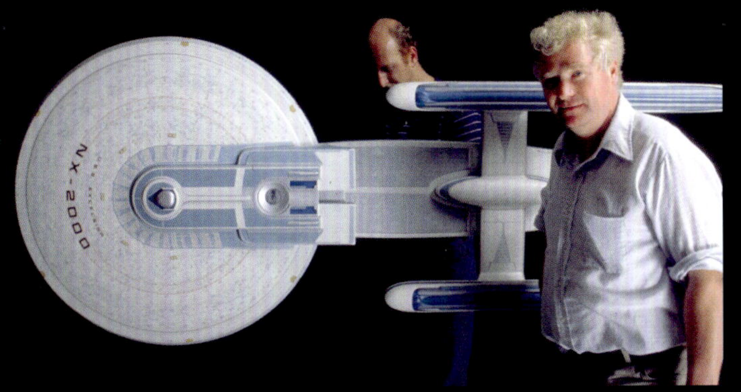

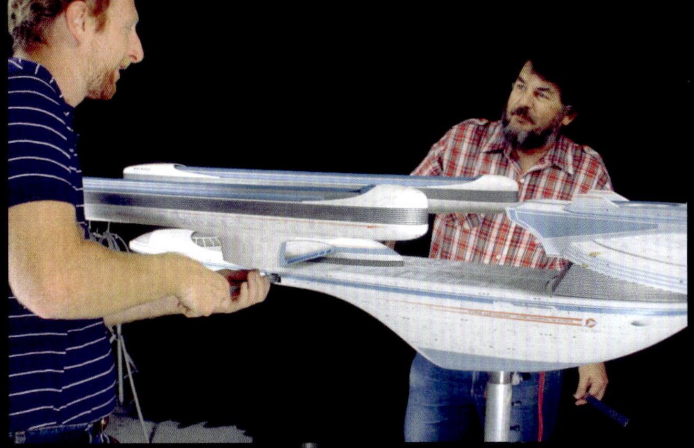

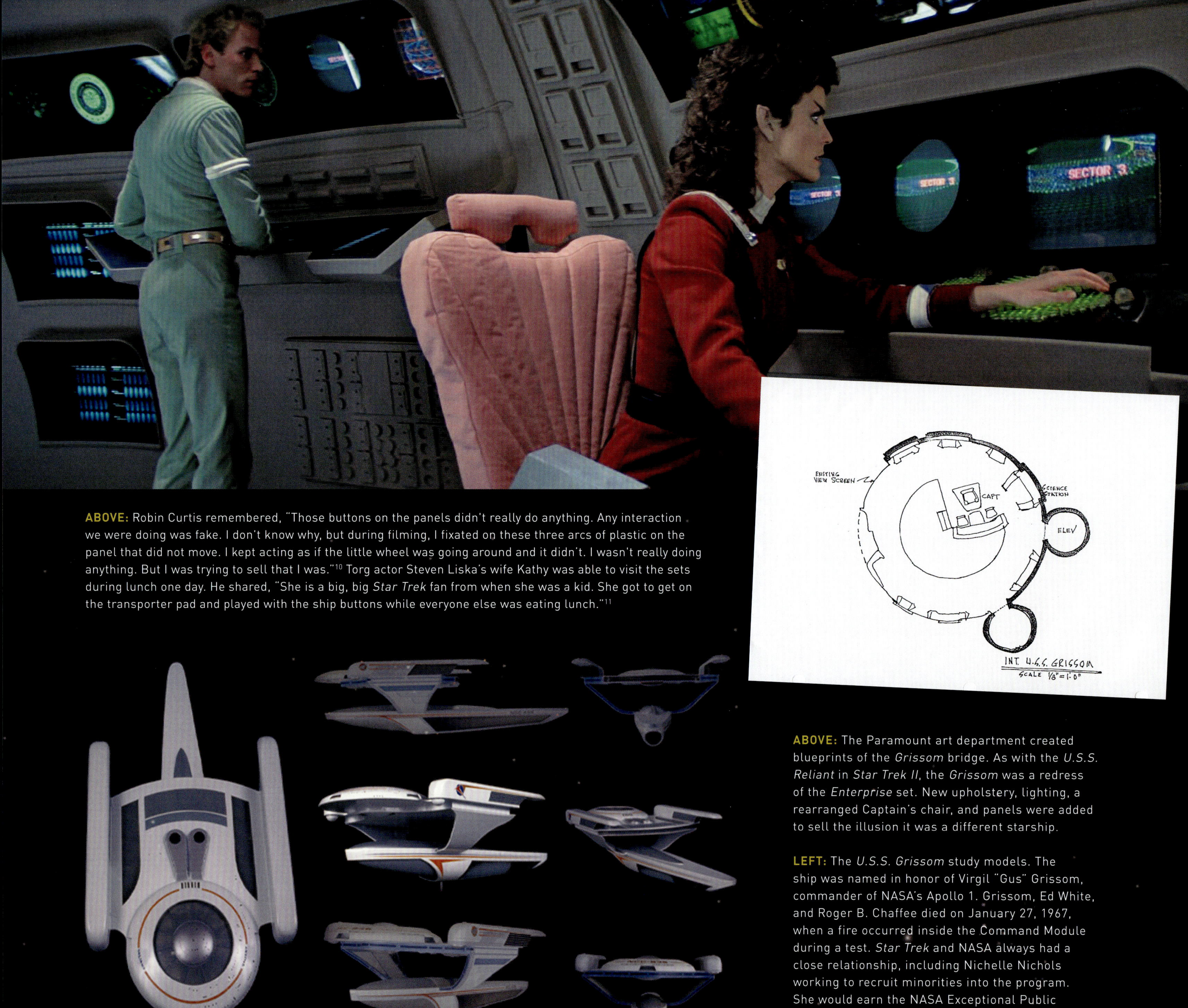

ABOVE: Robin Curtis remembered, "Those buttons on the panels didn't really do anything. Any interaction we were doing was fake. I don't know why, but during filming, I fixated on these three arcs of plastic on the panel that did not move. I kept acting as if the little wheel was going around and it didn't. I wasn't really doing anything. But I was trying to sell that I was."[10] Torg actor Steven Liska's wife Kathy was able to visit the sets during lunch one day. He shared, "She is a big, big *Star Trek* fan from when she was a kid. She got to get on the transporter pad and played with the ship buttons while everyone else was eating lunch."[11]

ABOVE: The Paramount art department created blueprints of the *Grissom* bridge. As with the *U.S.S. Reliant* in *Star Trek II*, the *Grissom* was a redress of the *Enterprise* set. New upholstery, lighting, a rearranged Captain's chair, and panels were added to sell the illusion it was a different starship.

LEFT: The *U.S.S. Grissom* study models. The ship was named in honor of Virgil "Gus" Grissom, commander of NASA's Apollo 1. Grissom, Ed White, and Roger B. Chaffee died on January 27, 1967, when a fire occurred inside the Command Module during a test. *Star Trek* and NASA always had a close relationship, including Nichelle Nichols working to recruit minorities into the program. She would earn the NASA Exceptional Public Achievement Medal for her service.

THE BAR

The bar scene was filmed on Stage 9 using a redress of the *Enterprise* sickbay set. One of the most memorable characters in the film is the Bar Alien who McCoy tries to hire for transportation to Genesis. The character is played by veteran actor Allan Miller. How Miller got the role is an example of Bennett's loyalty.

Miller recounted, "Around 1981, I was walking on the Paramount lot to the commissary and back. A guy on a bicycle comes gliding by, and I notice him. He says, 'Hey! Hi, Alan!' And I didn't initially know who he was, but he introduced himself as Harve Bennett. I said, 'Oh, Harve. Oh, I'm so sorry!' He said, 'It's okay. I see you more than you see me!'" Bennett had been producer on several shows that Miller had guested on. Bennett told Miller, "This is really coincidence, but your name just went on a list for some casting we're doing for a movie in Egypt. It has a nice part in there, we're thinking of you." A few days later, Bennett called to apologize because the decision had been made to cast an Egyptian actor instead. He ended the conversation by telling Miller, "So, I owe you one." In 1983, Miller would get a call from Bennett's office asking to see him. "I hiked over to Paramount," Miller said, "and Bennett was sitting there with Leonard Nimoy, whom I did know as an actor and a friend. There is some chuckling and small talk. Leonard leaned into him and said, 'Harve, are you gonna ask him or not?' And Harve went across and pulled up a drawing of the alien. He asked, 'Would you like to act him?' And I laughed. I asked, 'Does he speak?' Harve says, 'Oh, yeah, it is a key scene in the movie.' Leonard said, 'It is a very good scene, and we both thought you'd be wonderful in it.' And I said, 'I'd be happy too. How come you thought of me for this creature?' And Harve said, "I told you I owed you one!"[12]

Miller went immediately after for a costume fitting where he received his portion of the script. He thought it was a good scene and would be fun to do. He may have been less enthusiastic if he knew that the makeup would take five and a half hours to put on. The grueling makeup process

BELOW LEFT: The camera department and film crew get ready to start their day filming the bar sequence which was more ambitious than what audiences see in the final version, including a futuristic version of a Western bar brawl.

BELOW: Allen Miller as the 'bar alien.'

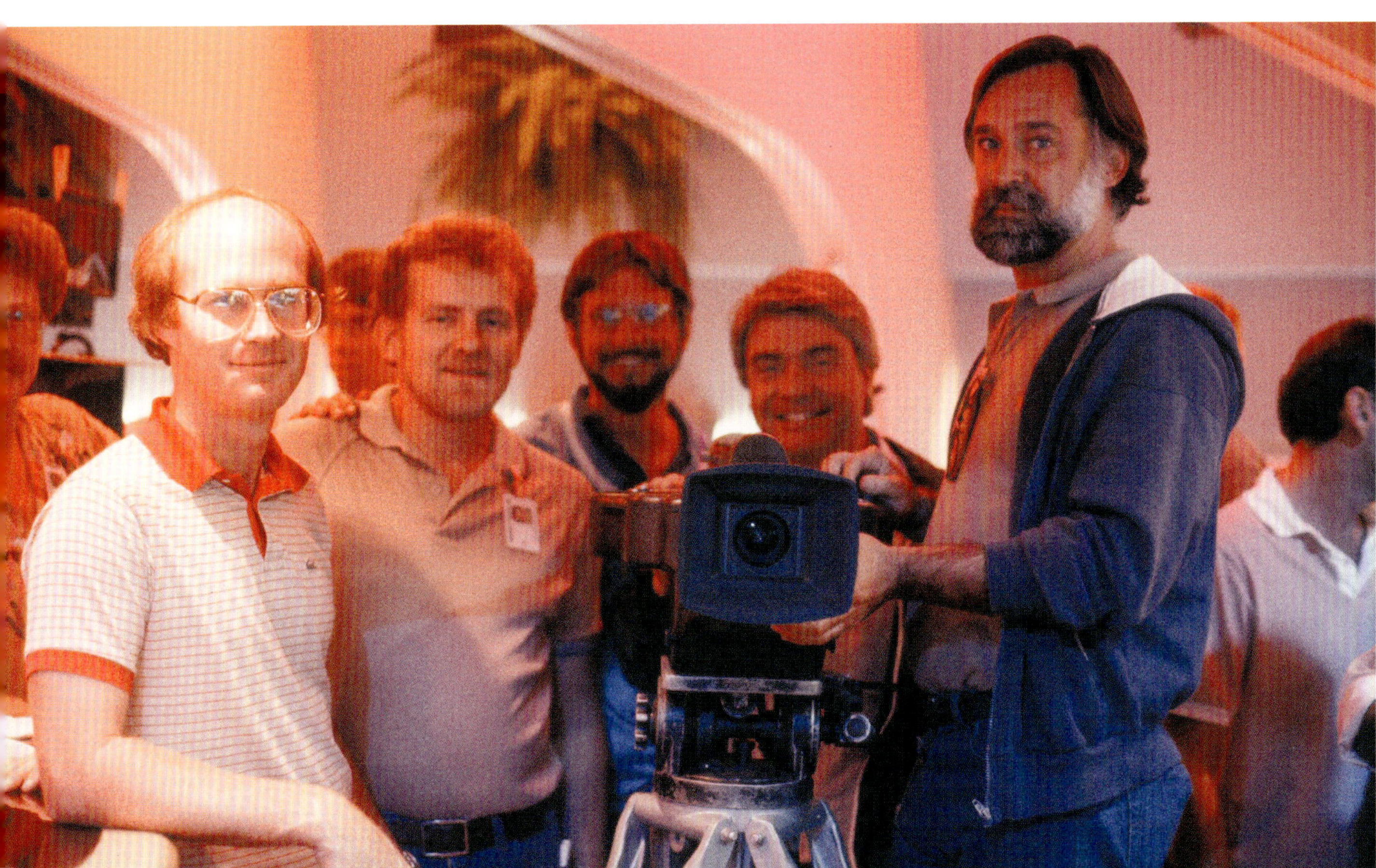

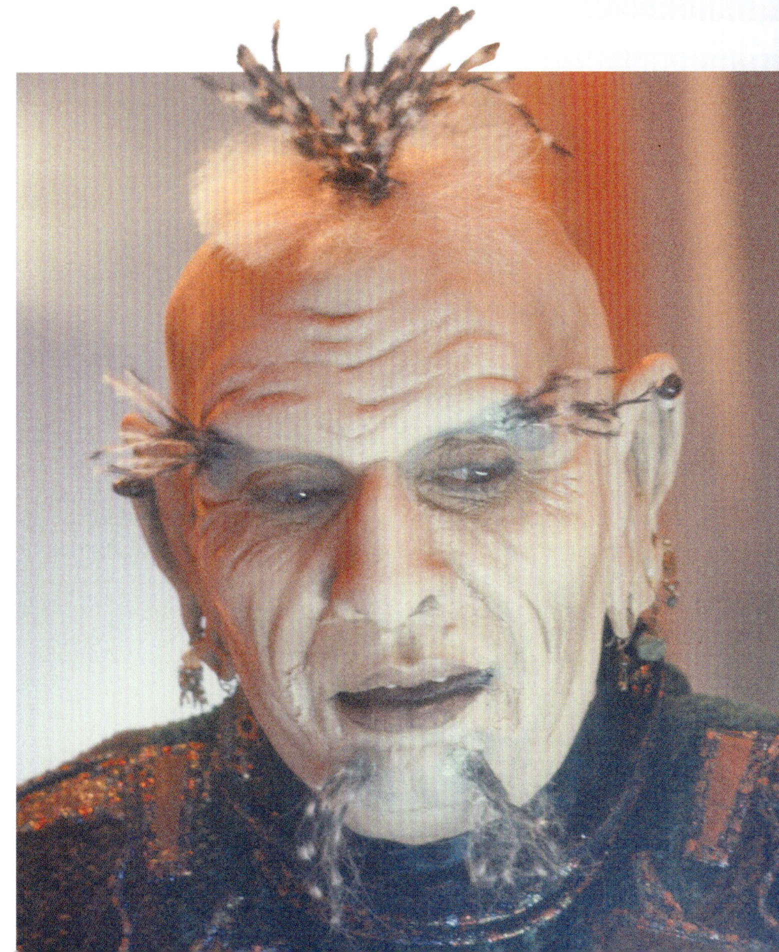

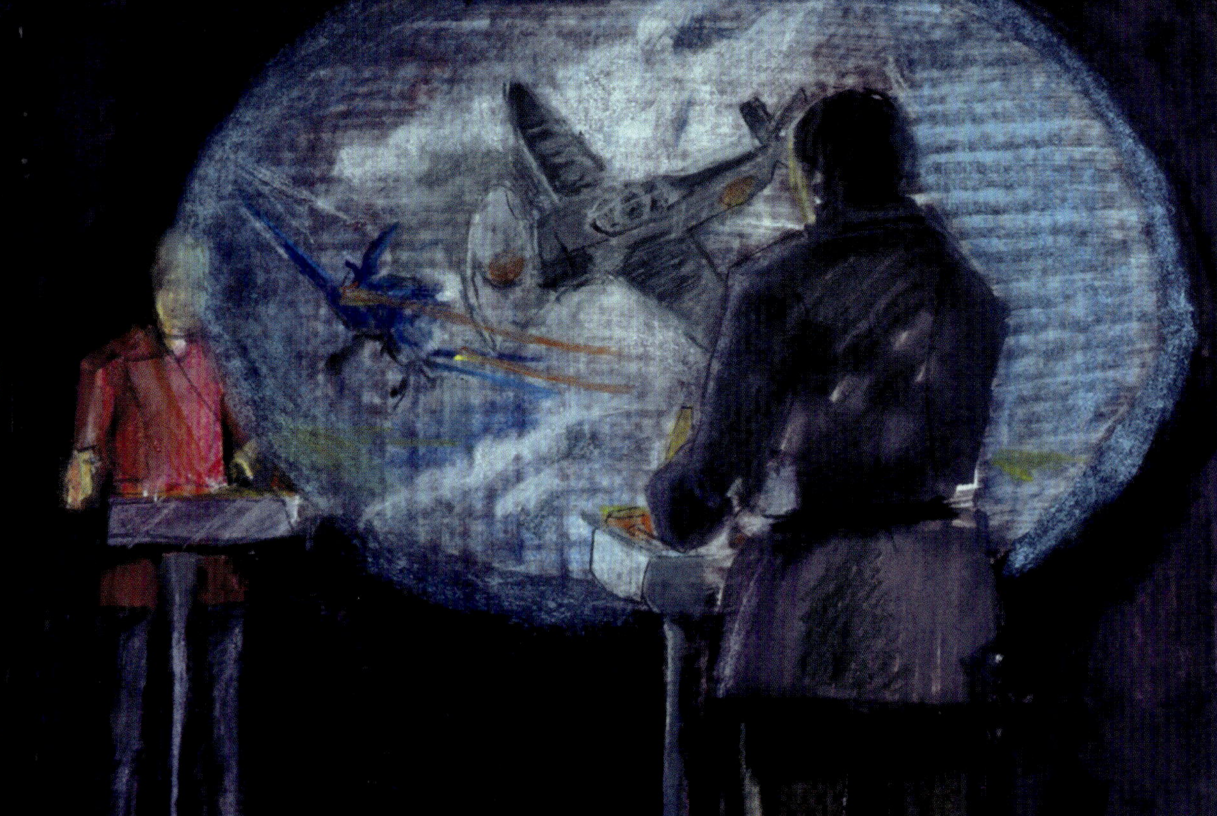

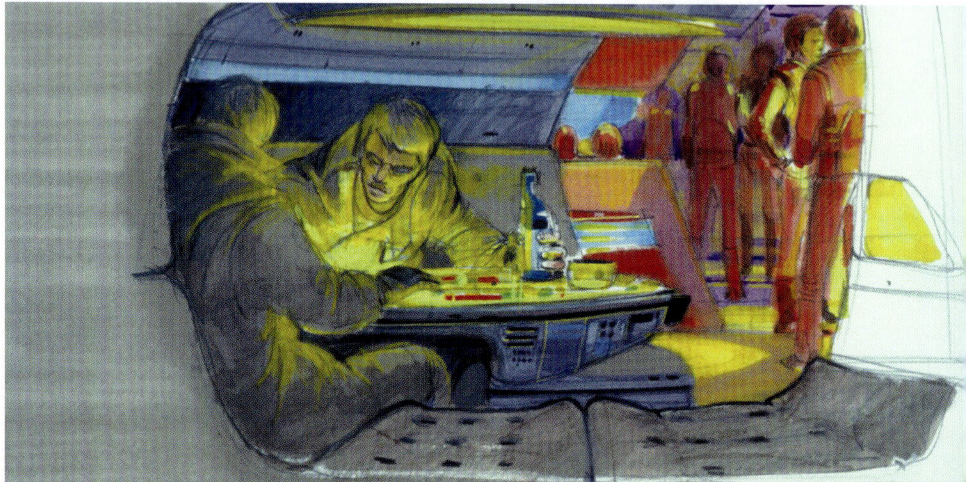

ABOVE: Bennett's script mentioned that the patrons of the bar were playing "twenty-third century equivalent of video games, darts." Carson thought it would be interesting if the game was a holographic of anachronistic airplanes. Electronic systems designer Jerry Jeffress created the wire frame animation, an example of early computer-generated effects in film. Cinematographer Charles Correll had wanted to add atmospheric smoke to the bar set, but could not because it would have hindered ILM's generation of the video game effects.

actually inspired a trait of the character's look, the Bar Alien's double lip. Miller explained, "There were three makeup artists who applied the eight appliances. I could only sip through a straw and couldn't eat anything. I was getting hot and claustrophobic. I said, 'Please, I can't do anymore.' One of the artists said, 'We're just finishing your lip.' And I said, 'What difference does that make with the rest of his face? So, I'll have two lips!' And I did. If you look carefully, you will see, I have two lips that look sort of mixed together. It was a nice look."[12]

To prepare for the role, Miller wondered how the character learned to speak English. He imagined that perhaps the Bar Alien had somehow learned from a machine that spoke English, but did not do so correctly, like "a wire recorder going backwards. It fit in perfectly with what I was doing so I just thought of that idea to back me up, and the way I was talking. I'm very musical, so some of the things are like playing music with my voice in a backward kind of way, and it went with the makeup, and that was the mixture."[12]

Actors sometimes suffer for their art, and that is true of Miller. He was given a choice by the makeup artists on how they could remove his appliances. One option would take several hours. The other was to literally rip it from his face, although it would hurt. After the twelve-hour filming day, hungry and exhausted, Miller chose the second option. The makeup team found a little piece of his appliance that was loose, and they pulled it off. "And the water poured off because the sweat had nowhere to go and accumulated. It was a deluge," Miller remembered. "It took me at least five, six, or seven days for my skin to recover. I swore I would never go through one of those battles of makeup again."

Despite this, Miller has great affection for his time on *Star Trek III* and the quotable character he helped create. He especially enjoyed working with Kelley. "I had seen DeForest on the show, so I was prepared for who McCoy was and how DeForest performed him," remembered Miller. "The whole scene felt nicely improvised with good choices on both our parts which emphasized the character differences. I loved it when, I don't know where it came from, where I said, 'Genesis!' Why, I went up high, I have no idea. It just happened, and it felt like the right choice."[12]

TOP AND ABOVE: Nilo Rodis art showcasing his imaginings of the San Francisco bar.

FLIGHT RECORDER VISUAL:

ALLAN MILLER, BAR ALIEN

Allan Miller, born February 14, 1929, never had any ambition to be an actor. Until, somewhat surprisingly, he was a seventeen-year-old serving in the United States Army assigned to driving a truck for the 14th Quartermaster Corps in Japan. Supply runs to Tokyo inspired him to try out for an Army acting assignment in the city mostly because he loved Tokyo and disliked driving the truck. "At the audition," Miller remembered, "it turned out that I could actually read although, sorry to say, most of the guys from the Army at that time couldn't. I was assigned to a Special Services company whose mission was to entertain our troops. The company was a small ensemble which had to produce a light comedy and one musical. Soon, I started thinking, 'What the hell am I going do with a musical? I can't sing, and I don't dance. So, I made up a musical called *Heavenly Daze*. I was dressed like Saint Peter at the gate, with a golden halo wearing a kimono. Everybody else in the cast had to audition for me to get into Heaven." His troupe of Army actors passed through Hiroshima only a year and quarter after the atomic bomb had been used on the city. Of his experience seeing the devastation, Miller said, "None of us could sleep that night, the officers, the enlisted men. We sat up making up death songs. When I returned to the States, I went back to college. I tried to do regular academic subjects. Because of what I saw in the military, there was no connection. I couldn't talk to any of the guys unless they were veterans. I had a rough time adjusting."[12]

Acting would help Miller express his feelings and became a passion. "I met, by chance, a guy who was in basic training with me. He said he was going to his acting class. I had no idea that they had actual classes for acting. That's how innocent I was. He said, 'If you're free this afternoon, come watch.' I went to watch the acting classes. People were free with their feelings, their thoughts, their behavior. It was like I came to life again. I found out I could sign up with the G.I. Bill."[12]

Miller would go on to star and guest star in more than 100 television programs, and he became a respected acting teacher. Perhaps the most famous of his many students was Barbra Streisand, who he taught from age fifteen and coached during the Broadway production of *Funny Girl*.

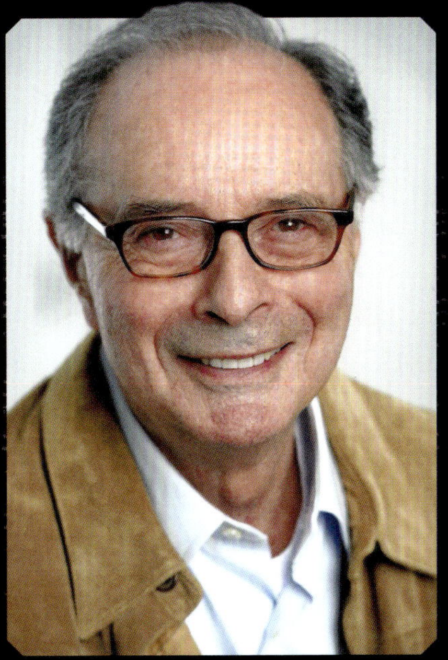

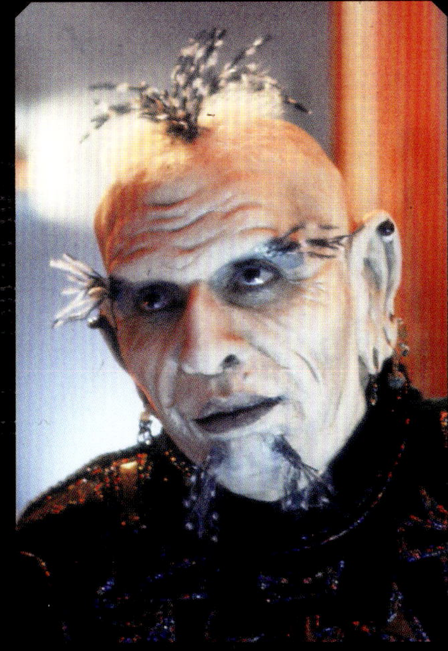

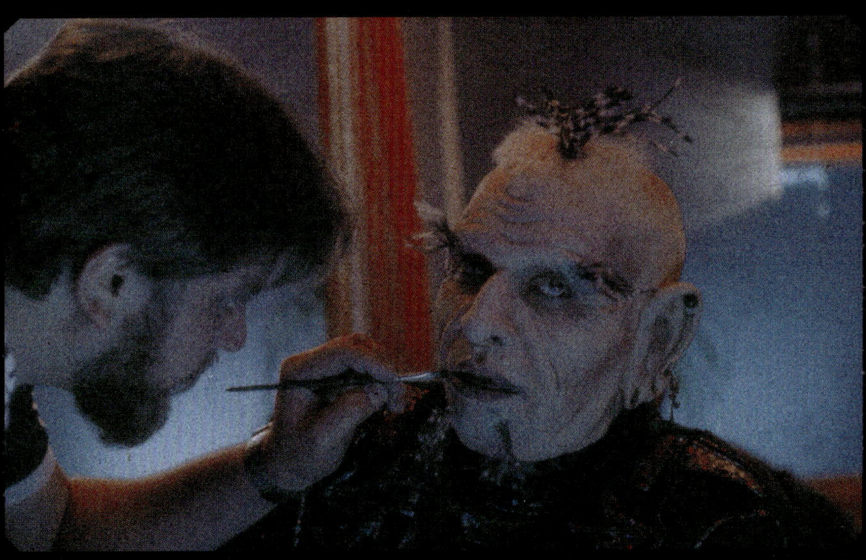

THIS PAGE: Miller with and without his character makeup.[13]

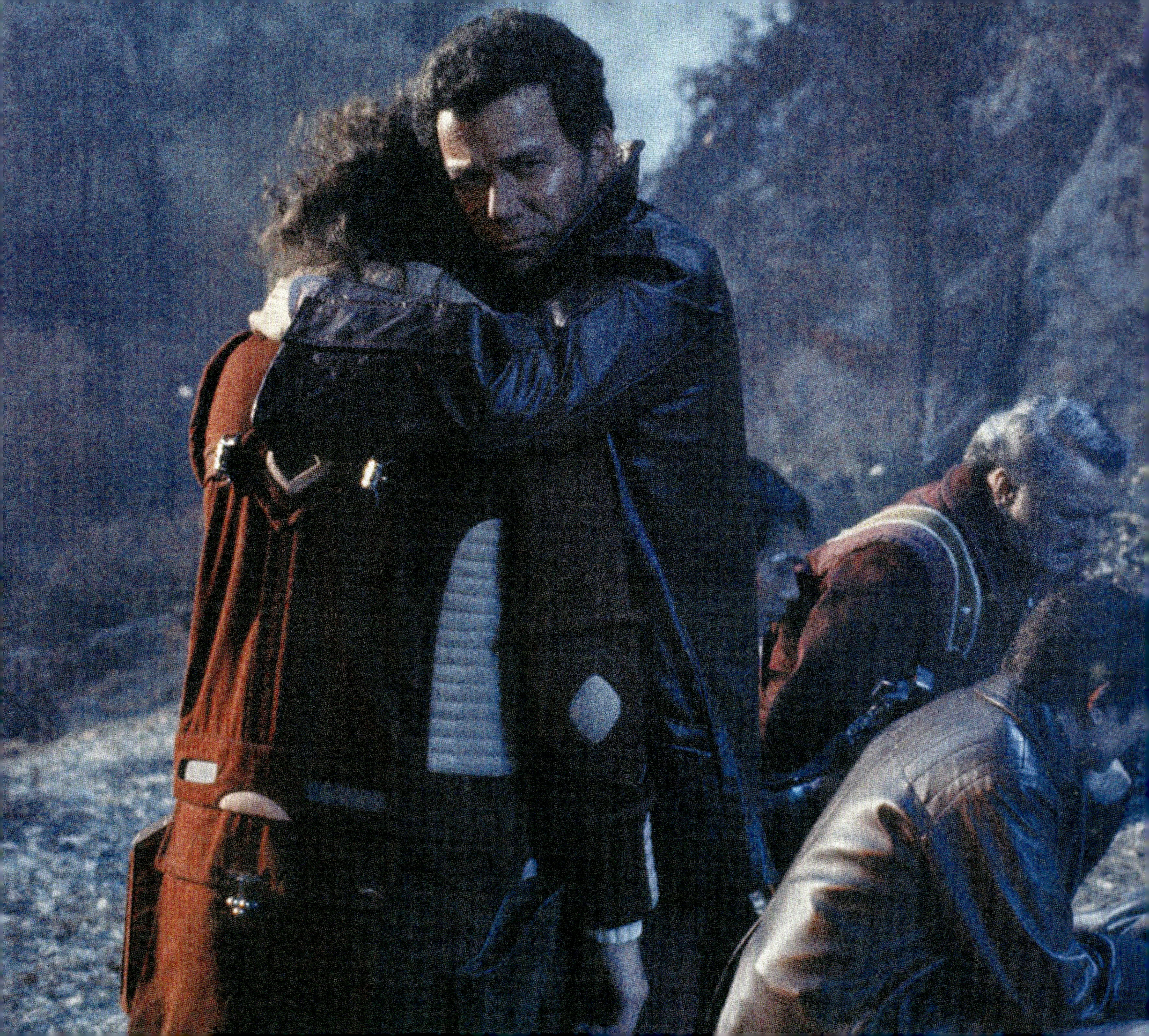

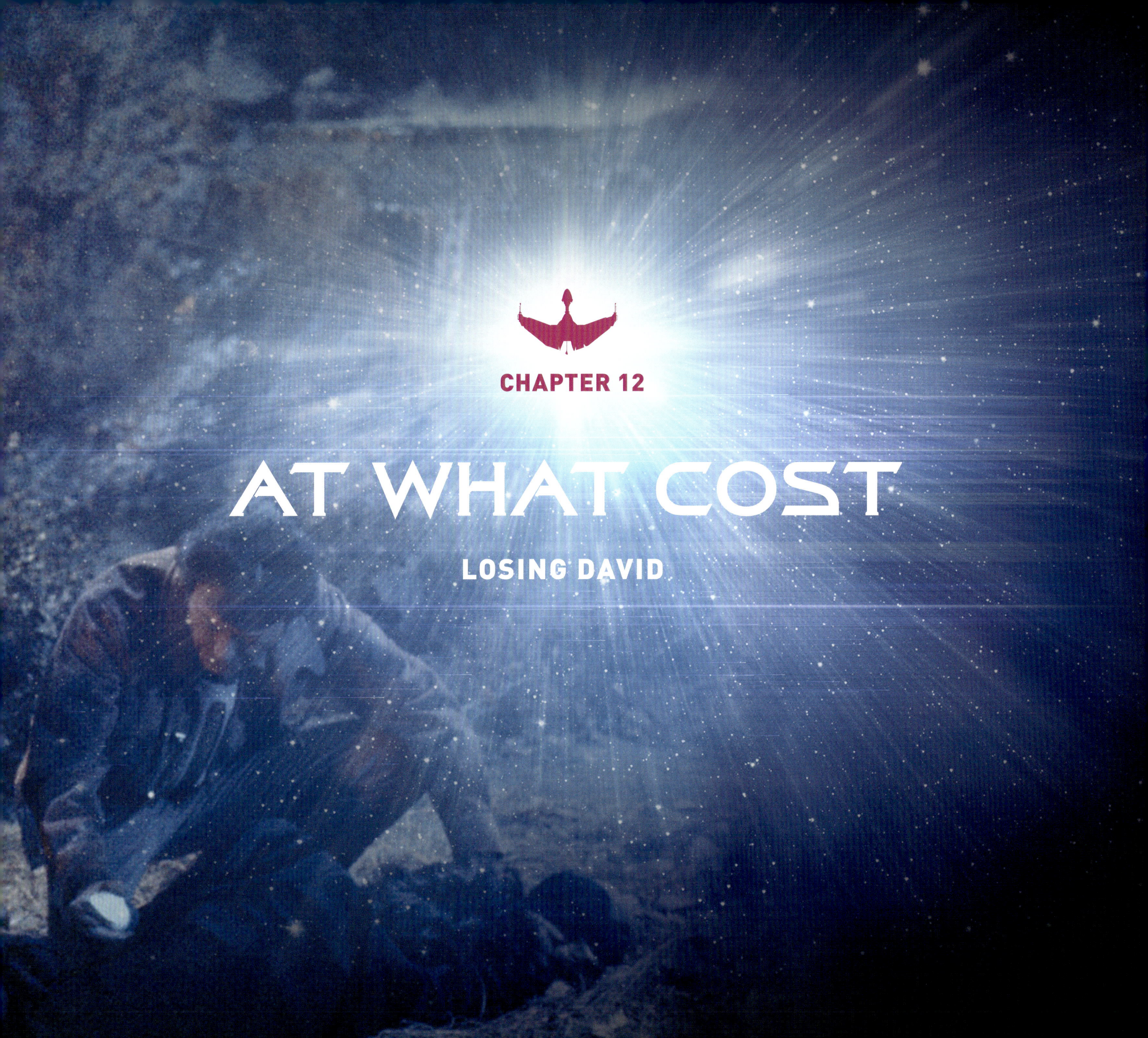

CHAPTER 12

AT WHAT COST

LOSING DAVID

"The death of David Marcus is a tragedy," Harve Bennett believed. "But truthfully speaking, we really didn't know what to do with the character; David Marcus was *not* very well defined. We discussed the matter and thought that he might best serve the story by being killed off. And that's what happens. Now, as it turns out, both the character and the young actor who plays him, Merritt Butrick, were so good in this film, so much better than *Trek II*, that I'm sorry we lost him."[1]

During scripting, Bennett realized his McGuffin had become a story problem. Now that the Genesis device existed, and had been deployed, it had the possibility of reshaping the galactic landscape, both figuratively and literally, placing the Federation at the apex of power. It wasn't theoretical as it had been for most of the previous movie. It was real. How could the film deal with Genesis without changing everything about intergalactic relationships and muddling the film with audience musings about how Genesis might be used in the future? The solution was provided by Roddenberry who recommended that Genesis should contain a serious flaw. This inspired Bennett to make Dr. David Marcus responsible for that flaw. When it was decided that David used protomatter to bypass certain problems, and that he was the only scientist who knew this and could replicate the production of another Genesis device, his fate was sealed. With David gone, so, too, was the future use of another Genesis device.

When Saavik says to David that protomatter is, "An unstable substance which every ethical scientist in the galaxy has denounced as dangerously unpredictable," two purposes were served. First, it is a bit of exposition to let the audience know why David's behavior was wrong. Second, however, it was included to assuage a worry Leonard Nimoy had about protomatter as a narrative element. Nimoy told Steve Swires of *Starlog*, "I thought we had better tread carefully there, because, in effect, we were saying that scientists can't always be depended upon to be – you should pardon the expression – *logical*. We were accusing a scientist of prematurely finishing an experiment with which he had become impatient. I checked with some very important scientists on this subject, and they told me it happens all the time."[2] By having Saavik chastise David for using something ethical scientists had denounced, Nimoy was satisfied.

Despite the demise of his character, Butrick was grateful to appear in *Star Trek*, being a fan of the show before being selected to play David in *Star Trek II*. Butrick shared, "*Star Trek* was really my big break. It was the first time I had ever had that much responsibility in a role. It was the first time that I was kind of put in a position of being a professional in the sense of having to deal with other professionals."[3]

THIS SPREAD: When Butrick first got the role and met William Shatner, he introduced himself by saying, "Hi, my name is Merritt and I'm your son!" Shatner laughed. Of the original cast, Butrick said, "...one of the things I had the most fun with, as an audience member watching *Star Trek III*, was watching the original cast. I don't think *Star Trek* is dependent upon anybody but them; they ARE *Star Trek*."[3] Butrick reunited with *Star Trek II* co-star Judson Scott for the *Star Trek: The Next Generation* episode 'Symbiosis' about a year before his death in 1989.

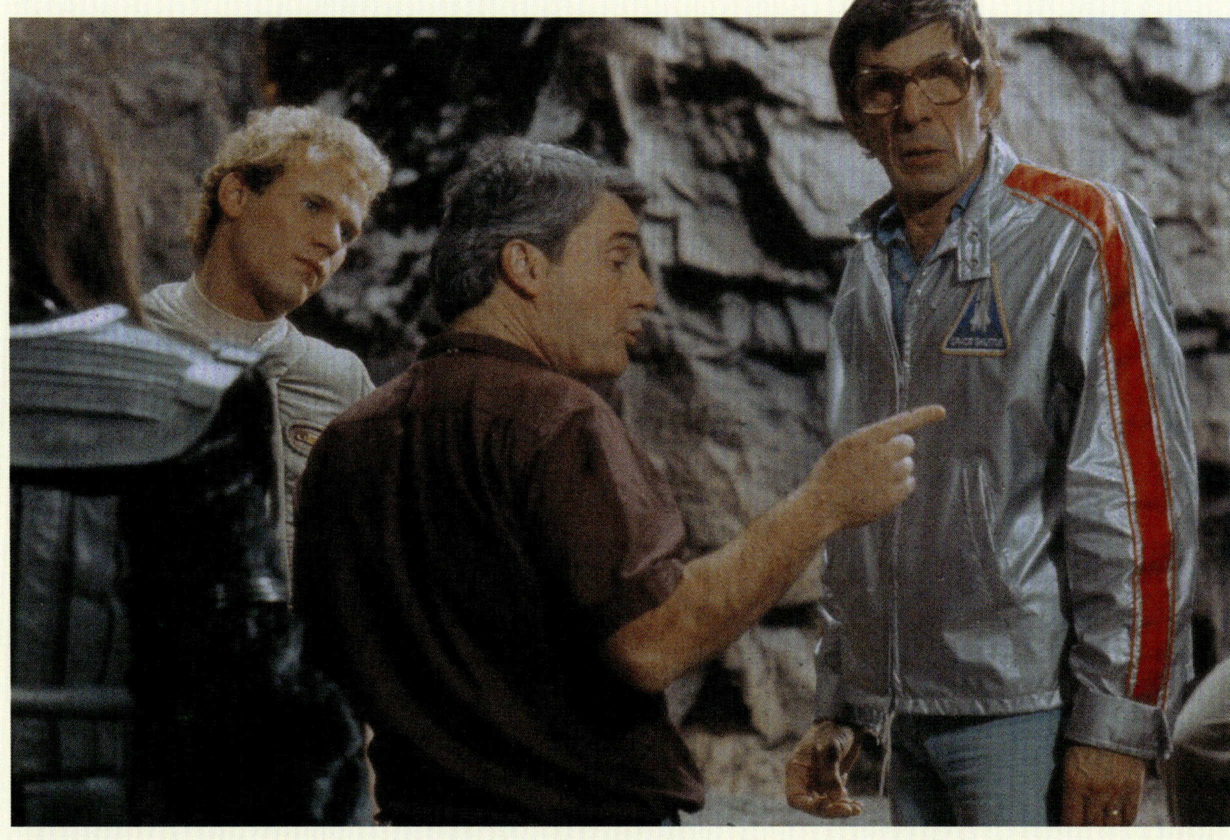

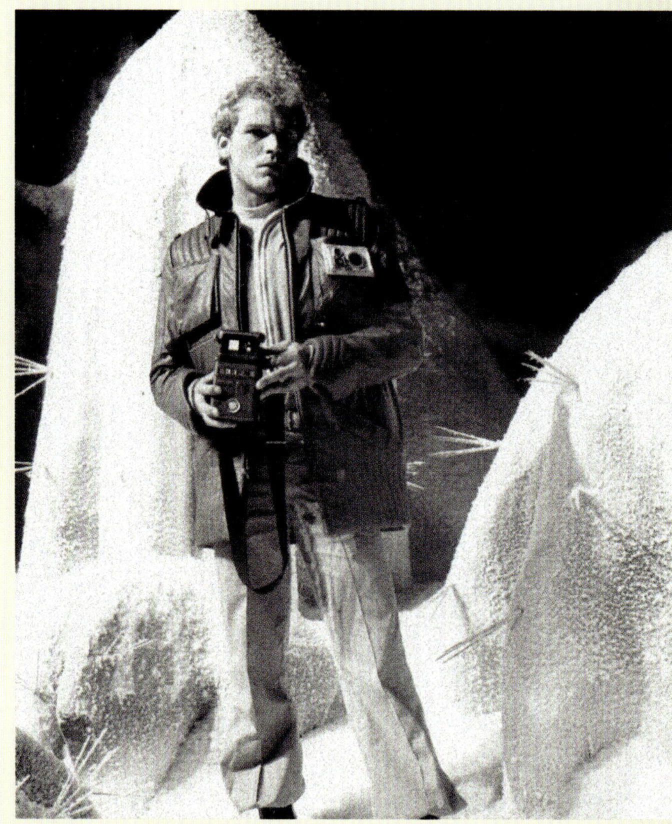

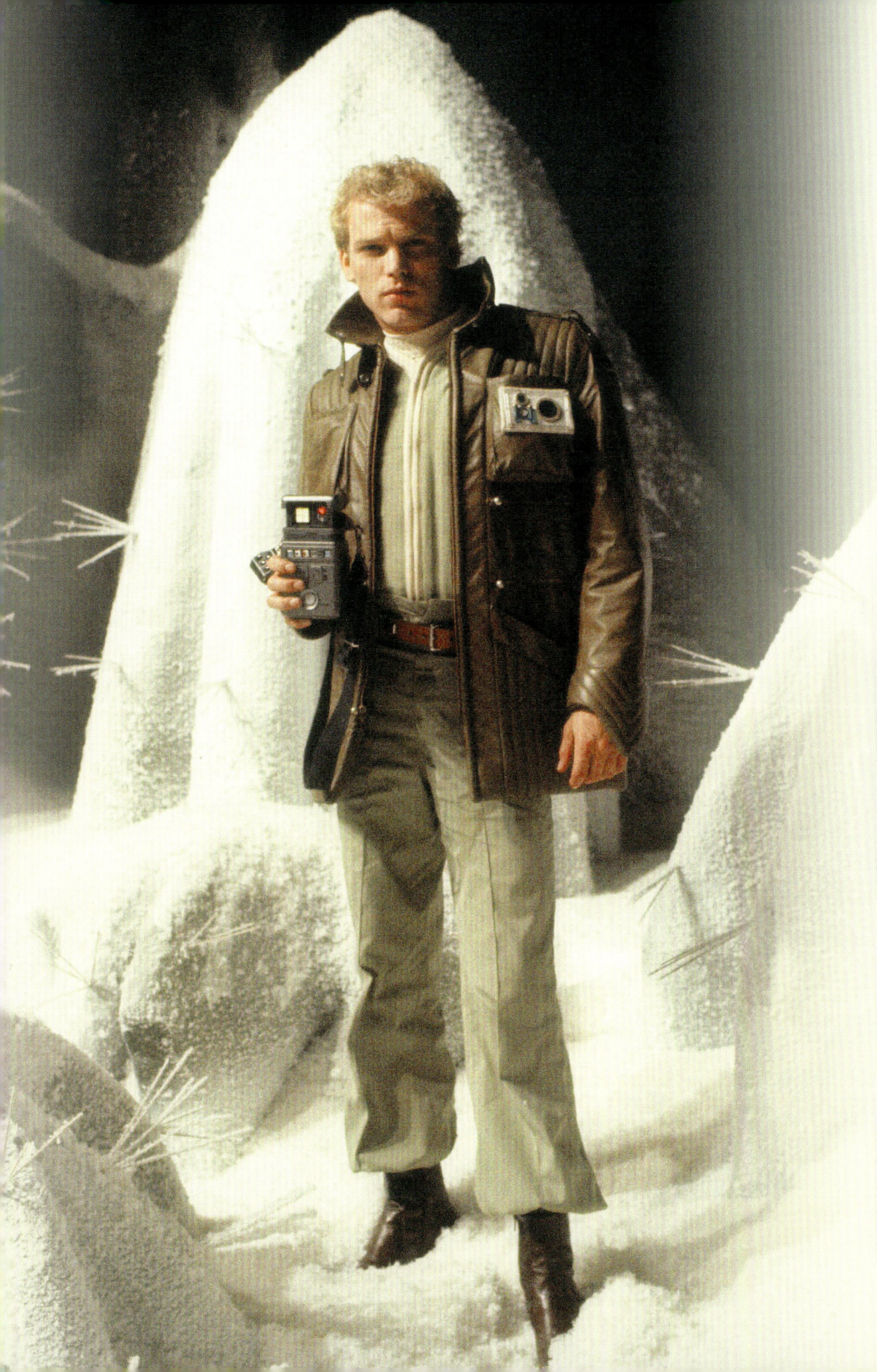

In 1983, Butrick had a phone chat with Bennett and Nimoy who told them about their plans for David. He was asked to go to Paramount to read the script due to the ongoing secrecy concerns. "I read the script and read David's death and it just seemed natural at the time," shared Butrick. "I loved the initial idea. I did not want to grow up just to be Captain Kirk's son. The way they had written his death was the perfect end for David. I never really thought about being a continuing new character in the *Star Trek* films."[3] One of the reasons that Butrick liked the script was that this time, David had a maturity and seriousness of purpose about him. Butrick explained, "He has grown up in this film, tempering his obnoxious attitude and impetuousness. We get to see him in much more dramatic situations which I like."[1] Butrick himself had a similar situation, maturing as an actor between the *Star Trek* productions, including both theater work and his first regular TV series, *Square Pegs*.

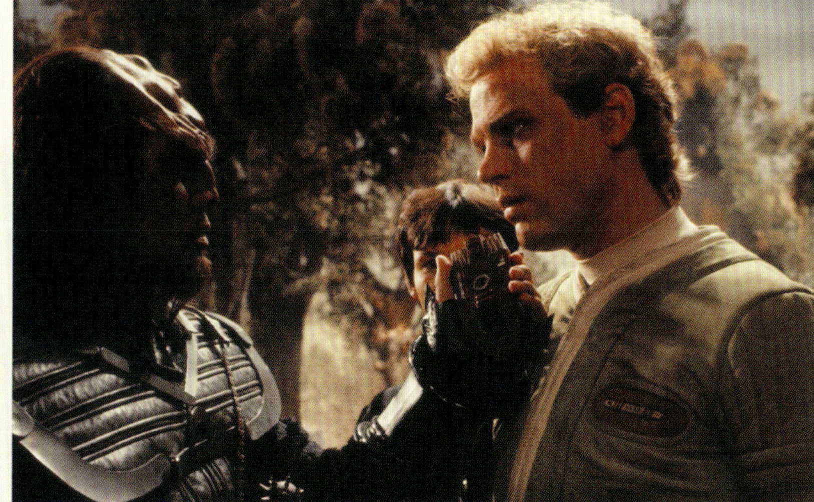

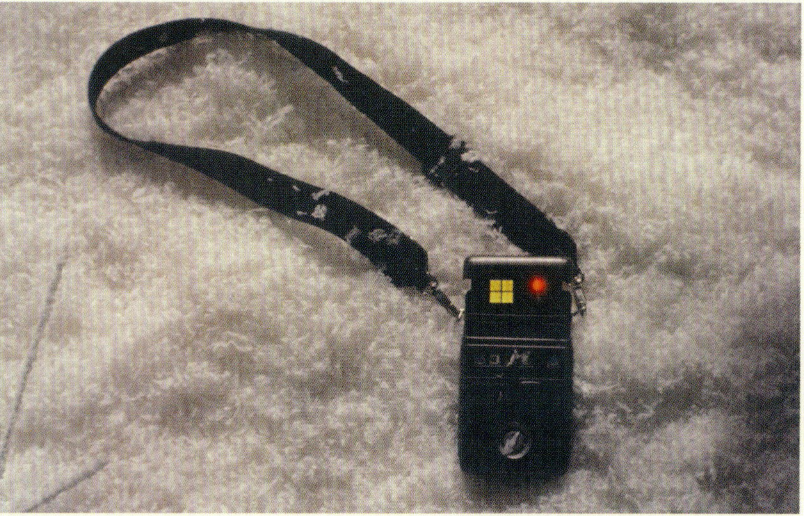

DELETED SCENES

DAVID'S EULOGY AND SAAVIK'S EXPOSITION

In the film, there is an emotional moment when Kirk places his jacket on David in repose. As originally planned and filmed, Kirk would have also delivered a short eulogy to David as he did so. Kirk said, "My son...'To thee no star be dark...Both Heaven and Earth...Friend thee forever,'" quoting William Shakespeare's *The Two Noble Kinsmen*. Butrick shared his disappointment at the moment being edited from the film, but understood why. He explained his feelings during an interview with Dan Madsen in 1986. "When they finally put a film together, they have to go for pacing more than sentimentality. I remember Kirk had a eulogy after David's death. I was a little taken back when they arrived on the Genesis planet and looked at David and said, "He's dead Jim, let's go fight some Klingons!" It seemed that short to me. I watched it again on cable not too long ago and it plays fine when you don't know what was left out. But, I knew what scenes were still filmed and I would say, 'But, there's more to this!' I think *Star Trek III* was edited very well, though. I have no qualms about that."[3]

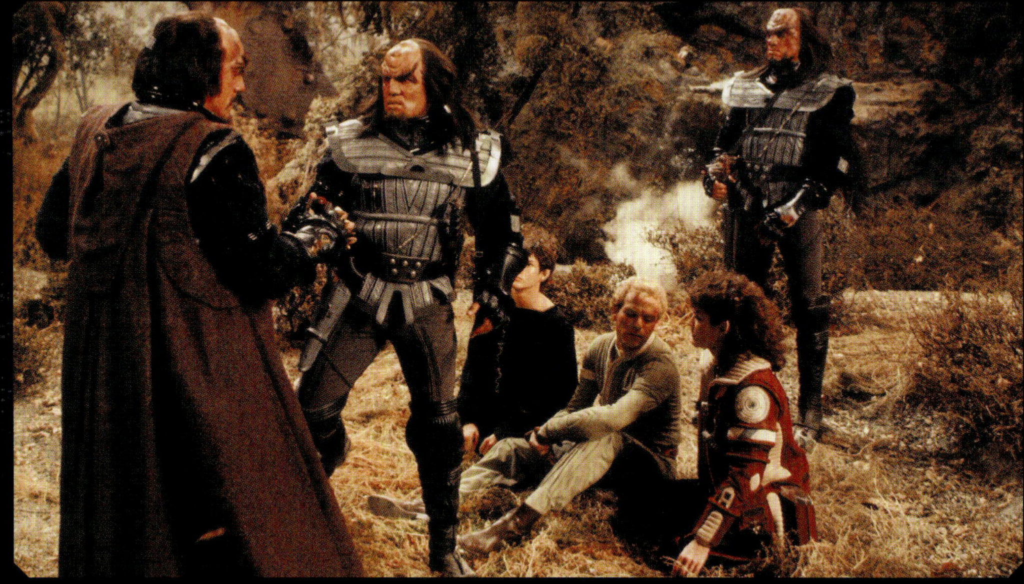

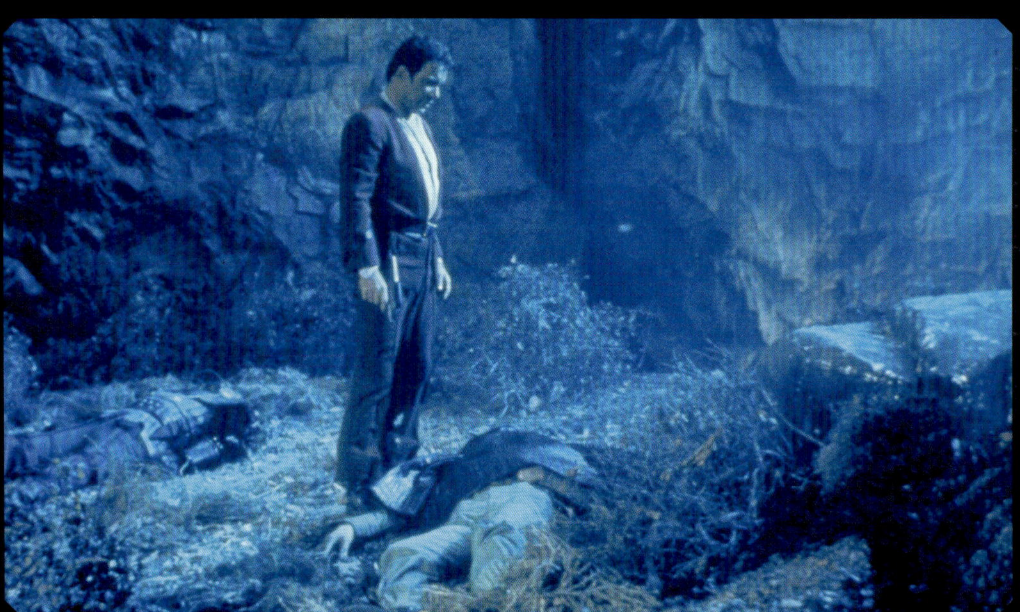

On board the Bird-of-Prey as it navigated to Vulcan, a scene was filmed of Saavik explaining the difference between the katra ritual meant to place a consciousness in the Hall of Ancient Thought and fal-tor-pan which is a refusion of the body and the mind. When Kirk asks what will happen to Spock if the refusion fails, Saavik warns, "He will remain always as he is." Because the scene is somewhat resonant of T'Lar's scene on Vulcan, the moment was edited from the film.

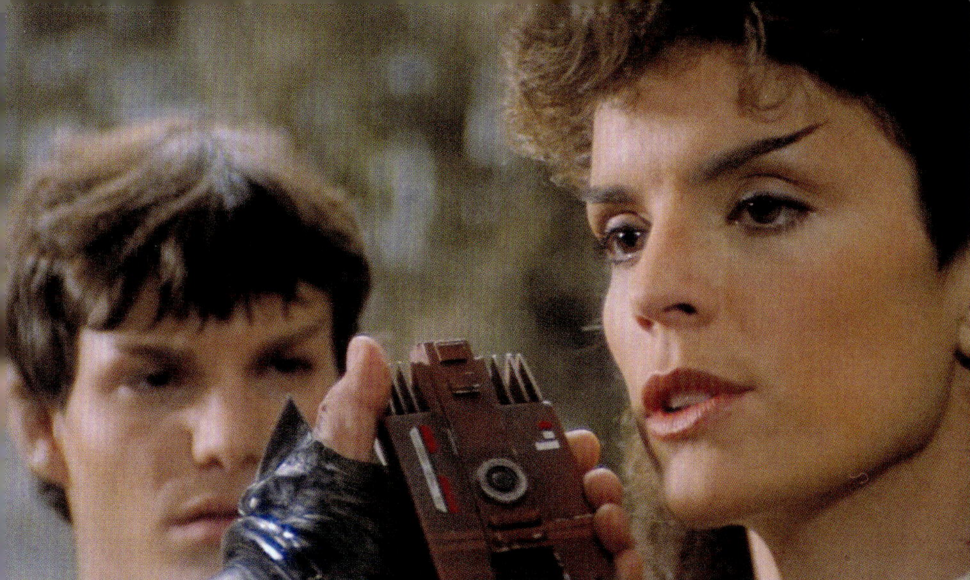

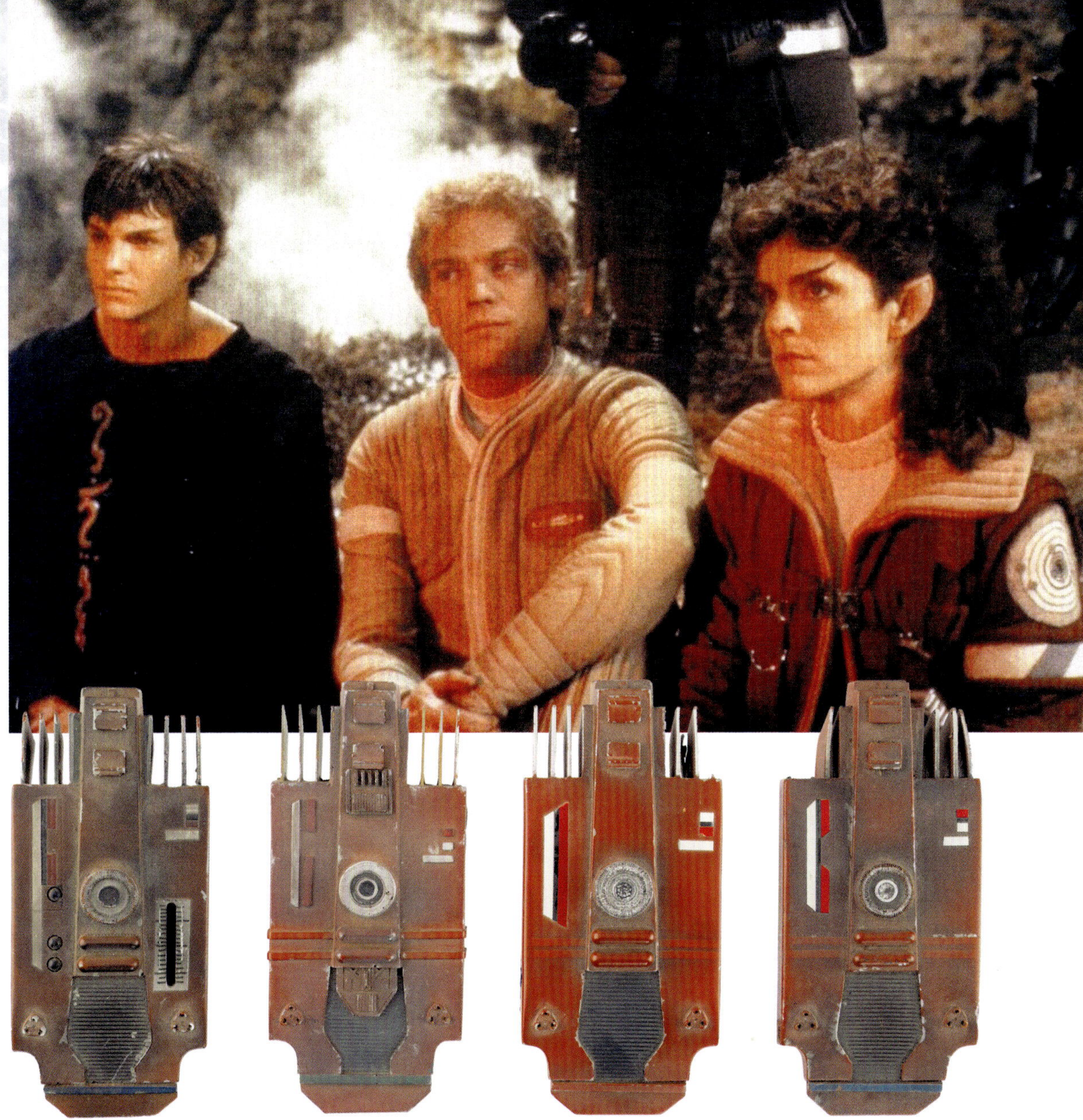

David's death was filmed on October 3, 1983. Spock actor Stephen Manley described the process that day. "Mr. Nimoy did a shot where the camera dollies along. He goes from Robin, to Merritt, and then to me, as the Klingon sergeant is being threatening. Leonard looked at me and said, 'You are standing there, not quite aware of your surroundings.'"[4] Manley, who was a *Star Trek* fan, was familiar with Spock's signature eyebrow raise. "We did a rehearsal and when the camera was hot on me," Manley continued, "I slightly raised that right eyebrow, while keeping that kind of lost gaze. Leonard said, 'I like that. It is just enough. Leave that in there. I get what you are doing.'" When they filmed David's death, with stuntman David Cadiente in his role as the Klingon sergeant and David Burton performing David Marcus' stunts, the fight was choregraphed and filmed. Butrick was brought in to play the character's final moment.

One of the challenges that Curtis faced was how to deliver the news to Kirk about David's sacrifice with the words, "Admiral. David is dead." Despite Bennett's script which described Kirk hearing "Saavik's shaken voice," Nimoy wanted a less emotional interpretation than the previous iteration of the character as played by Kirstie Alley, who Bennett had presumed would be playing the role when he wrote *Star Trek III*. Curtis shared, "No one talked about Kirstie with me. Not one word. I was never made to feel like I needed to mimic some aspect of the character that she'd established. It was as if the character never existed. [Apart from] Merritt, who was my fellow actor, he talked to me about it because actors help each other. He said, 'Kirstie and I, as Saavik and David, had this like full, flirtatious energy between us.' And I'm like, 'Okay, I get it.' However, I always deferred to Leonard's direction. There is some of that energy in the first scene together on the *Grissom* where we are focusing on the Genesis planet. There is a little bit of humor during that scene between David and Saavik, but that is the end of it."[5]

TOP RIGHT: Although already an experienced actor, Manley was grateful he was able to watch and learn from the other performers on set. He reminisced about the day filming David's death. "Robin and Merritt were talking. Merritt joked, 'I die today.' Robin said, 'Please don't die! Don't! I need you here!' They became close, good friends."[4] As part of his education, Manley snuck in to watch dailies of the scene where David observes Genesis transform from day to night. "I sat in the back so as not to disturb anyone," added Manley. "Harve, Charles Correll, and Mr. Nimoy were there watching. There was a big discussion about that scene for about thirty minutes. They talked about its implications, about Merritt's reaction, the lighting. They really cared. It was very important to them."[4]

ABOVE: Heritage Auctions / HA.com The Klingon communicator is essential to the plot, both when Saavik shares the news about David with Kirk, and when Kirk uses that same technology as a ruse to make Maltz think he is Kruge.

ABOVE LEFT: Nimoy guided Curtis through the scene with the advice that, "'It is about the eyes.' Leonard felt, even if I barely said the words, 'David is dead,' without any emotion in my voice, that my eyes would tell the truth."[5]

David's death was important not only to *Star Trek III*, but future films; in particular, it would have implications for Kirk's reactions to peace with the Klingons in *Star Trek VI: The Undiscovered Country*. Kirk's reaction onboard the *Enterprise* to news of David's death is easily one of the most emotional for the character in the pantheon of *Star Trek* adventures. When Kirk hears the news, he stumbles back and misses the Captain's chair. A few moments later, as Kirk continues to process the news, he literally leans on the *Enterprise* as he spins in his chair. William Shatner wrote in his book, *Star Trek Movie Memories*, that, "First, I'm really proud of that scene. Second, I really believe it might actually represent Kirk's finest celluloid moment ever. And third, it came together by accident."[6]

Kirk's reaction scene will play in the film interspersed with the action on Genesis. However, because all scenes occurring on the *Enterprise* were filmed together for cost and resource efficiency, Shatner's performance was filmed seven weeks before Butrick's. On August 23, 1983, as work on Kirk's reaction began, Nimoy asked for privacy on the bridge set so that he and Shatner could work on the scene. When everyone filed out, and before the discussion began, the two friends hatched a plan. Practical jokes stretch back to the filming during the original series, including the famous bicycle incident. In the 1960s, Nimoy brought a bicycle to set so as to more efficiently get to the commissary. As a joke, Shatner hid his friend's bicycle in the unlikeliest of places, including the set rafters, each day. For his part, Nimoy would try to keep the bicycle from Shatner, locking it in his own car. Of course, Shatner had Nimoy's car towed as the joke continued. By the time of *Star Trek III* not much had changed. Taking advantage of the privacy they had on the bridge set, but with colleagues waiting nearby, a new prank evolved.

"Bill and I started acting as if we were having a big fight," Nimoy revealed. "He started yelling at me, I'm yelling at him. And he's yelling things like, 'No, I'm not gonna do it that way!' And I'm yelling, 'You'll do it the way I tell you to!' And we're throwing things, slamming chairs on the floor to make noise." Nimoy laughed, "I don't think we fooled anyone at all, I think they knew exactly what we were doing, what was going on."[7]

Getting back to business, Shatner and Nimoy started to do the work that would eventually lead to what Nimoy considered a triumph for Shatner in his role, and a vulnerable, very human moment for Kirk.[7] When asked where the idea to have Kirk stumble came from, Shatner responded, "It dwells in the area of an unspoken heart, of un-thought. It dwells in the area of spontaneous art as an actor. Whatever it is you don't question it." Continuing, he added, "It's like when you're speaking. You don't say, 'The next word I'm going to say is...' The words are there, and if you were to analyze how the words got there, you might be stumbling... It's a conversation with yourself in effect and you are into whatever is the primary emotion or object and you allow it to flow. And it has to flow not only how you would do it, but how would the character you're playing do it? It's symbiotic. It's kind of like a free form. It's jazz."[8]

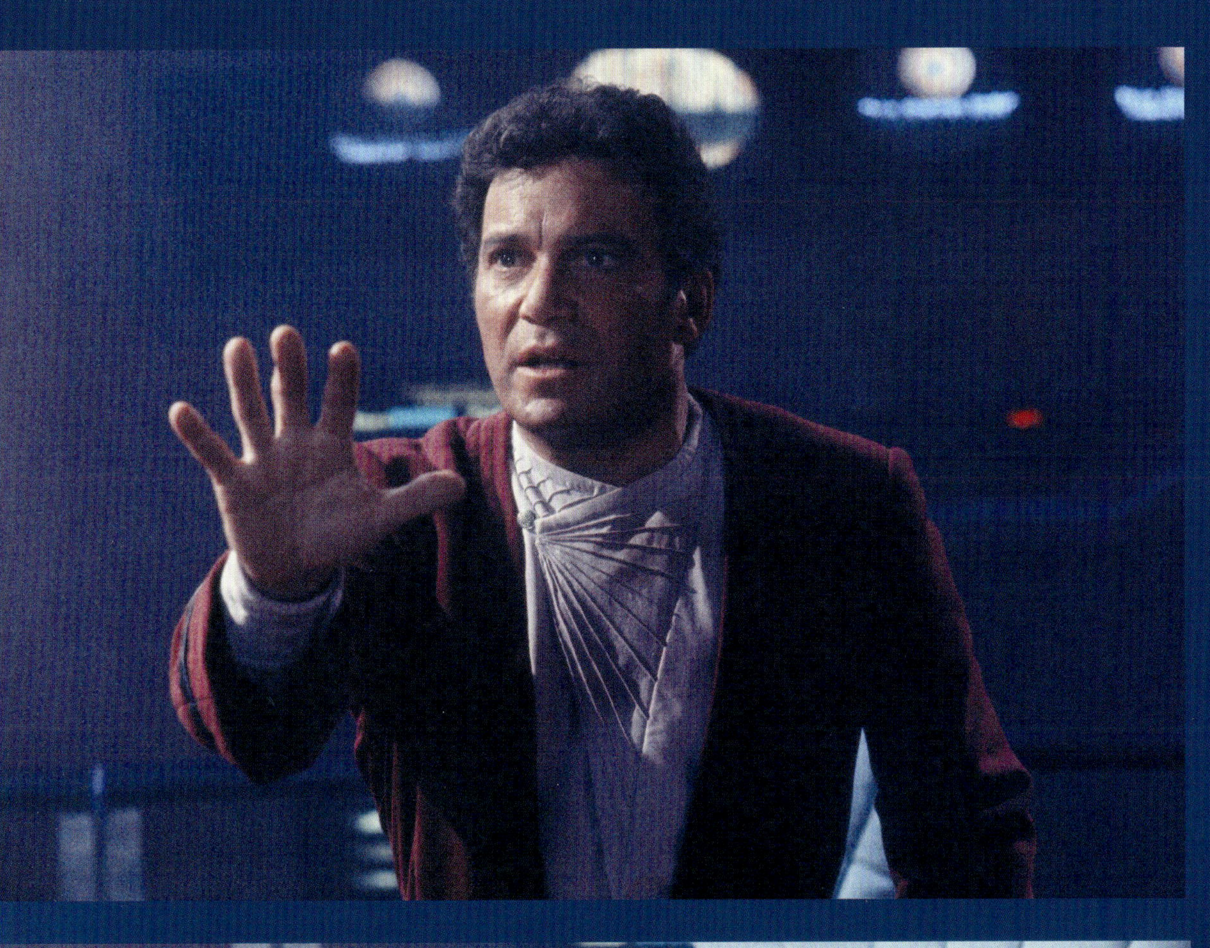

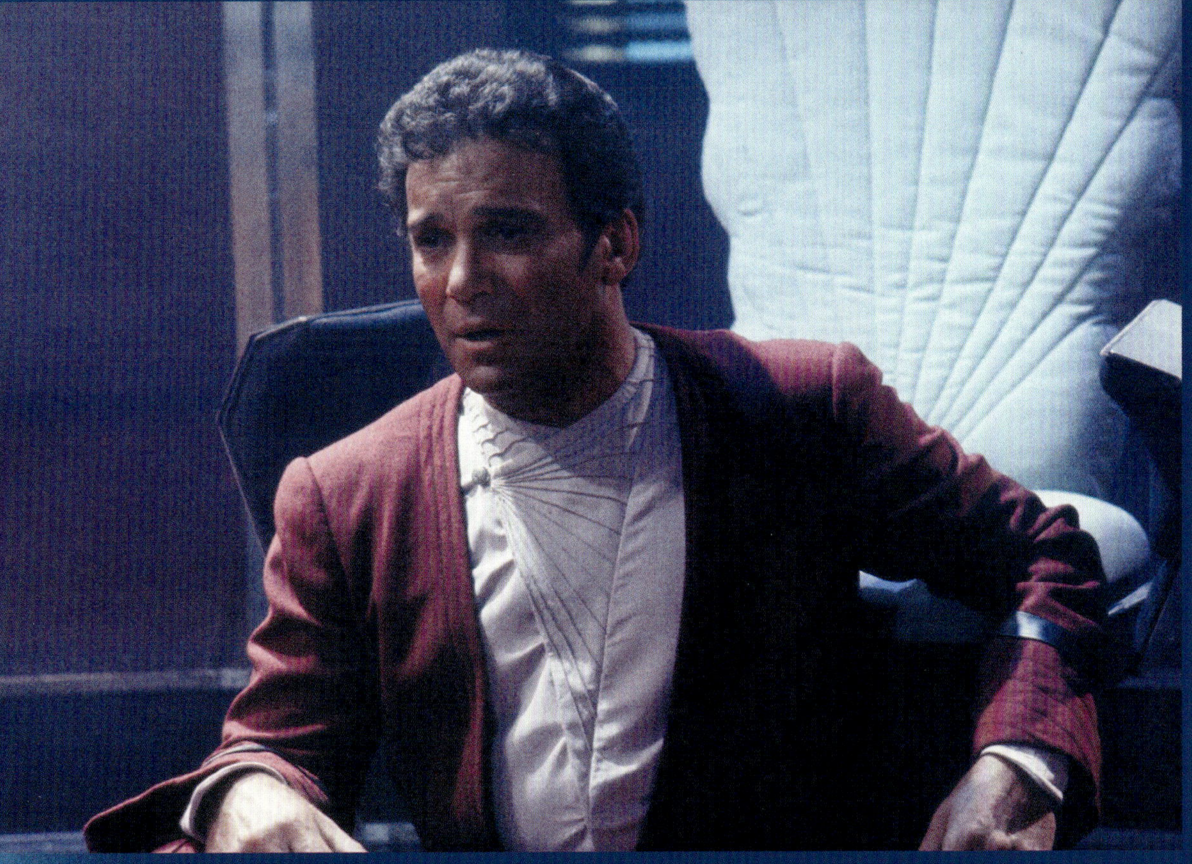

RALSTON'S JOKE

Continuing the tradition of practical jokes on set, ILM's Kenneth Ralston played one that he later vowed never to do again. "It was not the first time I've done this joke, but this was the last! It was the last day of shooting. And you know, everyone's always happy on the last day. We had filmed a lot with ILM's Empireflex camera which most people don't really understand how it works. I had hidden a 400-foot roll of useless raw stock in my jacket. Leonard was sitting in his director's chair. I said to him, 'Let me check the camera to make sure everything's okay.' I opened the camera, which in reality has a contained film magazine. There is no way to expose the film or even get to the film. No one outside of ILM really knows that. I open the top of the camera lid to hide what I am doing, and I reach into my pocket and grab one end of the roll of fake film I have there. It rolled all the way to Leonard." Ralston added, "He is looking at the film he thinks is from the camera and I remember him slowly looking up. That look on his face. Before I could get anything out, Charlie Correll, who I loved by the way, who did not know we were joking, said, 'I guess we have to start again.' There is this moment of silence. I started laughing and I said, 'Oh, no. I'm sorry.' Once I told them it was a gag, it was okay. Leonard was gracious about it. But that look he had on his face before, it was like, 'Oh, what have I done?' I figured I better not do that joke again!"[9]

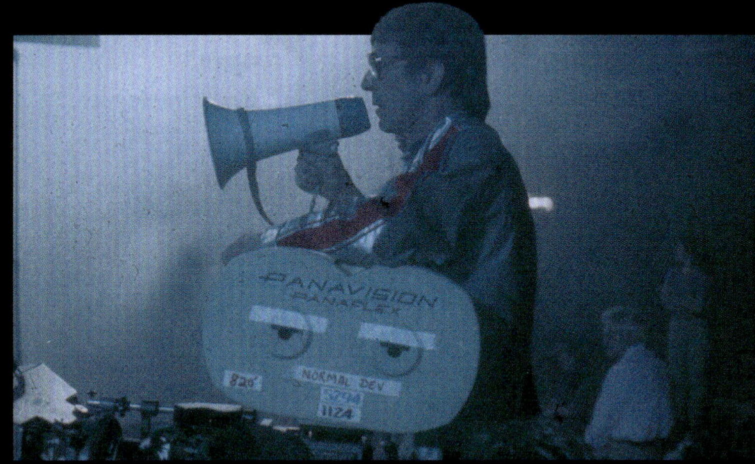

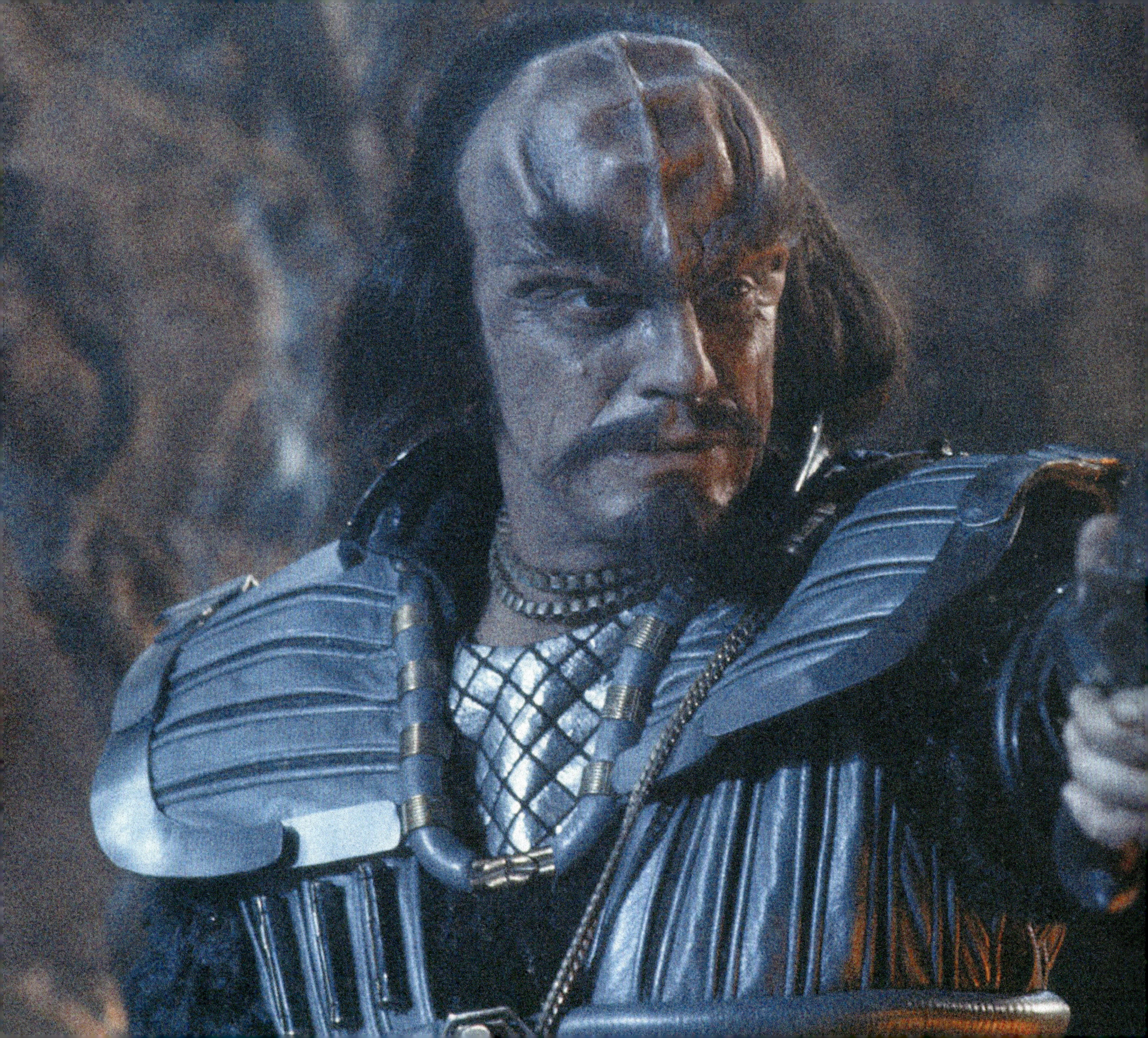

CHAPTER 13

A FIGHTING CHANCE

STUNTS AND STAND-INS

"I found the stunt people and those coordinators to be the most incredible professionals, and caring, cautious people that I've ever met," Robin Curtis said.[1] From a group bar fight, to the Kirk-Kruge mano a mano, to catapulting Klingons, the total stunts required of *Star Trek III* were exponentially greater than *Star Trek II*. Considering how action-packed the previous film was, this was an impressive feat. In fact, two coordinators, Ronald A. Rondell and Rob Stein, would be needed to hire stuntpersons, plan, and safely choreograph stunts.

One of the most important responsibilities of a stunt coordinator is to liaise with other department leaders. For example, costumes sometimes affect how stunts are performed, or which stunts are possible, requiring conversation between stunt coordinators and costume designers. That goes for makeup as well. Stuntman Thomas Morga illustrates, "I had been a Klingon in the first film, as well as *Star Trek III*. I had the right build for a Klingon, and was also used as one of the models for the Klingon uniforms. Fighting in Klingon wardrobe can be a challenge. They have big thick jackets with heavy shoulders that restrict arm movement. As far as makeup, any alien makeup with exaggerated brows and deep-set eyes can restrict vision."[2]

ILM and the stunt team also had a close relationship. Art director Nilo Rodis created several images outlining the Kirk-Kruge fight because miniature sets at ILM would be integrated with live action stunts filmed on the Paramount set. A miniature puppet of Kruge, designed and built by ILM, would transition from the stunt player to the model after Kirk wins the fight.

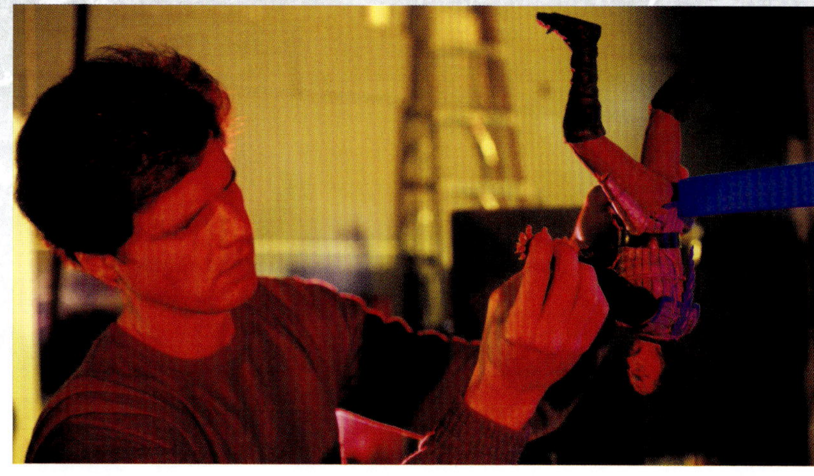

ABOVE: © Industrial Light & Magic. All Rights Reserved. Not all stunts are real. Some are created by special effects wizards like ILM's Tom St. Amand, pictured here with the finished Kruge puppet, connected to a rotator motion control device. The puppet was filmed against a blue screen and composited with a shot of the lava that engulfed Kruge. If fans watch the film carefully they will see the transition, aided by a flash of light, between the stuntman Al Jones and the Kruge puppet. Such a finished sequence required coordination between actors, the director, ILM, the Paramount camera crew, and the stunt team.

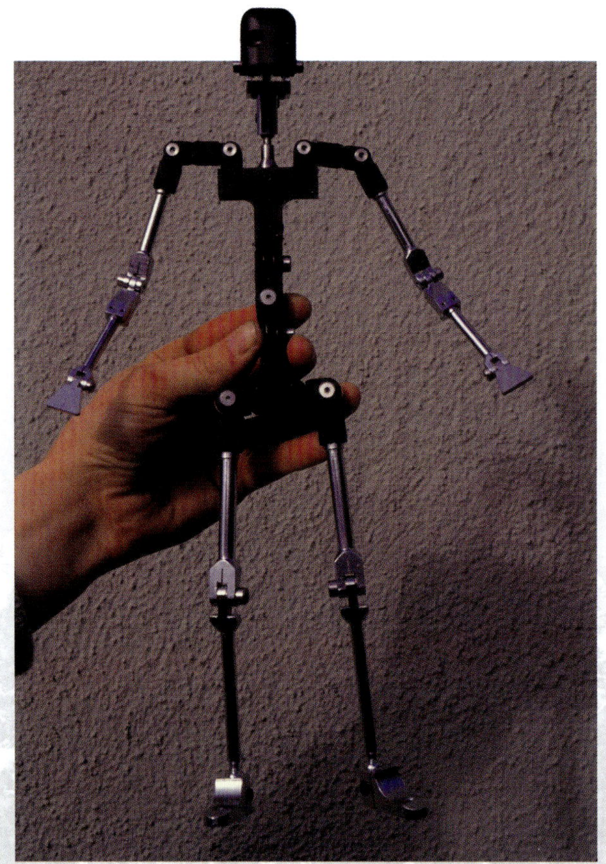

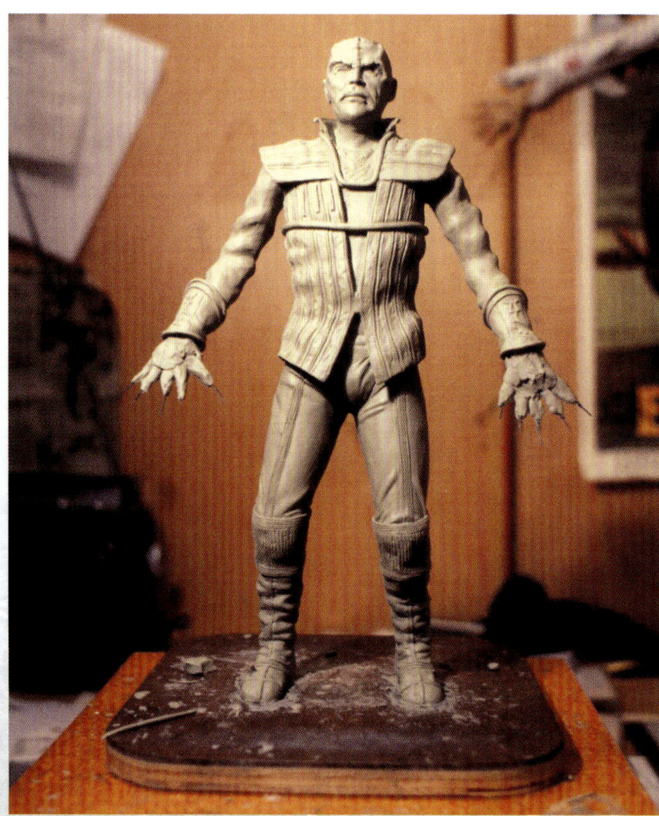

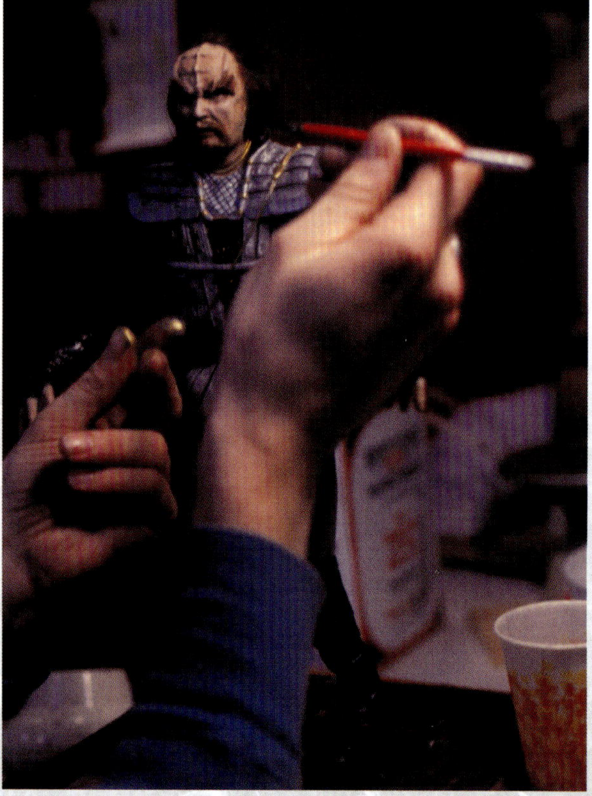

ABOVE: © Industrial Light & Magic. All Rights Reserved. Mini-Kruge from start to finish. St. Amand built the armature, David Sosalla sculpted the puppet, and it was cast by Sean Casey. The puppet movement was programmed by Denis Muren.

FLIGHT RECORDER VISUAL:

THOMAS MORGA, STUNTMAN

Thomas Morga is one of the most visible performers in *Star Trek* history, ironic, considering his job frequently is to stay invisible. As a stunt performer and coordinator, Morga has probably appeared on screen as more *Star Trek* characters than any other stunt person or guest star, playing more than eighty-five alien and human characters, and doubling for nearly forty guest stars as well as regular cast members that included Leonard Nimoy, Michael Dorn, and Jonathan Frakes. Morga began his action-oriented career not in Hollywood, but in Missoula, Montana with the United States Forest Service. Morga remembered when he was discharged from the Marine Corps in 1968, he got a job with the Forest Service at a tanker station in Southern California. After hearing about smokejumpers and their style of fighting fire, which consists of parachuting into remote areas to suppress fires while they're small, then packing back out to do it again, sounded appealing to Morga. "I applied to all the jump centers in the West and was accepted at the Missoula jump base. My very first season, an episode of the TV show, *Mutual of Omaha's Wild Kingdom* was scheduled to use the smokejumpers in their story about saving a Buffalo herd from a forest fire. I was fortunate to be on the shoot and was impressed with the experience. Of course, we weren't paid for it because we were working for the government. They just volunteer us!" Morga joked. "Following six seasons with the jumpers, I went to Hollywood hoping my background could help me become a stuntman, and it worked!"[2]

His first job as a stuntman on TV was on Harve Bennett's *The Six Million Dollar Man*. "I got one of my first feature films, and first *Star Trek* role, on *Star Trek: The Motion Picture*. When they were looking for a stunt double for Leonard Nimoy, I was recommended to the stunt coordinator Bill Couch, and he thought I looked enough like Leonard to make a good double. Sometimes it's just a matter of luck. And I had a good deal of luck with Leonard. Some actors, like Leonard, are very good to their stunt doubles." As an example, Morga explained, he was not a member of *Stunts Unlimited*, the stunt group that Rondell and Stein belonged to. "In most cases a stunt coordinator will pick stunt people, understandably so, from their group," Morga explained. "However, stunt coordinators try to honor the request of the actors if possible. When I first went to the production office and Leonard introduced me to Ron, he said, 'This is Tom Morga. He's my stuntman.' And that was just the beginning. Leonard proceeded to say, 'There is a scene with the merchant ship that has an alien. Tom can play that character. Oh, and the Klingons. Tom can be a Klingon. And in the bar fight scene, Tom can play a patron in the bar.' Ron said, 'Okay.' And that is how I got the four characters I played in *Star Trek III*."[2]

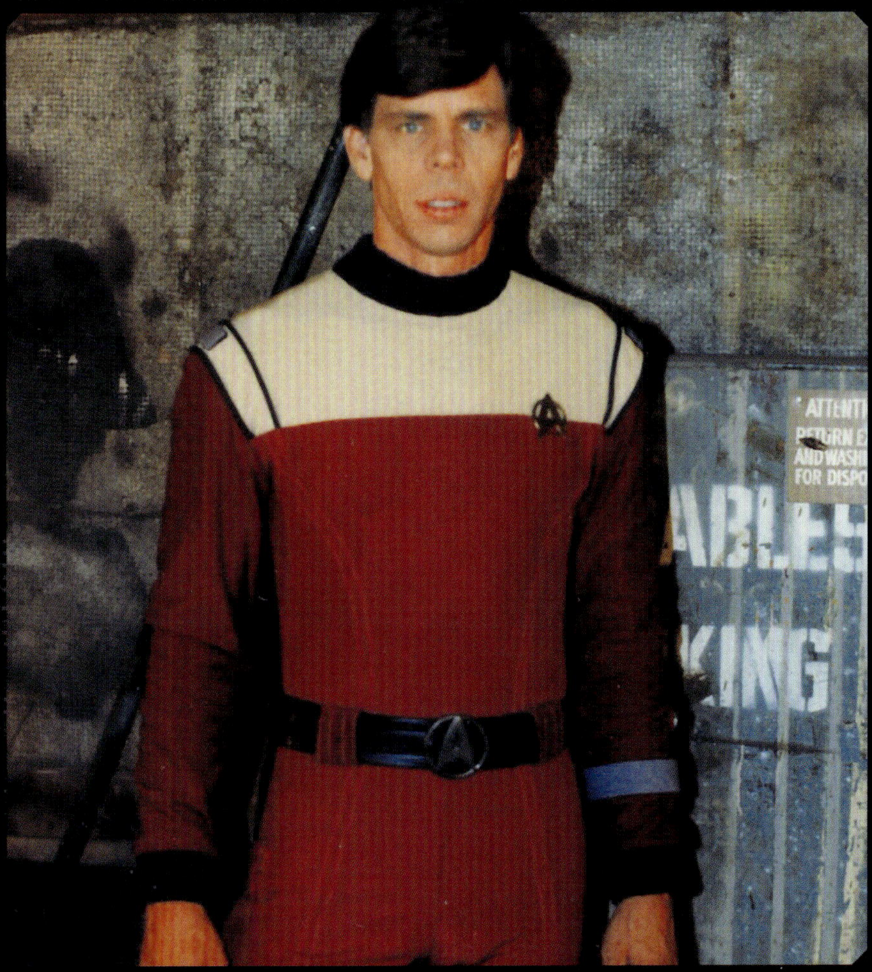

ABOVE: Ready for a fight! Morga in his bar patron costume.

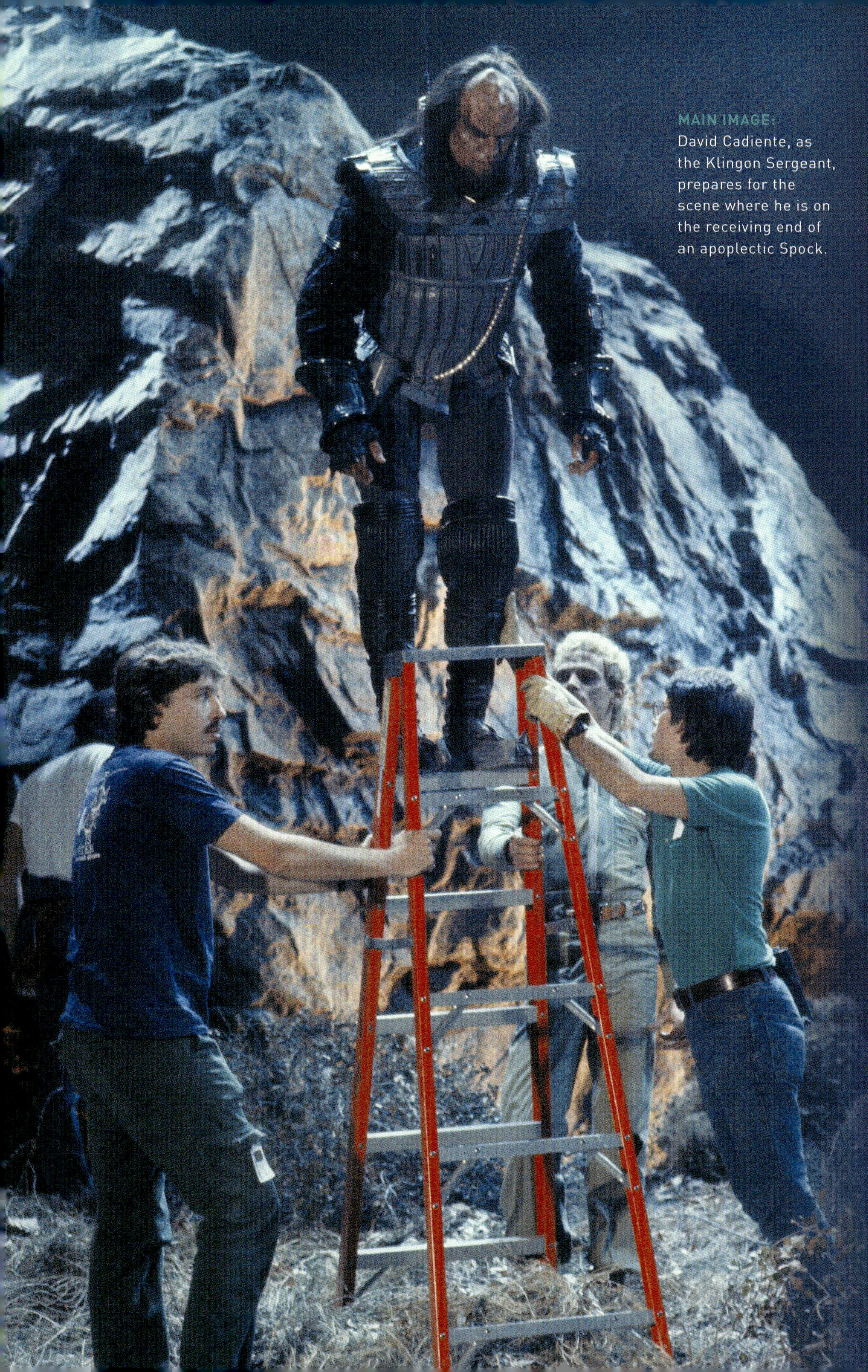

MAIN IMAGE: David Cadiente, as the Klingon Sergeant, prepares for the scene where he is on the receiving end of an apoplectic Spock.

The goal of all this coordination is to create not only spectacular stunts that enhance the story, but also to do so safely. Morga shared that the mantra of stunt coordinators is, "Always make it really exciting, make it look real, make it safe, and satisfy the director."[2] Spock actor Stephen Manley knows all too well the problems that can occur if a stunt goes badly after receiving second and third degree burns on his last day filming *The Hindenburg*. He was impressed by how concerned the stunt team

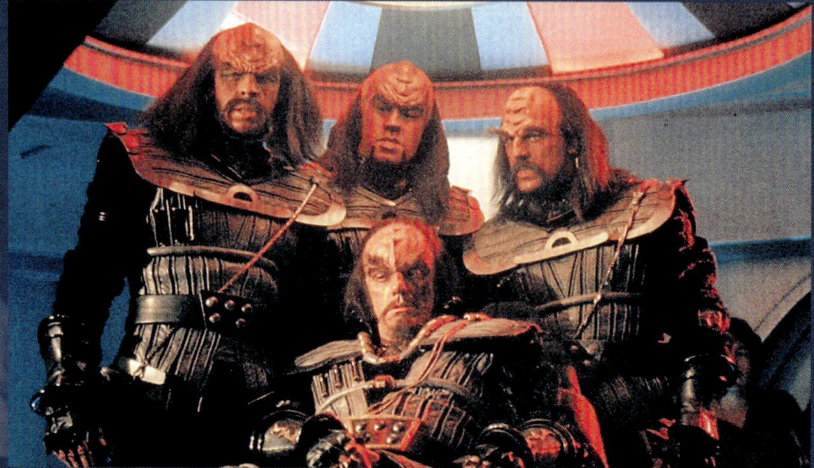

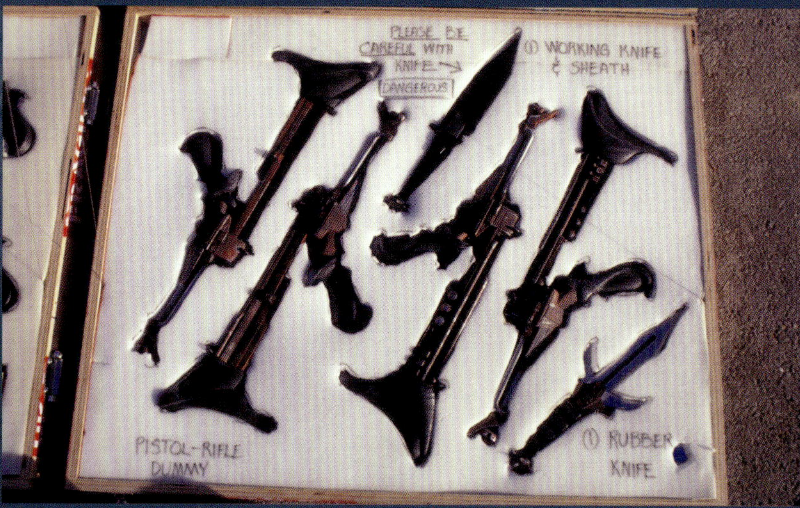

TOP: This image of Kruge surrounded by loyal Klingon soldiers serves also as a picture of Lloyd surrounded by stunt performers: Thomas Morga, Branscombe Richmond, and David Zellitti.

BOTTOM:
ILM helped design and build some of the props used in the film, including the phasers and disruptors. Stunt coordinators and performers frequently help actors learn how to safely handle props during fight sequences. The note "Please be careful" in this image of the Klingon weapons box is an example of the caution taken on set.

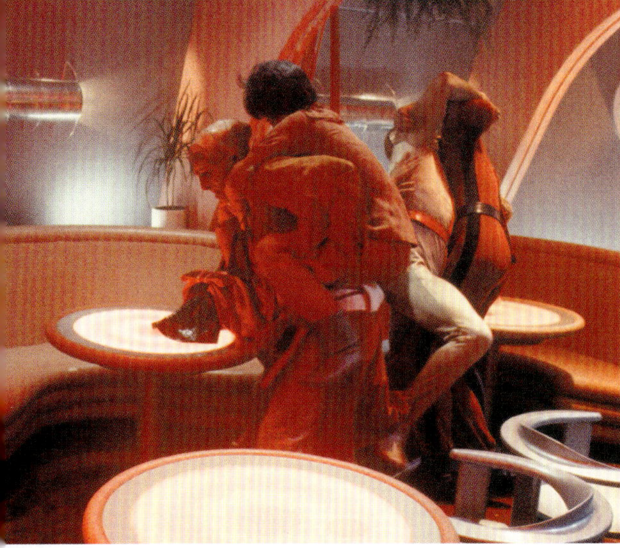

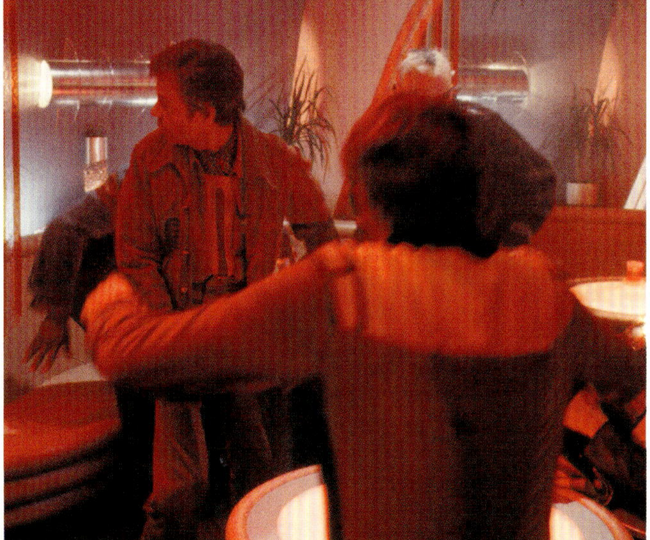

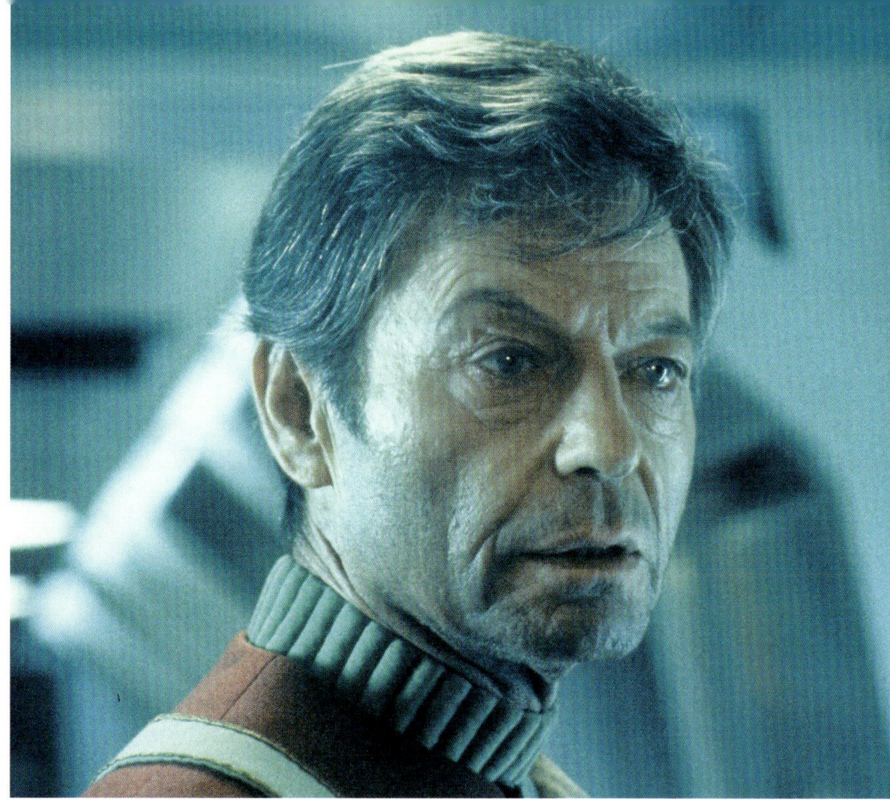

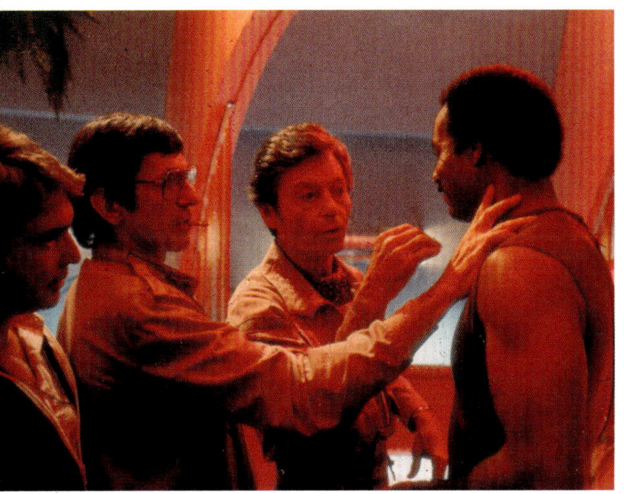

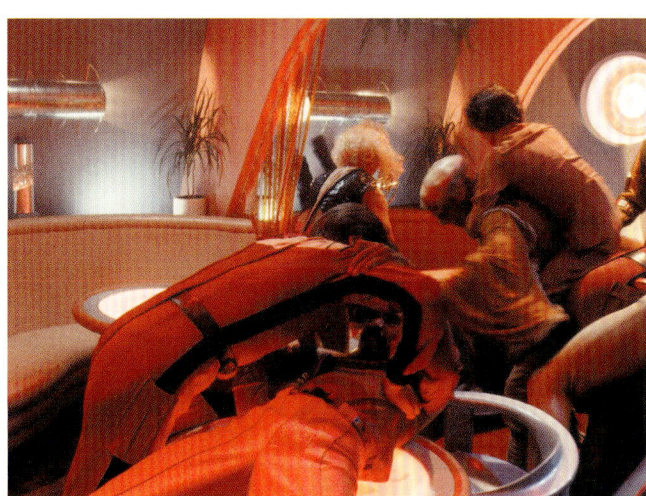

ABOVE: Kelly enjoyed filming the bar scenes more than any other in the film. He described his experience. "We had a great time with that scene... Something went wrong with the whole [fight] situation and the set was built in such a way that they couldn't redo the scene. But they let it go to the very end of the picture and we did a retake and came back. We then refilmed it and ended the scene at the table. We had a lot of fun doing that scene and I suppose that was the best for me."[5]

BOTTOM LEFT: Charles Correll watches as Nimoy teaches Kelley how to apply a Vulcan nerve pinch. The reason the group is rehearsing while standing, rather than in the booth as the scene appears in the film, is because in the original script McCoy applied the nerve pinch as he tried to leave the bar during the fight.

TOP LEFT, TOP MIDDLE AND BOTTOM MIDDLE: Pictured is the deleted scene showing the bar fight around McCoy and the Federation security agent.

on *Star Trek III* was about safety. "David Cadiente, who played the Klingon sergeant, knew that I had been terribly injured on the set of *The Hindenburg*. He took me around to show me what was going on with the set, showing me where not to stand or to watch out for the catapult that was spring loaded for the Klingon. The *Star Trek* stunt team took good care of me and all the actors."[3]

Stunt performers and coordinators need to be flexible because of changing conditions. An example is the San Francisco bar scene. The bar was a redress of the *Enterprise* sickbay set on Stage 9. As originally filmed, when the alien McCoy is negotiating with learns that he wants to go to Genesis, he starts to leave. McCoy grabs him and holds on during the entire time that the civilian agent talks with McCoy. When the agent reveals his identity, the alien will have no more of this and gets McCoy to release him. This causes the alien to accidently bump the waitress, which makes another patron think the alien had deliberately hit the waitress. A bar fight ensues, which Bennett described as "a general scuffle." McCoy tries to escape during the confusion, but is apprehended. The bar fight appears in both the novelization by Vonda McIntyre and the DC Comics adaptation.

There were two reasons why the extensive stunt work was edited from the film. First, the production ran out of filming time that day. Bar alien actor Allan Miller described the scene. "A big fight develops between these other aliens, about twenty, maybe twenty-five actors getting made up beautifully by all these makeup artists. The whole scene had to be removed because they ran out of time for that day. They couldn't go into overtime and there were no duplicate appliances available."[4] To restage and finish the fight the next day, all the alien makeup would need to be redone and the set rebuilt, which would have been prohibitively expensive. Second, Nimoy questioned whether the scene was actually necessary. Morga remembered, "I'm in the bar scene. I look like an extra because they took the fight completely out of the film. I think Leonard did not think the fight fit the storyline. It was more of a distraction. That scene worked without the need for the fight."[2]

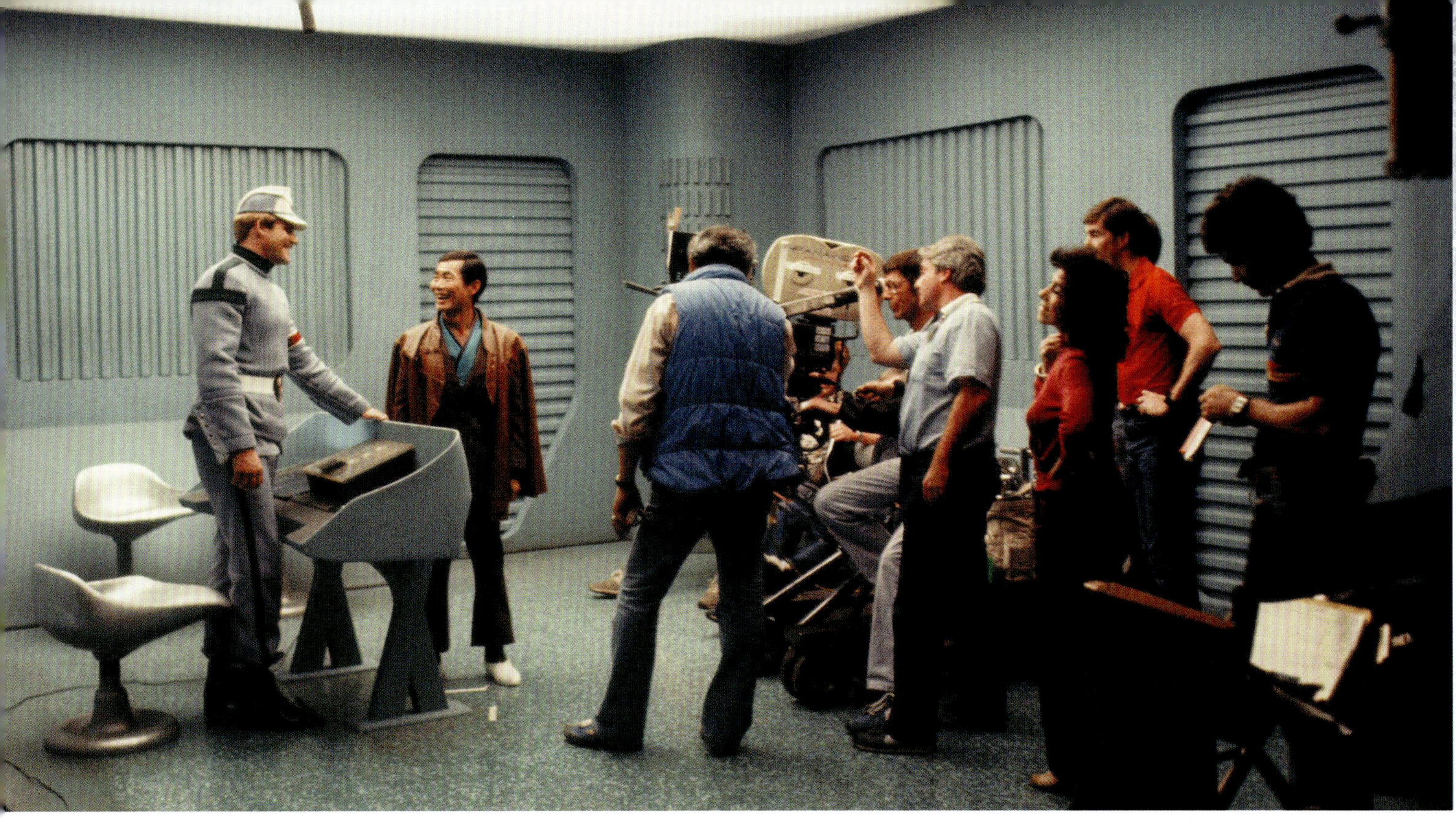

LEFT: On the last day of regular production, October 21, 1983, Nimoy and Correll film a scene that illustrates how movie magic creates a convincing stunt. While actor Douglas Alan Shanklin played Prison Guard #2, the flip the character does because of Sulu during the escape was performed by stuntman Jeffrey S. Jensen. Through careful alacrity, the editing hides the change from Shanklin to Jensen from theater audiences. Originally, George Takei had reservations about the scene because he worried about fan reaction to Sulu being described as "tiny." Bennett and Takei agreed to see what the other actors thought during a reading of the script at Nimoy's house. Their positive reaction and laughter convinced Bennett to keep the scene. Audiences, too, appreciated the scene, both for its humor and for how Sulu stands up for himself. "I have people who are shorter in stature come up to me at conventions and say, 'George, thank you, thank you for that line.'"[7]

A test for the stunt team was the fight scene between Kirk and Kruge, one that was met by drawing on years of experience, collaboration, and flexibility. As envisioned, the fight would have had Kirk and Kruge dealing more with the environment, dodging rocks and fire erupting from the Genesis planet, while they battled. Problems with the technology meant there was a need to rethink the fight. William Shatner wrote in his book *Star Trek: Movie Memories*, '...watch closely, and you'll notice that in our haste to rework the scene I even managed to dredge up a few of Kirk's well-worn TV moves. The giant windup into a left-handed haymaker, the roundhouse kick, the two quick jabs to the stomach followed by a right to the jaw, they're all in there.'[6]

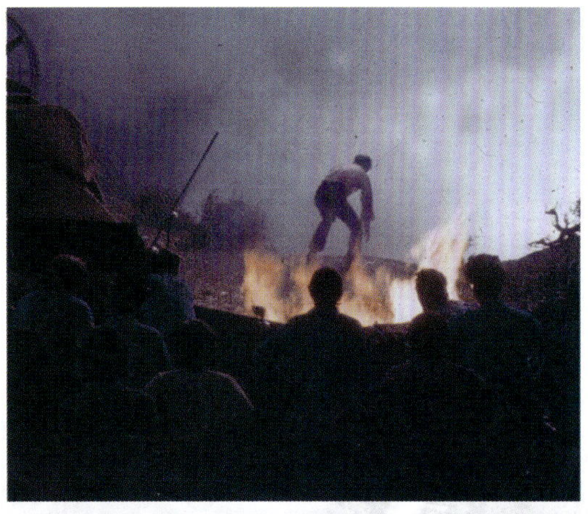

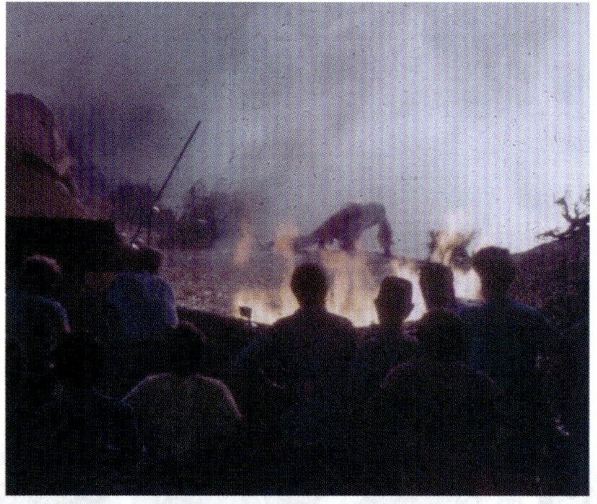

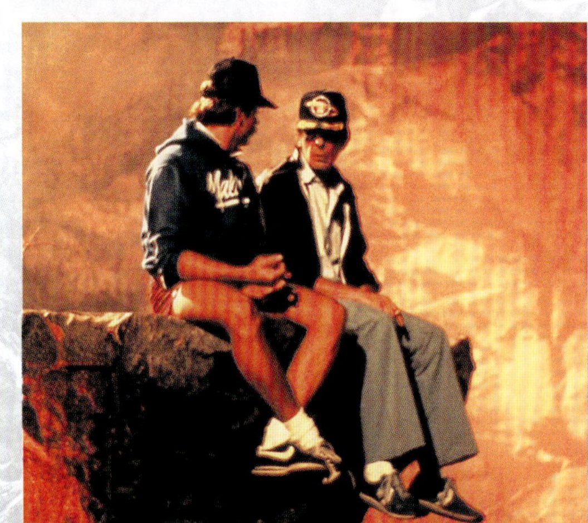

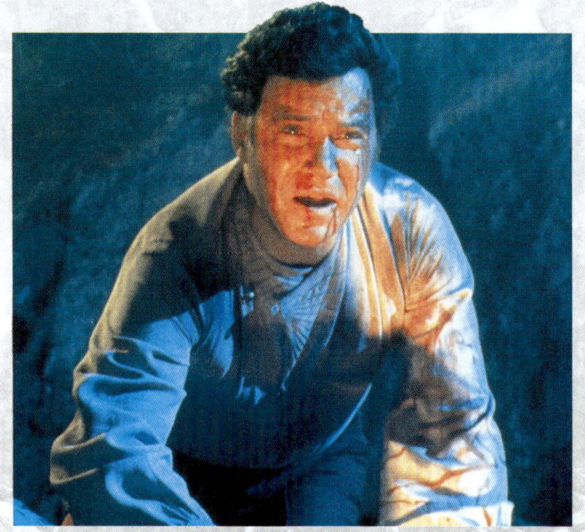

ABOVE RIGHT: Shatner performed some of his own stunt work, something he did in many of his roles. To ensure the safety of crew personnel, representatives of many different departments, from stunts to construction, are on hand to help if needed. For the more dangerous sequences, Johnny C. Meier would double for Shatner and Al Jones for Lloyd. Jones can also be seen as one of the Klingons who travel to Genesis with Kruge.

RIGHT: Rondell and Nimoy confer about the Kirk-Kruge fight.

FAR RIGHT: This picture demonstrates how preproduction art design, costuming, makeup, lighting, camera work, stunts, and acting combine to make an effective and emotional scene.

FLIGHT RECORDER VISUAL:

PHILIP WEYLAND, STAND-IN

Born April 20, 1948 in Wakefield, Massachusetts, Philip Weyland developed an early interest in both acting and directing. "I got a part in *Richard III* and after graduating college, I started doing dinner theater. I was in plays with Andy Devine, Linda Kaye Henning, and Nancy Kulp," Weyland said. It was his acting and directing of dinner theater that would lead him to boldly go to the 23rd Century. "I had directed a play *Beginner's Luck* starring DeForest Kelley at the Hayloft Dinner Theater in Lubbock during the summer of 1974. We became friends," explained Weyland. "A few years later, De called and asked if I wanted to be his stand-in for *Star Trek: The Motion Picture*. De warned me, 'You should think about it. You do that, you might get pigeonholed as a stand-in.' I said I would take my chances. I would be paid three times as much as I was making acting and directing."[8]

On Weyland's first day at Paramount, Kelley demonstrated why many people thought of him as a generous and amazing person. "DeForest looked for me that first day. He said, 'You know, my wife Carolyn and I were thinking about you this morning because it's the first time you are working on a movie and we were wondering what experience you were having.' That's the kind of guy he was. He would be thinking about other people and what they were thinking about." As Morga had experienced with Nimoy looking out for him, so, too did Kelley for Weyland. "On one of the movies, not *Star Trek III*, I was standing in for DeForest on the transporter pad which has a waffle grill floor with lighting that was really hot. Like *Cat on a Hot Tin Roof* hot! Myself and another stand-in were lifting our feet up and trying to cool them. This went on for hours. Our shoes melted. DeForest was not happy. I only saw him get mad a few times and he was really mad. 'How dare you make these guys do this without giving them breaks!' He was a great guy."[8]

By the time *Star Trek III* was to start filming, Shatner's stand-in Joel Marston was retiring. Weyland had been Shatner's stand-in on *T.J. Hooker* when he asked Weyland to take Martson's place. "I called DeForest and said Bill asked me to be his stand-in on *Star Trek III*, but that I wouldn't do it if he wanted me to be his," said Weyland. "DeForest told me, 'You have to go where the money is. I'm not going to work much. Bill will always be working.' De was correct, as I worked as a stand-in or dialogue coach on many of Bill's projects, from subsequent *Star Trek* films, *Sh*t My Dad Says*, *Boston Legal*, and numerous commercials. On the first day on the set, De gave me a signed picture. He wrote, 'So, you're leaving me for Shatner!' (Laughs)."[8]

What exactly are the responsibilities of a stand-in? According to Weyland, the most important rule is to be there when you are needed, to be ready to go. Stand-ins watch what actors do during rehearsals, from dialog to locations. "Productions mark the set floor with tape and the actor has to be at particular mark on a specific word so the camera and lighting is how it should be," explained Weyland. "So, if Bill is at the back of the bridge and he walks down to sit in the chair, then that is what I am going to do later. I will do that with the camera operator and cinematographer because they have to light it. They have to rehearse that with me because when the actor arrives, you want to do it fairly quickly. The reason is that 99% of the time, they don't want the actors getting tired, standing out there for hours with the lights on them."[8]

Of his many years working as Shatner's stand-in, Weyland shared, "Bill is a real professional, a great actor. I would help run lines whenever he had time between filming. In the makeup chair, usually. He had a good grasp of the entire script a few days into any episode or movie. It was a privilege to watch James Spader and Bill on *Boston Legal*; when they would be on that little balcony, rehearsing, I am standing there and it was the best live theater."[8]

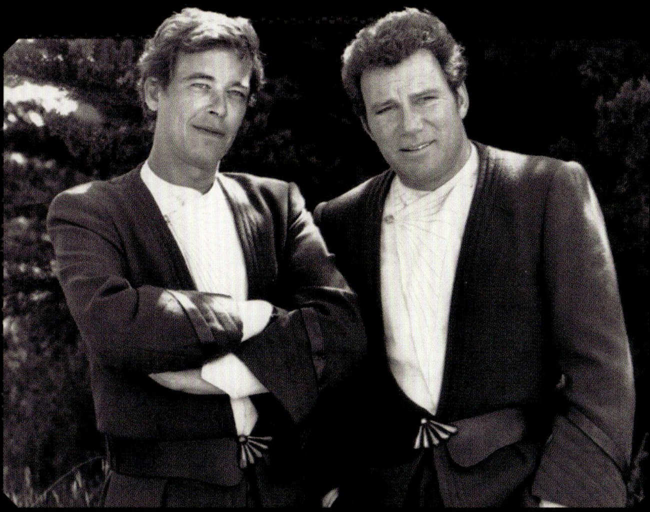

LEFT: Weyland and Shatner on location in San Franisco while filming *Star Trek IV*. Photo by Bruce Birmelin.[9]

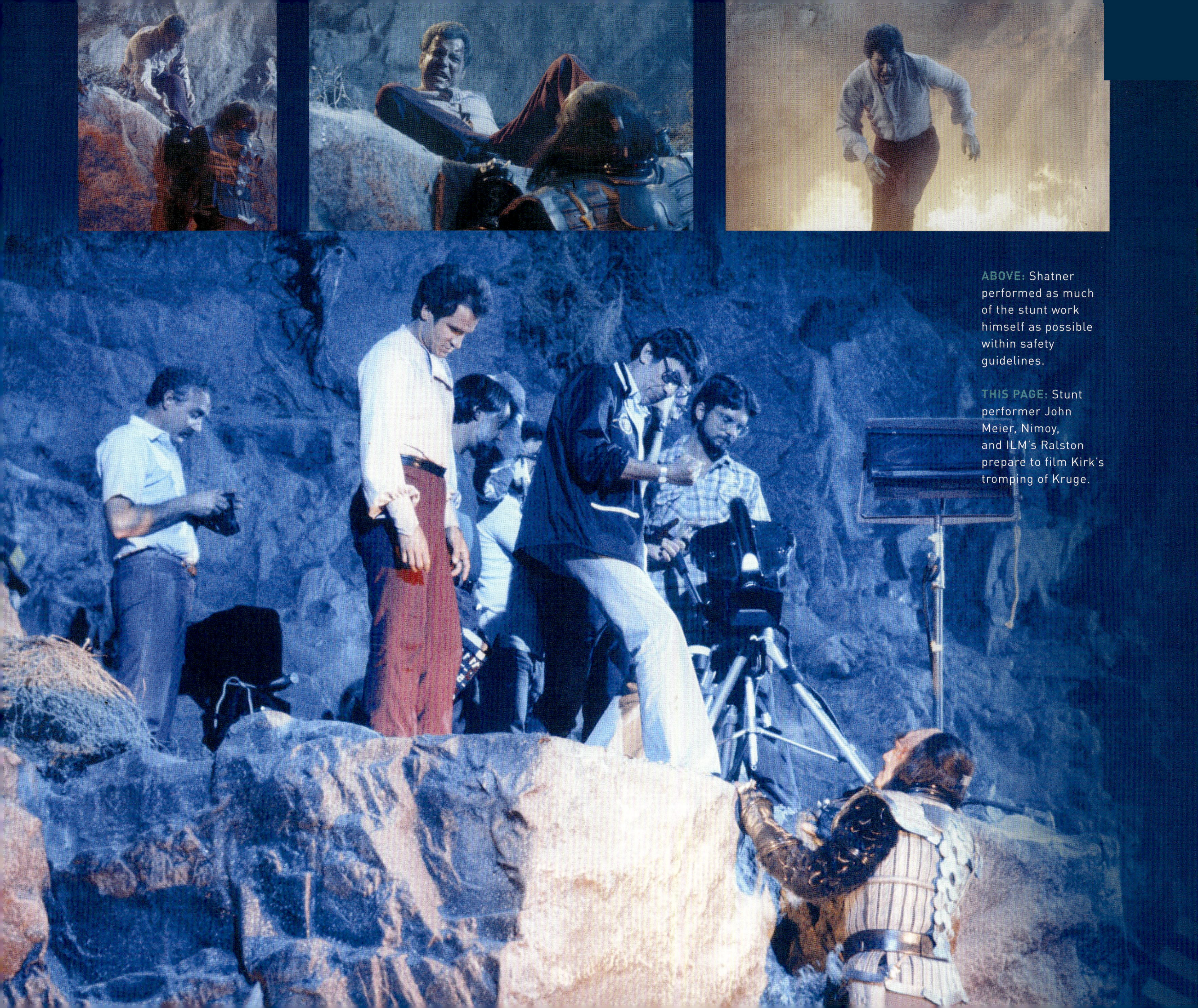

ABOVE: Shatner performed as much of the stunt work himself as possible within safety guidelines.

THIS PAGE: Stunt performer John Meier, Nimoy, and ILM's Ralston prepare to film Kirk's tromping of Kruge.

Communication is also an important factor in safety. No one knows this more than William Shatner. James T. Kirk is a character molded from the same clay as classic heroes of literature and mythology; he is a thinker and a doer. He balances thought and action in his explorations and adventures. To help make that balance believable to audiences, to make the jeopardy authentic, there are times when, if deemed safe enough by the coordinators, actors are permitted to do their own stunts. "It's a struggle between ego and machismo," observed Shatner about what drives some actors to want to perform their own stunts.[8] When considering when an actor versus a stunt double should take on a stunt, Shatner shared, "It has to be worthwhile, like somewhere in the middle of the stunt is a close-up that couldn't be shot any other way other than you actively falling or hanging onto something with your face in full view."[10]

Safety and the practicalities of insurance contracts are primary concerns when making the decision. "The factor against it is insurance," explained Shatner. "They won't insure you if you do something you're not insured to do, and actors are not insured to do stunts. They hire specialists who take the brunt."[10]

Shatner is no stranger to doing his own stunts, nor to their dangers. "I broke my leg doing a western at Paramount. There's a technique to make a horse fall called a 'Running W.' You pull on the reins to get the horse's head to the side he's trained to hit the ground on. I'm a horseman, and I thought, how difficult can that be? So, they dug up the ground to make a soft-landing spot, but they had watered down the whole western street to give it a look of usage rather than being dusty, dry, and non-trafficked. They watered everything down, including the dug-up place where I and the horse were going to fall on the soft ground. I did the 'Running W' and the horse fell. I forgot one small detail. That was to take my leg out of the way. So, he fell on my leg in the dirt, and now he's struggling to get up because I'm struggling to get out. And there was this whole mishmash. I don't know whether I broke my leg when he fell on it or when he stepped on it, but I got up and finished the scene trembling with pain. They took me to L.A. General hospital, which in itself was a trip."[10]

On *Star Trek III*, those kinds of problems were avoided by careful planning and communication. Even with a fast-turnaround on restaging the Kirk-Kruge fight, there were no serious problems because they took the time to rehearse with the actors and test props. "It's choreographed exactly like a dance," Shatner explained when describing how a fight like the one between Kirk with Kruge is staged.[10]

BELOW AND BOTTOM RIGHT: Art by ILM's David Carson demonstrates some of the original thoughts about the fight.

BELOW LEFT: Rodis envisions Kirk and Kruge's fight. The scene was a recycle and reimagining of a scripted fight between Kirk and Khan from *Star Trek II*. In that version, Kirk taunts Khan until he beams down and the two fight using swords, with Khan actually defeating Kirk, leaving him and his crew stranded on the planet. It was decided that the scene was not necessary and never filmed. Bennett, never one to waste a good idea, saw a need for the fight in *Star Trek III*.

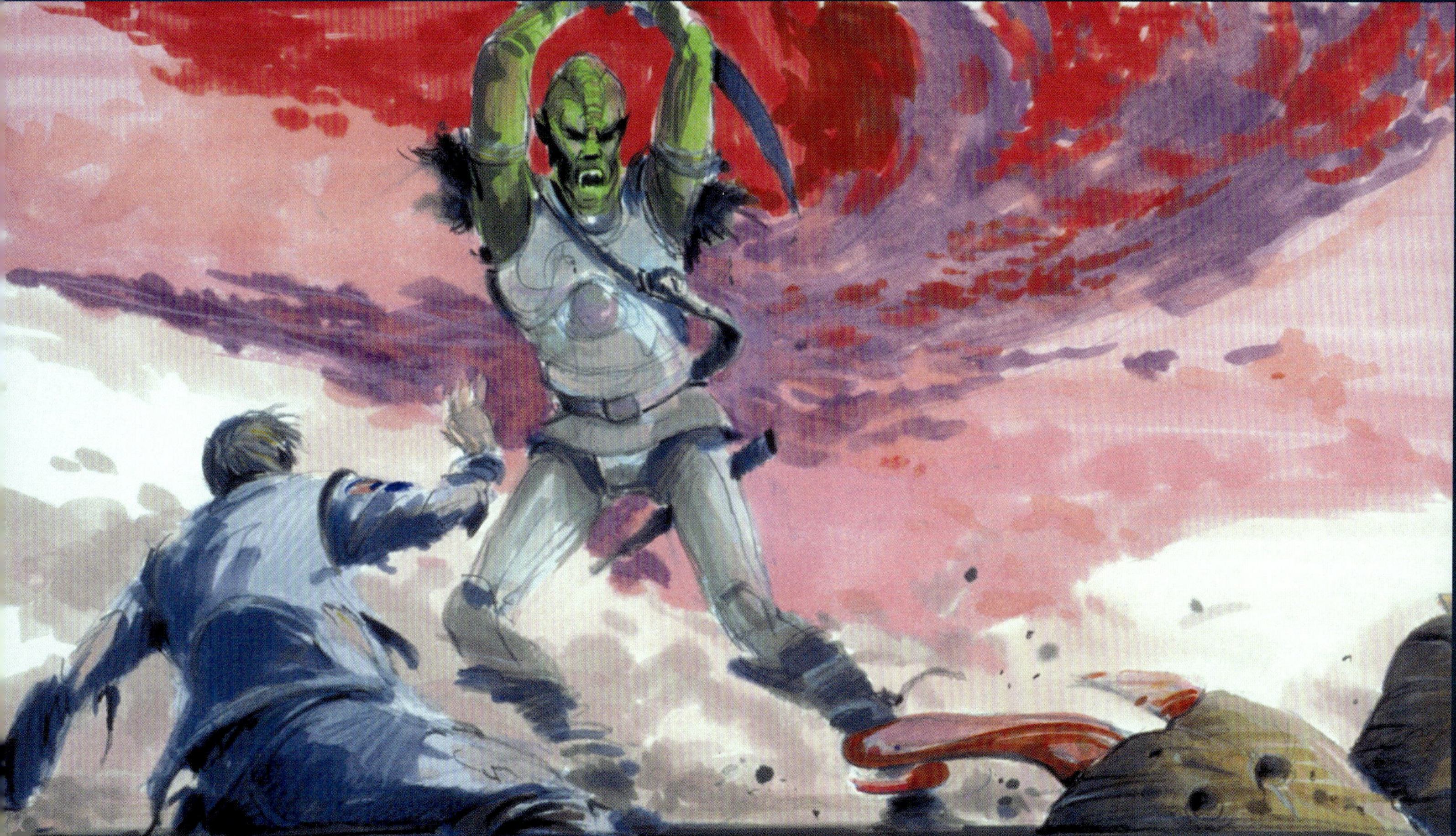

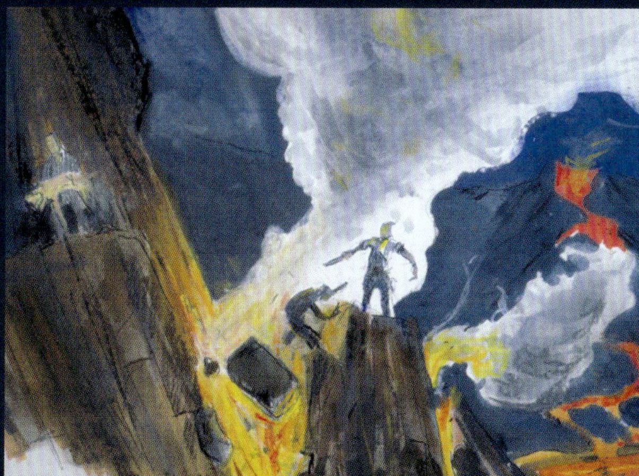

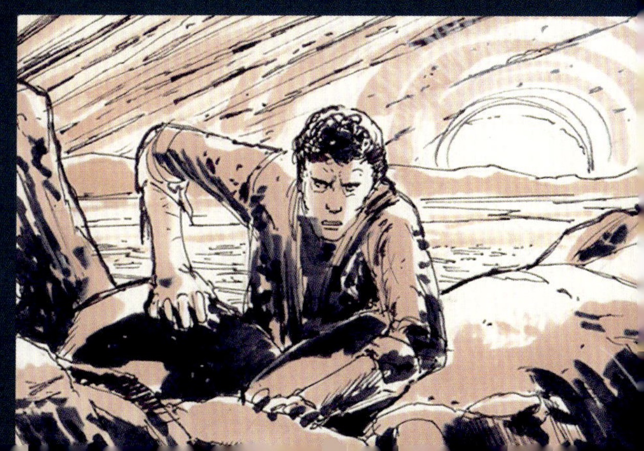

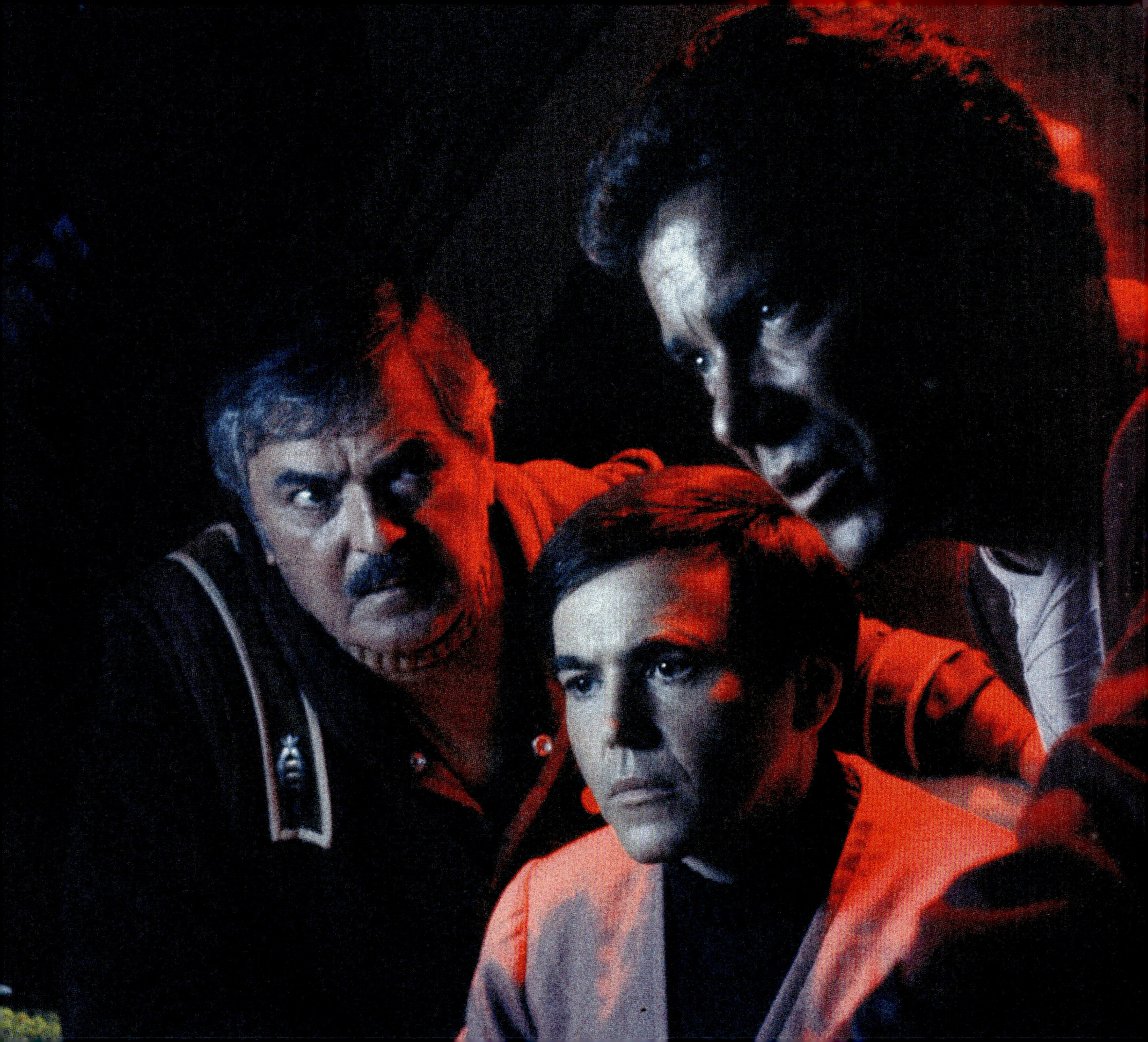

CHAPTER 14

ZERO-ZERO-ZERO DESTRUCT-ZERO

DESTROYING THE *ENTERPRISE*

"I remember an anecdote that Harve Bennett passed on to us," said ILM's David Carson. "He told us that he had sent the script to Paramount executives for comment about the destruction of the *Enterprise* scene. One of the executive's comments was 'Milk this.'"[1] There were reasons both artistic and prosaic for why the *Enterprise* was destroyed in *Star Trek III*. Thematically, loyalty is only tested when it means something, when those displaying it have something to lose. Kirk's loyalty to Spock and his responsibility to his crew was so great that he was willing to sacrifice the ship that meant almost everything to him. The previous *Star Trek* films, and many of the episodes, demonstrated the close bond Kirk had with the *Enterprise*, sometimes becoming, as McCoy warns in *Star Trek: The Motion Picture*, an obsession that could blind him to "far more immediate and critical responsibilities." Simply, Kirk's sacrifice of the *Enterprise* symbolized his growth and his commitment to his friends.

More practically, the prevailing wisdom then, and perhaps now, is that sequels must somehow justify themselves by besting the original or preceding film. The death of Spock in *Star Trek II* had become iconic immediately, capturing the emotion and imagination of moviegoers. *Star Trek III* needed something to surprise the audience, who would've strongly suspected that, somehow, Spock's return was guaranteed. Worried about preserving the surprise, many of the actors, including principals, were not initially let in on the secret when first given their scripts. George Takei shared, "When we first got the script, I was reading along and suddenly the script didn't quite seem to make sense. It was disjointed. I then started looking at the pages and there were about four or five pages missing. The numbers skipped suddenly. We didn't get those pages that involve the destruction of the *Enterprise* in the first draft..."[2] Ironically, despite the extraordinary secrecy, some of the marketing of the film would actually spoil Bennett's surprise before the film premiered.

As much as the *Enterprise* is more than a ship to Kirk, it was the same for fans. The original design of the starship by Matt Jefferies had captured the imagination of many for its unique look that diverged from the traditional sci-fi fare. From model making to studying blueprints, the *Enterprise* was an important character, even if inanimate. Gene Roddenberry had shared with Bennett and Nimoy his strong objections to the ship's demise. Bennett, however, was resolute about the scene, and wanted to make certain it was visually spectacular and emotionally resonant. For this, ILM would play an important role, one that would task all departments. Many at ILM had great affection for the original series; even George Lucas had attended *Star Trek* conventions before his fame made it impossible. They understood what it meant to destroy the *Enterprise* and shared the Paramount philosophy of why and how the shots should be achieved.

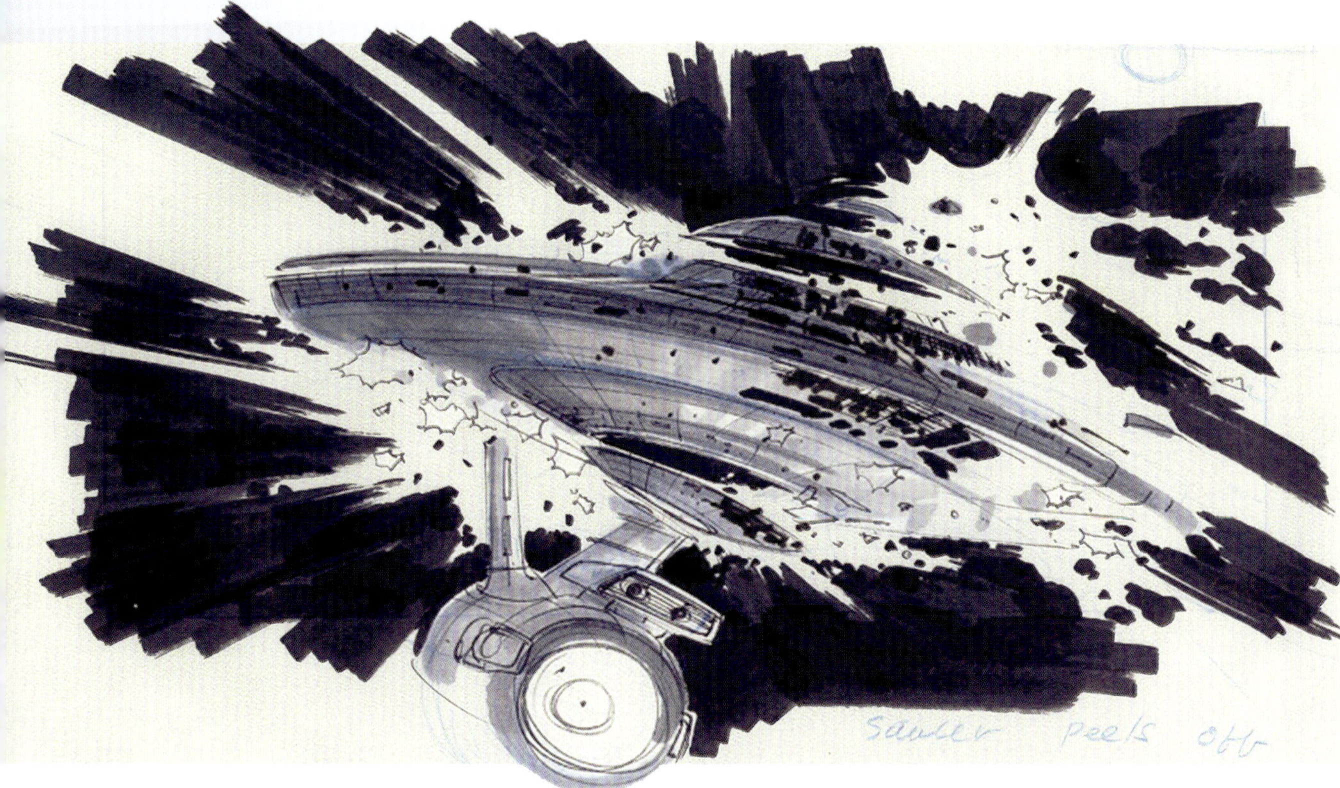

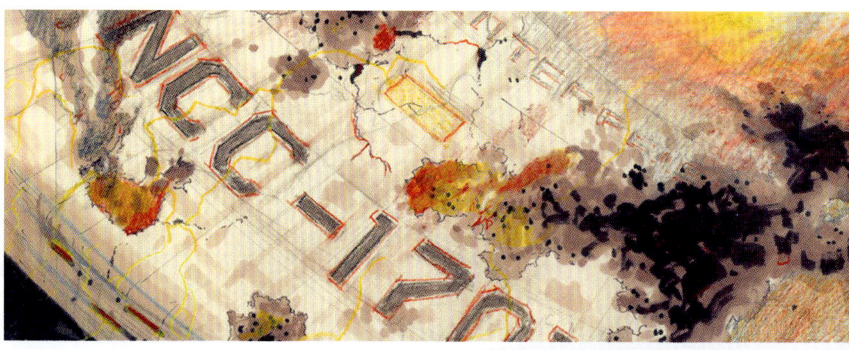

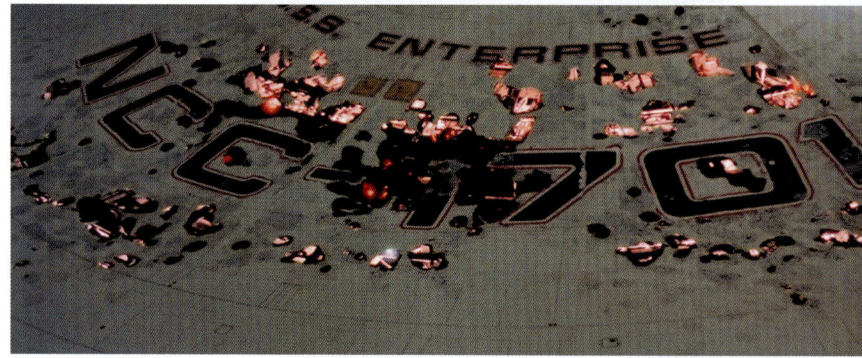

THIS PAGE: Preproduction art by ILM art director David Carson served as a blueprint for the final effects generated by the visual effects department.

GOODBYE FRIEND

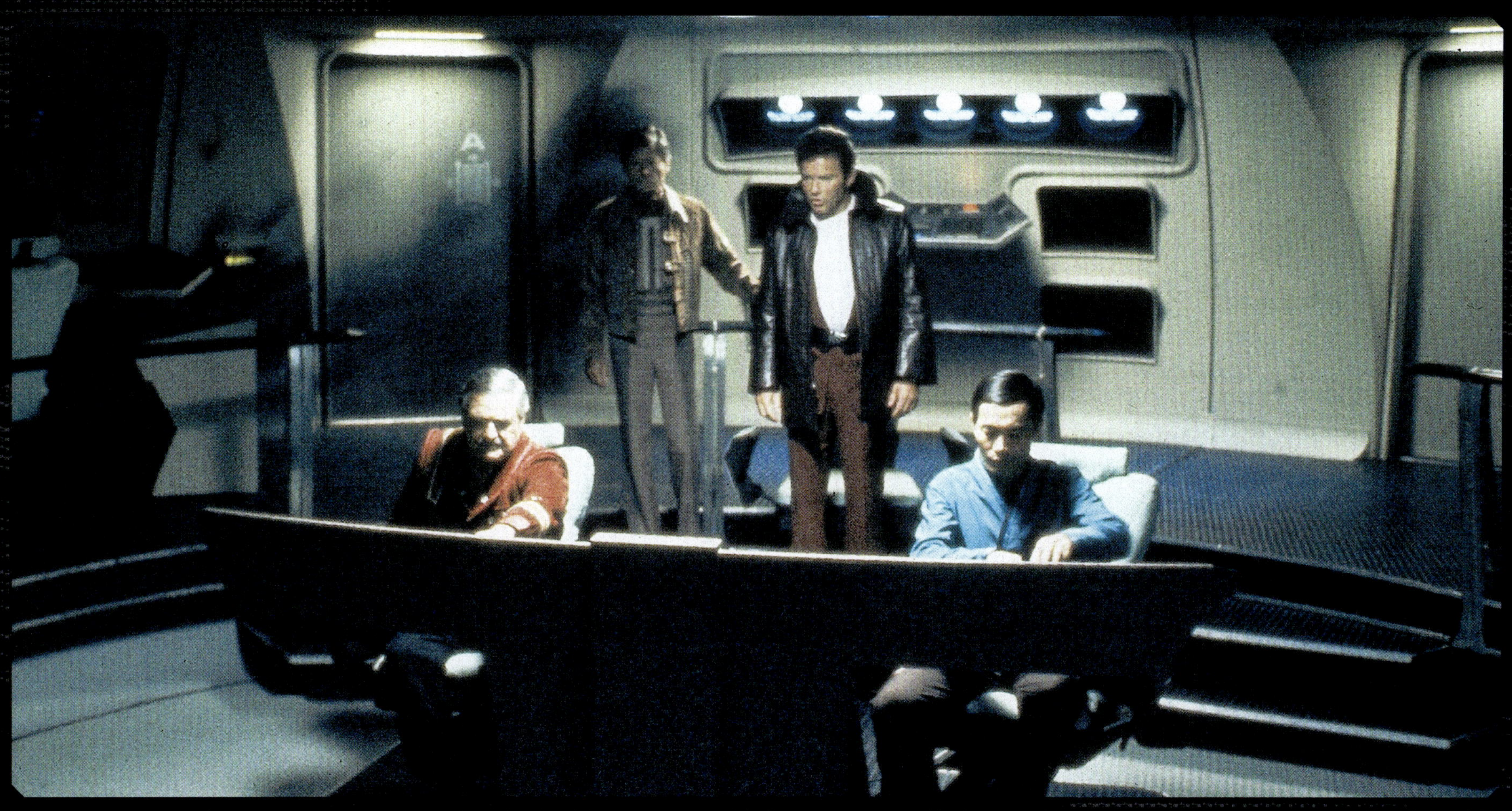

Dan Madsen, president of the *Official Star Trek Fan Club* and publisher of its concomitant magazine, asked *Star Trek III* actors to share thoughts and feelings about the destruction of the *Enterprise* in 1984.

William Shatner: "I thought the loss of the *Enterprise* was a very clever device used to create drama in a situation."

James Doohan: "If we can bring Spock back alive, we can certainly build another *Enterprise*. And I've got a few screws lying around from the last one! (Laughter)."

George Takei: "It was also a magnificent and noble way for that demise. And, you know, Star Trek does talk about change and loss which is part of life. So, in that respect, it was very much in keeping with the basic philosophy of *Star Trek*."

Walter Koenig: "I think the *Enterprise* is too strong a symbol of the show and what it's all about to dismiss it. That isn't to say that I didn't think the scene of its destruction was beautifully done and touching. I think it was worthwhile to film that scene. It was a very evoking sequence. I just think we've proven we are in the resurrection business and that if we can do it with animate organisms, we certainly should be able to do it with an inanimate object."

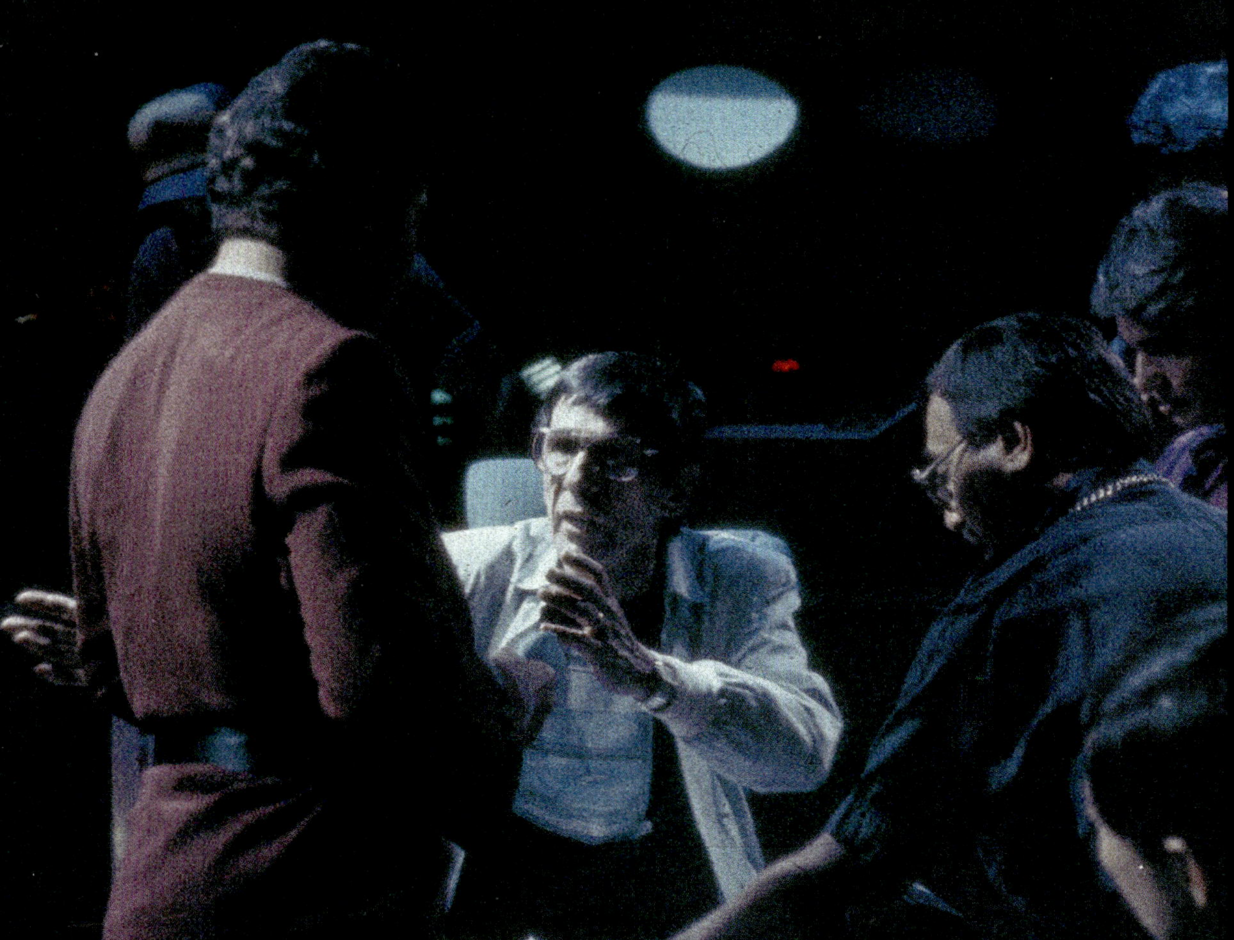

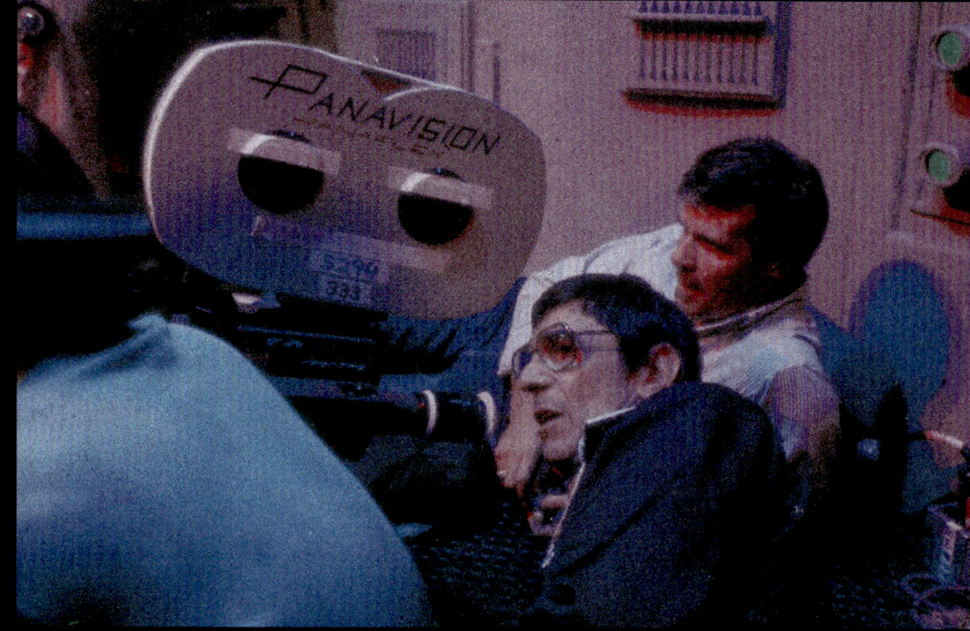

ABOVE: Positioning the camera lower than usual on the *Enterprise* bridge to showcase the stunts added to the drama and effectiveness of the scene.

LEFT: Nimoy directs Shatner as Kirk makes the decision to save his friends by starting the *Enterprise* self-destruct sequence. The same codes used to destroy the *Enterprise* in *Star Trek III* were used in the original series episode 'Let That Be Your Last Battlefield' where Kirk refuses to let Commissioner Bele control his ship. Luckily, in the episode, Bele relents and the destruct sequence is cancelled.

The finished sequence would require filming in Los Angeles on Stage 9 at Paramount on the bridge, corridor, and transporter sets. The bridge was located in a corner of Stage 9, while the transporter set was connected to the corridors. Additional filming would be done on the Genesis set with Kirk and company as they watched the fiery end of the beloved ship. Meanwhile, in San Rafael, ILM would film the visual effects.

Linguist Marc Okrand was a witness to movie history. "There was no real reason for me to be on set the day they were going to destroy the *Enterprise* bridge, but you've got to believe that I was going to be there that day! I wasn't going to miss that," he revealed. "The bridge set is a big circle with the viewing screen in front which was really a big hole. Behind the hole is a black curtain with glitter in it and behind that is another one, so when you look at it, there appears to be stars out there."[3] From within that nook, Okrand silently watched as the scene unfolded. "They did it in one take with four cameras. There was supposed to be a big fireball that rolled down the corridor, but they were having problems with it."[3]

The issues were eventually worked out. Okrand was impressed by the gymnastics of the stunt performers, who were catapulted across the set and dodged exploding consoles, all in one take. The reset of the bridge to its original condition would have been expensive to say the least.

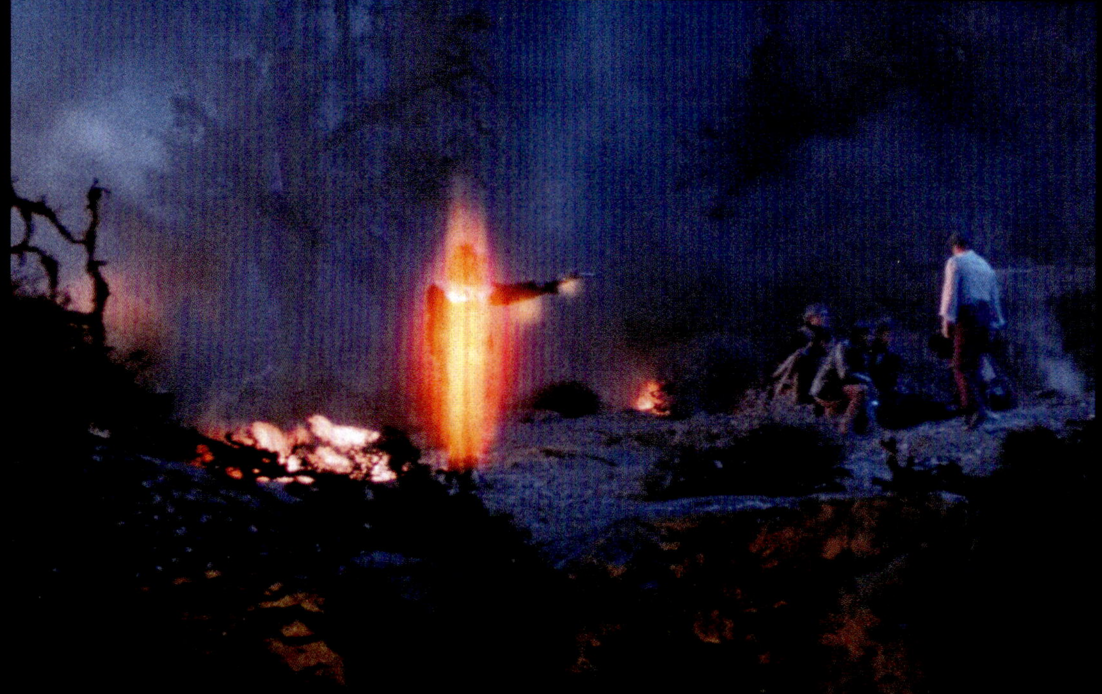

ABOVE: ILM's animation department, supervised by Charles Mullen, was frequently relied on to solve problems, earning the moniker ACFI, or "animation can fix it." Federation transporters had a different color palette than the Klingons, symbolizing their cultural differences.

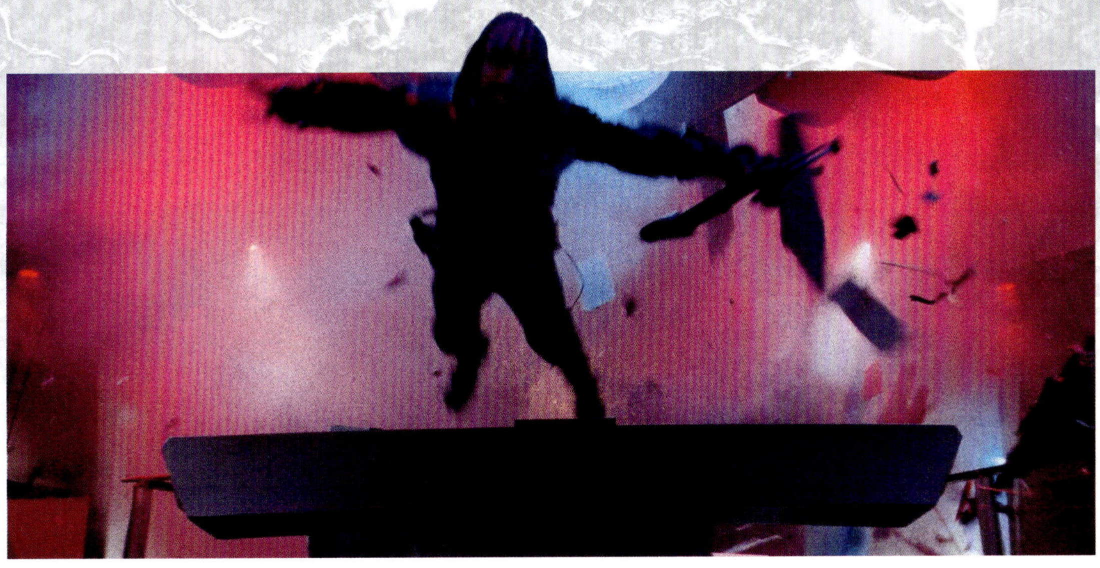

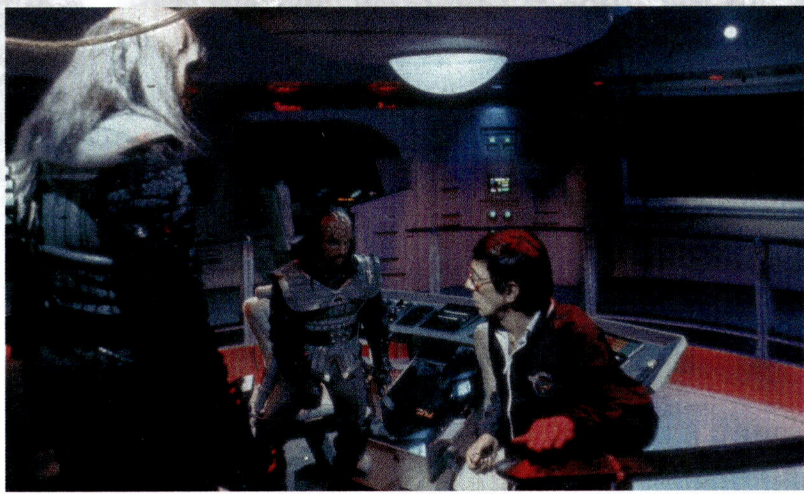

ABOVE RIGHT: Nimoy works with David Zellitti and other stunt performers as they prepare to film the destruction scene.

Actor Stephen Liska, who played Torg, spoke about the work of the stunt team. "When the explosions started, that was a situation where you had to be where you had to be, because everything is set. You had to be careful about that. They rehearsed that scene with the stuntmen a lot. They were never going to use the actors for the actual destruction part of the scene," he explained. "I had a fantastic stuntman who covered me the entire movie. After we had rehearsed, he said to me, 'Steve, as soon as this starts, don't wait. Dive under that desk because when it happens, it is going to happen quick, especially with you wearing all this makeup.' The best thing that can happen is to have a good stuntman covering you who is prepared. Wearing the makeup and the costume adds to the nervousness because it makes seeing and reacting more difficult. You have to be careful. They don't want anyone to get hurt, so they are careful with us."[4]

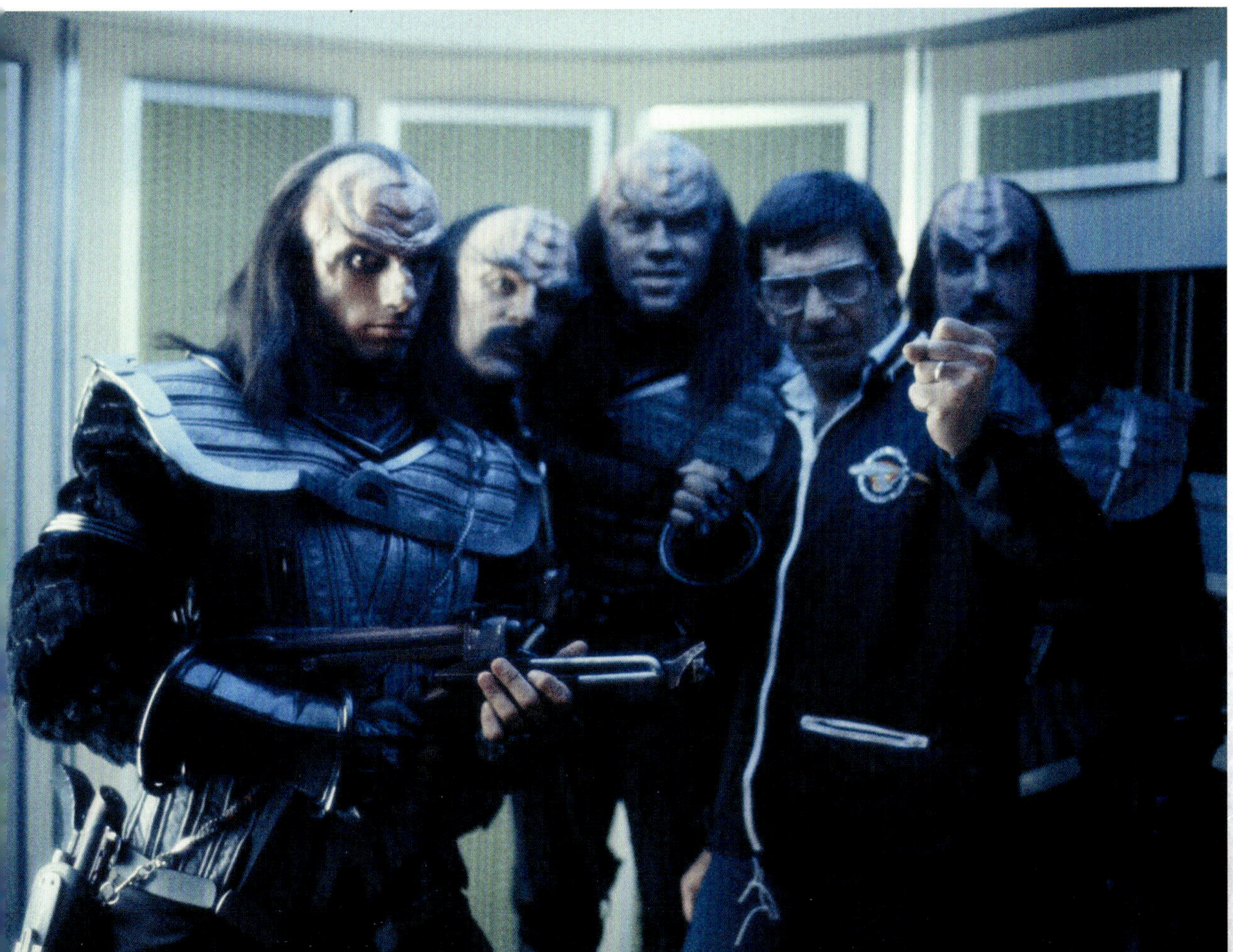

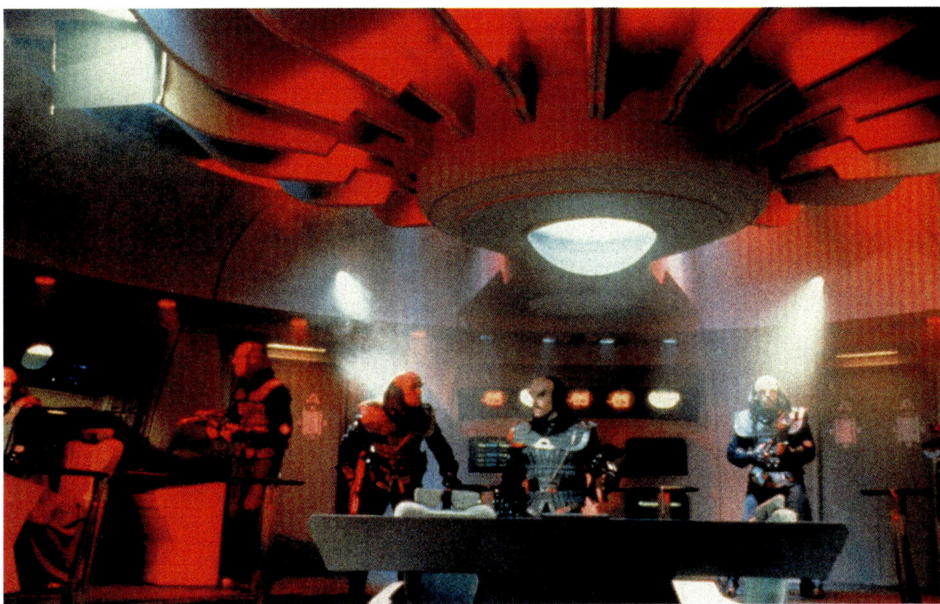

ABOVE: Actor Stephen Liska, as Torg, and the team comprising Kruge's rogue gallery get to their marks, ready to perform their stunts.

LEFT: Despite the seriousness of the stunt work, Nimoy takes time to have some fun with the Klingons, including Don Charles McGovern, Charles Picerni, Jr., Branscombe Richmond, and David Zellitti.

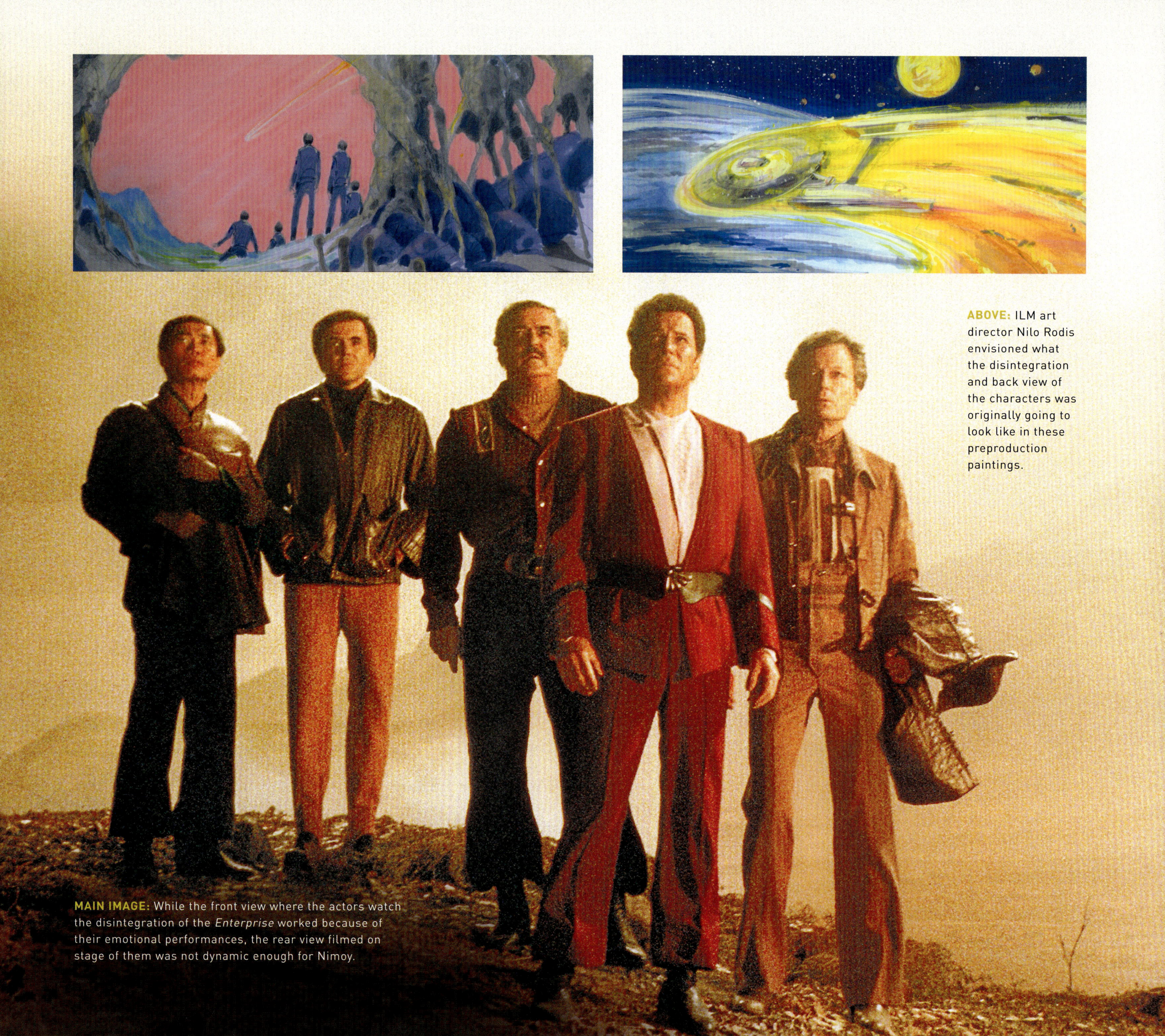

ABOVE: ILM art director Nilo Rodis envisioned what the disintegration and back view of the characters was originally going to look like in these preproduction paintings.

MAIN IMAGE: While the front view where the actors watch the disintegration of the *Enterprise* worked because of their emotional performances, the rear view filmed on stage of them was not dynamic enough for Nimoy.

At ILM, the destruction of the *Enterprise* was first plotted by art directors Nilo Rodis and David Carson, in concert with Bennett and Nimoy. Visual effects supervisor Kenneth Ralston and his team were then tasked with achieving the desired sequence of events.

One of the most daunting challenges faced by ILM was surrounding the scene where Kirk, McCoy, Scotty, Sulu, and Chekov, having safely escaped to Genesis, watch the *Enterprise* burn in orbit. The moment had been filmed at Paramount with the actors in front of a painted backing. While Nimoy was happy with the performances of the actors when filmed from the front, he thought the view from the back as they watched the starship was dull and listless because of the unconvincing background. Nimoy turned to ILM's matte department for help. In one of the fastest turn arounds on the film, they were able to add the now iconic visual to the film. Matte camera supervisor Craig Barron explained, "It was an important dramatic part of the movie and the destruction of the *Enterprise* was something fans were going to be emotionally connected to, so we wanted it to have more of a special treatment than what they had filmed on set. Nimoy asked the matte department to help with the moment instead."[5]

Added to the painting was a separate pyrotechnic element. Visual effects artist Tom Moehnke, supervising stage technician Patrick Fitzsimmons, and a team from ILM returned to the Cow Palace in Daly City,

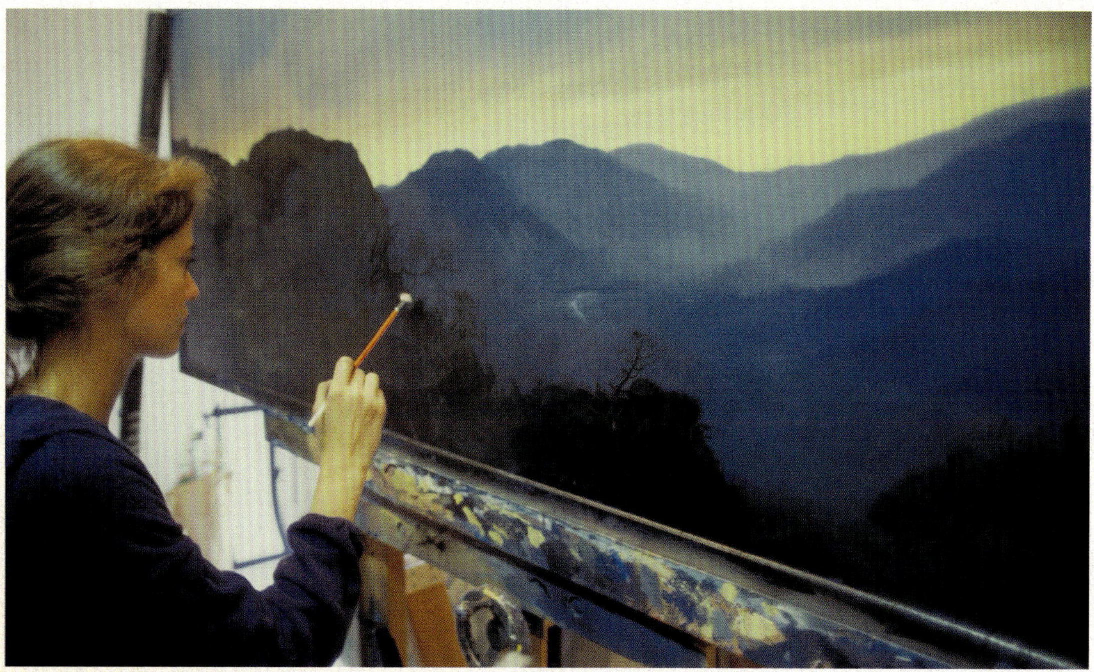

ABOVE: Barron praised Caroleen "Jett" Green, saying, "This is Jett's interpretation of the shot: the characters are now depicted as smaller and positioned on a hill, watching the deorbiting. It's a beautiful painting, featuring yellow clouds, a blue sky, and a sunset. We didn't have time to refilm the actors, so the characters are just painted in. Because they are small and stationary, it really worked and added drama. Jett completed this painting in just a week, whereas it would normally take us two to three times longer."[5]

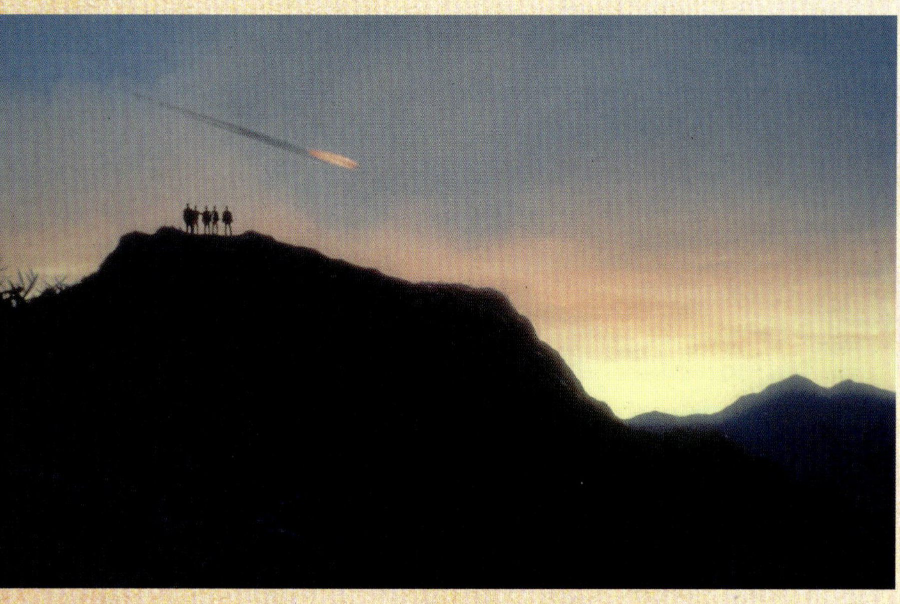

ABOVE: An early composite test by ILM.

RIGHT: After lighting adjustments, the ILM improved version met with the approval of Bennett and Nimoy.

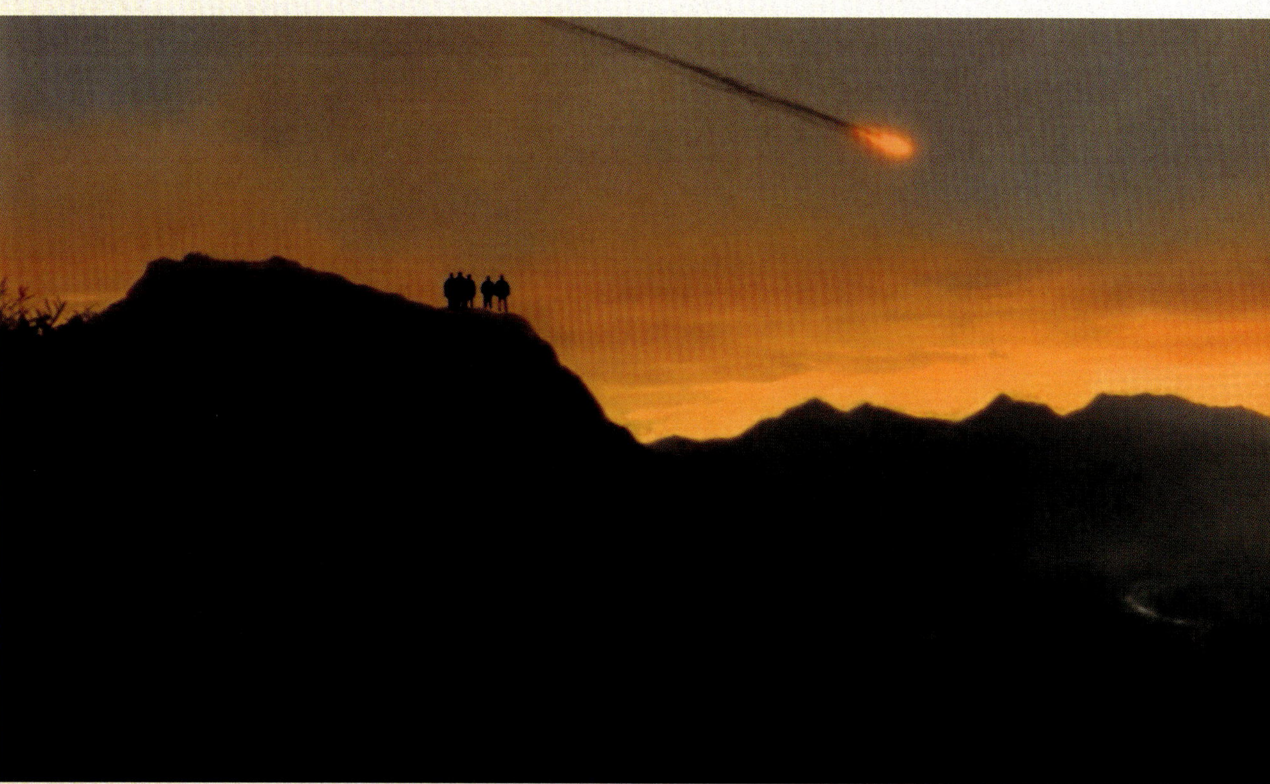

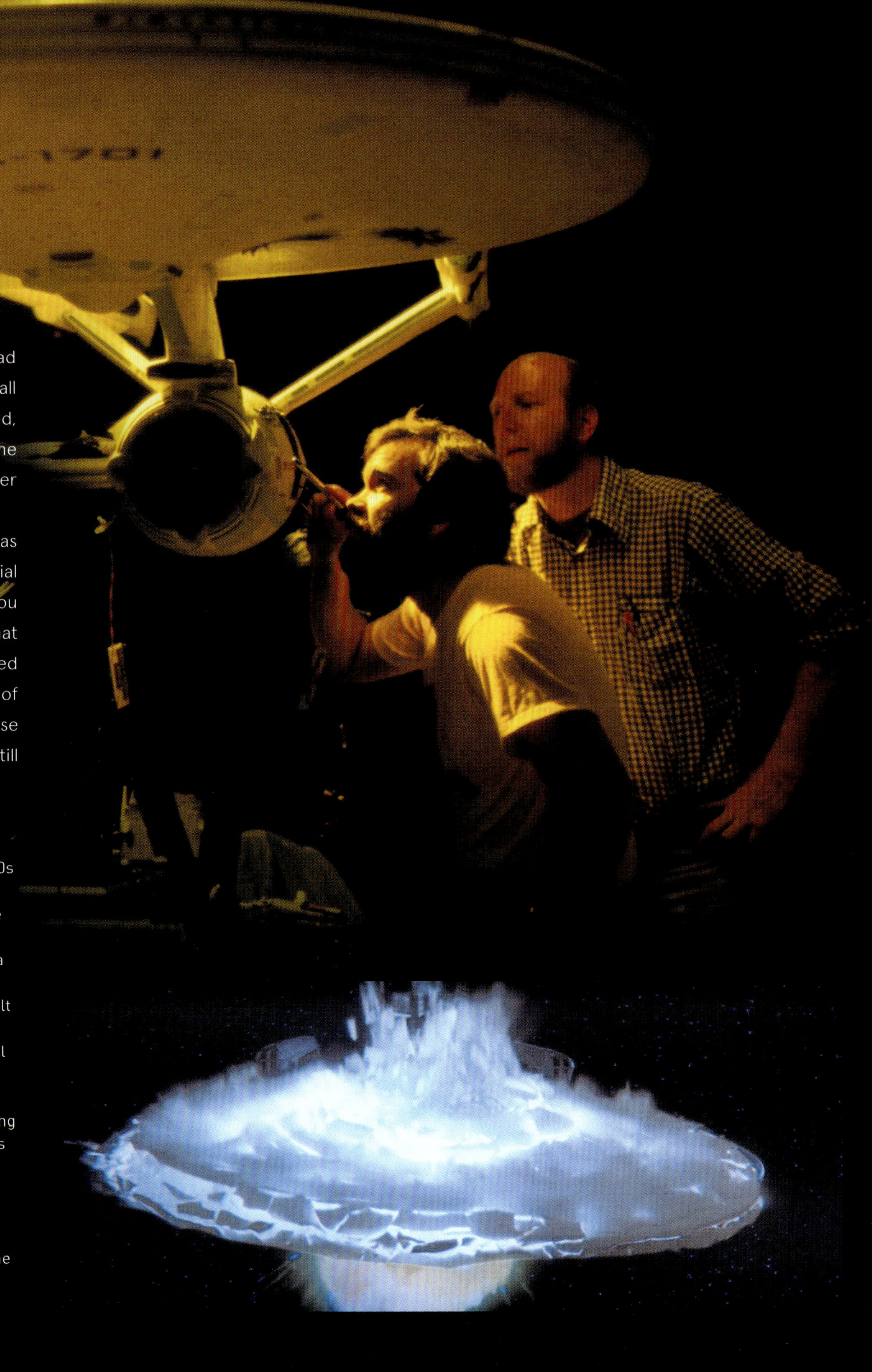

an event venue where the *Star Trek II* Genesis device explosion had been filmed. The high ceiling afforded ILM the space to film the fireball which was created using a torch on cables. Using a special high speed, high frame rate camera gave the illusion it was moving slowly and at the proper scale. ILM animators would also add a smokey trail to further sell the effect.

Stunt performer Tom Morga who played one of the Klingons was proud of how both the footage from Paramount and the special effects from ILM combined. "It was a great sequence because you felt it emotionally. You saw the whole bridge go up and you saw that explosion of the top of the *Enterprise* to start with, then it deteriorated in the atmosphere and they are watching as it is turned into a kind of asteroid. The whole idea of it was pretty cool. And I thought all those shots worked well. Even today I think you can look at that film and still believe it. You know that looks great."[6]

MAIN IMAGE:
The original hero model of the refit *Enterprise* was built during the late 1970s by Magicam's model supervisor Jim Dow – brother of ILM's Don Dow – and his team, and painted by Paul Olsen. At a build time of more than a year, the eight-foot-long model cost $150,000, and hence, it was never slated to be destroyed for the *Star Trek III* scenes. Instead, other models were built as a substitute. One was constructed from a commercially available AMG model kit of the *Enterprise* with a twelve-inch diameter dome. Another model, built by supervising model maker Steve Gawley and his team, was made at one-third the scale of the eight-foot hero model. In this image, Gawley and visual effects camera assistant Toby Heindel coordinate filming at ILM.

RIGHT: Ralston's favorite shot from the destruction is the main dish blowing up. "We had a high-speed camera and we were using a special kind of lens we borrowed from famed cinematographer John Hora. He wasn't on the *Star Trek III* team, but someone had borrowed a lens from him. I had the idea of sprinkling talcum powder on the dish because then, when it blows up, it will look like there's more fine material coming off of it." Ralston added, "Unfortunately, a piece of cardboard from inside that dish that came flying out of it during the explosion and it smacked right into the lens we borrowed. Oh, I don't think John was too happy about that!"[7]

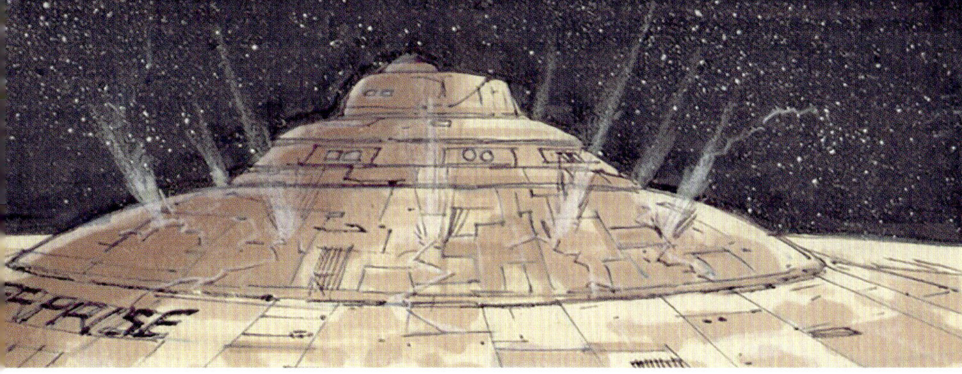

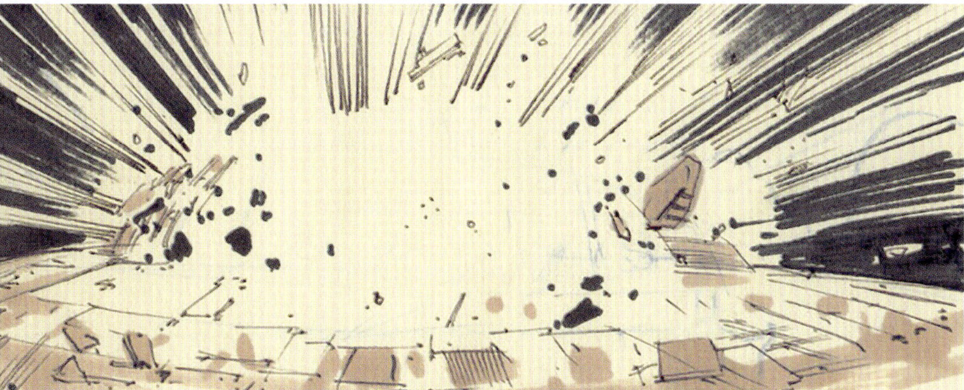

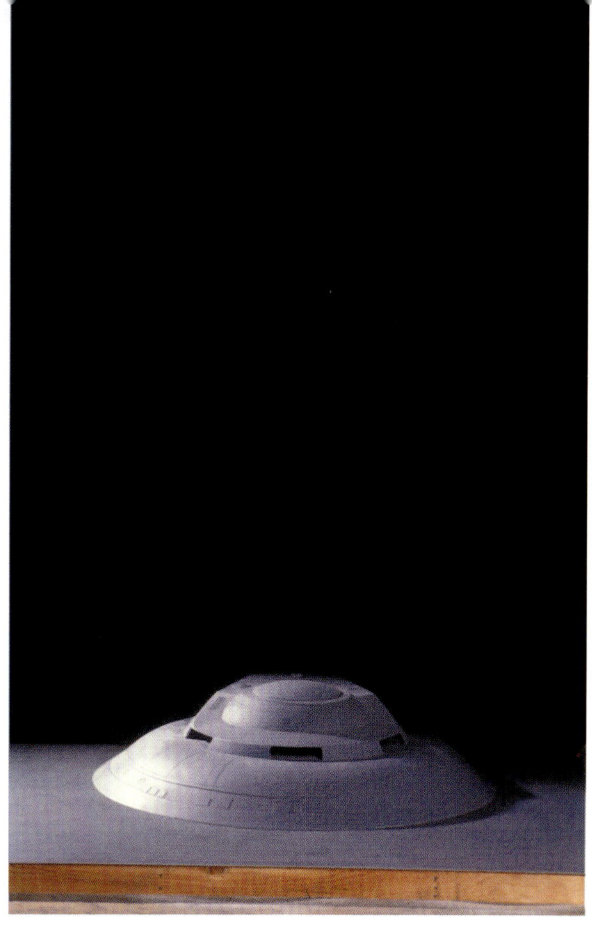

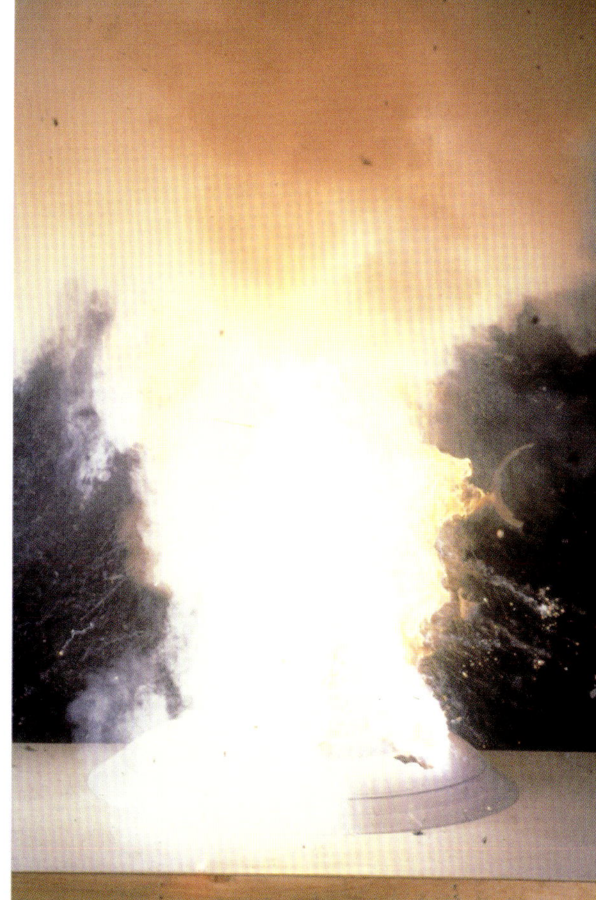

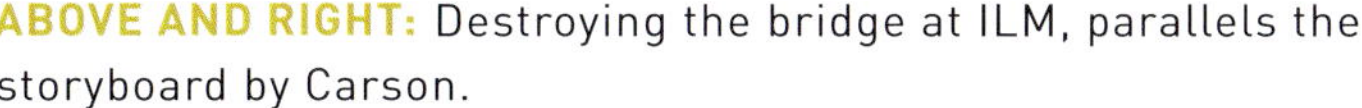

ABOVE AND RIGHT: Destroying the bridge at ILM, parallels the storyboard by Carson.

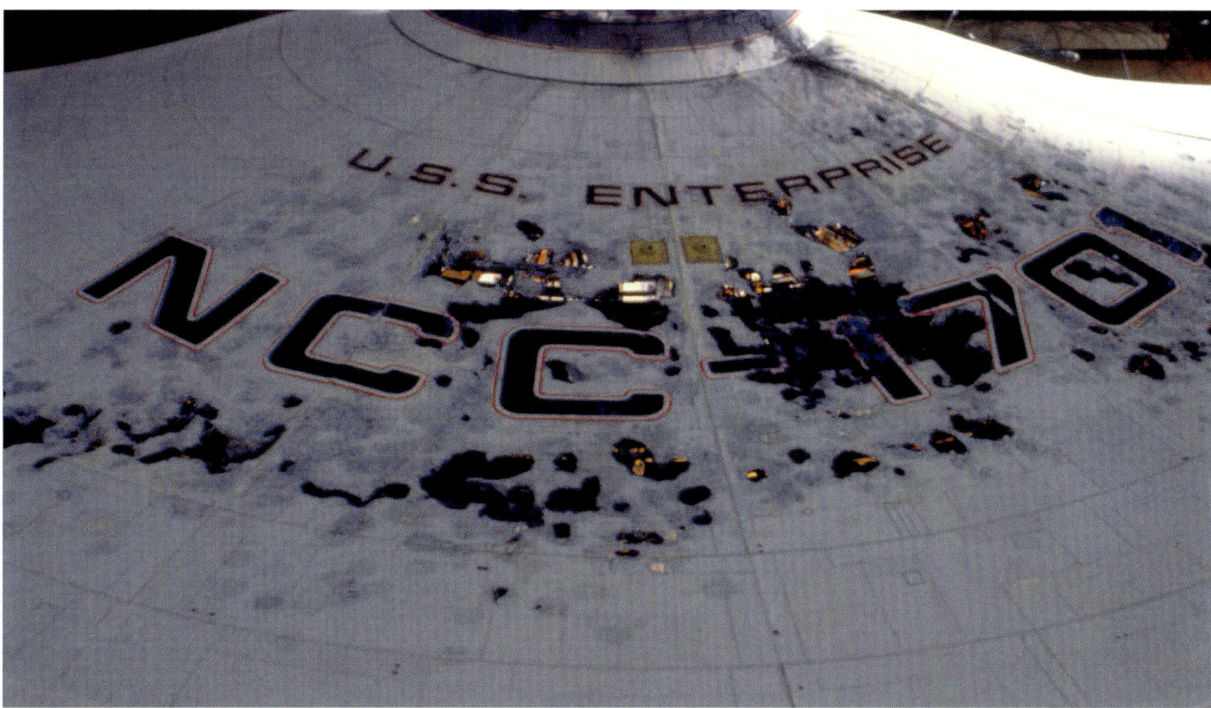

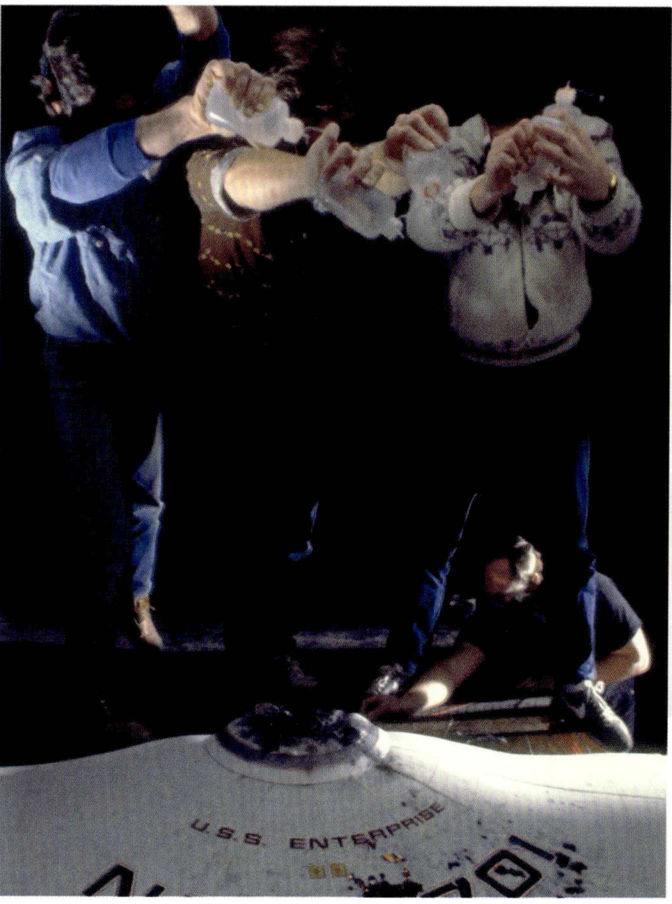

ABOVE AND RIGHT: The burning-through of the *Enterprise* saucer was inspired by the tragic events of the Hindenburg disaster of 1937. To achieve the effect, model makers created a six-foot saucer made of Styrofoam. Bill George then used colored pencils to add detail and built a fully realized interior that would be visible as the saucer disintegrates. George and other model makers dribbled the chemical acetone, dissolving the Styrofoam saucer section.

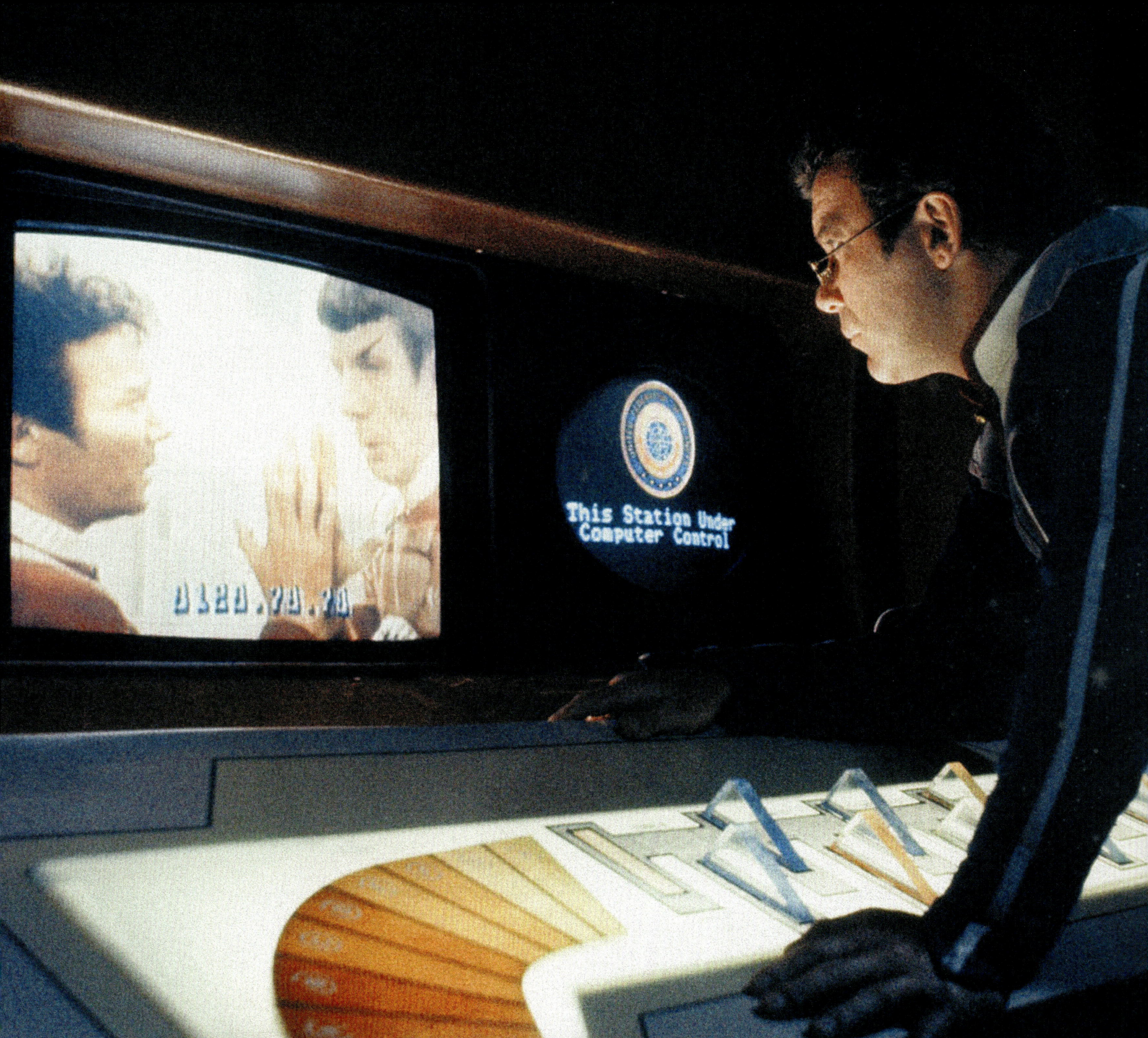
This Station Under
Computer Control

CHAPTER 15

FIXING THE BARN DOOR

POSTPRODUCTION

Editing is everything. Director Francis Ford Coppola believed, "The essence of cinema is editing. It's the combination of what can be extraordinary images of people during emotional moments, or images in a general sense, put together in a kind of alchemy."[1] The process of editing is an archetypal example of the idiom that the sum can be greater than its parts. Editors combine the disparate pieces filmed during production by the director and special effects artists, choosing which takes are the best and what order those scenes are best presented, all of which are enhanced later with sound mix improvements and music.

Trust and understanding between the editor, producer, and director are therefore requirements, or at least ideals, in the editing process. It is not unusual for editors, directors, and producers to have divergent thoughts on how a film should be assembled. Usually, studios and producers have the winning say, which is why director editions of films are sometimes released. Luckily, problems were avoided during postproduction of *Star Trek III* because director Leonard Nimoy, producer Harve Bennett, and editor Robert F. Shugrue, ACE, had already established good working relationships. A veteran editor who started his career during the 1960s, Shugrue had previously worked with Bennett editing *Salvage 1* and *A Woman Called Golda*, a production for which Nimoy, Bennett, and Shugrue would earn acclaim; Nimoy was nominated for a supporting acting Emmy, and both Bennett and Shugrue won Emmys, for producing and film editing respectively.

Good editing can solve problems that are unanticipated during production. As originally scripted and filmed, McCoy's escape and the theft of the *Enterprise* was meant to be presented, as Nimoy revealed, "in staccato bursts" interspersed between other scenes taking place simultaneously among the Klingons and the science team on Genesis.[2]

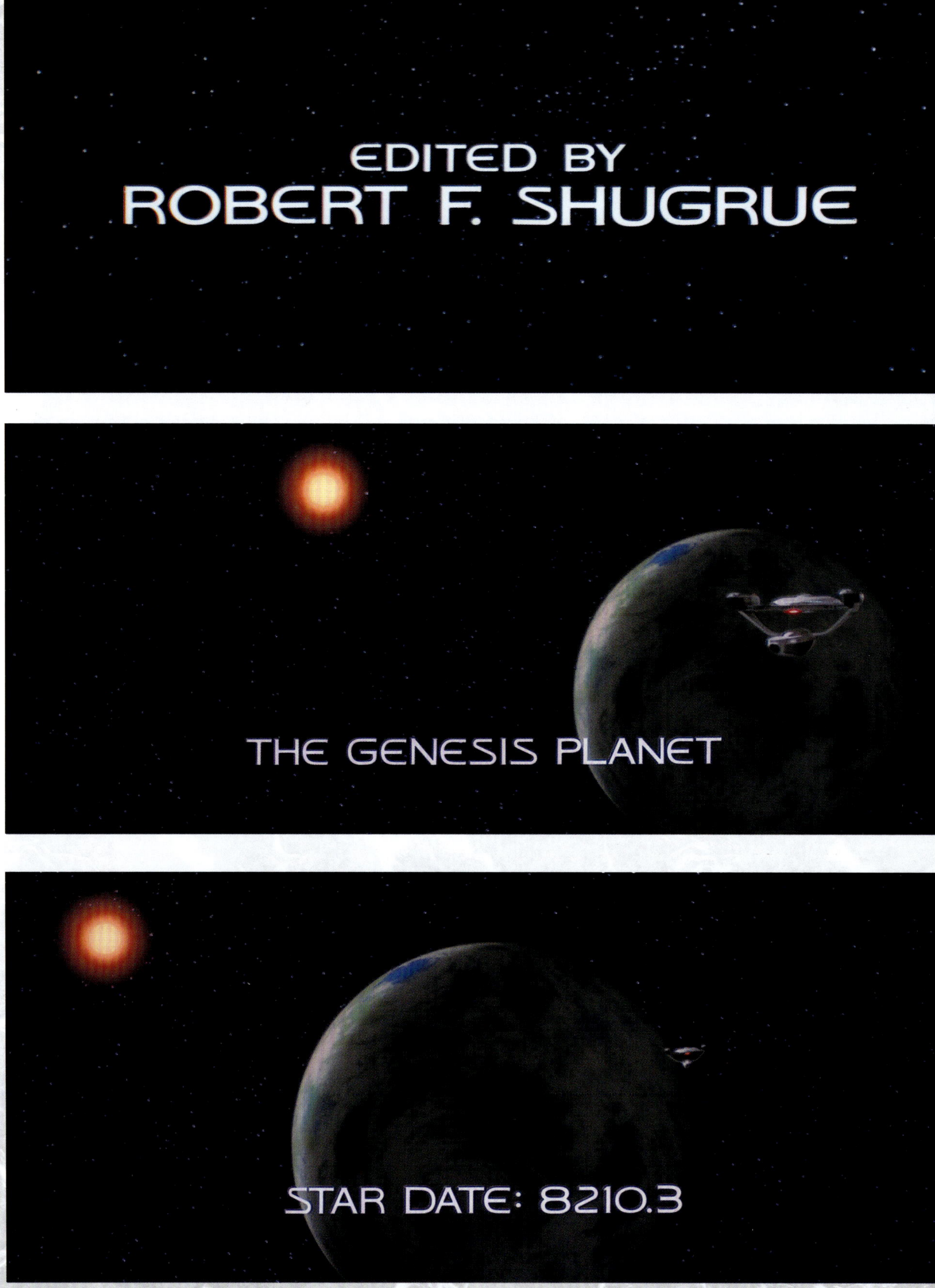

THIS PAGE: An example of the Nimoy, Bennett, and Shugrue's collaboration was Nimoy's decision to change how the film was scripted and planned to start by Bennett. "In the original script, the picture opened on the merchant ship in space, awaiting Kruge's arrival. Then, the Bird-of-Prey appeared, and destroyed the merchant ship," Nimoy told Steve Swires of Starlog. "But, when I screened it that way for myself, I became aware that it would be better to open with the *Enterprise*, establish the character, and get them on their way home."[3] Some watching the film in theaters the summer of 1984 may have wondered why the stardate is given not at the start of the film with Kirk's personal log, but several scenes later, which this edit explains. Note that the word is spelled in the film as "star date" rather than the now customary singular "stardate." It was also Nimoy's decision to leave his name out of the opening acting credits, with a longer time lapse between William Shatner and DeForest Kelley's names where his name usually appears, to preserve the secret of whether Spock returns.

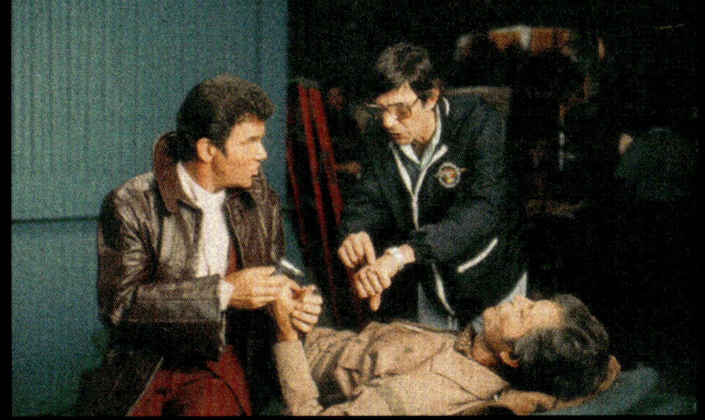
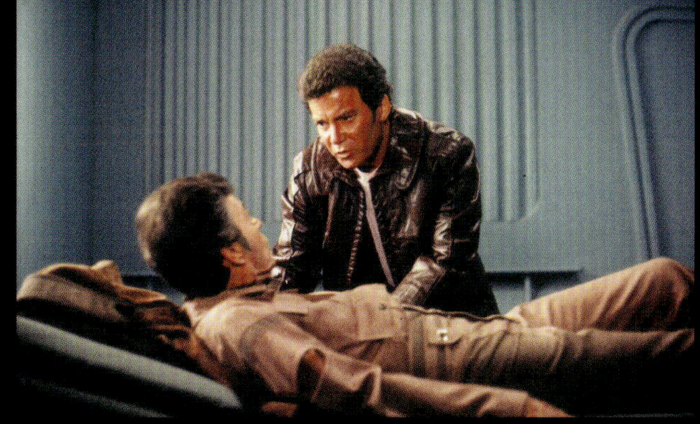
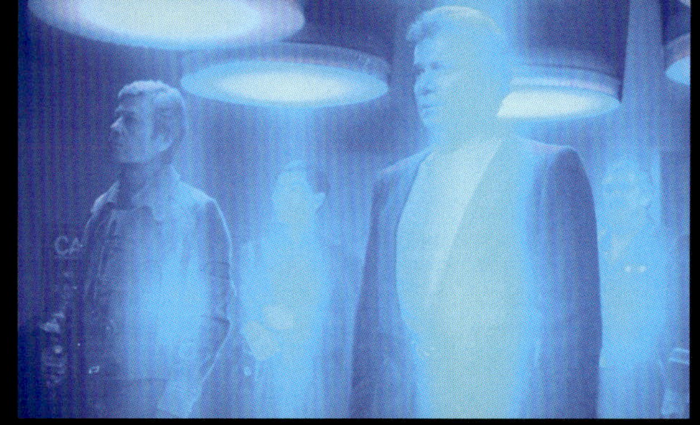

ABOVE LEFT: Nimoy prescribes how to administer lexorin on Stage 8 during the filming of McCoy's escape.

ABOVE RIGHT: When Kirk and company beam from the *Enterprise*, escaping its destruction, the transporter recycles to return them briefly for one last look.

However, during editing, it became apparent that these scenes were not working emotionally. Nimoy explained, "It interrupted the flow of it. The joy of watching these guys deciding to steal the ship and take it out and run away with it. So, we just glued some pieces together and told more of one story in a chunk and then more of the other, as opposed to what was on the page."[2]

Shugrue's editing both preserved the emotional performances of the actors during quieter moments and improved the action sequences; he utilized fast edits back and forth between Kirk and Kruge, in their space battle and their fist fight on Genesis.

Adding to these moments is the sound mix and effects created by the sound department. Supervising sound editor Cecelia Hall, reprising her role from *Star Trek II*, sound mixer Gene S. Cantamessa, special sound effects creator Alan Howarth, re-recording mixer David J. Hudson, and the entire team not only captured the sounds on set, but created otherworldly sound effects, from the din of Genesis to the ambiance of starships. Sound in film helps sell the special effects that exist without any native resonance and gives environments, especially those created on an artificial soundstage, a believability. Many sounds are added during postproduction and the editing phase, including the iconic *pew-pews*. Clarity of speech was also the responsibility of this team; ADR editor Ron Horwitz would record actor dialogue that needed to be added or be re-recorded due to any problems that interfered with the original sound.

Cantamessa, who a few years before *Star Trek III* had won an Academy Award for his work on Steven Spielberg's *E.T.: The Extraterrestrial*, would eventually share an Academy Award nomination for his *Star Trek IV* contributions. Stand-in Philip Weyland remembered a funny incident involving Cantamessa and Nimoy. "Gene began playing soft music while the lighting, etc. took place. He and I were on the bridge set.

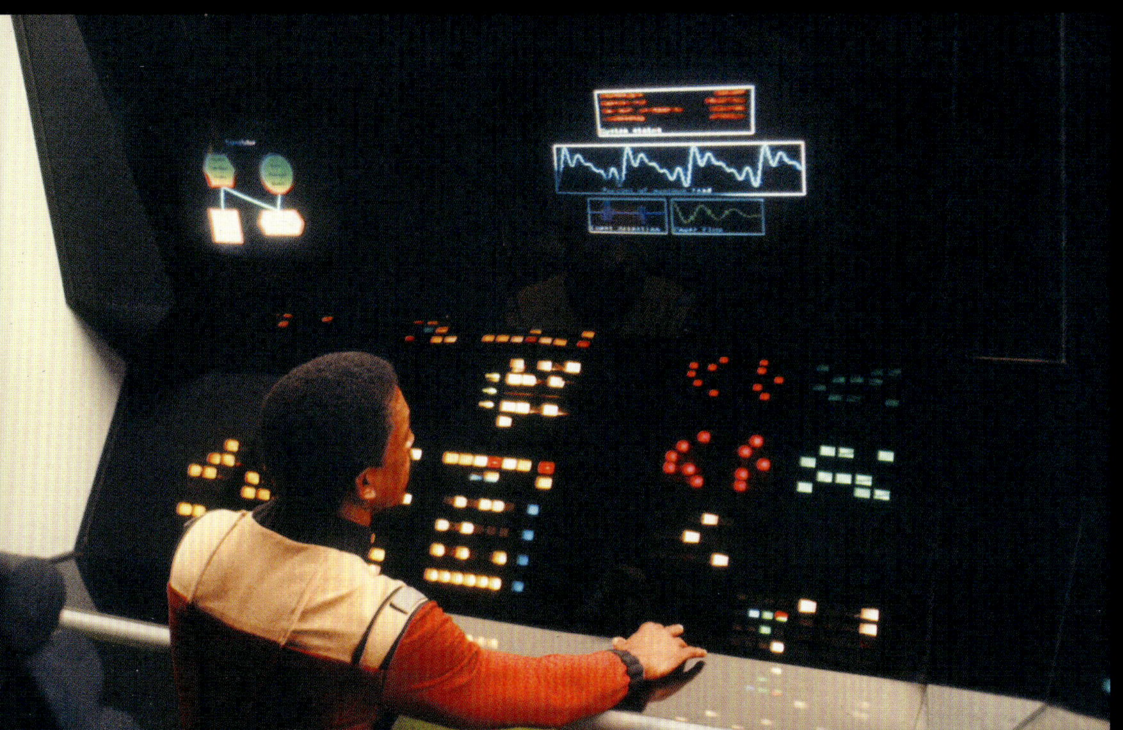
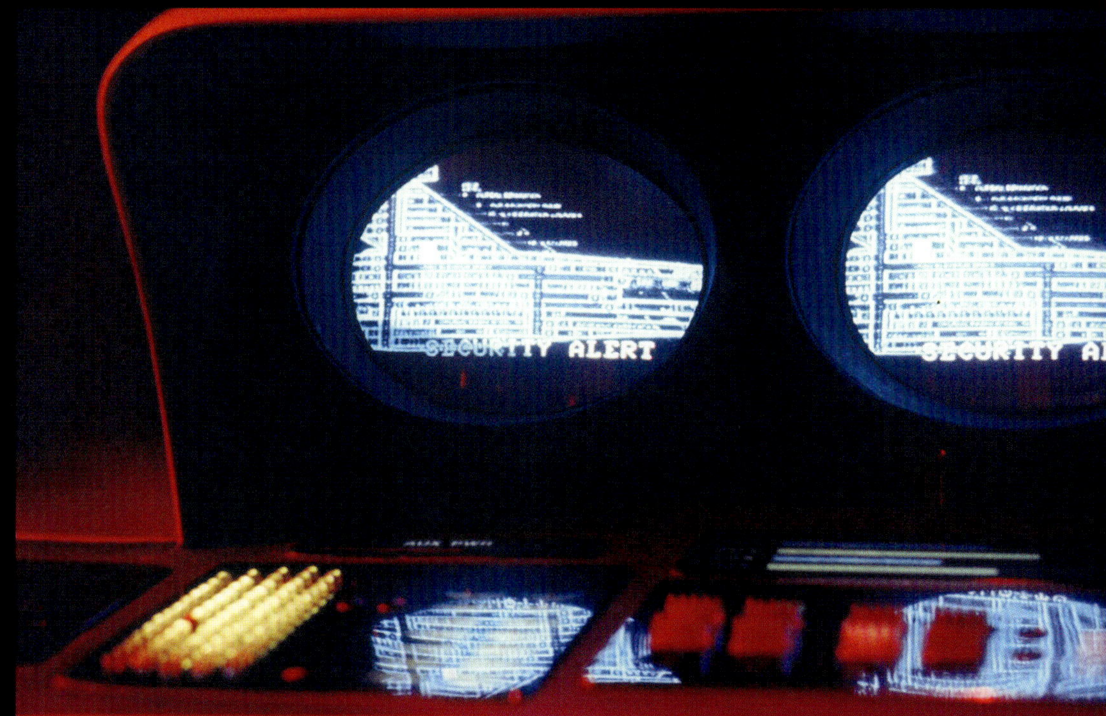

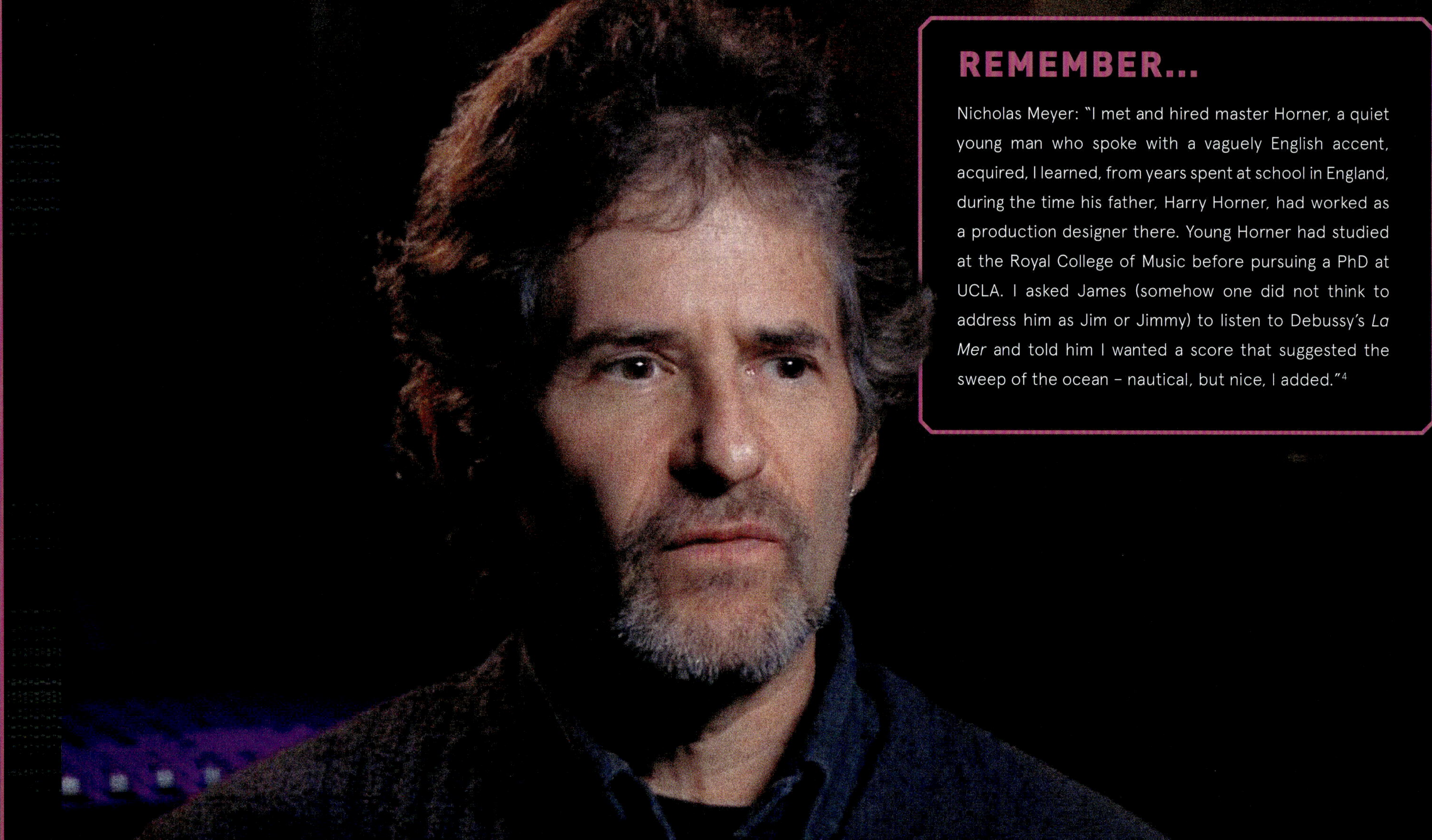

REMEMBER...

Nicholas Meyer: "I met and hired master Horner, a quiet young man who spoke with a vaguely English accent, acquired, I learned, from years spent at school in England, during the time his father, Harry Horner, had worked as a production designer there. Young Horner had studied at the Royal College of Music before pursuing a PhD at UCLA. I asked James (somehow one did not think to address him as Jim or Jimmy) to listen to Debussy's *La Mer* and told him I wanted a score that suggested the sweep of the ocean – nautical, but nice, I added."[4]

FLIGHT RECORDER VISUAL:

JAMES HORNER, COMPOSER

Born August 14, 1953, in Los Angeles, Horner seemed destined for a career in film. His father was Harry Horner, an Oscar® winning art director and set designer. From an early age, Horner was fascinated with music and started playing piano at age five. He was enamored with the music of film composers, especially the likes of John Williams and Jerry Goldsmith, who he shadowed as he began his career. Horner sat in during Goldsmith's *Star Trek: The Motion Picture* recording sessions in 1979. His *Star Trek II* audition tape was championed by producer Robert Sallin, director Nicholas Meyer, and Paramount music vice-president Joel Sill. Horner was only 28 at the time, and joked with Meyer when the director said that some passages of his *Star Trek II* score evoked Sergei Prokofiev's *Alexander Nevsky*, saying "'Whatdya want from me? I'm a kid. I haven't outgrown my influences.'"[4] Horner would eventually win two Academy Awards® and was nominated eight more times, including competing against himself when he was nominated twice in the same year for his scores to *Apollo 13* and *Braveheart*. An avid pilot, Horner died as the result of his plane crashing on June 22, 2015.

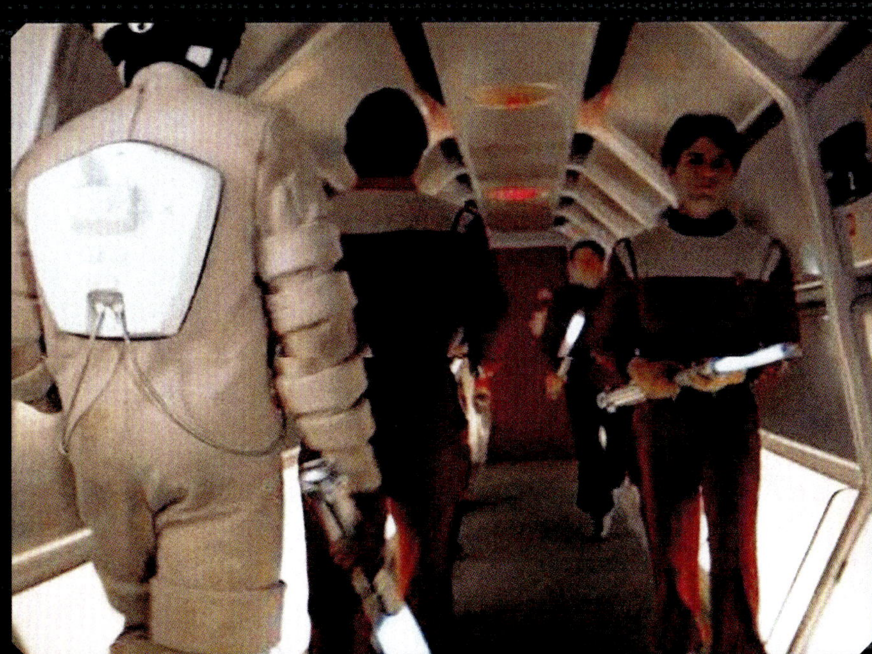

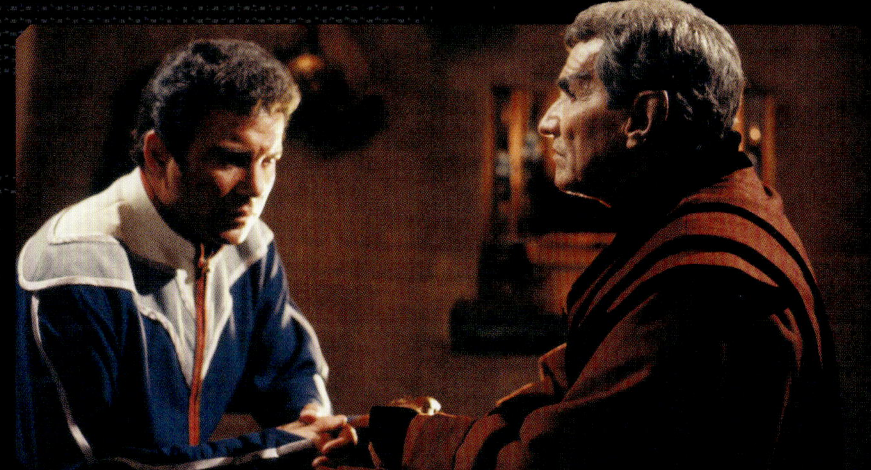

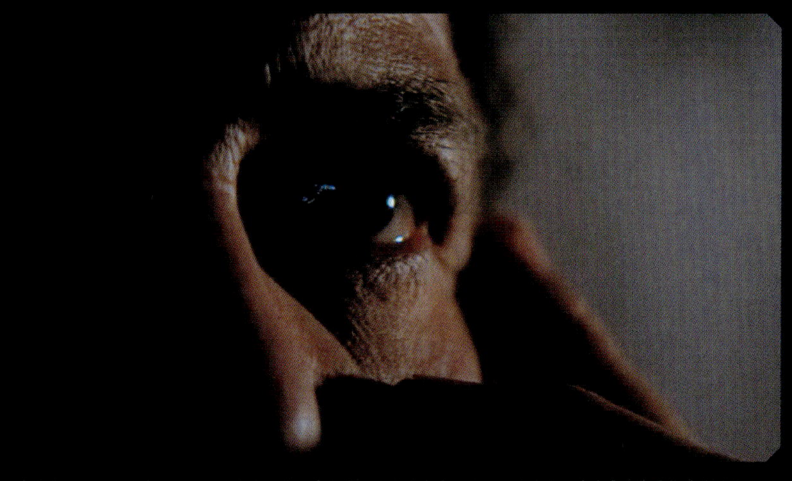

ABOVE: Horner has a cameo in *Star Trek II* during the battle between the *U.S.S. Reliant* and *U.S.S. Enterprise*.

RIGHT An example of collaboration is the mind-meld scene with Kirk and Sarek. Nimoy directed William Shatner and Mark Lenard whose performances were captured in extreme close-up by Correll; this choice made it easier for the audience to hear the words recorded by the sound department. Editing by Shugrue and the music by Horner complete the emotion.

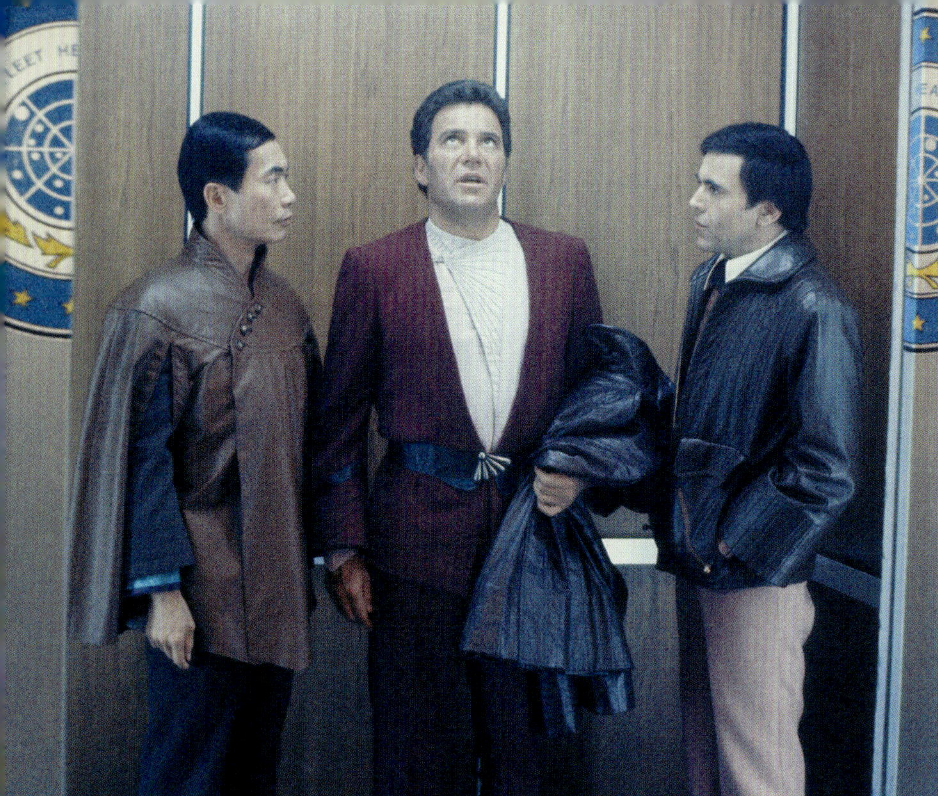

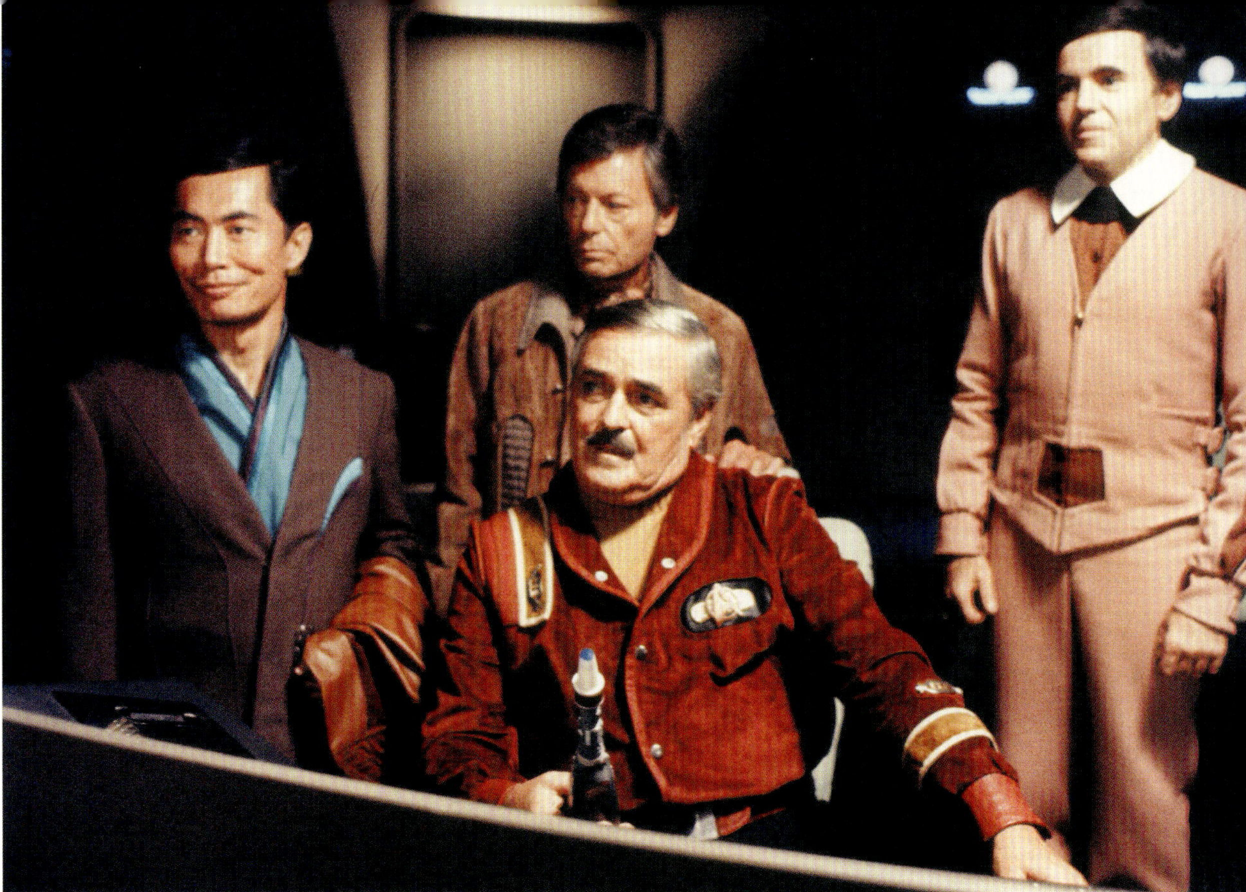

All of a sudden, we heard Leonard's voice saying very loudly and with an irritated vocalization, 'What is that noise? Who's playing music? Turn it off!' Gene turned it off, turned to me, laughing, and said, 'During pre-production, Leonard said he wanted some music played, like classical music, during the set-ups to help keep everyone relaxed. He told me to find a lot of appropriate music to play. I guess Leonard forgot!'"[5]

Some of the last sound added during postproduction to a film is the musical score. Merritt Butrick shared, "There is a magic feeling I get when I hear the *Star Trek* theme music play. I feel like, 'Hey, I was a part of that!'"[6] At first, Nimoy thought to hire his friend, pioneering composer Leonard Rosenman. This collaboration had to wait until *Star Trek IV*, for which Rosenman earned an Academy Award® nomination, as Bennett thought it better to keep the music stylistically similar to *Star Trek II*. He envisioned *Star Trek II* and *III* as two chapters of the same book so wanted to hire James Horner for a return composing effort. Bennett had already been thinking about this at the time of postproduction on *Star Trek II* and had elicited a promise from Horner to compose music for the next movie. "The seeds I was sowing in *Star Trek II* were now going to be able to bloom and work in *Star Trek III*," Horner said, understanding how connected the two films were thematically. "I had to change the end of *Star Trek II* musically, and they changed the cut so that it merged into the beginning of *Star Trek III*, and it actually held me in very good stead. *Star Trek II* was really to me, an emotional story between Kirk and Spock and that really paid off in a big way obviously in the next movie."[7]

Music is, without hyperbole, the emotional soul of a film. Horner spoke to how music and special effects interact during a 1984 interview with Steven Simak of *CinemaScore*. "The music is very hard pressed to keep up with the visuals and that is what's so challenging: to write something musically that is just as terrific on the ears as the visuals are on the eyes..."[8] Horner was able to meet that challenge, as witnessed by his eight-minute, thirty-three-second composition 'Stealing the *Enterprise*.' The music, which includes references to Alexander Courage's original *Star Trek* theme, serves as a stirring companion to Kirk and company's heroics.

Balancing quieter moments such as Kirk and Sarek's mind-meld with the bombastic action was something that Horner and Nimoy discussed during four hours of meetings. Of *Star Trek III* and Nimoy, Horner shared with Simak, "It's made by someone who knows the characters of *Star Trek* so much more intimately than anybody else involved, except maybe Gene Roddenberry. The fact that Leonard Nimoy directed this film gives it a whole interesting light that it would never have had with anyone else. It was fascinating working with him."[8] Horner was proud of his achievement, and preferred the music he composed for *Star Trek III* to that of his previous effort.

The music for the film was recorded during February 1984 at Paramount, with Horner conducting the 102-piece orchestra. Greig McRitchie orchestrated and Dan Wallin recorded the soundtrack.

THIS PAGE: When Admiral Kirk and crew bend the rules in *Star Trek III*, it harkens back to the episode "Amok Time" when Kirk risks his career to get Spock to Vulcan as he suffers the effects of pon farr. This time, Kirk's crew joins directly in his decision.

DISCO TREK

The wildly successful dance version of John Williams' *Star Wars* themes by musician and producer Meco Monardo – which was number one on the *Billboard* chart and sold more than two million copies – inspired a host of other disco-ized movie themes. Horner asked Group 87, a respected session group comprised of jazz and progressive musicians Mark Isham, Patrick O'Hearn, and Peter Maunu to work with him on creating an electronic dance version of the *Star Trek III* theme music. A 7" 45 RPM single was released by Capitol Records timed to the film's premiere. The A side was 'The Search for Spock' dance song, while the B side was the regular orchestral version of 'Returning to Vulcan.' The disco version also appeared on the regular soundtrack.

For those who purchased the 12" 33 RPM soundtrack album, also by Capitol, Group 87 and Horner's disco song was included as a bonus record, making *Star Trek III* the first double record *Star Trek* movie soundtrack. Interestingly, 'The Search for Spock' disco song is not mentioned on the album covers, front or back. It was only referenced on sales stickers affixed to the plastic wrap.

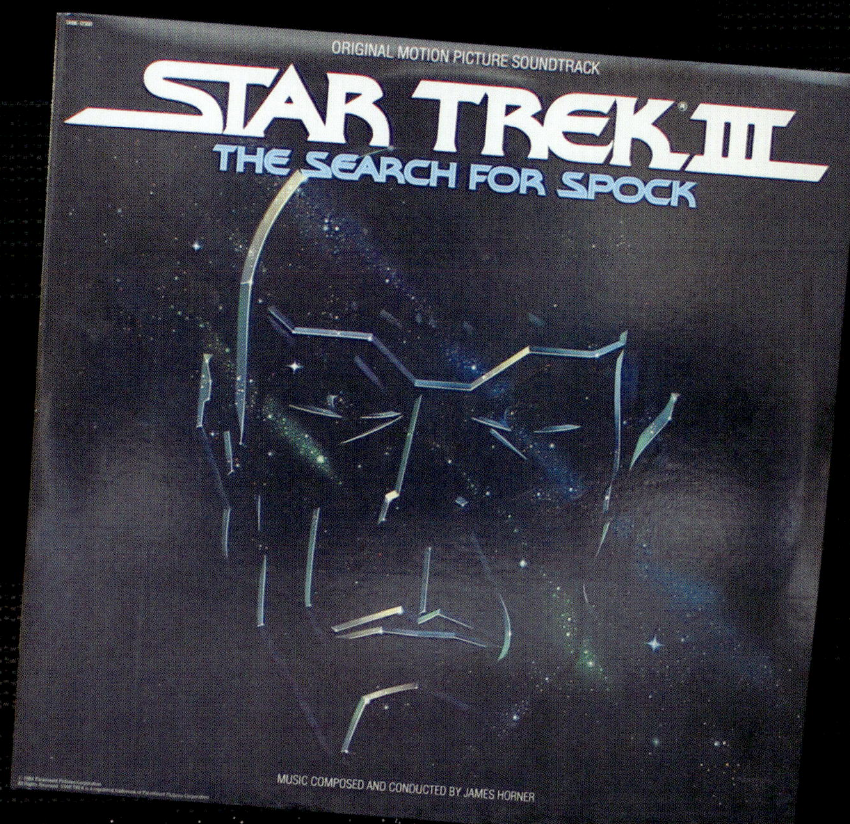

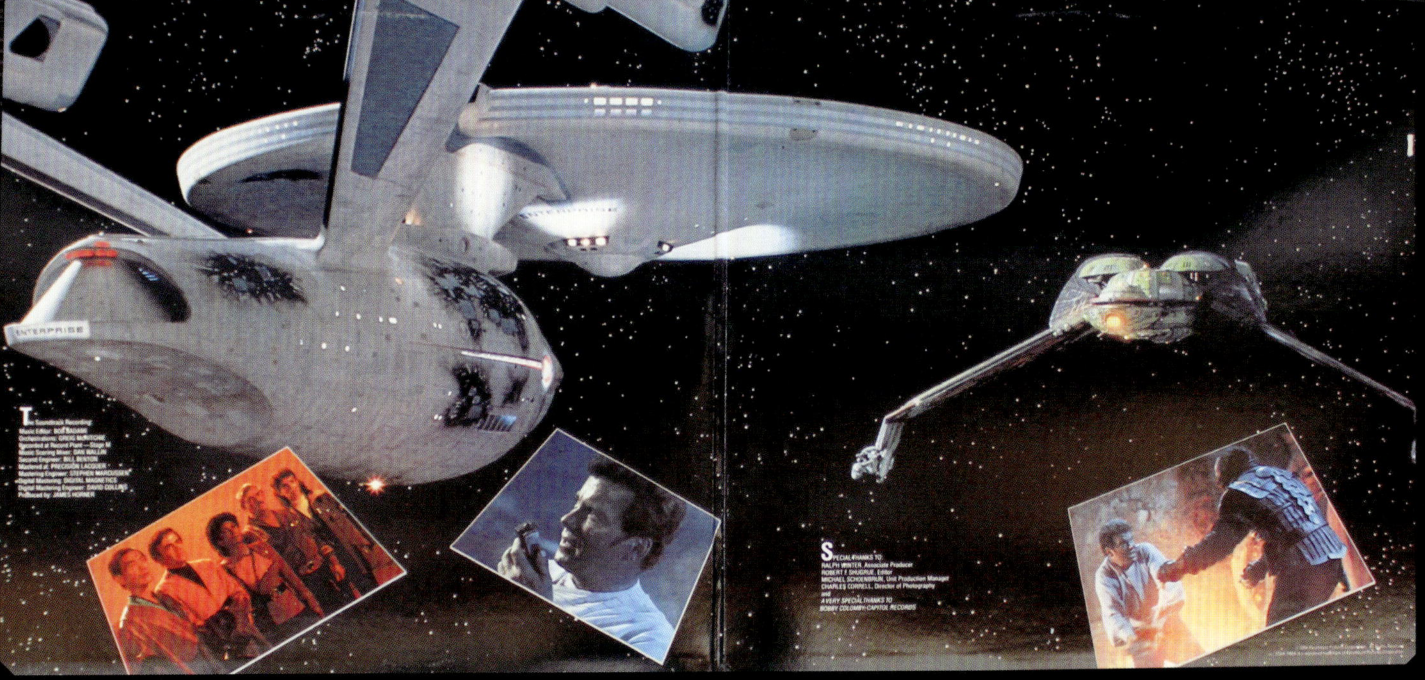

THIS PAGE: The soundtrack album gatefold included an impressive image of the *Enterprise* versus the Bird-of-Prey. Although a very similar moment occurs in the film, this exact image is really an ILM publicity composite.

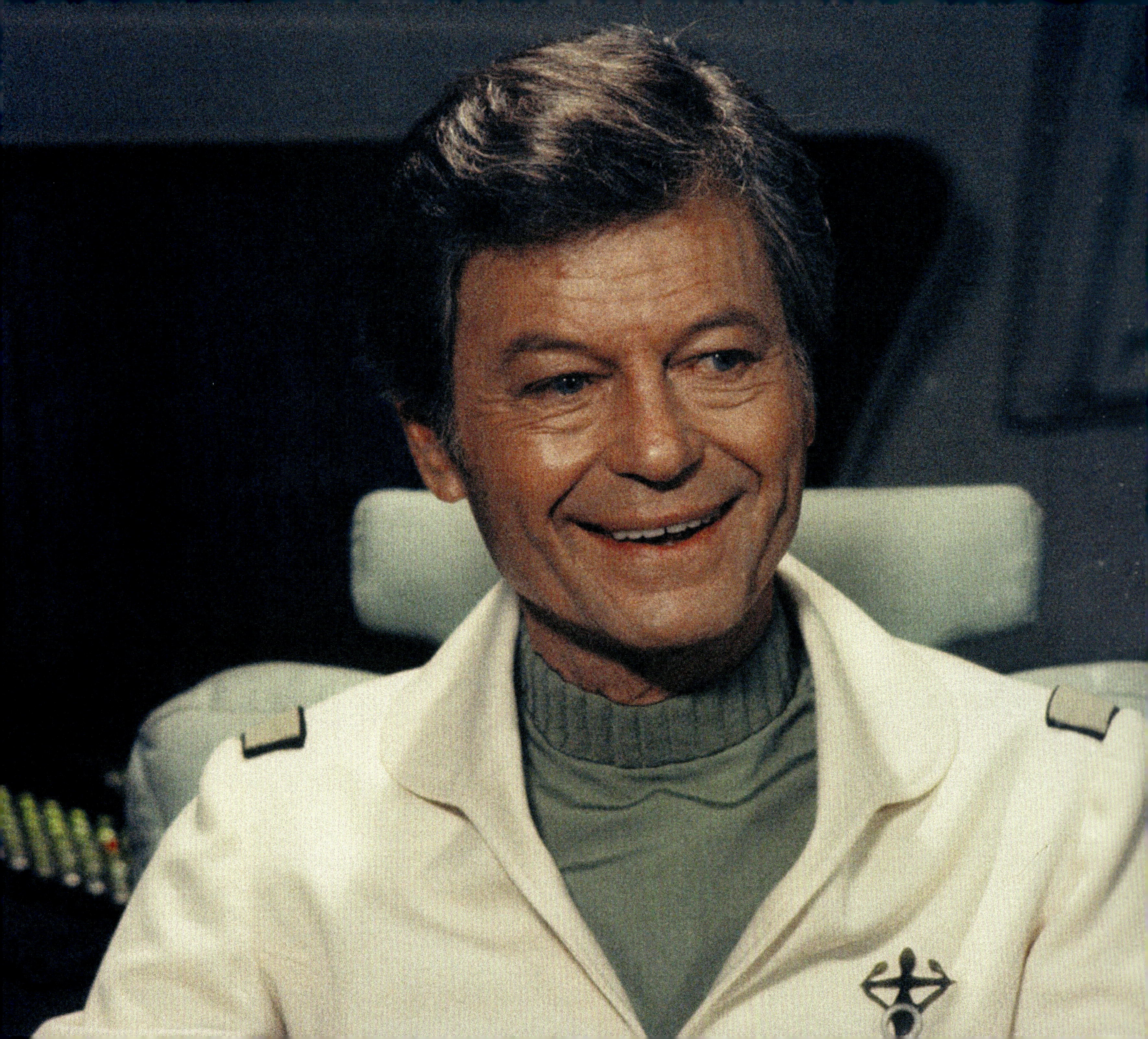

CHAPTER 16

AND THE ADVENTURE CONTINUES

THE PREMIERE AND REACTION

Almost two years after Harve Bennett first received the go ahead to make *Star Trek III*, with post-production complete, nearly all the challenges he and Leonard Nimoy faced had been met. For Bennett, writing *Star Trek III* had been a joy. "Because I've been a producer for twenty-five years, I'm much more comfortable in that function, but I do find writing more satisfying," he explained. "And I'm as proud of *Star Trek III* as anything I've ever done in my career."[1] For Nimoy, he had alleviated concerns by his fellow actors and Paramount executives about his directorial debut. George Takei praised Nimoy, saying, "Leonard did that extraordinary thing of bringing a major motion picture right in on schedule and a little bit under budget. That is unheard of in Hollywood. Leonard did that because he commands that kind of respect and cooperation from his people."[2] That Nimoy did so while facing production obstacles such as the Paramount fire added to the achievement.

One more test loomed for *Star Trek III*, however. How would fans and audiences react? Nimoy got an inkling of how that question would be answered when three weeks before the June 1, 1984 release he was asked to a meeting with Jeffrey Katzenberg. In *I Am Spock*, Nimoy wrote that Katzenberg said, "We know that *Star Trek III* is going to be a success – but there's something we want to tell you now, so that you know our decision has nothing to do with the box office. We want you to make another one for us. This time, the training wheels are off! Give us your vision of *Star Trek*!"[3] "It was the fact that Dad brought *Star Trek III* on time and under budget that was the reason Jeffrey Katzenberg gave him *Star Trek IV*," said Adam Nimoy, Leonard Nimoy's son. "That was the big test, and I'm not surprised that he did it. Dad knew what he was doing. He captured the spirit of what *Star Trek* was all about." Adam added, "I'm proud of the work he did. His work ethic, his creativity, and his artistic integrity. What he had achieved is amazing. He was a true artist. A guy who was trying to stay in the moment, never resting on his laurels, and always looking forward to the next project."[4]

Another sign of what audiences would think of *Star Trek III* was gleaned at the Paramount Studio Theater cast and crew screenings, a screening at ILM in San Rafael, and a New York test audience screening. The positive reactions of those in attendance heralded those of the general audience.

BELOW: Nimoy and Takei collaborate on how to most effectively play Sulu's scan of the Genesis surface.

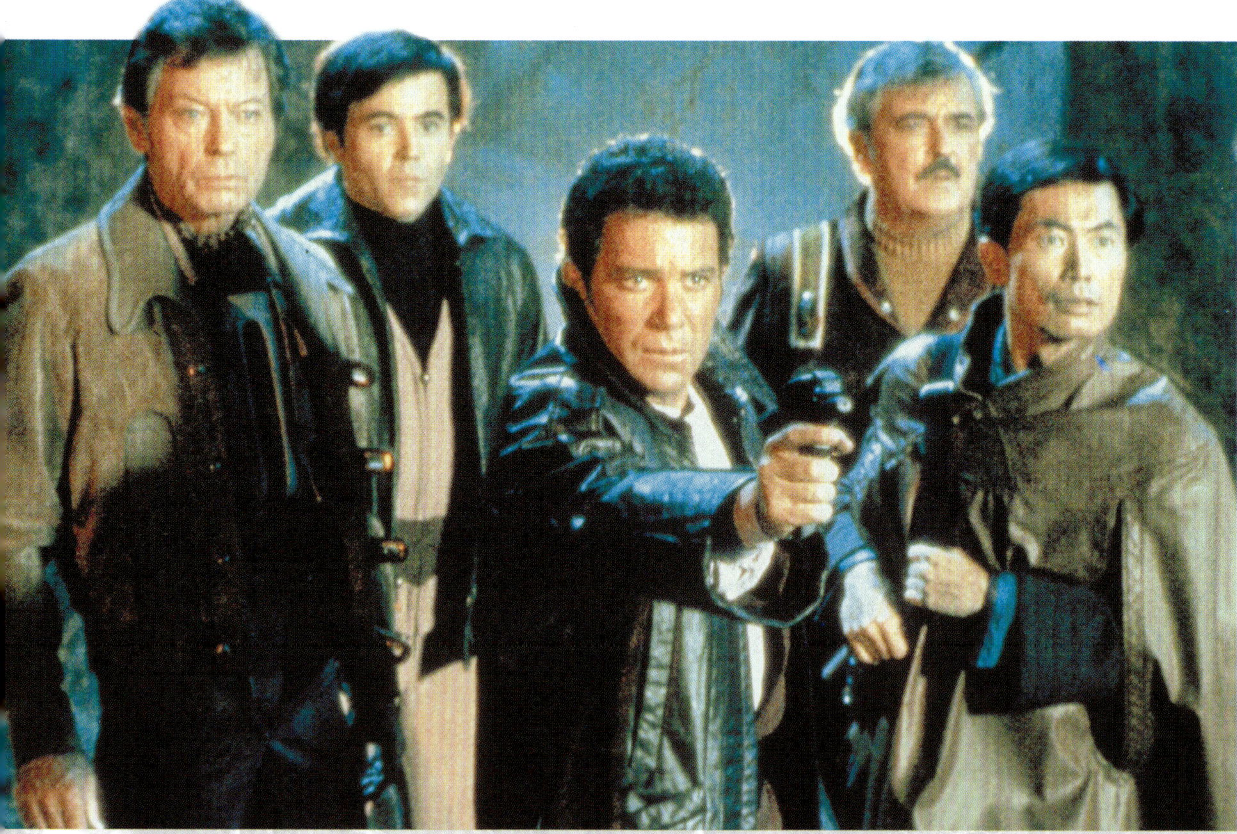

ABOVE: A publicity image featured in many newspapers and magazines at the time.

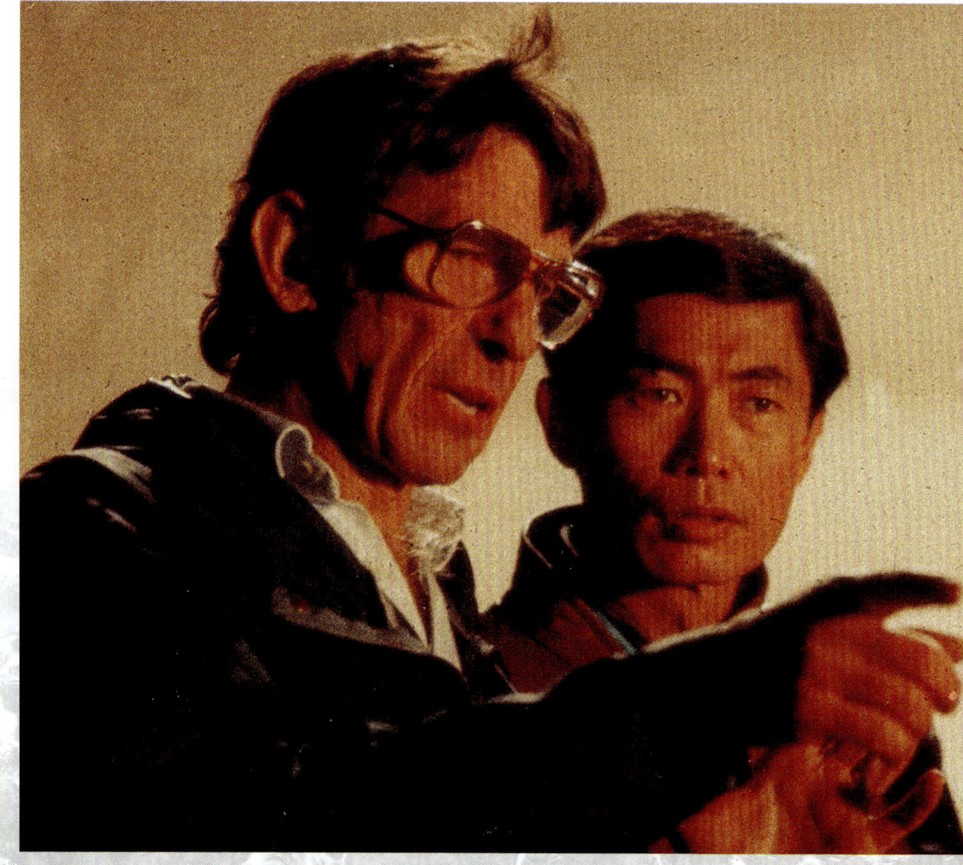

MEMORIES OF THE MAY 29, 1984 PARAMOUNT SCREENING

Robin Curtis: "Of course, I invited my brother, the *Star Trek* fan, and his wife to LA to accompany me to the premiere. Cinematically, there were many moments I loved and my favorite wasn't one of mine. It was with Kirk and Sarek, mind-melding. Leonard captured some visually stunning closeups. And Horner's music. These moments went right to my emotional core. Very effective."[5]

Christopher Lloyd: "I wish I was going to be in the fourth film. Of course, I got wiped out in the last one! See what you can do. I'd even like to come back as some other character. It would be fun to do another one. I would love to do it!"[6]

Stephen Liska: "My wife Kathy and I would always go to the cast screenings. I would sit in the back and watch and see, and try to take some notes and so forth to keep learning. There are so many people who love this series. Forty years later, I keep getting phone calls and requests, so that tells you something."[7]

Vadia Potenza: "I remember loving the film. So excited, calling my friends and being like, 'We gotta go see this!' I immediately wanted to turn around and see it again in the theater."[8]

Stephen Manley: "At the cast Paramount screening, Leonard introduced the film. On opening day, I also went to the Cinerama Dome on Sunset Boulevard with a friend to see it with an audience. There was a long line of people. Because people had not seen the film yet, and my eyes were really blue, they did not know I was an actor from the film. While I was waiting in line, I turned, and there was Walter Koenig, walking the line signing autographs for all the fans."[9]

Thomas Morga: "*Star Trek III* was great. You didn't have to clean up any of the rough ends. Kirk may have lost his career. Kirk lost his son. Kirk lost his ship. Would Kirk ever get command again? All those sacrifices were done in the Great Kirk style. He worked, moved on his own, made his own decision. And the way he did it, to save the day! It is like when Kirk asks McCoy, 'What have I done?' And McCoy tells him he gave them all a chance."[10]

Keegan Allen, son of Phillip R. Allen: "I had *Star Trek III* on VHS and the part where my dad's ship is blown up by the Klingons skipped a bit because I rewound it and watched it again and again. He was proud of playing Esteban, and I'm very proud of him for that, too. The film became a staple of that classic *Star Trek* linear storytelling. Those movies are fun, but at the heart of them, it's cosmogonic. It's human. It's humans wanting peace throughout the galaxy."[11]

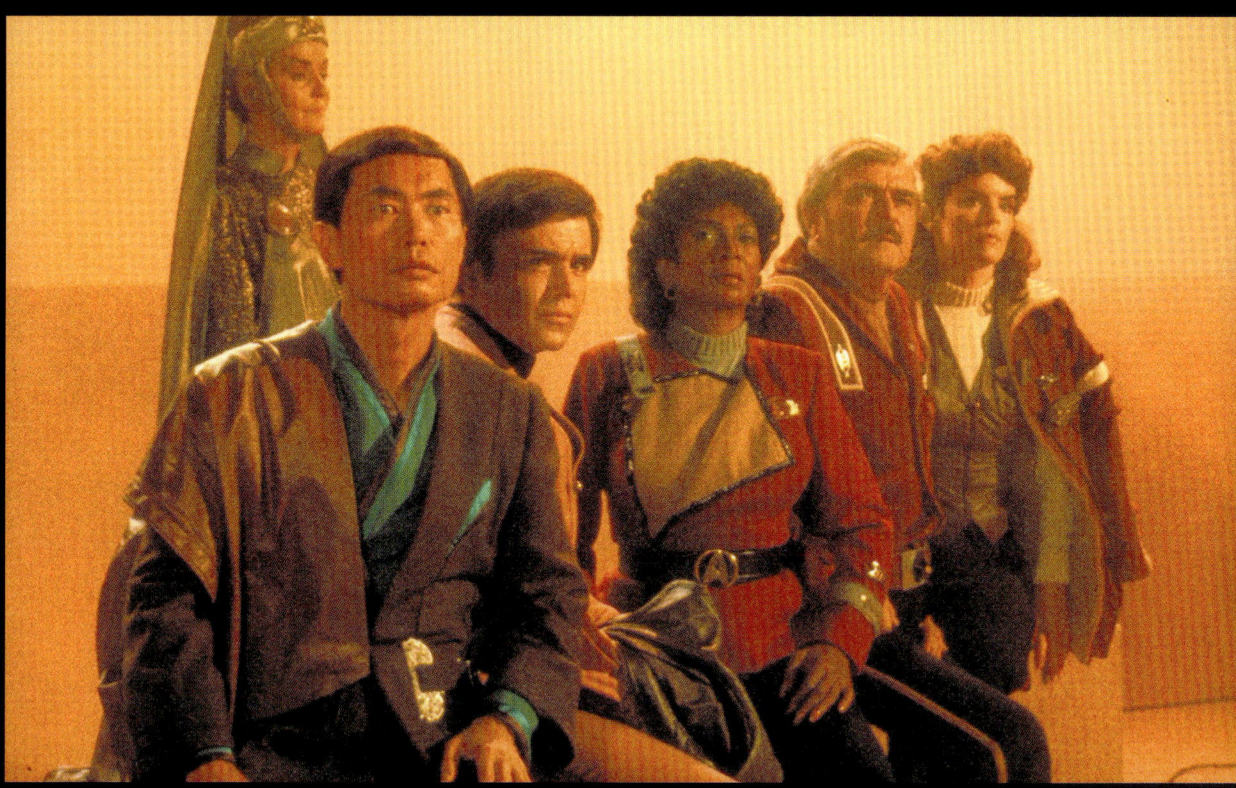

ABOVE: Curtis and her family have a special memory of seeing *Star Trek III*. "I didn't want to be anywhere else but with my family for the premiere. There we were in Utica, NY at the Riverside Mall, having arrived by the limousine a local funeral home lent to us so that my grandparents, mom and dad could attend together. Cherished family friends, the Petersons, hosted a celebratory party that evening while their son, Bill, stood in line early that morning to procure seats! What a thrill to watch with my family and neighbors! It was quite a night for this small-town girl. And several months later, that same funeral home honored my dad as he beamed up to heaven."[5]

MEMORIES OF THE ILM SCREENING

David Carson: "I was really happy to have something to follow *Jedi* because you had to keep working. *Star Trek III* was a good project. I ave very fond memories of that film."[12]

Craig Barron: "*Star Trek III* is much more character driven than a typical] big special effects picture. What was important was the loyalty of these friends getting together and bringing back Spock. I like seeing film at the cast and crew screening, because it's fun to see people. Harve told us thank you. But I wanted to see it with an audience, so I mmediately went to the theater when it premiered. You want to know how an audience reacts. I am very proud of the work on *Star Trek III*. The movie is part of an arc, a continuation of *The Wrath of Khan*."[13]

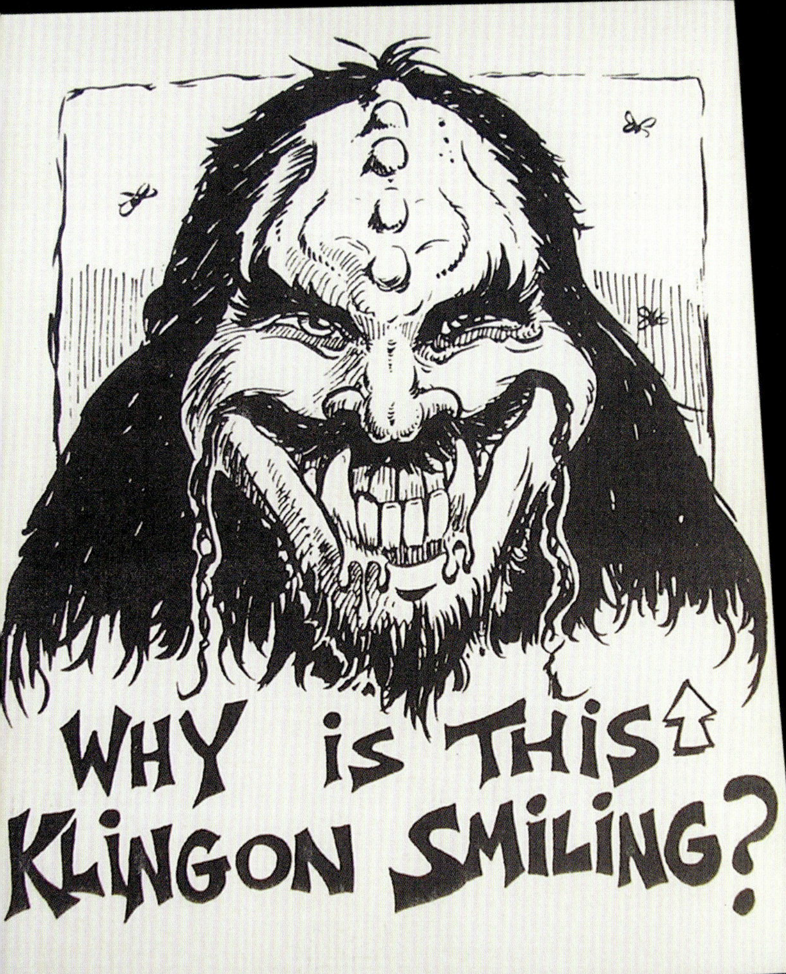

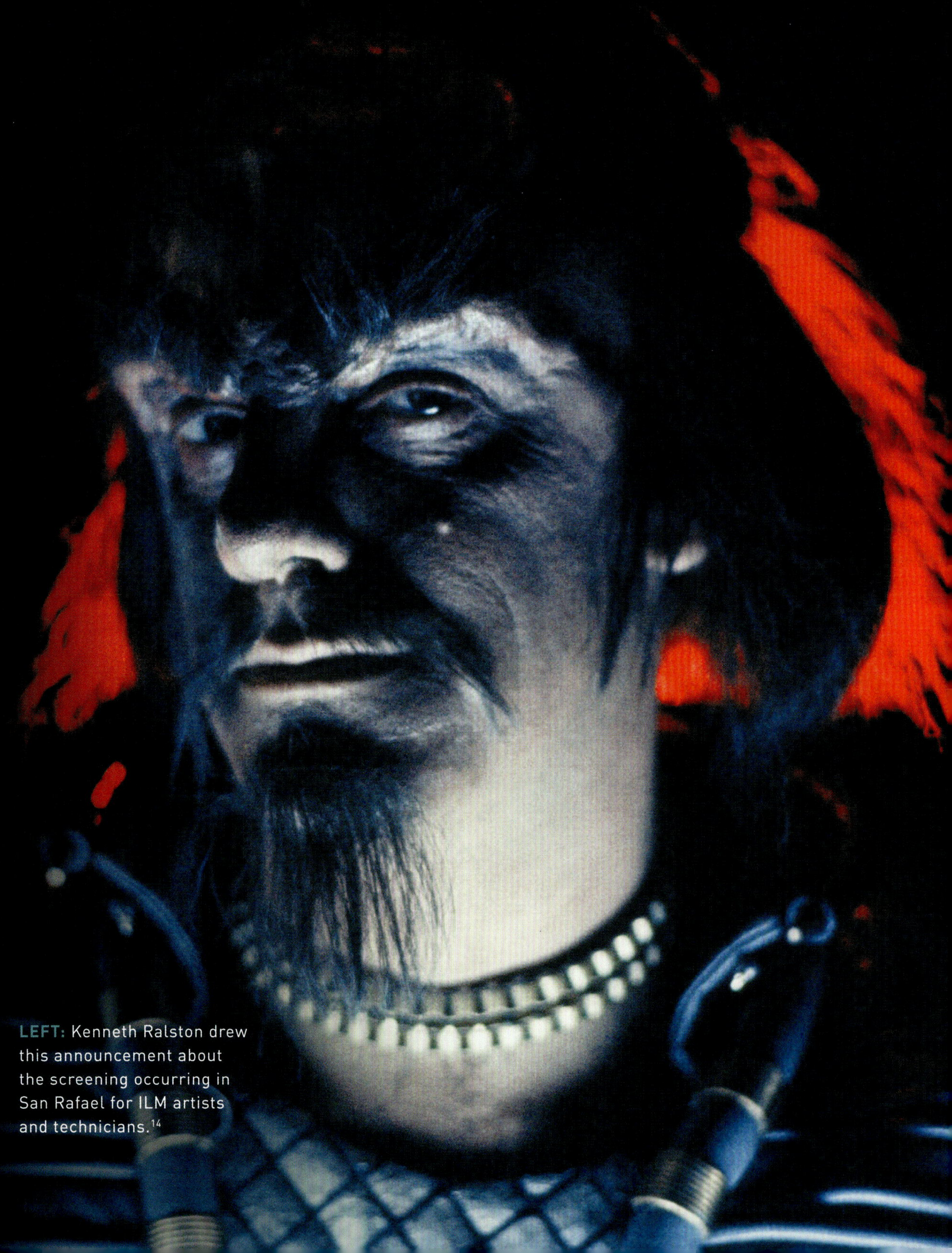

LEFT: Kenneth Ralston drew this announcement about the screening occurring in San Rafael for ILM artists and technicians.[14]

MEMORIES OF THE NEW YORK TEST AUDIENCE SCREENING

Leonard Nimoy: "The most exciting thing for me in the previews was the moment when Kirk has finally beaten Kruge on the burning planet; he picks up Spock; and they are both standing, and he is holding Spock with one arm around him. He calls up to the ship imitating Kruge, demanding that he be beamed up. There's an effects shot where the beaming effect takes place and Kirk and Spock start to disintegrate. As that happens, the very ground they have been standing on crumbles and starts to burn in a burst of flame. The audience broke into cheers and applause. And that told me that they had been with us for the story and that they'd felt relieved. It was quite thrilling, actually. Quite a wonderful experience."[15]

Marc Okrand: "Harve invited me to the New York preview audience screening. The audience responded favorably to the film. What impressed me most, given my role, is that the audience cheered when Kirk picks up the communicator near the end of the film while holding Spock. He repeats the Klingon words he previously heard Kruge used, saying, "Maltz, jol ylchu'!" There were no subtitles, but the audience understood it was Kirk tricking Maltz on the ship using his own language. Bill Shatner and I had practiced that line in his trailer. I wasn't there when he filmed it, so I did not know how it was going to be until I saw the movie. Bill did a good job. The audience really got it."[16]

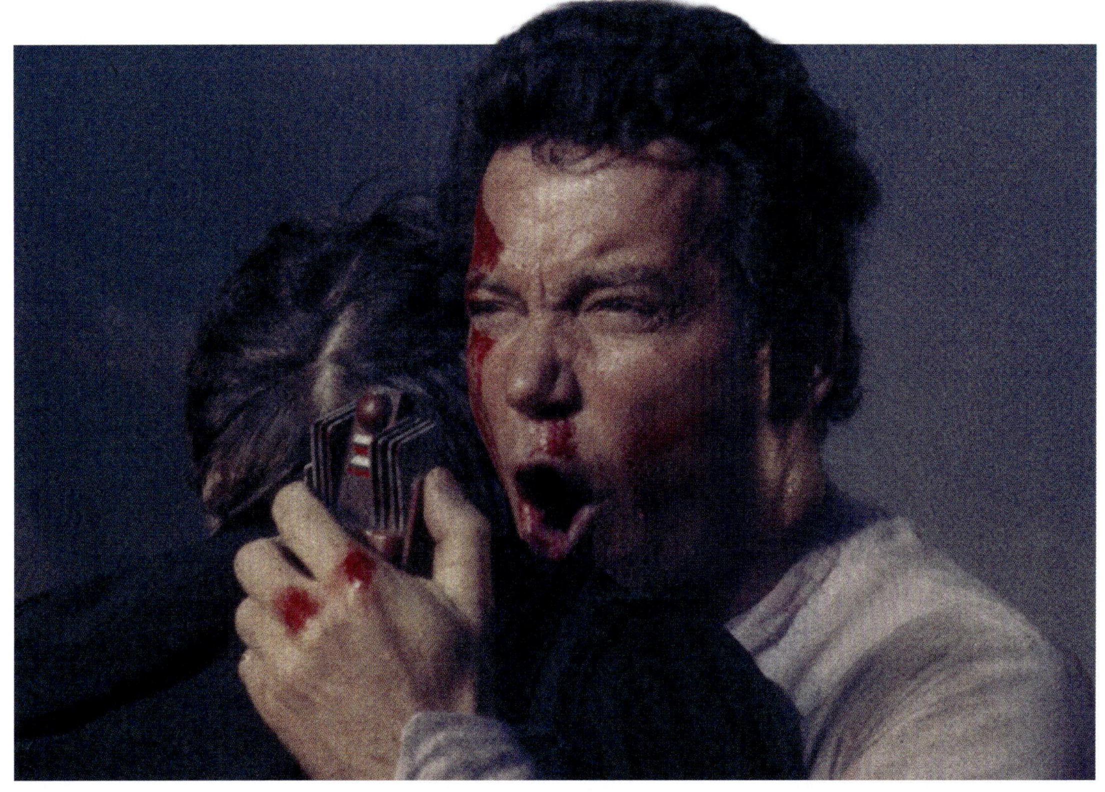

THIS PAGE: Although Kirk uses his brawn to defeat Kruge, he ultimately saves the day and Spock by using his intellect, strategically mimicking Kruge's commands to Maltz.

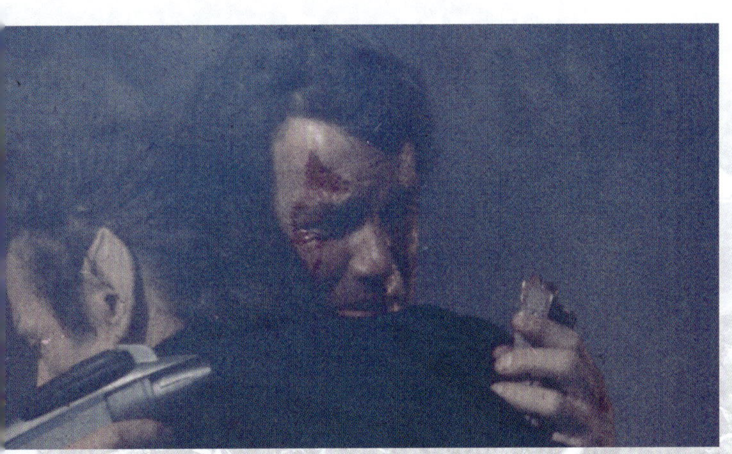

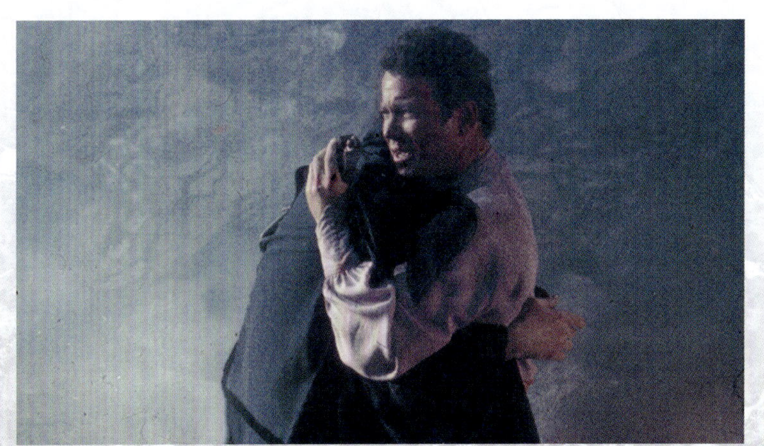

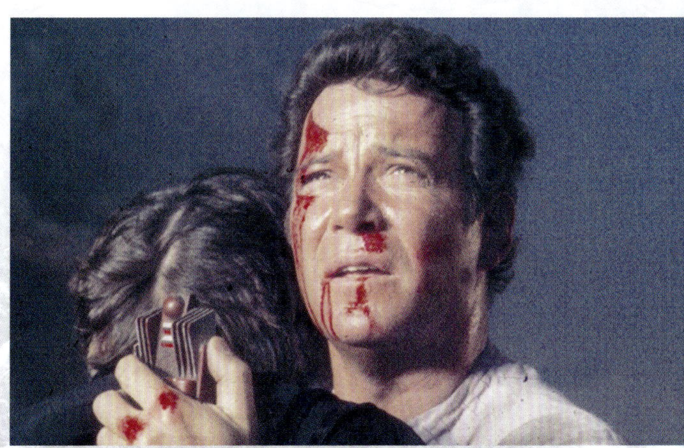

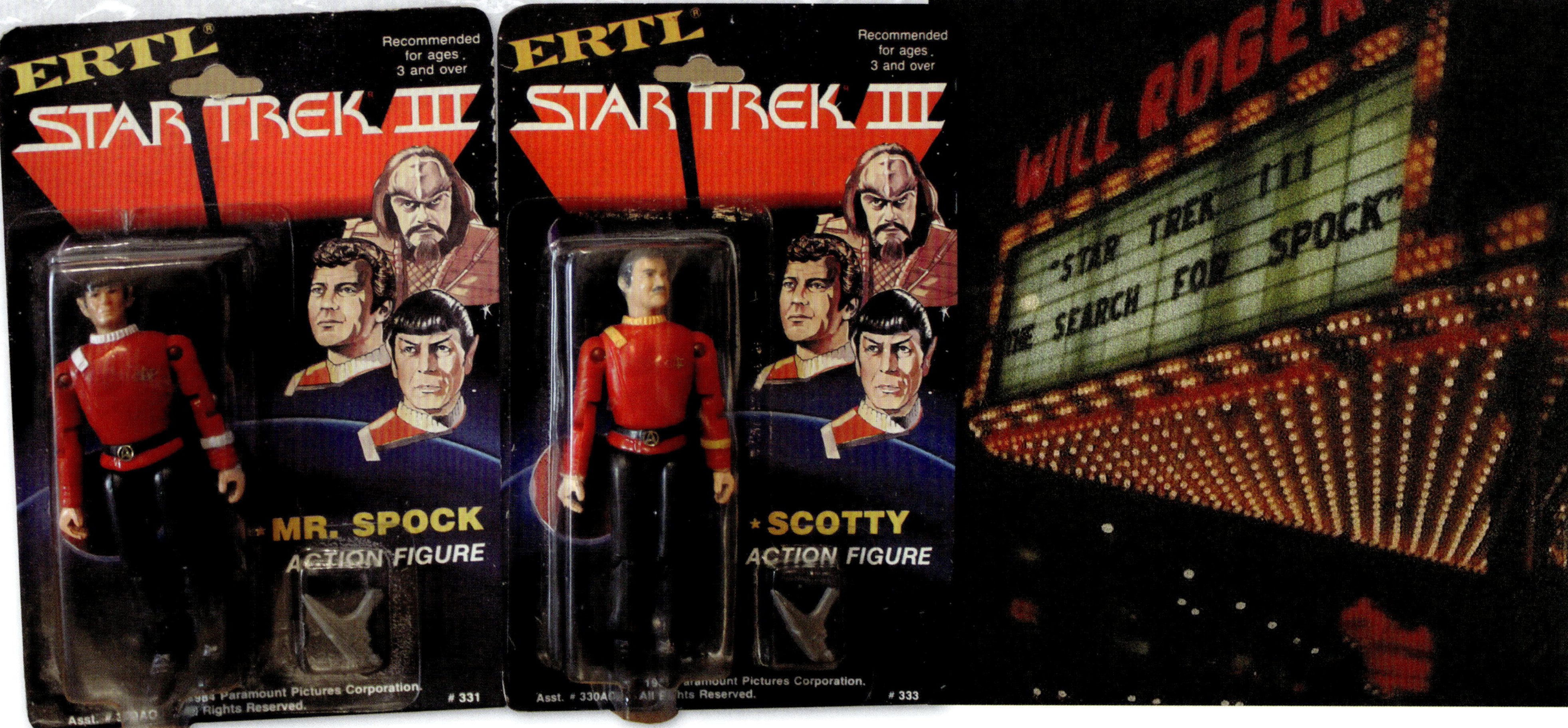

ABOVE LEFT: ERTL produced four action figures for the movie and three die-cast vehicles, including the first ever toy reproduction of a Klingon Bird-of Prey.

ABOVE RIGHT: Photograph of the June 1, 1984, first showing of *Star Trek III* at the Will Rogers Theater in Chicago by Mike Beyer.[23]

Movie reviews, as they are wont to be, were varied. Jack Mathews of *USA Today* called it "The best ride yet aboard the *Starship Enterprise*."[17] Kenneth Pilarski of the *Hattiesburg American* was also adulatory, writing that the film was "delightful fun and should not be missed."[18] Roger Ebert and Gene Siskel liked the film, giving it three stars. They both shared the opinion that the film was, as Ebert wrote, "a good but not great *Star Trek* movie, a sort of compromise between the first two."[19] They were also impressed by the Bird-of-Prey design. Other reviewers were not as kind. Whereas Siskel found the explanation of Spock's return believable, William Wolf of *Gannett News Service* thought it "less than convincing."[20] Brent Northup of the *Longview Daily News* believed that the theme of friendship saved the film, however, he was concerned that the "film does seem like a marketing ploy to set up future sequels. It does tend to negate Spock's sacrifice."[21]

Of the reviews that said the film was good, but not as good as *Star Trek II*, Nimoy was philosophical. "I'm aware that there are some people, here and there who say, *Star Trek II* was better. That's okay," commented Nimoy. "My feeling is, for me, this was the best *Star Trek* that we could do at this particular time based on the story that had to be told here. It had to be a continuation of *Star Trek II*. It had to deal with the fact that Spock died and what was going to happen about that."[22]

Audience reaction, however, was enthusiastic to say the least. *Star Trek III: The Search for Spock* premiered on June 1, 1984, in 1,966 theaters in the United States, the widest release of any of the prior *Star Trek* films. Coincidentally, the number of theaters was the same as the year the original series premiered and perhaps it was a good omen. The film broke box office records with a three-day opening of $16,673,295, which was to that date the highest non-holiday opening of any film in Hollywood history. After its thirty-week run in theaters was completed, the film would earn $87 million world-wide, which is all the more impressive considering its competition that summer included juggernauts like *Indiana Jones and the Temple of Doom*, *The Karate Kid*, and *Ghostbusters*. Of the over 180 films released by studios in 1984, *Star Trek III* was the eighth highest grossing.

The success of *Star Trek III* is measured by more than its box office success. More than forty-years later, much has changed, and many

THE SHELF FOR SPOCK

Marketing for *Star Trek III* started with publicity events such as newspaper trivia contests – with prizes ranging from posters to an all-expense-paid trip to see the premiere of the film – and a media blitz including newspaper, television, and magazine interviews with the actors. Merchandising was more robust than it was for *Star Trek II*, a sign of faith by licensees about the film's prospects.

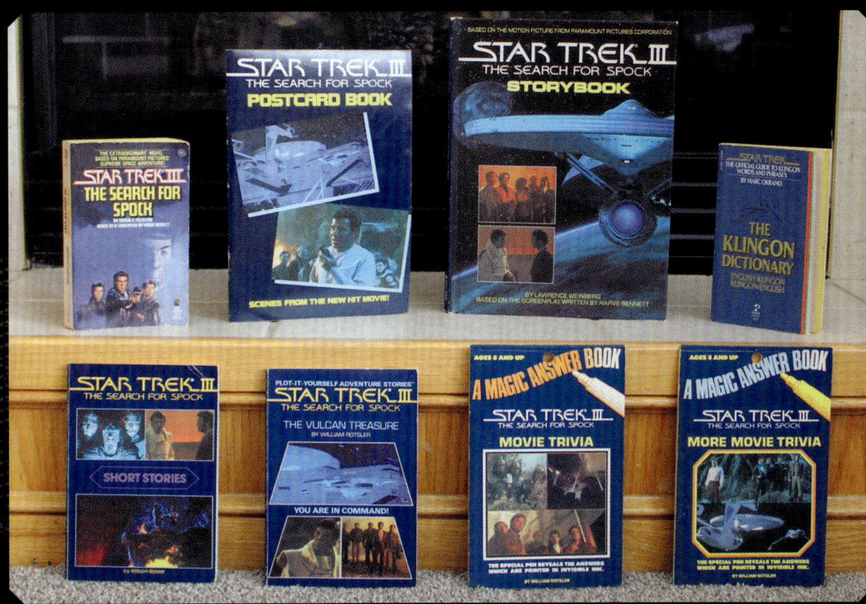

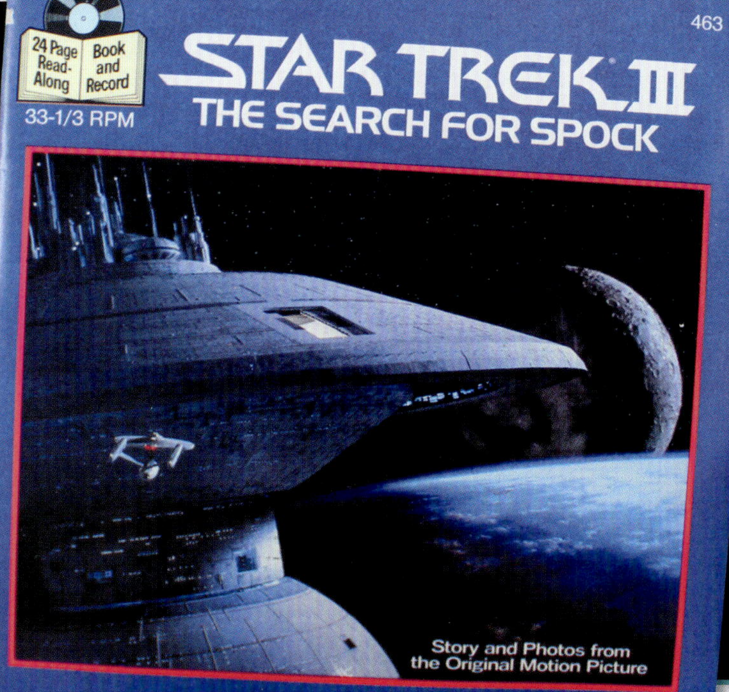

RIGHT: In addition to the Capitol Records release of James Horner's soundtrack, the story of *Star Trek III* was available from Buena Vista Records on a 7" 33 1/3 RMP long playing record accompanied by pictures from the film. Narration was provided by Chuck Riley, who also narrated the movie trailer.

ABOVE LEFT: Books of all varieties were produced. Both the novelization by Vonda McIntyre and the storybook by Lawrence Weinberg, prepared months before postproduction, included Valkris' reveal, the turbo-lift scene with Kirk and McCoy, and the bar fight.

ABOVE RIGHT: During June and July of 1984, Taco Bell sold four glasses featuring art and text at a price of 69 cents each, with the purchase of a medium or large drink. The accompanying television commercial revealed big secrets from the film, including that Spock lives and the fate of the *Enterprise*. Many young fans have fond memories of riding bicycles or asking parents to drive them to the restaurant each week to collect their glasses. Spock actor Vadia Potenza was one of those fans. "I first realized I was on the Taco Bell glasses when I saw the commercial. No one told me I was to be on the glasses! My mom bought a case of like 60 of them! It's pretty cool. It's a pretty weird fun, footnote of my life."[8]

THE STAR TREK III'S THAT WEREN'T

Contemporary *Star Trek* licensees were sent a letter in December 1982 by Paramount inviting them to propose merchandising ideas for the then titled *Star Trek III: In Search of Spock*. Most interesting among the information was that *Star Trek III* was going to be a 3-D movie, with the promise that brand awareness of *Star Trek* and 3-D were a perfect marriage for licensing possibilities. 3-D films experienced something of a renaissance during the early 1980s, with many adventure and science fiction films employing the technology, most especially *Jaws 3-D* (1983). While the three-dimensional ballyhoo was eventually abandoned, it is interesting to contemplate how *Star Trek III*, especially its visual effects and the destruction of the *Enterprise*, would have been different.

While Bennett prepared the *Star Trek III* that fans are familiar with, a parallel film idea was being considered. On January 21, 1981, a first draft script by writer John Hughes was delivered to Paramount for consideration. The story *The Rise of Khan* was a prequel to *The Wrath of Khan*, set during the twenty-first century, showing Lt. Khan and the machinations which brought about his control of Earth as emperor. The script ends with Khan's exile in suspended animation, defeated by his nemesis, the film's heroes John Pierce and Captain Thorpe. While the script review thought Khan was an effective character, few others were deemed believable or engaging. The script was determined to be more fantasy than science fiction, and there was a concern about the limited charm and humor that defined previous *Star Trek* productions. Because of these reasons, the project was abandoned.

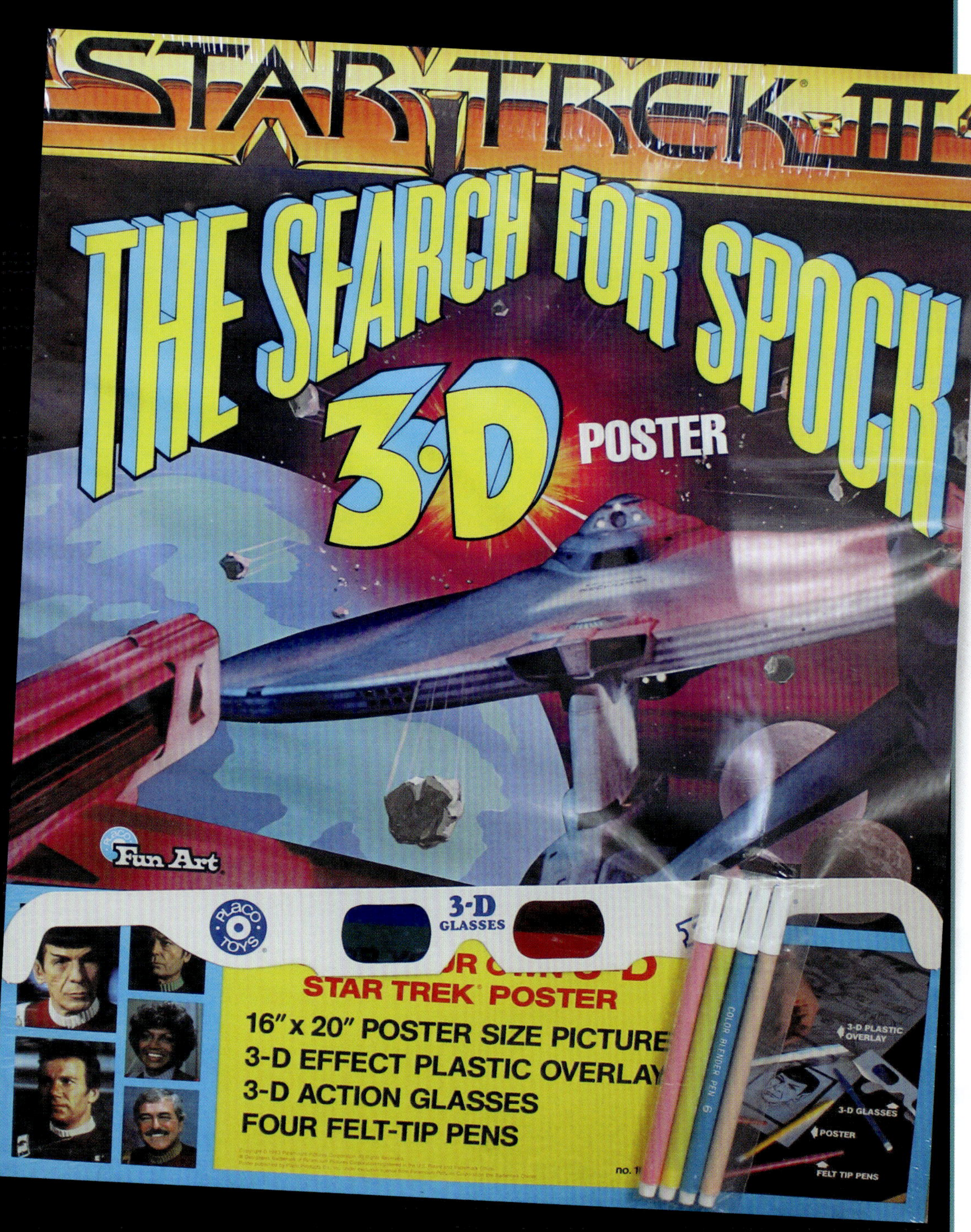

RIGHT: The closest fans got to a 3-D version of *Star Trek III* was this 3-D poster to color by Placo Products Co.

of those who worked on this film about death and resurrection have themselves been lost to their family, friends, and fans. Harve Bennett, Gene Roddenberry, Leonard Nimoy, DeForest Kelley, Nichelle Nichols, James Doohan, Merritt Butrick, Charles Correll, James Horner, and many other actors and behind-the-scenes artists from Paramount and ILM have died since the film's premiere.

Although only eighteen at the time, Spock actor Stephen Manley knew he was witnessing something poignant. "On my last day of filming, I was standing at the craft table getting a cup of coffee. The stage door near me was ajar, and the sunlight from outside was blinding. It looked like the end of *Close Encounters of the Third Kind* when the pilots who were lost in the Bermuda Triangle walk out of the spaceship. From the light emerges these figures. I see William Shatner, DeForest Kelley, James Doohan, Walter Koenig, and George Takei walk in wearing their costumes. I knew that, seeing all of them in one group, filtered through that light, one behind the other, and kind of congregated, that this was a moment I would not get to see again."[9]

Those who worked on *Star Trek III* left behind something enduring and emotional. Curtis spoke to this: "I hadn't watched *Star Trek III* in over three decades. And my overarching memory of the story was of sadness. And loss. My goodness, everything dies! Our illusions with the Genesis experiment. David? Dies. The *Enterprise*. Genesis! Destroyed! But having revisited the film recently, my lasting impressions were dead wrong. I categorized the story incorrectly in my mind. The film is hopeful. There are scenes filled with humor, friendship, and the promise of renewal. I can't explain my former impression. Perhaps it was the loss of my father. And the enormous seriousness with which I took playing the role of Saavik."[5]

The last image of the film is a Vulcan sun rise, created by ILM's matte department, with the words "...and the Adventure continues..." promising more. It is noteworthy that the word "Adventure" is capitalized because it encapsulates what *Star Trek* is about. For Bennett and Nimoy the promise was literal, as work began immediately on the next film. *Star Trek III* proved the sustainability of the franchise and helped ensure its future. Harve Bennett said of seeing *Star Trek III*, "For the first time, I remember expressing to Leonard, who totally agreed, 'You know what we've done? We've now completed act two of our trilogy.' That's really what carried us into *Star Trek IV*."[24]

At its heart, *Star Trek III* is about loyalty and friendship, which somehow despite the losses suffered by the characters, reminds the audience that there is always hope in those universal values. And it does so with a sense of fun. A wink, a nod, and an eyebrow raise.

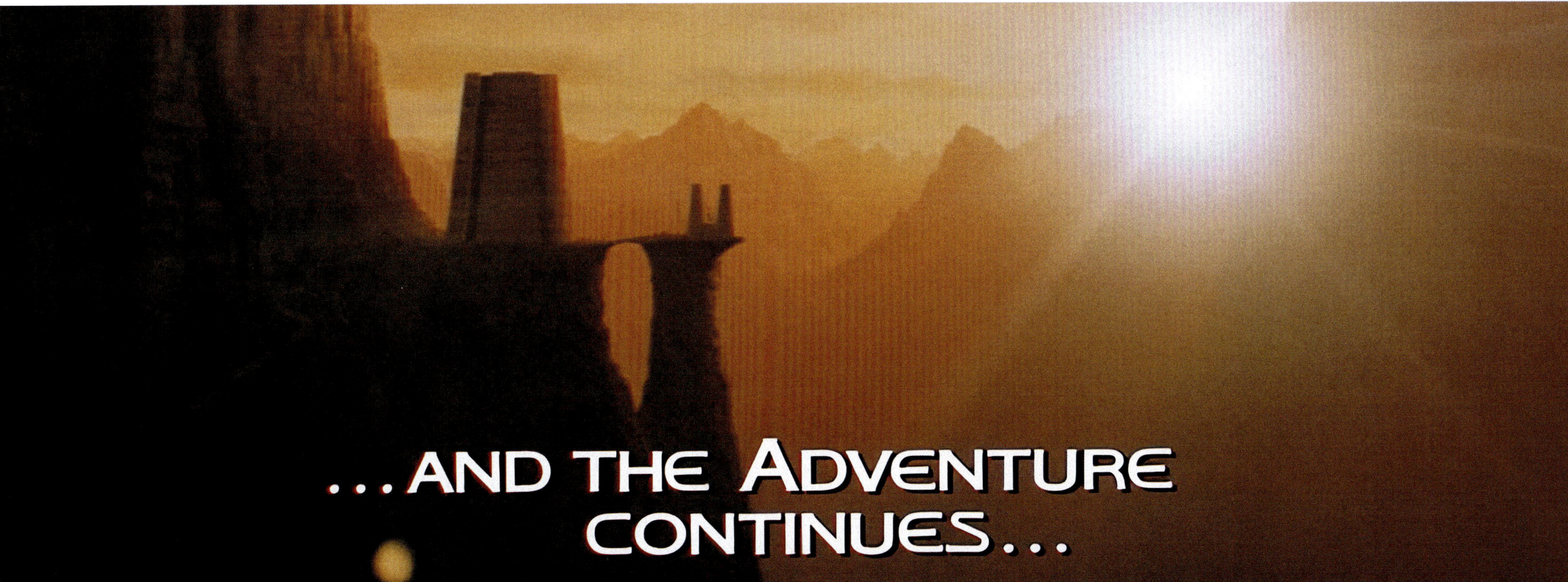

SOURCES

CHAPTER 1

1. "Captain's Log." Bonus feature. Mark Rance, Producer. *Star Trek III: The Search for Spock*. 4K Ultra HD Blu-ray Plus Blu-ray Plus Digital Edition. 2022.
2. McDonnell, David, ed. *Star Trek III: The Search for Spock: The Official Movie Magazine*. 1984. *Starlog*.
3. *The Oregonian*. 1946 August 6. Pg. 9.
4. Nimoy, Adam. Interview. 2024 August 15.
5. Manley, Stephen. Interview. 2024 August 30.
6. "Harve Bennett." *Star Trek: The Magazine*. Vol. 3. Issue 8. December 2002.
7. Scapperotti, Dan. "Leonard Nimoy." *Cinefantastique*. May 1984.

CHAPTER 2

1. Coppola, Francis Ford. Quote. *The Chicago Movie Magazine*. https://www.chicagomoviemagazine.com/
2. Meyer, Nicholas. *The View from the Bridge: Memories of Star Trek and a Life in Hollywood*. Viking Penguin, 2009.
3. Madsen, Dan. "Leonard Nimoy: Directing the Continuing Saga." *Star Trek III: The Official Fan Club Magazine*. Number 43. 1984.
4. Shatner, William. Interview. 2024 July 8.
5. "Captain's Log." *Star Trek III: The Search for Spock* Blu-ray. Paramount Pictures Corporation. Producer Mark Rance. 2023.
6. Shatner, William, with Chris Kreski. *Star Trek Movie Memories*. Harper Collins, 1994.
7. McDonnell, David, ed. *Star Trek III: The Search for Spock: The Official Movie Magazine*. 1984. *Starlog*.
8. "Harve Bennett." *Star Trek: The Magazine*. Vol. 3. Issue 8. December 2002.
9. Madsen, Dan, and John S. Davis. "Merritt Butrick: The Life and Death of David Marcus." *Star Trek: The Official Fan Club*. Number 49. April May 1986.
10. Madsen, Dan. "Gene Roddenberry: The Father of Star Trek." *Star Trek III: The Official Fan Club Magazine*. Number 44. 1984.
11. Carson, David. Interview. 2024 August 16.
12. Nimoy, Leonard. *I Am Spock*. Hyperion, 1995.

CHAPTER 3

1. McDonnell, David, ed. *Star Trek III: The Search for Spock: The Official Movie Magazine*. 1984. *Starlog*.
2. Photos courtesy of Kenneth Ralston.
3. Ralston, Kenneth. Interview. 2024 July 30.
4. Munson, Brad. "The Final Voyage of the *Starship Enterprise*." *CineFex: The Journal of Cinematic Illusions*.
5. Morga, Thomas. Interview. 2024 August 2.
6. Shatner, William. Interview. 8 July 2024.
7. Madsen, Dan. "Leonard Nimoy: Directing the Continuing Saga." *Star Trek III: The Official Fan Club Magazine*. Number 43. 1984.
8. "Production Designs." *Star Trek: The Magazine*. Vol. 3. Issue 8. December 2002.
9. Ralston, Kenneth. Interview. 2024 July 30.

CHAPTER 4

1. "Harve Bennett." *Star Trek: The Magazine*. Vol. 3. Issue 8. December 2002.
2. Nimoy, Leonard. *I Am Spock*. Hyperion, 1995.
3. Curtis, Robin. Interview. 2024 July 19.
4. Potenza, Vadia. Interview. 2024 August 1.
5. Manley, Stephen. Interview. 2024 August 30.
6. Nimoy, Adam. Interview. 2024 August 15.
7. Welker, Frank. Interview. 2024 August 6.
8. Allen, Keegan. Interview. 2024 August 9.
9. Madsen, Dan. "Leonard Nimoy: Directing the Continuing Saga." *Star Trek III: The Official Fan Club Magazine*. Number 43. 1984.
10. Photos courtesy of Vadia Potenza.

CHAPTER 5

1. Shatner, William, with Chris Kreski. *Star Trek: Movie Memories*. Harper Collins, 1994.
2. Madsen, Dan, and John S. Davis. "Christopher Lloyd: A Man of Character." *Star Trek III: The Official Fan Club*. Number 47. September October 1984.
3. McDonnell, David, ed. *Star Trek III: The Search for Spock: The Official Movie Magazine*. 1984. *Starlog*.
4. "Captain's Log." *Star Trek III: The Search for Spock* Blu-ray. Paramount Pictures Corporation. Producer Mark Rance. 2023.
5. Liska, Stephen. Interview. 2024 August 14.
6. Nimoy, Adam. Interview. 2024 August 15.
7. Murray, Will. "John Larroquette: Klingon Comedian." *Starlog*. Number 138. 1989.
8. *The Twilight Zone Magazine*. August 1984.
9. Okrand, Marc. Interview. 2024 August 9.
10. "Designing the Klingon Bird-of-Prey." *Star Trek: The Magazine*. Vol. 3. Issue 8. December 2002.
11. Ralston, Kenneth. Interview. 2024 July 30.
12. Carson, David. Interview. 2024 August 16.
13. "ILM: Visual Effects." *Star Trek: The Magazine*. Vol. 3. Issue 8. December 2002.

CHAPTER 6

1. Madsen, Dan, and John S. Davis. "Christopher Lloyd: A Man of Character." *Star Trek III: The Official Fan Club*. Number 47. September October 1984.
2. Curtis, Robin. Interview. 2024 July19.
3. Robert Fletcher, *Costume Sketch of Hines in the Paramount Pictures Production of 'Star Trek III: The Search for Spock'*, 1984; Chalk, pen on paper, 13 x 19 3/4 in.; Los Angeles County Museum of Art, Gift of Robert Fletcher.
4. Liska, Stephen. Interview. 2024 August 14.
5. Image credits from left to right:

Robert Fletcher, *Costume Sketch of Mark Lenard as Sarek on Vulcan in the Paramount Pictures Production of 'Star Trek III: The Search for Spock'*,1984; Pastel, ink on paper, polyester, 20 x 12 3/4 in.; Los Angeles County Museum of Art, Gift of Robert Fletcher.

Robert Fletcher, *Costume Sketch of Cathie Sherriff as Valkris in the Paramount Pictures Production of 'Star Trek III: The Search for Spock'*, 1984; Colored pencil, pen on paper, lamé, 19 x 12 3/4 in.; Los Angeles County Museum of Art, Gift of Robert Fletcher.

Robert Fletcher, *Costume Sketch for the Paramount Pictures Production of 'Star Trek III: The Search for Spock'*, 1984; Colored pencil, pen on paper, 20 5/8 x 12 3/4 in.; Los Angeles County Museum of Art, Gift of Robert Fletcher.

Robert Fletcher, *Costume Sketch for the Paramount Pictures Production of 'Star Trek III: The Search for Spock'*, 1984; Colored pencil on paper, 19 3/4 x 12 3/4 in.; Los Angeles County Museum of Art, Gift of Robert Fletcher.

Robert Fletcher, *Costume Sketch of High Priestess in the Paramount Pictures Production of 'Star Trek III: The Search for Spock'*, 1984; Colored pencil, pencil on paper, 19 7/8 x 12 7/8 in.; The Los Angeles County Museum of Art, Gift of Robert Fletcher.

6. Photos courtesy of The Burman Studio.
7. Madsen, Dan, John S. Davis & Shelley Davidson. "Robert Fletcher: Designing 23rd Century Fashions." *Star Trek III: The Official Club Magazine*. Number 45. March April 1984.
8. Madsen, Dan. "Mark Lenard." *Star Trek III: The Official Fan Club Magazine*. Number 42. 1984.
9. Manley, Stephen. Interview. 2024 August 30.
10. Potenza, Vadia. Interview. 2024 August 1.
11. Photo courtesy of Vadia Potenza.
12. Okrand, Marc. Interview. 2024 August 9.

CHAPTER 7

1. Nimoy, Leonard. *I Am Spock*. Hyperion, 1995.
2. McDonnell, David, ed. *Star Trek III: The Search for Spock: The Official Movie Magazine*. 1984. *Starlog*.
3. Madsen, Dan. "DeForest Kelley: Still the Real McCoy." *Star Trek III: The Official Fan Club Magazine*. Number 44. 1984.
4. Okrand, Marc. Interview. 2024 August 9.
5. Shatner, William. Interview. 8 July 2024.
6. Ralston, Kenneth. Interview. 2024 July 30.
7. Weyland, Philip. Interview. 2024 August 5.

CHAPTER 8

1. Scott, Vernon. "Nostalgia Bonfire: Historic Sets Lost in Movie Studio Blaze." *Ventura County Star*. 26 August. 1983. Pg. 20.
2. Associated Press. "Paramount Fire Destroys Sets From Famous Films." *The Baltimore Sun*. 26 Aug. 1983. Pgs. 1 and 3.
3. Associated Press. "Paramount Fire Ruled Arson." *Lancaster New Era*. 6 Oct. 1983. Pg. 58.
4. Weyland, Philip. Interview. 2024 August 5.
5. Shatner, William. Interview. 2024 July 8.
6. "Captain's Log." *Star Trek III: The Search for Spock* Blu-ray. Paramount Pictures Corporation. Producer Mark Rance. 2023.
7. Munson, Brad. "The Final Voyage of the *Starship Enterprise*." *CineFex: The Journal of Cinematic Illusions*.

8. McDonnell, David, ed. *Star Trek III: The Search for Spock: The Official Movie Magazine*. 1984. *Starlog*.
9. Nimoy, Adam. Interview. 2024 August 15.

CHAPTER 9

1. Barron, Craig. Interview. 2024 September 9.
2. "Production Designs." *Star Trek: The Magazine*. Vol. 3. Issue 8. Dec. 2002.
3. Madsen, Dan. "Mark Lenard." *Star Trek III: The Official Fan Club Magazine*. Number 42. 1984.
4. "Swires, Steve "Leonard Nimoy: A View from the Bridge." *Starlog*. Number 106. May 1986.
5. "Captain's Log." *Star Trek III: The Search for Spock* Blu-ray. Paramount Pictures Corporation. Producer Mark Rance. 2023.
6. Carson, David. Interview. 2024 August 16.
7. Munson, Brad. "The Final Voyage of the *Starship Enterprise*." *CineFex: The Journal of Cinematic Illusions*.
8. *Star Trek: The Magazine*. Vol. 3. Issue 8. December 2002.

CHAPTER 10

1. Barron, Craig. Interview. 2024 September 9.
2. Curtis, Robin. Interview. 2024 July 19.
3. Potenza, Vadia. Interview. 2024 August 1.
4. Madsen, Dan, and John S. Davis. "Merritt Butrick: The Life and Death of David Marcus." *Star Trek: The Official Fan Club*. Number 49. April May 1986.
5. Manley, Stephen. Interview. 2024 August 30.
6. "Leonard Nimoy." *Star Trek: The Magazine*. Vol. 3. Issue 8. Dec. 2002.
7. Ralston, Kenneth. Interview. 2024 July 30.
8. Okrand, Marc. Interview. 2024 August 9.
9. Liska, Stephen. Interview. 2024 August 14.
10. Nimoy, Leonard. *I Am Spock*. Hyperion, 1995.
11. Nimoy, Adam. Interview. 2024 August 15.

CHAPTER 11

1. Carson, David. Interview. 2024 August 16.
2. Munson, Brad. "The Final Voyage of the *Starship Enterprise*." *CineFex: The Journal of Cinematic Illusions*.
3. Ralston, Kenneth. Interview. 2024 July 30.
4. "Production Designs." *Star Trek: The Magazine*. Vol. 3. Issue 8. Dec. 2002.
5. Whitney, Grace Lee, with Jim Denney. *The Longest Trek: My Tour of the Galaxy*. CA: Quill Driver Books, 1998.
6. "Industrial Light & Magic: The Visual Effects of *Star Trek*." *Star Trek III: The Search for Spock* Blu-ray. Paramount Pictures Corporation. Executive Producer Tim King. 2023.
7. Madsen, Dan. "Gene Roddenberry: The Father of *Star Trek*." *Star Trek III: The Official Fan Club Magazine*. Number 44. 1984.
8. Madsen, Dan. "Leonard Nimoy: Directing the Continuing Saga." *Star Trek III: The Official Fan Club Magazine*. Number 43. 1984.
9. "ILM: Visual Effects." *Star Trek: The Magazine*. Vol. 3. Issue 8. Dec. 2002.
10. Curtis, Robin. Interview. 2024 July 19.
11. Liska, Stephen. Interview. 2024 August 14.
12. Miller, Allan. Interview. 2024 July 19.
13. No makeup photo courtesy of Allan Miller.

CHAPTER 12

1. McDonnell, David, ed. *Star Trek III: The Search for Spock: The Official Movie Magazine*. 1984. *Starlog*.
2. Swires, Steve "Leonard Nimoy: A View from the Bridge." *Starlog*. Number 106. May 1986
3. Madsen, Dan, and John S. Davis. "Merritt Butrick: The Life and Death of David Marcus." *Star Trek: The Official Fan Club*. Number 49. April May 1986.
4. Manley, Stephen. Interview. 2024 August 30.
5. Curtis, Robin. Interview. 2024 July 19.
6. Shatner, William, with Chris Kreski. *Star Trek: Movie Memories*. Harper Collins, 1994.
7. "Captain's Log." *Star Trek III: The Search for Spock* Blu-ray. Paramount Pictures Corporation. Producer Mark Rance. 2023.
8. Shatner, William. Interview. 2024 July 8.
9. Ralston, Kenneth. Interview. 2024 July 30.

CHAPTER 13

1. Curtis, Robin. Interview. 2024 July 19.
2. Morga, Thomas. Interview. 2024 August 2.
3. Manley, Stephen. Interview. 2024 August 30.
4. Miller, Allan. Interview. 2024 July 19.
5. Madsen, Dan. "DeForest Kelley: Still the Real McCoy." *Star Trek III: The Official Fan Club Magazine*. Number 44. 1984.
6. Shatner, William, with Chris Kreski. *Star Trek: Movie Memories*. Harper Collins, 1994.
7. Madsen, Dan. "George Takei: A Man of Many Talents." *Star Trek III: The Official Club Magazine*. Number 45. March April 1984
8. Weyland, Philip. Interview. 2024 August 5.
9. Photo courtesy of Phillip Weyland.
10. Shatner, William. Interview. 2024 July 8.

CHAPTER 14

1. Carson, David. Interview. 2024 August 16.
2. Madsen, Dan. "George Takei: A Man of Many Talents." *Star Trek III: The Official Club Magazine*. Number 45. March April 1984.
3. Okrand, Marc. Interview. 2024 August 9.
4. Liska, Stephen. Interview. 2024 August 14.
5. Barron, Craig. Interview. 2024 September 9.
6. Morga, Thomas. Interview. 2024 August 2.
7. Ralston, Kenneth. Interview. 2024 July 30.

CHAPTER 15

1. Rivka, Sarah. "Navigating Coppola's Maze." *TheSeventies.Berkeley.Edu*. 13 June 2018.
2. "Leonard Nimoy." *Star Trek: The Magazine*. Vol. 3. Issue 8. Dec. 2002.
3. "Swires, Steve "Leonard Nimoy: A View from the Bridge." *Starlog*. Number 106. May 1986.
4. Meyer, Nicholas. *The View from the Bridge: Memories of Star Trek and a Life in Hollywood*. Viking Penguin, 2009.
5. Weyland, Philip. Correspondence. 2024 September 19.
6. Madsen, Dan, and John S. Davis. "Merritt Butrick: The Life and Death of David Marcus." *Star Trek: The Official Fan Club*. Number 49. April May 1986.
7. "James Horner: Composing Genesis." Bonus feature. *Star Trek II: The Wrath of Khan*. 4K Ultra HD Blu-ray Plus Blu-ray Plus Digital Edition. 2022.
8. Simak, Steven. "James Horner on Scoring *Star Trek III: The Search for Spock*." *CinemaScore*. Issue 13 and 14. Fall 1984 and Summer 1985.

CHAPTER 16

1. McDonnell, David, ed. *Star Trek III: The Search for Spock: The Official Movie Magazine*. 1984. *Starlog*.
2. Madsen, Dan. "George Takei: A Man of Many Talents." *Star Trek III: The Official Club Magazine*. Number 45. March April 1984.
3. Nimoy, Leonard. *I Am Spock*. Hyperion, 1995.
4. Nimoy, Adam. Interview. 2024 August 15.
5. Curtis, Robin. Interview. 2024 July 19.
6. Madsen, Dan, and John S. Davis. "Christopher Lloyd: A Man of Character." *Star Trek III: The Official Fan Club*. Number 47. September October 1984.
7. Liska, Stephen. Interview. 2024 August 14.
8. Potenza, Vadja. Interview. 2024 August 1.
9. Manley, Stephen. Interview. 2024 August 30.
10. Morga, Thomas. Interview. 2024 August 2.
11. Allen, Keegan. Interview. 2024 August 9.
12. Carson, David. Interview. 2024 August 16.
13. Barron, Craig. Interview. 2024 September 9.
14. Photo courtesy of Kenneth Ralston.
15. "Leonard Nimoy." *Star Trek: The Magazine*. Vol. 3. Issue 8. Dec. 2002.
16. Okrand, Marc. Interview. 2024 August 9.
17. Mathews, Jack. Quoted in *The Baltimore Sun*. 1984 June 22. Pg. 35.
18. Pilarski, Kenneth. "'Star Trek III' stresses emotions." *Hattiesburg American*. 1984 June 7. Pg. 9.
19. Ebert, Roger. "*Star Trek III: The Search for Spock*." 1984 June 1. https://www.rogerebert.com/reviews/star-trek-iii-the-search-for-spock-1984
20. Wolf, William. "'Star Trek' saga continues in 'The Search for Spock.'" *Fort Meyers*. 1984 June 1. Pg. 6D.
21. Northup, Brent. "'Star Trek III' Friendship Saves This Sequel." *Long View Daily News*. 1984 June 7. E6.
22. Madsen, Dan. "Leonard Nimoy: Directing the Continuing Saga." *Star Trek III: The Official Fan Club Magazine*. Number 43. 1984.
23. Photo courtesy of Mike Beyer/ChiTownSoundz.
24. "Harve Bennett." *Star Trek: The Magazine*. Vol. 3. Issue 8. Dec. 2002.

ACKNOWLEDGMENTS

DEDICATED TO

Dan Madsen, chronicler of the final frontier

and

Nicholas Jose Tenuto, the next generation

THANK YOU TO ALL INTERVIEWEES FOR THEIR TIME AND SPECIAL MEMORIES:

William Shatner
Keegan Allen
Craig Barron
David Carson
Robert Greenberger
Allan Miller
Stephen Liska
Stephen Manley
Thomas Morga
Adam Nimoy
Marc Okrand
Vadia Potenza
Kenneth Ralston
Rod Roddenberry
Frank Welker
Philip Weylan
and with heartfelt thanks,
our inspiration **Robin Curtis**

WITH APPRECIATION FOR YOUR HELP, PERMISSIONS, AND RESOURCES:

David Adler
Mike Beyer/ChiTownSoundz
Julia Borcherts
Jo Boylett
Paul Camuso
John Champion
Sherilyn Connelly
Marian Cordy, Star Trek Archive
Patricia Rose Duignan
Judy Elkins
Chris Hawkinson
Kathleen Hays
Julia Hydar and *The Stuntmen's Association of Motion Pictures*
Industrial Light & Magic
Michael Kmet and Maurice Molyneaux
Lucasfilm, Ltd.
Dan Madsen
Nicholas Meyer
Kevin Motley
Julie Nimoy
Denise Okuda
Michael Okuda
The team at Paramount
The archivists of Trekcore.com
Carrie Shaw and *Stunts Unlimited*
Ashlei Tave and *The International Stunt Association*

And, finally, much appreciation to the late **Bob Peak** for the spectacular cover art,
William Robinson, graphic artist extraordinaire, and
Laura Burgess, our editor who improved everything.

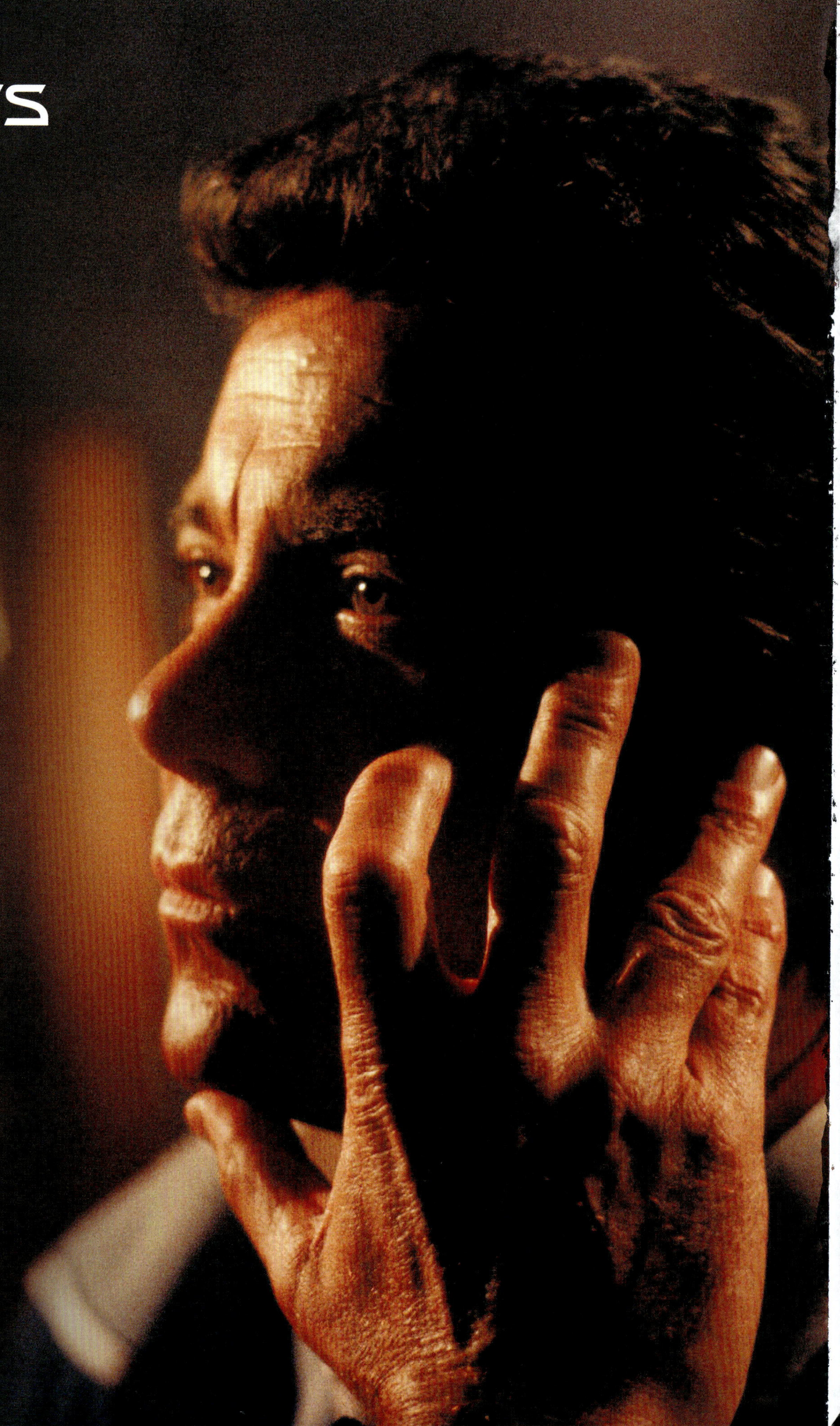

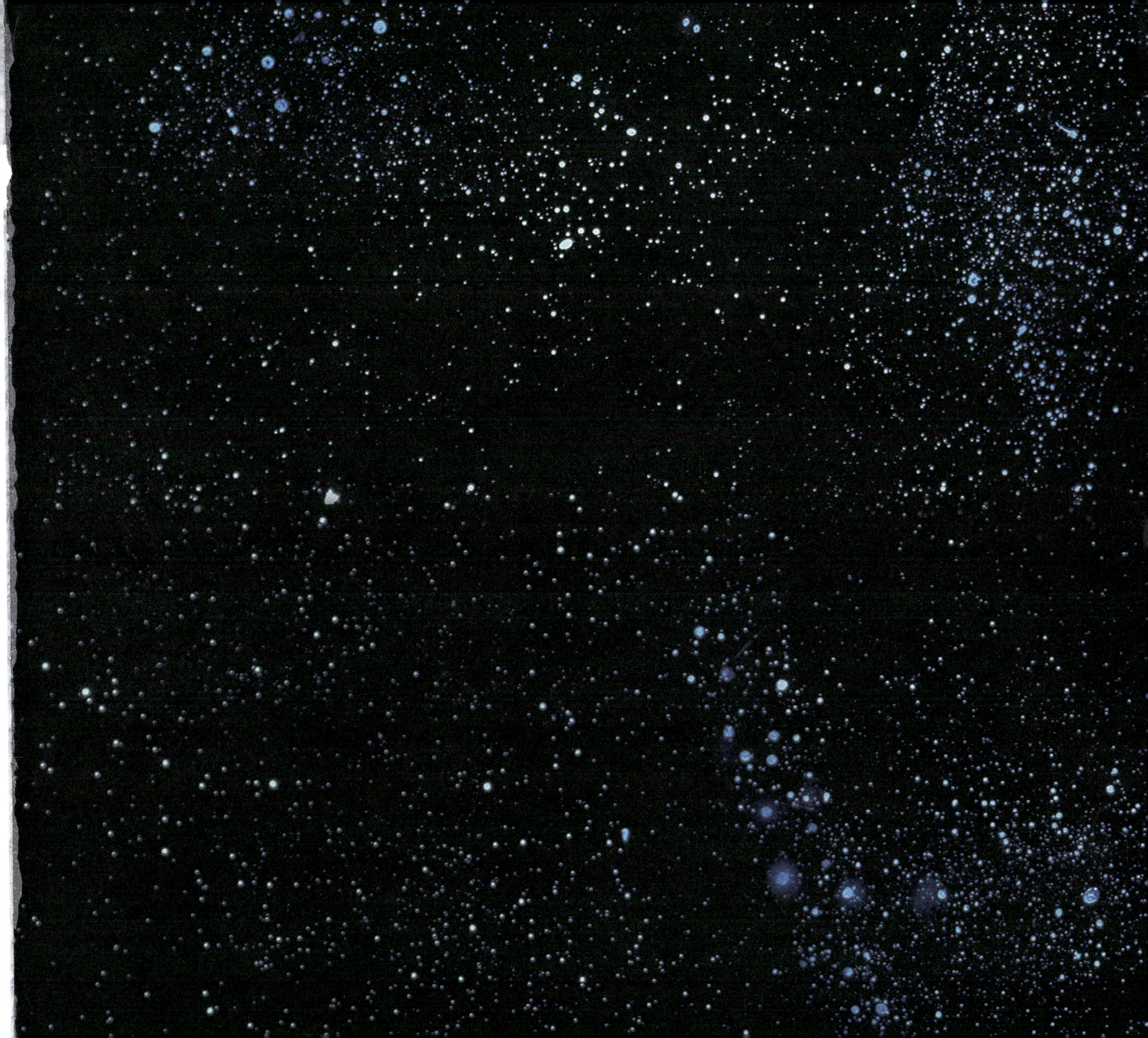

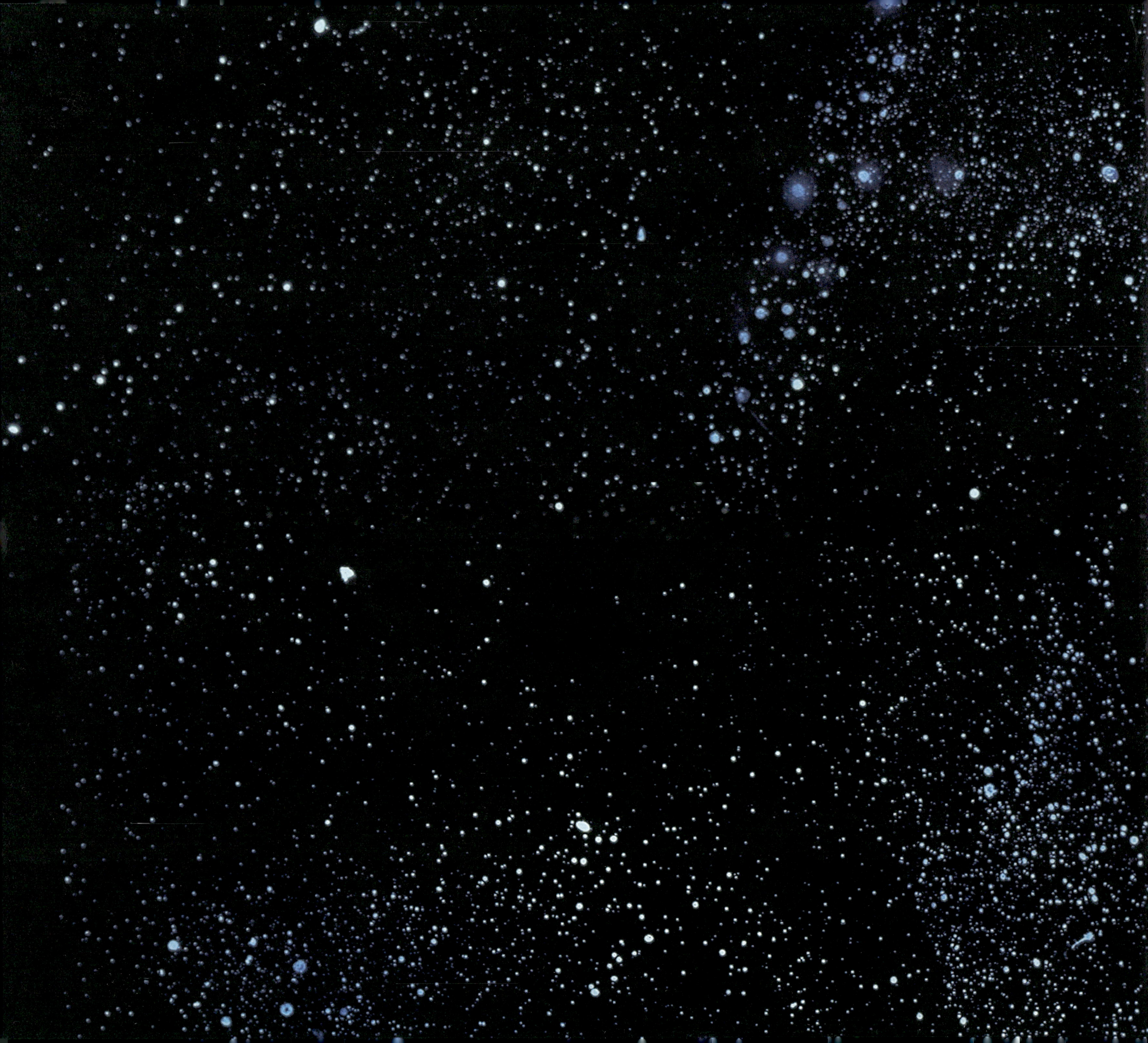